HATCHER'S
NOTEBOOK

0 11557 00350 5

JULIAN S. HATCHER

Technical Editor, *The American Rifleman*, Member, The National Board for the Promotion of Rifle Practice. Member, The United States Olympic Games Committee. Director, The National Rifle Association of America, 1922 to 1946.

"Distinguished Pistol Shot" U. S. Army. Winner, Webley & Scott Pistol Trophy, Bisley, England, 1931. U. S. International Rifle Team, Switzerland, 1925; Rome, 1927; Antwerp, 1930. Captain, U. S. International Rifle Team, Bisley, England, 1931.

Editor, "The Dope Bag," Pistol Section, *Arms and the Man* and *The American Rifleman*, 1922 to 1933. Life member, United States Revolver Association.

Officer in Charge, Experimental Department, Springfield Armory, 1917. Chief, Machine Gun and Small Arms Section, Engineering Division, Ordnance, Washington, 1918. Works Manager, Springfield Armory, 1919-1921. Officer in Charge of Small Arms Ammunition Manufacture, Frankford Arsenal, 1923-1928. Chief of Small Arms Division, Technical Staff, Ordnance Department, Washington, 1929. Chief of Small Arms Division, Manufacturing Service, Ordnance Department, Washington, 1929-1933. Assistant Commandant, The Ordnance School, 1937-1940. Commanding General, The Ordnance Training Center, 1941-1942. Chief of Ordnance Training Service, 1942-1943. Chief of Field Service, 1943-1945. **Distinguished Service Medal, Legion of Merit.**

HATCHER'S NOTEBOOK

A STANDARD REFERENCE FOR SHOOTERS, GUNSMITHS, BALLISTICIANS, HISTORIANS, HUNTERS AND COLLECTORS

JULIAN S. HATCHER
Foreword by Ned Schwing

STACKPOLE
BOOKS

Copyright © 1947 by The Military Service Publishing Company
Copyright © 1952–1957 by The Telegraph Press
Copyright © 1962 by The Stackpole Company

Published by
STACKPOLE BOOKS
5067 Ritter Road
Mechanicsburg, PA 17055
www.stackpolebooks.com

Printed in the United States of America

10 9 8 7 6 5 4 3 2 1

Third edition

Cover design by Wendy A. Reynolds

ISBN-13: 978-0-8117-0350-5
ISBN-10: 0-8117-0350-9

Cataloging-in-Publication Data is on file with the Library of Congress

CONTENTS

PART ONE

FOREWORD

I received a copy of *Hatcher's Notebook* on my fifteenth birthday. The math was a little over my head, but the information contained in this remarkable work was to guide me through the sometimes mystifying task of learning the finer points of firearms and how they functioned as they did. General Hatcher's book opened my youthful eyes to the fact that a lot of things have to happen for a firearm to discharge properly. I also found his observations on military firearms interesting and instructive. Over the ensuing five decades, *Hatcher's Notebook* has continued to be an important source of historical and technical information to me both professionally and personally.

Hatcher's is really two books in one. In the first part of the work, Hatcher discusses the 1903 Springfield, the 1917 Enfield, .30 caliber cartridges, the design and function of automatic firearms, the history of machine guns, and military semi-automatic rifles from the early designs to the M1 Garand. Each chapter and firearm is described in great detail with historical background as well as technical information. Much of General Hatcher's observations are based on actual hands-on experience, which adds authority to his commentary. What I found most useful about these early chapters was the author's personal comments on various aspects of each firearm discussed. Hatcher's personal experience spans from before the outbreak of the First World War to the end of World War II. General Hatcher has handled and fired the weapons he writes about, which brings color and vibrancy to what otherwise might be a dry recitation of technical data. For example, his assertion that a machine gun would get red hot when fired extensively was challenged by a military official who claimed it was impossible to fire a gun that long without it jamming. Hatcher then demonstrated the firing of a Benet-Mercie machine gun thousand-round without stopping. After seven hundred rounds, the barrel became red hot, and after one thousand, the receiver began to glow. The official who questioned Hatcher stood corrected.

Perhaps the most insightful part of Hatcher's work is the second part of his book where he describes a wide variety of firearms-related topics. These topics help establish a foundation of greater understanding for the reader. General Hatcher discusses subjects such as receiver steels, headspace, recoil theory, gunpowder, ammunition, set triggers, and his invaluable "Random Notes" on various subjects. He begins this section with his personal recollections of legendary gun designers he has known and worked with over the years. Included are John M. Browning, John C. Garand, J.D. Pedersen, Colonel Townsend Whelen, Melvin Johnson, and several others. The balance of "Random Notes" covers subjects from National Match ammunition to cartridge dimensions and identification tables. Just about every aspect of internal and external ballistics, bullet comparisons, chamber and bore measurements, wind deflection, and many other constructive topics are covered without complicated theory.

There is no doubt in my mind that General Hatcher's book is a timeless study in all aspects of firearms, both internally and externally. Its width and breadth have never been surpassed.

NED SCHWING

PREFACE TO THE 1962 EDITION

IT is gratifying to me to note the continued interest in HATCHER'S NOTEBOOK and the increased demand for this collection of reference material which I have found so useful.

This 1962 edition includes new material in Chapter 19 on recent progress in military small-arms research, specifically project "Salvo" of the U.S. Army, which resulted first in the Remington .222 Magnum cartridge, and then in two experimental lightweight rifles, the .224 Winchester Military Rifle and Colt's AR-15 "Armalite" rifle shooting the Remington .223 Military cartridge.

Also in Chapter 19 I have added some notes on commercial hunting cartridges that have appeared since the 1957 edition—the .222 Remington Magnum, the .22 Winchester Rim Fire Magnum, the .338 Winchester Magnum, and the .264 Winchester Magnum; also, in revolver cartridges, the .22 Remington Jet and the .256 Winchester Magnum.

A new and rather comprehensive chapter (22) has been added on a subject of fundamental interest to every shooter: "How Far Will My Gun Shoot?" Some of this material, written by me, is quoted from the September 1961 issue of the magazine *The American Rifleman*, on whose staff I serve as Technical Editor. In preparing this chapter I gathered about everything that is known on the subject, including tabular ballistic data, then boiled it down to basic essentials. I am glad to include such helpful data here in permanent form for future reference.

JULIAN S. HATCHER
Major General, U.S.A., Retired

Falls Church, Virginia,
January, 1962.

PREFACE TO THE 1957 EDITION

WHEN in 1946, after 41 years service, I retired from the Army and became Technical Editor of *The American Rifleman*, I collected together a number of reference notes for my own use. These proved so useful to me that I thought it would be nice to have them permanently available in book form, so I arranged for their publication under the title of HATCHER'S NOTEBOOK.

As the supply on hand sold out, the book has been reprinted from time to time; now, nine years after the book's first appearance, the publisher's stock is again nearing exhaustion, and it again becomes necessary to print a fresh supply. For that reason this seems an appropriate time to add some chapters covering additional subjects which my experience as head of the National Rifleman's Technical Service has shown to be of interest to members of that association and to readers of the *Rifleman*.

Accordingly, all of the original material of HATCHER'S NOTEBOOK has now been reprinted without change as Part One, and four new chapters have been added as Part Two which will give much important information not included in the original volume. The original index is retained at the end of Part One and an index of the new material appears at the end of Part Two.

First of the new chapters covers the development and adoption of a new non-corrosive primer, a new rifle and machine gun cartridge, a new service rifle, and a new all-purpose machine gun by the Army, as well as the development and marketing of a number of new rifle cartridges by the commercial ammunition companies.

The second new chapter covers the subject of explosions and powder fires, as well as the behavior of ammunition when it is exploded, accidentally or otherwise, while it is not in a gun. The many inquiries on this subject that I received from Police and Fire Departments, state and municipal authorities, and from readers of the magazine caused me to make a large number of interesting experiments to be able to answer their questions with certainty. The information thus developed is of great value, and is so important that it should be preserved permanently in convenient form for reference.

The third new chapter covers the fascinating and little understood subject of what happens when a bullet is fired straight up. Many experimenters have fired bullets vertically upwards and tried to note their return to earth; but in most instances such bullets simply disappear into the wild blue yonder and no sign of their return is ever detected. The reason is here explained and well documented by the results of official tests taken from Ordnance files.

The fourth chapter, on the subject of exterior ballistics, is again the result of my urgent desire to have available a handy bound reference book for which I can reach when I want to make any of a number of simple but necessary ballistic calculations arising out of such questions as—What is the ballistic coefficient of a newly designed bullet of which I have just received a sample? If the chronograph shows a certain velocity at 25 feet in front of the gun, what is the real muzzle velocity? If it loses 125 feet of its original velocity in the first 100 yards, how much will it lose in the next hundred and the next? What will be its time of flight over any given distance and how much will the bullet drop below the line of departure at various ranges? And other similar questions.

As technical Editor, I often receive requests for the name of a book on exterior ballistics that will give such information; and I am always distressed to have to reply that the books that I use for that work are out of print and unobtainable. The ballistic tables and references that I use are contained in six different books, and in this new chapter I have endeavored to include material that will enable me to throw those six books away and never miss them.

The best exterior ballistic tables for use in small arms work are those of Ingalls, published years ago by the Ordnance Department in the now out-of-print Artillery Circular M. Ingalls' highly useful Table I has been included in full, together with an abridged form of his Table II. In addition the history and principles of exterior ballistics have been stated in a simplified form, together with a comparative tabulation of the hard-to-find basic retardation functions as determined by several different experimental firings in various countries.

Mr. Walter J. Howe, editor of *The American Rifleman*, on whose great knowledge and excellent judgement I rely greatly, has been most helpful. Col. E. H. Harrison, Ordnance Corps, U.S. Army, retired, of *The American Rifleman* editorial staff, has made numerous valuable suggestions, and has pointed out several errors in my work that without his help would have gone undetected. Mr. Homer S. Powley, of Shaker Heights, Ohio, who is extremely accomplished in the field of exterior ballistics, has been of incalculable help to me in my efforts to obtain a better understanding of this subject, and has furnished me valuable material which I have included. To these three men I offer my sincere thanks for the assistance they have so generously given.

Falls Church, Virginia.
July, 1957.

JULIAN S. HATCHER,
Major General, U.S.A., Retired

ACKNOWLEDGMENTS

It is a pleasure to acknowledge my indebtedness to the many friends and associates who have so willingly answered my requests for assistance in the preparation of this work.

Charles B. Lister, Editor of *The American Rifleman*, spent much time and labor in reading the first draft of the manuscript, and made a number of extremely valuable suggestions which resulted in a complete re-arrangement and rewriting of the book. Richard Gordon McCloskey made a number of highly constructive suggestions as to form and contents which were most gratefully received and put into execution.

Invaluable technical information and assistance was freely given by a number of my friends who will be mentioned in alphabetical order as follows: Alvin H. Barr, of the National Rifle Association Technical Staff; Lt. Col. Calvin Goddard; Maj. J. C. Gray and Col. Samuel G. Green, of the Ordnance Department; my son, Lieut. Robert D. Hatcher, now on active duty in the Navy; Mr. Stanley F. Hood, Small Arms Maintenance Expert for the Ordnance Department; Col. G. B. Jarrett, of Aberdeen Proving Ground; Capt. F. J. Jervey, retired hero of the Marne fight in World War I, now Ordnance Engineer and ammunition expert; Capt. Melvin M. Johnson, U. S. M. C. R., eminent arms designer; Mr. Frank J. Kahrs, of the Remington Arms Co.; Mr. Edwin Pugsley, of the Winchester Repeating Arms Co.; Maj. J. J. Reen; Capt. Philip B. Sharpe; Col. Rene R. Studler, Chief of the Small Arms Division, Ordnance Research & Development Service; and my longtime friend and counselor, Col. Townsend Whelen.

It should be understood that the opinions given herein represent my own views, and are not necessarily the views of the Chief of Ordnance or of the War Department.

JULIAN S. HATCHER,

Falls Church, Va.,   Major General, U.S.A., Retired.
July 8, 1947.

PART ONE

I

Brief History of the Springfield U. S. Rifle, Caliber .30, Model of 1903

IN the Spanish American War of 1898, our Army was armed partly with Krag Jorgensen .30 caliber repeaters and partly with the old .45 caliber Springfield single shots, while the Navy used the Lee Straight Pull rifles in a caliber called 6 mm U.S.N., which in inches was equal to .236 caliber.

The Mauser rifles used by the Spaniards proved to be formidable weapons, and gained a reputation which caused our weapons to be regarded so critically that immediately after the war the Chief of Ordnance ordered the preparation of the pilot model of a new rifle. This gun had a 30 inch barrel and was fitted with a rod bayonet housed in the stock beneath the barrel. The mechanism was a modification of the Mauser action; it had two locking lugs at the front of the bolt instead of one at the rear as did the Krag. The rimmed cartridge was fed from 5 shot clips into a single row magazine extending below the stock.

The pilot model was forwarded to the War Department on August 25, 1900 for examination, after which it was tested at Springfield by a board which on October 2, 1900, recommended that the form of the magazine should be changed "to allow the cartridges to lie in a zig-zag manner, thus avoiding the necessity of having the magazine project below the stock" and that the rifle should use cannelured cartridges. A new model was then made which was basically the same as the M 1903 Springfield except that the barrel was 30 inches long and the rod bayonet was used. After test, this rifle was approved for experimental manufacture as the Model of 1901.

The construction of 5000 of these guns was authorized, but first the machinery had to be changed, and this took a long time, so it was not until April 7, 1902 that an appropriation of $1700 was made for the manufacture of 100 experimental rifles. (Thirty years later an order was given for the production of 80 experimental Garands at $1000 apiece.)

The 100 rifles were tested at Springfield Armory on Feb. 16, 1903, by a board which recommended that the barrel and bayonet each be shortened six inches to permit the gun to be used by the mounted services as well as by the Infantry, and thus avoid the necessity for a carbine.

On the recommendation of Brigadier General William Crozier, Chief of Ordnance, this new model was on June 19, 1903, approved as standard by the Secretary of War and designated as the U. S. Magazine Rifle, Model of 1903, Caliber .30.

On June 20, 1903, orders were given to begin immediately the manufacture of the fixtures, dies, tools gauges, etc., required for making 225 of these rifles per 8 hour day at Springfield Armory and 125 per 8 hour day at Rock Island Arsenal. The following month these instructions were changed to direct the manufacture of sufficient fixtures, etc., for making 400 rifles per 8 hour day at Springfield Armory.

These fixtures, etc., were made with such rapidity that quantity production of the rifles was begun in November, 1904, and continued without interruption until after the close of World War I.

Various changes were made from time to time in the components of the rifle and the methods of manufacture, some of the more important of which were as follows:

During the fiscal year of 1904, the first year of manufacture, 30,503 rifles were made. These had the rod bayonet and claw-hammer rear sight. During this period the cocking piece and safety lock were redesigned so that the rifle might more satisfactorily meet the requirements imposed by the Infantry Drill Regulations of that time.

During the fiscal year 1905, (starting July 1, 1904) 43,905 rifles with rod bayonets were made. On Jan. 11, 1905, work on the rod bayonet was stopped, following a letter dated Jan. 4, 1905, from President Theodore Roosevelt to the Secretary of War, which stated in part: "I must say I think the rod bayonet about as poor an invention as I ever saw. As you observed, it broke off as soon as hit with even moderate violence. It would have no moral effect and mighty little physical effect. . . . This ramrod bayonet business does not make me think we can afford to trust too much to theory . . ."

The Army was then experimenting with a trowel shaped combination bayonet and intrenching tool, but this idea was dropped, and a knife bayonet was approved on April 3, 1905 by Secretary of War Howard Taft as the Model of 1905. All rifles were altered to take this new bayonet.

In this period also, all work on the rear sight was suspended pending the outcome of trials of an improved sight, which was finally adopted. All rifles equipped with the old sight were changed so as to have the improved model.

The cartridge used with this gun was known as the Ball Cartridge, Caliber .30, Model of 1903. It had a rimless case and a 220 grain round nosed full metal jacketed bullet, with a muzzle velocity of 2300 feet per second. In the meantime, experiments had been underway with a sharp pointed bullet of lighter weight and higher velocity.

On October 15, this improved cartridge was approved by the Secretary of War, under the designation of Cartridge, Caliber .30, Model of 1906. It had the same case as the older one, except that the neck was shortened .07 inch; the bullet was of the sharp pointed or so-called spitzer type, weighing 150 grains, and having a muzzle velocity of 2700 feet per second.

This sharp pointed bullet did not extend as far forward as did the older round nosed one, and it therefore became necessary to alter the design of the bullet seat in the barrel of the rifle to fit the changed bullet contour. During the months of November and December 1906 and January and February 1907, no rifles were assembled, owing to the necessity of rechambering the barrels to fit the changed ammunition. All rifles previously made were afterward brought back to the Armory and rechambered. This was done by taking out the barrels, cutting them off at the rear end for a distance of two threads of the breech screw (two tenths of an inch), rethreading, putting back the barrels, and then reaming the chamber to the new size.

Up to the beginning of World War I, there had been manufactured at Springfield Armory a grand total of 606,924 rifles. In addition there had been manufactured nearly a third as many at Rock Island Arsenal, using tools, fixtures, gauges, etc., made at Springfield Armory and furnished to Rock Island.

The production of the M 1903 Springfield Rifle from its adoption up until the beginning of World War I was as follows:

Fiscal Year of	1904	(July 1, 1903 to July 1, 1904)	30,503	rifles
"	"	"	1905	43,905	"
"	"	"	1906	97,603	"
"	"	"	1907	102,116	"
"	"	"	1908	62,565	"
"	"	"	1909	25,662	"
"	"	"	1910	46,797	"
"	"	"	1911	49,697	"
"	"	"	1912	35,179	"
"	"	"	1913	38,070	"
"	"	"	1914	26,545	"
"	"	"	1915	25,977	"
"	"	"	1916	13,631	"
"	"	"	1917 to declaration of War, Apr. 6, 1917	8,674	"

Production by months during the War of 1917-1918 is given on Page 6.

On February 20, 1918, at rifle No. 800,000, a major change was made in the heat treatment of the receiver and bolt, which resulted in a rifle of far greater strength than before.

On May 11, 1918, at receiver No. 285,507, Rock Island Arsenal

adopted an improved heat treatment for carbon steel M 1903 receivers and bolts. Around August 1, 1918, at about receiver No. 319,921, that arsenal began using nickel steel for part of the production of receivers and bolts, but at the same time continued to make these parts of carbon steel also.

On April 1, 1927, at rifle No. 1,275,767, Springfield Armory changed the material in the bolt and receiver to nickel steel. The receivers in this series, while not quite as strong as the double heat treated ones which preceded them, still had ample strength, and the manufacture was simpler, as the complicated double heat treatment was avoided. In changing to the nickel steel, another advantage of the double heat treated receivers and bolts was lost, and this was the surface skin of very hard metal which gave a superb wearing surface, and made for a very smooth working action, without the "stickiness" of the relatively soft nickel steel. These nickel steel actions, are, however, highly satisfactory, everything considered. In the rare event of a failure, it occurs by a gradual stretching rather than by a sudden rupture.

Nickel steel receivers and bolts of rifles numbered in the 3,000,000 series made by the Remington Arms Co. during World War II were surface carburized, making them quite hard on the outside and thus avoiding the stickiness above mentioned.

During the years after World War I, it was the custom to make up each year several thousand rifles which were especially selected for use at the National Matches. In general these were the regular rifles, with star-gauged barrels, which simply means that the barrels were measured with a device called a star-gauge, so that any not within

---

MAKERS OF RIFLE HISTORY

"Major Hatcher, explaining to Expert Stock Maker Taylor, the details of the new .22 caliber Springfield.

"About the time that Europe blazed into war, a young officer of the United States Army was becoming known as an authority on rapid firers. As the war progressed, he turned his attention to military small arms, and having been interested in rifle and pistol shooting all his life, soon became even a more prominent human factor in the development of our army rifles than he had been in his work with machine guns.

"For the three years past, which have seen the greatest strides made in perfecting the most accurate of weapons for our riflemen, Major Julian S. Hatcher has been actively concerned with the production of super-accurate rifles at Springfield Armory. He has served with the Ordnance branch of the National Match Staffs of 1918, 1919, 1920 and 1921, has personally competed in the matches and applied his practical knowledge of the needs of the rifleman, thus gained, to the problem of producing for the National and International Matches the best possible weapons. In addition, Major Hatcher has been a member of three boards appointed to select ammunition for the National Matches, and has contributed scientific articles to the 'Encyclopedia Britannica,' 'The Saturday Evening Post,' 'The Scientific American' and "Arms and the Man.' "

From the February 1, 1922 issue of "Arms and the Man."

tolerances could be thrown out. In addition, the actions were carefully fitted for good trigger pull and the best possible functioning.

At one time the National Match rifles were made with headless cocking pieces, the idea being to get a faster firing pin action. The regular firing pin required .0057 second to travel through its six-tenths inch fall, while the headless pin required .0049 second; an advantage which was very likely more imaginary than real. It was found that the lessened inertia of these headless firing pins encouraged ruptured primers or primer blow-backs, and they were declared dangerous by the Ordnance Department and discontinued.

Several different kinds of pistol grip stock were tried on the National Match Springfields, and eventually one of these, which had undergone extensive tests by the service boards was adopted as standard in place of the old straight grip stock. This new stock was the one submitted for test under the designation of "Type C." Besides having a pistol grip, it omitted the finger grooves on the sides of the stock.

This was standardized on March 15, 1928, by Ordnance Committee Minute No. 6860, and the rifle so altered was known as the M 1903 A1. A1, of course, stands in Army nomenclature for Alteration 1.

Alteration 2 is one which is not seen by the ordinary user of the M 1903. It is a stripped barrel and action used inside a tank cannon for subcaliber practice; the only interest it has here is to let the reader know what the M 1903 A2 is, and so fill the gap in the record.

Along about the 1930's, the Ordnance Department made up a few thousand Springfield rifles with sporting stocks and Lyman No. 48 rear sights for sale to the members of the National Rifle Association. This was known as the Rifle, Caliber .30, M 1903, Style N.R.A.

Some heavy barrelled target rifles were also made up on sporting type stocks. These were known as the Rifle, Caliber .30, M 1903, Style T.

Occasionally a Springfield M 1903 will be seen that has an ejection port in the left side of the receiver, and the words Mark I on the receiver ring. This is one of the rifles that was made up for use with the Pedersen Device during the latter part of World War I.

During the early 1930's, the rifle production at Springfield Armory was confined to replacement parts for use in overhaul, plus a few National Match Rifles assembled in those years when the matches were held. By 1936, the Armory was being tooled up for the production of the Garand, and no Springfields were made that year, though a few were made after the tooling was completed.

Ordnance records show that in each of the calendar years in which these rifles were made at Springfield, receivers produced at the beginning of January had serial numbers according to the list which follows:

Year	Serial number of receiver Produced at start of Year	Year	Serial number of receiver Produced at start of Year
1907	269,451	1922	1,239,641
1908	337,862	1923	1,252,387
1909	358,085	1924	1,261,487
1910	398,276	1925	1,267,101
1911	456,376	1926	1,270,301
1912	502,046	1927	1,274,765
1913	531,521	1928	1,285,266
1914	570,561	1929	1,305,901
1915	595,601	1930	1,338,406
1916	620,121	1931	1,369,761
1917	632,826	1932	1,404,026
1918	761,758	1933	1,425,934
1919	1,055,092	1934	1,441,812
1920	1,162,501	1935	1,491,532
1921	1,211,300		

In 1936, during the tooling up for the Garand, production of the Springfield was suspended, but it was resumed in a small way in 1937. The last receiver made was in October 1939, and it had the number 1,532,878.

On November 12, 1941, the production of Springfields was again resumed at the plant of the Remington Arms Co., Ilion, N. Y., and the first rifle produced by them under this contract was 3,000,001. There are therefore no Springfields with numbers between 1,534,878, the last one made at Springfield Armory, and 3,000,001, the first one made on commercial contract during World War II.

At first, Remington made the ordinary M 1903, with some options as to the form of stock and other details. They started making receivers and bolts with the same 3½% nickel steel used in the Springfields, afterward changing to a chrome-nickel-molybdenum steel with only .20% to .40% nickel, or on the average, about one tenth as much as had been used formerly, but with the same amount of chromium, that is, .20% to .40%, plus a small percentage of molybdenum.

In the effort to gain increased production, this firm immediately began studies and experiments on design changes to make manufacture simpler and easier. One change was to omit two of the four grooves used in rifling the barrel. As it was found that there was little difference in the performance of the two grooved barrel and the four grooved one, this was approved. There were a number of other changes, and one which was a distinct improvement was the provision of a receiver peep sight.

On May 21, 1942, this simplified form of Springfield was approved for manufacture under the name of Rifle Caliber .30, Model of 1903 A 3.

Other changes on the A 3 model are:

Stock. Similar to that on the '03, except that the pistol grip is optional

Barrel Guard. Replaces the handguard of the '03, also covers the space formerly occupied by the rear sight.

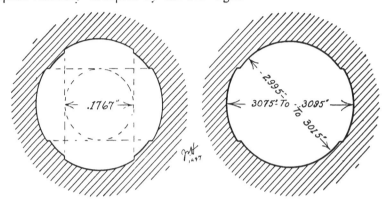

Forms of rifling used in the M1903 Springfield rifles.

Left: standard four groove rifling used previous to 1943. The grooves are three times as wide as the lands, and the twist is one turn in ten inches, right handed.

Nominal dimensions are: bore diameter, .300 inch, groove diameter .308 inch; width of grooves, .1767 inch. However, these exact dimensions are rarely encountered, as the manufacturing tolerances permit the bore to be anything from .2995 inch to .3015 inch, with grooves from .167 inch to .177 inch, and a groove diameter from .3075 to .3095 inch.

Right: two groove rifling approved in 1943 for use in the M1903 A3 rifle and for replacement barrels for the M1917 Enfield. This is simply the four groove rifling with two of the grooves omitted.

Upper Band Assembly. Is made of sheet metal stampings. The bayonet stud band, which replaces the upper band of the '03, is shorter, solid on top, and has two bayonet mounting stud bands on the bottom. The stacking swivel and its band are stampings.

Lower Band and Lower Band Swivel. These are made from sheet steel stampings.

Trigger Guard Magazine Assembly. This is the new nomenclature for the stamped, staked, and welded magazine, trigger guard and floor plate.

Front Sight Group. This is composed of a flat front sight pinned in a slot in a ring type sight base which is keyed and pinned to the barrel near the muzzle. The front sight blades are furnished in five heights from 0.477 to 0.537 inches. In targeting the rifles the proper height of blade is used to make the gun shoot as nearly as possible in agreement with the rear sight graduations.

U. S. Rifle, Caliber .30, M1903A4—Sniper's.

Weight (without sight)—8 pounds, 10 ounces. Sight magnification—2½ power.
Weight (with Model 330 Weaver Sight)—9 pounds, 2 ounces. Eye Relief—3 to 5 inches.
Weight (with Lyman Alaskan Sight)—9 pounds, 6 ounces.

Butt Plate Group. This is made of stampings.

Butt Swivel Group. This is made of two plates welded together with the swivel between them.

Bolt Group. While it is basically the same as that for the 1903, some parts differ in design and will not interchange with the 1903.

Follower Group. This is made from a stamping, but will interchange with the same part from the 1903.

Serial Numbers of the 1903 A 3. Before the approval of these changes the Remington Arms Co. had produced 348,085 M 1903 Springfields with serial numbers lying between the numbers 3,000,001 and 3,348,085. They continued to produce rifles, but these were now of the M 1903 A 3 type lying within blocks of serial numbers assigned to this firm. These blocks of numbers, not all of which were used, however, are as follows:

> 3,348,086 to 3,607,999 inclusive
> 3,708,000 to 4,707,999   "
> 4,992,001 to 5,784,000   "

Rifle Caliber .30 Model 1903 A 4. On June 14, 1943, the 1903 rifle similar to the A 3, but fitted with a telescopic sight was approved as the Rifle Caliber .30, Model of 1903 A 4. The sight used was the Weaver 330 3-power telescopic sight, slightly modified, and called by the Army the M 73 B 1. Redfield Junior Mounts were used to attach these Weaver Telescope sights to these Sniper's Rifles.

The rifle, caliber .30, M 1903 A 4, with Weaver telescopic sight and Redfield Junior Mounts was made by the Remington Arms Co., with serial numbers in the blocks given below:

> 3,407,088 to   3,427,087 inclusive
> 4,992,001 to   4,997,045   "
> Z4,000,000 to Z4,002,920   "

Springfield Made by L. C. Smith-Corona Typewriters, Inc. This firm was the only other besides Remington which produced Springfield Rifles during World War II. This plant started on the production of M 1903 A 3 rifles on Oct. 24, 1942, and actually began to turn out rifles in volume early in 1943. Blocks of numbers were assigned to this firm as follows:

> 3,608,000 to 3,707,999 inclusive
> 4,708,000 to 4,992,000   "

Production at this plant stopped February 19, 1944, with rifle No. 4,845,831, after a total of 234,580 rifles had been produced. Again it will be noted that not all the numbers were actually used, as the total produced does not agree with the difference between the serial number of the first and the last rifle. This is because of the loss of numbered receivers through rejections, experimental tests, etc.

Principal Dimensions and Weights of U. S. Magazine Rifle, Model of 1903

Barrel:	Dimensions	Inches
Diameter of bore		0.30
Exterior diameter at muzzle		0.619
Exterior diameter at breech		1.14
Length of chamber and bore		23.79
Length of barrel, total		24.006
Length of travel of bullet in bore		21.697
Diameter of chamber, rear end		0.4716
Diameter of chamber, front end		0.442
Diameter of neck of chamber, rear end		0.3425
Diameter of neck of chamber, front end		0.3405
Length of body of chamber		1.793
Length of shoulder of chamber		0.16
Length of neck of chamber		0.396
Length of chamber, total		2.3716

Rifling:

Number of grooves, 4.

Twist, uniform, one turn in		10.00
Width of grooves		0.1767
Width of lands		0.0589
Depth of grooves		0.004
Height of front sight above axis of bore		1.05
Distance from top of front sight to rear side of leaf, leaf raised		22.1254

Stock:

Length, with butt plate		40.166
Crook, i.e., distance from axis of bore to heel of butt		2.089
Distance from trigger to butt plate		12.74
Length of gun complete		43.212
Sight radius		22.1254
Width of single division on windage scale		0.0267

	Weights	Pounds
Barrel		2.79
Barrel, with rear sight base and front sight stud		3
Butt plate		0.26
Receiver		0.98
Bolt mechanism		1
Magazine and trigger guard		0.44
Magazine mechanism, including floor plate		0.17
Bayonet		1
Stock		1.58
Hand guard		0.13
Front and rear bands, including swivels		0.25
Rear sight, not including base		0.20
Total weight of metal parts		7.30
Oiler and thong case		.19
Total weight of arm, including oiler and thong case, with bayonet		9.69
Total weight of arm, including oiler and thong case, without bayonet		8.69
Weight to compress mainspring		16 to 18
Trigger pull (measured at middle point of bow of trigger)		3 to 4½

II

Brief History of the Enfield, U.S. Rifle Caliber .30, Model of 1917

IN 1907 the British adopted the Lee-Enfield rifle that now is known as the Short Model Lee-Enfield, (S.M.L-E.), using a rimmed cartridge of .303 caliber that somewhat resembled our old Krag cartridge.

Three years later, they began the development of a new rifle to permit the use of a higher powered rimless cartridge with improved ballistics. By 1914 the new rifle and cartridge had been perfected and had undergone the official trials and was about to be adopted under the name of Rifle, Enfield, Caliber .276, Pattern of 1913.

The name Enfield came from the fact that the rifle was developed at the Royal Small Arms Factory at Enfield Lock, in Middlesex, 11 miles north of London Bridge.

At that period Britain became involved in World War I, and time limitations prevented the intended change to a new caliber of small arms cartridge. As the need for rifles was urgent, existing plants in England which had previously made the .303 S.M.L-E. were put into high gear and production of the old model was stepped up to the maximum possible.

This, however, did not seem to be enough, so Britain turned to the U. S. for further supplies of small arms, and placed contracts for the establishing of three huge rifle plants.

These were the enormous plant built at Eddystone by a newly incorporated firm, the Remington Arms Company of Delaware, to have a capacity of 6000 rifles per day; the Winchester Repeating Arms Company, New Haven, Connecticut, 2000 rifles a day; and the Remington Arms Company, Ilion, N. Y., capacity, 3000 rifles per day.

The rifle to be made in these factories was the Enfield, Pattern of 1914 (the .276 Pattern '13 converted to take the .303 cartridge) which, while it did not work as well through the magazine as the rimless cartridge, was and still is a good military small arms cartridge.

These plants proved to be more or less of a disappointment to the British, for they were slow getting tooled up and into full production, and by the time a satisfactory volume was achieved, the British had overcome their rifle shortage by production in their home plants. By the early part of 1917, the British had started reducing these contracts, and before the U. S. entered the war on April 6 of that year, large lay-offs were taking place, and the remainder of the

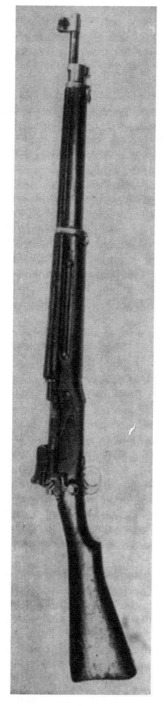

U. S. Rifle, caliber .30, M1917.

work on these contracts was to be terminated by about June 1, June 21, and July 21, for the three plants respectively.

The rifle that was being produced for the British was of highly advanced design, making it the best military rifle used in World War I. Though it was basically a typical Mauser, it was improved in several respects, and had a bolt and receiver of high grade nickel steel that gave it a superbly strong action. The well protected peep sight, mounted on the receiver, close to the shooter's eye, with a front sight likewise protected by strong steel ears, gave a sighting combination that was far superior to that on the Springfield, and by a considerable margin the best and most practical of any seen in that war.

The bolt mechanism, like that of the S.M. L.-E., was designed to cock on the closing motion. This was to make the extraction easier in rapid fire, when the heat always tightens things up. With the Springfield, the work of cocking the firing mechanism is added to that of extracting the cartridge, with the result that unless very hard brass is used, the bolt becomes very difficult to open after a few rounds of rapid fire. This feature, considered a great advantage by the British, was in general not liked by our people who were thoroughly used to the Springfield, which cocks on the opening of the bolt.   .

The .303 Enfield had a set of auxiliary long range sights for musketry work at extreme ranges. These were attached to the left side of the rifle, but were omitted in our M. 1917.

When we entered World War I on April 6, 1917, we had on hand about 600,000 M 1903 Springfields, and some 140,000 Krags. Springfield Armory had a capacity of 1000 rifles per day, and Rock Island Armory could turn out 400 Springfield Rifles per day.

With the rapid mobilization of our forces, the need for rifles was urgent; our newly inducted soldiers were actually using broomsticks instead of rifles for their basic drill instruction.

It was obvious therefore that these three great rifle plants should be gotten into production at the earliest possible moment, making rifles for our own use. To convert them to make the Springfield rifle would take months; therefore it was decided that we would use the Enfield, but that first it would be converted to use our .30-'06 cartridge.

The only really poorly designed feature on the rifle was the ejector, which had the ejector spring formed integral with it by milling a slot in one side and letting the thin part thus separated act as the spring. This often breaks in service, but fortunately the ejector with its spring is cheap and easy to replace.

For this rifle the British used the Enfield type of rifling, with wide lands and deep grooves, which had been adopted as a result of years of research to obtain a form of rifling that would best resist the severe erosion and barrel wear of the hot nitro-glycerine powder used in the British service. This had a left hand twist, with five lands and five grooves of equal width, the grooves being .0058 inch deep in a bore of .303 inch diameter.

We retained the Enfield form of rifling, but changed the bore and groove dimensions to suit our own bullet diameter of .3086 inch. To accomplish this we changed the bore from .303 inch to .300, and made the grooves .005 inch deep instead of .0058 as in the .303.

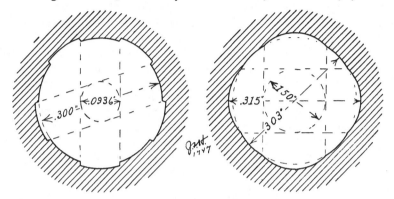

Left: Form of rifling used in the M1917 Enfields. There are five lands and five grooves, and lands and grooves are of equal width. Nominal dimensions call for a bore of .300 inch, the same as for the Springfield. Grooves are .005 inch deep, and have a twist of one turn in ten inches, left handed. During World War II, many 1917 Enfields were rebarrelled with two grooved barrels, with right hand twist, the same as used in the M1903 A3 as to form and dimensions of rifling and direction of twist.

Right: Rifling of the "Metford" type, as used in the Model 99 (1939) 7.7mm Japanese rifle. Grooves are .006 deep in the center, and have a twist of 1 turn in 9.5 inches, right handed. Other Japanese rifles and pistols use a similar form of rifling. This Metford rifling was developed in England, and was used in the Lee-Metford Rifle, but was superseded by the Enfield form of rifling to permit longer barrel life.

This gave a somewhat tighter barrel than was used on the Springfield, as will be seen when it is remembered that in the M 1903 the grooves are three times as wide as the lands, while in the 1917 the lands and grooves are equal.

In the M 1903 Springfield the bore diameter is .300 inch, but only one fourth of it is left this size. The other three fourths has the groove diameter of .308 inch, so that the average diameter is .306 inch.

In the 1917 the bore is likewise .300 inch, but this comprises one half of the entire inside surface, instead of only one fourth as in the Springfield. The other half consists of grooves, and as they are .005 deep, the equivalent groove diameter is .310 inch though as each groove is opposite to a land there is no actual place where the groove diameter can be measured directly. With half the bore having a diameter of .300 inch and half having a diameter of .310 inch, the average would be .305 inch as against .306 inch for the '03 Springfield.

While this is, as shown above, somewhat tighter than the rifling we had been using on the M 1903, it was adopted because after careful tests it seemed to give the best results for that form of rifling with the diameter of bullet we were already using.

This has been gone into at some length because we so often see in print the erroneous statement that the 1917 has a bore that is too loose for our bullet, because we "used the British dimensions" when we took over the manufacture of the Enfield.

The statement that this is not so is from first hand knowledge, because during a large part of the First World War, I was Chief of the Machine Gun and Small Arms Section, Engineering Division, Ordnance, or in other words, Chief of Engineering and Design for Small Arms for the Army, and had personal contact with this matter at the time these rifles were being made.

It is interesting to note in this connection, that many tests made during the years since then have shown that the 1917 barrels will always outwear the '03 Springfield barrels. At this writing, March, 1947, there is serious consideration being given to adopting some such form of rifling as that on the Enfield for all future small arms manufacture.

At the present time, not all 1917 Enfield Rifles have barrels of the type described above, for some were rebarreled with 4 groove barrels having a right hand twist, of which the Hi-Standard Manufacturing Co., of New Haven, Conn., made 61,250, and some were rebarreled with 2 groove barrels, of which Johnson Automatics, Inc., of Providence, R. I., made 81,571. Recent Ordnance tests show that the accuracy of all these barrels is comparable, but that the 2 groove barrels give slightly lower pressures with high powered hunting loads. The difference is not, however, great enough to give these two-groove barrels much advantage over the four groove type.

During the First World War the three plants mentioned above turned out a total of 2,202,429 Model 1917 Enfields, at a cost of approximately $26 each.

Principal Dimensions and Weights of United States Rifle, Cal. .30, Model 1917

Barrel: Dimensions	Inches
Diameter of bore	0.30
Exterior diameter at muzzle	0.60
Exterior diameter at breech	1.32
Length of chamber and bore (from face of bolt to muzzle)	26.
Diameter of chamber, rear end	0.4716
Diameter of chamber, front end	0.442
Diameter of neck of chamber, rear end	0.3425
Diameter of neck of chamber, front end	0.3405
Length of body of chamber	1.785
Length of shoulder of chamber	0.16
Length of neck of chamber	0.396
Length of chamber, total	2.341

Rifling:

Number of grooves, 5.

	Inches
Twist, uniform, left hand, one turn in	10.
Width of grooves	0.0936
Width of lands	0.0936
Depth of grooves	0.005
Height of front sight above axis of bore (mean)	1.06
Distance from top of front sight to rear side of leaf, leaf raised	31.76

Stock:

	Inches
Length, with butt plate	42.62
Crook, i.e., distance from axis of bore to heel of butt	2.12
Distance from trigger to butt plate	13.5
Length of gun complete	46.3
Sight radius	31.76
Sight radius (battle sight)	31.69

Weights

Bayonet	1	lb.	2 oz.
Oiler and thong case			3 oz.
Total weight of arm with oiler and thong case and bayonet	10	lbs.	5 oz.
Total weight of arm with thong case without bayonet	9	lbs.	3 oz.
Weight to compress mainspring	16 to 18	lbs.	
Trigger pull (measured at middle of bow of trigger)	4½ to 6½	lbs.	

RIFLE PRODUCTION TO NOV. 9, 1918

Months	Eddystone	Winchester	Ilion	Springfield Armory	Rock Island Arsenal	Total
Before August, 1917	....	....	....	14,986	1,680	16,666
Aug. 1, 1917 to Dec. 31, 1917 ..	174,160	102,363	26,364	89,479	22,330	414,696
1918						
January	81,846	39,200	32,453	23,890	7,680	185,069
February	98,345	32,660	39,852	6,910	2,460	180,227
March	68,404	42,200	49,538	120	420	160,682
April	87,508	43,600	36,377	2,631	....	170,116
May	84,929	41,628	54,477	3,420	550	185,004
June	104,110	34,249	52,995	6,140	619	198,113
July	135,080	35,700	60,413	14,841	2,038	248,072
August	106,595	20,030	65,144	27,020	1,597	220,386
September	110,058	31,550	58,027	29,770	3,813	233,218
October	100,214	33,700	53,563	35,920	3,256	226,653
Nov. 1-9, 1918	30,659	9,100	16,338	10,500	808	67,405
Total	1,181,908	465,980	545,541	265,627	47,251	2,506,307

Note: Eddystone, Winchester, and Ilion plants turned out the Enfield, while the Springfield Armory and the Rock Island Arsenal produced the Springfield. The months marked by a drop in the production at Springfield and at Rock Island were months in which the components manufactured were not assembled but were used for spare parts.

III

A Brief History of the .30-'06, the .30 M1 and the .30 M2 Cartridges

W HEN the M 1903 rifle was first adopted, the cartridge designed to go with it had a rimless case, which, except for very minor changes, is the same as that we have now. The bullet was of round nosed shape, weighing 220 grains, with a muzzle velocity of 2300 feet per second.

In 1906 we adopted a lighter bullet weighing 150 grains, having a sharp or "spitzer" point, and with a muzzle velocity of 2700 feet per second. This bullet had a cupro-nickel jacket, and a core composed of 1 part tin to 39 parts of lead. The maximum range was given in the handbooks as 4700 yards.

For use in long range matches, the commercial companies furnished a cartridge with a 180 grain bullet, having better wind bucking qualities, and longer range.

In 1911 to 1913, when I was a lieutenant of Artillery stationed in Florida, I did a lot of shooting, and one of the things I tried was to see how far I could shoot a Springfield rifle along the beach. To my disappointment, I just never could seem to get it to shoot as far as the book said it would.

As Chief of the Machine Gun and Small Arms Section, Engineering Division, Ordnance, during World War I, I decided to solve this mystery, so I got one of my Mexican Border Machine Gun School assistants, with whom I had often collaborated in similar experiments, and set him to check the range tables. This was the late Lt. Col. Glenn P. Wilhelm, and the work was started at Borden Brook Reservoir, near Springfield Armory, and later was continued at Miami, then at Daytona Beach. The late noted firearms writer, Capt. Edward C. Crossman was one of Col. Wilhelm's assistants in this work, as was my brother, Major James L. Hatcher, 65th Artillery, who was firing his 9.2 inch howitzers on the fortress of Metz the day of the Armistice and returned to this country immediately afterward. The troops he was to take back to France were cancelled in view of the Armistice, and while waiting for another assignment he worked on this project with Col. Wilhelm. This started him on a long and brilliant career in the Ordnance Department as a small arms expert.

Col. Wilhelm and his crew soon found, as I had suspected from my Florida experience, that the .30-'06 bullet would not go anywhere nearly as far as the book said it would The maximum range was found to be 3300 to 3400 yards at an angle of about 29 degrees, and the same up to about 45 degrees, after which the range began to shorten.

When the reason for this discrepancy was investigated, it was found that the original tables of fire had been made at Springfield Armory as a result of test firings at Longmeadow, along the Connecticut River not far from the Armory. Up to 1200 yards, the results were quite accurate; beyond this range, the target became harder and harder to hit, and had to be made larger and larger. Then, even with the largest practicable targets, some bullets would be on and some off, and the center of impact had to be more or less estimated. When the range went beyond 1800 yards, it became impossible to get results, and the figures on out to extreme range were then calculated according to the best information available in those days, which, however, was not good enough. The figures for the extreme range were about 38% too big.

Beginnings of the investigation to check the small arms range tables, Borden Brook Reservoir, Mass., 1918. Center, Lt. Col. Glenn P. Wilhelm. Right, nearest the camera, Lt. Col. Wallace L. Clay.

When this long range firing program was initiated, I felt certain that sooner or later our forces in France would demand greater range in the Small Arms cartridges, as the Heavy Machine Gun was being much used at that period and extreme range was an important characteristic. I had been head of the Machine Gun Schools, first

on the Mexican Border, then at Sandy Hook and later at Springfield, and had just written a book, with Wilhelm and Malony on
Machine Guns, their tactics, fire control, etc., and felt that when the
users of these guns in France found that their bullets were inferior
in striking power at long ranges to some others, trouble would start.
So to be ready with some kind of solution, I ordered 100,000 rounds
of 180 grain match ammunition, and made range firings with that also.

Col. Wilhelm's Ballistic Station at Miami in 1918. Officer in center of top
platform under range clock is Major (now Colonel) James L. Hatcher, brother
of the author.

Our Army had practically no machine guns when the war started,
so we armed our first troops in France with British Vickers guns
and with the French Hotchkiss. The Vickers used the .303 Mark VII

Col. Wilhelm's Ballistic Station, Daytona, Fla., 1919. Firing the .30 Caliber rifle with Swiss boat tailed bullets for maximum range.

cartridge, having a 174 grain flat based bullet, and the French Hotch-kiss used the "Balle D," a solid bronze boat tailed bullet weighing about 198 grains.

Very soon the users of these guns found that these bullets had an extreme range nearly 50% greater than did our .30-'06. When the Vickers and Hotchkiss guns gave way to the new Brownings, and the troops found that they could no longer lay down barrages at the same long ranges as before, cablegrams came back hot and heavy demanding that something be done about it. Fortunately we were already well along toward finding out what our ammunition would really do and what it wouldn't, and the reasons for the condition. An officer from my office who was in France on temporary duty told them about the 180 grain Match bullets we were trying, and immediately a demand was cabled back for some of this to try, and it was sent. We were then told that a longer range for our small arms cartridges was necessary and work was started on developing such a cartridge. Not long afterward the Armistice of November 11, 1918 put and end to the work for the time.

In France, the Fiske Board, with Col. Earl McFarland, Maj. Lee O. Wright, and Lt. Col. J. S. Hatcher as Ordnance Members, visited each Division, Corps, and Army headquarters and interviewed the Commanding General as to the actual charactertistics that should be embodied in the new cartridge. It was determined that the same ammunition should be provided for both rifle and machine gun, and that it should have the longest possible range and the flattest possible trajectory that would still permit it to be used in the rifle.

After the end of the War, the development of this new ammunition proceeded, with much advice from the Infantry Board and the Cavalry Board, and with some of the experimental types being tried out at the National Matches at Camp Perry each year.

In connection with these tests we had our attention directed by Col. Lucian B. Moody to the Swiss Service Ammunition, which had a 174 grain boat tailed bullet of the same diameter, as our own service bullet, that is, .308 inch. Very early in the game Col. W. L. Clay, Commanding Officer of Frankford Arsenal conducted a series of firings with this ammunition that showed it to be immensely superior to ours at long ranges. Conveniently enough, these Swiss bullets could be loaded into our own cases and fired in our guns.

Col. Townsend Whelen succeeded Col. Clay in command of Frank-ford Arsenal, and made up a series of bullets with boat tails from 2 degrees on up to 12 degrees taper. These were fired at Aberdeen Proving Ground, and it turned out that the 9 degree bullet gave the best performance.

Meantime, in 1923, I succeeded Col. Whelen in charge of the Frankford Small Arms Ammunition Plant, and in 1925 the type E 9 degree boat tailed bullet was adopted as standard for both rifles

The Ballistic Station at Daytona, Fla., 1919. Arrangement for obtaining the actual angle of departure by firing through a screen and measuring the height of the bullet hole above that of the bore.

and machine guns, and the ammunition was called the .30 caliber M 1. The bullet had a gilding metal jacket, and a new and improved ogive, of 7 calibers radius, giving it a slightly better form factor than the very similar looking ogive on the 1906 bullet. The muzzle velocity was 2700 feet per second, and the extreme range was 5900 yards, as against 3400 for the 1906.

To get 2700 feet per second muzzle velocity with this heavy bullet and still keep within a desirable pressure range was found to be so difficult that many lots of powder were eliminated; as a result, Col. Clay, Chief of the Small Arms Division, pushed through a reduction of the velocity to 2640 f. s. at the muzzle or 2595 at 78 feet. This reduced the extreme range to about 5500 yards.

The old .30-'06 bullet had been made with a core of 29 parts lead to 1 part tin; this was found to be too soft for the boat tailed bullet, which, in the early samples at least, seemed to require a very hard core, so the metal used was 1 part antimony to 7 parts lead. The .30-'06 bullet had a cupro-nickel jacket; the M1 had one of gilding metal, hence there was no difficulty in distinguishing between them by appearance. The bullet on the '06 looked silvery, the M1 looked like gold.

At this time we had on hand about two billion of the war-time .30-'06 cartridges, and as ammunition is perishable, the policy was to use up the oldest ammunition first, keeping the newer for war reserve. Thus the shooters on Army, National Guard and Civilian rifle ranges had to use the old war time stuff, while wishing for the happy day to come when they could get some of the good new ammunition to use.

Finally about 1936 that wished-for day arrived, and with it trouble of an unexpected sort. The new ammunition had so much longer range and carrying power that it began to shoot beyond the previous danger zones of the existing ranges. The National Guard Bureau then requested the War Department to make up some ammunition like the old 1906, to use on the restricted ranges, and the order was given to make up 10,000,000 rounds of it.

This short range ammunition was made as much like the 1906 as possible. It had a 150 grain flat base bullet, but the jacket was of course made of gilding metal instead of the old cupro-nickel. It was, however, colored to look like the 1906 by the use of a stannic stain, so it could be de distinguished from the M 1. The ogive was of the same shape as the M 1, and differed a bit from the shape of the 1906, but the difference was so slight as to be imperceptible.

Some of this ammunition reached the Service Boards, which by now had lost all of the old World War I machine gunners who so keenly felt the inadequacy of our ammunition in 1918. Our soldiers liked the lessened recoil of the new ammunition. More rounds could be carried for the same weight, etc., so the suggestion was made and carried through that it should be substituted for the M 1. In 1940 this ammu-

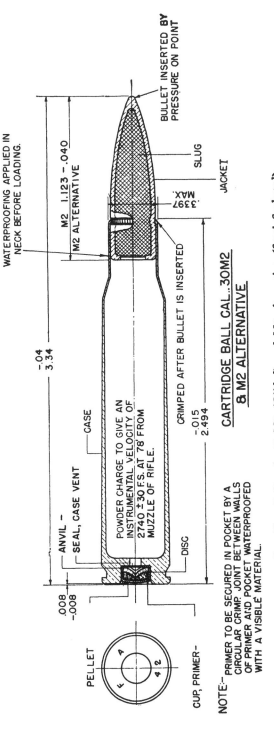

CARTRIDGE BALL CAL..30M2 & M2 ALTERNATIVE

WATERPROOFING APPLIED IN NECK BEFORE LOADING.

BULLET INSERTED BY PRESSURE ON POINT

M2 1.123 −.040 M2 ALTERNATIVE

SLUG

.3397 MAX.

JACKET

−.04 3.34

CASE

POWDER CHARGE TO GIVE AN INSTRUMENTAL VELOCITY OF 2740 ±30 F.S. AT 78' FROM MUZZLE OF RIFLE.

CRIMPED AFTER BULLET IS INSERTED

−.015 2.494

ANVIL −

SEAL, CASE VENT

DISC

.008 −.008

NOTE:− PRIMER TO BE SECURED IN POCKET BY A CIRCULAR CRIMP. JOINT BETWEEN WALLS OF PRIMER AND POCKET WATERPROOFED WITH A VISIBLE MATERIAL.

PELLET

CUP, PRIMER−

F A 4 2

Cartridge, Ball, cal. .30 M2 (Gilded) and M2 alternative (Steel Socketed).

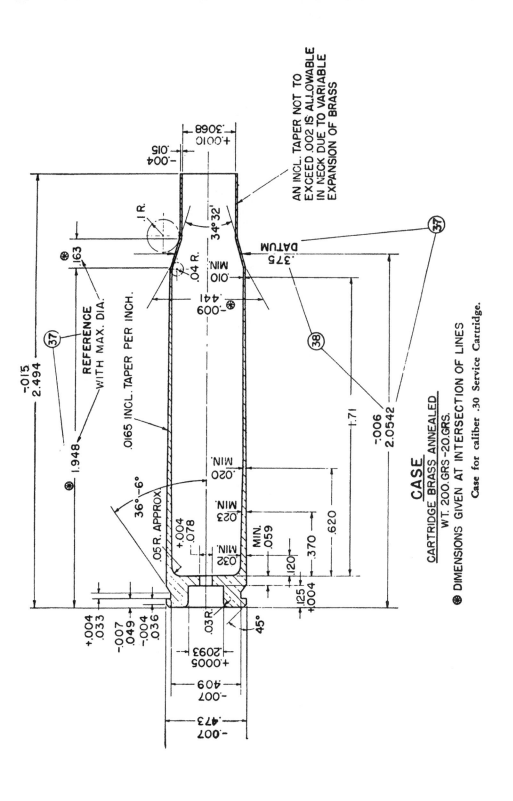

CASE

CARTRIDGE BRASS ANNEALED
WT. 200.GRS-20.GRS.

⊛ DIMENSIONS GIVEN AT INTERSECTION OF LINES

Case for caliber .30 Service Cartridge.

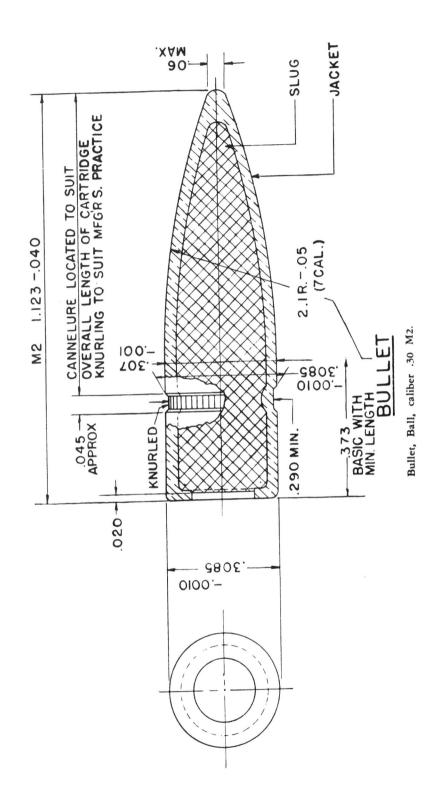

Bullet, Ball, caliber .30 M2.

nition with some slight further changes, was standardized as Cartridge, Ball, Caliber .30 M 2.

By the time this ammunition was standardized, tin and antimony were getting scarce, and it was found that it was satisfactory to make the bullet core of lead without the addition of any alloying material. As the lead used is secondary lead, that is, reclaimed from batteries, etc., it will have some hardening material in it, but not much. This results in a slightly increased bullet weight of 152 grains instead of 150. The muzzle velocity was also boosted from 2700 f. s. to 2805 f. s.

While we were going backward, the Germans were going to the opposite extreme. During the first World War, their standard infantry bullet weighed 154 grains, and was a flat based type, with a cone shaped depression in the base.

For machine gun use during that war, they developed a boat tailed bullet weighing 196 grains. This was adopted by them as standard and was the one used in the recent war.

In our own Army, the tendency is definitely to use armor piercing ammunition for everything, and to do away with plain ball. The Armor Piercing Ammunition that we use now is nearly identical with that developed immediately after World War I by Col. Clay, known as the M 1922. Our present type is known as Cartridge, Armor Piercing, Caliber .30, M 2. A black tip on the bullet indicates that it is armor piercing. The bullet weight is 168.5 grains.

Characteristics of the Various Types

Type	Bullet weight grains.	Muzzle Velocity foot seconds.	Instru- mental velocity @ 53 Ft.	Instru- mental velocity @ 78 Ft.	Muzzle Energy Ft. lbs.
Cal. .30-'06	150	2700	2655	2640	2429 Ft. lb.
Cal. .30 M 1	174.5*	2647	2620	2600	2675 Ft. lb.
Cal. .30 M 2	152*	2805	2755	2740	2656 Ft. lb.
Cal. .30 A.P. M 2	168.5*	2775	2730	2715	2780 Ft. lb.

*Maximum weight minimum 3 grains less.

Tables of Fire

Range, yards.		Cal. .30-'06 Angle of Departure, Minutes.
100	....	2.6
200	....	5.2
300	....	8.3
400	....	11.7
500	....	15.8
600	....	20.7
700	....	26.33
800	....	32.4
900	....	39.8
1000	....	48.3

Cartridge, Ball, Caliber .30, M1

Range Yards	Angle of elev. minutes	Time of flight seconds	Maximum ordinate feet	Angle of fall minutes
100	2.7	0.12	...	2.7
200	5.4	0.25	0.3	6.1
300	8.4	0.39	0.6	10.1
400	11.8	0.54	1.17	14.9
500	15.9	0.70	2.01	20.25
600	20.25	0.88	3.09	27.3
700	25.31	1.07	4.56	35.8
800	30.7	1.27	6.45	46.2
900	36.8	1.50	9.00	95.9
1000	43.5	1.75	12.3	74.3

Cartridge, Ball, Cal. .30, M2

Range Yards	Angle of elev. minutes	Time of flight seconds	Maximum ordinate feet	Angle of fall minutes
100	2.4	0.12	...	3.4
200	5.1	0.25	0.3	6.8
300	8.1	0.38	0.6	10.1
400	11.5	0.53	1.2	13.5
500	15.5	0.70	1.8	20.3
600	20.3	0.89	3.0	30.4
700	26.0	1.11	5.1	40.5
800	32.4	1.35	7.2	57.4
900	40.2	1.62	10.8	74.3
1000	49.3	1.91	15.3	94.5

Cartridge, Ball Caliber .30 Armor Piercing M2

Range Yards	Angle of elev. minutes	Time of flight seconds	Maximum ordinate feet	Angle of fall minutes
200	5.1	0.24	0.3	5.7
400	11.5	0.52	1.2	14.5
600	19.6	0.87	3.0	29.7
800	30.7	1.30	6.9	54.0
1000	46.2	1.82	13.5	90.1

Table of Fire for the .22 Caliber Long Rifle Cartridge

Range, yards	Velocity, f. s.	Energy, ft. lbs.	Time of flight sec.	Drop at target, inches	Mid range ordinate inches	Angle of departure, minutes
0	1,100	102				
25	1,070	95	0.068	0.89	0.24	3.5
50	1,020	89	0.140	3.17	0.98	7.6
75	980	84	0.214	8.06	2.28	11.7
100	950	79	0.292	14.82	4.08	15.8
125	920	75	0.372	24.73	6.78	20.5
150	890	71	0.455	36.64	10.02	24.9
175	860	67	0.541	50.80	14.20	29.6
200	840	64	0.630	72.93	19.10	34.3
225	810	61	0.720	93.04	28.30	39.7
250	790	58	0.812	118.21	31.87	44.7
275	770	55	0.911	147.20	39.87	50.8
300	750	52	1.005	177.12	48.69	55.7

Table of Fire for the Cartridge, Ball, Cal. .45 M1911

Range, Yards	Time of Flight Seconds	Drop, Inches	Deflection due to drift, inches (To the Left)
10	0.037	0.3	0.1
20	0.75	1.1	0.2
30	0.113	2.4	0.3
40	0.151	4.4	0.4
60	0.229	9.9	0.8
80	0.308	18.0	1.3
100	0.388	28.0	2.0

IV

Automatic Gun Mechanisms

AN automatic firearm is one which fires, throws out the empty
cartridge, and reloads itself when the trigger is pulled. Strictly
automatic firearms will also keep on firing as long as the trigger is
held down; but the term automatic pistol, or automatic shotgun, etc.,
is often used to designate what is more properly called a *semiautomatic*
or *self-loading* gun, which is one that unloads and reloads itself but
which fires only one shot for each pull of the trigger. Thus on the
Government automatic pistols the trigger must be released and pulled
again for each shot fired.

The first automatic firearm was the Maxim machine gun. Machine
guns were known for many years before the advent of the Maxim
gun in 1884 but these older machine guns were hand-operated. In
other words, they were worked with a crank like a sausage grinder,
the cartridges being fed into a hopper, or feed-way, by one hand
while the other one turned the crank. In 1880 Sir Hiram Maxim
constructed a mechanism in which the barrel of the gun was allowed
to kick back for about three-quarters of an inch when the shot was
fired, and this backward motion was utilized to unlock the breech,
eject the empty cartridge and feed a new one in. Maxim's gun was,
therefore, what is known as a *recoil-operated* gun.

It was not very long after this that John M. Browning, a gunsmith
of Ogden, Utah, conceived the idea of making an automatic gun that
would operate like a little gas engine. He bored a hole in the barrel of
the gun about a foot from the muzzle and fitted this hole with a
piston on the end of a swinging lever. When the gun was fired, the
bullet first passed this little hole in the barrel, then the gas under very
high pressure struck on the piston resting in this hole and drove it
downward with great force. This piston was on the end of a lever
which was swung downward and to the rear by the force of the gas,
operating a connecting rod which worked the breech mechanism.
This gun was said to be *gas-operated*. The invention of the Colt gun
by Browning in 1889, was almost immediately followed by the invention by Baron Von Odkolek, in Austria, of a gun in which the
gas acted on a piston moving straight to the rear in a tube under the
barrel. This gun, also gas-operated, was subsequently developed into
the Hotchkiss. More about these inventions will be found in a later
chapter.

As soon as the first successful machine gun was produced, this very
fact turned the attention of inventors to the subject of automatic

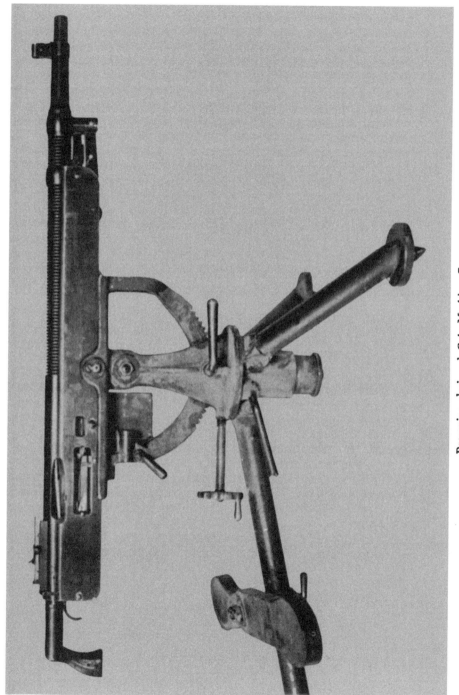

Browning designed Colt Machine Gun.

firearms and almost immediately there were a large number of inventions produced along this line. Many of the early efforts turned to pistols and some successful ones such as the Mauser, Luger, and Colt, were soon produced. All these guns worked on the recoil-operated principle.

During the half century that has elapsed since the automatic machine guns first demonstrated their success, there have been hundreds of attempts to make machine guns, semi-automatic rifles and automatic pistols, and the patent offices and war departments of the world have been inundated by a constant flood of inventions of this general category. It is really amazing to see the different ingenious devices that were thought of in an effort to produce a successful semiautomatic shoulder rifle. Most models of such guns were either recoil-operated or gas-operated, but there have been dozens of models based on novel principles, such as operation by the movement of the primer in the cartridge case; inertia-operated shoulder guns in which a sliding weight remains relatively stationary while the gun recoils; guns with movable butt plate resting on the shoulder of the firer and operating through a system of rods to unlock the gun when the kick pushed the butt plate against the firer's shoulder; guns in which the breech was held stationary and the barrel allowed to move forward; and many others, the principal ones of which will be described in detail later.

Much of the mechanism of the machine gun is involved in the locking and unlocking of the breech block. A high-powered rifle cartridge generates a pressure of 50,000 pounds to the square inch when the gun is fired, and this pressure, acting on the head of the cartridge case, tends to force the breech block to the rear. Accordingly, when high pressure cartridges are used, the breech block must be securely locked to the rear end of the barrel in order to hold the cartridge in the chamber of the gun during the explosion. However, the force of the explosion of a cartridge is gone in a very small fraction of a second. The high pressure of 50,000 pounds to the square inch lasts less than one-thousandth of a second and then drops rapidly off to zero.

If we had a fairly heavy breech block, it would not move enough to do any harm during the very short time the pressure lasts. If the weight of the breech block could be chosen correctly, it would be possible to make a breech mechanism in which no locking device would be necessary. The pressure on the cartridge case would be just sufficient to give the heavy breech block enough movement so that the breech would open after the cartridge is fired, and if the proper spring were put behind the breech block it would close again, pushing a new cartridge in at the same time.

Blow-back Mechanisms

Actually this type of breech mechanism, called the *straight blow-back* system, is perfectly practical for low-powered cartridges, and such mechanisms are used on almost all pocket automatic pistols and on caliber .22 pistols and rifles. The breech block is simply held against the head of the cartridge by a spring, and when the gun is fired, the powder pressure blows the bullet out through the muzzle with very great rapidity, and at the same time pushes the breech block back with just the right speed to extract the fired case after the powder pressure has fallen to zero. If the breech block is made too light, it will open too quickly, and if it opens while pressure is still in the cartridge case, the cartridge case will be ruptured and gas will escape to the rear.

Calculations and experiments have shown that for the caliber .30 cartridge, such as is used in the Springfield rifle, the breech block would have to weigh in the neighborhood of twenty-seven pounds to operate satisfactorily on the blow-back principle. As the Springfield rifle itself weighs only nine pounds, the use of this kind of breech mechanism is obviously impracticable for a semiautomatic shoulder rifle using the Springfield cartridge, where the weight must be kept down to the lowest possible figure. Moreover, such a breech block is entirely too heavy for even a machine gun using the full powered Army rifle cartridge.

However, straight blow-back guns powerful enough for hunting have been produced but these guns are considerably less powerful than the Army rifle. The most powerful hunting rifle built on the blow-back principle is the Winchester self-loading rifle which was made in .32, .35, .351 and .401 calibers, with a straight cartridge shaped somewhat like a large pistol cartridge.

Even though the mechanisms of the blow-back type do not seem to be suited for military machine guns or semiautomatic rifles, the straight blow-back principle was applied to the Springfield rifle in the production of the Pedersen device, described elsewhere in this volume. This remarkable weapon was an automatic bolt for the Springfield rifle, enabling the rifle to be converted in a few seconds into a semiautomatic gun capable of firing forty shots with one reloading and having detachable magazines so that after the forty shots were fired new magazines containing forty more cartridges could be attached almost instantly.

The application of the blow-back principle to the military rifle in this case was made possible by the fact that instead of using the full powered military cartridge, the device used a caliber .30 pistol cartridge of very much the same size and dimensions as the cartridge for the caliber .32 automatic pocket pistol but considerably more powerful. The device was in reality nothing more or less than an automatic

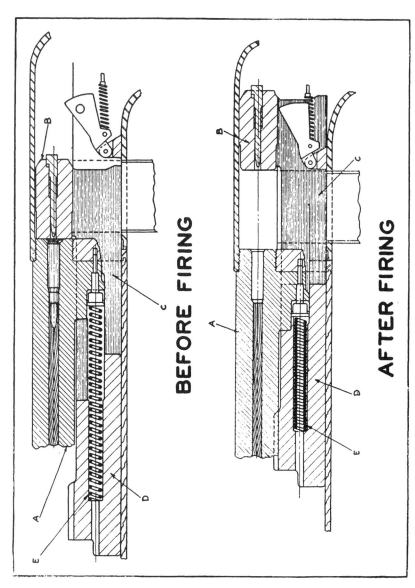

BEFORE FIRING

AFTER FIRING

Fig. 1. Diagram of straight blow-back breech closure principle as used in the Winchester self-loading rifle.

pistol specially shaped so that it could be attached in the breech of the rifle in place of the regular bolt. The additional power of the cartridge was taken care of by a weight attached to the breech block of the device.

Fig. 1 is a diagram showing the principle of the Winchester self-loading rifle, the most powerful blow-back gun. In order to handle the powerful cartridge used in this rifle, the breech block must have a considerable amount of weight, which is provided by attaching to it a large bar of iron which lies inside the hollow wooden forearm under the barrel. The weight of this large piece of metal lying inside the forearm of the gun, gives a rather curious balance to these self-loading rifles, but aside from this they are very satisfactory guns.

Referring to Fig. 1, B is the breech block proper, but B, C, and D are all one piece of metal, as the sliding weight, D, lying inside the hollow wooden forearm of the gun is connected to the breech block, B, by the slotted section, C, which straddles the magazine well and the hammer. When the gun is fired the breech block slides to the rear, ejecting the empty cartridge case and at the same time compressing the return spring E. This return spring then forces the breech block forward again, feeding in a new cartridge from the magazine. The rearward motion of the breech block also serves to force the hammer down into the cocked position. The straight blow-back guns are the simplest of all automatic firearms as regards mechanism.

Submachine Guns

Submachine guns are called machine pistols by the Germans. They are weapons larger than a pistol and smaller than a rifle, intended to be fired from the shoulder or with two hands from the hip. They use high powered pistol cartridges, and can usually be fired either full or semi-automatically.

These weapons were much used during World War II, and there are numerous types in existence. They have one thing in common, and that is the fact they are built on the straight blow-back principle, with no locking mechanism for the breech, an exception being the early model Thompson which had a retarding wedge. This however was removed in later models.

It requires little or no ingenuity or engineering ability to build a submachine gun, and the existing models exhibit so few design features of interest that not much space will be given to them in this work.

There is just one outlet for really fine engineering in the field of submachine guns, and that is in simplifying the manufacturing processes as was done by Col. Studler in the U. S. M3 type.

"Blow-Forward" Mechanisms

We have seen above that some method must be provided to hold the breech block against the barrel when the gun is fired, because otherwise the pressure of the powder gas pushing back on the cartridge case would drive the breech block back away from the barrel and let the cartridge out while the explosion was going on. With the blow-back gun the breech block is allowed to move in this manner, but is made heavy enough so that the movement does not occur too quickly.

Instead of allowing the breech block to move back, it would be quite possible to attach the stock and all the frame-work of the gun firmly to the breech block and then allow the barrel to move forward when the gun is fired.

In 1917 an inventor appeared at Springfield Armory with a machine gun made to fire the Krag army cartridge, having the framework of the gun solidly fixed and the barrel loosely mounted so that it could move forward against the action of a spring when the gun was fired. This gun operated, but it was necessary to grease the cartridge case to prevent the front part of the case, expanded by the pressure, from sticking to the barrel as it moved forward.

While nothing came of this effort, it should be noted that several automatic pistols, notably the Schwarzlose and a model by Von Mannlicher have been constructed on this principle.

Retarded Blow-back Mechanism

We have mentioned above that with light cartridges giving low pressure it is quite possible to use what is known as the straight blow-back breech mechanism, which depends entirely on the weight of the breech block to keep it from opening too quickly. We also stated that with the full power army cartridge the breech block would have to weigh about twenty-seven pounds to prevent it from opening too soon if we depended on weight alone.

There are other things that we can depend on besides weight to retard a blow-back action. In a straight blow-back the cartridge merely pushes the breech block directly to the rear so that the full thrust is exerted in the direction of the motion. Instead of using extra weight to slow up the action, we can slow it up by arranging so that the thrust is working at a mechanical disadvantage; in other words, so that it takes more push to produce the same amount of motion or the same push to produce less motion.

If we arrange the breech block like the piston of a gas engine so that it is attached to a crank and connecting rod, it is quite obvious that if the crank and connecting rod are exactly on dead center the breech block will be prevented from moving, and all the force will be transmitted to the crank shaft. If the gun were made like this it would never operate at all. However, if it is made so that the crank, instead of being on dead center, is just slightly to one side or the other of it, then most of the thrust of the breech block will be transmitted to the crank shaft, or in this case, the pin supporting the connecting rod; but there will be a certain component of it that will tend to drive the crank pin around in a circle just as the explosion does in the cylinder of an automobile. If the crank is almost exactly on dead center when the explosion starts, so little of the force in the breech block is directly applicable at once to moving the crank away from dead center that the motion is retarded sufficiently to enable the explosion to be largely completed before the breech block moves away far. The further away the crank goes from dead center, however, the more power the breech block has to accelerate the motion.

The Schwarzlose machine gun is made on this principle of the retarded blow-back, with the crank and connecting rod attached to the breech block as described above. In addition, the breech block is made fairly heavy and there is a very strong spring behind it. All these elements combine together to retard the motion enough so that full powered military cartridges can be handled successfully, though the breech is not actually locked to the barrel.

The diagram of the Schwarzlose machine gun (Fig. 2) shows how the crank and connecting rod work.

There is one queer thing, however, that is common to almost all blow-back and retarded blow-back guns, and that is that there is a tendency to rupture the cartridges unless they are lubricated. This is because the moment the explosion occurs the thin front end of the cartridge case swells up from the internal pressure and tightly grips the walls of the chamber. Cartridge cases are made with a strong solid brass head and a thick wall near the rear end, but the wall tapers in thickness until the front end is quite thin so that it will expand under pressure of the explosion and seal the chamber against the escape of gas to the rear. When the gun is fired the thin front section expands as intended and tightly grips the walls of the chamber, while the thick rear portion does not expand enough to produce serious friction. The same pressure that operates to expand the walls of the case laterally, also pushes back with the force of fifty thousand pounds to the square inch on the head of the cartridge, and the whole cartridge being made of elastic brass stretches to the rear and, in effect, gives the breech block a sharp blow which starts it backward. The front end of the cartridge being tightly held by the friction against the walls of the chamber, and the rear end being free to move back in this manner under the internal pressure, either one of two things will happen. In the first case, the breech block and the head of the cartridge may continue to move back, tearing the cartridge in two and leaving the front end tightly stuck in the chamber;

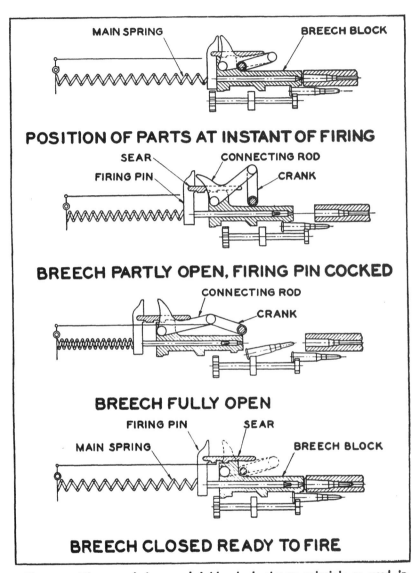

Figure 2. Diagram of the retarded blow-back closure principle as used in the Schwarzlose machine gun.

or, if the breech block is sufficiently retarded so that it does not allow a very violent backward motion, the result may simply be that the breech block moves back a short distance and the jerk of the extractor on the cartridge case stops it, and the gun will not operate.

However, this difficulty can be overcome entirely by lubricating the cartridges in some way. In the Schwarzlose machine gun there is a little pump installed in the mechanism which squirts a single drop of oil into the chamber each time the breech block goes back. In the Thompson Auto-Rifle there are oil-soaked pads in the magazine which contains the cartridge. In the Pedersen semiautomatic rifle the lubrication is taken care of by coating the cartridge with a light film of wax.

Pedersen Semiautomatic Rifle

About the year 1927 Mr. J. D. Pedersen perfected a semiautomatic rifle on the retarded blow-back principle, which rifle gave an especially satisfactory account of itself in trials. It also has a crank and connecting rod as does the Schwarzlose gun, but the mechanical arrangement is somewhat different. The operation of the Pedersen rifle is shown in Fig. 3. *A* is the breech block which is held against the head of the cartridge by the blocks *B* and *G* which are in line with each other and which transmit the thrust of the breech block to the heavy pin, *D*, which goes through the receiver. These three parts, *A*, *B* and *G*, form a toggle joint, and *C*, the point of contact between *B* and *G*, is just slightly above the line of thrust between the head of the cartridge case and the pin, *D*. Thus when there is a very heavy pressure on the front end of the breech block, *A*, there is tendency for the toggle joint to "break" and the piece, *B*–*G*, to move upward as shown in the cut marked "After Firing." If the point of contact at *C* were directly on the line of thrust, the toggle joint would remain locked and the breech would not open, but as this point, *C*, is just above the line of thrust the breech does fly open as soon as the pressure comes on the head of the bolt, but this opening is retarded because the two pieces, *B*–*G*, roll on each other in starting to open in such a manner that the contact point, *C*, continues for some little time to remain near the line of thrust. The shape of the rolling surface is worked out very skillfully in order to insure this result. As the breech opens the spring, *F*, is compressed and as soon as the motion is completed this spring causes the breech to close again.

However, like the Thompson gun, this mechanism starts to open while the high pressure is still on, and therefore it was necessary to lubricate the cartridges. Instead of lubricating them with oil, each cartridge was coated with a very thin film of hard wax which had a very high melting point, so that the cartridges would not pick up dirt when dropped as they would if oily or greasy.

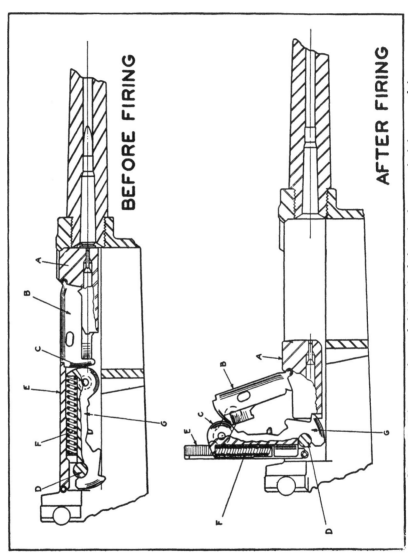

Figure 3. Diagram of retarded blow-back breech closure principle as used in the Pedersen semiautomatic rifle.

There was a good deal of talk about the disadvantage of "lubrication" in this gun; but after all, it seems that this disadvantage is more fancied than real, as the cartridges are not greasy or oily. Moreover, it has been found that corrosion is one of the greatest causes of season cracking in brass cartridge shells, and if this wax prevents the cartridge brass from corroding it may be quite possible that it would eliminate deterioration of cartridges from season cracking.

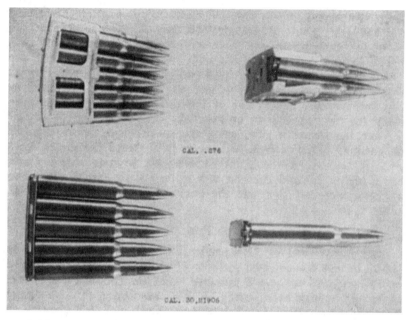

Pedersen .276 cartridges in his ten shot "en block" clip designed by him for his semiautomatic rifle. U. S. cal. .30 clip for comparison.

Up to that time, all the semi-automatic rifles submitted for test had been required to be of .30 caliber, adapted to use the service cartridge. Mr. Pedersen presented very convincing arguments to the effect that the .30 caliber cartridge was more powerful than was required for the shoulder rifle, and that to reduce the caliber to the ballistically ideal 7 mm or .276 would result in a number of advantages, to wit; saving in weight; saving in material, reduction of heating in rapid fire; ability of the soldier to have a larger number of cartridges available; etc.

The Army made an extended study of this question, including a series of firings at live animals with .256, .276, and .30 caliber bullets. It was found that the .256 was apparently the worst killer, on account of the fact that the bullet had less diameter, hence less gyrostatic stability, and would yaw badly upon impact, and make very lethal woulds. The .276 was found to be about as effective, and as it had certain advantages over the .256, its adoption was decided on for the new semi-automatic rifle that it was hoped would soon be adopted.

The cartridge selected had been designed by Mr. Pedersen with features making it especially suitable for automatic firearms, such as an increased taper for easy extraction. The ammunition was first made with a solid bronze bullet weighing 125 grains; later with a 126 grain jacketed boat tail bullet. The bullet diameter was .2845. The charge was about 30 grains of duPont IMR No. 25. At one time a small lot of this ammunition was made with flat base bullets.

The Pedersen gun was made with what is called the block clip. This is an arrangement whereby a packet of ten cartridges is shoved bodily into the magazine, clip and all. After firing ten shots, the clip automatically jumps out of the rifle and the bolt stays open, ready for the next clip to be inserted.

After the Pedersen rifle, using the special .276 caliber cartridge designed by Mr. Pedersen, had successfully passed the severe Army tests, it seemed on the point of adoption by our armed forces; but a high command decision was made not to change the caliber of the service cartridge, and the final action to adopt this gun was never taken.

Blish Principle

Some experiments by Commander Blish, U. S. Navy, retired, led him to believe that inclined surfaces which would slide on each other under light pressure would not slide when the pressure was heavier. He is said to have been started on this investigation through observing that when heavy naval guns were fired with full charges the breech remained locked, whereas when they were fired with light charges the breech had a tendency to unscrew by itself. Accordingly he took out U. S. Patent No. 1,131,319, dated March 9, 1915, covering the application of this principle to firearms and describing his findings in detail with elaborate diagrams.

Utilizing this theory, the Thompson Autorifle is constructed so that the breech block is locked to the barrel by a steep thread. The pitch of this thread is made just steep enough so that the gun will not unlock too quickly under the full pressure of the explosion. The supposition is that while the full pressure is on the breech block, adhesion of the threads on the breech block to the threads in the receiver will prevent any motion, but as soon as the pressure drops slightly this adhesion will no longer operate and the threads will then unscrew, allowing the breech block to open.

A diagram of this breech closure is shown in Fig. 4. The breech block, *B*, has steep threads, *D*, engaging the receiver, *C*. When the

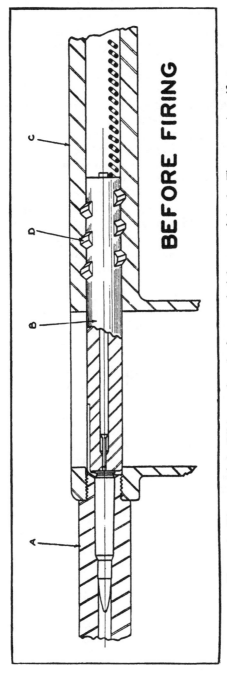

BEFORE FIRING

Figure 4.   Diagram of the Blish type breech closure principle as used in the Thompson Autorifle.

gun is fired the breech block unscrews from the pressure and opens against the action of the return spring which immediately shuts the breech block again and causes it to rotate into the locked position when the threads engage each other. The locking of the breech block is assisted by the action of a knob on the end of the bolt handle which adds a sort of flywheel effect to the motion of the bolt and thus assists in locking it securely.

There is no doubt that this mechanism can be made to operate as described, provided the cartridges are lubricated, but there has been some dispute among engineers as to whether or not the Blish principle really exists. Some of them claim that this is merely a retarded blow-back breech mechanism and that as soon as the pressure comes on the end of the bolt it starts to unscrew; but on account of the fact that the angle of the thread is so slow it takes a great deal of pressure to unscrew it, and for this reason the bullet is gone before the bolt has unscrewed enough to do any damage. That this type of mechanism actually opens while there is still considerable pressure in the cartridge case is evident from the fact that the gun does not operate satisfactorily unless the cartridges are lubricated.

Thompson Sub-Machine Gun

The Thompson sub-machine gun, utilized to fire pistol cartridges at a rapid rate from magazines holding 20, 30, 50 or 100 cartridges, was also constructed on the Blish theory, but instead of having a screwed breech block with a steep thread as does the Thompson Auto-rifle, it simply has the breech resting against a vertical sliding wedge held in its upper position by spring pressure. When the breech block is pushed backward a sloping surface on the rear end of the breech block resting on a similar surface of the wedge, cams the wedge downward as the breech block moves to the rear. This downward motion of the sliding wedge is supposed to retard the breech block in its rearward motion and thus assist in reliable functioning. Owing to the low pressure involved in the pistol cartridge, it is not necessary to lubricate the case.

Recoil Operated Guns

It has already been mentioned that the first machine gun, the Maxim, was recoil-operated, and that the barrel moved back about three-quarters of an inch. A gun in which the barrel moves only a short distance and the breech block moves through the rest of its travel from the momentum imparted to it by this motion of the barrel, is called a "short-recoil" gun.

There is another kind in which the barrel moves all the way to the rear along with the breech block and then leaves the breech block back in the rearward position while the barrel goes forward. This is called the "long-recoil" type.

Both of these will be described in turn, and as the simplest example of the short-recoil type of action we will take the Service automatic pistol shown in Fig. 5.

Colt Automatic Pistol

In this mechanism the barrel and breech are locked together, and when the gun is fired the recoil drives them both back at one time. However, it takes only about one-quarter of an inch of motion to unlock the breech block from the barrel and as soon as this one-quarter inch has been completed, the barrel strikes sharply against a stop and remains in position while the breech block continues on back through the momentum imparted to it by the one-quarter inch kick, coupled with a residual pressure that may remain in the case.

The action in detail is as follows: (Refer to Fig. 5)

Referring to the diagram marked "Before Firing," it will be observed that the barrel, A, is locked to the slide, B (which is in one piece with the breech block), by the locking shoulder, C, formed on top of the barrel and fitting into the recesses, D, in the slide. When the gun is fired the recoil pushes the slide and breech block, B, to the rear and as the slide is locked to the barrel, the barrel is also carried to the rear. However, the barrel is pivoted to the frame of the pistol by means of the link, E, and as the barrel continues its rearward motion, the top end of this link first moves backward in the arc of a circle and then downward around the lower pin as an axis. This motion swings the back end of the barrel downward, and disengages the locking shoulders in the slide, which continues to the rear, leaving the barrel in position with its bottom lug against the stop shoulder in the frame. This rearward motion of the slide throws out the empty cartridge and at the same time compresses the return spring, F, which immediately returns the slide to its forward position, at the same time feeding a new cartridge into the chamber from the magazine in the handle (not shown in the drawing). As the slide completes its forward motion, it strikes against the rear end of the barrel and as the barrel goes forward it swings upward through the action of the link, causing the locking shoulders, C, to engage in the recesses, D, in the slide.

Maxim and Browning Machine Guns

These two guns are also examples of the short-recoil type of mechanism, but in a much more refined form. As described above for the Colt pistol, the barrel goes back about one-quarter of an inch carrying the breech block with it and stops with a bang against the solid shoulder and lets the breech block go on to the rear by its own momentum. This will work with a low-powered cartridge like that used in the pistol, but even so the shock to the action of

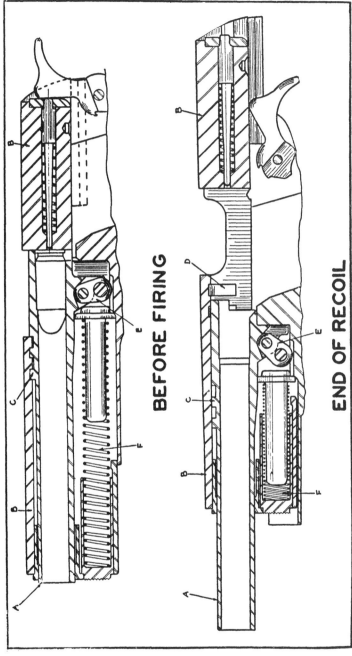

BEFORE FIRING

END OF RECOIL

Figure 5. Diagram of the short-recoil type breech closure principle as used in the Colt automatic pistol.

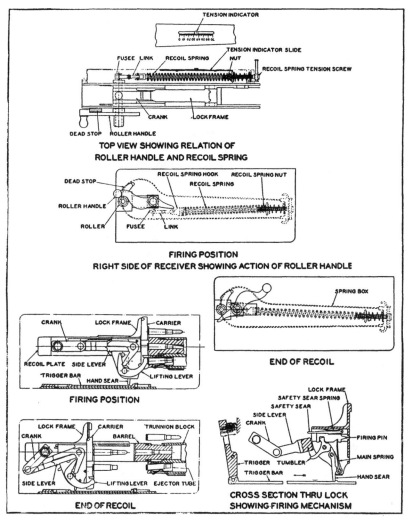

Figure 6. Diagram of the short-recoil type breech closure principle as used in the Maxim machine gun.

the gun is severe, and with a high powered cartridge it is necessary to resort to some device by which the barrel is gradually brought to a stop through transferring its energy to the breech block and then allowing it to be gradually absorbed through a fairly long travel of the breech block against the return spring.

In the Maxim machine gun (Fig. 6) the locking of the breech is accomplished by having the breech block (called in this gun the "lock") attached to the barrel extension (called in this gun the "recoil plates") through the medium of a crank and connecting rod (called in this gun the "slide lever") as was discussed under the subject of retarded blow-back guns. However, in the Maxim gun the crank is on dead center when the explosion comes, so that the lock cannot move back in relation to the barrel, and the thrust of the cartridge on the lock is transmitted through the side lever and crank to the crank axle and thence to the recoil plates through which the crank axle passes. Hence the barrel, lock and recoil plates all move back together as a unit, under the force of the recoil.

On the right-hand end of the crank axle is a handle with a convex shaped bottom, and this handle rests on a roller attached to the side of the gun. As the barrel, lock and recoil plates move back together, this handle, which is on the axis of the crank, also moves back, while the roller is fixed in position on the side of the gun. An examination of the figure will readily show that this backward motion of the roller handle against the roller causes it to rotate so that the back end of the handle moves upward. This rotation of the crank axle by means of the roller handle throws the crank and connecting lever off dead center and draws the lock away from the barrel. In other words, as soon as the roller encounters the cam on the roller handle, the action of the cam is to slow down the barrel and transfer its motion into an accelerated rearward motion of the breech block. However, as the rotation of the roller handle continues, the tail of the roller handle strikes on the roller and by the action of these two surfaces on each other the rotation of the roller handle is checked and the recoil plates are pushed forward, shoving the barrel to battery.

On the left-hand side of the gun there is a strong spring attached to the extension on the end of the crank axle. This recoil spring tends to do two things; first, to keep the barrel pulled into battery and resist any rearward motion, and second, to keep the roller handle rotated so that the lock is in the closed position. As soon, therefore, as the barrel has been returned to battery by the reaction of the tail of the roller handle against the roller, assisted by the pull of the recoil spring, a further pull of the spring rotates the handle back into the original position, and closes the breech of the gun, putting the lock back in the firing position. This action can be very easily understood from the diagrams.

However, the drawing does not show the method of feeding the cartridges into the gun. They are supplied in a fabric belt and there is a feed crank operated by the recoil of the barrel which advances a fresh cartridge into position each time the barrel moves to the rear.

The Browning gun accomplishes the same thing in a somewhat different manner. In this gun the barrel moves to the rear about five-eighths of an inch. There is a frame screwed onto the back end of the barrel. This frame is called the barrel extension, and the heavy breech bolt is locked to this frame through the medium of a

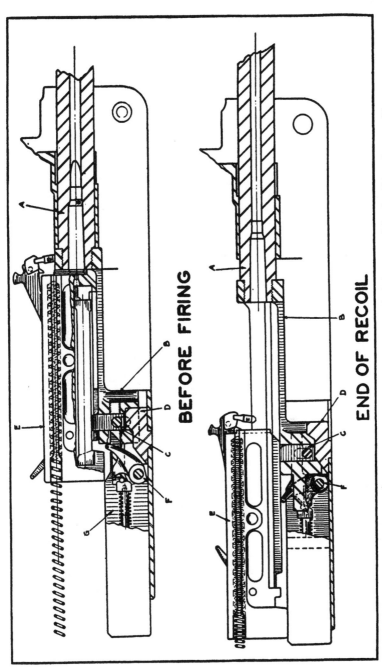

Figure 7. Diagram of short recoil type breech closure principle as used in the Browning machine gun.

vertical sliding bolt, called the breech lock, which is actuated by a cam on the bottom of the gun. Thus when the barrel and barrel extension are in the forward position, the bolt is locked securely to the barrel extension. However, when the barrel recoils about one-half inch the breech lock cam is drawn down out of engagement with the bolt and the bolt is entirely free from the barrel and barrel extension. As the barrel continues its backward motion it strikes against the convex side of a curved lever, the point of which rests against the breech block. The continued motion of the barrel to the rear swings this lever backward in such a manner as to separate the breech block from the barrel; in other words, to slow up the barrel and speed up the breech block, throwing it forcibly from the barrel and at the same time extracting the cartridge case. Of course the breech block already had a rearward motion imparted to it while the barrel was recoiling, but this motion is increased or accelerated by the action of the curved lever which is accordingly called an accelerator.

The mechanism of this gun, which is shown in Fig. 7, will now be described in detail. The barrel, A, is screwed into the barrel extension, B, which extends to the rear for several inches and carries in a slot in its rear end the vertical sliding breech lock, C. In the closed position the breech lock cam, D, in the bottom of the gun, holds the breech lock up so that its top end engages in a slot in the bolt, E, and locks it to the barrel extension.

When the gun is fired, the barrel, A, recoils about five-eighths of an inch carrying with it the barrel extension, B, the breech lock, C, and the breech bolt, E, all locked together. However, as the parts move to the rear the breech lock moves off the high surface on the breech lock cam and a transverse pin through the breech lock strikes a slanting surface on the lock frame, G, which forces the breech lock down out of engagement with the breech block.

Just under the breech bolt there is an accelerator, F, pivoted on a horizontal axis. As the barrel extension, B, moves to the rear it swings this accelerator backward and the point of the accelerator catches in a notch in the bolt and throws the bolt forcibly to the rear, compressing the return spring which immediately returns the bolt to its forward position.

While the bolt is in the rearward position, the barrel extension and lock frame are fastened together by the accelerator in such a position that the barrel cannot move forward. However, when the bolt goes forward far enough to strike the accelerator, it disengages the barrel extension from the lock frame and allows the barrel and barrel extension to move forward with the bolt as it completes its motion. The forward motion of the barrel extension carries along with it the breech lock which rides up the sloped surface of the breech lock cam and again locks the bolt to the extension ready for firing.

The backward motion of the bolt extracts the empty cartridge case and the forward motion feeds a new one in. The top of the bolt has a cam slot in it which actuates the lever which feeds the belt of cartridges in, the width of one cartridge each time the bolt moves to the rear.

Long-Recoil Type

The long-recoil type of automatic mechanism, in which the barrel and breech bolt, locked together, recoil for several inches, and then the breech bolt is held back while the barrel goes forward, is used for the Remington auto-loading rifle, the Remington, Winchester and Browning automatic shotguns, and the Chauchat machine rifle.

In a typical gun of this type there are two return springs, one to return the barrel and a separate one to return the breech block. The breech block being locked to the barrel when the cartridge is fired, the pressure on the head of the breech block drives it three or four inches to the rear until it is arrested by striking a stop provided for this purpose. The barrel being locked to the breech block, also goes to the rear and this rearward motion compresses both the breech block return spring and the barrel return spring. When the breech block has reached the limit of its rearward motion, it is caught and held in that position by a latch. The barrel return spring then pushes the barrel forward and the lock on the breech block is so constructed that when the breech block is held and the barrel is pulled forward, the bolt will unlock itself from the barrel and allow the barrel to go forward. As the barrel goes forward, the empty cartridge, held to the breech block by the extractor, is ejected. As the barrel reaches its forward position, it strikes a lever which drops the latch and allows the breech block to come forward, feeding in a new cartridge.

Remington Auto-Loading Rifle

The action of this type of breech closure can be followed in detail by reference to Fig. 8 showing the Remington auto-loading rifle. The barrel, A, is supported in a barrel jacket, B, and is held forward by the coil spring, I, surrounding the barrel. The breech block, E, has a turning bolt head, D, arranged to be rotated by the action of two pins, F, working in cam slots cut in the sides of the bolt head, D.

This bolt head is arranged to lock in the barrel extension, D, by the action of the pins, F, in the cam slots, turning the bolt head. There is a separate return spring, G, for holding the breech block in the forward position.

When the gun is fired, the parts recoil into the extreme rearward position, as shown in the figure marked "End of Recoil." At this point the breech block is locked in its rearward position by the latch, H, and the barrel then starts forward under the impulse of the barrel return spring, I. As the barrel moves forward it draws with it the bolt head, D, but this forward motion of the bolt head causes the pins, F,

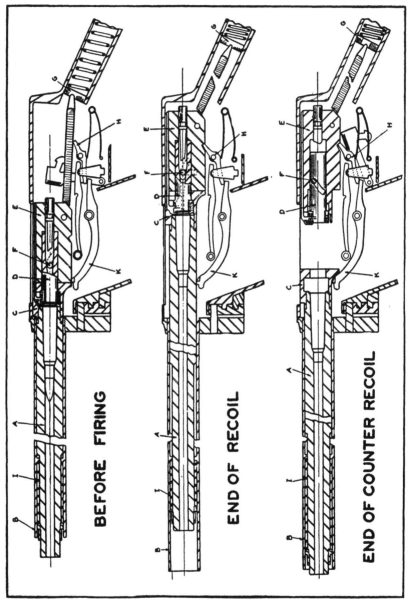

BEFORE FIRING

END OF RECOIL

END OF COUNTER RECOIL

Figure 8. Diagram of the long-recoil type breech closure principle as used in the Remington autoloading rifle.

to act in the cam slots so as to turn the bolt head and release it entirely from the barrel. As the barrel continues forward it leaves the empty cartridge case held by the extractor and when the barrel is entirely off the cartridge case a spring ejector in the bolt head kicks the cartridge out of the gun. At this moment the parts have reached the position marked "End of Counter-recoil" and the curved surface on the bottom of the barrel at the rear end strikes against the lever, K, which in turn disengages the latch, H, allowing the breech block to be pushed forward again by the spring, G. As the breech block goes forward it feeds a new cartridge into the barrel from the magazine (not shown). As the bolt approaches its forward position, the bolt head, D, enters the recess, C, in the barrel and then a further motion of the bolt causes the pins, F, to act on the cam slots in the bolt head in such manner as to turn the bolt head and lock it to the barrel so that the gun is again ready for firing.

Gas-Operated Type

While the original machine gun was built on the recoil-operated principle and while nearly all automatic pistols are made on that principle, the gas-operated system has also been a great favorite, especially with inventors of semiautomatic shoulder rifles, as it does away with the necessity for mounting the barrel so that it can slide, which is a great complication in making a rifle.

One of the earliest successful machine guns, the Colt, invented by Mr. Browning in 1889, was gas-operated. The Hotchkiss gun, invented about the same time, was also gas-operated, and both of these guns have been used extensively ever since. During World War I the Colt gun was modified somewhat by the Marlin Arms Corporation, of New Haven, though the breech mechanism remained the same in principle, as did the construction of most of the parts.

A light form of the Hotchkiss, known as the Benet-Mercié, was adopted as the standard of the U. S. Army in 1909 and remained standard until 1916. This also was a gas-operated gun.

Then at the beginning of the World War, Mr. Browning submitted a model of what he called a light machine gun built on the gas-operated principle. This gun, afterward known as the Browning Automatic Rifle, was adopted and many thousands of them were used during the World Wars I and II. While it is called an automatic rifle, the reader should clearly distinguish between this type of automatic rifle which is really a light machine gun, and the semiautomatic rifle which is a self-loading shoulder rifle to take the place of the Springfield. Bear in mind that the "automatic rifle" and the "machine rifle" are really light machine guns.

While the recoil-operated principle as embodied in the Maxim, Vickers and Browning guns was more widely used than any other, the gas-operated type as exemplified in the Colt, the Hotchkiss and

the Marlin machine guns and the Browning, Bren and other auto
matic rifles, have been a close second in popularity.

As mentioned above, the gas-operated system has been the favorite
for semiautomatic shoulder rifles, but while a great many guns have
been produced which operate on this principle, none of them prior
to the Garand attained any lasting popularity or wide use. Among
the more prominent early ones may be mentioned the Mondragon,
adopted by the Mexican Government in 1911 but never very extensively used; the "Standard" automatic shoulder rifle manufactured
about 1915 as a sporting rifle, and the St. Etienne semiautomatic
shoulder rifle used to a limited extent by the French during the
first World War.

In the conventional gas-operated system there is a hole drilled in
the barrel, and some of the gas of the explosion passes through this
hole and acts on a piston driving it to the rear with sufficient force
to unlock and open the breech. One of the great troubles with rifles
of this kind has been the fact that it is difficult to control this gas
under extremely high pressure so as to prevent it from operating
too quickly. In the Army tests of the 1930's an inventor named
White submitted a gas-operated shoulder rifle in which the front
end of the gas piston is hollow and the gas port is bored not
only through the barrel and through the gas cylinder, but through
the walls of this hollow piston so that as soon as the piston starts
to move the gas port is cut off after the manner of the slide valve
in a steam engine. Thus gas can go into the hollow piston only
before it starts its motion; as soon as it begins to move the gas
supply is shut off and the gas which is already in the piston is supposed to act by expansion, therefore producing a less violent action
than would otherwise occur. So reasons the inventor. However, other
designers state that inasmuch as the gas pressure in the barrel lasts
only about a thousandth of a second, it makes no difference whether
this cut-off action is used or not.

Another inventor who attempted to get away from the brusque
action of the gas is Mr. Hudson, who invented a machine gun in
which he used the gas to compress a spring which then operates
the mechanism.

In order to give the reader an opportunity to study the mechanical
action of the gas-operated breech closure in detail, three different
examples of this type of mechanism will be illustrated with drawings
and descriptions. The guns chosen for illustrations are the modified
Colt, known as the Marlin, the Browning automatic rifle and the
Garand semiautomatic rifle.

Marlin Machine Gun

The mechanism of the Marlin machine gun, shown in Fig 9,
operates as follows: The barrel, *A*, has a gas port, *D*, drilled in it

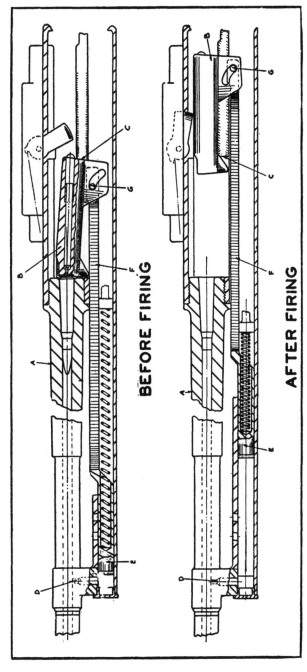

BEFORE FIRING

AFTER FIRING

Figure 9. Diagram of the gas-operated type breech closure principle as used in the Marlin machine gun.

at some distance from the muzzle. This gas port communicates with a gas cylinder lying under the barrel containing a piston held in its forward position by a spring. This piston is attached to the bolt, B, through a connecting rod, F, which is fastened to a pin, G, riding in a cam slot in a wing on the bottom of the bolt. When the piston is forward the bolt is forward and the rear end of the bolt is drawn down by the action of the pin, G, in the cam slot, until the back surface of the bolt rests against the locking shoulder, C, cut in the receiver. When the gun is fired the cartridge is held firmly in place by the bolt, which is locked in position against the shoulder, C. After the bullet passes the gas port, D, near the muzzle of the barrel, some of the gas rushes into the gas cylinder and impinges on the head of the piston, D, driving it violently to the rear, together with its connecting rod, F, and the pin, G, which is in the slot in the bolt. As the pin, G, goes to the rear, the first action is to press on the top of the cam slot and raise the bolt up out of engagement with the shoulder, C, after which the bolt is carried to the rear as shown in the cut marked "After Firing." This rearward motion of the bolt ejects the empty cartridge. The compressed return spring immediately causes the piston to move forward, carrying the bolt with it, until the shoulder, C, is reached, when the action of the pin, G, in the cam slot again locks the bolt down behind this shoulder and the gun is ready for firing once more.

Browning Automatic Rifle

The operation of the Browning automatic rifle is shown in Fig. 10. In this gun the barrel, A, has a gas port, B, and there is a piston, C, lying in the gas cylinder under the barrel. This piston connects with the bolt, G, by means of the connecting rod, D. However, instead of being connected to the bolt by means of a pin in a cam slot, the connection in this case is by means of a linkage consisting of the bolt link, E, and the bolt lock, F. In the firing position the bolt lock, F, presses against the shoulder, H, in the top of the receiver and this holds the bolt firmly in position against the head of the cartridge. When the gas impinges on the end of the piston, C, and drives it to the rear, the bolt link, E, draws the bolt lock down out of engagement with the shoulder, H, and then draws the bolt to the rear, as shown in the cut, "After Firing."

Garand Semiautomatic Rifle

The principle of the Garand rifle is shown in Fig. 11, which illustrates the gas take-off used in the first examples of this gun. These early Garands, instead of having a conventional gas port drilled in the barrel, had a muzzle cap, B, screwed on to the end. After the bullet had left the rifled portion of the barrel, some gas went down

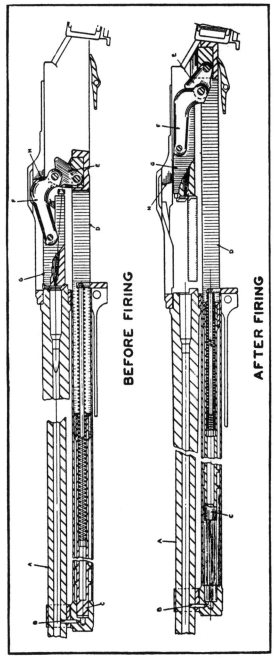

BEFORE FIRING

AFTER FIRING

Figure 10. Diagram of gas-operated type breech closure principle as used in the Browning automatic rifle.

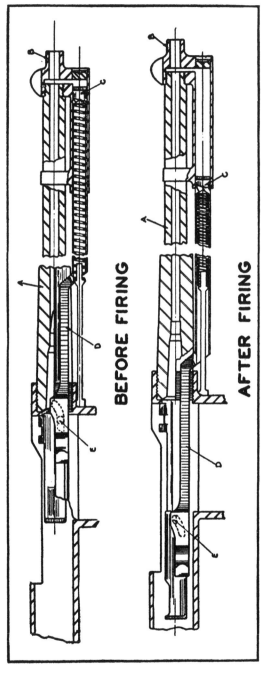

Figure 11. Diagram of gas-operated type breech closure principle as used in the Garand semiautomatic rifle.

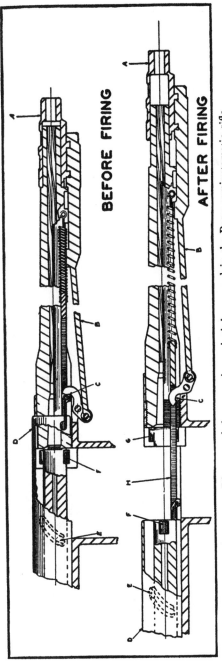

Figure 12. Diagram of the operating principle as used in the Bang semiautomatic rifle.

between this muzzle cap and the end of the barrel, to strike on the piston, C, driving it to the rear, together with the operating rod, D, which works the bolt through a cam slot and a lug, E.

The bolt is of the ordinary rotating type, locked to the receiver by locking lugs engaging in suitable recesses. As the piston goes back, the cam slot, working on the lug, E, first rotates the bolt, then carries it to the rear.

As soon as the rearward motion is completed, the return spring pushes the operating rod forward, closing the bolt and rotating it into the locked position.

This muzzle cap arrangement was soon abandoned in favor of a convential gas port drilled near the muzzle. Otherwise the principle of the gun remains the same.

Bang Principle

In 1911 Soren H. Bang, of the Danish Recoil Rifle Syndicate, presented a semiautomatic shoulder rifle to the United States Government for test, and this rifle functioned exceptionally well. The principle on which it operated is shown in Fig. 12.

The barrel had a sliding cap, A, fitting over the muzzle. When the bullet passed out, some of the gas acting in the space between this cap and the end of the barrel, pulled the cap forward as shown in the figure marked "After Firing." The cap, A, was fastened to a connecting rod, B, which operated a lever, C. This lever in turn acted against a sliding breech cover, D, having in it a cam-cut acting with a lug, E, on the bolt. In the position of rest, the bolt is locked to the barrel by the locking lugs, F, in the locking recess, G. When the gun is fired, the gas escaping from the muzzle pulls the muzzle piece, A, forward, thus causing the lever, C, to throw the sliding breech cover, D, quickly to the rear. As this cover goes to the rear, the cam slot acting on the lug, E, turns the bolt so as to unlock it and then carries the bolt to the rear along with the breech cover. There is a return spring under the barrel which is connected to the breech cover through a rod, H. As soon as the rearward motion is arrested, the spring pulls the breech cover forward again and when the forward motion of the bolt is completed the cam slot in the cover acting on the lug, E, again locks the bolt to the rear end of the barrel.

Primer Actuated Type

Among the many novel ideas for operating a semiautomatic rifle, is the scheme for allowing the primer to move enough in the cartridge case to unlock the breech mechanism. If the head of the cartridge were supported around the edge only, leaving the primer free, the primer would move back under the pressure of the gas when the gun is fired, and if it were allowed enough freedom it would be blown entirely out of the cartridge case. However, it is possible to control this motion and allow the primer to move back just a few hundredths of an inch, utilizing this short but powerful motion to impart energy enough to the moving actuator to cause it to unlock the breech.

Garand's Invention

In the first World War, John C. Garand, a machine designer living in New York, began working on the design of a light machine gun to be operated by the set-back of the primer in its pocket. The primer was to be allowed to move back slightly, and in so doing, it was to transmit this motion through the firing pin to an actuator which would open the breech and extract the empty cartridge, after which the gun would be reloaded by the action of a spring which had been compressed during the first motion. The United States Bureau of Standards at Washington being anxious to aid the war effort, employed Mr. Garand and provided him with facilities to work on the invention.

When the gun was examined by the Ordnance Department in 1919, it was seen to be exceptionally well designed, and was considered to have such promise that Mr. Garand was hired and sent to Springfield Armory, where he has remained as an Ordnance Engineer ever since.

Early models of Mr. Garand's gun worked well in tests, but just about the time he had his second and much improved model nearly perfected and ready for adoption, the type of powder was changed from the old fast burning pyro to the progressive burning Improved Military Rifle power, in which the first rise in pressure was not nearly so rapid.

Mr. Garand was much disappointed when his mechanism, which up to now had done so well, failed to function reliably with the new type of powder. He thereupon dropped the primer actuated system and switched over to the gas operated type of gun for his future work along this line which eventually resulted in the production of the present U. S. Rifle Cal. .30 M 1.

In spite of the fact that this rifle is not now being used, a description of the mechanism is included here because the novelty of this principle makes it interesting to any student of firearms.

Referring to Fig. 13, A is the barrel screwed onto the receiver, B. C is the breech block containing inside of it a moving actuator, G, arranged to have motion imparted to it by a slight motion of the firing pin, F. When the gun is fired the firing pin moves back about three-hundredths of an inch. This motion is very quick and imparts a considerable blow to the actuator, G, which travels rapidly to the rear.

The bolt up to this time has been locked to the receiver, by the locking block, D, bearing on the shoulder, E. As the actuator goes

Garand's first semiautomatic rifle, a primer actuated model built at Springfield in 1920. It used the service .30 caliber cartridge.

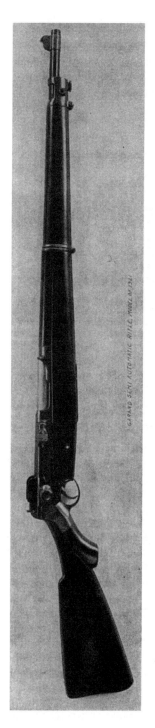

GARAND SEMI-AUTOMATIC RIFLE MODEL M1921

Garand's second primer actuated .30 caliber model, produced at Springfield Armory in 1921. It did not use a turning bolt, as did the first model. The bolt, which moves back and forth in a straight line, was locked by a piece of steel hinged at its rear end, and fitted to be lifted or depressed by the motion of an actuator inside the breech block. When the gun was fired, the primer was allowed to move back .035 inch, and this motion, transmitted through the firing pin to the actuator, operated the gun.

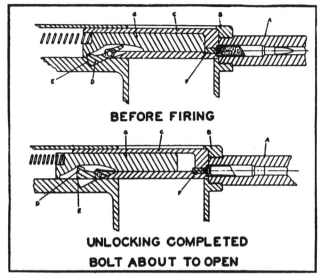

BEFORE FIRING

UNLOCKING COMPLETED
BOLT ABOUT TO OPEN

Figure 13.   Diagram of primer-actuated type breech closure principle
used in an early experimental Garand semiautomatic rifle.

to the rear the cam surface lifts this locking block out of engagement
with the receiver and the bolt then moves to the rear with the actuator against the action of the return spring, which causes the parts
to move forward again as soon as the rearward motion is completed.

Caliber .22 Machine Gun

While most of the principal methods of operating machine guns
and semiautomatic rifles have been described above, one can never
be sure when an inventor will come in with something entirely
new and different. For example some time ago a desire was expressed by the Army for some means of shooting caliber .22 cartridges in a machine gun. It was desired to do this for two reasons;
first, because it was thought that by using the very cheap and in-
expensive caliber .22 cartridges for machine gun practice in time
of peace, a great deal of training could be obtained without expend-
ing the expensive full powered cartridges and, consequently, much
money would be saved; and in addition, it was desired to find some
safe method of allowing troops to obtain antiaircraft practice with
machine guns, which in most military posts cannot be accomplished
with full powered cartridges because the great power and range of the
Army cartridge makes it dangerous to fire at high elevation.

At first glance it seemed very difficult to construct a machine gun
that would work with the low powered caliber .22 cartridge, but a
young mechanic, David M. Williams, of Godwin, North Carolina,
appeared in the Ordnance Office and offered, not to make a special

machine gun for .22's, but to take a heavy Browning gun and operate its massive mechanism with the .22 cartridge. This feat appeared so absolutely impossible that the arms experts had not even given it any consideration, but when this young inventor outlined his proposed method of doing the job he was given the order to proceed. In six weeks he modified a Browning machine gun so that it operated in a normal manner with the caliber .22 cartridges with never a malfunction. The Browning gun is a recoil-operated gun and the caliber .22 cartridge does not have a fraction of the recoil power to operate this gun, but Mr. Williams accomplished his job by making the chamber of the gun in a separate piece from the barrel, somewhat in the same way as the cylinder of the revolver is separate from the barrel. The separate chamber, however, instead of being outside the barrel is in the form of a hollow piston fitting into the rear end of the barrel. When the gun is fired the gas of the explosion gets into the space between the face of the chamber and the rear end of the barrel, and the pressure of the gas is sufficient to force the separate chamber backward with more than enough recoil to operate almost any mechanism.

The Colt Service Model Ace .22 Caliber Pistol

This is another well known adaptation of the Williams Floating Chamber. It is a replica of the Army .45 Pistol, M. 1911 A1, only it is made to shoot the ordinary .22 long rifle cartridge. Through the action of the floating chamber, the .22 caliber cartridge is given enough power to function the slide with enough energy to give a very good imitation of the recoil experienced with actual .45 caliber cartridges.

The utility of this gun is to give practice in handling the service sidearm, including rapid fire practice, without the expense of using the full powered loads. The action of this gun will be readily understood from the accompanying illustrations.

The Short Stroke Piston Principle

In 1940 the Winchester Repeating Arms Co. submitted for test a 9⅓ pound Cal. 30 semiautomatic rifle operating on the short stroke piston principle, patented by Mr. David M. Williams.

The gas is taken off near the breech, where the pressure is very high. The piston is completely housed in the cylinder, and is permitted to move through a stroke of only about a tenth of an inch. At the rear of its stroke, it acts as a valve, and prevents the gas from escaping from the gas cylinder except by going back into the barrel through the port by which it entered the gas cylinder.

The operating slide rests against the projecting end of the piston, which, under the impact of the gas, strikes the operating slide a sharp blow. Even the short piston stroke imparts to the operating

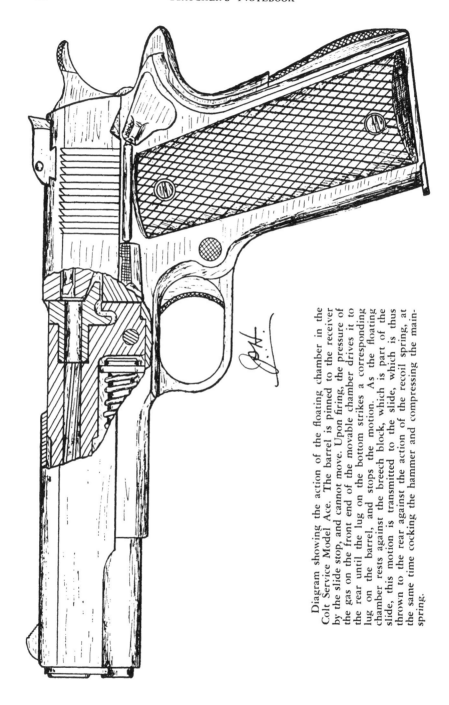

Diagram showing the action of the floating chamber in the Colt Service Model Ace. The barrel is pinned to the receiver by the slide stop, and cannot move. Upon firing, the pressure of the gas on the front end of the movable chamber drives it to the rear until the lug on the bottom strikes a corresponding lug on the barrel, and stops the motion. As the floating chamber rests against the breech block, which is part of the slide, this motion is transmitted to the slide, which is thus thrown to the rear against the action of the recoil spring, at the same time cocking the hammer and compressing the mainspring.

slide sufficient energy to cause it to carry through and operate the mechanism.

It is something like the action of a croquet ball held under the

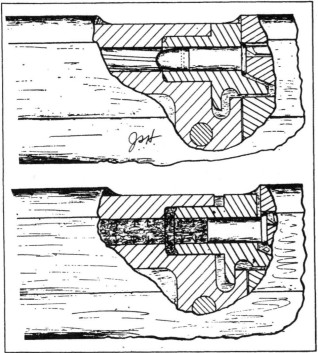

Action of the floating chamber in the Colt Service Model Ace.

Upper: Position of the parts at the instant of firing. The floating chamber with the cartridge, is held forward by the slide under pressure of the recoil spring. The barrel is held fast to the receiver and cannot move.

Lower: The gun has just been fired, and gas pressure (indicated by arrows) acts on the inside surface of the cartridge head and on the front face of the chamber to drive the chamber, cartridge case and slide to the rear. When the floating chamber has moved a short distance to the position shown, its motion is arrested by a lip on the bottom, which strikes a corresponding lip on the barrel. The momentum which the slide has acquired carries it on to the rear.

foot and struck a sharp blow with a mallet while another ball rests freely against the far side. The second ball will be driven swiftly away by the elastic impact.

This same principle was used in the Winchester Carbine which was adopted by the Army in 1941 as the U. S. Carbine Caliber .30, M 1.

This system has the great advantage of doing away with the long operating rod; moreover, the power of the gas impact on the piston is so great that there is little or no danger of having the piston stick from fouling or other cause. The gas impact slaps the piston to the rear 1/10 of an inch; then the operating slide, driven forward by the return spring, slaps it back again.

V

Notes on Machine Guns and Their Development

GUNS which are capable of delivering continuous fire as long as the trigger is held and while the ammunition supply holds out are in the main called machine guns, though there is another nomenclature used in our army for the very light fully automatic guns capable of being fired from the shoulder, which are called "automatic rifles," as distinguished from the semi-automatics which require a separate pull of the trigger for each shot.

The mechanical principles used to operate these automatic weapons will be described in the following chapter. Here we propose to set down a very brief history of the development of the machine gun, together with some information on the various types which have been or still are standard weapons of our army, as well as some information on the principal foreign types.

Machine guns as a class are not a very new invention, for some type of gun capable of firing more than one shot at a time has been the goal of inventors ever since the beginning of firearms history, and many inventions of this class were tried out in the days of muzzle loaders, and perhaps even before that, for it is said that there was a cross-bow used at the Battle of Hastings in 1066 A. D. which was capable of firing ten arrows at one time.

From the earliest days of firearms until the present time, the effort to increase the volume of fire obtainable from a single weapon has been continuous, and this has resulted in the production of an innumerable host of contrivances, most of which were merely curios but a few of which were useful.

In the era of the muzzle loader, the machine guns of that time usually took the form of a row of musket barrels mounted side by side in a frame like the pipes of an organ, and arranged so that they could be fired one at a time or all together. These contrivances were called "organ guns." In general they were not much of a success. In the first place they were heavy and clumsy to handle, but this was not their greatest disadvantage. That was the fact that after all the barrels had been fired in rapid succession, thus gaining quite a volume of fire for a short time, this period of usefulness was immediately followed by the long interval of inaction necessary to reload separately each of the muzzle-loading barrels.

A much improved gun of this general type, called the "Requa battery," was used in the late stages of the American Civil War.

The gun had a sliding breechblock which could be operated by a lever, and when the breechblock was opened the gun could be charged with special cartridges which were held in a long strip, behind which the breechblock was closed by the lever handle. Each cartridge had in the back end a hole which communicated with a vent in the breechblock. The vents were all connected together by a hole extending through the entire length of the breechblock and arranged to be filled with fine powder. In the middle of the breechblock was a regular percussion lock with a hammer, and a nipple for a cap. When this cap was fired the flame spread from the center toward each end of the breechblock, and the cartridges were ignited successively. The reloading could be done with reasonable rapidity as all that was necessary was to replace the strip of cartridges, place some powder in the communicating channels, cock the hammer, and place a new cap on the nipple.

Another old Civil War machine gun embodied the principle of the revolver. This gun used cap and ball ammunition which was loaded in steel containers, which served the double purpose of cartridges and explosion chambers, as the containers did not enter the barrel of the gun at all but during the explosion were held close behind the barrel but in line with it, like the chambers of a revolver.

To prepare the gun for action, a number of the containers were loaded with powder and ball and each was primed by placing a percussion cap on the nipple. The loaded containers were then placed in a hopper on top of the gun, and upon turning the crank the charges were fed down into grooves on the edge of a revolving cylinder which carried them past the breech end of the barrel, where they were successively fired, each empty container being rolled out on the far side of the breech as a fresh one was being fed up. This gun had only one barrel, which was consequently subject to overheating and excessive fouling from the residue of the black powder which was used in those days.

The Gatling Gun

The first really practical and successful machine gun was invented on November 4, 1862, by Dr. Richard J. Gatling. The Gatling gun was somewhat similar to the revolver gun described above, in that it used the same general type of steel cartridges which were fed from a hopper into grooves in a cylinder which was revolved by a crank on one side of the gun. At one point in the travel the charge was held firmly against the back end of the barrel by a cam mechanism, and fired as in the early revolver gun; but the Gatling gun differed importantly from the other gun in that instead of having only one barrel, it had six, one for each of the grooves in the feeding cylinder at the breech. These six barrels revolved with the cylinder so that each cartridge, after once entering the mechanism, remained

The Gatling gun.

in line with its respective barrel until it was fired and finally ejected from the gun. In this way each barrel was fired only once for each revolution, and the heating and fouling effects were greatly reduced. An additional advantage was the fact that hangfires were rendered comparatively harmless, as the cartridge was always in line with the barrel.

As this invention occurred during a war, the promoters found an easy way to demonstrate it by bringing the gun out on a battlefield, and firing at an actual enemy.

As soon as the self-contained metallic cartridges were invented, great improvements in the Gatling mechanism were made and the number of barrels was increased, usually to ten.

The Gatling gun was adopted by many nations and enjoyed a long period of popularity. It was really a most effective weapon and had some very good features. In our own service it was the standard machine gun as lately as during the Spanish-American War. In the Santiago campaign both automatic machine guns and the Gatlings were used side by side, and the Gatlings seemed to be the more effective at that time.

The Mitrailleuse

During the Civil War many experimental guns were tried, but as this was before the days of metallic cartridges, none were very successful and all were considered freaks or experiments, as indeed they were. As the Gatling came out near the end of the war, it passed practically unnoticed. After the war it gradually became popular, but before it reached this popularity the Franco-Prussian War occurred, and the French invented a machine gun called the "mitrailleuse," which created a great sensation at that time.

The word "mitrailleuse" comes from the French word *mitraille*, meaning small cannon balls or grape shot. The French now call all machine guns by this name, and they also call a machine gunner a *mitrailleur* (or grape shooter). The name originated, however, with the weapon which Napoleon III used against the Prussians in 1870. This consisted of 25 rifle barrels fastened together into a parallel bundle and encased so as to resemble a field gun. The breech of the gun could be opened to allow a block containing 25 cartridges to be inserted. Each of the holes in the block registered with one of the barrels. After the breech was closed, a turn of the handle released the 25 firing pins, one after the other, thus firing a volley of 25 shots, which could be made slow or fast according to the speed of the firing handle. The gun was capable of firing about 125 shots a minute.

The advent of brass cartridge cases had removed many difficulties attending the invention of machine guns, and the mitrailleuse was really a formidable weapon. This gun was adopted a year or two before the Franco-Prussian War, and its construction and operation were kept a deep secret. Though efforts were made to keep the actual details of the guns secret, their existence was widely heralded, and the French were told that they had a weapon which would make them invincible, and would render victory easy and sure.

The fame of this invention and the secrecy surrounding its actual use proved its undoing. The Prussians heard of the wonderful new gun, and from what they knew of the Gatling and other machine guns they were sure that they had a formidable antagonist. Therefore they set about with characteristic energy and strategy to compass its downfall, in which they were most successful. They realized that the French were well supplied with these weapons, and that what few machine guns they themselves could obtain would not be sufficient to counteract it. Accordingly, for the purpose of producing a moral effect, they scorned the Gatling and such other machine guns as they could have obtained, and fostered a contempt for all weapons of this class. At the same time, they carefully instructed the artillery to concentrate on the mitrailleuses whenever they appeared, and to insure their destruction at all costs.

In addition to this handicap, the mitrailleuses went into the war practically unknown to the army that was to use them. They were kept about as much a secret from the army as from the public, and the result was that the personnel was unfamiliar with the mechanism, and that no proper tactics had been worked out. When the guns were finally brought into action they were used as artillery, and not as infantry weapons, and the usual result was that they were quickly destroyed by the German artillery. In one or two instances they were used with effect, but in general they were a failure. The German strategic fiction that machine guns were useless soon came to be believed not only by the Germans themselves but by everyone else, and the adoption of machine guns by all nations was delayed for years by the fiasco of the mitrailleuse, the machine gun field for some years following being largely filled by the Gatling gun.

It will be observed by the reader that up to this time all the guns described were hand-operated guns, or guns in which the muscular power of the operator was used by means of a crank or lever to do the loading or unloading. For example, in the Gatling, one man put the cartridges into the gun while another man turned the crank continuously as long as he wanted the gun to shoot.

The Maxim Gun

It was inevitable that sooner or later some inventor would discover a way to make the gun fully automatic, that is, to utilize part of the force of the explosion for throwing out the empty shell, operating the mechanism of the gun, and putting in a new shell. This was accomplished in 1884 by Sir Hiram Stevens Maxim, who produced the first successful automatic gun; and today in nearly its original

A machine gun of 50 years ago. A very early model of the Maxim at the end of a 20,000 round endurance test at Springfield Armory. Firing was into a sand pile in the room in front of the gun. The cartridges are the rimmed type of .30 caliber used in the then new Krag Model of 1892. It is interesting to note that there is very little difference between this early machine gun and some that were used in World War II.

A group of World War I officers witnessing a demonstration of the Vickers machine gun, Model of 1916. Photo taken in May, 1917.

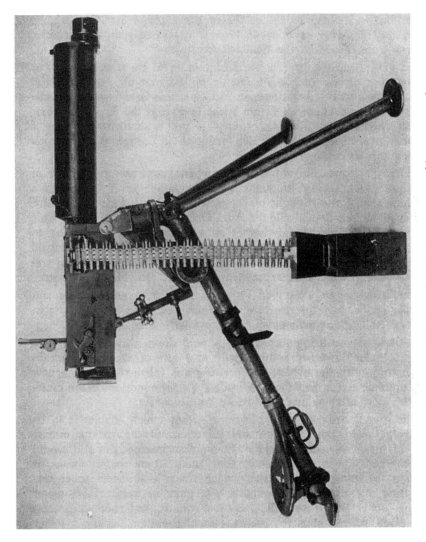

Maxim machine gun model of 1904. This heavy type machine gun was in use by our Army from the time of its adoption up until the beginning of World War I.

form it remains one of the leading machine guns of the world, though it is now known principally by the name of Vickers, from the firm which made it for so many years. This firm was first known as Vickers Sons & Maxim, but is now Vickers, Limited.

Maxim was an American, traveling in Europe at the time of this invention. In a letter to the editor of the *London Star*, in 1915, he gives the following account of how it happened that his inventive efforts were turned to the field of firearms:

"In 1881 I visited the Electrical Exhibition in Paris, and was made a Chevalier of the Legion of Honor on account of some electrical and chemical work I had done; and about a year later I was in Vienna where I met an American whom I had known in the States. He said: 'Hang your chemistry and electricity! If you wish to make a pile of money, invent something that will enable these Europeans to cut each other's throats with greater facility.'

"This made me think of the time when I was about 14 years of age and was making drawings for my father of a handworked machine gun. I also thought of the powerful kick I got the first time I fired a United States military rifle. On my return to Paris I made a very highly finished drawing of an automatic rifle. Happening to meet a Scotchman in Paris whom I had known in the States, I showed him my drawings. He invited me to come to London. I did so; and shortly after I started an experimental shop at 57d, Hatton Garden."

The Maxim gun, described on page 247, has a very simple and reliable action, and for many, many years has given extremely satisfactory functioning wherever it was properly used.

As long as the firing mechanism is held down this gun will continue to reload and fire automatically at a rate of about 450 rounds per minute until the belt of 250 cartridges is exhausted, when a new belt must be fed in and the gun loaded with the motion of the crank on the side, after which it is ready to fire again.

The gun is ordinarily fired from a tripod which enables it to be controlled for both elevation and direction. Owing to the intense heat of firing so many cartridges in rapid succession, the gun would become red hot in a very short time unless some special means of cooling were adopted. For this reason there is a water jacket surrounding the barrel, which holds 7½ pints of water. The water in the jacket begins to boil after 600 rounds, and then evaporates at the rate of 1½ pints for each thousand rounds.

The Vickers gun weighs 38 pounds, including the water in the jacket, and the tripod weighs 35 pounds.

In 1904 the heavy Maxim gun was adopted as standard for the United States Army, to be superseded in 1909 by the Benet-Mercié, which will be described later. In 1916 the Vickers gun, which was a lighter edition of the same type of mechanism as the Maxim, was adopted as the Army standard, and many Vickers guns were used during World War I.

The Colt Machine Gun

The invention of the Maxim machine gun was followed by the design of a gun by John Browing, of Ogden, Utah, which afterward became known as the Colt. Mr. Browning produced the first model of this gun in 1889.

In this connection, the following letter will be of interest as establishing the date when Mr. Browning made this invention.

Hartford, Conn.,
Dec. 20, 1917.

Capt. J. S. Hatcher,
Springfield Armory,
Springfield, Mass.

Sir:

In regard to our recent conversation, would say that the application for the first machine gun patent granted to my father was filed Jan. 6, 1890.

This arm was, more properly speaking, of the machine rifle class, weighing less than 12 pounds, and meant to be fired from the shoulder.

The mechanism was operated by means of a lever, or "flapper," which was pivoted near the forward end of the barrel; this lever being actuated by the gases at the muzzle. The gun took the .44 Winchester black powder cartridge, and fired at the rate of about 16 shots per second. A model of this gun was made early in the year 1889.

As far as I can learn, this was the first effort of my father's in the machine gun line, his time previous to this being taken up in designing the Winchester repeating and single shot firearms which are still on the market.

Thanking you for your courtesy extended to me at Springfield Armory, I am,

Respectfully,
V. A. Browning

About 1892, Mr. Browning brought an improved version of this invention to the Colt factory at Hartford, where it was perfected and put into production as the Colt Machine Gun, Model of 1895. This gun was adopted by the Navy, and then by the Army, and was used in the Spanish American war of 1898, along with a number of the old hand operated Gatlings.

This gun did not have a water jacket for cooling, as did the Maxim. Instead, it had the barrel made as heavy as practical, to enable a number of shots to be fired before the barrel would become too hot for operation. One disadvantage of this gun was that when the finger was removed from the trigger, the breech remained closed on a live cartridge. If a long burst of shots had been fired, the barrel would be so hot that the round thus left in the hot chamber would go off from the heat in a short time. The remedy was for the gunner to unload the gun at each interruption of fire.

One of the original Browning designed Model 1895 Colt machine guns in use during the Spanish American War of 1898 on board the U.S.S. Aileen.

The weight of the Colt gun was about 35 pounds, and it used a tripod weighing some 56 pounds. Like the Maxim and the Vickers, it was fed from belts holding 250 rounds. However, these belts were much simpler and cheaper to make than the ones used by Maxim type guns.

When World War I broke out in 1914, the Russians placed a large order for Colt guns with the Marlin-Rockwell Co., of New Haven, and when we entered that war in 1917, we purchased some 2500 of these Colt guns from Marlin. These were used during the early part of that war for training, then became obsolete as far as our army was concerned. No Colt guns of that type have been made since 1917. However, this gun, in a modified form known as the Marlin, saw very extensive service in both aircraft and tanks in 1918.

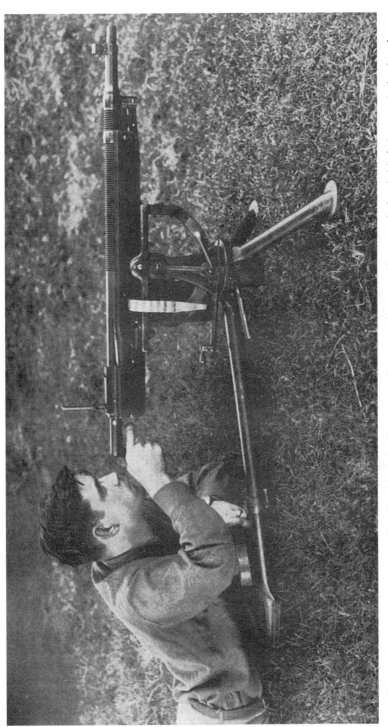

Colt machine gun, invented by Bowning in 1889. The gas passing through a port about six inches behind the muzzle impinged on a lever pivoted under the gun, swing it downward and backward to actuate the mechanism. The present author is shown firing one of these guns in 1917, when they were being made for the Russians by Marlin-Rockwell.

The Marlin Machine Gun

When we entered the first world war we were desperately in need of machine guns of any kind, but especially of a type that could be mounted on the aircraft of that day and synchronized so as to fire through the propellers without hitting them. The engineers of the Marlin Rockwell Co. therefore decided to attempt a conversion of the Colt gun to one that would be suitable for this purpose. The action is described on page 56.

The swinging lever under this gun, while it had the advantage of giving great smoothness of operation and exceptional reliability to the action, had the very obvious disadvantage of being quite in the way. Marlin therefore did away with this lever, and substituted a straight line piston. This became a very difficult feat of engineering indeed. The piston, instead of giving a slow and accelerating backward thrust through a connecting rod, was slapped back at maximum speed right at the beginning of its stroke, with the result that as often as not, it simply tore the heads off the cartridges instead of extracting them. One thing that was done to modify this action was to add a sizeable weight to the piston, which slowed up the initial rearward motion.

Another difficulty was that the final closing motion, which with the swinging lever, acting through a connecting rod, had been slow but powerful, now became a simple and terrific slam, which drove the cartridges in so fast that they were resized enough to make them too short for the chamber, and thus give the effect of excess headspace. To counteract this effect, the chamber was made 11 thousandths of an inch shorter than standard.

The work of making this redesign was done principally by Mr. A. W. Swebilius, who accomplished a most difficult task in a few weeks, and produced a gun that was used throughout the war as the principal synchronized gun of the U. S. air force, and was also used in tanks.

The Marlin Gun was discontinued at the end of World War I, and with its disappearance the old Browning Colt Machine Gun made its final bow.

The Hotchkiss Machine Gun

It was about the time that Mr. Browning was doing his first work on the Colt Machine Gun that an Austrian Army Officer, Baron Von Odkolek, also invented a gas operated gun. There was this difference, however; instead of using a swinging lever, he employed a simple reciprocating piston, and overcame his extraction difficulties, etc., by making the parts heavy and massive.

The heating problem was attacked by the use of very heavy barrels which would heat up slowly; moreover, the barrels were made so that they could be changed in an instant, even while hot. The danger of "cooking off" a cartridge in the hot barrel was overcome by so arranging the mechanism that when the trigger was released, the breech remained open, with no cartridge in the chamber.

Marlin tank machine gun of World War I shown mounted in a tank of that period. This was the Marlin aircraft gun fitted with a hand trigger and an aluminum radiator on the barrel.

Instead of feeding the cartridges from belts, as do the Maxim, Colt and Browning Guns, the Hotchkiss feeds them from steel or brass strips holding 30 cartridges each. The cartridges are held in place by spring fingers from which they are stripped by the breech block as it goes forward. When the gun is operated, these strips can be fed in one after the other without interrupting the firing.

The gun gets its name from the fact that the Odkolek invention was perfected and put into manufacture by Mr. Ben B. Hotchkiss, an American living in Paris. The Hotchkiss Company founded by him became one of the major factors among the armament makers of the world. The gun was adopted by the French Army in 1905, and has been used by them ever since. Hotchkiss machine guns of one model or another became the standard armament of many nations, and have been noted for their ruggedness and reliability.

The Marlin aircraft machine gun of World War I. This was developed from the old Browning designed Colt machine gun by Mr A. W. Swebilius of the Marlin Rockwell Co. The gun was used as a fixed aircraft machine gun synchronized to fire through the propellers. It is shown on the tripod merely for convenience in photographing.

During World War I, when we had almost no machine guns of our own, our early divisions in France were armed with the French Hotchkiss, Model of 1914, using the 8mm Lebel cartridge, and these guns gave a splendid account of themselves in action and were very popular with our troops. During World War II, the Standard Japanese heavy machine gun was a Hotchkiss called the Model 92 (1932). Model 92 refers to the year 2592 since the founding of the Japanese

The Hotchkiss machine gun; an old reliable performer of World War I, used by many of our divisions in France in 1918.

Empire, which occurred 1660 years before the beginning of the Christian Era; hence their year 2592 is our 1932. For a fuller explanation of the rather complicated system of model chronology used by the Japanese, see the note in Random Notes.

The Schwarzlose Machine Gun

A heavy machine gun which was prominent before and during World War I, and was even used to a considerable extent in the late war, was the Schwarzlose, Model 1907/1912, designed by the Austrian, Andrea Schwarzlose. It has a retarded blow-back mechanism which has already been described under "Mechanical Principles." It was adopted by Austria and several other countries, and was used very extensively during the war of 1914-1918. During that period the Italians captured a number of these guns from the Austrians,

Schwarzlose Machine Gun, M 1907/1912. This was the standard heavy machine gun of Austria-Hungary before and during World War I. It was also used by several other European nations. During World War II Italy used large numbers of these guns that they had captured from the Austrians during the previous World War

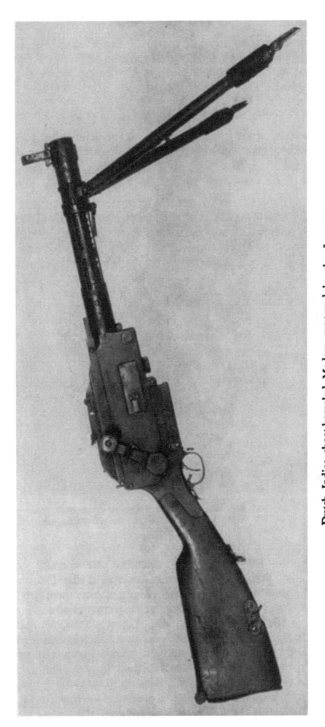

Dutch Indies short-barreled Madsen captured by the Japanese.

and these were used to some extent during World War II, and hence have again come into public notice.

The Madsen Machine Gun

About 1903 there appeared on the scene a machine gun which was very much lighter and more portable than any full automatic gun had been before that time, and which was really the first of the Machine Rifle class that became so popular during World War I.

Madsen Machine Gun. The photo was taken at Springfield Armory about 1908, at the time of the tests which resulted in the adoption of the Benet-Mercié Automatic Machine Rifle, Model of 1909.

This was the 21 pound recoil operated, air cooled, magazine fed Madsen gun, invented by Captain Madsen of the Danish Army.

The Madsen was tested in this county about 1909, but was passed over in favor of the Light Hotchkiss, tested at the same time, and adopted as the Automatic Machine Rifle Cal. .30, Model of 1909.

In spite of the fact that this gun was not successful in the U. S. Army trials, it was adopted and used with great success by several nations, including Denmark and Holland. It was used to some extent in Germany, and after World War I, it was for a time seriously considered by Great Britain as a successor to the Lewis, but finally gave way to the Bren, which was adopted instead.

The Benet-Mercié Gun

Our first standard machine gun of the automatic type, as compared to the hand operated type like the Gatling, was the Colt Automatic Machine Gun, Model of 1895. Note the word "Automatic" in the name. That was put in to distinguish this new type of gun from the simple "machine guns" like the Nordenfelt or the Gatling, which did not supply their own power.

Our second standard machine gun was the Maxim Automatic Machine Gun, Model of 1904. Both these were heavy guns, mounted on tripods. Our next standard machine gun was of an entirely different type, which today would be known as a light machine gun, but in those days was called a Machine Rifle. It was the light Hotchkiss, designed by Benet, son of an American Chief of Ordnance who had gone to Paris and become an engineer with Hotchkiss, in collaboration with another Hotchkiss engineer named Mercié. This gun was adopted by our Army in 1909 after extended trials, and was called the Automatic Machine Rifle, Caliber .30, Model of 1909.

Now if at that time we had known the least thing about the tactical role of machine guns, we would have realized that we ought to have had two kinds in the Army at the same time; the heavy type for one kind of action, and the light type, for a totally different use. We didn't, however, realize this or anything else much about these matters, so we adopted this light gun as THE machine gun of the Army. In those days every regiment had a machine gun platoon, made up by detailing men from regular companies for temporary duty in the machine gun platoon. This platoon had four guns. It wasn't a regular authorized company, but just a scraped together aggregation of the men who could best be spared from other places. Many times the temptation to get rid of unwanted problem children was solved by company commanders by sending them to the machine gun platoon. A pretty sorry outfit it was, as a rule.

When we had gone through all these trials and had finally settled on the gun we wanted, and had adopted it, we gave the Hotchkiss Company an order for twenty-nine of these guns. I repeat, *twenty-nine only* of these guns at a time when nations like Germany were buying thousands of machine guns. The reason was that the funds allowed the army in those days would pay for twenty-nine guns and no more, so we got twenty-nine.

Then we put the gun into manufacture at both the Colt's Patent Fire Arms Manufacturing Co., and at Springfield Armory, and in the next few years, we made a total of 670 of these Benet-Mercié guns. That many, divided between two factories was not enough for either of them to learn and overcome the usual production and heat treating difficulties.

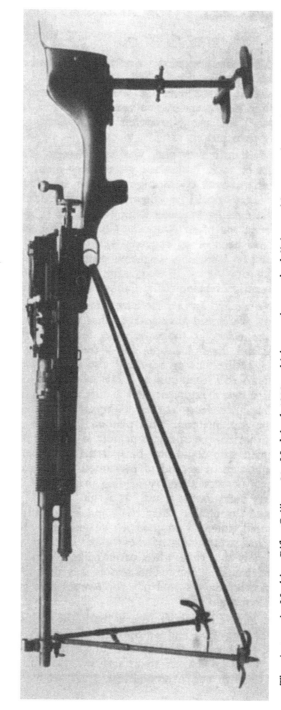

The Automatic Machine Rifle, Caliber .30, Model of 1909, which was the standard light machine gun of our Army at the beginning of World War I. This light Hotchkiss gun, known also as the Benet-Mercié, from the names of two Hotchkiss Company engineers who developed it, was superseded by the Browning Automatic Rifle.

This Benet-Mercié gun remained standard from 1909 until 1916, when the Vickers was adopted as a result of another set of tests and trials.

The Lewis Machine Gun.

Beginning in 1912, and at intervals thereafter the Army tested a machine gun invented by Col. I. N. Lewis, Coast Artillery, U. S. Army. This gun resembled the Hotchkiss in that it was gas operated, and employed a straight piston which was driven to the rear by a jet of gas from a port drilled in the barrel. The cartridge feed was from flat pan shaped magazines holding 47 shots each, or later, in the air-craft type, 97 shots. This was placed on top of the receiver, and was fed around and around like a cog wheel as the firing progressed.

The barrel of the gun was surrounded by an aluminum radiator, outside of which was a sheet steel casing something like a section of stove-pipe. This casing was open at the rear end, and at the front it extended past the muzzle of the gun so that the blast of gas from each shot had a tendency to create a draft of air through the steel casing over the aluminum radiator around the barrel, thus keeping the barrel reasonably cool as firing progressed.

In the first several tests of the Lewis gun, it failed to handle our powerful .30-'06 cartridge successfully, and while further develop-ment was under way, the world War I broke out in Europe. Lewis submitted his gun to the British, and with the relatively low powered .303 cartridge it made a much better performance than it did with our heavy high-pressure ammunition.

In England this gun was made by the Birmingham Small Arms Co., as the Model of 1915, and it was used with great effect by the British from that year until the end of World War I.

In this country a high pressure publicity campaign was started to force our Army to adopt this gun. Repeated tests, however, did not produce a Lewis gun that would satisfactorily shoot our ammunition.

In April, 1916, the Army held a formal test to select a new machine gun as a standard to replace the Benet-Mercié. The Lewis gun, made in this country for the British by the Savage Arms Company, was naturally a strong contender in these tests, and the proponents of this gun made the most of the reputation which this gun had made for itself in the British Service, and accused the U. S. Army of the worst kind of reactionary stupidity for allowing an American invention to go unappreciated at home, only to be adopted abroad. The fact that the gun had repeatedly failed in tests with our ammuni-tion was of course not mentioned, or was even denied.

In these April tests of 1916, a Lewis gun was submitted for the U. S. ammunition which finally put up a creditable performance and showed great promise of being capable of further development to handle our ammunition with complete satisfaction. In the test, this

Lewis Machine Gun, Model of 1917. This was the ground type Lewis gun which the Army and Navy purchased at the beginning of World War I. The Army bought 2500, and the Navy and Marines 9270. After this initial purchase the entire production of the factory was devoted to the Lewis Aircraft machine gun, of which the Army bought some 47,000.

new Lewis gun jammed 206 times, had 35 parts broken, and had 15 other parts which bent or got out of shape so that they had to be replaced. This was during the firing of the 20,000 shots which comprised the endurance test given machine guns in the usual Army trials.

In this test there was also the Vickers gun, which had no parts broken, and none that had to be replaced, and suffered only 23 jams as against 206 for the Lewis. Naturally this Vickers won the test over the Lewis, and was adopted as the Automatic Machine Gun, Caliber .30, Model of 1916.

In this same month of April, 1916, there occurred an incident that touched off a renewed and redoubled campaign of villification of the Ordnance Department and of the Army. The town of Columbus, in New Mexico, was raided by a bandit named Pancho Villa, and in this raid some civilians and soldiers were killed. It happened that this town was garrisoned by a cavalry troop and a machine gun platoon, and there were four Benet-Mercié guns available. The raid was in a way a miniature Pearl Harbor as far as the surprise element was concerned; there did not seem to be any reason to anticipate any such occurrence, and the little garrison was caught completely off guard.

The members of the machine gun platoon, routed from their beds in the middle of the night, hauled out their guns in the dark, hunted for the ammunition, and in some way got the guns to shooting.

The following is quoted from an article that I wrote for the Saturday Evening Post in the issue of Nov. 10, 1917 "The night was dark, and naturally some trouble was experienced with the guns. Occasional jams occurred; but in each case the trouble was overcome and the guns continued in the fight. At least two of the four guns were always in action. These guns were not always firing, though, as they frequently had to stop for lack of a suitable target.

To fire machine guns in the dark streets of a town without a well-defined target is to risk killing friend as well as foe.

There were many highly excited people present, however, and to these it no doubt seemed that all the guns should be firing, regardless of whether an enemy was in sight or not. Thus it happened that a report was started that the machine guns at Columbus had jammed, and the impression was created that they had not figured in the fight. This impression was false, for the machine guns were a decisive factor in saving the town; and in spite of occasional jams, they fired nearly 20,000 rounds of ammunition in the fight."

After this incident, General Pershing was sent on an expedition for the capture of Villa, and the Regular Army and the National Guard were mobilized along the Mexican Border. The old orphan machine gun platoon was done away with, and each regiment was given a machine gun company with four guns. The machine gun company thus had its own tables of organization, with officers, non-coms, etc.,

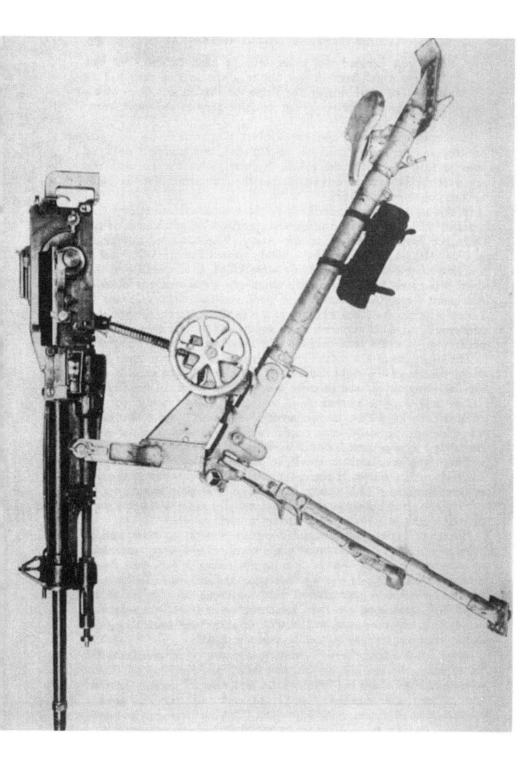

and the system of making the machine gun outfit a catch-all for undesirables came to an end.

The Ordnance Department, lacking enough guns to arm the newly organized companies for all the border regiments made an emergency purchase of 350 Lewis Machine Guns from the Savage Arms Co. These were for the .303 British ammunition, as the gun for our own high powered ammunition had not yet been perfected and put into production. We of course had to buy ammunition as well as guns, and Ford trucks were also bought to act as machine gun cars. Up to this time all machine guns had been packed on mules, so this was quite an innovation for that day.

The Ordnance Department, of course, had nothing to do with the training of soldiers in how to use the guns. The guns and ammunition were furnished by the Ordnance, together with handbooks on how to operate the guns, but the actual training of the combat troops was not an Ordnance function. This was done by the School of Musketry at Fort Sill. Unfortunately, there was never enough of an ammunition allowance to permit that organization to indulge in sufficient function firing to give the gunners familiarity with the mechanical operation of their weapons. The result was just the same as a flying school would have in training pilots without any gasoline. Much attention was given to the tactics, and to the theory of how to use the guns, but no one actually knew how to keep them firing.

General Crozier, the Chief of Ordnance, was a powerful and determined man, and he decided forthwith that the gunners should have training that would eliminate the talk of machine guns that jam, and that if the people who should give this training were not doing it, he would do it himself, whether they liked it or not. He therefore gave me instructions to accompany this shipment of 350 Lewis .303 Machine guns, and to go to each organization which was armed with this gun and teach them how to use the guns, and thus prevent the guns from getting an undeservedly bad name. It is rather ironical that the first gun whose reputation he thus undertook to guard was the Lewis, whose backers were already carrying on a publicity campaign to the effect that this gun was the only one that wouldn't jam.

After a lot of fine instruction and many spectacular demonstrations from the Lewis people on the virtues of their gun, I went from regiment to regiment along the border, giving intensive instruction in just how to get the best performance, and how to avoid trouble.

French St. Etienne machine gun of World War I. It is a gas operated air cooled machine gun, using the 30-shot Hotchkiss feed strips. It has several novel features such as the front sight with a compensating mechanism to change the sight elevation as the gun barrel heats up. The gas piston is blown forward instead of backward as is usual in guns of this kind.

The Moore centrifugal machine gun, set up for test at the U. S. Bureau of Standards at the time of World War I.

The grooved rotor was driven at high speed by a powerful electric motor. Steel ball bearings were fed into the center of rotor through the flexible pipe, and were delivered at a speed of about 1200 f.s. through the slot at left. The accuracy was extremely poor, but the inventor insisted that the gun would be useful in the trench warfare on the Western Front of 1918. The gun was not used.

In doing this I expended large quantities of ammunition, as I believed that the only way to learn how to shoot a gun is to shoot it. On this job I was accompanied by Col. John J. Dooley, of the National Guard, State of Maine, retired, who was employed as an expert by Savage Arms Co.

I had received intensive indoctrination on the Lewis, and everyone I saw praised it and condemned all the others, so that knowing nothing about the other guns, I was inclined to believe the propaganda that I had been reading about how bad the other guns were in comparison.

After all the 350 Lewis guns had been distributed, I was directed to set up a school and teach all machine gunners on the border, no matter what gun they had, how to use their guns. At Harlingen, Texas, near the mouth of the Rio Grande, there was a newly established Ordnance Depot commanded by Captain Everett S. Hughes, now Major General, Chief of Ordnance. Here I set up a school for instruction in the Colt, the Maxim, the Benet, and the Lewis.

I soon found, much to my surprise and chagrin, that every one of the other three was a far better and more reliable gun than the Lewis I had been praising so highly. The Lewis had some parts that broke and others that bent easily, and after a few hundred miles of being carried around in those Ford trucks, the gun was loose at the joints, the magazine rims were deformed so that they would skip shots, and the feed fingers that guided the cartridges in to the feedway would bend and cause jams; etc., etc. In short, it was just about impossible to keep these guns in firing condition. The other three were strong, rugged, well tempered, and would stay in shape indefinitely if not abused.

In the school everyone in the company, from Captain to cooks, had to learn how to keep the guns going under every kind of adverse condition. The course lasted two weeks; during the first part, the reason for every part and how it worked was explained, also what troubles could happen. Then everyone had days and days of actual firing. First the gun would be fired in good condition; afterward, a bad part would be put it, and the firer would be given ammunition, and when the gun misbehaved, he was given all the time he wanted to find out the trouble and fix it. It was amazing what a difference that two weeks would make in a company.

Typical is the case of a captain who wrote to the Chief of Ordnance telling him that his Benet-Mercié guns were utterly worthless, and asking to have them exchanged for the new Lewis gun. When he came in for his course, I told him that he could have his guns exchanged for any of the other three kinds, but that first he would have to take the two weeks course with all four kinds.

He was dissatisfied with this; wanted to change immediately. Said he had been using his guns four years, and had never been able to get more than two shots out of any gun without a jam. I said that we would make the exchange, but first I wanted him to fire each of his four guns 300 shots just to see how they worked. That really gave him a laugh. He assured me that no one could get any of his guns to shoot more than two shots.

His guns were placed on a table, and he was told to have his men gather around and pay close attention as we were going to explain the function of each piece. My assistants and I then took the guns to pieces, and explained just how each piece worked, but at the same time casually pointed out some defects. We would say, for example, "Now the firing pin must have a good rounded point, so that it will indent the primer properly without puncturing it. This firing pin has no point at all. Naturally the gun would not fire in that condition, so let's put in this new firing pin. On this other gun the actuator is badly bent—see, right here. That will keep the breech block from closing and of course the gun will not fire, let's replace that bent part with a new one." By the time the guns had been put together again, the bad parts had been replaced. Also, the Captain was doing a bit of thinking, no doubt.

We then had his own gunners load the gun, but two of them started to put the feed strips in wrong. There is a little trick to loading, if it is done wrong, the gun will fire just two shots and then jam. This is all explained in the instructions, but nobody had read them, it seems. So his gunners fired three hundred shots each, with no jams or trouble of any kind. The Captain said that he just wouldn't have believed it; he said he saw that there was a lot to learn about this business.

After he had completed his two weeks he was asked which of the three other makes of gun he wanted in exchange for his. He said "No one is going to get those guns away from me; they are the best guns in the world, and I'm going to sit right down and write to the Chief of Ordnance and tell him so." And he did: I saw the letter afterward in Washington.

During the nine months that this school ran, it trained one company a week; it was a two weeks course, but there were two companies present all the time, one taking the first week, of mechanical instruction, the other taking the second week, of actual firing. The men that were trained in this border school and one that I later ran at Sandy Hook for all the young regular Ordnance officers and at Springfield Armory for reserve officers and emergency officers became the key machine gun men in the entire Army during World War I.

This school kept going until the first of April, 1917, when war with Germany seemed imminent, and I received a telegram ordering me to Washington. War was declared on April 6, 1917, and among

The Berthier machine rifle submitted for test in 1917. It passed an excellent test, but was not adopted, as the Browning was then being put into production. The officer firing the gun is the present author.

my notes there is an old Ordnance Office memo sheet on which I have written; "War Declared; on hand 670 Benet, 282 Maxim, 143 Colt, 353 Lewis." Believe it or not, those figures represent all the machine guns this great nation owned when we went to war with Germany in 1917. None of the new Vickers had yet been delivered.

A little further down on that memo is the entry; "April 12; 1300 Lewis Guns Ordered." It seems that while all this border instruction

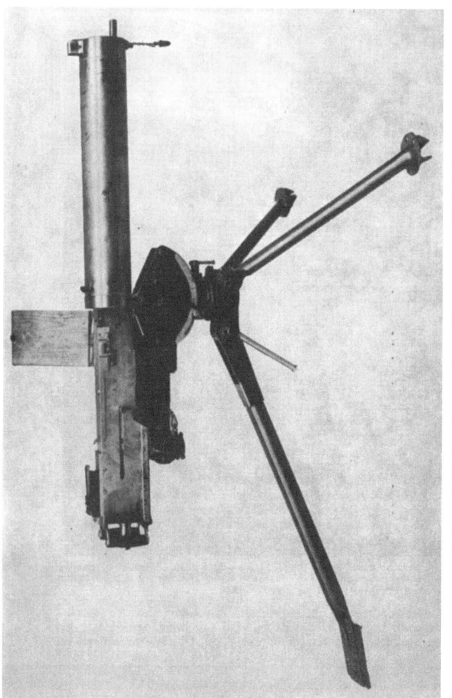

Early model of the Browning .50 caliber machine gun made by Colt in 1924.

The Browning .30 caliber water cooled machine gun.

had been going on, the Savage Arms Company had been perfecting the Lewis for our ammunition, and we ordered these 1300 without a formal trial. We really needed guns by then.

In May 1917, the War Department held a machine gun test before a board composed of Army officers, Navy officers, and civilians, called the United States Machine Gun Board. At this test the Lewis gave a good account of itself, and more were ordered by the Army to a total of 2500. The Navy and Marines got 9270. The Army then adopted a stripped and lightened version of the Lewis as the standard flexibly mounted gun for aircraft use, and purchased 47,000 of them. This Lewis Aircraft gun did not have the barrel jacket or the aluminum radiator.

The Browning Machine Gun

A gun which gave a sensational performance before this United States Machine Gun Board was a heavy water cooled gun submitted by Mr. John Browning, of Ogden, Utah. It was built on the recoil principle, with a very much simplified action. As it was much easier to manufacture than the then standard Vickers, none of which had yet been delivered, it was decided to concentrate on the simpler and more easily made Browning. The Colt Co. which was already getting into production on the Vickers, produced 9327 of the water cooled type, and 7502 of the aircraft model during the war, while Westinghouse and Remington produced 71,019 heavy Browning machine guns during World War I.

Like the Vickers, the Heavy Browning is water cooled and belt fed, but the belt is of much simpler and cheaper construction. In fact, it is exactly the same as Browning used on his Colt Machine Gun Model of 1895. The weight of the Heavy Browning is 36½ pounds with water in the jacket, and the tripod weighs 48 pounds. The rate of fire is about 550 shots per minute.

The Browning machine gun with water jacket removed and with the barrel made heavier and shorter was used for arming tanks, and was also adapted to ground use on a tripod as a light machine gun. Stripped of its water jacket it was used during World War I as a synchronized aircraft gun for fixed mounting on the aircraft of that day, firing through the propellers. Much improved and lightened after the war, and fitted with right and left hand feed, it became the standard .30 caliber aircraft machine gun.

A similar series of Browning guns was made up in .50 caliber. These are used for both aircraft and ground use, and have been widely copied all over the world, and were used not only by the U. S., but by many other nations during World War II.

Light Machine Guns

During the early part of the first World War, the Germans were armed only with the heavy Maxim machine gun, and had no light machine gun to compare with the British Lewis. These lighter guns could readily be carried forward with advancing troops, and after the men had attained an advanced position, they could lie flat with these guns, and produce bands of fire to stop a counter attack.

The Germans soon felt the need for such a gun, and produced a lightened version of the Maxim gun, known as the '08/15. This was simply a Maxim with a smaller water jacket, and mounted on a bipod support so that it could be used in the prone position, the same as the Lewis could. Feeding was from 100 round belts carried in small boxes arranged to attach to the side of the gun. This was a most effective weapon, and produced many casualties among our forces.

Toward the end of that war the Germans produced another light type of Maxim, called the '08/18, which was the same as the other, except that the water jacket was omitted entirely, and a perforated barrel supporting tube was substituted for it. Naturally the ability

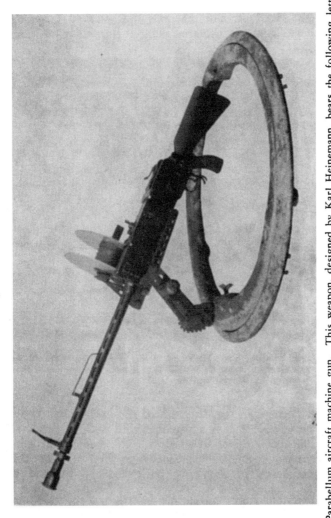

German Parabellum aircraft machine gun. This weapon, designed by Karl Heinemann, bears the following lettering on the left side, "S. M. Gew. Mod. Parabellum 1913. Berlin." It was used as a flexible machine gun in German World War I aircraft.

to produce sustained fire was less, as the barrel would heat up after
about a hundred rounds so that it was too hot to shoot.

This use of light guns by the British and Germans caused a need
for such a gun to be acutely felt by the French, and the result was
the development of a new gun called the "Chauchat," weighing only
about 25 pounds. With this gun a new type of machine gun firing
became much talked of, and that was the so-called "walking fire."
The gunner was supposed to carry the gun forward with him during

German Maxim machine gun, Model of 1908. It was the standard heavy machine gun of the German Army in World War I, and was used as a reserve and
home defense weapon in World War II.

his advance, point it in the direction of the enemy, and fire it from
the hip. The Chauchat was a machine rifle with a bipod, and was
of the "Long-recoil" type mechanism. The barrel and all of the
breech mechanism recoiled several inches to the rear inside the barrel
casing. These heavy parts moving backward and forward weighed
almost as much as the rest of the gun, and the result was a violent,
jerky motion of the gun when firing. The mechanism was crude,
but it was simple, and for this latter reason the guns could be made
in almost any fairly well equipped machine shop. Many thousands of
them were used, not only by the French but by the American Army
as well, those used by the Americans being chambered for our own
cartridge. This gun was much disliked as a crude makeshift, and was
discarded as soon as possible after the war.

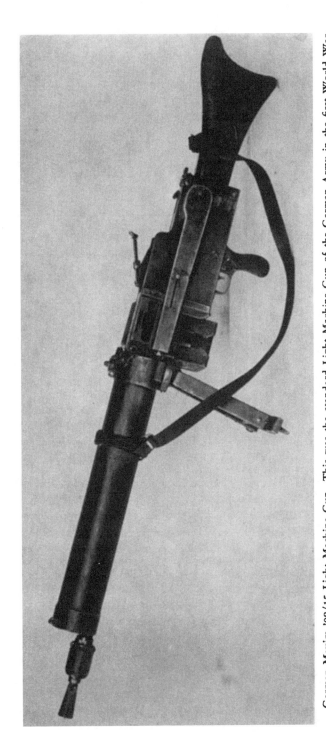

German Maxim '08/15 Light Machine Gun. This was the standard Light Machine Gun of the German Army in the first World War, and did enormous execution. It was continued in use as a standard gun by the Germans up to about 1936, and was used to a considerable extent as a substitute in World War II.

A German machine gun crew of World War I. This picture was found on the soldier at the right when he was captured in 1918.

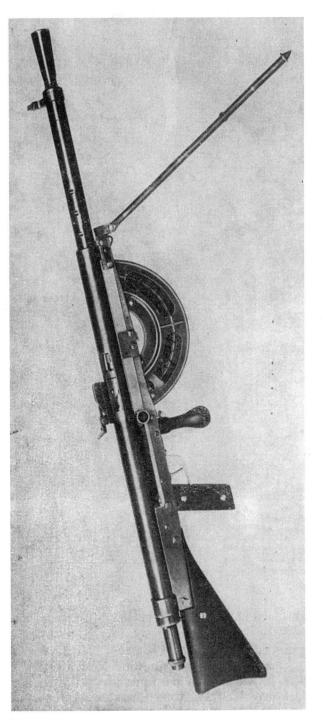

The French Chauchat machine rifle as used by the American Army in 1918. The gun shown was made for use with the 8 mm Lebel cartridge. The semi-circular magazine held 30 shots.

The Hotchkiss machine rifle submitted for test in 1917. It had in the mechanism a clockwork device like that in an electric toaster, to keep it from firing too fast. "Walking fire," shooting the gun from the hip, as shown, while advancing across the "No Man's Land" of the 1918 trench warfare was a favorite way of using the automatic weapons of that day.

The British incorrectly call this gun the "Chauchard."

The instruction pamphlets in French that accompanied the 8mm Chauchat guns that we used in 1918 spelled it "Chauchat". Col. Calvin Goddard, of the Historical section, Army War College, traced the word back to its origin from the name of Chauchat. The French call it Model 1915 C.S.R.G., from Chauchat, Suterre, Ribey Rolle and Gladiator, who developed this gun.

The Browning Automatic Rifle

Another gun that Mr. Browning submitted to the United States Machine Gun Board in May, 1917 was the Browning Automatic Rifle. This gun was so different in characteristics from the conventional Machine Gun or Machine Rifle of the day that it created a sensation when it was submitted to the Board. I was present, and well remember the excitement it produced.

It was the first weapon light enough to be fired from the shoulder and at the same time sufficiently heavy and rugged to permit fairly long bursts of full automatic fire. It was a 15 pound gun made on the lines of a large shoulder rifle. It was gas operated, and was fed from detachable box magazines holding 20 shots each. It could be arranged to deliver either full automatic fire or single shots at will, by changing the position of a lever on the side of the gun. It was well adapted for the marching fire in vogue during the trench warfare of those days, as well as for full automatic fire from the prone position, using any rest that might be available for the muzzle of the gun. The action is described on page 58.

This gun can be fired full automatic from the shoulder, but it requires practice to do this without losing control of the gun. When this is attempted by someone who does not know the trick, the rapid succession of recoils, coming at the rate of 450 a minute, will quickly throw the firer off his balance, and he will usually allow the muzzle to swing around to the right, or up into the air, or both. A serious tragedy was narrowly avoided at an early demonstration of this gun when an inexperienced person tried to fire it this way, and the muzzle swept rapidly toward the group of persons standing at the firer's side. It is really the surprise effect more than anything else that is responsible, for if the firer will just lean heavily into the rifle as he starts firing, this motion can be controlled.

This gun passed a magnificent test before the board, and was immediately adopted, and 85,277 of them were produced during the year and a half that elapsed before the end of that war. This gun, officially called the "Browning Automatic Rifle, Model of 1918," but more commonly known as the BAR, was the standard weapon of its type in our Army during World War II. The Germans called BAR's captured from Poland the Maschinengewehr 28(p), and those captured from Belgium the 127(b).

During the years since its adoption there have been several changes or modifications to this gun. The Browning Automatic Rifle, Cal. .30, M 1918 A1, which is limited standard at this writing, has a gas cylinder with spiked feet attached to the gas cylinder tube just forward of the forearm, and a hinged butt plate extension designed to rest on top the shoulder of the firer. The gas cylinder has been changed to have a larger diameter, and to incorporate a relief valve in the head. The forearm is shorter, and is cut away from the barrel.

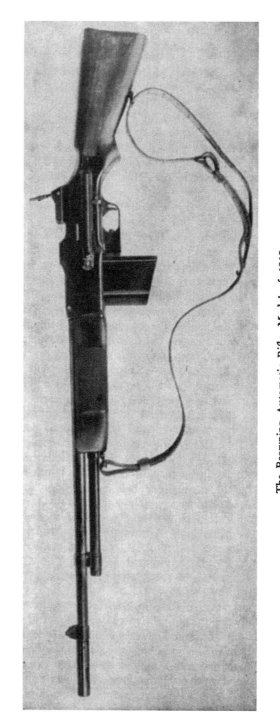

The Browning Automatic Rifle, Model of 1918.

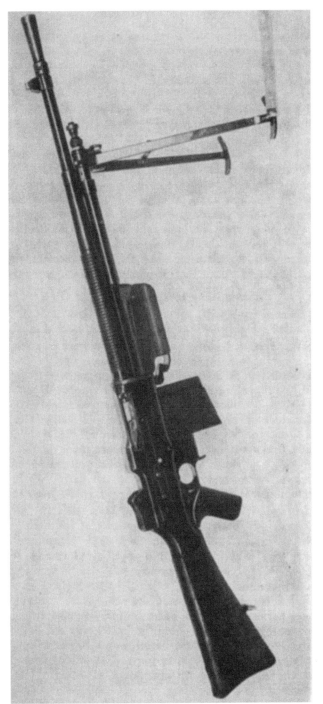

Browning machine rifle made by Fabrique Nationale, at Herstal, Liege, Belgium.

The M 1918 A2 has the forearm cut away even more, with a metal shield incorporated to protect the recoil spring from the heat. A bipod with skid type shoes is assembled to the flash hider and a stock rest is fitted into a recess in the buttstock. This model also has a device for slowing the rate of fire when desired. It also has a hinged butt plate extension, which is shorter than that on the A1. The rear sight has been changed to include click adjustments for both elevation and windage.

The Browning Machine Rifle, M 1922 has a bipod and a heavy flanged barrel. This modification of the B A R which was used for a time as a light machine gun has been superseded for this use by the Browning Machine Gun, M 1919 A4, and is now obsolete.

Those nations which do not use the B A R all use some other gun of similar characteristics. Examples of other guns on the same general principle or at least of similar dimensions and designed for the same tactical use are the British Bren, the French Chatellerault, the Japanese Year 99 Model, (M 1939), the Mexican Mendoza, and others.

General Observations on Machine Guns

It will be seen from what has been written above that machine guns can be divided roughly into two classes, water cooled and air cooled.

In the water cooled guns, whenever the trigger is released during firing, the mechanism stops with a live cartridge in the chamber. Most air cooled guns are made so that trigger is released, the gun stops with the breech open and the chamber empty. When the trigger is again pulled, it releases the mechanism, which closes, pushing in a fresh cartridge at the same time, and fires as it locks. The Hotchkiss Machine Gun, the Lewis, the Benet-Mercié, the Browning Automatic Rifle, and most other similar guns are made in this way. The reason for this is obvious. With an air-cooled gun the barrel gets very hot, and if a live cartridge were left in the barrel when the firing was interrupted it might explode in a few seconds from the heat.

At a lecture at Sandy Hook in the early part of 1917, after I had just previously been conducting a series of machine gun schools along the Mexican border, the fact was mentioned that the barrel of a gun would get red hot when fired extensively without stopping. An official who was present said that it was impossible to fire a gun that much without a jam. Accordingly a demonstration was arranged for a class of students who were studying machine guns, and I personally fired a Benet-Mercié machine rifle 1,000 shots without stopping. After 700 shots the barrel was red hot, and at the end of the thousand shots the barrel was a bright cherry red, and part of the receiver had begun to glow. The official who had started the argument was dancing up and down, shouting: "I see it but I don't believe it."

Of course, in practice a barrel is never fired enough to make it

Mexican Mendoza machine gun. This gas operated, air cooled light machine gun weighs about 20 pounds, and has the barrel arranged so that it may be changed almost instantly when hot.

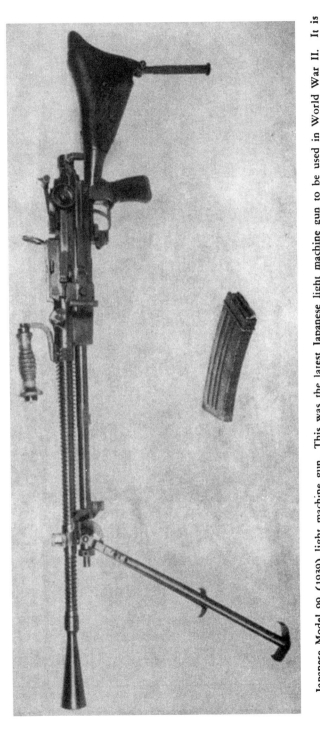

Japanese Model 99 (1939) light machine gun. This was the latest Japanese light machine gun to be used in World War II. It is gas operated, weighs about 20 pounds, and is simple and effective in design.

French 7.5 mm Chatellerault light machine gun Model 1924-29.

The author, protected by asbestos gloves, is removing the barrel from a Colt machine gun during World War I. These air-cooled guns heated up rapidly when fired, and a hot barrel could be replaced with a cool one as shown.

red hot, but several hundred shots will make the barrel of an air-cooled gun too hot for safety in case of a jam. In working with air-cooled guns some very exciting experiences will be had when a jam occurs with a very hot barrel and a cartridge stuck in the chamber, and with the breech partly open.

Once on the Mexican border I saw a student get a cartridge jammed in a hot gun with the breech partly open. He was looking right in it and I had visions of having the cartridge explode in his face, so I snatched him away from the gun and grabbed up a cleaning rod so as to knock the hot cartridge out before it had time to go off. The effort was just a little too late, however, for as I shoved the rod down the muzzle, the cartridge went off. This apparently happened just about the time the rod touched the bullet, for the bullet did not go out of the barrel. The cartridge case was blown to bits but no damage was done, as the breech, being open at the back, allowed the explosion to dissipate itself to a large extent. I knocked out the bullet and found that it was somewhat flattened where the point had rested against the cleaning rod. I still have this bullet and the remains of this cartridge case among my rather large collection of cartridge curios.

At the test of the Berthier machine rifle at Springfield Armory in 1917, a jam occurred, and when the handle of the gun was drawn back the hot cartridge was ejected but exploded in the air just in front of the group of men who were holding the gun. The bullet stuck in the cuff of one of the spectators.

Another time at Springfield Armory a cartridge exploded while I was extracting it from a hot Browning automatic rifle, but fortunately it was all the way out of the breech; and when a modern military rifle cartridge explodes in the open air it does not have much force, so no damage was done. Usually the explosion is just sufficient to tear open the cartridge case and send the bullet with very low velocity. Of course there is danger of getting pieces of brass blown into hands or eyes.

The greatest danger in a case like this is in having an explosion when the breech is jammed in a position very nearly closed. In this case the pressure is high and the explosion is violent, and some parts of the breech mechanism are likely to be blown out with sufficient force to do great damage. In this way, an extractor blew out of a Marlin gun and struck a soldier in the abdomen inflicting a wound from which he afterward died.

Submachine Guns or Machine Pistols

During World War I, the Germans introduced into actual and rather extensive use a type of machine gun which up to that time had been very little known, but which was very widely used in World War II. This is the machine pistol, or submachine gun, firing pistol ammunition, or in some cases, ammunition intermediate in

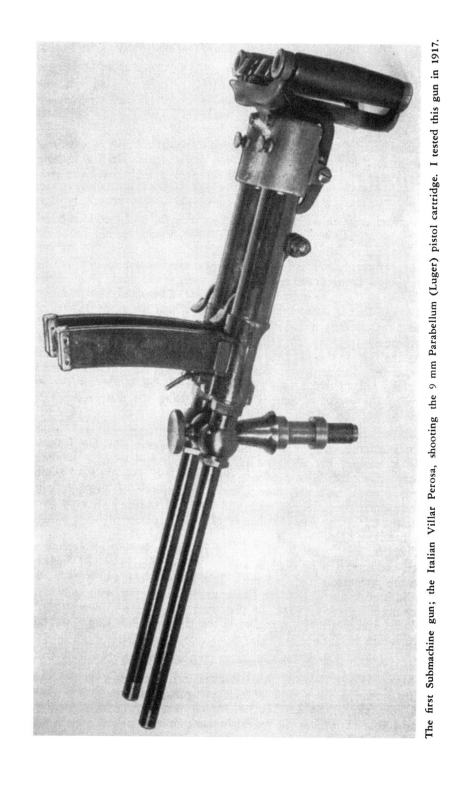

The first Submachine gun; the Italian Villar Perosa, shooting the 9 mm Parabellum (Luger) pistol cartridge. I tested this gun in 1917.

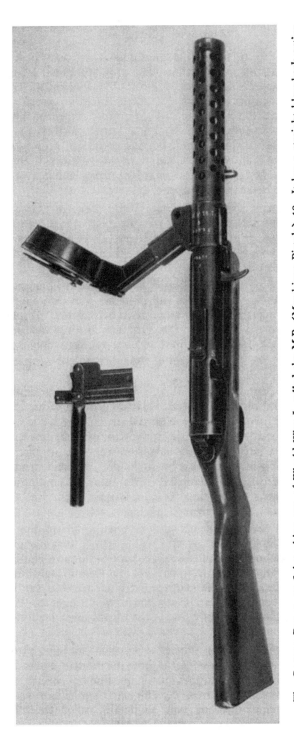

The German Bergmann Submachine gun of World War I, called the M.P. (Maschinen Pistole) 18. It has a straight blow-back action and shoots the 9 mm Luger pistol cartridge from a snail shaped magazine. The World War II submachine guns are no advance over this except in cheapness of manufacture due to their flimsy construction of tubing and stampings.

power between pistol and rifle ammunition. It was in 1917 that my first acquaintenance with submachine guns occurred in testing the Italian Villar Perosa gun, (sometimes called the Revelli). This was a two-barrelled weapon, shooting the 9 mm Luger pistol cartridge, and intended at that time to be used in arming airplanes. There were fifty cartridges in each of the two magazines, and on pressing the trigger, they were all fired in a little over a second, making the speed of the firing so rapid that the sound of the individual shots could not be distinguished at all. The sound of firing this gun was much like that of tearing a strip of canvas.

During the latter part of the first World War, the Germans used a number of submachine guns of a type called the Bergmann. This was straight blow-back gun used the Luger pistol ammunition from a so-called snail magazine, that is, one in which the cartridges lie in a spiral or snail shaped drum.

After the end of the first World War, General Thompson, a retired Army officer invented a submachine gun shooting the .45 automatic pistol cartridge. This weapon, known as the "Tommy Gun" became a favorite weapon of the gangsters during the prohibition era in the United States, and in this way received much publicity. It was adopted by the Army, and was a standard weapon during World War II.

Every nation that fought in World War II had some kind of submachine gun, and some had several varieties. Owing to the low power of the cartridge involved, these required no locking device, and they were therefore constructed on the straight blow-back principle. None of them showed any particular advance over the original German Bergmann of World War I, except in simpler magazine arrangements and cheapening of manufacture by the use of simple turned or stamped out parts. Examples are the British Sten, the Australian Austen and Owen, the German Schmeisser, etc.

Col. René R. Studler of our Army contributed to this field the U. S. Submachine gun Cal. .45 M3, which was a real advance in this category of weapons. It is characterized by the utmost simplicity and cheapness of manufacture. It is made so that by the substitution of a barrel and magazine together with some other parts, it can be almost instantaneously converted to shoot the 9 mm Luger or Parabellum ammunition almost universally used as the pistol cartridge by European nations.

In 1943, the Germans introduced a so-called machine pistol which was entirely out of the class of the guns mentioned above. It was in reality a full-automatic carbine, made to shoot a special shortened version of the standard German 7.9 rifle cartridge. There were several models of this gun, differing only in details, called the MP 43, the MP 43/1 and the MP 44.

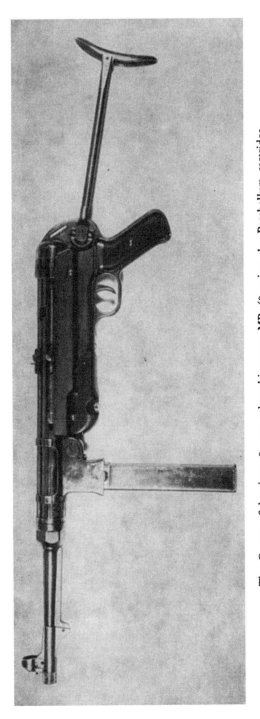

The German Schmeisser 9 mm submachine gun MP 40 using the Parabellum cartridge.

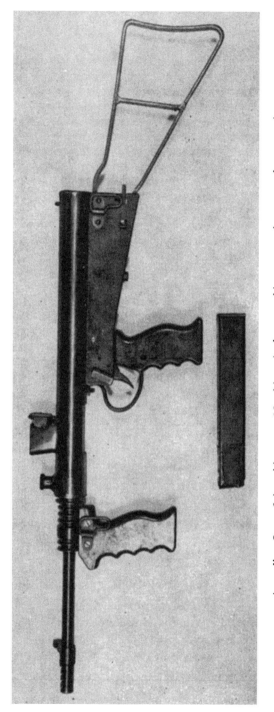

Australian Owen Submachine gun. Notable only for one thing: utter cheapness of construction.

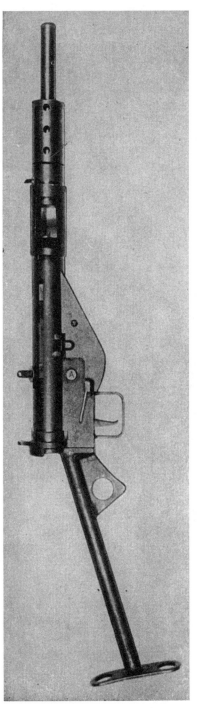

British Sten Submachine gun Mark II. Essentially this is the Bergmann of World War I cheapened as much as possible. Like the Bergmann, it uses the 9 mm Luger cartridge. On account of its utterly crude construction and its clumsiness it was usually called by our soldiers the "Stench" gun.

The Russian Sudiaev 7.62 mm machine pistol or submachine gun called PTS 1943.

German MP 44. This is a full automatic carbine shooting a shortened version of the 7.9 rifle cartridge. There were three variations of this weapon which differed only in unimportant details, called the MP 43, the MP 43/1, and the MP 44.

Machine Guns in World War II

During World War II, the standard American ground type heavy machine gun was the Browning in essentially the same form as that used in the first World War, and mounted on the same tripod. It is the Browning heavy belt fed water cooled machine gun, called the M 1917 A1, and the tripod is likewise the M 1917 A1. The only im-

Ammunition for the MP 43 and MP 44 (left) compared with the regular German rifle cartridge (right).

portant change in the gun from the original design is the strengthening of the water jacket end cap, and an improvement of the fastening of the water jacket to the trunnion block. The receiver is also reinforced. The general appearance and functioning of the gun remain identical.

The light machine gun, called the Browning Machine Gun M 1919 A4, on ground tripod M 2, is a modification of the Browning Tank Machine Gun used in World War I. This gun has the usual Browning mechanism, but instead of a water jacket, it has a perforated barrel jacket or support, and a rather heavy barrel. It is air cooled.

During the recent war, a whole series of .50 caliber Browning machine guns was employed. They were used in both the water jacketed and the air cooled varieties, for both aircraft and anti-aircraft, in combat vehicles and tanks, and for other uses. The varieties most used were: The Browning Machine Gun, Caliber .50, M 2, aircraft, basic; an air cooled, recoil operated, alternate feed gun, suited for any type of installation in aircraft.

The Browning Machine Gun, Caliber .50, water cooled, flexible,

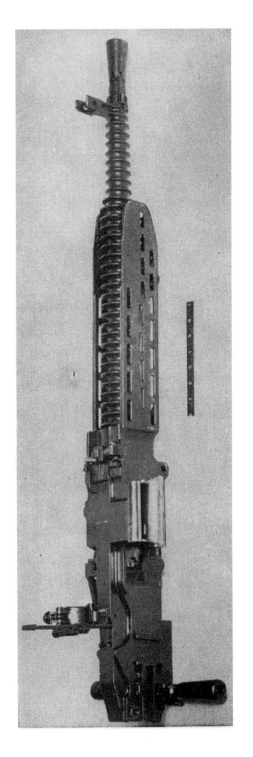

The Besa machine gun. This was a heavy air cooled gas operated gun used by the British and the Germans in armored vehicles. The one shown in this cut is the Czech version called ZB 53.

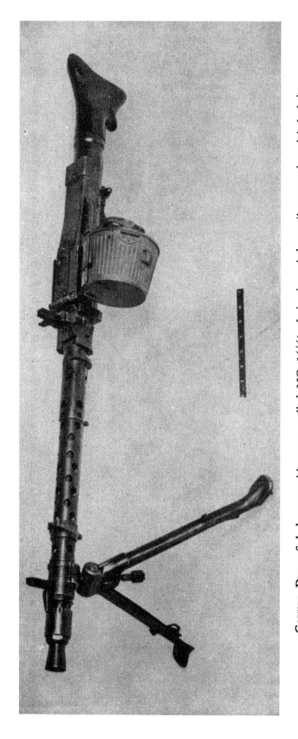

German Dreyse-Solothurn machine gun, called MG 34/41. It is air-cooled, recoil operated, and belt fed.

type; a recoil operated, water cooled, alternate feed gun. There is a water chest with a pump for supplying a circulation of water through the jacket. This permits firing long bursts without cooling. This gun was used extensively for anti-aircraft work.

The Browning Machine Gun, Cal. .50M2, HB, fixed type; an air cooled, recoil operated, alternate feed gun, adapted to fixed mounting in tanks or combat vehicles.

The Browning Machine Gun, Cal. .50, M 2, heavy barrel, flexible; the same as the fixed gun except that it has a spade-grip back plate assembly, and is fitted for flexible mounting in tanks, combat vehicles, or on the Machine Gun Tripod Mount, Cal. .50, M 3.

Most of the Allies of course used .50 caliber Brownings furnished by the United States. Great Britain used the Bren as the principal light machine gun, with the Vickers still taking the heavy machine gun role. For use in combat vehicles, they used the Besa, in 7.92 caliber, an almost exact copy of this gun as originally made in Czechoslovakia.

The Germans also used the Besa, though in slightly different form from that used by the British. As ground machine guns they used light recoil operated guns, very similar in general characteristics to the '08/18 Vickers of World War I, but with smaller and lighter breech mechanisms. These guns were air cooled and belt fed, and were developed from the Dreyse MG 13 of World War I. The earlier model was the MG 34. A later development and refinement of this model was the MG 42.

An amazing light full automatic and semi-automatic rifle using the full powered 7.9 German service ammunition is the Fallschirmjaeger Gewehr or FG 42/44, intended, as the name indicates, for use by parachute troops. With its folding bipod it weighs only 11 pounds. This gun is a clear indication of the future trend in light machine guns, and will well repay study by designers of automatic weapons.

The Russians used, besides their old Maxim Model of 1910, a new heavy air cooled belt fed machine gun called the Degtyarev, Model 1939. With its heavy flanged air cooled barrel, this gives much the appearance of a Hotchkiss. Another gun of the same general type and appearance is the Guryonov, Model of 1943.

In the field of light machine guns, the Russians had a 20 pound gas operated air cooled gun, fed from a flat pan magazine holding 47 shots, called the Degtyarev Model DT, which has been in service since 1926.

The Japanese used weapons of the Hotchkiss type as their principal heavy machine guns. They were called the Model 92 (1932) 6.5 mm machine gun, and the Model 01 (1941) 7.7 mm machine gun. Following the usual Hotchkiss principles, they were gas operated, air cooled and strip fed. They used the same 30 shot feed strips that we used in our old Benet-Mercié, that was standard in our Army

German Fallschirm Jaeger Gewehr 42, or F.G. 42, automatic rifle. Intended, as indicated by the name, for use by parachute troops. An extremely light weight gun of advanced design, weighing, complete with bipod, only a little over 11 pounds.

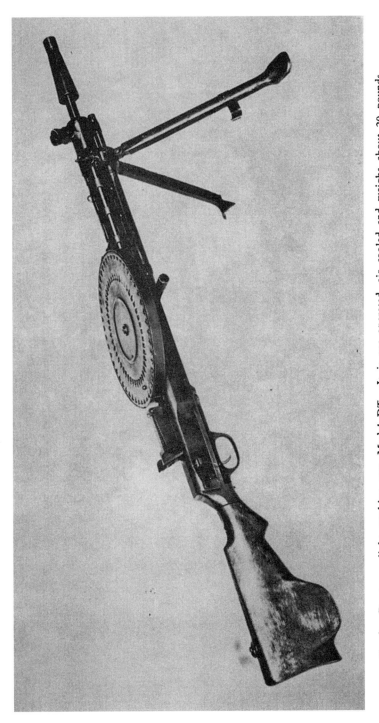

Russian Degtyarev light machine gun, Model DT. It is gas operated, air cooled and weighs about 20 pounds. In this photo the Flash Hider is reversed.

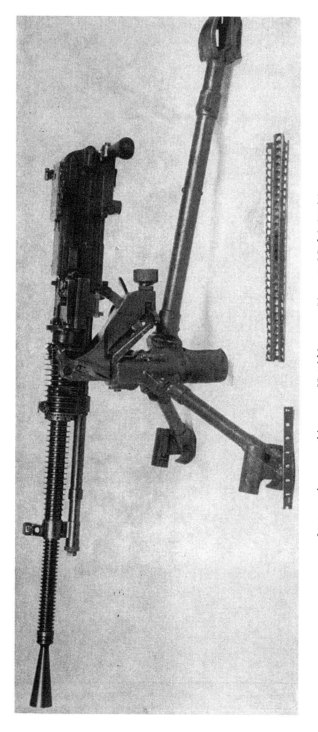

Japanese heavy machine gun, Hotchkiss type, Year 01 Model (1941).

Japanese Nambu machine gun, Model 11 (1922). Except for the hopper feed, it follows the Hotchkiss principle of design.

Japanese copy of Browning aircraft machine gun.

from 1909 to 1916. When I saw hundreds of these familiar looking feed strips strewn along the beach at Saipan in 1944, it reminded me of my Mexican Border Days of 1916 as machine gun instructor.

A lighter gun of the general type of a Hotchkiss was the Japanese Nambu Model 11 (1922) 6.5 mm Light Machine Gun. It looks a lot like the old Benet-Mercié, but uses a hopper for the cartridges instead of feed strips. It is air cooled, gas operated, and weighs about 22 pounds. It was largely superseded by the later light machine guns.

The model 96 (1939) 6.5 mm light machine gun is a lot like the Bren in appearance, but different in mechanism. It is gas operated, air cooled, and weighs 20 pounds. It is a very effective weapon.

The Model 99 (1939) 7.7 mm Light Machine Gun is a weapon similar to that just described, except that it is made for the newer 7.7 mm (or .303 inch) cartridge. It also is a highly effective weapon. The Japanese also made and used excellent copies of the Browning and Lewis machine guns.

Johnson Light Machine Gun

A gun that showed great promise, but never attained any wide use in the War is the recoil operated light machine gun designed by Captain Melvin M. Johnson, of the United States Marine Corps Reserve.

This gun, which has some quite novel and desirable features, had the bad luck to make its appearance just at a time which made it most difficult for it to attain the recognition that it otherwise probably would have received. It was adopted by the Dutch in 1941, but before it had gotten well into production, the Dutch Colonial possessions passed to the Japanese, and this market for the new gun passed out of existence.

It is a short-recoil operated air cooled light machine gun weighing, without magazine, only 12.3 pounds. The barrel can be removed and replaced in 8 seconds while the gun is hot.

It is fed from removable box magazines weighing 14 ounces and holding 20 rounds. The feeding lips which guide the cartridges into the chamber are machined out of the solid metal of the receiver, instead of being shaped out of the thin metal of the magazine, which is easily deformed. This feature removes a common cause of malfunctions. The gun can have additional cartridges clip fed into the magazine from the right side of the gun while the magazine is in place. Thus a partly empty magazine can be replenished, or a different type of cartridge, tracer, for example, can be brought into use in an instant.

A clever arrangement of the breech mechanism makes the gun fire from an open breech when executing full automatic fire, thus removing the danger of having a cartridge "cook off" if fire is interrupted while the gun is hot; but when the gun is used as a semi-automatic,

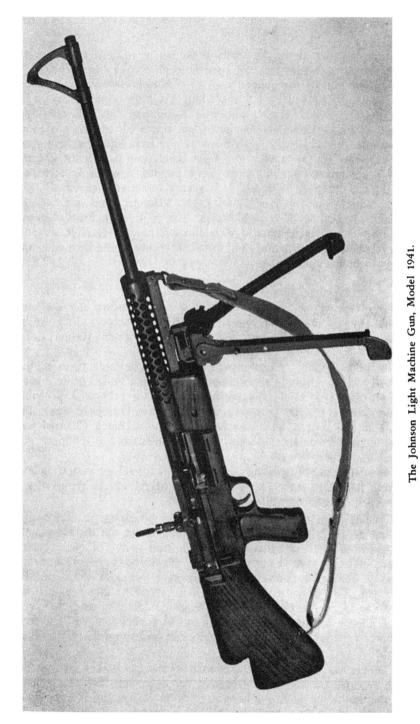

The Johnson Light Machine Gun, Model 1941.

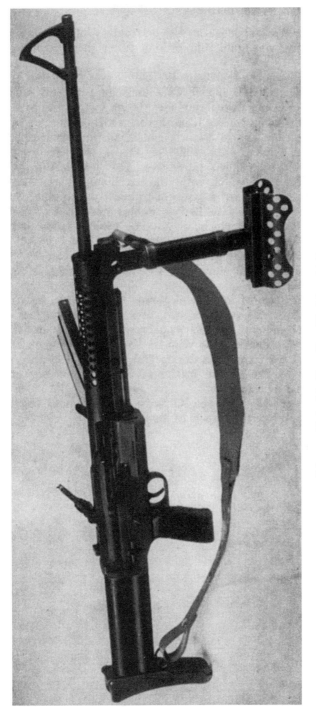

Johnson Light Machine Gun, Model 1944 E 1.

the breech closes and locks on the cartridge, after which a pull on the trigger fires the gun, thus making easier the attainment of accuracy.

The gun that was adopted by the Dutch was called the Model of 1941, and guns of this model were used by parachute troops and raiding parties in our own Army and Marine Corps, uses to which its unusually light weight made it particularly adaptable.

About the time World War II ended, an improved experimental model called Model 1944 embodied some new features shown to be desirable by combat experience. This was further developed into the Model 1945, which with attached monopod rest weighs only 15.5 pounds. This gun has a gas assist to boost the recoil of the barrel and increase the cyclic rate. Barrels on this model can be changed in six seconds, and this should be done every 1000 to 1200 rounds when firing at the rate of 50 shots per minute.

Commencing with the gun empty, one man can load and fire 180 shots in 1 minute full automatic, and 60 aimed shots in 1 minute semi-automatic.

A two man team of loader and gunner can load and fire 100 shots in 18 seconds or 200 in 37 seconds, thus maintaining a rate of over 300 shots per minute. A three man crew, with spare magazine and spare barrel can deliver 1000 shots in six minutes, though they will have changed barrels 9 times during that period. Of course, unless it is necessary to fire at the maximum rate, the number of barrel changes would be much less.

It will be seen that this gun has some very advanced features, and it is a highly effective weapon of its type.

VI

The Military Semiautomatic Rifle

WHAT is the reason for a semiautomatic rifle, was not the Springfield good enough? A very little reflection will answer this question. Consider a soldier engaged in a skirmish. He is lying prone on the ground with his rifle, trying to make himself as inconspicuous as possible. Somewhere in the distance one of the enemy soldiers shoots at him. The chances are he does not know where the bullets are coming from. In World War I one of the things that surprised our soldiers at first was the fact that many of them went through several entire battles without seeing any of the enemy soldiers. Suppose our soldier does locate an enemy's helmet, barely distinguishable against the landscape 200 or 300 yards away. He has detected some movement and he knows that this is all he can see of one of the enemy soldiers, so he decides to use it as a target. He takes careful aim and fires, and a puff of dust a little in front of and a little to the right of the point of aim shows where his bullet struck. Then, in his excitement, he yanks back the bolt, shoves it forward again, turns it down and locks it, and what happens? The chances are that the resulting movement of his rifle has disturbed his line of sight for the moment, and when he looks back he can no longer locate the object. Then, again, he has made quite a movement himself and the alert eyes of the enemy may have detected this, and he may, in turn, be serving as a target.

Consider, however, that this soldier has a semiautomatic rifle. He takes careful aim, presses the trigger, and observes a puff of dust a little in front of and a little to the right of where he was aiming. Immediately, without taking his eyes from the sights, he shifts his point of aim a little to the left and a little higher, presses his finger to the trigger, and this time his bullet will probably find its mark.

Many years ago, the Army recognized the desirability of having the service rifle operate on the self-loading principle, and sent out frequent invitations to inventors to submit models for test; but during a period of some thirty years, little success attended these efforts.

For a while, the recoil operation seemed to be a favorite with inventors, but they ran into several difficulties, such as trouble in attaching a bayonet. At this writing, the bayonet may be considered as obsolete, but that was not so a few years back. The fact that the barrel cannot be fixed rigidly to the receiver or stock, but must be free to slide back, posed a problem. Some inventors met it by encasing the barrel in a tube, but while this is all right for a hunting rifle,

The Remington autoloading rifle, model 8 (now model 81) fitted for military use. During the years around 1930, when we were trying to find a suitable semiautomatic rifle for adoption, a number of these Remingtons, in .35 caliber were fitted up like this and issued to the Army for tactical tests to determine the best way to use a semiautomatic rifle in various situations.

which is fired only occasionally, it will not do for a military gun, which must stand continued firing; the hearing of the barrel is too severe.

Finally a recoil operated gun was designed by Capt. Melvin M. Johnson, U. S. Marine Corps Reserve, which overcame the previous objections to this method of operation. This came after the Garand had already been adopted by the Army, but the Netherland Indies government ordered a large number of these guns, and some of them saw service with our forces in the Southwest Pacific. In actual service they were not liked as well by their users, the U. S. Marine Corps, as were the Garands. The Johnson gun was nevertheless, a fine serviceable weapon, probably second only to the Garand among the semiautomatics of World War II.

Early Ordnance Designs

In 1916 our Ordnance Department attempted to design a semiautomatic rifle at Springfield Armory, and another at Rock Island Arsenal. Both of these guns were gas operated, and the already difficult problem of gas operation was complicated by the requirement laid down by our thrifty government that the guns must be made so that if possible the regular hand operated Springfields could be converted.

Both of these guns were extremely crude, though the Rock Island model was better than that produced by Springfield. This Rock Island gun had a sort of sliding cage over the breech, with a cam in it to operate the bolt handle, and when I showed this to Mr. Browning in 1917, he remarked with a dry smile, "Where do you put on the cheese?" We saw the point at once, for the resemblance to a rat-trap was rather marked.

Many of the models submitted by inventors were of the gas operated type, and the presence of a gas cylinder under the barrel, or at the side of it, or on top of it, inevitably added quite a bit of weight and bulk.

Then another trouble with these guns was that gas was tapped off the barrel at such tremendous pressure that it was hard to handle it without introducing severe strains on the gun. When the bullet passes the gas port in the barrel, the pressure at that point will be anywhere from 40,000 down to 5,000 or 10,000 pounds per square inch, depending upon where the port is located. The closer to the breech it is, naturally, the higher will be the pressure. Assuming that the port is at the point where the pressure is 25,000 pounds to the square inch, a sudden application of this enormous pressure on the head of the piston slams the breech-block open with extreme violence, and the result is not only undesirably quick opening, tearing the heads off the empty cartridge cases, and such troubles as these, but also excessive breakage of parts.

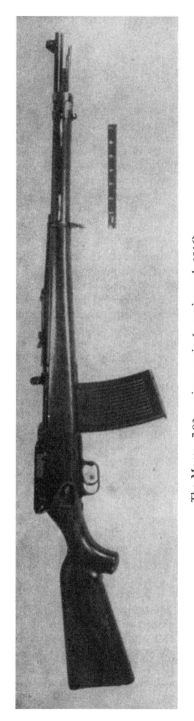

The Mauser 7.92 semiautomatic (experimental, 1916).

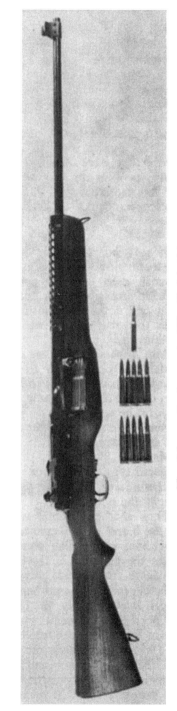

The Johnson Semiautomatic Rifle Model 1941.

Left: Farquhar-Hill rifle, tested at Springfield Armory in 1917.
Middle: Gas operated semiautomatic rifle designed at Springfield Armory, 1916.
Right: Gas operated semiautomatic rifle designed at Rock Island Arsenal, 1916.

The logical thing to do was to move the gas port as far forward as possible, where the pressure would not be so great, and reduce the area of the port so that the gas was throttled down to a lower pressure before striking the piston. By doing these things a number of very successful gas-operated guns have been made; but there is another disadvantage to the gas-operated system, and that is the hole bored in the barrel to form the gas port. It is difficult to clean this

Top: Rychiger recoil operated rifle. This rifle, made in Switzerland, was based on the straight pull Schmidt Rubin action, and was chambered for the Swiss service ammunition.

Middle: Rychiger type rifle, made for the U. S. Service ammunition by Major Elder of the Ordnance Department during 1918.

Bottom: Bommarito recoil operated rifle submitted for test during 1918. It has a toggle jointed breech lock, like that on the Luger pistol.

hole, so that it is always a point where rust and corrosion are likely to start.

Gas operation was successfully applied to machine guns long before it was to shoulder rifles. In machine guns, the moving parts can be made heavy enough to absorb the sudden and powerful impact of the gas. Moreover, the pressure of the gas on the piston endures for only a very small time interval, and if the piston can be made rather heavy, it will have a better chance to absorb enough energy during this very brief interval to carry it through its stroke.

With the shoulder rifle, conditions are very much more difficult.

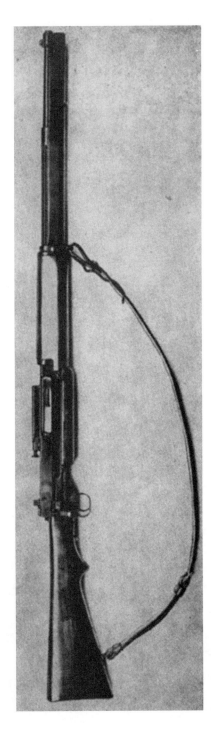

An early example of the semiautomatic rifle submitted for test by the United States Machine Gun Company. Based on a Berthier design.

The Bang semiautomatic rifle, model of 1911. This gun is operated by the pull of the muzzle blast on a sliding cap over the muzzle. The pull is transmitted to a lever in the breech through a thin rod. This gun passed a most creditable test, but failed of adoption principally because the very thin barrel heated up too much in rapid fire. The gun is shown with a muzzle protector in place over the end of the barrel. It must be removed before firing.

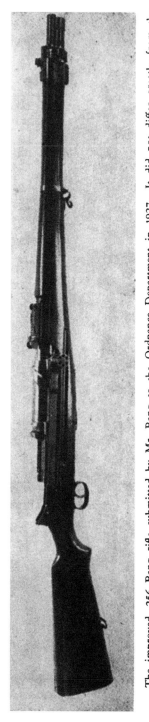

The improved .256 Bang rifle submitted by Mr. Bang to the Ordnance Department in 1927. It did not differ greatly from the original Bang. The action is shown closed.

The piston and other moving parts cannot be made heavy or the gun will weigh too much; and light parts do not have enough inertia to carry through the rearward motion after the gas pressure is gone unless the impact of the gas is made extremely violent. The result has been that in most gas-operated shoulder rifles the light piston gets up energy enough to open the breech against the spring action by being slammed to the rear with very high speed, and this violent action is conducive to very high breakages.

The Bang Rifle

In 1911, Soren Hansen Bang, of the Danish Recoil Rifle Syndicate, Copenhagen, submitted a rifle which passed a remarkably satisfactory test. Its performance was better than that of any other semi-automatic rifle submitted up to that time or for many years to come. It is described on page 62.

The Bang gun was big and bulky, but very light. The lightness was obtained by hollowing out the stock so that in some spots it was little more than a shell, and by turning down the barrel so that it was reduced to the minimum in diameter.

While this gun passed a splendid test as far as the functioning was concerned, the barrel was far too light to stand the heat.

The muzzle cap used by Bang was much like one patented by Sir Hiram Maxim in 1885. Such a principle was experimented with by John Browning in 1889 on a model gun built by him. It was used, but not patented by Bang, probably on account of Maxim's patent. It was used in an auto-loading rifle built by Mr. Garrison of the Remington Arms Co., about the time of World War I, using the breech action of the Remington auto-loading rifle. Grant Hammond also patented some modifications of this principle. The rifle submitted for test at Springfield in 1921 by General Liu of China had the Bang muzzle attachment in almost the identical form in which Bang used it. The Puteaux Machine gun, used by the French for some years used a similar type of gas take-off. The Rheinmetall Semi-automatic rifle, designed by Karl Heinemann, and tested at Aberdeen Proving Ground in 1929 in the Pedersen .276 caliber had a muzzle cap almost exactly like the one used by S. H. Bang.

Hatcher Self Loading Rifle

In 1920, Major James L. Hatcher, (now Colonel; brother of the writer) built a semiautomatic rifle at Springfield Armory, which had the same general type of muzzle cap gas take-off that Bang used, but which was a big improvement on the Bang as far as ruggedness was concerned, and eliminated the defects formerly noted in the original Bang. He completed his first model rifle in the phenomenally short time of four months, and while this rifle passed an excellent preliminary test, breakages eventually developed, indicating the need

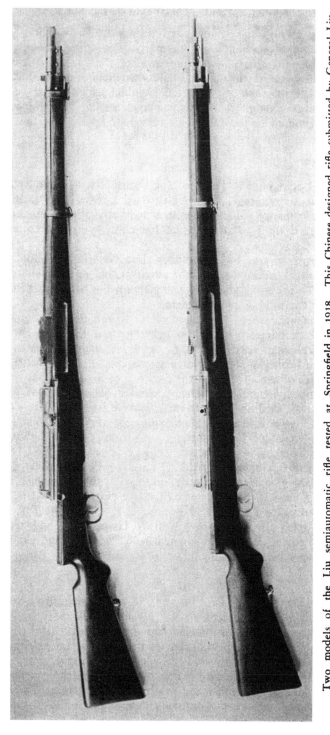

Two models of the Liu semiautomatic rifle tested at Springfield in 1918. This Chinese designed rifle submitted by General Liu follows the Bang principles very closely.

The Heinemann rifle, another modification of the famous and popular Bang, designed by Karl Heinemann and submitted by Rheinische Metallwaren und Maschinen Fabrik. The muzzle attachment and gas operation are the same as in the Bang, but the breech closure is a toggle joined breech block opening horizontally on the right side of the receiver. This gun embodies a neat device for overcoming the tendency of the breech block to bounce open slightly after slamming shut. The finger lever for opening the action by hand is pivoted loosely on the side of the breech block. When the breech block slams shut, the finger lever, which has been following along behind, catches up, and just as the block starts to bounce open, strikes a blow which kills the bounce completely.

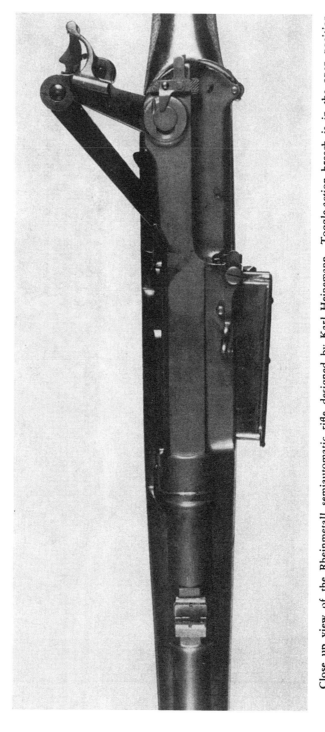

Close up view of the Rheinmetall semiautomatic rifle designed by Karl Heinemann. Toggle-action breech is in the open position. Note the loosely pivoted piece of metal attached to the finger hook to kill the rebound when the breech block slams shut.

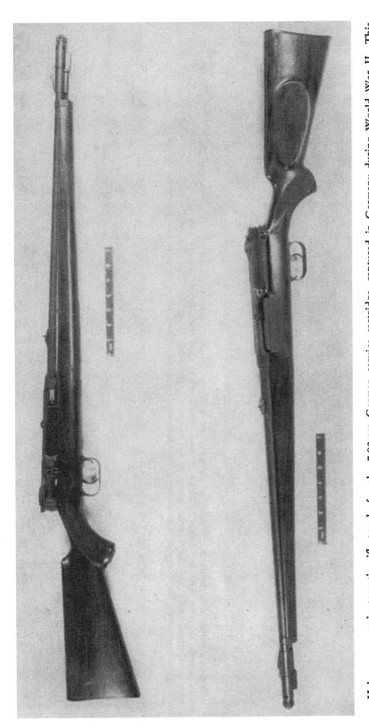

Heinemann semiautomatic rifle, made for the 7.92mm German service cartridge, captured in Germany during World War II. This is very similar to the .276 model of this gun that was tested in Aberdeen Proving Ground in 1929.

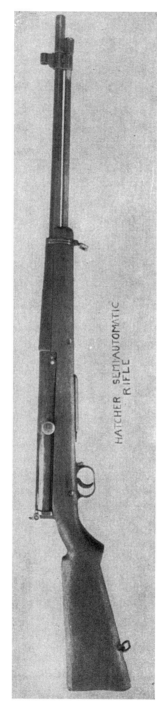

Semiautomatic rifle built at Springfield Armory in 1920 by Major James L. Hatcher. It employed a sliding muzzle cap actuator, similar to that used by Bang. Though it was produced in the remarkably short time of four months, it was extremely simple, performed well, and gave great promise of success. Unfortunately, as the rifle was undergoing some changes found desirable in a preliminary test, the designer was ordered to other duty, and never had an opportunity to perfect the design.

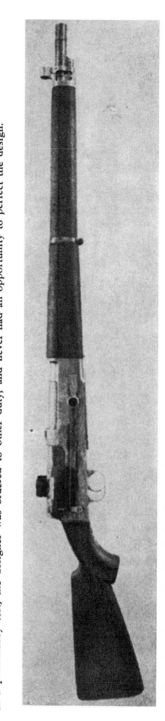

Second semiautomatic rifle designed by Major (now Colonel) James L. Hatcher, constructed by him while stationed at Aberdeen Proving Ground in 1923, it used a muzzle sleeve actuator, of the Bang type as did his earlier model.

for redesign of some of the parts, as usually happens with an inventor's first model. The board which tested the gun suggested certain changes, but before they could be gotten underway, the designer was ordered to another station, thus effectively putting an end to this effort.

This gun business in those days was something like a horse race. There were a couple of favorites which seemed to be coming into the home stretch, and they had very heavy backing in some quarters, and certain information which came to me in a highly confidential way at that time led me to conclude that the change of station which interrupted this work was not accidental.

Major Hatcher was given permission to work on an improved model at his new station "in addition to his other duties." He did succeed under very great handicaps, in turning out a second model, but as far as I know, never did actually have it tested by the official board.

Thompson Autorifle

Another scheme for a semiautomatic rifle was based on the so-called Blish principle, already mentioned on page 44.

It was on this principle that the Thompson semiautomatic rifle was built by General J. T. Thompson, retired, formerly Chief of the Small Arms Division of the Ordnance Department.

The Thompson autorifle that I tested at Springfield Armory in 1921 worked as long as the oiled pads were used, but it opened with extreme speed and ejected the cartridges with such force that the empty shells in one test were actually stuck into a heavy wooden door about twenty feet to the right of the ejection port.

Anyone standing to the right of this gun could have been very severely injured by these flying missiles. Moreover the bolt handle came back with such speed that it would simply have sheared off the thumb if the operator had been so unwary as to put his thumb up alongside the receiver. Obviously the Thompson guns, of which a number of models were tested, never had a chance of adoption.

World War I Designs

During World War I, the French quietly placed on the firing line a long, heavy gas-operated rifle, using the 8 mm Lebel cartridge, which then was the standard French Service cartridge. This rifle, called the St. Etienne, was rather simple but effective. It used the cartridges in clips of five, which were placed, clip and all, in a hinged magazine under the receiver. The bolt was a straight-pull affair, and the thrust of the gas piston simply shoved the bolt handle to the rear, causing it first to rotate the bolt to the unlocked position by means of a cam, then to pull it open. The rifle had a rather violent opening action, owing to the uncontrolled thrust of the gas. The gun was used in the war, but not much was heard of it.

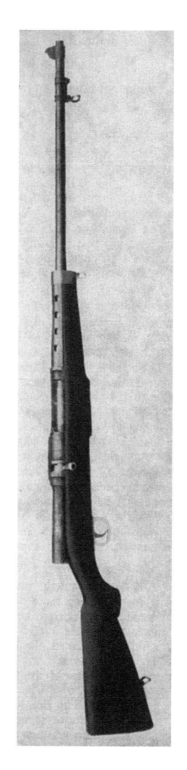

The Thompson Autorifle, Colt model 1921.

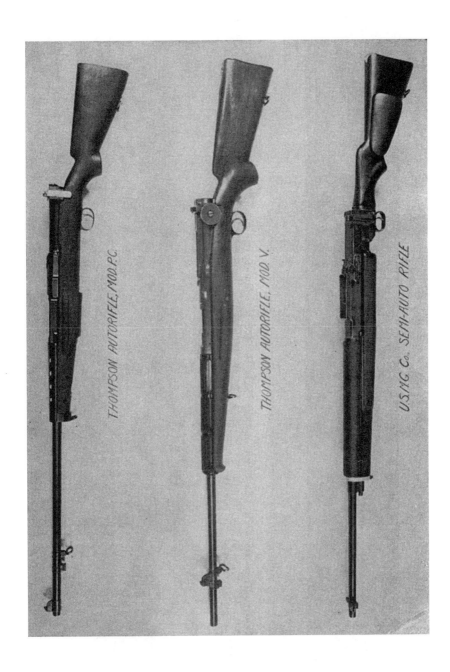

THOMPSON AUTORIFLE, MOD.P.C.

THOMPSON AUTORIFLE, MOD. V.

U.S.M.G. Co. SEMI-AUTO RIFLE

The Thompson semiautomatic rifle called Autorifle Style D. The breechblock was held shut by steep screw threads engaging in a bronze nut. The angle of the threads was so steep that the pressure of the discharge caused the bolt to unscrew and fly open, but the unscrewing retarded the opening sufficiently so that the gun would operate satisfactorily provided the cartridges were oiled. The ammunition rubbed against oil saturated felt pads built into the sides of the magazine.

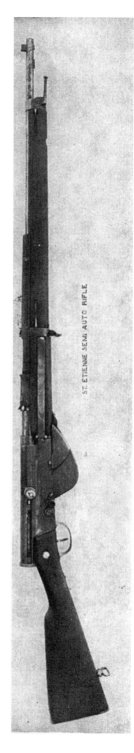

ST. ETIENNE SEMI AUTO RIFLE

St. Etienne semiautomatic rifle. This simple gas operated arm was used by the French in World War I, and was copied in our .30 caliber by Major Elder in 1918.

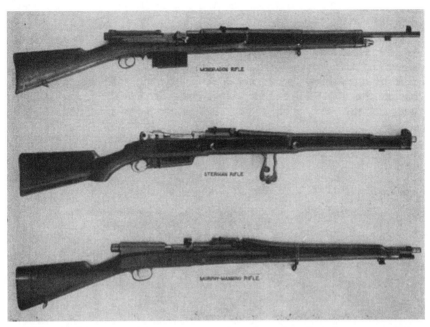

Top: Mondragon semiautomatic rifle, a gas operated design patented by Manuel Mondragon of Mexico, August 8, 1904, and adopted by Mexico in 1911. It was made in Switzerland by the Schweizerische Industriel Gesellschaft at Neuhausen, on the Swiss-German border. With the advent of World War I the production was diverted to Germany, and the use of the gun by Mexico was discontinued.

Middle: The Stergian rifle. This was not semiautomatic, but was manually operated in the same manner as a pump action shotgun, by means of the hand grip under the forearm. This was jointed so it could be folded into a slot in the stock when not in use.

Bottom: The Murphy-Manning gas operated semiautomatic, designed and built by two Springfield Armory employees about 1915.

During the war of 1914-1918, the Germans used quite a few gas operated rifles of the kind called the Mondragon, which had been adopted by the Mexican Government in 1911. This rifle was developed by the Mexican General Mondragon at the plant of the Sweizerische Industriel Gesellschaft, at Neuhausen in Switzerland. This is only a few miles from Germany; in fact it is so close that when I went there to investigate this rifle the train from the next Swiss town wandered back and forth across the border. The train went straight while the border wound in and out. As stated above, this gun had been adopted by the Mexicans just before World War I. When the war broke out, it was no longer possible to send the guns to Mexico, and the entire production was diverted to Germany. The Mondragon compares rather favorably with some of the gas operated semi-automatics used in World War II, such as the Tokarev and the Gew. 43.

During the early months of our war with Germany in 1917 and 18, the Ordnance Department commisssioned as Major an arms designer of the Stevens Arms Co., named Elder, and gave him the task of attempting to get out a semiautomatic rifle that we could use in the war. Major Elder copied the St. Etienne in .30 caliber and did the same with a very promising Swiss short recoil rifle

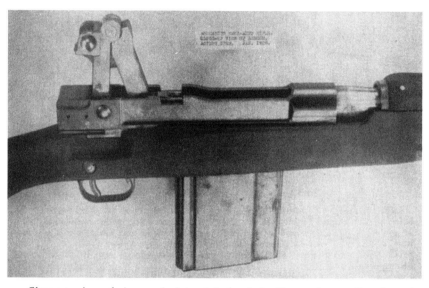

Close up view of the toggle jointed lock of the Bommarito recoil action. A downward projecting arm on the rearward member of the breech block meshes in a depression in the frame, and is geared up so that as the barrel moves to the rear, the breech action is forcibly moved to the open position shown.

called the Rychiger. Major Elder, who worked under my supervision when I was Chief of the Machine Gun and Small Arms Section, Engineering Division, Ordnance, in 1918, produced some very creditable models, but the war ended before any of them had been actually put into production for war use.

The Pedersen .276

A rifle which is neither gas operated nor recoil operated was built by Mr. J. D. Pedersen. Mr. Pedersen is a gun designer of immense experience. Years ago he designed the Remington pump shotgun, which attained great commercial success, and afterwards he designed numerous rifles for the Remington Arms Company, including the slide-action .22. He also designed the Remington auto-

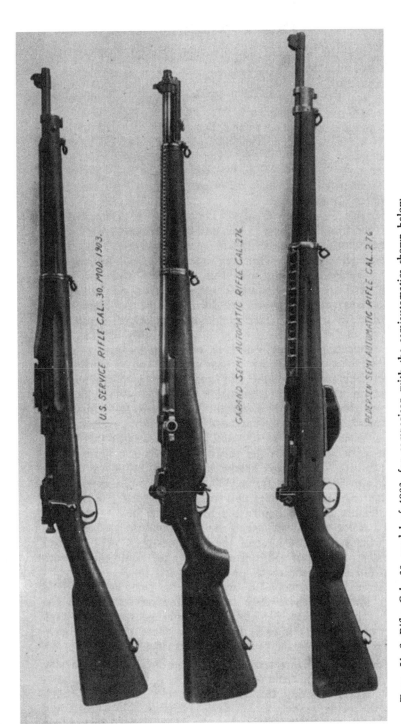

U.S. SERVICE RIFLE CAL. 30. M1906. 1903.

GARAND SEMI AUTOMATIC RIFLE CAL. 276.

PEDERSEN SEMI AUTOMATIC RIFLE CAL. 276

Top: U. S. Rifle, Cal. .30, model of 1903, for comparison with the semiautomatics shown below. Middle: Garand's third model, a gas operated gun built to shoot the Pedersen 276 cartridge. This gun, later changed to .30 caliber, became the present M1.

Bottom: The Pedersen .276. A retarded blowback gun, which eliminated all the complications of gas operation or recoiling barrel by an exceedingly clever method of opposing the opening tendency of the breech by the inertia of the parts acting through a favorable leverage. It passed a highly satisfactory test, but used waxed cartridges, a fact which weighed against it, more on theoretical than on practical grounds.

matic pistol, and the Pedersen device which was one of our most closely guarded secrets of World War I.

Along about 1922 Mr. Pedersen approached the Ordnance Department with a plan for a semiautomatic rifle on an entirely new design. The design was so promising and Mr. Pedersen's reputation as a designer so great, that the Ordnance Department decided to build the rifle. As a result Mr. Pedersen was employed and his rifle was built at Springfield Armory. The first test was successful, and twenty samples were built, which went out to the infantry and cavalry for service test. Some of these twenty rifles were also demonstrated from time to time at Camp Perry.

Mr. Pedersen's rifle, like General Thompson's is what may be called a delayed blow-back, but in this gun there are no screw threads on the breechblock. The breechblock is a toggle joint, or crank, very much in principle like what was described in connection with the Maxim machine gun, but with this difference, that this crank is never on dead center. It is always just a little bit out of line, so that the moment pressure comes on the cartridge the toggle joint begins to open. If it were merely a hinged crank with a pin joint where the connecting rod joins to it, it would open too fast. The crank and connecting rod are, however, not hinged together with a simple hinged joint, but each has a cam surface, and as the breechblock moves back and the toggle joint breaks, these two cam surfaces roll together in such a way as to delay the speed with which the line of thrust gets away from a straight line. Thus again this blow-back mechanism, while it does not have much weight, is as *hard* to move and as *slow* to move as if it did have the weight there. It is hard to move because, when the thrust comes on the head of the breech-block, it is transmitted almost in a straight line to the big pivot pin in the back of the frame. When this thrust is exerted, the center of the toggle joint moves upward, but this center must move up a considerable distance before the head of the bolt moves back appreciably. A *lot* of upward speed must be put into the center of the toggle joint before the head of the bolt goes back very far, and this delays the opening of the gun sufficiently to enable the powder pressure to fall before the cartridge case can get out.

Mr. Pedersen finally completed twenty of his rifles at Springfield Armory in 1927, and these were sent out for service test. In the meantime Frankford Arsenal had been experimenting with .276 cartridges, and several hundred thousand of these cartridges were made up for use in testing the twenty Pedersen rifles.

In 1927 the Pedersen rifles were tested by the Infantry and Cavalry and were found to be suitable for military use. It was decided, however, that before adopting this rifle, we would make a thorough test of all the other models which were available, and accordingly notice was sent out to inventors that the War Department would

The Pedersen .276, shown with action open.

Pedersen .276 semiautomatic, showing action in closed position.

Japanese copy of the Pedersen semiautomatic rifle. Unlike the Pedersen, this rifle uses a rotary magazine similar to the Schoenauer type, or to that used in the Savage Model 1899, and is arranged to be loaded by stripping cartridges from a clip like that of the Springfield or Mauser.

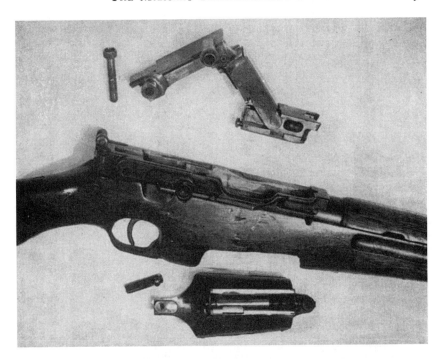

Close up of the mechanism of the Japanese copy of the Pedersen semiautomatic rifle, showing rotary or spool type magazine. Only two samples of this rifle were found. They were in an arsenal about 7 miles from Tokyo, and were marked No. 1 and No. 2, respectively, so it is likely that they were experimental models, and that they were the only ones made.

hold a test of semiautomatic rifles in July 1929. These rifles were to fire the new .276 ammunition which by that time had been approved for adoption as the service cartridge for any new semiautomatic that met the final tests.

The Improved Garand

In 1928, Mr. Garand had started to work on an improved model, in which he had abandoned his primer operation in favor of gas operation. His new rifle was, of course, of the .276 caliber.

Mr. Garand's new gun, contrary to the usual practice in gas operation, did not have a gas port in the barrel. Instead, he used a cap over the muzzle, similar to the cap used by Bang, with this important difference; the Garand cap did not move. See page 58.

There is an entry in my notebook, made some years ago as follows: "Garand's muzzle cap patented by L. Silverman of Crayford, Kent, assigned to Vickers Sons and Maxim, U. S. Patent 618,743, Jan. 31, 1899."

Czech semiautomatic rifle tested at Aberdeen Proving Ground in 1929. It was designed by Holek, and submitted by the "ZB" firm, (Ceskoslovenska Zbrojovka, of Brno.) It was chambered for the Pedersen .276 cartridge.

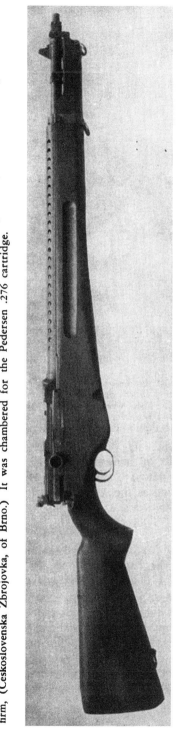

The White semiautomatic .276. This was one of the rifles tested at Aberdeen in 1929. It had an unusually short compact action, and a system of admitting a small portion of gas into a hollow piston and then cutting off the supply, after the manner of a slide valve in a steam engine, so the gas could act by expansion and thus soften the blow of the piston.

Garand used this arrangement on his early production of M 1 rifles, but soon changed to the conventional gas port near the muzzle.

The Garand gas operated gun was characterized by extreme simplicity and clean design of all the parts. It had only about 60 pieces, which is considerably less than the number in the Springfield '03. The first of these guns weighed about the same as the 1903 Springfield. The gun had a ten round magazine, with an "en bloc" clip; a receiver peep sight, with clicks for both elevation and windage; a pistol grip stock, with more length that that of the Springfield '03, and with a higher comb for more comfort in prone shooting.

The official test, held at Aberdeen Proving Ground in 1929, included the Pedersen and Garand rifles, the Thompson rifle, a Browning of the short-recoil type made by the Colt's Patent Fire Arms Manufacturing Co., and three European rifles—the Brauning, invented by a Belgian (which should not be confused with the American-invented Browning guns made in Belgium), a Czechoslovakian gas-operated rifle, and a rifle invented by Karl Heinemann, who designed the German Parabellum aircraft machine guns during the first world war.

As a result of this Aberdeen test of 1929,—which I attended, as it came under my direct supervision as Chief of the Small Arms Division, Technical Staff,—the Garand .276 came out on top, and it was decided to make twenty of them for an extended service test, as had already been done with the Pedersen. The test was completed in 1932, and it then remained to determine which of these two highly satisfactory rifles would be adopted for service use by the army.

In the meantime the British apparently had shown a disposition to adopt the same rifle we finally chose, so Pedersen went to England and worked with Vickers, Ltd., tooling up for his rifle, which most people apparently thought it certain we would adopt.

Apparently the Japanese thought so too, for recently I have seen a rifle of the Pedersen type, with variations such as a rotary magazine, two of which were found in an arsenal outside of Tokyo. These were marked 1 and 2, respectively. Most likely they were experimental models, and they may have been the only two made.

However, the decision of the Army board was to adopt the Garand .276 instead of the Pedersen, and the report recommending this action was laid on the Chief of Staff's desk, when a sort of a figurative atomic bomb burst in the semi-automatic rifle business. General MacArthur, U. S. Army Chief of Staff, disapproved the report, and stated that the recommendation had been made under a misapprehension; there would be no change in the caliber of the service ammunition.

This decision, which as proved by later events was eminently sound, ended the many years of work on the .276 rifles, and required a new

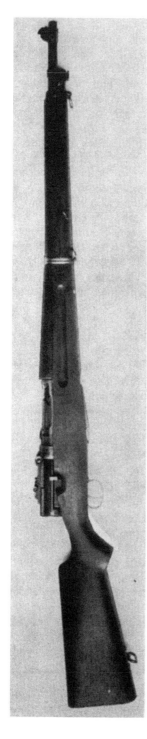

Thompson semiautomatic rifle in the .276 Pedersen caliber, submitted for test at Aberdeen in 1929.

Colt semiautomatic rifle tested in 1929. It was designed by a member of the Browning family, and was in the caliber .276 Pedersen.

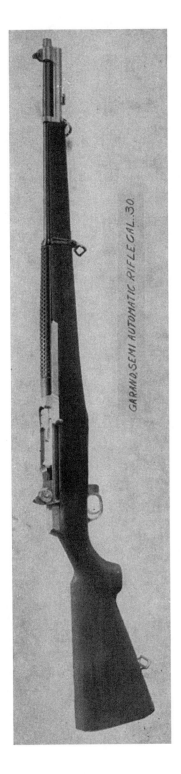

GARAND SEMI AUTOMATIC RIFLE CAL. 30.

First model of the present .30 caliber M1 rifle. Garand first built two successive models of primer actuated .30 caliber guns, then a .276 gas actuated gun to take the Pedersen .276 cartridge. The gun shown above duplicates his .276 in .30 caliber. Photo taken September 10, 1930

Japanese copy of the U. S. Garand M1 rifle. Guns like this, differing from the U. S. M1 only in minor details were found in the Japanese service towards the close of the war. Main differences were the caliber, which was the standard Japanese 7.7mm; the rear sight, which was of the ramp type, and the magazine, which was arranged for loading by having the cartridges stripped out of a clip as is done in the M1903 Springfield.

start to be made in the matter of the selection of a semi-automatic shoulder rifle. Fortunately Garand had already been working on a .30 caliber model, and he proceeded to submit it for test. Twenty of these rifles were submitted for service test, and the rifle was standardized Jan. 9, 1936, as the U. S. Rifle, caliber .30, M 1.

Soon after this an allottment of $80,000 was given to Springfield armory for the construction of 80 of these rifles, together with a considerable amount of tooling up for making them by production methods.

The first actual quantity production of parts started at Springfield Armory in January, 1937, and completed rifles started coming off the production lines in August of the same year.

During World War II, the Garand was produced by the Winchester Repeating Arms Co., as well as by the Springfield Armory, a total of 4,028,395, being produced.

Johnson vs. Garand

In 1936, Capt. Melvin M. Johnson, U.S.M.C. Reserve, started work on a much improved type of short recoil action, which he incorporated in both a semiautomatic rifle and a light machine gun. This gun was ready for production about the end of 1939, and was adopted by the Netherlands Indies Army and by the Royal Netherlands Navy.

There is no doubt that both the Johnson Automatic Rifle and the Johnson Light Machine Gun were excellent weapons, with many attractive and useful features. Some people thought that we should abandon the Garand and adopt the Johnson, though there was nothing to show that the Johnson was any better than the Garand, or for that matter, as good. The tooling up for the Garand has been completed at great expense, and some 50,000 of the new guns had been manufactured, so that even if the Johnson had been better, a change at that time was out of the question. Finally, experience by the Marines with both types in the Southwest Pacific demonstrated the fact that the Garand was unquestionably a better battle rifle than the Johnson. The Johnson rifles that the Marines had acquired were turned in and Garands obtained to take their place. The Johnson is nevertheless a splendid semiautomatic rifle, and Captain Johnson is entitled to a world of credit for his outstanding accomplishment in developing it in a very short time.

European Semiautomatics

Both Germany and Russia used a certain number of semiautomatic shoulder rifles during World War II. The best of these is probably the German Gewehr 43, later called K-43.

This is a gas operated gun, with a gas piston and operating rod lying on top of the barrel, under a wooden handguard. Contrary

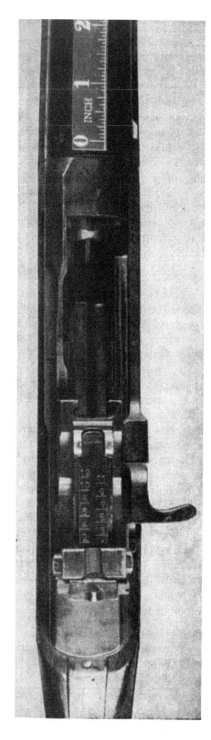

Top view of the Japanese copy of the U. S. Garand M1, showing the ramp type rear sight and the magazine arranged to use the Springfield type clip.

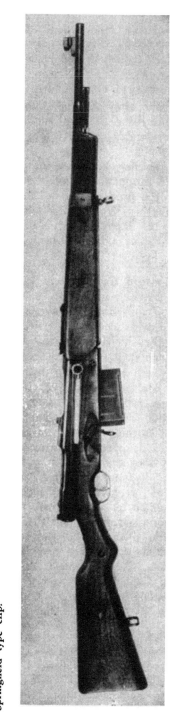

Czech 7.92 ZH-37 semiautomatic rifle captured in Germany during World War II.

to usual practice, the piston is the fixed member; the cylinder is arranged to telescope over the fixed piston.

The gas is taken off ten inches from the chamber, and must pass through the port and then back through the 4 inch length of the fixed piston before it comes out at the rear of the piston and strikes the moveable cylinder. Thus the action of the gas is softened considerably.

The locking arrangement comprises two wing-like pieces pivoted in the breech block. As the firing pin goes forward, it wedges these pieces out into recesses in the receiver, thus locking the action. As the gun is fired, the operating rod is driven backward by the gas, striking the bolt carrier, and driving it to the rear. It, in turn, pushes back the firing pin, first camming the two locking wings inward and out of engagement with the locking shoulders, then carrying the bolt to the rear.

I have seen samples of this gun in both 22 and 24½ inch barrel. The longer barrel model weighs 9 lbs. 13 oz. with magazine, and is 46¾ inches overall. It has a ten shot detachable box magazine, inserted from the bottom. It has a base for telescope mounting on the right side of the receiver.

Previous German models were the Gewehr 41, the Gew. 41 M, and the Gew. 41 W. These were operated by a piston driven to the rear by gas action, but there was no gas port in the barrel; instead, there was a muzzle cap over the end of the barrel, something like that used by Garand on his first gas operated models. The gas is trapped inside this cap long enough to act on the piston. In the Gew. 41 and the 41 W, the breech action is almost a duplicate of the Gew. 43; the Gew. 41 M has a turning bolt with a straight-pull action.

The Russians had a Simonov semiautomatic in 1936, called Avs 36, which was both semiautomatic and full automatic. It was gas operated, with the piston and gas cylinder on top of the barrel. The lock is a hollow rectangular member which is cammed downward out of engagement with the breech block when the breech block carrier is driven to the rear by the backward stroke of the piston. As it was intended for optional full automatic fire, this gun had a muzzle brake or compensator to control the climb. This was continued on the later Tokarev models, though the full automatic feature was dropped.

Following the Simonev was the Tokarev, Model 1938 and later, Model 1940. This weapon, the invention of an engineer named Feodor Vasilyevitch Tokarev, is a gun of neat and effective design. It is chambered for the regular 7.62 mm cartridge, and is fed from a ten shot detachable magazine, inserted from the bottom. The magazine may also be clip fed while in place in the gun.

The gun is gas operated, with a gas cylinder on top of the barrel near the muzzle. The operating rod passes through a hole in the rear sight instead of straddling it as in the Simonev.

Another view of the Czech ZH-37 7.92mm semiautomatic rifle found in Germany in World War II.

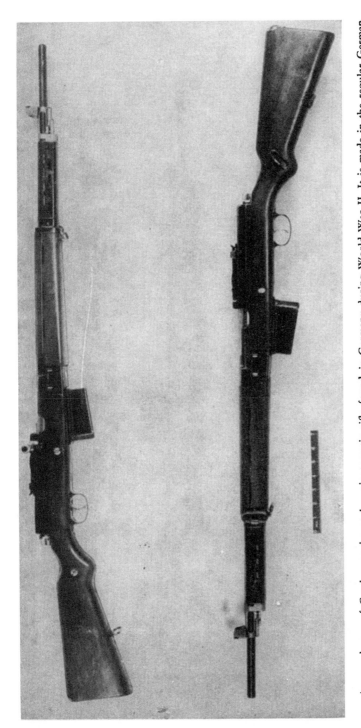

A second type of Czech experimental semiautomatic rifle found in Germany during World War II. It is made in the regular German 7.92 caliber, and is gas operated.

German semiautomatic rifles of World War II: 1. Gewehr 41M. 2. Gewehr 41W. 3. Gewehr 43. 4. Gewehr 43 with stock removed to show gas cylinder

Russian Tokarev semiautomatic rifle Model SVT 1940.

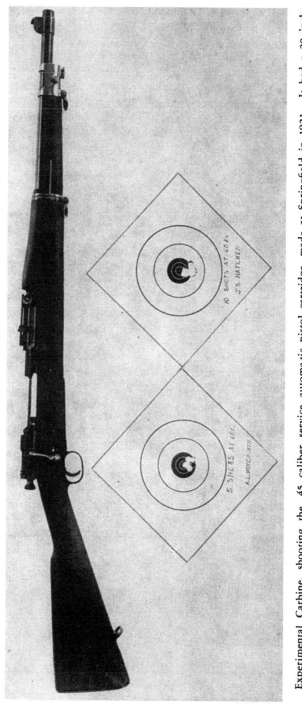

Experimental Carbine, shooting the .45 caliber service automatic pistol cartridge, made at Springfield in 1921. It had a 20 inch barrel.

The bolt is of the rocking type, similar in locking principle to that on the old Colt Machine Gun, or the Winchester Model 12 shotgun. As the bolt carrier moves forward under the action of the return spring in closing the action, a cam tips the rear end of the bolt downward, locking it in front of a shoulder in the receiver. As the operating rod is driven to the rear under the impulse of the gas, it pushes the bolt carrier back; this action cams the rear end of the bolt up out of engagement with the shoulder in the receiver, thus permitting it to be carried to the rear.

The gun is remarakably light, weighing only 8½ lbs., with magazine. The barrel, including the integral muzzle brake, is 27 inches long; if the muzzle brake is not included, the length is 24½ inches. The overall length of the gun is 48 inches.

The U. S. Carbine, Cal. .30 M 1 and M 2

During 1940 the Ordnance decided to produce a very light semiautomatic rifle to take the place of the pistol in the armament of company officers, non-commissioned officers, communication units, engineers, tank units, artillery, etc.

The cartridge was developed in conjunction with the Winchester Repeating Arms Co., from their .32 self-loading rifle cartridge. It has a round nosed 110 grain bullet, driven at a muzzle velocity of 1975 f.s. by a charge of approximately 12.4 grains of Hercules Carbine Powder, called by the Army, Hercules Flake, or by a suitable charge of the Western Cartridge Company's Ball Powder.

The gun was to weigh not over 5½ pounds, and was to be capable of either semiautomatic action or full automatic fire.

An Ordnance test in 1941 was followed by a service test, which I was fortunately able to attend. A number of models were tested, submitted by Springfield Armory, Winchester, the Auto-Ordnance Co., Woodhull, Hyde, Savage Arms Co., and Harrington and Richardson. The Winchester model was adopted in the latter part of 1941.

The gun, which weighs 4¾ lbs. and has an overall length of 35 inches, with an 18 inch barrel, has a breech mechanism like that of the Garand, operated by a short stroke piston with gas take-off near the breech. For description of this system of operation see the previous chapter. A modification of the carbine called the M 1 A 1 has a folding skeleton stock in combination with a wooden pistol grip, to lighten the gun for use by parachute troops.

A further modification called the M 2 is arranged for either full automatic or semi-automatic fire at the option of the user, according to the position of a selecting lever.

Italian Beretta Moschetto, or carbine, Model 1938-A, using the 9mm Parabellum cartridge.

European Carbines

The Germans produced a so-called Machine Pistol, the MP 43, which has already been mentioned under Submachine guns. This is not properly either a submachinegun or a machine pistol, but instead is a full automatic or semi-automatic carbine, arranged to shoot a shortened version of the 7.9 mm German service cartridge. This was by a big margin the most advanced European weapon in the carbine class.

Another gun which comes closer to being a carbine than a submachine gun is the Italian Beretta *Moschetto* or *little musket*. This is a carbine shooting the 9 mm Parabellum pistol cartridge.

VII

Experiments With Barrel Obstructions

THERE are some things about guns and shooting that are usually the subject of hearsay rather than of accurate first hand knowledge on the part of most of the shooting public, and one of these is the effect of the various abuses that are popularly supposed to result in a blown-up gun.

Perhaps the reason is that most people would rather hear about trouble than experience it, and so play safe; and the small minority who have enough curiosity to want to find out haven't the time or facilities.

It happens once in a while, however, that some individual is so placed by circumstances as to afford him an opportunity to investigate some of these things without too much trouble. That is just what happened to me. One thing alone that would guarantee me an opportunity to see a lot about how guns behave is the fact that I have been either Ordnance Officer or Ordnance Technical observer at nearly every National Match that was held between World Wars I and II.

The point of all this is that in all those years, I have rarely ever seen a gun failure cause any injury to the user, and what few injuries I have seen could mostly have been avoided by the use of shooting glasses.

I have tried almost everything I could think of, and in my early shooting days, I didn't know enough to wear shooting glasses, but I was lucky, and never received an eye injury. Now I wouldn't fire a shot with any kind of gun without shooting glasses on, or lacking special shooting glasses, ordinary eyeglasses would prevent the majority of eye injuries.

I have seen high powered rifles blown up by all kinds of fool tricks, such as buying a new gun and then firing it without ever looking in the barrel to see if it happened to be full of cosmoline; getting a cleaning patch stuck, with a rod wedged in the patch, and then trying to shoot both rod and patch out of the gun with a ball cartridge; loading a ball cartridge with blank cartridge powder, which just cannot be confined without causing a detonation; etc.

Lots of these incidents resulted in very narrow squeaks for the perpetrator of the stunt, but none that I have witnessed ever really hurt anyone. Once, for example, when I was in charge of the Experimental Department at Springfield Armory, we were trying to develop a blank cartridge attachment for the service .45. The special barrel had a plug in the muzzle with a very small hole in it, and the chamber was made too small to accept a regular ball cartridge, but would take the special blank. These blanks worked all right when the closing wad could be made hard and brittle so it would break up in passing through the small hole at the muzzle. One lot, however, failed to dry out properly, and the wads, instead of being brittle, were gummy, and the first one choked the vent. I was firing at the time, and the next shot with that sensitive blank powder confined in the barrel, simply detonated, and blew the barrel and slide all to pieces, leaving me holding the handle of the gun and wondering why I hadn't been hurt.

I certainly don't want the statements made above to be construed as any encouragement to take chances with dangerous overloads, etc.; anyone who keeps on with that long enough is sure to be hurt. What I do mean is that if you take reasonable care and wear glasses, your chances of being hurt by your gun are slight. Also, when you look at the wrecked guns pictured in this book, remember that most of them didn't hurt anyone, after all.

Now getting to the subject of this chapter, barrel obstructions, I suppose that all of us have had accidental experiences along this line. I remember very well a certain .22 of childhood days (the days when cleaning a gun had not been heard of), which one time failed to bring down a sparrow at very close range; not only that, but it failed to even make him fly; and still worse, the whole contents of the magazine, shot in rapid succession, did not obtrude itself on his consciousness in any way, or produce any visible or audible result at all. The puzzled feeling of surprise occasioned by this unusual circumstance prompted an investigation which disclosed the astonishing fact that the barrel did not have a hole through it. The gun was taken to the village bicycle man, who acted as gunsmith, locksmith, and general utility man, to have the dozen or more bullets bored out.

The operation was conducted with expedition and economy, and while I have never inquired into how he conducted the boring out operation, or how he got out the remnants of lead that might have remained between the lands, I can say that the result was entirely satisfactory and was well worth the quarter it cost, and the old Winchester is still kicking around to prove it. Of course, the accuracy, measured by modern standards, is nil, but you can't expect much from a barrel that has endured many damp summers with little or no cleaning. The incident seemed to indicate that the .22 short has not power enough to blow up a gun, no matter what you do. This conclusion encouraged me to try shooting under water with a .22, an experiment that was completely satisfactory. The gun was loaded entirely under water, so that the barrel was filled. Good practice was had at tin cans some ten feet away, and the worst damage to the gun was the wetting.

Another incident that is equally well impressed on my memory refers to a time some years ago, when I was trying out for a certain rifle team, and another member of the squad in pistol practice had the side of the cylinder on his .38 revolver lifted out by what seemed to be an extra heavy explosion. Investigation finally showed that the trouble was caused by a double charge of powder in the cartridge. It was factory loaded stuff, put up by one of our largest makers, and we heard a story of how it happened, which ran this way. The machine for putting in the powder charge was arranged to handle fifty cartridges at a time. Now this particular machine just once made two strokes instead of one, thus putting a double dose of powder into all fifty of the shells of that batch. When the lot of cartridges containing these fifty bad ones got onto the market, trouble started for both the revolver makers and the cartridge company, for soon complaints began to come in from widely separated points. After several such cases had been reported, and it was found that in each case a revolver had blown up while "A" ammunition of lot "B" was being used, the company realized where the trouble lay, and withdrew the whole lot of cartridges from their dealers, and also replaced all the revolvers that were damaged from this cause. Incidentally, they fixed the loading machines so that they could no longer put in more than one load of powder.

The damaged revolvers had the cylinder wall blown out, which is the way a revolver fails under very high pressure. Apparently no personal injuries resulted from any of these blow-ups. The lessons of this incident are, first, that a double charge of Bullseye doesn't do a revolver any good, and second, that an overcharge in a revolver may blow out the cylinder, but cannot injure the barrel. Damaged barrels result from other causes. For example, I once knew a young man who was annoyed one night by an owl. He was an excellent revolver shot, so he got out his .45 Model 1917, and took careful aim by the bright moonlight, and fired, without disturbing his feathered friend in the least. He took better aim, and fired again, and when the owl only opened his big eyes and looked puzzled, he took a quick shot with lots of temper behind it, and finally threw the revolver, which at least gave him the satisfaction of seeing the feathered pest flap away into the darkness. When he retrieved his gun and went to clean it, it wouldn't clean, and on examining for the reason, he found that the barrel was plugged. A steel drift and a hammer removed three service bullets. The barrel was slightly bulged.

Again, I have seen a .38 military model revolver with the barrel absolutely full of bullets (I think there were nine), and a .32-20 the same way. These were jacketed bullets. The barrels were sawed lengthwise for examination, so that there is no doubt that the bullets were there. The .32-20 was badly bulged, and .38 only slightly.

The chances are that such accidents are caused by a cartridge having a weak charge, or none at all. Perhaps in some cases the powder has been deteriorated from a trace of oil that in some way got into the case during manufacture. A weak charge might drive the bullet only part way into the barrel of the revolver, and the next bullet would be stopped by the obstruction.

Many cases like this have occurred with model 1917 revolvers, and in some cases the barrels are split along the line of lettering "U. S. Property" under the barrel, which forms a weak section. As far as has been heard, these accidents have not caused any injury to personnel. This trouble does not seem to occur with the automatic pistol. Perhaps it is because the barrel of the pistol is closed for its whole length, instead of having an opening, as the revolver does between the barrel and the cylinder, which would allow the escape of gas. With the closed barrel, even the defective charge will usually drive the bullet clear, and thus avoid trouble on the next shot.

If the head of the cartridge used in the automatic pistol is very soft, it is possible for it to blow out at the bottom, where the barrel is chamfered to permit easy feeding. This may split the grips of the pistol in the older model having wooden stocks. With the steel cartridge cases used in the recent war this would not happen.

I have rarely seen the service .45 pistol badly wrecked by an accident in service, but finally one came in, which is shown in a picture with this chapter. It seemed as if this must certainly have been due to a terrific overload. This result was duplicated experimentally by a charge of Bullseye powder of nearly three times the proper amount.

I have already mentioned my experience with the blank cartridge in the .45. The barrel had no locking lugs, so that the pressure could blow the action straight back, and there was a choke, or plug, screwed into the end of the barrel which reduced the bore at this point to about an eighth of an inch, so as to confine the gas and give more power to work the action. A charge of about five grains of blank cartridge powder was used, which worked very well, except when the choke got stopped up by a wad. The first time this happened, a bulge occurred in the barrel, at the front end, just behind the choke, though there was no bullet, only powder, and the place where the bulge occurred was not the weakest part of the barrel, as there was a thin section over the chamber which was not nearly as strong.

Another barrel was then made, and it was tempered much harder. This time when the wad jammed, the barrel split wide open, blowing the slide off at the same time, but leaving the grip intact.

In speaking of blank cartridges, it may be remarked that the * E. C. blank cartridge powder used in this test burns with extreme speed.

---

* E. C., for "Explosives Company."

The reason is clear when it is remembered that there is no bullet to confine the gas and cause a report, so that reliance must be placed on a powder that will burn all at once and give a sharp report even when it is not heavily confined.

This question of blank cartridges brings to mind the case of an enthusiast who once got hold of some of this powder, and being familiar with E. C. Shotgun powder, failed to realize that E. C. Blank cartridge powder is different, and loaded a batch of shells with

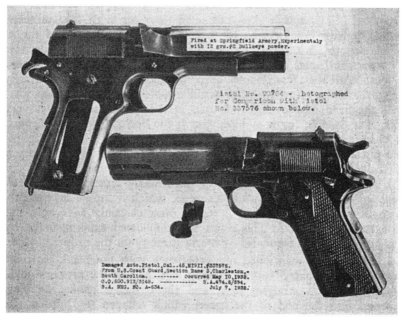

Effect of a heavy overcharge of Bullseye powder. The lower pistol was blown up in service. Springfield Armory duplicated the accident by using a charge of 12 grains of Bullseye instead of the normal charge of about 4.6 grains. As is usual in accidents of this kind, the firer was not injured.

this fast-burning stuff. To try out his new load he got out his fine Lefever gun, and put up a target in the shooting gallery to get the pattern. Some of the loungers in the vicinity were watching, and they saw him swing up his gun and fire. There was a terrific detonation, and a big piece was blown out of the side of the barrel near the breech, and flew across the room, glancing off the wall and striking a bench, where it buried itself in the wood.

The owner of the gun was an inveterate experimenter, who had gotten into trouble once or twice before. Whether the shock dazed him, or whether he felt that he had better hide his mistake to prevent his friends from laughing at it, will never be known, but what hap-

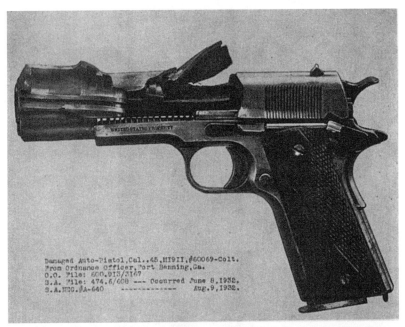

Damaged Auto-Pistol,Cal.,45,M1911,#60069-Colt.
From Ordnance Officer,Fort Benning,Ga.
O.O. File: 600.913/3167
S.A. File: 474.6/608 --- Occurred June 8,1932.
S.A.MIG.#A-640 ------------- Aug.9,1932.

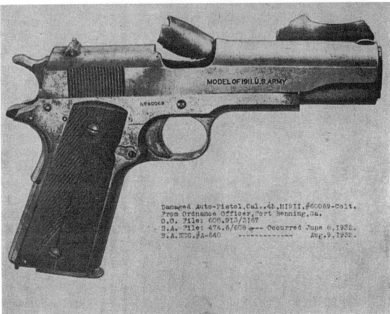

Damaged Auto-Pistol,Cal.,45,M1911,#60069-Colt.
From Ordnance Officer,Fort Benning,Ga.
O.O. File: 600.913/3167
S.A. File: 474.6/608 --- Occurred June 8,1932.
S.A.MIG.#A-640 ------------- Aug.9,1932.

This shows what will happen if the charge of pistol powder is increased to
about three times the normal amount. Even so, there is not much danger to the
firer.

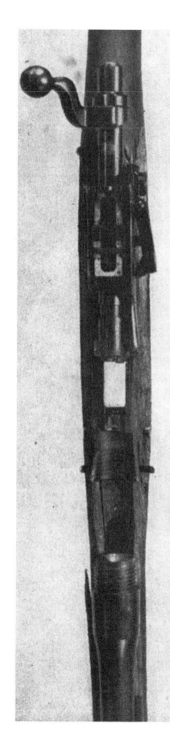

The magic term "Nickel Steel" does not mean that the receiver cannot burst. This 1917 Enfield had a cleaning patch wedged in the barrel about 2 inches in front of the chamber, and the owner tried to shoot it out. The top of the receiver was blown away, but the bolt remained in place, held by the bottom lug, and no one was hurt.

pened is that he at once put on an indescribably ludicrous air of unconcern, as if he were perfectly unconscious that anything had happened, and marched down the room humming a snatch of song and swinging the gun in time to the tune. Quickly, and with a covert glance to be sure that no one had noticed, he slipped the gun into his locker and started to walk off to another part of the room.

But this would never suit the audience, who at once wanted to know "What's the trouble?" To which the victim replied that there was no trouble, he was just tired of shooting for a while. When his attention was drawn rather forcibly to the piece of gun sticking in the bench, he saw that he hadn't gotten away with anything. He blushed and stammered as he admitted that there must have been an accident, and tried to convince his now thoroughly amused audience that he hadn't noticed it before. The material lesson of this episode is plain. Don't use blank cartridge powder behind lead. The psychological lesson is not so plain, but was interesting to the observers.

Machine guns are a big source of experience in the behavior of small arms, for they are shot so much that many things can happen. This recalls an incident on the Border in 1916, when the Ordnance Department had sent some Lewis guns to the troops, and they were being instructed in the use of them. A factory expert was demonstrating, and had just fired several shots, when the gun stopped. He pulled back the handle, and out came an empty shell. I called to him not to shoot, but he had already pulled the trigger, and apparently nothing happened, for the gun went on shooting, but when it was dismounted that evening the barrel was found to have a lump on it the size of an egg. The shot that failed to work the gun had stuck in the barrel, and the next shot had caused the bulge. Perhaps the fact that the barrel was surrounded by the thick aluminum radiator had kept it from bursting.

As was mentioned in a previous chapter another peculiar incident occurred with the Benet Machine Rifle, when a student, who had fired the gun until it was nearly red hot, managed to get the breech mechanism jammed partly open with a live cartridge in the chamber. Hoping to be able to dislodge the cartridge before it exploded from the heat, I pushed a ramrod quickly down the barrel from the muzzle, and just as the rod came sharply against the bullet, the cartridge exploded. The breech was open, and the impact of the heavy rod prevented the bullet from moving forward as long as the cartridge case was perfectly free to move backwards. The result was that the cartridge case was blown out of the breech and torn to bits, without doing any harm, while the bullet remained in place.

This naturally brings up the question of what would happen if such a cartridge were extracted from the breech and should then explode from the heat. I have seen this happen, as most people have who have handled the old air-cooled machine guns to any large extent. The result is only a very mild explosion, just sufficient to burst the brass case open and scatter burning grains of powder around. The reason that the explosion is not more violent is that the pressure necessary to rupture the cartridge case is not sufficient to cause the powder to burn rapidly enough to develop its full force. These accidents are not very dangerous, except for the possibility that small bits of brass may be blown into the eyes.

A hang-fire gives a similar result when it occurs after the cartridge has been entirely ejected, but if it should occur just as the bolt has been unlocked, and while the cartridge is still in the chamber, the result is likely to be serious, as the pressure will be held in sufficiently to develop a powerful explosion, which may blow the bolt back with violence.

One of the best ways to become acquainted with the causes of rifle trouble and their results is to have to examine, study and report on the various damaged rifles that are sent in from the service from time to time for post-mortem. On two separate occasions, once before the war and once afterwards, I have been stationed at Springfield Armory in charge of the experimental department, where this work is done. Many of the wrecks bore eloquent testimony to the destructive power of the improvised cleaning patch and the unsuitability of the old style service hat-cord for use as a pull-through. The hat-cord will pull, but it will not push, and when a soldier who is trying to clean his gun with one of them gets it all the way into his rifle barrel and then tries to dislodge it with a cleaning rod, trouble starts. No matter how you push it, the woozy, wobbly thing wedges together and cannot be moved an inch. Of course, if you had something like a corkscrew, and could get hold of the end to pull, it would come out easily enough, but ordinarily no such object is at hand, and some friend, with a quick but not cautious brain, sees a way out of the difficulty, and says "Let's shoot it out." "Of course! Why didn't I think of that before?" says the owner. In goes a cartridge, the trigger is pulled, and the next moment the air is full of flying splinters of the stock, and after the victim picks himself up and looks to see if he is all there, he glances at his rifle and finds the barrel split and the rest of the outfit looking pretty sick from the blast.

The shirt-tail cleaning patch is another trouble maker. The rifleman who has no cut patches and tears off an irregular piece of cloth to swab out his rifle often finds himself in a worse fix than he would if he made no attempt whatever to clean his gun. The ill-fitting piece of cloth requires undue force to push it through, so that frequently the cleaning rod pierces the patch and wedges so tightly that it is a problem to get it out at all. If the shooting-out method is employed, the results are the same as with the hat-cord, only more pronounced.

The wrong way of using the regular cleaning patch may also cause trouble. To prevent the cleaning rod from piercing and wedging it, the corner of patch should be turned over, and the tip of the rod should be placed against the double thickness. If this is not done, but the rod is merely placed in the center of the patch against the single thickness of cloth, it may punch through and wedge.

An officer in charge of a company on the firing range will usually encounter cases where men will get obstructions in their rifles which cannot be removed by ordinary methods. A number of years ago when in charge of a rifle range, I employed a method of removing obstructions, which may be interesting, though for reasons which will appear later, it is distinctly not recommended now. I read in an old Ordnance manual printed in the days of muzzle loaders the results of a series of experiments to determine the effect of failing to ram the ball all the way down onto the charge before firing. The early experiments tried the effect of pushing the bullet nearly onto the charge and ring the piece. The pressure was found to be less than normal. The next time the ball was rammed only half way down, and this gave a pressure much less than before. Lastly, the ball was inserted near the muzzle and on firing a very low pressure was recorded. None of the barrels were harmed in the least by these experiments, and the conclusion was that firing a gun with the bullet not entirely seated on the powder could not injure the gun. But when two balls were employd at one time, one near the breech and another some distance away in the barrel the gun was burst.

This information seemed to indicate that if an attempt were made to blow out an obstruction with powder gas the pressure would be less than with a service charge, and no harm would result if the bullet were first removed from the cartridge. After a few cautious experiments along this line I applied this method as will be described. When a rifle was brought up with an obstruction in it, I removed the bullet and half the powder from a cartridge and then holding the muzzle elevated so that the powder would stay against the primer, I fired, blowing out the obstruction. Success was uniform for the few times this method was employed during several seasons on the range. Still I always had some misgivings as to just what might happen in unusual cases, so that I was quite pleased when an opportunity was presented to test out this matter thoroughly under proper experimental conditions.

The first question taken up was the removal of rags and cleaning patches stuck in the barrel. These were easily blown out with a cartridge from which the bullet had been removed, and no injury to the barrel resulted. Then several rags were tried at a time, as well as patches wedged tightly in place, but all were removed without difficulty. Next we tried pieces of nat-cord which were wetted to make them stick more tightly. When these were successfully removed it began to look as if the method would prove worthy of recommendation as a standard method to be used for removing obstructions.

Finally, as a last grand demonstration as regards rags, a cleaning rod was filed off on a slant, and with it a couple of patches were wedged tightly in place. A cartridge minus bullet was then inserted and fired with all the confidence in the world that the cleaning rod and patch would go flying down the range, but strange to say no such thing happened. Instead, the only result was a loud prolonged hiss, as of escaping steam, and on cautiously opening the bolt it was found that the powder had all burned up without moving the obstruction in the least. Also it was noted that the cartridge case was partly filled with a thick black sludge, or mud, the residue of the powder when burnt under these peculiar conditions, and there was an acrid smell which was not at all like the regular smell of powder gas. The next thing that was tried was a heavier charge of powder, all that could be put into a cartridge case. Result, just the same as before. It appeared that with the regulation powder, which burns slowly like celluloid unless closely confined, the loosely woven porous cloth patch did not furnish enough resistance to make the powder burn quickly, so that the pressure leaked out as fast as it was generated. The obvious remedy was to use a quick powder, such as black. As a can of King's semi-smokeless was close at hand, a shell full of it was tried without success. Then a cartridge full of fine-grained black powder was used which finally blasted the obstruction loose, without injury to the barrel. After this experience the method did not look quite so good.

The next thing tried was dislodging bullets stuck in the barrel. It was found that a bullet lodged at any point was easily blown out, using the full charge of powder. This experiment was tried on an old discarded pressure gun and it was found that the pressures ran very much less than normal, as would have been expected, especially after reading the old experiments referred to above. When the bullet was seated at the muzzle, the pressure, with a cartridge case full of powder, was about half service pressure. No swelling or other injury to the barrel could be detected.

These results did not indicate any danger in this procedure, but there has been talk of the possibility that gas, in rushing down the barrel at high speed and being suddenly arrested at the base of the stationary bullet, might pile up at this point and expend its dynamic energy in a local ring of pressure that would not show on the pressure gage, but would still be capable of doing damage. To try out this idea a bullet was wedged tightly into the muzzle so that it would offer considerable resistance to being expelled. Then the gun was loaded and the trigger was pulled, but nothing happened; not even the hissing that had been experienced with the tightly wedged rags. We wondered whether it was a misfire or whether the cartridge had gone off and all the gas was remaining penned up in the barrel ready to come out with a bang as soon as the breech was opened. In order to avoid casualties we pointed the breech in a safe direction and opened the bolt by tapping the handle with a piece of wood. No sooner was the bolt handle driven to a vertical position than the bolt suddenly flew open with a loud "pop" like a champagne cork, and the empty shell was ejected smartly. As the obstruction had not been removed a heavier charge was tried, then a mixture of black and smokeless, without success, though with plenty of fun opening the bolt each time. Finally, after two tries with black powder the bullet was blown out, but on examination the muzzle of the barrel was found to be slightly swelled. It was hard to tell just what had caused the swelling, for if the piling up of a gas pressure at this point had done it, it would seem that the swelling would be found just behind the bullet. In fact it was at the very end of the muzzle, almost at the front end of the wedged bullet!

The only thing that this test settled was the fact that more tests were needed to enable proper conclusions to be drawn as to just what was happening. It was therefore decided to go ahead and do some of the things that usually cause damage, so as to determine exactly how the various forces produce their effect. We knew that firing out an obstruction with a bullet usually results in disaster, so the next experiments were planned to show more plainly just what happens in this case.

The first thing tried was the effect of loose drops of water in the barrel, as might happen in case of rain. No effect could be detected. Apparently the mass of the water drops does not check the bullet enough to do damage. Next, small pieces of brass, such as are punched from the vent holes of cartridges in manufacture, were laid in the bore in front of the bullet in the position that might be occupied in case one of these punchings should be left in the cartridge in manufacture (as sometimes happens), and should follow the bullet a short way down the bore in firing, and then lodge and wait to cause a disturbance on the next shot. These punchings, singly or several at a time did not cause any trouble that could be detected. It seems clear that they cannot bulge or burst a barrel with the present service rifle and cartridge. After this an investigation of the effect of bullet *jackets* lodged in the barrel was undertaken. It was found that they always caused a slight bulge in the barrel. In one case the new bullet passed completely through the lodged jacket, and in so doing, pressed it slightly into the steel, so that it could not be dislodged. After this a number of other bullets were fired without moving the lodged jacket, which became bedded down into the metal of the bore so that it could hardly be seen from the inside. In being pressed into the steel, it raised a slight bulge in the barrel, which could be detected from the outside.

Cleaning patches lodged loosely in the barrel gave a very slight bulge, or none at all, but two heavy patches jammed tightly in place gave a large bulge, and if the barrel had happened to be a seamy one, it would probably have split from end to end. A light piece of paper placed loosely in the barrel gave no effect.

These results suggested very forcibly the question, "Just what causes a bullet to ring a barrel?" Some people say with great confidence that it is the pressure of the air which is suddenly compressed between the moving bullet and the stationary obstruction. This theory seems extremely unlikely. Then other theorists say that checking the bullet as it strikes the obstruction causes the rapidly moving column of gas to be arrested suddenly on the base of the bullet, so that it spreads out sideways, changing its dynamic energy into static pressure which is momentarily exerted in a ring of local pressure which may cause the swelling. This theory is better than the first, but still it does not seem good enough. It is more likely that the "ring" seen so often in a barrel which has been fired with an obstruction is due entirely to the bullet, as a rough calculation will show that at any point in the barrel the moving bullet possesses about twelve times as much dynamic energy as the rushing gas behind it. The bullet is made of a plastic material of very great density. If the forward motion of the front end of this rapidly moving bullet is suddenly checked the inertia of the lead in the rear portion of the bullet, coupled with the pressure of the gas on its base, will cause it to "upset," or expand sideways, which is what I think must cause the ring. Any obstruction, such as a patch, causes the point of the bullet to wedge, and thus checks it, and the resulting ring is proportional to the amount of the checking effect.

It was argued that if this theory were true no bulge would be caused in shooting out a cleaning patch or other light obstruction, provided that the wedging could be prevented. To try this out it was decided to lodge a rag in the bore and then shoot it out with a bullet which was square in front and did not have any pointed end to wedge. The quickest way to do this seemed to be to use the back end of a regular bullet, so one was pulled out of the cartridge and put in again, back end forward, and a rag was shot out without a sign of a bulge, which may be taken as an indication in confirmation of the wedging theory, though it is of course by no means conclusive.

After this experiment with rags, it was decided to try the same thing with bullets as obstructions, to see what could be learned or deduced. A bullet was lodged in a condemned barrel, near the muzzle,

and a regular cartridge was inserted and fired, with the inevitable result; the barrel forward of where the bullet was lodged was blown
completely away. It was not possible to tell whether the damage
originated just at the location of the obstructing bullet, or behind
it, as the barrel was too completely destroyed at this point. At least
one thing was certain, though, and that was that this attempt to
shoot out a bullet with another one caused terrible havoc. In order
to see if the wedging effect had anything to do with it, the experiment
was repeated with the remaining portion of the same barrel, and
the bullet in the cartridge was reversed, as described above, so as to
attempt to sweep out the stationary bullet without allowing any
wedging effect. As was expected, the result was the same as if the
bullet had been shot sharp end first; the barrel was "sawed off," so
to speak, at the point of obstruction. There is really no contradiction
between this result and the one obtained when the rag was shot out
successfully with the square end of the bullet, for in the last experiment the mass of the stationary bullet was sufficient to cause the
lead of the two bullets to expand, merely from the impact, without
the necessity of any wedging effect to help the action along.

In this connection it should be noted that in all the experiments
conducted with light obstructions, such as cleaning patches, etc., even
where everything possible was done to make the conditions favorable
for the greatest damage, the worst results obtained were rings or
bulges, while with heavy obstructions, the destruction was complete.

To determine more definitely whether or not the gas pressure on
the base of the bullet had anything to do with the damage, another
experiment was decided on. A plug of cotton waste was put in the
center of a condemned barrel, and some melted lead was poured in
so as to form a slug about four inches long at about the middle of
the barrel's length.

On firing the gas was all retained, as has been described before.
This firing was repeated once or twice, when to our great interest
a distinct bulge was observed at about the middle of the space occupied by the lead slug. Measurements showed that the lead had
not moved. In attempting to account for the formation of the bulge
at this point, it was thought possible that the lead might have been
poured in so as to leave cavities or vacant spaces which would give
the effect of two or more slugs separated by a certain space, which
could be driven together by the force of the explosion, and thus
ring the barrel as two bullets would when driven together. To eliminate this possibility, as well as to verify the result of the experiment,
the test was repeated, taking great care to pour the lead so as to
form a solid obstruction, without cavities or pockets. On firing, the
ring again occurred, which would seem to indicate that the bulging
of barrels is principally due to the upsetting, or sidewise expansion
of the lead in the bullet. The hammering of the gas pressure on the

base of the lead plug is what caused the upsetting in this case, which leads to the conclusion that in firing a bullet with an obstruction in the barrel, the gas pressure on the base of the bullet aids the wedging effect in causing the bullet to upset sufficiently to ring the barrel.

During World War I an officer of the Ordnance Department conducted a series of experiments at one of the big commercial rifle plants to determine the effect of various barrel obstructions. These experiments, which were made with 1917 model rifles, should prove very instructive. At the time these tests were made, there was a lot of trouble with loose bullets in service cartridges, and it some times happened that when a gun was unloaded without firing, the case would be extracted, but the bullet would stick fast in the rifling. It was feared that if this should happen on a misfire, and another cartridge should be inserted and fired, the rifle would be blown up from the effect of the two bullets.

It was found that in no case could a bullet without any cartridge be forced into the rifling far enough to allow the insertion of another cartridge and the closing of the bolt. However, a bullet was inserted in this manner, and a cartridge was prepared by forcing the bullet down into the case until the base of the bullet rested hard on the powder, filling practically all the air space and projecting out of the cartridge case only about three-sixteenths of an inch. This prepared cartridge was inserted in a rifle behind the stationary bullet and fired without damage to the rifle, though the cartridge case showed evidence of excess pressure, as the primer was blown and the cartridge base was distorted.

A bullet was driven into the rifling just far enough to permit another cartridge to be inserted and the bolt to be closed. On firing both bullets were ejected without damage to the gun, but the case showed evidence of high pressure.

A bullet was seated in the barrel with the base one inch ahead of the point of the bullet in the cartridge seated in the chamber. On firing both bullets were ejected without apparent damage to the barrel.

A bullet was then seated in the barrel at a point one inch further ahead than the one just described, or so that the base was two inches ahead of the point of the bullet seated in the chamber. On firing the barrel was burst from the receiver to the lower band.

In a barrel and action without stock, a bullet was forced into the rifling to a point one inch forward of the lower band and a cartridge was inserted into the chamber. On firing the barrel was split into three sections.

A bullet was seated in the barrel at a point one and three-fourths inches from the muzzle. On firing the barrel was bulged badly at the point of obstruction and the part forward of the bulge was split into four parts.

The barrel of this rifle burst on the first shot when the owner fired it with the barrel full of cosmoline. The low-numbered receiver No. 478,579 with its bolt, both of the old heat treatment, did not fail.

A dry cleaning patch was inserted one and one-half inches in the muzzle. On firing no apparent damage was done.

A dry cleaning patch was inserted to a point three inches to the rear of the lower band. On firing the barrel was split from the receiver to above the lower band and the lower part of the stock and the lower hand-guard were blown away. The front sight carrier was blown entirely off.

A cleaning patch of cotton cloth soaked with oil was rolled up and inserted in the muzzle for a length of about one and a half inches, as it would be in the case of a man inserting a plug or tompion in his piece to keep out the dirt or rain and forgetting to remove it before firing. On firing the muzzle was split about one inch, the front sight carrier was blown entirely off and the muzzle was slightly bulged.

A cleaning patch soaked in oil was made into a roll and pushed into the bore to a point about the lower band. On firing a decided bulge was made at this point, which is visible on the outside, but there was no rupture of the barrel.

The piece having been fouled by firing a few shots, the muzzle was inserted in sand and then shaken out, leaving a very small amount of sand or dirt in the muzzle. On firing no visible result was produced.

The same test as the preceding one was again made, leaving a greater amount of sand in the muzzle. No effect was evident.

One inch of sand was inserted in the muzzle, forming a solid plug. On firing the sand was blown out without apparent effect.

The test just described was repeated, putting one and one-half inches of sand in the muzzle. On firing the barrel was split in two pieces to below the lower band, blowing away the forward end of stock, handguard and front sight carrier.

The barrel was filled with warm cosmoline and allowed to drain naturally for a few moments, and the gun was then fired without cleaning. No damage whatever was apparent to the rifle or cartridge case.

The barrel was filled with warm cosmoline and allowed to cool over night, leaving a maximum of cosmoline in the barrel. On firing no effect whatever was visible on either the barrel or the cartridge case.

A fairly heavy dose of cold cosmoline was distributed through the barrel, not enough, however, to fully obstruct it at any one point. On firing no effect was visible.

The muzzle was filled solid with cosmoline to a depth of approximately one inch. On firing the barrel was split in two pieces to below the upper band, and the front sight carrier was blown entirely off.

A small wad of chewing gum was inserted in the muzzle, as on inspection a number of instances have developed where a man has put a wad of gum in the muzzle of his rifle and it was desired to see what would result if such a wad should be left in while firing. A decided bulge was caused, but no fracture.

A study of the experiments that have been described will at least partly remove this subject from the realm of conjecture and will often enable the observer to tell from the examination of a wrecked gun the general cause of the trouble and will also enable one to know what to expect under certain circumstances. For example, some years ago a new front sight cover and protector was designed, which consisted of a cup-shaped steel stamping arranged to slip over the front end of the gun and protect both the muzzle and front sight. A rifleman, on being shown the design, objected that it would burst the barrel if the shooter forgot to remove it before shooting. In order to prove it the gun was fired with the muzzle cover on, with the expected result, which was that the bullet pierced the cover neatly and then proceeded on its way with no harm done to the rifle. In this case it could be stated with certainty that the rifle would not be injured because it was known that the service bullet could pierce a one-sixteenth-inch piece of sheet steel with such ease that it would not be checked seriously, and if the bullet were not checked the barrel would not be harmed. Thus besides having an academic interest, experiments of this nature give the designer reliable information that is at times invaluable.

VIII

The Strength of Military Rifles

ONE September day in 1920, I happened to be standing on the firing line at Camp Perry during a match, when the competitor directly in front of me fired a shot—and then couldn't see his rear sight! He rubbed his eyes incredulously, and looked again, then let out a howl that brought me to his side. It happened that I was the Ordnance Officer of the Matches, and thus was responsible for the condition and performance of the issue National Match rifle he was using. What was this about no rear sight? I dropped to my knees beside him and took a look. No rear sight at all—not even the sight base, but in the newly exposed barrel where the sight had been, a nice crack about an inch or more long. Then we began finding little bits of the sight lying around. It had broken into a dozen or more pieces, the breaks occurring on the lines that formed the range graduations.

So we issued him a new rifle and sent the damaged one back to Springfield for the investigation that was always made whenever a rifle failed from any cause. This one was due to a hidden seam in the metal of which the barrel had been made.

Of the damaged rifles which were returned to Springfield when I was in charge of the Experimental Department in 1917, and later, when I was Works Manager in 1919, '20 and '21, a fair per cent showed barrel failures. This might lead naturally to a question whether the barrel is properly designed as to strength, so let's look further into this subject.

Before any barrel is accepted for service it is proof fired with a high pressure test cartridge, or "blue pill," which gives about forty per cent higher pressure than the service load. These test cartridges are tin plated to make them look different from the regular cartridges, and this gives them a bluish white color, hence the name "blue pill."

When I was at Springfield, the regular service load gave a pressure of around 50,000 pounds per square inch, and the blue pill at first gave 70,000 pounds; which we later raised to 75,000 pounds, as will be explained further along.

Each finished rifle was given one high pressure proof charge, and this was followed by five service loads to test the functioning.

It would seem that this test should eliminate any barrel with a tendency to weakness of any kind; but, as we have seen, even National Match barrels can burst in service. What is the explanation?

As was stated above, every gun that failed in service was returned

to Springfield for examination, which almost always showed clearly
the cause of the failure.

The object of this examination was, of course, to correct any
faulty methods or design features that might be responsible. When,
as was true in a large number of cases, the barrel showed a decided
annular bulge or ring near the origin of the fracture, there was not
much the Armory could do; the damage was plainly due to an
obstruction in the bore.

A large and heavy obstruction, such as a bullet, will often make
a lump as big as a walnut, and may split the barrel to pieces in addition, while a small or light obstruction, such as a cleaning patch,
may leave a barely perceptible ring.

As intimated above, the barrel does not always burst when it is
fired with an obstruction in it, though it generally does if the obstruction is a solid object.

Twice I have seen a machine gun fired with a bullet already in the
bore, and in neither of these cases did the barrel burst. In one case
the accident was not even discovered until several hundred additional
shots had been fired and though a large lump had been formed on
the barrel, the functioning or the accuracy were apparently not
affected.

I have seen a Springfield rifle, which, though it had a pronounced
bulge near the muzzle, still shot very well indeed.

Besides obstructions there are two other occasional causes of
barrel failure. One of these is seamy metal. Before any machine work
is done on the barrels they come to the factory in the shape of
billets of steel which are afterward heated and rolled to the approximate shape of the barrel. In this barrel steel, as in any other
metal, flaws will occur. When the pieces of barrel steel are rolled
out to a long shape to make the barrel blank, any flaws that they
may contain are also stretched out in the same direction, so that
instead of a bad spot, we get a bad streak.

Most of these streaks are discovered during the machining operations. After every turning operation on the outside or reaming operation on the inside, the barrels are carefully inspected, and any with
flaws are thrown out. Once in a great while, however, it happens
that a seam or flaw may be entirely inside the walls of the finished
barrel. Luckily, the high pressure test eliminates most of these barrels.
Some which the flaw does not greatly weaken may stand the high
pressure test and get into the service. Then if by using grease on
the neck of the cartridge, or by improper handloading, or in some
other way an excess pressure is obtained, the barrel may fail.

Another trouble that was experienced after World War I was
burnt steel. Before the war, the billets of steel were rolled into barrel
blanks at Springfield Armory. But during the production rush of
1917 and 1918 outside sources were called on to do this work, and

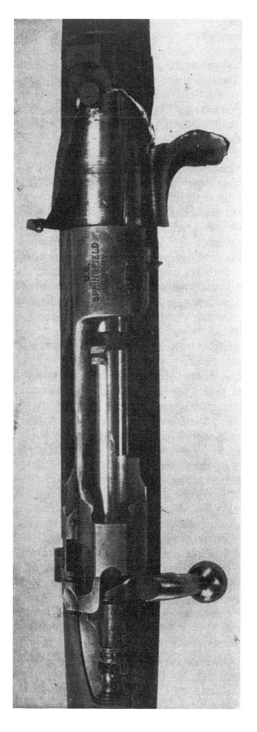

Result of a hidden seam in the barrel. After the adoption in 1918 of a double heat treatment for the receiver and bolt, it was the practice to select a rifle occasionally from production and subject it to the highest pressure that could be obtained in a test cartridge. This rifle, selected at random from production on May 3, 1918, was first tested with ten 70,000 pound test shots, then was fired with a 125,000 pound test cartridge. The receiver and bolt held, as they invariably did with this double heat treatment, but the hidden seam in the barrel opened up, with the results shown.

the barrel blanks were bought from the steel makers already forged to shape. These factories, instead of rolling the barrel blanks to the finished shape, as Springfield did, took bars of steel which were of the right diameter for the main part of the barrel blank and formed the enlarged breech end by heating this part of the blank very hot and then upsetting or bumping up the large part.

In order to get quantity production, a great many of these blanks were heated at once, and in order to make them forge up easily and quickly, they were made good and hot. For this, as well as all other work, the steel companies had to contend with the shortage of skilled help that was felt everywhere during that War, as well as during the recent one. Under such conditions it was natural that once in awhile a piece was left too long in the furnace and became too hot.

When steel becomes too hot, the fine crystalline structure that gives it its strength becomes ruined, and the metal separates into large, coarse grains with a gaseous film between them which takes away their power of cohesion and makes the steel weak and brittle. This condition is very hard to detect, because burnt steel looks like any other steel, and in automatic machinery any difference in the machining qualities could not be noticed. If such a blank should be made up into a barrel and pass the proof test it might, from the repeated shock of firing, gradually get worse in service until a break occurs.

Of course, this condition only occurs in an extremely small percentage of the blanks; perhaps one in two or three thousand, and most of these are detected by inspection or fail on proof. That the danger from this cause is small is evident from the fact that though all guns manufactured at Springfield Armory immediately after World War I had barrels made of this steel, several years passed before a barrel failure occurred which led to the discovery of this condition.

As there were several hundred thousand barrel blanks on hand at the end of the War, it meant that all barrels to be made for a long time had to be made from this steel. However, once the trouble was understood, every possible step was taken to prevent any defective barrels from being sent out. For the sake of greater safety, Springfield raised the proof charge to 75,000 pounds, instead of 70,000, to be more certain of eliminating all faulty barrels.

In the course of experiments on receivers some years ago, I used pressures up to 130,000 pounds without any apparent ill effects on the barrels. The late Sir Charles Ross, whom I knew well, had told me about his experiments on the thickness of barrels, and I had read some remarks by Newton on the same subject, but I couldn't get sufficiently authentic facts to satisfy me, so I collected some first-hand information by turning a Springfield barrel to 1/8 inch wall thickness and firing it with regular and high pressure cartridges. As the results were not visible, I turned the barrel down so that it was only 1/16 inch thick over the chamber. It held three regular service cartridges perfectly. I then put a 75,000 pound shot through which blew a piece out of the side, as can be seen in the photograph. As

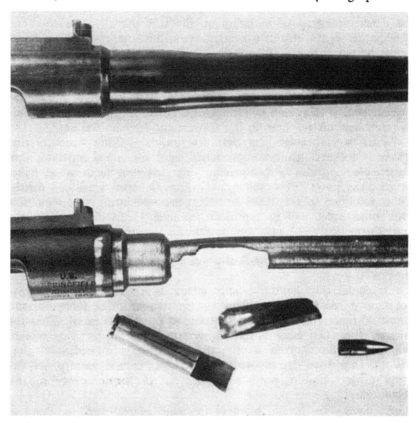

The upper barrel was turned down until it was reduced to the size shown. Three regular service charges were fired with no effect, but a 70,000 pound blue pill (high pressure test cartridge), lifted out a piece as shown. Lower barrel is for comparison to show size before any metal was removed.

the thickness of the regular barrel at this point is 5/16 of an inch, it is plainly evident that the strength should be sufficient.

Failures in the Action

Now that we have disposed of the barrel, lets consider the action. I once received a letter in which the writer inquired about the strength of the bolt. He stated that he had read in a magazine that the Springfield bolt was much weaker than that of the Krag-Jorgensen, and that the Springfield bolt was dangerous because of a tendency to blow out of the rifle, which the Krag would not do. Of course, anybody who has any conception of rifle construction knows that either the Springfield bolt or the Enfield bolt with double lugs is far stronger than the Krag bolt with only one lug.

Even so, the Krag has entirely satisfactory strength for the range of pressures for which it was designed, that is, about 40,000 pounds maximum. In connection with its loading of Krag cartridges, the Ordnance Department determined that the pressures should never be allowed to go over 42,000 pounds per square inch.

These guns have been used by many persons with little regard for this limitation, and consequently we occasionally see a Krag with one locking lug cracked, or even broken entirely off; other Krag bolts have broken in two just back of the locking lug. However, these bolts *did not blow out of the gun;* there is a rib on the right side of the bolt that bears against a shoulder on the receiver, and this acts as a safety lug, and in addition, the bolt handle turns down into a slot at the rear, which acts as a further safety feature.

The Krag rifles have been in use since October, 1894, when the first issue of the so-called Model of 1892 was made. During the intervening period of over 50 years this fine rifle has made a great reputation for itself.

The 1917 Enfield will occasionally shed its lugs. One such case came to my attention in March, 1947. The bolt had both lugs cracked entirely off, but, as usual, stayed in the gun. The cartridge showed every evidence of extreme pressure, and was covered with a spotty black deposit of caked material which indicated that perhaps it had been covered with grease when fired, which would readily account for the high pressure. The owner sent along the damaged bolt and the cartridge case, accompanied by a letter which stated in part:

". . . This shot blew the bolt and locked it in the gun so that we couldn't get the empty shell out. On taking it down, we found the bolt had blown apart; that is, two pieces had blown off the shell extractor end. It looks to me like a person could have been hurt if the bolt could have come out. . . ."

While I don't believe the writer of the letter intended it as ironical, the last sentence is certainly a magnificent understatement. Fortunately for him the bolt, as usually happens, was held in place in spite of the loss of its lugs.

For a good many years most of the rifles damaged in service were returned to Springfield, and as far as I know, no one has ever seen a case where the bolt was actually blown out. I have heard people speak of cases where the "bolt blew out" but investigation or closer questioning has always shown that the statement was not accurate. I have never been able to run down one authentic case. In some of the low numbered Springfields, made before the heat treatment was revised, lugs have been known to crack off, but in all cases the safety lug kept the bolt from actually coming back.

Just how strong the lugs really are in relation to their normal load was very well shown by an experiment I made at Springfield some years ago. The lugs of the bolt, which have a standard length of four-tenths of an inch, were reduced to one-half that amount, and firing tests were conducted with both service cartridges and high pressure loads with no bad effects. The lugs were then reduced in thickness to one-tenth of an inch, or one-fourth of their original dimensions. Shots with service cartridges caused no trouble, but a 75,000 pound blue pill broke off the weakened lugs. Still, the safety lug held, and the bolt did not move.

This test indicates that the lugs on the bolt are about four times as strong as necessary to hold the service cartridge. Still, this test did not satisfy us. We thought we might as well find out exactly what the safety lug would do by itself, so we took another bolt and removed both lugs. The service shot crushed the safety lug slightly, but did not move the bolt. The high pressure shot sheared off the metal of the safety lug which was already crushed, and allowed the bolt to move back slightly. However, the bolt did not move far, for the safety lug sheared off at an angle, and the remaining part wedged under the right-hand wall of the receiver, bringing the bolt to rest after it had moved back about half an inch. If a bolt with the locking lugs entirely removed requires a blue pill to move it half an inch, the regular bolt, with all its lugs, must be pretty safe.

The Strength of the Receiver

The next subject, and perhaps the most important one of all, is the strength of the receiver. A broken receiver makes a bad mess, and once in a while we do see cases of this kind. It was in the spring of 1917 that I first came actively into contact with the question of receiver strength. I had just come to Springfield Armory from the Mexican border, and had been placed in charge of the Experimental Department, where one of my first duties was to examine two burst rifles and report on the cause of the trouble. Both rifles had failed while using a certain make of wartime ammunition. This, on the face of it, pointed to defective ammunition as the cause of the trouble, but only a cursory examination of the steel in the receivers was required to show that it was coarse grained, weak and brittle. I reported that soft cartridge cases had probably contributed to the failure, but that the real underlying cause was poor steel in the receivers. At first this report was received with skepticism. It was argued that the Springfield rifle had been used for years with no complaints, and that as both accidents had occurred with the same ammunition, the cartridges were to blame. The answer to this was, that aside from any fault in the cartridges, the steel was susceptible to a very considerable improvement, which should be made in order to give the rifle the greatest possible factor of safety, even with bad cartridges. Finally this view prevailed; the Armory obtained the services of a highly skilled metallurgist and a staff of assistants, and completely revised the heat treatment of the receiver and bolt, as will be described in detail later on. Meantime, as Chief of the Experimental Department, I proceeded to find out all that I could about receiver strength and related matters.

One of our first steps was to try the effect of soft-headed cartridge cases. To do this, we took out the bullets, powder, and primer from a number of cartridges and annealed the heads of the cases, thus making the brass very soft. We then reloaded these cases and fired them.

We found that they were more dangerous than the high pressure cartridges. When they were fired, these soft-headed cases would spread out at the back end, or give way entirely, letting the gas at high pressure out into the receiver, with disastrous results. When gas at 50,000 pounds is pressing on the inside of the barrel, it does not have much surface to work on, and the total load is not great, but when it gets out into the bolt-well of the receiver, whose diameter is about an inch, it has more surface to push against, and the total load is enormous. A failure of this kind may burst a weak receiver, and even if the receiver is not injured, escaping gas is likely to do damage of other kinds, such as blowing off the extractor, splintering the stock, or blowing out the magazine floor plate. An extreme case of this nature occurred with soft cartridge case in a 1919 National Match rifle in which the receiver, bolt and barrel were too strong to be injured, but the stock was badly splintered.

Besides soft cases, we tried the effect of high pressures. As the rifles were constructed at that time, the average gun would stand about 80,000 or 90,00 pounds, but a 100,000 pound shot could be pretty well depended on to burst the receivers of almost any of the rifles then coming off the production line

One thing made evident by these tests is the fact that the weakest feature of most modern military actions is in the cartridge case itself. In the Springfield rifle the head of the cartridge case projects out of the rear end of the chamber a distance of from .147 to .1485 inch; in other words, there is a space of well over an eighth of an inch where the pressure is held in only by the brass. This is the weak point of the M 1903 Springfield, the M 1917 Enfield, the M 98 Mauser, and other high powered rifles using rimless cartridges.

When very high pressures are encountered, this brass wall either spreads or blows out, and the gas under high pressure gets loose and wrecks things. If the receiver is weak or brittle, it may be fractured; if it is strong, then the extractor may be blown off, the magazine well may be bulged, the stock may be splintered, and other damage may be done.

In the design of the U. S. Rifle Cal. .30, M1, Mr. Garand took great pains to eliminate this source of weakness by arranging the rear end of the chamber and the front of the bolt so that the metal of the cartridge case is surrounded right down to the extractor groove by the chamber walls.

In spite of the fact that there were over four million Garand M1 rifles made during World War II, there has never yet been a case reported of a blown receiver or bolt on this rifle. It is true that as a result of firing grenades, the rear wall where the bolt is arrested in its backward stroke has cracked out in a few instances, but there has never at this writing, (June, 1947) been a case reported where the receiver has failed at the front end where the locking is accomplished.

In trying to determine the ultimate strength of the gun, Mr. Garand built up progressively higher proof loads in increments of 5000 pounds pressure, from the regular proof load of 70,000 lbs. to the extreme figure of 120,000 lbs, per square inch.

At this latter figure, cracked left lugs on the bolt began to be encountered. A gun in which the bolt had the left lug cracked by one of these excessive high pressure overloads was then fired an endurance test of 5000 rounds of service ammunition, using the cracked bolt, which showed no further deterioration. The U. S. M1 Rifle thus has perhaps the strongest action of any military shoulder rifle in existence at this time.

The M 98 Mauser and the Model 99 (1939) 7.7 Japanese rifle are safer than the Springfield in this regard, because in each of these guns the supporting metal of the chamber comes to the forward edge of the extractor groove instead of leaving some of the actual cartridge case wall hanging out in the air, as do the Springfield and Enfield.

The Krag, which uses a rimmed case, does not have this weakness. The case enters the chamber right up to the rim, and there is little chance for the cartridge to fail at the head. That is the main reason why we never, or at least hardly ever, hear of a burst Krag receiver. A nearly similar condition is true of the Japanese Model 38 (1905) 6.5mm Arisaka rifle. It uses a semi-rim cartridge, which has only a very slight extractor groove, and the cartridge head is thus quite strong. As the cartridge walls are also particularly well supported near the head, the action of this rifle is harder to wreck than those of the Springfield, Enfield, or Mauser, all of which use the truly rimless cartridge with its weaker head construction.

Some Reasons for Cartridge Failures

As has been stated above, the modern military bolt action rifle is no stronger than the cartridge case; or stated another way, the first thing to fail is usually the case.

A serious weakness in poorly made cases is softness of the metal near the head of the cartridge. Brass gets soft when it is heated, or *annealed;* and it gets hard when it is worked. In order to be able to draw the brass from sheets into long tubes, it is heated and thoroughly softened. After the tubes are drawn, the head must be hardened. This is done in the process of giving it its final shape, during which process the metal must flow into the shape given it by the dies. Forcing the primer pocket into the solid metal aids considerably in the hardening or working process. Another thing that helps is imprinting the lettering that gives the make and date. I remember in one series of cartridges where we wanted the heads particularly strong, to hold some high-intensity loads, we carefully changed to bigger and deeper

Cartridge case with longitudinal split in head and rear end of body. Note the off-center position of the ring crimp around the primer. The case was not held centrally on the supporting stem during the primer crimping operation, and the crimping punch struck harder on one side than on the other, thus over-stressing the metal on the high side, and making it too hard and brittle. The prevalence of this defect in cases of 1934 Frankford Arsenal manufacture led to a study which revealed the cause and led to a correction of the process to avoid a recurrence.

The case illustrated was sent in April 24, 1947, after the text describing such defects had already gone to press; thus it furnished excellent confirmation of the previously written material.

The shooter reported that he got "quite a blast of hot gas," but as he was wearing shooting glasses, he was not injured.

letters stamped on the head, and gained quite a bit of additional hardness and strength this way.

After the head is formed, the cartridges under process of manufacture must be heated again, so that the body can be tapered and the neck formed. This heating is often performed with the head of the case standing in water, so that it cannot absorb heat and thus become softened. If one of these should by some accident during manufacture have the head heated after it is formed, the head may spread and the primer pocket open out during the stress of firing, and damage to the gun may result. Thus in cartridges a soft head is a dangerous defect.

Another defect that is quite dangerous is a longitudinal split in the body of the case. The rear end of the case is rather thick, and the rear end of the chamber is made a little loose, so that cartridges can feed and extract easily. The thin front of the cartridge, that can expand and hug the walls of the chamber is depended on to keep the gas in. If the case should split near the back end, where the metal is too thick to hug the walls closely, gas will come back, and if

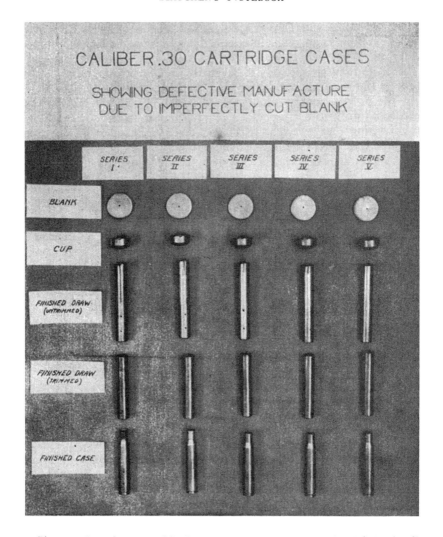

Photograph made at Frankford Arsenal to show how a slight nick in the disc from which a cartridge is drawn may cause a body split in the finished cartridge when it is fired. The nick is more pronounced in Series I and decreases in the others.

the shooter is not wearing glasses, serious eye injury may result. Always wear shooting glasses!

In well made cartridges, this defect of a longitudinal body split is not very common; but at one time Frankford Arsenal was having quite a bit of trouble from this cause. Master Mechanic Andrew H. Hallowell undertook to find out why the condition was occurring, and he finally traced it to the fact that when the discs from which the cartridges are made were being cut from the sheet brass, they were spaced too closely together, so that occasionally there was a bit of overlapping, and the edge of one of the discs might be nicked slightly.

"Andy" found that when this occurred, the nicked place caused a tiny crack that extended some distance down along the side of the drawn cartridge case, and sometimes opened up under the pressure of firing. This is shown in the photo made at the time from blanks that were found to have a slight piece cut out of the edge.

As soon as the cause of this trouble was found, it was of course eliminated but some time later, the same defect cropped up again. This time it was found that the presses had been speeded up in an effort to gain more production per day; evidently if the cases were drawn too fast, the metal was worked and hardened more than was good for it, and became brittle. When the presses were returned to their former slower pace, the trouble again disappeared.

Once more, however, the defect of lengthwise splits in the rear part of the cartridge case body appeared, this time in the 1934 .30 caliber M 1 ball ammunition. Once more the shop "detectives" were put on the trail to find out why. After some cases were cut up and micro-photographs were made it was seen that on one side the brass crystals were smaller than they were on the other side, indicating harder brass there. It was also seen that the metal of the head was thicker on that side. Cases that had not yet had the primers crimped in did not show the streak of hardness down one side.

It was finally determined that the crimping-in of the primer was responsible for making a streak of hardness down one side of the cases that sometimes gave way in the form of a crack. In crimping-in the primers, the cases are held on a stem which acts as an anvil for supporting the case against the crimping punch. When one side of the head was thicker than the other, this supporting stem made contact with the inside of the case only on the high side, and when the ring-shaped crimping punch came down, this thick section was pinched, and a streak of hardness, and consequently, of brittleness also, extended down this side of the case, and it was at this place that the splits appeared.

In the cartridge making business, there is never a dull moment!

As stated above, longitudinal splits in the body of a cartridge case are dangerous, because they allow gas to come to the rear through the mechanism, and there is danger of injury to the firer, especially to the eyes. One thing that encourages such splits is a chamber which is very loose fitting at the rear.

It so happens that the Model 99 (1939) 7.7mm Japanese rifle has a bore only a little bit larger than ours; three thousandths, to be exact, as this rifle is a .303. The cartridge is a few thousandths larger than ours is at the rear end, and is shorter than ours. Therefore it is quite easy to convert these Japanese rifles to shoot our ammunition by deepening the chamber; or our .30 caliber cartridges can be necked down to work in these guns. Unfortunately, however, the rear of the chamber is too big, and every time a U. S. .30-'06 cartridge is fired in one of these guns, there is a strain on the rear of the cartridge case, inviting it to split. If the brass is perfect with no flaws or

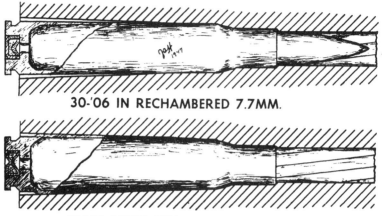

30-'06 IN RECHAMBERED 7.7MM.

SAME AFTER FIRING

GAS LEAKS IN CASE

Top: .30-'06 cartridge in rechambered Japanese 7.7mm. Note the clearance around the rear of the cartridge case, which for reasons of clarity is slightly exaggerated in the sketch.

Middle: .30-'06 cartridge case in rechambered 7.7mm Rifle after firing. Note that the thin walls of the case have expanded to fit the chamber, but the head of the case, where the metal is thick, has not expanded.

Bottom: When this .30-'06 cartridge was fired in a Japanese rifle, two longitudinal splits developed in the case as shown, permitting hot gas at high pressure to escape violently to the rear. The case, sent in by the member to whom the accident happened, is head stamped F.A. 39. Fortunately no serious injury resulted.

planes of weakness, there is slight chance of having this happen, but if the weakness is there, such a split will happen more easily than it will in the tighter chamber of the M 1903 rifle; and more gas will come back, as the loose chamber gives more room for it. So far, (March, 1947), I have seen only one case where this happened with the Model 99 (1939) 7.7 rifle chambered for our cartridge, but I expect to see more.

These Jap rifles are good strong rifles, but they are by no means proof against blowing up if abused. Recently some boys tried shooting .35 Remington cartridges in one of these guns. The bolt closed so hard that the boys used a mallet to get it shut, and they actually fired two shots with no damage to the gun; but on the third shot the receiver gave way completely and the firer had a piece of steel embedded in his brain. I am happy to be able to state, however, that after a delicate operation, the life of this intrepid young experimenter was saved.

IX

Receiver Steels and Heat Treatment

The trouble with weak receivers that occurred in 1917, and which has already been mentioned briefly, led to a complete change in the heat treating methods at Springfield Armory, and to change of heat treatment and afterward, a change of steel at Rock Island. Both these important changes were later followed by others. In order to understand just what happened and the reasons for what occurred, it is necessary to go back into history a bit.

From the time the Springfield Rifle went into production in 1903, and up until 1927, the receiver and bolt were made of Springfield Armory Class C Steel, afterward W. D. 1325, having a composition as follows:

	Min.	Max.
Carbon	.20%	.30%
Manganese	1.10%	1.30%
Silicon	.15%	.35%
Sulphur		.05%
Phosphorus		.05%

The receiver was forged under a 2,000 pound drop hammer, hot trimmed, and then while hot was given one blow in the forging dies under the hammer to straighten it. It was next put in charcoal and allowed to cool very slowly. It was then pickled to remove the scale, and again put under the drop hammer cold to bring it to size, after which it went to the receiver shop where all machine operations were performed.

After machining was finished, the receivers were heated in bone, four in a pot, to 1500° F. and kept at this temperature four hours. This was in a muffle type oil furnace. The receivers were then quenched in oil.

At Rock Island receivers were made from the same steel until 1918. The treatment was as follows:

Pack in charred leather in pots. Heat to 1475 to 1500° F. and hold at this temperature for 3½ to 4 hours. Quench in oil.

This quenching from a high temperature made the receiver fairly hard all the way through, though the surface and the material near the surface into which the carbon from the charred leather had penetrated were harder than the interior, so that the piece was actually case-hardened.

Now the harder the steel, the greater its tensile strength, and these receivers, being quite hard, were very strong and highly resistant to a *slowly* applied load. Also, the harder the steel, the more brittle it is when subjected to a *sudden shock*.

The very hard surface had excellent wearing qualities, and made a fine smooth working action. When properly headspaced and used with ammunition of good quality, these receivers gave excellent re-

Springfield rifle with low numbered receiver, burst at Sandy Hook, N. J., October 24, 1921, by having a 7.9 German service cartridge fired in it. Such a cartridge fired in a Springfield rifle results in a pressure of over 75,000 lbs. per square inch. It may burst a low-numbered receiver, but tests have shown that the double heat treated receivers will stand this mis-treatment without giving way. For full report see Chapter 18, p. 458.

sults. The Springfield rifle had then been in use for some fourteen years, and there were about 700,000 of them in existence, and there had never been any complaint, though it was later found that some of them, while showing a high static strength, would shatter under a sudden blow.

The maximum working pressure for the service cartridge was 50,000 pounds per square inch. Each finished rifle was proof fired with a test cartridge or blue pill giving a 40% overload, or 70,000 pounds per square inch, after which it was function fired with five service cartridges. This eliminated most of the weak ones. Very rarely one would break in service, but usually this could be traced to some abuse, and anyway, it happened so seldom that it caused no comment.

When World War I came along, the production of rifles was stepped up to the maximum possible, both at Springfield and at Rock Island, and at the same time several new companies tried their hand at making ammunition, and some of the new cartridges were far from satisfactory in quality.

This was the situation when, as already described, I was given the job, in the spring of 1917, of investigating the cause of the damage to two rifles sent in from the new cartridge factory of the National Brass and Copper Tube Co., at Hastings-on-Hudson. In both of these rifles the receivers has been demolished, but the barrels were intact, with the cases, or what remained of them, still in the chambers.

This was only a year after my graduation from the Ordnance School of Technology at Watertown Arsenal, where I had taken, among other subjects, a course on the metallurgy of iron and steel under Dr. Fay of Massachusetts Institute of Technology. I was by no means a skilled metallurgist, but at least I thought I knew burnt steel when I saw it and this is what the fractured surface of the first rifle looked like to me.

The gun had been fired only 252 rounds when it gave way. The engineers who examined the rifle at the cartridge factory where it failed sent along a note which stated: "It is the judgment of everyone who has seen the broken edges of the receiver that the steel most emphatically is not properly case-hardened as per specifications, and that it has been heated too hot before quenching, creating crystallization and resulting in the greatest weakness. There is no wonder it burst."

I could quite agree that the steel appeared to have been weakened by overheating. Pieces of this receiver placed in a vise and tapped with a hammer simply fell apart.

On these two guns there was also evidence that the heads of the cartridge cases had been soft, and had expanded before the receiver failure, thus letting gas under high pressure get out into the receiver ring where it had such a large surface to work on that the load on the receivers was greatly increased.

My experiments resulted in a report which stated in effect that the damage had been caused by a combination of soft headed cartridge cases and receivers which were weak and brittle; and further, that similar weak and brittle receivers were still coming off the production line. Half a dozen new receivers were taken at random from the assembly room and fastened in a vise and struck with a hammer. Several of them shattered to pieces.

As has been stated above, this report led to the employment by the Armory of the best obtainable metallurgical staff, headed by Maj. W. H. Bellis, a well known specialist on the heat treatment of iron and steel.

One fact that this staff quickly developed was that the forging temperature was not being sufficiently controlled. Too much reliance was being placed on the knowledge and experience of the furnace men who heated the receiver and bolt steel in the forge shop.

These men thought that they could tell when a piece had the right heat just by looking into the furnace. They were proud of their experience, skill, and ability, and believed that it took years of practice to become expert in judging the forging temperature. They were highly paid craftsmen, who were jealous of their exclusive skill, and who both hated and feared these new fangled pyrometers which threatened to make useless their special knowledge.

The first step taken by the metallurgists was to install pyrometers, when it was quickly found that the "right heat" as judged by the skillful eye of the old timers was up to 300 degrees hotter on a bright sunny day than it was on a dark cloudy one. This variation was of course made much worse by the fact that production had been stepped up to such a degree that many less skillful men had to be employed on this and all other critical jobs. The production rush had, as always happened, caused a drop in the quality of a product which even at best was not up to what could be obtained by the most modern controlled methods.

A further result of the fine work on the metallurgical improvement of the bolt and receiver by Major Bellis and also by Lieut. Col. W. P. Barba, Chairman of the Ordnance Department Board on Steel, and others, was the development of an entirely new so-called double heat treatment for the Springfield Armory Class C Steel, as follows:

The receiver was forged under a 2000 pound drop hammer, hot trimmed, and then given one blow under the hammer to straighten it, after which it was allowed to cool in an open pan. It was then pickled to remove scale, cold trimmed, and brought to size cold, under the drop hammer. It was then annealed by packing in charcoal, heating to 1500 degrees F. for 2 hours, and cooling in the furnace, after which it was pickled, inspected, and machined.

After machining, the receiver was heated in bone in an American Gas Company Carburizing Furnace at 1500 degrees F. for 2½ hours, then quenched in oil. It was re-heated to 1300 degrees F. in a salt bath for 5 minutes, and again quenched in oil. It was next drawn at 350 degrees F. in an oil bath and air cooled, and tested for hardness with a Scleroscope, which should give a reading between 45 and 60. This would correspond roughly to from 33 to 44 Rockwell C.

The difference in the resulting receiver (and bolt) structure between the old and the new treatment can be outlined briefly as follows:

In both methods, the receivers (and bolts) were carburized so that the metal on and near the surface had a higher carbon content than did the inside. In the old method the receiver was simply heated above the hardening temperature of the steel and then quenched. This made the receiver hard all the way through, though the carburized surface, having a higher carbon content came out harder than the lower carbon interior, which, however, was still hard enough to be brittle under shock.

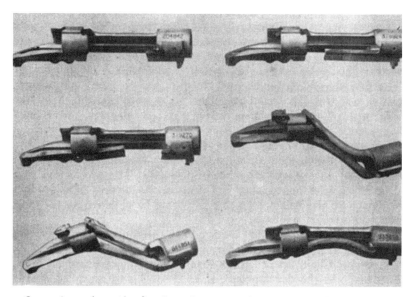

Comparison of case hardened receivers as made at Springfield and Rock Island up to 1918, with the double heat treated receivers made at Springfield between 1918 and 1927.

Top left: Receiver No. 204,842. Top right: Receiver No. 318,924. Middle left: Receiver No. 319,270. These were all of the old case hardened type A light blow with a steel rod shattered the side rib of the receiver, showing that the steel, while strong, was too hard to resist impact.

Middle right: Receiver No. 808,549. Bottom left: Receiver No. 811,951. Bottom right: Receiver No. 833,698. These receivers, numbered above 800,000, all had the double heat treatment, giving a hard surface and a soft tenacious core. When repeated blows with a steel rod failed to shatter the side rib, which is the weakest part of the receiver, they were fastened in a heavy vise and belabored unmercifully with a heavy iron bar. Note that while cracks appeared in the hard surface where it was bent, the soft interior held the metal together. These double heat treated receivers fitted with bolts having the same treatment produced the strongest rifle actions ever made.

The new treatment was based on the fact that the higher the carbon content of the steel, the lower the temperature to which it must be heated to make it harden when quenched from this temperature.

As the reader is no doubt aware, the hardness of carbon steel is largely dependent on the form in which the carbon exists in the steel. If the carbon is in a form called Pearlite, the steel will be soft. If it is in a form called Martensite, the steel will be hard. If it is part one and part the other, the hardness will be intermediate. When steel is heated, a point is reached at which it seems to absorb heat. At this so-called decalescence point, the Pearlite turns into Martensite. This is one of the "critical" points of steel. If the steel is heated to this point and then cooled slowly, another critical point, called the recalescence point, is reached some 200 to 250 degrees lower, where the steel stops cooling for a time and actually seems to give out heat as the Martensite turns back to Pearlite. Steel cooled slowly in this way will come out soft. But if, when the steel has reached the first critical point, it is cooled suddenly, as by quenching in brine or oil, the Martensite is trapped before it can change back and the metal becomes very hard. This operation is called hardening.

If the hardened steel is then heated, it begins to soften. If heated a little, it is softened slightly. If heated nearly to the critical point, it becomes very soft.

Now the newer double heat treatment takes advantage of the fact that, as noted above, the higher the carbon content of the metal, the lower the temperature to which it must be brought to make it harden when cooled suddenly.

Thus if the piece is quenched from a temperature just high enough to permit hardening the carburized outside surface, the lower carbon inside core will remain very soft.

In the revised heat treatment, heating to 1500 degrees and quenching hardens the receiver through and through, and refines the grain. Re-heating to 1300 degrees draws the temper and softens the metal. This temperature is above the hardening point of the high carbon outside surface but not hot enough to cause the low carbon inside core to harden when quenched. When the piece at 1300 degrees is then plunged into oil, the outside surface becomes very hard, and the inside core remains soft and tough. Afterwards the receivers are heated to 350° F., which slightly reduces the hardness of the surface layer and adds to its toughness.

Typical of the old single heat treatment is the following test of three receivers:

After firing ten rounds of 70,000 pounds per square inch the increase in headspace was found to be from .003 inch to .006 inch. One of the three receivers tested was blown up with one round of 80,000 pounds per square inch and the other two receivers broke with the firing of one round each of 100,000 pounds per square inch.

On the other hand, receivers with the double heat treatment could not be broken with the highest proof loads that could be made up for this caliber, namely 125,000 pounds per square inch.

In 1926 a Board investigating this subject took from stock 24 rifles made in 1918 having double heat treated receivers and tested them with results as given below:

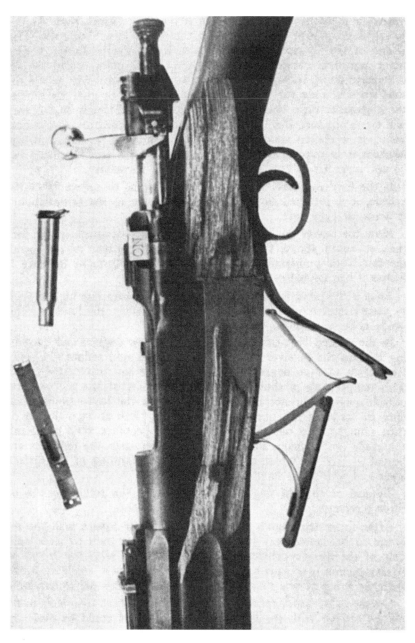

This double heat treated receiver and bolt withstood a destruction charge of 45 grains of bullseye behind a 170 grain flat based proof bullet, giving a pressure of around 133,000 pounds per square inch. The head of the case practically melted away, letting the gas out into the receiver well, where it messed things up a bit, and blew splinters off the stock, but the action held firm.

HEADSPACE

Receiver No.	At Start	After 10 70000 # sq. in. proof shots	After 1 80000 # sq. in. proof shot	After 1 125000 # sq. in. proof shot
853,398	1.945	1.946	....	O.K.
853,347	1.942	1.945	....	O.K.
859,213	1.942	1.945	....	O.K.
856,789	1.942	1.945	....	O.K.
857,661	1.942	1.944	....	O.K.
858,771	1.941	1.942	....	O.K.
859,576	1.941	1.945	....	O.K.
855,485	1.942	1.944	....	O.K.
859,797	1.942	1.944	1.944	O.K.
860,825	1.946	1.948	1.950	O.K.
860,995	1.942	1.944	1.944	O.K.
861,038	1.944	1.946	1.946	O.K.
862,031	1.941	1.942	1.945	O.K.
861,534	1.942	1.944	1.945	O.K.
862,747	1.942	1.945	1.945	O.K.
862,564	1.941	1.942	1.942	O.K.
860,651	1.942	1.945	1.945	O.K.
861,049	1.945	1.947	1.948	O.K.
863,998	1.940	1.940	1.940	O.K.
865,717	1.943	1.946	1.946	O.K.
866,906	1.940	1.941	1.942	O.K.
876,523	1.944	1.950	1.951	O.K.
868,526	1.940	1.941	1.941	O.K.
868,622	1.941	1.944	1.944	O.K.

Receivers made at Rock Island Arsenal as well as at Springfield Armory had been involved in the accidents occurring in 1917 and 1918 which caused the revision of heat treatment. Rock Island was using the same steel that Springfield specified, and they made some experiments that verified the Springfield results. Accordingly on May 11, 1918, beginning with receiver No. 285,507 they adopted an improved heat treatment, as described later on for the carbon manganese steel receivers and bolts. In addition, on August 1, 1918, but receiver No. 319,921, they adopted a nickel steel similar to that being used at the time for the 1917 rifles under manufacture by Winchester, Remington and Eddystone.

This .35% carbon, 3.5% nickel steel was given the following treatment:

Heat in salt bath to 1500° F., quench in oil, and draw in sodium nitrate at 600° F. for 30 minutes. Then test for hardness with Sclerscope which must be between 55 and 70 (this corresponds roughly to 41-52 Rockwell C.).

Tests made on these Rock Island nickel steel receivers gave the following results:

Treatment: Oil quenched from 1600° F. Reheated to 700° F.

Head Space	At Start	After 10 70000 lbs. sq. in. proof shots	After 1 80000 lbs. sq. in. proof shot	After 1 125000 lbs. sq. in. proof shot
Nickel Steel	1.941	1.944	1.949	O.K.
" "	1.941	1.942	1.951	O.K.
" "	1.942	1.948	Bolt jammed	
" "	1.940	1.941	Bolt jammed	
" "	1.940	1.946	Bolt jammed	

Treatment: Oil quenched from 1500° F. Reheated to 650° F.

Head Space	At Start	After 10 70000 lbs. sq. in. proof shots	After 1 80000 lbs. sq. in. proof shot	After 1 125000 lbs. sq. in. proof shot
Nickel Steel	1.941	1.943		O.K.
" "	1.940	1.943		Blew up
" "	1.941	1.943		Blew up

Treatment: Oil quenched from 1425° F. Reheated to 650° F.

Head Space	At Start	After 10 70000 lbs. sq. in. proof shots	After 1 80000 lbs. sq. in. proof shot	After 1 125000 lbs. sq. in. proof shot
Nickel Steel			Broke	
" "				Blew up
" "				Blew up

Some time after World War I the question arose as to just how receivers with the old heat treatment could be identified. Springfield stated: "The exact date of the change from the old to the new method is not known. Between receivers number 750,000 and 780,000 there seems to have been a shifting in heat treatment. Receivers No. 800,000 was completed on February 20, 1918, and it is known that all receivers after 800,000 received the double heat treatment."

While for practical purposes the division between the old and the new heat treatment at Springfield Armory may be taken as receiver number 800,000, this cannot be considered completely accurate, as it has been said that a few receivers of the old treatment, which had been set aside for some reason were put back in the assembly line just after number 800,000. It is significant that out of the 68 accidents reported between 1917 and 1929 in which receivers of the M 1903 rifle were shattered or fractured only one was supposed to be of the new Springfield double heat treatment, and that one, which occurred in 1929, involved receiver number 801,548. I have no doubt that this was actually a receiver having the old heat treatment.

As to Rock Island receivers, on September 24, 1926, Rock Island replied as follows: "There are no records to show the serial number at which a change was made from carbon to nickel steel. Miscellaneous shop memoranda indicate that this change occurred shortly after August 1, 1918. The serial numbers in August, 1918, run upward from 319,921. One fact seems clear and that is that all finished receivers of nickel steel were stamped 'NS' on the face at the front end. This stamping is covered by the assembly of the barrel but can be seen on disassembled receivers. A fairly sure test can be made with a file as all nickel steel receivers cut easily, while filing makes no impression on the file-hard carbon receivers."

On September 27, 1926, the following supplemental information was furnished by Rock Island Arsenal: "Stock movement records have been found showing *both carbon and nickel steel* receivers being made *each month to include December 1918 and July 1919*. No separation of serial numbers was made.

"In February, 1918, the heat treatment of carbon steel receivers was changed to the following:

"Annealed at 1500° F. for 2 hours, dropped to 1050° in the furnace, then removed and air cooled. Hardened by heating to 1550 to 1600° F. for 15 minutes and quenched in Houghton's No. 2 quenching oil. Reheated to 1425° F. followed by quenching in oil. Washed in soda kettle. Drawn in oil at 500° F.

"Instructions were issued on March 2, 1918, to destroy all carbon steel receivers *having the old heat treatment* remaining on hand and to assemble only receivers having the new heat treatment after that date. Some 16,000 receivers were destroyed.

"The serial numbers of receivers manufactured at Rock Island Arsenal prior to February 1, 1918, run from No. 1 to No. 285,506. Manufacture was suspended on January 30, 1918, and none were made during February, March or April. On May 11, 1918, manufacture of receivers was resumed with serial number 285,507.

"It would seem that if it were necessary to replace those of Springfield Armory manufacture bearing serial numbers below 800,000 it it would be desirable to do the same thing with those of Rock Island Arsenal manufacture of serial numbers less than 285,507 as the heat treatment was the same at both arsenals."

After World War I was over and the Army was demobilized, the War Department began to consider the question of what, if anything, should be done about the low numbered receivers in service.

On December 2, 1927, a Board, consisting of Major Herbert O'Leary, Major James Kirk, Captain James L. Hatcher and 1st Lieutenant René R. Studler, was convened to recommend the policy to be adopted governing the use of Model 1903, caliber .30, rifle receivers of Springfield Armory manufacture bearing serial numbers below 800,000 and Rock Island receivers below 285,507.

The following extracts from the proceedings of the Board are of interest:

A statement by Frankford Arsenal, June 25, 1925; "In view of the large number of accidents occurring with rifles having serial numbers below 800,000, this Arsenal considers that all such rifles should be withdrawn from service and not used for any firing."

And a statement from Frankford Arsenal on April 23, 1926: "This Arsenal thinks that not only the firing of grenades in rifles manufactured at Springfield Armory with receiver serial numbers below 800,000 should be prohibited, but that the firing of all small arms ammunition in such rifles should be prohibited, and this opinion has been expressed by this Arsenal upon several occasions."

Springfield Armory on June 23, 1926, stated, referring to the above: "This Armory agrees. Receivers manufactured at Springfield Armory with receivers below 800,000 are known to be weak. The use of a rifle with such a receiver is dangerous if the pressures are above normal or the headspace is excessive."

In 1923 Springfield Armory undertook an investigation to determine the practicability of re-heat treating receivers with numbers below 800,000 to determine if they could thus be given strength equal to receivers of later manufacture. One hundred receivers were re-heat treated and tested. The result indicated a considerable variation in carbon content, many receivers being low enough to require re-carburizing before heat treating.

The test showed that while the old receivers were improved by re-heat treating, they were still likely to burst at pressures slightly in excess of 50 percent above normal, while the later double heat treated receivers would successfully withstand very high pressures. The Board stated: "The test brings out quite clearly the fact that uniform results cannot be obtained by re-heat treating old receivers which vary widely in chemical composition."

It may be noted that one trouble encountered with the low numbered receivers was that some of them were dangerously weak by reason of having been overheated, or burnt, during the forging process. *No amount of re-heat treating would cure this trouble.*

In one of the experiments at Springfield Armory, 48 receivers were carefully re-heat treated, after which 16, or one-third, failed on high pressure test.

The Board found:

(1) That low numbered receivers are not suitable for service use in their present condition.

(2) That means have not yet been determined for making such receivers suitable for service use.

(3) That it is considered impracticable, if not impossible, to re-heat treat these receivers in such a manner as to make them serviceable.

The Board recommended that the receivers be withdrawn from service and scrapped.

After considering the proceedings of the Board, the Chief of Field Service, Brigadier General Samuel Hof, on February 7, 1928, made the following recommendation to the Chief of Ordnance, which was approved as a policy:

"Our ammunition is getting worse and accidents may be somewhat more frequent. On the other hand, some of these early rifles have been in use for many years and undoubtedly some of them have worn out several barrels. I do not think the occasion merits the withdrawal of the rifles of low numbers in the hands of troops until the rifle is otherwise unserviceable. On the other hand, I do not think we are justified in issuing such rifles from our establishments. I recommend that we instruct our Ordnance establishments to no longer issue rifles with these questionable receivers, that such rifles be set aside and considered as a war reserve and the question of the ultimate replacement of the receivers be deferred. When rifles are turned in from the troops for repair the receivers having these low numbers should be scrapped."

During the twelve years from 1917 to 1929 inclusive, 31 receivers of Springfield manufacture are recorded as having blown up, together with 25 of Rock Island manufacture and 5 listed as unknown. Of these, one Rock Island receiver, No. 445,136, was definitely of new manufacture. Of the Springfield Armory receiver, No. 801,548, which oddly enough is the last one on the list in 1929, was *recorded* as having the new heat treatment. This, however, is doubtful because as above stated, it is known that just about No. 800,000 a small lot of old receivers which had been set aside for some reason were found and put in process, and the number, together with the fact that no other case is recorded of the breakage of a receiver of double heat treatment, indicates that this was probably one of this special lot. This receiver incidentally was burst by firing it with a 7.9mm German service cartridge.

Two Springfield receivers, with the double heat treatment, Nos. 946,508 and 951,718, were "deformed" and "bulged," respectively. This is typical of the double heat treated receivers when exceptionally high pressures are encountered. They will always hold together, even though the cartridge head may open up and allow enough gas to escape to bulge the magazine wall and splinter the stock.

In this latter case the report of the accident stated: "Damage was caused by excessive pressure which was sufficiently high to cause the cartridge case to fail suddenly and allow gas under very high pressure to escape into the action. The *receiver* was evidently properly heat treated because *it did not fracture*."

The complete tabulation and record of the investigation of all accidents to the U. S. Rifle Caliber .30, Model of 1903 which were reported between the years of 1917 and 1929 inclusive will be found in the last chapter.

Receivers and bolts for the Springfield rifle continued to be made of the carbon steel, double heat treated, until April 1, 1927, when a change was made to nickel steel with rifle No. 1,275,767.

While Rock Island had, as noted above, been using nickel steel for part of their production since August 1, 1918, Springfield first approached a change to this material in 1926. In March of that year, after the manufacture of rifles had been discontinued at Rock Island, 25,600 unfinished nickel steel receivers, together with a number of other unfinished parts, were shipped to Springfield Armory to be finished. These Rock Island receivers were forged of steel stated to be Hot Rolled Nickel Steel, S. A. specification 35-NS. The analysis furnished at that time was as follows:

Carbon	.30%— .40%
Manganese	.45%— .50%
Phosphorus	.05% or less
Sulphur	.05% or less
Silicon	.10%— .25%
Nickel	3.25%—3.75%

Springfield Armory completed the manufacture of these receivers, the first one being finished about April 1, 1927, and numbered 1,-275,767.

In August, 1926, Colonel Schull, Commanding Officer of Springfield Armory, asked the Chief of Ordnance to approve the manufacture of an experimental lot of 100 receivers, bolts and cut-offs for the M 1903 rifle to be made of nickel steel, WD 2340.

In his letter, Colonel Schull stated that this experimental lot of bolts, receivers and cut-offs would be used in a comparison test with corresponding parts manufactured of the plain carbon steel, WD 1325. He further said, "It is believed the manufacture of this number of components would yield valuable experience in drop forging and heat treating and develop the necessary physical qualities, and in addition aid in determining whether or not machining operations with this higher grade of steel will be materially increased using present jigs, fixtures and methods." The same file also states, "Attention is invited to numerous complaints which have been made during the past few years concerning the manner in which bolts and cut-offs become unserviceable."

Approximately 100 receivers and bolts were manufactured from the WD 2340 steel, assembled into rifles and tested. The results of the tests performed were studied by the Ordnance Office, and on March 6, 1928, a letter was received from that office which stated: "It is directed that a suitable alloy steel be substituted for carbon steel heretofore used in the components named." Chemical composition of WD 2340 is as follows:

Carbon	.35%— .45%
Manganese	.50%— .80%
Phosphorus	Max. .04%
Sulphur	Max. .04%
Nickel	3.25%—3.75%

It will be noted that this steel differed slightly from the first nickel steel receivers made by Rock Island Arsenal and Springfield Armory between 1918 and 1927.

Except for the annual assembly of National Match rifles, the production of the 1903 rifle was suspended from the early 1930's until the beginning of World War II. The few rifles that were made during this period had receivers and bolts made of nickel steel WD 2340.

Likewise the WD No. 8620 Steel used in the bolts and receivers of the M1 Garand rifle and the M 1903 A3 and A4 rifles is a nickel-chromium molybdenum steel having about 60 points (.40% to .70%) of nickel and about 20 points (.15% to .25%) of carbon.

Recapitulation

For ready reference, the information given above as to steel compositions and heat treatments is collected together here along with some other material not already given, so as to present in easily available form the information on the material used in the various military rifles used in the Army over the last fifty years.

Krag Jorgensen Rifle. (U. S. Rifle Cal. .30, Model of 1898)

The Barrel was made of Ordnance Barrel Steel having the following composition:

Carbon	.45% to	.55%
Manganese	1.00% to	1.30%
Sulphur	Not over	.05%
Phosphorus	Not over	.05%

The Receiver was made of Springfield Armory Class C Steel.

Carbon	.20% to	.30%
Manganese	1.10% to	1.30%
Silicon	.15% to	.35%
Sulphur	Not over	.05%
Phosphorus	Not over	.05%

The Bolt appears to have been made of carbon steel having around .55% to .65% carbon with .45% to .55% manganese.

The Springfield Rifle, Model of 1903, with its alterations A1, A3, and A4

The Barrel, for rifles of Springfield Armory make, from serial No. 1 to serial No. 1,532,878. (This includes all the rifles made at Springfield Armory, and refers to the original barrel only, as some were rebarrelled in the course of repair using barrels of commercial make.)

Material: Ordnance Barrel Steel with composition as given above under the Krag.

Treatment: Quench in oil at 1600° F. and temper for 2 hours at 1200° F.

The Barrel for rifles having serial numbers over 3,000,000, made during World War II.

Material: War Department (WD) Steel No. 1350 Special, (resulphurized), Alternate, WD Steel No. 1350 Modified; with compositions as given below:

	WD No. 1350 Special		WD No. 1350 Modified	
Carbon	.45% to	.55%	.45% to	.55%
Manganese	1.10% to	1.35%	1.10% to	1.35%
Silicon	.25% to	.35%	.25% to	.35%
Resulphurized	to	.06% Sulphur	Not over	.05%
Phosphorus	Not over	.06%	Not over	.06%

Treatment: Before machining, heat to a temperature of 1525° to 1600° F.; oil quench, and temper to Brinell hardness of 229 to 285. Stress relieve not less than 900° F. after straightening if necessary.

Receivers and Bolts of Springfield Armory make, from serial No. 1 to serial No. 800,000.

Material: Springfield Armory Class C Steel as given under Krag.

Treatment: Carburize in bone, 4 in a pot at 1500° F. for 4 hours in a muddle type furnace, then quench in oil.

Springfield Receivers and Bolts from serial No. 800,000 to 1,275,767.

Material: Springfield Armory Class C Steel as given under Krag.

Treatment: Heat in bone in an American Gas Company Carburizing Furnace at 1500° F. for 2½ hours, then quench in oil. Reheat at 1300° F. in a salt bath for 5 minutes, and again quench in oil. Draw at 350° F. in an oil bath and air cool. Test for hardness with a Scleroscope, which must read between 45 and 60. (Roughly equivalent to Rockwell C 33 to C 44.)

Springfield Receivers and Bolts from Serial No. 1,275,767 to No. 1,532,878.

Material: Nickel Steel WD 2340.

Carbon	.35% to	.45%
Manganese	.50% to	.80%
Nickel	3.25% to	3.75%
Sulphur	Not over	.04%
Phosphorus	Not over	.04%

Treatment: Quench from 1600° F. and draw in sodium nitrate at 600° F. for 30 minutes.

Receivers and Bolts for rifles having serial numbers over 3,000,000, of World War II manufacture.

Material: Until March, 1942, Nickel Steel WD 2340, as above.

Treatment: Anneal in charcoal at 1450° F., cool in furnace. Heat in carburizing salt, 1425° to 1450° F.; quench in oil. Temper. Case depth, .003 inch to .005 inch. Rockwell C 42 to C 47 for core.

On March 4, 1942, the use of WD Steel No. 4045 was authorized; this had the following composition,

Carbon	.40% to	.56%
Manganese	.70% to	1.00%
Molybdenum	.20% to	.30%
Sulphur	Not over	.05%
Phosphorus	Not over	.04%

Treatment: Anneal in charcoal, cool in furnace. Heat in carburizing salt at 1475° to 1500° F.; quench in oil. Temper. Case depth, .003 inch to .005 inch. Rockwell C 42 to C 47 for core.

On July 5, 1942, the use of an additional steel, namely WD No. 8620 Modified, was authorized. The composition of this steel was:

Carbon	.18% to	.25%
Manganese	.70% to	1.00%
Nickel	.20% to	.40%
Chromium	.20% to	.40%
Molybdenum	.15% to	.25%
Sulphur, resulphurized	to	.07% max.
Phosphorus	Not over	.04%

Grain Size 5 to 8 ASTM

Hardenability, Jominy C 20 Rockwell, minimum, at $\frac{3}{8}$ inch from quenched end.

Treatment for bolt: Normalize before machining. Carburize .012" to .015"; oil quench. Temper at 350° F. Hardness, Rockwell D 62 to D 70 on barrel of bolt.

Treatment for receiver: Normalize before machining. Carburize .009" to .015"; oil quench. Temper at 350° F. for 1 hour at heat. Rockwell D 62 to D 70 on side rail.

M 1903 Rifles of Rock Island Make

The Barrel was made of Ordnance Barrel Steel as given above.

Receivers and bolts from serial No. 1 to serial No. 285,507.

Material: Springfield Armory Class C Steel

Treatment: Pack in charred leather pots. Heat at 1475° to 1500° F. for 3½ to 4 hours. Quench in oil.

Receivers and bolts from serial No. 285,507 to 319,921.

Material: Springfield Armory Class C Steel.

Treatment: Anneal at 1500° F. for 2 hours; drop to 1050° in the furnace, remove and air cool. Harden by heating at 1550° to 1600° F. for 15 minutes and quenching in Houghton's #2 quenching oil. Reheat to 1425° F. followed by quenching in oil. Wash in soda kettle. Draw in oil at 500° F.

Receivers and bolts over serial No. 319,921.

Material: *Both* Class C Steel *and* Hot Rolled Nickel Steel Specifications WD 35 NS. WD 35 NS had the following composition:

Carbon	.30%	to	.40%
Manganese	.45%	to	.50%
Nickel	3.25%	to	3.75%
Silicon	.10%	to	.25%
Sulphur	Not over		.05%
Phosphorus	Not over		.05%

Treatment: For nickel steel bolts and receivers: Heat in salt bath at 1500° F., quench in oil, and draw in sodium nitrate at 600° F. for 30 minutes. Scleroscope hardness must be between 55 and 70 (Roughly C-41 to C-52 Rockwell).

1917 Enfield Rifles

Barrel made of "Smokeless Barrel Steel" specified in Ord. Pamphlet No. 3098.

Carbon	.45%	to	.55%
Manganese	1.10%	to	1.35%
Silicon	.20%	to	.30%
Phosphorus	under		.06%
Sulphur	under		.06%

Receiver and Bolt made of "3½% Nickel Steel" specified in Ord. Pamphlet No. 3098. This could be either made by the Acid Process or the Basic Process with compositions as follows:

	Acid Process			Basic Process		
Carbon	.30%	to	.40%	.35%	to	.45%
Manganese	.50%	to	.70%	.50%	to	.70%
Nickel	3.00%	to	3.75%	3.25%	to	3.75%
Silicon				.10%	to	.20%
Phosphorus	under		.05%	under		.035%
Sulphur	under		.035%	under		.05%

U. S. Caliber .30 M-1 Rifle (Garand)

Barrel.

Material: WD Steel No. 4150 Modified, with composition as given below:

Carbon	.45%	to	.50%
Manganese	.60%	to	.90%
Chromium	.80%	to	1.10%
Molybdenum	.15%	to	.25%
Silicon	.15%	to	.35%
Phosphorus	Not over		.04%
Resulphurize to	.04%	to	.09%

Treatment: Before machining normalize if necessary. Oil quench from 1575° to 1675° F. Temper not less than 2 hours to meet physical properties as follows:

Tensile Strength, 130,000 lbs. per sq. in.
Yield Strength, 110,000 lbs. per sq. in.
Elongation in 2 inches, 16% minimum.
Reduction of area, 50% minimum.
Brinell hardness, 269-311 (Equivalent to Rockwell C-28 to C-34).
Process stress relief if required not less than 1 hour at 1000° F.

Bolt.

Material: (Prior to March, 1942)—WD Steel No. 3312.

Manganese	.30%	to	.60%
Nickel	3.25%	to	3.75%
Chromium	1.25%	to	1.75%
Carbon	Not over		.17%
Sulphur	Not over		.05%
Phosphorus	Not over		.04%

Material: Authorized July 5, 1942, WD Steel No. 8620. Modified, with composition as given above under M1903 rifle.

Treatment: Normalize before machining. Carburize .015" to .020" at 1600° F.; oil quench. Temper 1 hour at 325° F. Rockwell C 55 to C 59 on locking lugs and rear end of bolt.

Receiver.

Material: Early production: WD Steel No. 3115.

Carbon	.10%	to	.20%
Manganese	.30%	to	.60%
Nickel	1.00%	to	1.50%
Chromium	.45%	to	.75%
Sulphur	Not over		.05%
Phosphorus	Not over		.04%

Material: Intermediate Production: WD Steel No. 3120.

Carbon	.15% to .25%
Manganese	.50% to .80%
Nickel	1.00% to 1.50%
Chromium	.45% to .75%
Sulphur	Not over .05%
Phosphorus	Not over .05%

Material: After July, 1942, WD No. 8620 Modified, same as for the bolt.

Treatment: Carburize .012″ to .018″ at 1600° F.; oil quench temper 1 hour at 480° F. Rockwell D 59 to D 67.

U. S. .30 Caliber Carbine M-1

Barrel.

Material: WD No. 1350 Special—(Carbon .50 to .60%; resulphurized to .04% to .10%; Fine grain, gun quality, billets macro-etch inspected). Alternate, WD No. 1350 Modified.

W. D. No. 1350 Special as Specified Above.

Carbon	.50% to .60%
Manganese	1.35% to 1.65%
Silicon	.15% to .35%
Resulphurized	.04% to .10%
Phosphorus	Not over .045%

Treatment: Normalize before machining if necessary. Oil quench 1350° to 1375° F. Temper not less than 2 hours at heat to physical properties specified in U. S. Army Spec. 57-107-25. (Tensile strength, 110,000 lbs. per sq. in.; yield point 80,000 lbs. per sq. in.; elongation in 2 inches, 18% minimum; reduction in area, 45% minimum; Brinell 229-277.)

Receiver and Bolt.

Material: WD 4140 Special—(Resulphurized .04% to .09%; fine grain, gun quality, billet macro-etch inspection required.)

Carbon	.35% to .45%
Manganese	.70% to 1.00%
Phosphorus	Not over .04%
Sulphur	.04% to .09%
Chromium	.80% to 1.10%
Molybdenum	.15% to .25%

Treatment, Bolt: Normalize before machining. Preheat 700° F.; oil quench from 1550° F. Temper 2 hours at heat, not less than 375° F. and not more than 450° F. Rockwell C 48-54.

Treatment, Receiver: Same as bolt except temper 1 hour at heat to Rockwell hardness specified, that is C 38-45.

German Mauser Gew 98

Analysis of the metal taken from several bolts and receivers indicates that they are made of plain carbon steel similar to SAE No. 1035, which has carbon .30% to .40% and manganese .60% to .90%.

Japanese 6.5 mm. Arisaka

Several bolts and receivers analyzed appear to be made of ordinary carbon steel similar to SAE No. 1085 which has carbon .80% to .90% and manganese .60% to .90%.

Steel Specification Numbers

The reader has noted that the steels used in recent years for rifle manufacture are defined above in terms of SAE or WD numbers.

The SAE numbers refer to standard specifications issued by the Society of Automotive Engineers and published in the SAE handbook and in other engineers handbooks such as *Machinery's Handbook* and *Kent's Mechanical Engineer's Handbook.*

Much valuable information on the composition, physical properties, recommended uses, and appropriate heat treatments of alloy steels may be obtained from the SAE handbook and the mechanical engineers handbooks mentioned above.

The steels defined under War Department or "WD" number have in general the same composition as steels with the corresponding SAE numbers. However it is the practice to use WD numbers in official specifications, as SAE compositions, not being under the control of the War Department might be changed without their knowledge, thus involving a change in the War Department specifications over which they would have no control. In addition under the WD specifications the percentage of one or more of the constituent alloys may be varied or held to closer limits to meet the exacting requirements of gun manufacture.

The numbers themselves are assigned according to a system in which the first digit refers to the type of steel, the second indicates the percentage of the main alloying ingredient while the last two figures give the carbon content in points, that is in hundredths of a per cent.

The key to the meaning of the first digit is as follows:

1. indicates carbon steel
2. indicates nickel steel
3. indicates nickel-chromium steel
4. indicates molybdenum steel
5. indicates chromium steel
6. indicates chromium-vanadium steel
7. indicates tungsten steel
8. indicates nickel-chromium-molybdenum steel
9. indicates silico-manganese steel.

Applying the system given above, it can be deduced that WD steel No. 2340 of which so many M 1903 bolts and receivers were made is a nickel steel with some 3% (3.25% to 3.75%) nickel and some 40 points (.35% to .45%) carbon.

X

Headspace

WHEN I first became acquainted with sporting rifles, hunters were plagued with a certain very distressing malfunction, which would often occur right in the middle of a hunting trip, and would usually put the gun out of action until the user could get back to a gunsmith.

This trouble was a separation of the cartridge case, usually about a quarter to a half an inch ahead of the rim. When the breech was opened, the head of the cartridge would be pulled out by the extractor, but the body of the case would remain tightly wedged in the chamber, effectively preventing the insertion of another round of ammunition.

The remedy that was most often resorted to was to carry in the kit a small device called a broken shell extractor, sold by most sporting goods stores. When by bad luck a cartridge separated the user would insert the broken shell extractor into the chamber and close the bolt; on opening it again, the extractor would pull out the broken shell extractor, together with the front half of the ruptured cartridge case. This was of course a cure but not a prevention.

In every instance, the cause of this trouble was what is known as excess headspace, but the term "headspace" was rarely heard in those days, and nobody ever talked or wrote of it. However, styles change in the shooting world as fast as they do anywhere else, and in the last few years a lot of things have been blamed on headspace.

In the years just before World War II, it became the fashion for gunsmiths all over the country to originate "wildcat" cartridges by "improving" some factory cartridge, and then giving it a fancy designation with the originator's own name added.

The improvement frequently involved necking down the standard case to take a smaller bullet, and it almost always provided increased powder capacity by expanding the case into an enlarged chamber. Usually in the process the shoulder was made considerably sharper than it was in the original. This sharper shoulder is supposed to hold back the powder as the bullet moves forward in the bore, thus giving the powder better burning characteristics.

Making the shoulder sharper does, of course, add powder space, and thus make possible higher velocities, accompanied of course by the inevitable higher pressure. It is conceivable that the sharper shoulders do help the burning of the powder, but as far as I can see, this has not been proved. Very carefully conducted experiments, using chronographs and pressure gauges, with cases of the same caliber and cubic capacity, but with shoulders of different slopes have failed to show that the shape of the shoulder makes any difference at all.

With the increased powder capacity that these wildcat cartridges had, it was inevitable that increased pressures would be obtained. Usually the originator of one of these cartridges had no facilities for taking pressures, and depended entirely on the notoriously unreliable method of judging pressures by the appearance of the primer.

In many of these wildcats, the actual pressures obtained with some of the recommended loads must be fantastic, and it was no wonder that the usual crop of troubles with gas leaks and blown cases oc-

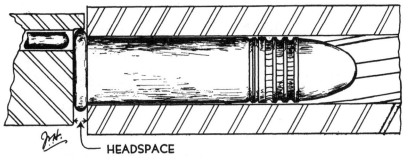
Figure 1. Headspace in a rifle using a .22 rimfire cartridge.

curred. For these the mysterious headspace formed a convenient scapegoat, and the term became a fashionable explanation for almost anything unpleasant connected with shooting these souped up loads.

Just what is this business of headspace that so many shooters are worried about these days? Let's get back to fundamentals a bit, and follow the thing through from the beginning of the term.

Early cartridges all had a rim, like the .22 caliber long rifle cartridges shown in Fig. 1. When such a cartridge is placed in the barrel of a rifle or pistol, the rim is the only thing that keeps it from going all the way in. As can be seen in the diagram, the rim stops against the rear face of the barrel. When the bolt is closed it comes up against the head of the cartridge. In front of the cartridge rim is the rear face of the barrel and behind it is the front face of the bolt. Between the bolt and the barrel there must be enough space to accommodate the head or rim of the cartridge, and this is the headspace.

Ordinary revolver cartridges are mostly of the rimmed variety, though there are some notable exceptions, such as the rimless .45 automatic pistol cartridge used in the Model of 1917 Colt and S. & W. revolver. In some revolvers the cartridge rims rest against the rear face of the cylinder, and in these the headspace is the distance from the cylinder to the recoil plate, which is that part of the frame which supports the cartridge head during firing.

Some revolvers, especially those made for rim-fire cartridges and for the ultra-high-pressure center-fire loads, have the chambers counter-bored so that the cartridges go in almost flush with the rear end of the cylinder, and the cartridge heads are each surrounded by a solid ring of metal. In these the headspace is the distance from the recoil plate to the shoulder against which the rim seats when the cartridge is in the chamber. In other words, just the rim thickness plus the necessary tolerance to accommodate ammunition of different makes.

Most revolver cartridges, such as for example the .38 special, are straight sided, just like the .22 rim-fire, and in these there is nothing

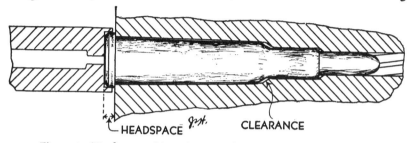

HEADSPACE   *g.p.t.*   CLEARANCE

Figure 2. Headspace with a rim cartridge, such as the .30-40 Krag.

but the rim to prevent the cartridge from going all the way into the cylinder. On the other hand, most high powered rifle cartridges of the rimmed variety, such as for example the .30-40 Krag, otherwise known as the .30 U. S. Army, shown in Fig. 2 are tapered or bottle-necked so they couldn't go very far in even if they didn't have a rim. These always have a clearance at the shoulder, as shown in the sketch, so that the rim will be sure to bear on its seat before the shoulder can come into contact. When such a cartridge is fired, the brass expands until the case fits the chamber at all points, hence in reloading, the clearance, above mentioned, does not exist. As long as the reloaded cases are used in the same rifle this makes no difference. However, if used in another gun of the same caliber, they might bear at the shoulder before the rim seats, and difficulty would then be experienced in closing the bolt.

When repeating rifles having box magazines first came into use it was found that the rims on the cartridges made it difficult to produce magazines that would feed the cartridges smoothly. To overcome this difficulty, two new types of cartridges were produced, which look much alike to a casual inspection, but which really are quite different in principle. These are the rimless type, and the semi-rim, or as it is sometimes called, the semi-rimless.

The semi-rim type is seen in such well-known cartridges as the

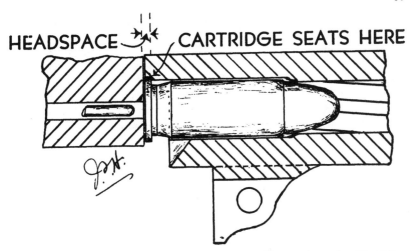

HEADSPACE **CARTRIDGE SEATS HERE**

Figure 3. Headspace with a semi-rim pistol cartridge, such as the .38 ACP.

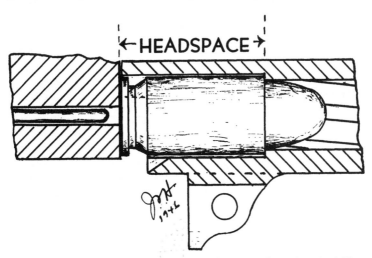

← HEADSPACE →

Figure 4. Headspace with a rimless pistol cartridge—the .45 ACP.

.351 and .401 Winchester self-loading and the .25, .32 and .38 A.C.P., the latter of which is illustrated in Fig. 3. The rim is made very little larger than the body of the cartridge, and there is a groove or cannelure cut into the body just forward of the rim, for the extractor to fit into. The semi-rim type works just like the rim cartridge. Even though the semi-rim is ever so little larger than the body of the case, this little is still enough to stop it positively at the right place.

Here also headspace is a distance equal to the thickness of the rim plus the necessary tolerances to enable different makes of gun and cartridge to fit together.

The true rimless cartridge has a head which is no larger than the body of the cartridge is at some point further forward. It has a groove or cannelure cut around it just forward of the rim, for the extractor to hook into. As the rim is no larger than the body, it cannot be used to limit the forward motion of the cartridge when it is seated in the chamber, and this must be accomplished in some other manner. With the .45 A.C.P. cartridge this is done by leaving the forward end of the cartridge, that is, the mouth, square, instead of crimping it onto the bullet as is done with most other pistol or revolver cartridges. A square shoulder or ledge is left at the front end of the chamber and the mouth of the case seats against this square ledge. See Fig. 4.

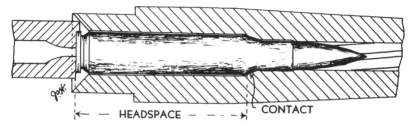

|← — HEADSPACE — — — →| CONTACT

Figure 5. Headspace with a rimless cartridge, such as the .30-'06.

As there is nothing for the head or rim to seat against, the true headspace in the old meaning of the term has no significance, and when we want to determine tolerances as to cartridge seating we have to measure all the way from the breech block to the shoulder at the front of the chamber. For convenience, we now call this distance "headspace" also, when speaking of guns using rimless cartridges.

When the Mauser repeating rifles were designed, the inventor introduced the well-known rimless rifle cartridges, of which the .30-'06 is an example. As shown in Fig. 5, these cartridges seat on the tapered shoulder which connects the body of the cartridge to the neck. Hence, in the high powered rimless rifle cartridge the distance from the face of the closed bolt to some reference point on the shoulder in the forward part of the chamber is, for convenience and for want of a better term, called the "headspace." Note that the principal contact which positions the cartridge in the chamber is at the same point where a clearance is purposely left in the rimmed variety.

As a practical matter, it is impossible to measure this kind of headspace without special gauges, because the shoulders both on the cartridge and in the chamber blend into the slopes ahead of and behind them, and there are no sharp edges to measure from. Actually

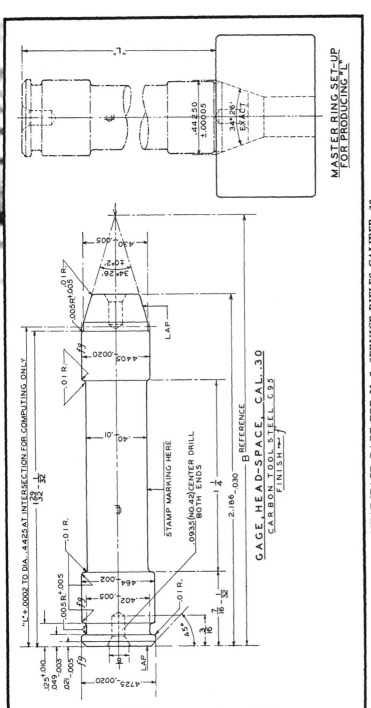

GAGE, HEAD-SPACE, CAL. .30

CARBON TOOL STEEL C 95

FINISH

MASTER RING SET-UP
FOR PRODUCING "L"

HEADSPACE GAGE FOR U. S. SERVICE RIFLES CALIBER .30.

"L" is the headspace, and "B" is the breeching space, used for purposes of computation only; it is equal to "L" plus .714 inch.

Values of "L" are as follows:

For manufacture of the U. S. Rifle Caliber .30 M 1: minimum, 1.942; maximum, 1.944.

For the manufacture of other rifles: minimum, 1.940; maximum, 1.944.

As a maximum gage for inspection of overhauled rifles: 1.946.

For inspection as a field headspace limit for serviceable rifles: 1.950.

If desired, a semi-circular groove may be cut in the head of the gage to clear the ejector in the M 1 Rifle, and thus avoid having to remove the ejector when headspacing these rifles.

the 1.940 inch minimum to 1.944 inch maximum headspace of the
'03 Springfield rifle is measured to a hypothetical intersection which
does not exist and can only be located by measuring to a given point
on a ring gauge that fits over the tapered shoulder of a steel gauge
shaped like a cartridge. This will be better understood by reference
to the official drawing for the .30-06 headspace gauge, which is shown
herewith in simplified form, retaining the essential dimensions but
omitting many confusing cross references.

There is still another variety of cartridge, and that is the belted
type, such as is used in the H. & H. Magnum and other similar rifle
cartridges. As shown in Fig. 6, it is really a modified rimmed
cartridge, having a very wide and very shallow rim. The rim is not

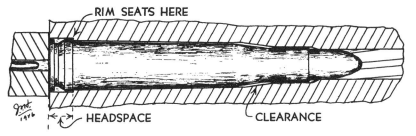

Figure 6.   Belted cartridge showing headspace.

high enough to give a good place for the extractor to take hold, so
there is an extractor groove cut into the rim itself. To explain it
another way, it is like a rimless cartridge with a slight step just ahead
of the extractor groove. In seating the cartridge this step comes to
rest against a slight corresponding ledge in the chamber. This gives
the same effect as that of a rimmed cartridge, and like it, always has
a clearance at the shoulder until after it has been fired once.

I have tried above to show just what headspace is. The next question is how does it vary, and what do the variations do to the functioning of the gun.

Taking the rim fire cartridge first, it should be quite obvious that
the headspace must not be less than the thickness of the rim. If it is,
the rim of the cartridge will be squeezed when the bolt is slammed or
forced shut, and premature discharge may result.

With the rim fire cartridge, excess headspace will result, in effect,
in a shorter firing pin blow, and thus in poor ignition. As the .22
rim fire cartridge is notoriously sensitive to irregular ignition, excess
headspace may result in variations in ignition that will have a very bad
effect on accuracy.

With straight sided cartridges of the center fire variety, such as
the usual pistol cartridge, headspace that is too small, that is, less
than the minimum specified, will usually make it impossible to close

the breech of the gun after it is loaded. Naturally this condition does not often occur as a gun defect, though the same result will follow the use of a cartridge with a head that is too thick, which is a trouble sometimes seen.

With these cartridges, the principal result of excess headspace is to let the cartridge move further away from the breech block when it is struck by the breech block. This, in effect, gives a shorter firing pin blow, and if it is very excessive, it may cause hang-fires or misfires.

Thus it is quite possible to fire the .45 A.C.P. cartridge in the .455 Webley & Scott selfloading Pistol, even though with this gun and cartridge combination there is about ⅛ inch excess headspace. If the cartridges are loaded into the chamber singly, they go in so far that neither the firing pin nor the extractor can reach them, and they will not fire; but if they are loaded from the magazine, they rise up under the extractor hook and this holds them close enough to the breech block so that the firing pin can strike the primer, and they fire, extract, eject, and reload just as if they were intended for this gun, in spite of the ⅛ of an inch excess headspace. I have fired many rounds of this .45 Automatic Colt Pistol ammunition through the .455 Webley and Scott Selfloading Pistol.

Likewise the 9 mm short, or .380 A.C.P. cartridge, which is .080″ shorter than the proper 9 mm Parabellum cartridge, may be fired from the magazine in the Luger or the P-38, but this little cartridge has insufficient power to eject and reload, so the slide must be pulled back by hand after each shot. I have fired many of these cartridges in both these guns with no trouble as long as they feed up from the magazine. If loaded in the chamber by hand, they will not fire because the extractor will not catch them at all in the Luger, and only part of the time in the P-38.

I have also fired the .455 Webley Revolver Cartridges Mark II in the .45 caliber Colt New Service Revolver with an excess headspace of .037″, and I have fired the .455 Automatic Webley & Scott Pistol Cartridge in this same Colt New Service .45 with an excess headspace of .025″.

Likewise, in trying everything I could think of, I have fired quite a few .45 Automatic Colt Pistol Cartridges in a Colt New Service Revolver Caliber .455, with an excess headspace for this combination of .051″.

In all of the above shooting, accuracy was excellent, and no bad results of any kind were observed. The only trouble to be expected was a possibility of hangfires or misfires from having the primer too far away from the firing pin, but even this did not occur.

Shotgun shells come in the category mentioned above, of rim cartridges with straight sides and giving low maximum pressures; usually not over 8000 to 10,000 pounds per square inch. A moderate amount of excess headspace in shotguns seems to make little or no difference, but a large amount, say a tenth of an inch or more, is dangerous, as there is nothing but the internal base wad of rolled cardboard and the thin brass wall to hold in the pressure where the shell is unsupported in the space between the end of the barrel and the face of the breech.

An acquaintance once told me that his pump action shotgun

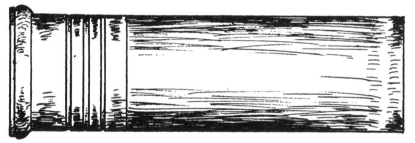

Figure 7. Upper: Shell after firing with normal headspace. Lower: Shell fired in gun with one-tenth inch excess headspace.

worked hard, and that after he had with some difficulty extracted the shells, they were badly bulged just ahead of the rim. I found that he had assembled his gun with the barrel just two threads forward of being fully seated in the receiver, and as the barrel had twenty threads per inch, this gave him just 1/10 inch more headspace than the gun would have had if it had been put together properly.

On November 1, 1946, Al Barr of the *American Rifleman* staff was helping me to pattern some shotguns, and we got to discussing this question, so we assembled a pump gun in this manner, and fired several shots with Federal Monark and also with Federal HiPower loads. I fired these loads myself from the shoulder, but was careful to wear my Rayban shooting glasses, and also to keep my forearm out from under the ejection opening, just in case the head of one of those shells should fail to hold the pressure. Patterns were the same as usual, and everything worked all right, except that extraction was a trifle hard, though not excessive. The fired shells were swelled out as shown in Figure 7, but they held together, in spite of the 1/10 inch excess headspace, and no harm was done. These particular shells have a high and very strong inside base wad, and this helped.

It should be noted that most pump action guns, such as the Winchester and Remington models cannot be mis-assembled this way; the designers have put in mechanical devices to prevent it. There is one high grade pump gun in which this can be done, but this will be corrected in the near future.

With bottlenecked cartridges, whether rim or rimless, the matter is quite different. The powder gas pushes back on the base of the cartridge with several thousand pounds pressure, and exactly the same total pressure is exerted in a forward direction, part of it on the base of the bullet and the rest on the tapered inside of the case body and shoulder. This pressure forces the forward part of the cartridge case tight against the shoulder of the chamber and at the same time drives the head of the case back against the face of the bolt. If there is excess headspace, the case will be stretched; if the headspace is too excessive, the case will be separated or ruptured at a point about ½ inch from the head where the thick brass in the base of the case begins to thin out as it joins the walls. When the gun is opened, the base of the cartridge will come out with the extractor, but the forward part of the case will remain wedged in the chamber and the gun cannot be used again until this is removed.

Lever action rifles are rather more subject to this trouble than are bolt action, as the lever actions stretch and spring more. With good strong actions and moderate pressure loads, and especially if the shooting glasses are worn, this trouble is not particularly dangerous, but is annoying and inconvenient. Very little, if any, gas escapes to the rear, because the back end of the cartridge, which remains in the chamber, acts as a seal. In fact, it is just such short brass cups that the Germans have for years used as the breech seals in their heavy artillery, instead of the "mushroom head" and gas check pad of our big gun system.

It just happens that I have had an unusual amount of personal experience with this matter of excess headspace and separated cases. In 1916 and '17 as Captain of Ordnance, I had charge of the Army Machine Gun Schools, first on the Mexican Border, then at Springfield. In those days, Frankford Arsenal made the .30-'06 cartridge case of very hard brass to make extraction easier and to improve the functioning in machine guns. These hard, brittle cases gave marvelous operation when the headspace was normal but would separate in a hurry if the headspace got the least bit over the limit. The automatic machine rifle, Caliber .30, M 1909, had detachable barrels, held on by a nut which could be tightened with a spanner. Let this nut get the least little bit loose and the case ruptured and the gun jammed because the following cartridge could not chamber fully. The ruptured case extractor was about the most important part of each gunner's kit. I experimented until I found how to fix the guns so they would fire a few shots, then chop off a case and jam.

Figure 8. Results of excess headspace. Top: Stretched case due to moderately excessive headspace. Center: Incipient separation due to greater headspace than top picture. Bottom: Rupture due to very excessive headspace.

Every student had this situation thrown at him repeatedly until he could correct it in the dark. In my own experimental firing I encountered at least a couple of hundred such separations, and every one of my several thousand students had to experience and correct this situation several times and I never saw enough gas escape to hurt any one. However, bear in mind we were using the old .30-06 cartridge with 150 grain bullet, 2700 feet per second and not over 50,000 pounds pressure. With some of the super high intensity loads that are being used today, any headspace over the normal can be dangerous.

In 1917, Frankford Arsenal began making the cases much softer, just to get away from these separations. The soft cases have been continued up to the present time, except for a few lots marked "R" (for rifle), and intended for the National Matches.

These softer cases stick badly in a hand-operated rifle when it heats up in rapid fire, but will stand a tremendous amount of stretching without an actual rupture.

Symptoms of excess headspace can be plainly seen on the cartridge case if you know what to look for—see Fig. 8. The first thing that happens is a stretch, which is a bright zone extending all round the case about a half inch from the base. As the headspace gets worse, the stretching shows up in a more pronounced manner, and the beginning of a crack running around the case may be seen. The next step is the actual separation.

One situation in which excess headspace can become dangerous is when the receiver and bolt are glass-hard and very brittle, as was sometimes the case with Springfield receivers of the old heat-treatment made before 1918. Like a razor blade, these are strong to any direct pull, but have low resistance to shock. Excess headspace allows the bolt to have a certain amount of play. When the explosion occurs, the bolt can move back and then stop suddenly against the locking shoulders, striking them a smart blow which, with one of these old glass-hard receivers, may cause it to shatter.

On the other hand, with receivers which, instead of being hard and brittle, are tough and elastic like the double heat-treated Springfields numbered over 800,000 and the nickel steel Enfields and late Springfields, such a hammering by the bolt, due to excess headspace, may cause a gradual stretching, but cannot cause either the bolt or the receiver to shatter.

Of course the very toughest problem as far as headspace is concerned is presented by the service cartridge, and other cartridges which like it, seat on a conical shoulder of thin brass. This does not form a very definite stopping surface, for it is quite possible if force is applied to drive the cartridge further in after it has seated itself, and any over-drive is in effect so much excess headspace. In World War I we had an aircraft machine gun in which the breech was slammed home rather violently by a strong spring, and in order to prevent this overdrive of the cartridge from causing headspace difficulties, the chamber of this gun was made eleven thousandths shorter than the specifications for the minimum chamber of the service rifle. That meant that the slam of the breech mechanism had to drive the cartridge in at least eleven thousandths beyond its first contact with the seating shoulder before the breech could even close.

Our riflemen are used to measuring the headspace of their rifles by thousandths, and are prone to become very much alarmed if the headspace gauges two or three thousandths of an inch more than the normal maximum. This is a good safe attitude to take, but it is something like measuring cordwood with a micrometer. When you have measured your headspace down to the last thousandth, you may load your gun with a slam of the bolt and drive the cartridge five or six thousands beyond the point where it first seats. Moreover, the minimum service cartridge is six thousandths shorter than the maximum; in effect that gives you six thousandths more headspace than you would have with a maximum cartridge under the same gun conditions.

Captain Melvin M. Johnson of the United States Marine Corps, the inventor of the famous semi-automatic rifle and light machine gun that bear his name, first called my attention to the variation in seating of the cartridge and the consequent variation in accuracy that can result from differences in the speed and force with which the bolt is manipulated in loading.

In an authoritative article on this subject in *The American Rifleman* for March, 1947, Captain Johnson stated in part:

"Now when the bolt or breechblock reaches the point of full locking, it may still go *forward* until it is stopped by the barrel shoulder or some other stopping point. The rear surfaces of the locking lugs bear on the shoulder surfaces in the receiver to prevent the bolt from being blown backward, but there is necessarily some clearance on the forward side of the locking lugs. Assuming the achievement of a perfect condition, i.e., no clearance forward of the locking lugs, the forward motion of the bolt would be stopped exactly at the point where the lugs were completely engaged. To obtain this perfect condition, the forward clearance on the bolt would have to be *exactly* zero. Rather a job of work to hold this clearance to precisely zero in mass production. Assume therefore a clearance of .006 inch forward of the locking lugs. The mechanical headspace of the .30 caliber M 1903 rifle is specified as 1.940 to 1.946, or an allowance of .006 inch. In addition we have the clearance of .006 inch just mentioned, and moreover there is allowed a tolerance of .006 inch in the length of the cartridge from head to shoulder.

"Therefore, what? The answer is that a rimless cartridge slammed forward with force will be driven into the chamber until the bolt stops. Then the bolt will lock. The forward clearance may permit the bolt to drive the cartridge a distance up to .006 inch beyond its intended stopping point, forcibly deforming or resizing the cartridge shoulder in the process. The result may be a working headspace of up to .012 inch above the theoretical minimum.

"Now take the case of a gun with greater headspace and clearance figures than those mentioned above. Consider mechanical headspace of 1.950 inch, or .010 inch above minimum, and forward clearance of .020 inch. Such a combination, when the bolt is slammed home with force, can produce a total of .030 inch, or a full thirty second of an inch above minimum headspace."

This drive-in condition is obviated to some extent because the bolt is arrested and commences to rotate on the extracting cam shoulder before the cartridge is fully chambered. This tends to squeeze the cartridge slowly home. Nevertheless, if the bolt is slammed home with full force, some drive-in can take place. A well made Mauser, and a National Match Springfield were tested for drive-in. Both weapons, caliber .30-'06 had a mechanical headspace of approximately 1.940 to 1.941 inches. A cartridge was very carefully and gently loaded into each weapon and a basic measurement was taken. The cartridges were then loaded with full force from the magazine by rapid manual operation.

In the Mauser it was found that the cartridge had been driven in .0045 inch, and in the Springfield the cartridge had been driven in .012 inch. This actual drive-in corresponded quite closely with the apparent forward clearance in the two weapons, the Springfield having over twice the clearance found in the Mauser.

The sum total of mechanical headspace, plus forward clearance, amounts to an operating or firing headspace quite beyond that indictated by headspace gauges. This is especially true of rimless ammunition. The rim or semi-rim case cannot be driven in beyond the headspace limit, while the average rimless case can be slammed forward very appreciably. A steep or abrupt shoulder on the rimless case is of decided advantage in this connection.

Captain Johnson proceeds to point out that the condition described above constitutes an open invitation to variations in cartridge chambering and consequently to variations in accuracy. If the operator loads each round carefully by hand, does not drive the cartridge home with any force, gently closes and locks the bolt with the lugs of the bolt rubbing the shoulders in the receiver as the motion is completed, then even with a mechanical headspace plus forward clearance of as much as .030, inch, he states that there would probably be no serious loss of uniformity between rounds and no serious trouble with inaccuracy traceable to this cause.

Suppose, however, that he loads one round slowly and gently, and then slams the next one in with speed and force. It is to be expected that he will vary the seating of the case and bullet in the chamber. The ignition and combustion may vary from a lack of uniform primer blow, and because the powder may be more or less piled up in the front of the case. This lack of uniformity would certainly be expected to show up in the group.

If these factors can affect the accuracy of the bolt action rifle, they may be expected to show up in much more pronounced form in self-loading or semi-automatic arms like the Garand M1, and especially in those made under the stress of wartime production. Tolerances must be as liberal as possible, and the forward clearance of the bolt may be expected to be rather large.

It might be expected that in such a gun, operating always under the same spring tension, the various rounds in the magazine would all be chambered with equal force, but a little reflection will reveal that this is not so. Assume that the magazine is full and the chamber is empty. The first round is chambered partly by the spring and partly by the operator, and is not slammed home as it is on subsequent shots when the breechblock opens at high speed and rebounds with great force.

Moreover, as successive rounds are fired from the magazine, there is' less and less friction from the round lying under the breechblock, because as the magazine empties, the magazine spring has less and less tension. Therefore the breechblock closes faster and harder, and the final round is chambered with maximum speed and force.

If we can get a combination of minimum headspace and the smallest possible forward clearance, in a semi-automatic firearm, the loss of accuracy from the causes described above would be held to the minimum.

Headspace Specifications

In the Garand M1 rifle, the headspace is held to unusually tight specifications, only two thousandths of an inch being allowed between the minimum of 1.942 inches and the maximum of 1.944 inches, measured between the face of the locked bolt and the reference point on the shoulder of the chamber. For the M1903 Springfield, the minimum is 1.940 inches, and the maximum, 1.944 inches for newly manufactured rifles after proof firing. On rifles returned to the arsenal for overhaul, the maximum is 1.946 inches. When rifles in the hands of troops are inspected, those having a headspace of 1.950 or over are returned for overhaul.

After the end of World War II, there were a large number of Model 1917 Enfields sold to members of the National Rifle Association through the Director of Civilian Marksmanship. Before being passed for sale, these rifles were inspected with the 1.946 inch gauge, and if this would not go in, they were passed. If this gauge did go, they were again tried with the 1.947 gauge, and if this did not go, they were passed for sale. If, however, the 1.947 gauge did go, they were rejected, and held for overhaul.

There is quite a technique necessary in testing the headspace of any rifle, and particular care must be used with the 1917, on account of the fact that it is possible to exert a powerful leverage on the gauges through the closing cams.

The proper procedure is to remove the firing mechanism and the extractor, and then insert the gauge, after which the bolt is pushed home and very gently turned down toward the closed position. If it goes all the way shut without resistance, the headspace is greater than the gauge. If, on the other hand, resistance is encountered, the headspace is less than the gauge. Under no circumstances should any force be applied in closing the bolt on the gauge. As soon as resistance is felt, stop, open the bolt, and push out the gauge with a cleaning rod.

When the 1917 rifles were placed on sale right after World War II, a lot of misinformation about headspace in these rifles was circulated. Numbers of ex-service personnel, casting about for employment, decided to capitalize on the knowledge of weapons they had gained in the service, and went into business as gunsmiths. Many of these men, unfortunately, did not have enough of the right kind of experience to make them experts in this line, and a lot of very bad advice was given by some of them.

The purchaser of an Enfield would often take it to a gunsmith to be checked, and would be told that it had excess headspace, and was dangerous to shoot. Some of these owners wrote that information in to gun editors, and it was printed, and soon the rumor grew that it was dangerous to fire a 1917 rifle purchased from the D.C.M.; this in spite of the fact that these rifles had all been in use on and off ever since World War I, and had an exceptionally clean record.

I received a number of letters from purchasers, complaining that they had received Enfields having headspace of over 1.950. I personally checked a number of these cases, and all those checked had headspace well within safe limits. Of course that does not prove that there were no 1917's sold which had excess headspace; on the contrary, I am confident that there were some just at first, before the order was issued that all had to be gauged as described above. But the fact that some self-styled gunsmith says a gun has too much headspace does not necessarily mean that it does.

As to gunsmiths, let me say that most of them, no doubt, are good sound operators, and know what they are doing; I am not by any means condemning the whole tribe, nor even those who made honest mistakes at first; in gunsmithing, as in most other skilled trades, experience is the best, and sometimes the only, satisfactory teacher. Those who started in a year or so ago without adequate knowledge have probably either learned the business or quit by now. But right after the war there were certainly a lot of men in the business who had not yet had enough experience. Let's take an actual example. In 1946, the owner of a shop which was just starting into the business of converting Enfields to sporters came in and asked to have their headspace gauges checked, as they had found that all the Enfields they had received for conversion were over the 1.950 limit, and they were afraid to convert them. But the fact that they were *all* that way made them suspicious of their gauge.

After the gauges were checked and found to be okay, the guns themselves were tried. First, the firing mechanism was removed, then the extractor was taken off, leaving the extractor collar in place. The 1.950 gauge was inserted and the bolt was pushed forward, and the handle was turned down very gently. Resistance was encountered about halfway down; obviously the headspace was considerably less than the supposed 1.950. This was repeated with a smaller gauge; the handle went almost all the way down, but not quite, the bolt finally closed on the 1.943 gauge in one rifle; the 1.944 gauge in the next; the 1.942 gauge in the following one, and so on. All were well within limits; in fact, better than that, or nearly perfect.

The shop foreman said that as he knew nothing about headspace, he had asked two gunsmiths to show him how to take it. Their system was to insert the gauge, then close the bolt as hard as possible, with the extractor and firing mechanism in place, and try to pull the trigger. If the trigger could be pulled, they considered that the gun had accepted the gauge. About like using a micrometer caliper by squeezing it down as hard as possible with a Stillson wrench before taking the reading.

In the latter part of 1946, a purchaser of an Enfield wrote in that his 1917 had "blown up" on the fourth shot, using a well known make of factory loaded extra high power hunting cartridge. This he felt sure was due to the excess headspace he had been reading so much about.

I doubted that the rifle had "blown up" at all; the trouble sounded more like a gas blow back from a soft head or an expanded primer pocket, not excess headspace. I wrote and offered to give him a new Enfield if he would send me the old one with the cartridge that had done the damage. I considered it well worth that much to find out about the trouble at first hand.

When the gun came in, it was in excellent shape, except that the extractor was blown off and the extractor collar bent. The offending cartridge was still stuck tightly in the chamber, and it was a typical soft head, with the primer pocket expanded to about twice its normal size and ripped wide open on one side. The cartridge was driven out, the extractor collar and extractor replaced, and the rifle appeared as good as new. The headspace was then taken, and after all this hullabaloo it was found to be only 1.943, in spite of the fact that the rifle had been "blown up."

On Nov. 1, 1946, Al Barr and I took this rifle to the range and reamed the headspace out to 1.955, or fifteen thousandths above the normal minimum, and I sat down at the bench rest and fired five shots with 172 grain boat-tail M1 ammunition, getting an excellent group at 100 yards. We then reamed it to 1.960, and I fired ten shots, getting a considerably larger group, possibly due to the fact that Al was telling me all the time that I was taking a terrible chance. After these ten shots, the headspace was again measured, and was found not to have changed at all. We then reamed it to 1.965, and I fired five more shots. The group was better, but not as good as the first one; but I don't put too much store by the group sizes, as we had to stop and chase horses from behind the target, and moreover, we had to watch out for a couple of boys driving up the cows, and besides it was getting very dark anyhow. This last we regretted, because we wanted to go on until we began to get separated cases. We will do that next time.

Up to this figure of 1.965, or twenty-five thousandths over the normal minimum, we had gotten no reaction whatever, and the cases themselves showed only a very slight indication of stretching, and were nowhere near a rupture.

What does this prove? Not very much, to be sure. One lone test doesn't prove anything in the gun business, and this was not even one test; it was only part of one. Why? Because headspace can occur in several different ways, with different effects. In this test we had only one kind.

Headspace, like that we have when we fire the .380 A.C.P. cartridge in the Luger pistol is really never any greater than the distance the extractor lets the case go away from the face of the bolt. Without the extractor holding it, the case might go quite a way in, but when it is held by the extractor, it cannot go very far, and this limits the headspace, and holds the cartridge close enough so that the firing pin can set off the primer. On the other hand, if we should cut back the locking shoulders on the bolt, the cartridge might go in snugly and fit right up to its shoulder, and he held close to the bolt face, but when the explosion occurred, the head of the cartridge would not be properly supported, and while the front part of the case would be held in place by the pressure, the back part could move back along with the bolt, and thus stretch or rupture the case.

In this 1917 Enfield, we had headspace of the first kind. It would make little difference, in all likelihood, if we had reamed the head-space some distance further. It would simply mean that there would be a clearance in front of the shoulder of the cartridge. The cartridges would not go any further forward than they already had, as they would be held by the extractor. When the explosion came, the head of the cartridge would be supported by the bolt, and could not move back much; but the shoulder would be expanded to fill the space made by the reaming.

I doubt very much if we would ever get a rupture this way, no matter how much we reamed the headspace. We would just move the shoulder further and further forward.

On the other hand, if we had produced this headspace by grinding off the bolt lugs, we would have a condition where ruptures would be more likely; if we got one, it would mean that the shooter would open the bolt and only the back part of the shell would come out. He would be unable to insert a new cartridge until he somehow got the other piece out.

Velocity as a Function of Headspace

Lieut. Robert C. Wyckoff, U.S.N.R. in an article in *The American Rifleman* for May, 1947, reported some very interesting tests that he made at the Des Moines Ordnance Plant in 1943 to determine the effect that variations in headspace would have on the muzzle velocity of the bullet.

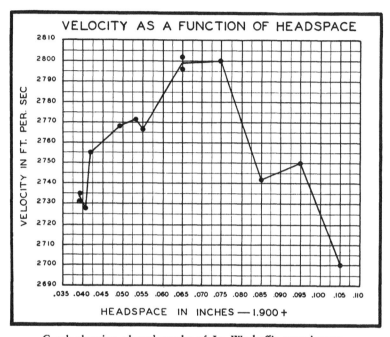

Graph showing plotted results of Lt. Wyckoff's experiments.

He selected a number of cartridge cases which all gauged 1.940 from head to shoulder. The bullets, caliber .30 ball, M2 were carefully gauged by hand and selected to have the same diameter and overall length, and were also selected as to weigh within 0.1 grain.

The cases were then loaded with carefully hand weighed charges of IMR 4676 powder. The accuracy of the weighing was such that the final balancing of the scales was determined by the addition of one or two sticks of powder, of which it requires about sixty to weigh one grain.

The bullets were all taken from one machine, in order to insure uniformity of ogive. The loaded cartridges were held to the same overall length. In short, every precaution was taken to achieve uniformity.

These cartridges were then fired in ten round groups in a standard

.30 caliber velocity rifle. The instrumental velocities were taken at 78 feet with a carefully adjusted LeBoulongé chronograph. After each group the chamber was reamed out a definite measured amount.

For the first group, the headspace was made as close as possible to 1.940 inches, which was also the length of the cartridges from head to shoulder. The bullet seat was made such that the bullet just touched it when the cartridge was seated home on the shoulder. Thus for the first group, there was no play between the head of the cartridge and the face of the breech.

After the first group, the chamber was reamed a certain definite amount to increase the headspace, and the next group was fired. This was continued until the headspace was 2.005, or some .065 inch more than the minimum of 1.940.

In order to obtain sufficient firing pin blow to dent the primer correctly, the cartridges were inserted in the chamber so that they projected to the rear, and had to be pushed gently into the chamber by the wedge shaped sliding breech block of the Modern Bond Universal Receiver which was used for the velocity gun. As the firing pin protrusion was .075, it would have dented the primer only .010 inch if the last cartridges had been shoved into the chamber until they seated on the advanced shoulder which had been moved forward .065 inch from its first position.

The test gun had no extractor, to hold the cartridge against the face of the bolt, hence the inertia of the cartridge was depended on to permit the firing pin to dent the primer, but this worked well enough so that satisfactory primer functioning was had throughout the test.

Results Obtained

The results of this test are shown in the tabulation given below, from which it will be seen that increased headspace does not of itself result in lower velocities. On the contrary, the velocity increased with increase in headspace up to some .035 above the minimum.

Tabulated Results

Headspace in inches	Velocity in feet per second at 78 feet
1.9395	2733
1.9406	2728
1.9419	2755
1.9495	2768
1.9530	2771
1.9550	2767
1.9650	2799
1.9750	2800
1.9850	2742
1.9950	2750
2.0050	2700

Lieut. Wyckoff commented that the increase in velocity with headspace, followed by a decrease was difficult to explain, but he thought that the increase might be due to the fact that as the head space is slowly increased from the 1.940 value, the bullet has a space to pass over before the ogive and sides encounter the lands and begin to be engraved by them. This is right at the time when the bullet is experiencing its greatest acceleration, and thus the bullet gains an increasing amount of momentum before the engraving and consequently, the retarding forces begin to act. This could easily account for the initial increase in velocity.

However, as the headspace is pushed to extremes, two things happen that have the opposite tendency. First, there is a space provided for some of the gas to escape around the bullet. Second, the density of loading is decreased; in other words, the powder has more space to expand into as it starts to burn, and this would tend to slow down the initial rise in pressure.

It is quite interesting to note that even with the fantastically excessive headspace used in this test gun, there were no ruptured cartridges, and the fired cases showed only very slight signs of stretching.

In closing his report, Lieut. Wyckoff states: "Many sportsmen are too concerned with excessive (that is, over the mythical limit set by the manufacturer of the gun) headspace. Increased headspace, even 30 or 40 thousandths of an inch over the maximum does not, in itself, result in lower velocities. What does, however, is erosion of the throat and bullet seat, and that should be the first thing to check when considering a used gun, instead of yelling for a set of headspace gauges. Even when the bullet seat and throat are badly eroded, it is possible to return the gun to its original velocity by cutting off an inch or so of the chamber end and re-chambering."

XI

Block That Kick!—
Some Observations on Recoil

I was raised on a farm about seven miles northwest of Winchester, Va., in a little valley between Hunting Ridge and the Great North Mountain. Around 300 acres was in cleared land used for crops or pasture, while the remaining half square mile was in timber.

In those days that was indeed a happy hunting ground for a small boy. There may have been game laws but if so, I never heard of them, or of a hunting license either, for that matter, and the only guns I ever saw or heard of were the double-barrel muzzle loader over the mantel, and later, when I was ten years old, the new breech loader that stood behind the dining room door.

Shells could be had at two cents each at the village store three miles away, and at the same store rabbits sold for ten cents each, skinned and dressed. I had seven rabbit traps and in the winter season it was a poor morning indeed that didn't find at least one or two cottontails waiting for me when I made my rounds.

There were a couple of the horses that were tame enough for me to catch any time I wanted to, and I could usually make them stand near a rail fence long enough for me to climb on.

I was between 10 and 11 when via rabbit, horse, and village store I acquired some 12 gauge shells. I quietly borrowed the double-barrel breech loader, proudly put in two of my new shells, and fared forth to see what the day would bring forth. After an hour or so of stalking unknown game through the woods back of the hill pasture I came suddenly face to face with what to me was the most terrifying of all wild animals, a large snake coiled up in the branches of a wild grape vine just waist high right beside the path. Up to this time I had been decidedly afraid to fire that big loud shotgun, but at the sight of the snake all misgivings vanished and I let him have *both barrels* at the same time! The results were instantaneous, gratifying and enlightening. The snake was made into a good imitation of mincemeat. I was knocked head over heels and landed flat on my back. But in spite of this rough treatment all my fear of shooting a shotgun vanished, never to return. I soon had a regular routine of getting up before daylight and making my way down to the river bottom through the early morning mist to sit under the tall hickory tree and listen to the dew dripping from the leaves until the sound of a falling nut told me that Mr. Squirrel was up there at work, waiting to be bagged for breakfast.

253

All I knew when I let the snake have both barrels was that my shoulder had gotten quite a wallop—"I can feel the place in frosty weather still!"—but later on I was told that one barrel of a shotgun gives a kick containing about 28 foot pounds of energy, so that the two of them fired at once must have kicked me about four times as hard as a Springfield rifle is supposed to kick.

Now it seems to me that there is quite a difference between "recoil" and "kick." The shotgun recoiled, and I got a kick on the shoulder. The recoil is mechanical, while the kick, or at least the effect of it, is mostly physical and psychological. The amount of kick resulting from the recoil force applied by the gun is largely dependent on the weight and conformation of the shooter, whether he holds the gun tightly or loosely, the presence or absence of a recoil pad or padded coat, and many other things. The location and shape of the shooter's bones and the texture of his flesh seem to have a big effect in some cases.

I first qualified as Expert Rifleman in 1908 on the Navy range at Annapolis, using the Krag. There was one chap shooting with us who took the most cruel punishment from the kick. In spite of the fact that he put a folded bath towel inside his shirt to act as a recoil pad, his shoulder was black, blue, and green after each day's shooting, while no one else on the line used padding of any kind and none seemed to suffer from recoil to amount to anything.

We did our qualification firing with the Krag, but after I was picked to try for the Camp Perry team I got acquainted with what was then known as the new Springfield. It made a sharper report than the Krag and kicked worse, and generally was looked on with suspicion and distrust. But it did shoot well, especially at 1000 yards. This advantage was at least partly offset by the pesky metal fouling to which it was subject. However, that great rifle shot, then known as Captain, and later as Major K. K. V. Casey, came down from DuPont to show us how to use the Springfield to best advantage and how to get rid of metal fouling. He had with him a book known as Ordnance Pamphlet No. 1923, *Rules for the Management of the Springfield Rifle Caliber .30, Model of 1903*. He very kindly let me read it, and I saw several interesting items, among them the following:

"Weight of rifle 8.69 pounds. Energy of free recoil 14.98 ft. pounds." I took this to mean that the rifle tends to hit the shoulder with nearly the same energy that a 15 pound weight would have if dropped a foot; or a one pound weight if dropped 14.98 feet.

I wondered if it really did kick harder than the Krag, so I found the Krag book, and for the old .45-70 as well. From these books I gleaned the following data:

RECOIL DATA TAKEN FROM ORDNANCE PAMPHLETS

Gun	Wt. Gun	Wt. of Charge	Wt. of Bullet	Bullet Travel	Muzzle Velocity	Energy Free Recoil
45 Cal. Rifle	9.3 lb.	70 gr.	500 gr.	32 inches	1315 f. s.	14.4 ft. lb.
45 Cal. Carbine	7.9 lb.	55 gr.	405 gr.	22 inches	1150 f. s.	7.5 ft. lb.
Krag Rifle	9.187 lb.	35 to 42 gr.	220 gr.	28.23 inches	2000 f. s.	10.025 ft. lb.
Krag Carbine	8.075 lb.	35 to 42 gr.	220 gr.	20.23 inches	1920 f. s.	11.827 ft. lb.
.03 Rifle	8.69 lb.	50 gr.	150 gr.	21.697 inches	2700 f. s.	14.98 ft. lb.

Below for purposes of comparison I append the following data reported by Aberdeen Proving Ground when I was chief of the Small Arms Division Technical Staff in 1930:

Gun	Wt. Gun	Wt. of Charge	Wt. of Bullet	Bullet Travel	Muzzle Velocity	Energy Free Recoil
Garand .276	8.625	37 gr.	125 gr.	20.625 inches	2700 f. s.	7.25 ft. lb.
Garand .30	8.83	50 gr.	172 gr.	21.76 inches	2653 f. s.	15.18 ft. lb.
.03 Rifle	8.68	50 gr.	172 gr.	21.76 inches	2653 f. s.	15.55 ft. lb.

That is quite an impressive tabulation, but just what does it mean? Why did the shotgun bowl me over so fast? I began to wonder just how much of an actual push I had sustained. So I went at it another way. The 12 gauge shotgun has a bore .73″ in diameter, which gives a cross section area of .424 square inch, and the maximum pressure of ordinary shotgun loads is said to be somewhere around 10,000 pounds per square inch. Thus for a brief instant the rearward push by one barrel of a 12 gauge shotgun is some 4240 pounds, or over two tons; and when I fired both barrels at the snake there were some 8400 pounds or over 4 tons pushing me back. Lucky that pressure didn't last more than a few ten thousandths of a second.

Let us look now at the service rifle. The bore has four narrow lands with a diameter of .300″ and four grooves three times as wide with a diameter of .308″. The average diameter is .306″ and the cross section area is .074 square inch. The maximum pressure with the '06 ammunition is around 50,000 pounds per square inch, so the gun for a brief instant receives a backward push of 3700 pounds. The pressure falls rapidly from its maximum, so that by the time the bullet leaves the muzzle the gas pressure is perhaps 7000 pounds, and the backward pressure on the gun is still 518 pounds. It should be noted that the rate of rise to the maximum and the rate of fall to the muzzle pressure, as well as the amount of the muzzle pressure itself, all vary with the type of powder. With quick burning powder the pressure of the gas when the bullet leaves is less than with a progressive powder. A typical curve, showing the time-pressure relation for '06 ammunition with 150-grain flat base bullet and pyro powder, is shown on Page 322. This gives a good idea of the magnitude of the backward thrust on the gun and just how long it lasts. Note that *after the bullet starts to move* it leaves the muzzle in less than one thousandth of a second. Recent tests (1946) show that from the time the firing pin actually touches the primer until the bullet leaves the muzzle is .0015 second. That agrees very well with the curve, for it takes an appreciable fraction of a second for the primer to ignite and in turn for it to ignite the powder and then for the pressure to rise sufficiently to start the bullet. It has been estimated (Major J. C. Gray, Ordnance Engineer, Research and Development Service) that it requires some 4000 pounds per square inch to start the bullet into motion.

We know from experience that a heavy gun kicks less than a light one; both tests and calculations show that with a given bullet weight, powder charge and muzzle velocity, the energy of free recoil is inversely proportional to the weight of the gun; that is, a gun weighing twice as much would have half the recoil.

In 1917, as a Captain of Ordnance in charge of the Experimental Department of Springfield Armory, I had to provide facilities for

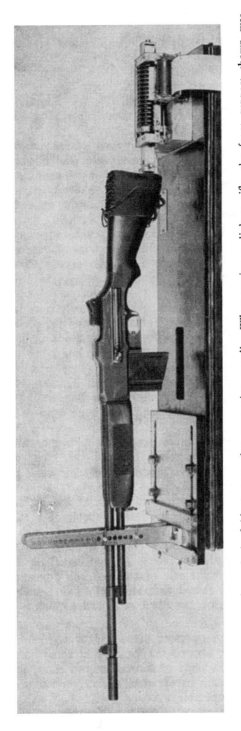

Dynamometer used at Springfield Armory for measuring recoil. When testing a lighter rifle, the front support shown was not used; the rifle was supported by a wire attached at the balance. This apparatus gives a result slightly less than the true value of the recoil energy, as the attachment to the butt of the gun, while it is made as light as possible, still adds some weight, and to this extent slows up the recoil. This effect must be compued and the results must be corrected accordingly.

the War Department test of machine guns and machine rifles held there in May of that year. In connection with the tests we measured the recoil of the shoulder rifles on a dynamometer constructed in the Experimental Department. It was interesting to note that with the Browning Automatic Rifle weighing 17 pounds with loaded magazine, the measured recoil was just half that of an 8½ pound Springfield rifle tested at the same time.

During this period every inventor with a semi-automatic shoulder rifle was referred to Springfield Armory for preliminary examination and test. One claim frequently put forth by inventors was that the kick was lighter with a recoil action semiautomatic because the mechanism absorbed the blow. This may sound all right when you say it fast, but it doesn't stand up under analysis.

In 1911 and thereabouts when I was a Lieutenant stationed in Florida, living in the edge of the woods with alligators right in my back yard, I used to read everything Lieutenant Whelen wrote in the outdoor magazines, and I managed some way to buy most every new rifle.

I bought ammunition by the case, and hardly ever left the house without a rifle, and a .22 target revolver as well for plinking at water moccasins, shells along the seashore, or what not. Among my rifles were two Remington Model 8 Autoloaders, one a .25 and the other a .35. These rifles really did kick! And they had long recoiling barrels that should have absorbed the kick if any such mechanism could. At the same time I was shooting a Belgian Browning Autoloading shotgun that had very much the same kind of action and a noticeably strong recoil.

This experience didn't agree very well with the theory that the recoil operated automatic action reduced the kick, so the recoil dynamometer was brought into action and some very plausible sales talk went out the window.

Here is a quotation from my notebook of the period 1917-1919:

"Now as to kick in connection with recoil operated small arms of automatic design—

"The silencers reduce recoil a certain amount, but they are not in general used to any great extent. (Those issued by the Army for the Springfield rifle at the rate of two to each company have been withdrawn as it was found that although they do silence the explosion, they cannot stop the crack of a bullet moving at supersonic velocity.)

"Some of the recoil operated automatic or self-loading rifles are supposed to absorb a part of the kick by reason of the motion of their recoiling parts. In many of those guns this is not so. They may, and often do, kick much harder than if the mechanism were locked so that it could not operate.

"This is easily understood. Consider for example a certain autoloading rifle weighing about seven pounds. The more a rifle weighs the less it kicks. But in this autoloader our calculations would be in error if we used seven pounds as the weight which resists the recoil, for the whole seven pounds does not stand up against the kick of the powder gas and help absorb the shock.

"The barrel and breech bolt are locked together and held in place in the frame of the rifle by springs, so that when the gun is fired they are free to move backward several inches independently of the rest of the gun. These recoiling parts comprise only about half the weight of the rifle.

"When the gun is fired, the stock and frame of the gun stand still against the shoulder while the barrel and bolt with their mere four pounds of weight are alone opposing the kick of the explosion. As far as resistance to kick is concerned you might almost as well be firing a four pound gun.

"The lighter the parts that oppose the thrust of the explosion, the greater the energy they acquire. Thus in the gun mentioned, the light recoiling parts, driven backward at high speed inside the barrel casing take up a heavy load of energy, then come to a stop against the inside of the receiver and transmit a large part of this energy to the shoulder of the shooter. The result is that the gun has a particularly vicious kick. Shooting this rifle is what first called our attention to the fact that in a self-loading gun of the recoiling barrel type the whole weight of the gun is not utilized against the recoil.

"Going into the physics of this proposition, it was found that theoretically, if the two parts of the gun were entirely inelastic, as for example if they were made of lead or putty, this effect would not occur, for after the two parts came together, the recoil energy would be reduced to what it would have been if no independent motion of the barrel had taken place. On the other hand, if the parts were perfectly elastic, they would act like two ivory billiard balls, and there would be an interchange of velocity, so that the recoiling barrel and bolt would stop and most of the energy in these parts would be transmitted to the stock and then to the shoulder. As the steel gun parts have a high degree of elasticity, this is just what happens.

"This reasoning was checked by firing well-known types of self-loading and autoloading hunting rifles in the recoil dynamometer.

"The guns were first fired with semi-automatic action and the recoil was measured. Then the action was blocked so that the self-loading action could not function and the test was repeated. In the guns tried the actual measured recoil was found to be much less when the semi-automatic action was out of operation."

Some time before this the Army had issued 300 .45 caliber Savage automatic pistols, and when they were withdrawn and sold as surplus I bought one of them. On firing this the recoil was found to be

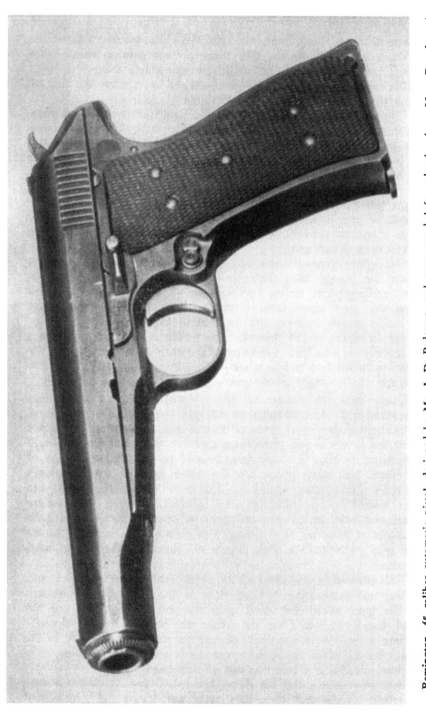

Remington .45 caliber automatic pistol, designed by Mr. J. D. Pedersen, and recommended for adoption by a Navy Board at the beginning of World War I. The pistol was never adopted because all available factories were already being tooled up for the M1911. This pistol, because of its clever design, gives a recoil which is relatively light.

excessive—much worse than that of the M 1911 pistol. Then some firing with the Remington .45, designed by my close friend J. D. Pedersen, had revealed that this gun had a notably mild recoil.

The excessive recoil of the Savage .45 is accounted for by the fact that the breech is not locked and the barrel does not move back at all with the slide. The rearward motion of the slide is supposed to be retarded by a cam arrangement forcing it to rotate the barrel slightly to the right before it can move to the rear. The reaction of the bullet against the twist of the rifling is supposed to hold the barrel to the left and resist the right-hand rotation necessary to allow the breech to open. Actually, however, the bullet has left the barrel before the slide has moved back far enough to rotate the barrel, so the supposed locking cannot take place.

Going again to my 1919 notes we find:

"The same thing that causes the nasty kick of semi-automatics actuated by barrel recoil or by straight blow-back also accounts for the rather disturbing recoil of the automatic pistol. You can easily verify this by shooting one with the slide blocked, and noticing how docile it is.

"The inventor of a new automatic pistol that one of the large arms companies has just brought out takes this fact into account and controls the recoil very nicely through an ingenious arrangement.

"When the explosion occurs, the breech block is allowed to move a very short distance to the rear, carrying the slide with it. The breech block then stops against a shoulder in the receiver, while the slide continues to the rear under the momentum imparted to it during the short stroke of the breech block. After it has gone some distance to the rear the slide, through a cam arrangement again engages the breech block, unlocks it from the receiver, and carries it on back, extracting and ejecting the empty shell. By controlling the length of the initial power stroke of the breech block, the designer has arranged so that the momentum transmitted to the moving parts is just enough to operate the mechanism with certainty, but not enough to make the recoil disagreeable."

If allowing the barrel of the gun to recoil independently of the stock is bad, there is one thing that is worse; that is, to allow the stock to recoil independently of the barrel. The worst kicking gun that I ever saw was one that an inventor brought in to Springfield Armory sometime in 1917. The breech block was not locked to the barrel at all. Instead, it was firmly fixed to the stock, while the barrel was free to slide forward against the push of a spring.

When the gun was fired, the barrel moved forward and the breech moved back keeping the empty cartridge with it. The empty was kicked out of the way, a new cartridge rose from the magazine, and the barrel slammed back, chambering the cartridge ready for another shot. The gun was made up for the Krag cartridge in full charge. It functioned well enough, but one shot was enough for me. The kick of a mule was mild by comparison. I handed the gun back to the inventor, and told him that *he* would have to do any further shooting that he wanted done. It seems that one can get used to anything, even the kick of a mule, for the inventor explained that he was "used to it," and proceeded to fire a number of additional shots without showing any unusual signs of discomfort.

Recoil in Gas Operated Semiautomatics

While, as has been stated above, some recoil operated self-loaders seem to have the recoil increased by the movement of the parts, this does not seem to be so in gas operated guns like the Garand M1 and the Browning Automatic Rifle. Both these guns give the impression of a softer and lighter recoil than that given by the M 1903 Springfield.

With the B A R, the additional weight of the gun would of course greatly reduce the recoil; but this is not so with the Garand, which weighs about the same as the Springfield. Nevertheless, many users of this gun remark about the lack of unpleasant kick. Captain John S. Rose of the National Rifle Association Technical Staff states that when he was instructor in the weapons section of the Infantry School during World War II, there was never a class that went through that did not have one or more members who raised the question of why the Garand kicked less than the Springfield. Strangely enough, there were also a few who insisted that it kicked worse.

Captain Rose thought that this inconsistency might be due to the fact that no rifle stock can fit everyone the same, and that the excellent fit of the stock with some men and the poor fit with others might account for the difference. This may well be so, but the fact remains that the general impression of the M1 Garand is that the character of the kick is less unpleasant to the average man.

It seems to me that this reduced kick with gas operated guns is to be expected. While the bullet is still in the barrel, and before the muzzle blast, which accounts for a sizeable percentage of the kick, can take place, a jet of gas enters the gas piston, and there pushes vigorously in two directions. It not only pushes the piston back, but it also pushed *forward* against the inside of the gas cylinder, giving the gun a powerful forward impulse which is in the opposite direction to the natural motion of recoil.

Moreover, the gas then goes on back and out of the rear end of the gas cylinder, acting like jet propulsion, tending to push the gun forward. Of course the operating rod and bolt do pick up quite a bit of rearward momentum, which has to be stopped by the shooter's shoulder eventually; but most of the energy in these parts is transmitted more or less gradually through the action of the operating rod spring.

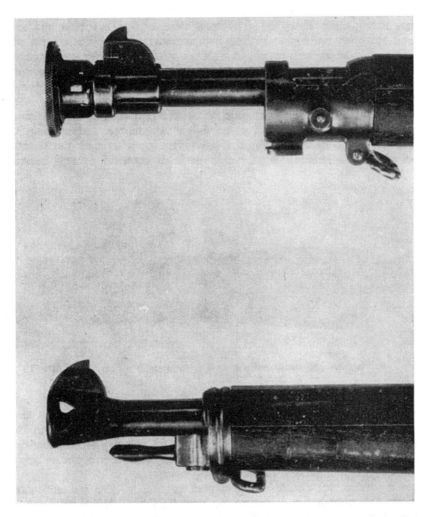

Upper: Thompson's experimental recoil reducer. Lower: an experimental model similar in principle to the type used on the Lewis aircraft machine gun. It was tested at Springfield Armory in 1904. Note the rod bayonet in the original 1903 Model Rifle.

Mr. Garand, in discussing this matter with me in June, 1947, stated that the M1 rifle gives about the same measured recoil as the M1903, but that it feels milder because the rate of application is different.

Reducing the Kick

A trip through the Springfield Armory Museum would convince any close observer that a good many people have been trying for

a long time to do something about making the kicking gun feel
less like a mule. Even before World War I, muzzle brakes and recoil reducers were one of the favorite subjects for the efforts of
inventors and experimentors. A number of these devices were tested
at Springfield Armory as far back as 1903, and some of those found
in the test reports are shown in the illustrations which accompany
this discussion.

All of the devices tested worked on the principle of intercepting
a part of the muzzle blast after it left the muzzle and turning it
sideways or backward. This is a promising idea, for over one-fourth
of the recoil velocity of the average high powered rifle is caused

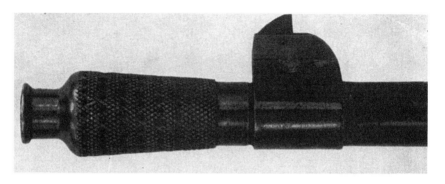

An experimental recoil reducer tried at Springfield before World War I.

by the rocket-like thrust of the jet of powder gas that rushes out
at high speed as soon as the bullet leaves. If we could suppress this
effect entirely, we would reduce the recoil velocity of the gun by
approximately one-fourth, and as the recoil *energy* is proportional
to the *square* of the recoil *velocity*, anything that reduces the velocity
one-fourth will reduce the energy by nearly 44 per cent.

Of course we could hardly expect to trap all the gas and take
away its reaction as it leaves the muzzle, for we have to leave a
hole for the bullet to go through, and a large part of the gas is
sure to follow the bullet out at high velocity.

However, that portion of the gas that we do catch can not only
be stopped from giving its rearward push, but can, in addition, be
made to do work in the opposite direction and give an actual forward push on the gun. This is accomplished by so shaping the
vanes of the muzzle brake that they will turn the gas back toward
the rear. If the blades of the muzzle brake are shaped like the blades
of an ideal turbine, they could in theory absorb up to twice the
momentum of the gases they trap. First they could extract all the
momentum by bringing the gases to a stop, then they could absorb
an equal amount of work in giving the gases the same momentum in

World War I Lewis aircraft machine guns with muzzle brakes.

The muzzle brake on the German high velocity 7.92mm anti-tank rifle.

a rearward direction. Of course no brake is this efficient in actual practice.

While many muzzle brakes were tested in those early days, none were adopted, the reason being that all of them, without exception, intensified to a disagreeable degree the noise and blast experienced by the gunner, and especially by those persons on each side of him.

However, with the advent of the aircraft machine gun in World War I, it was found important to reduce the recoil of machine guns as much as possible, and a muzzle brake was adopted and used as standard equipment on the 40,000 or more Lewis Aircraft Machine Guns that we bought in the war. As far as I know, this was the first actual adoption by the military of a muzzle brake on small arms.

The first World War also brought the introduction of full automatic rifles which were light enough to be fired from the shoulder. The most popular and widely used of these was the Browning Automatic Rifle, weighing fifteen pounds, and firing at the rate of about 550 rounds per minute from a twenty round magazine. When fired full automatic from the shoulder, the muzzle had a powerful tendency to climb as a result of the repeated impulses. It was soon found that this could be completely nullified by filing the front upper edge of the flash hider at an angle so that some of the gas could escape in an upward direction. This flash hider was simply a tube about four inches long and three-fourths of an inch in diameter inside, that was screwed onto the muzzle.

Only a very little bevel was enough to neutralize the climb; by using more, the muzzle could be deflected downward.

The Cutts Compensator

Shortly after the first World War, Colonel Richard M. Cutts of the U. S. Marine Corps appeared at Springfield Armory with a muzzle brake which he called the Cutts Compensator. I was present at several trials of this device, which did have some considerable effect on the recoil. It was sent to Ft. Benning for trial by the Infantry Board, but failed of adoption on the service rifle, because of the disagreeable side and back blast. It was, however, made standard on the Thompson Sub-machine gun. On this weapon, the Cutts compensator had the slots cut in the top, to neutralize the climb. As the muzzle pressure of the .45 A.C.P. cartridge used in this gun is much less than that of the service rifle, the blast was not so noticeable.

This device was afterwards applied to shotguns by the Lyman Gunsight Company, and is used in connection with interchangeable choke tubes which are screwed onto the front of the compensator. Like the pistol or the sub-machine gun, the shotgun has a low muzzle pressure, and the blast is not very noticeable. Various tests have indicated that the Cutts Compensator on shotguns may reduce the recoil by from fifteen to thiry per cent.

A somewhat similar looking device, with the same object, is the Weaver Choke. This is a cylinder which screws onto the muzzle of a shotgun, and which is fitted at its front end with threads for interchangeable choke tubes. In the Cutts Compensator, there are a number of parallel slots on each side of the cylinder. On the Weaver Choke,

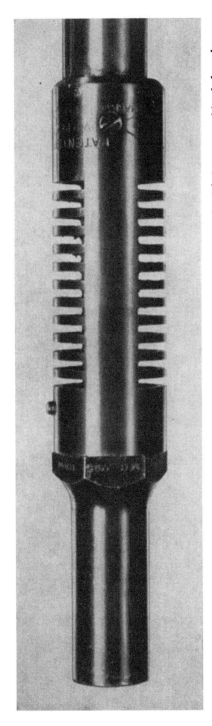

A Cutts compensator for shotguns. The slotted portion reduces the recoil. The portion at the left is a removable choke tube.

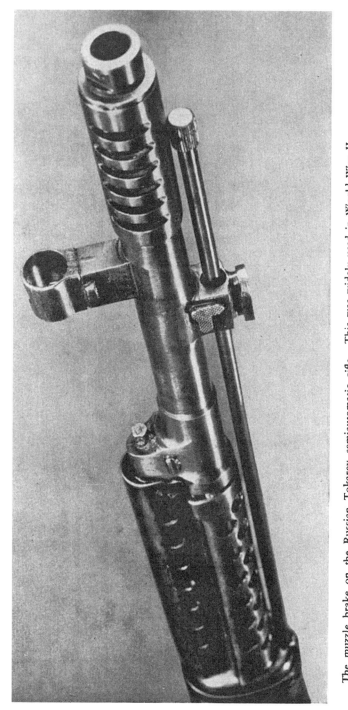

The muzzle brake on the Russian Tokarev semiautomatic rifle. This was widely used in World War II.

the cylinder simply has a number of round holes bored in it. The Weaver Choke reduces recoil also, but not as much as the Cutts Compensator. The reduction claimed for the Weaver Choke is from eight to thirteen per cent.

The Tokarev Semiautomatic

During the second World War, one service rifle appeared with a muzzle brake as regular equipment, and that was the Russian Tokarev. The muzzle brake on this gun is quite effective, but it still has the old trouble of a rather disagreeable side blast.

The Johnson Muzzle Brake

As soon as their war work ended at the close of World War II, the firm of Johnson Automatics, of Providence, R. I., makers of the

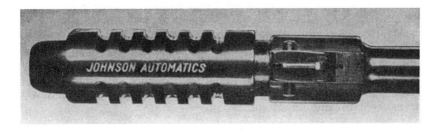

The Johnson muzzle brake. This reduces recoil from forty to fifty percent by actual test.

Johnson Semiautomatic Rifle and of the Johnson Light Machine gun, began putting out converted German Mauser rifles as well as Sporting Type 1903 and 1917 conversions. For use on their featherweight models Captain Melvin M. Johnson developed a very efficient muzzle brake, which weighs only two ounces, yet reduces the recoil as much as forty per cent by actual test.

Captain Johnson told me that tests made at the Massachusetts Institute of Technology, by having the butt of the gun drive a steel ball into a lead plate, and then calculating the recoil from measurements of the resulting indentation, showed a forty-one per cent reduction; while tests made at one of the large arms factories using a recoil dynamometer of the pendulum type indicated a reduction of some fifty-one per cent.

I have used this device quite a bit myself, and can state from personal experience that it does decidedly reduce the recoil. Captain Johnson stated that an unexpected dividend resulting from the use of this muzzle brake is an increase in accuracy as shown by his tests. He attributes this to the damping of barrel vibrations by the mass of metal attached to the end of the featherweight barrel. I have not had the opportunity to make any tests of this feature, but it seems reasonable that the muzzle brake might have this effect.

The Johnson Muzzle Brake, according to several users with whom I am well acquainted, does intensify the noise to a degree which is quite noticeable to some persons. Others complain that it kicks the muzzle down, and as a result, kicks the butt up against the cheek. I have not been bothered by either of these effects; but my imagination is perhaps not quite as vivid as is that of the average shooter.

Recoilless Cannon

During World War I, Commander Cleland Davis, U.S.N., invented a non-recoil cannon intended for use on airplanes, small boats, etc.

This consisted of a cannon open at both ends, and arranged with a loading gate in the middle. On the front end, the powder charge had the regular projectile, while on the rear end it had a charge of lead dust and vaseline, weighing as much as the projectile. On firing, the projectile went forward and the mass of lead and vaseline went backward at the same speed, while the gun stood still in the middle. This gun had the two serious practical disadvantages of clumsiness, and of shooting in both directions. It was true that the charge of lead dust would not carry to any great distance, but it inhibited a space directly behind the gun. As was to be expected, this gun was never used to any important extent.

The Bazooka

During World War II, very considerable use was made of an anti-tank weapon known as the Bazooka, which was a rocket discharger operated by two men, one of whom held the weapon on his shoulder and aimed and discharged it, while the other stood by his side to load. The projectile carried in its nose a so-called hollow charge, which gave a remarkably effective action against thick armor plate. This action was based on what was known as the Monroe Effect, a peculiar performance of high explosives under certain conditions, which was discovered this way:

For setting off charges of high explosive at a distance almost instantly in demolition work there is a kind of cord fuze known as detonating fuze, which consists of a lead tube containing a thin core of T.N.T. When a detonation is started in a piece of this fuze, it travels at a speed of around 7000 meters, or nearly four miles in a second.

In making tests on this type of fuze, someone happened to lay a piece down in a circle, and where the ends joined, a blasting cap was inserted and detonated, starting a detonation in both ends of the piece of fuze at the same time. Where these two waves met, a deep gash was cut in the steel plate on which the fuze was lying. Evidently where two detonation waves come together, so that one bucks the other, as it were, something very extraordinary happens.

57mm recoilless rifle M18.

Cartridge, 75mm, M 310, for 75mm recoilless cannon M 20. Note pre-engraved rotating band; perforations for escape of gas, and impregnated paper liner inside of case visible through perforations.

The forward end of the Bazooka projectile carries a high explosive charge hollowed out in front. Thus the detonation from all around the edges of the charge meets in the center, and when that happens, something just has to give way. To add to the effectiveness, the cup of explosive in the front of the bazooka is lined with a thin piece of steel, which is blown into a cylindrical slug by the explosion, and is then driven right through anything that happens to be in contact with at the time. This peculiar device will penetrate the thick armor on any tank or armored vehicle used during the war.

The velocity of the Bazooka projectile was low; 265 feet per second, with a range of 700 yards. The projectile was not spun, but had to depend for stabilization on fins at the rear, like those of a bomb. Consequently its accuracy was not great. The efficiency of the projectile was low, because instead of carrying only that part which was effective on impact, it carried also the propelling charge, the powder chamber, and the stabilizing fins.

Colonel Studler's Idea

One day during the early part of World War II, Colonel René R. Studler, Chief of the Small Arms Division, Research and Development Service, Ordnance, was considering the shortcomings of the Bazooka, and in consulting his notebook, he came across some data on the Davis Non-recoil Gun that he had made years ago. This started a train of thought that led him to make some calculations that convinced him that a truly recoilless cannon of very light weight but great power could be achieved.

The development that Colonel Studler envisioned was of such magnitude that there seemed little possibility that it could be accomplished in time to be used in the war then in progress; but Colonel Studler was head of a tremendous and highly efficient small arms development organization, so he called in a few selected assistants and explained what he wanted done.

The result was the design, test, and actual production in time for vitally important use in the war of one of the most fantastic weapons ever conceived; a full sized cannon that could be fired from the shoulder of one man, and that could throw a three pound high explosive shell with a muzzle velocity of 1200 feet per second to a range of over 4000 yards with an accuracy comparable to that of the M1 rifle.

This is the 57 millimeter recoilless cannon. In addition there is also the 75 mm fired from an ordinary machine gun tripod, and giving its fourteen pound shell a muzzle velocity of about 1000 feet per second for a range of some four miles.

In an article in *The American Rifleman* for September, 1945, Lieutenant Colonel B. B. Abrams of the War Department General Staff says: "Recoilless rifles were used against the Germans early in

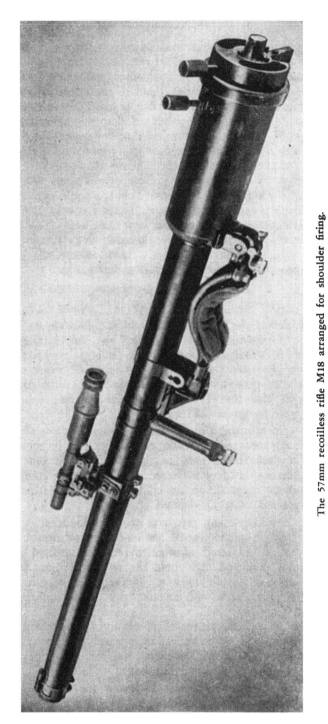

The 57mm recoilless rifle M18 arranged for shoulder firing.

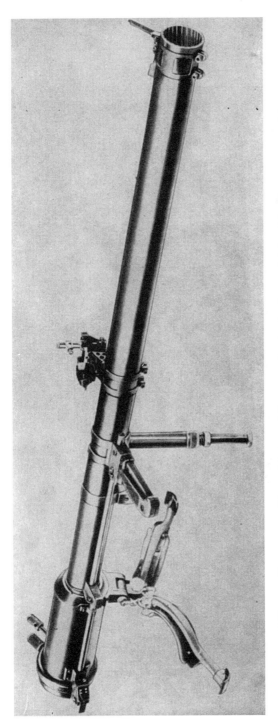

Rifle, recoilless, 57mm, M18, with iron sights erected and tripod extended for firing from prone position.

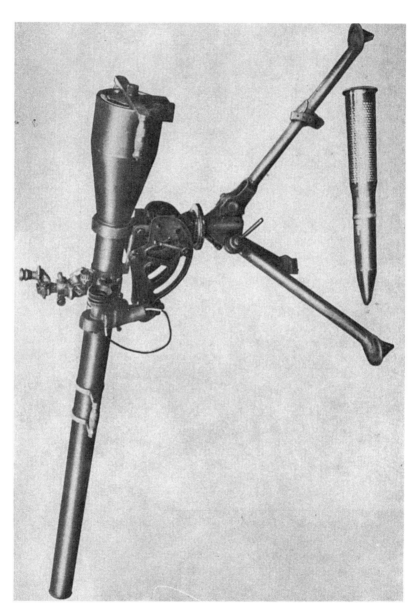

The 75mm recoilless cannon M20 on a machine gun tripod, with sighting equipment and a complete round of ammunition.

the spring of 1945, and were especially well adapted for use by airborne units because of their light weight and simplicity of operation. During one airborne operation on the Rhine River in March, 1945, two rounds from a 75mm recoilless rifle knocked out two German 88's and two 20mm guns concealed in a building. Both 88's were destroyed and about one hundred Germans captured."

In the same article, Colonel Abrams states further: "In the Pacific War the recoilless guns have been of inestimable value, particularly in blasting the Japanese from caves and bunkers, and in bringing fire to bear against the enemy from sites where it would be impossible to transport and emplace the conventional artillery.

"The 57mm gun weighs about 55 pounds complete with accessories

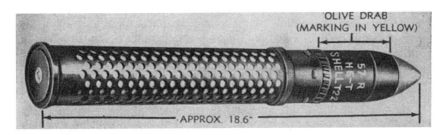

Cartridge, HEA-T, (High Explosive Anti-Tank), T22. 57mm Rifle. Note pre-engraved rotating band, perforated cartridge case, and headspacing band at mouth of case.

and can be carried by one man for short distances or by two men over long distances. The 75mm gun weights about 166 pounds complete with mount and sighting instruments, and is carried by five men. Compare these weights with the weight of the smallest type of conventional field artillery, weighing over a ton, in use by the United States Army.

"Both types of recoilless rifles are usually fired by a two-man team consisting of a gunner, who actually fires the gun, and an assistant gunner who loads the ammunition. However, it is possible for one man to operate the 57mm gun by himself. The gunner alines the sights and fires the piece. The assistant gunner opens the breech and inserts the projectile, and removes the empty case after firing.

"The doughboys claim that the recoilless rifles are as accurate as the M1 Rifle, and can easily hit a tank at ranges of from 60 to 1000 yards. They also advise against using the 57mm rifle for hunting any wild game other than Japs! A hunter armed with this weapon has no difficulty in hitting his target, but there is nothing left of the target to take home!"

How It Is Done

The fundamental idea back of this development was to provide several openings in the breech of the gun, and to allow some of the gas to squirt out of these openings, after the manner of the jets of a jet propelled plane. These jets will, of course, tend to drive the gun forward at the same time that the usual recoil is trying to drive it back.

Of course this idea took a tremendous amount of working out. The chamber of the gun was made much larger than the cartridge case. The case itself had its walls perforated with hundreds of small holes, to let the gas out into the chamber. The breech block had several orifices or venturi tubes to form the gas jets and direct them not only to the rear, to neutralize the recoil, but also at a slight angle to counteract the turning effect or reaction from the rifling, which tends to cause the gun barrel to rotate as well as to recoil.

Because the resistance of forcing the copper rotating band of the projectile into the rifling is high, and is quite variable even when the greatest care is taken in making the bands, it was decided to make grooves for the rifling beforehand; or in other words, to pre-engrave the rotating band of the projectile. That means that the loader has to turn the projectile slightly when he inserts it, until he feels the rifling enter the grooves already cut for it.

In order to cover up the holes in the walls of the cartridge case, there is a liner inside of the case, made of impregnated paper which will blow through the holes just after the pressure has risen enough to start the projectile from the mouth of the case.

Obviously, the jets of gas escaping to the rear of the rifle result in a danger space behind it, which must be kept clear of personnel. The danger zone is a triangular space about fifty feet to the rear of the breech and extending to some twenty-five feet on each side. The blast will throw up particles for a distance of about 100 feet behind the gun.

It has been found that as the venturis in the breech block wear from gas cutting, the recoil becomes over-compensated, and the gun will tend to move forward on discharge. When this becomes apparent, replaceable elements are used to bring the venturis back to their proper size.

Colonel Studler, who fathered the idea, and who, utilizing all the resources of his organization, drove it through to a successful conclusion, modestly refuses to claim any large share of the credit. He says that it was the work of the organization, not of any one man, and in *Army Ordnance* for September-October, 1945, he gives credit to a number of persons whose efforts were jointly responsible for the results obtained. In the same issue of *Army Ordnance*, General Barnes, former Assistant Chief of Ordnance, called the recoilless rifle "One of the Ordnance Department's more spectacular pieces of research . . . outstanding as a development, placing weapons of unprecedented power in the hands of the individual soldier . . . ."

XII

The Theory of Recoil

IT IS obvious that the weight of the gun is an important factor in determining how much it will kick. If the gun and bullet weighed the same, the gun would come back as fast as the bullet went forward, so that breech and muzzle would be about equally dangerous.

In practice, however, guns are always much heavier than the bullets they fire. The Springfield rifle is some four hundred times as heavy as its bullets, and over three hundred times as heavy as the combined weights of bullet and powder charge, so that the recoil energy is in the order of one three hundredth of the combined energy of bullet and products of combustion as they leave the muzzle.

We can say, therefore, the heavier the gun, the less the recoil, and conversely, the heavier the bullet and powder energy, the greater the recoil. Thus, anything that adds weight to the gun, or in effect adds such weight, is a help in preventing kick.

When the gun is held tightly against the shoulder, part of the weight of the shooter's body is in effect added to the weight of the gun, and the result is somewhat like that of using a heavier gun. The recoil has more mass opposed to it, so never does develop to as great an extent as it would if the rifle were free.

In measuring or calculating recoil, it is usual to obtain what is termed the "Free Recoil;" that is, the recoil velocity or recoil energy developed by the gun alone, with no other mass added to it that will help oppose its rearward acceleration. In practice some kind of additional weight or resistance almost always comes into play, hence we seldom encounter as violent a kick as the free recoil would give, but we still find it convenient to use this figure as a measure of the kicking potentialities of one gun as compared to another.

In the course of an excellent discussion of recoil, the *British Textbook of Small Arms*, 1909 edition, states.

"The physiological sensation produced by the recoil is generally termed the 'kick.' It is probable that the kick is intensified by the rapidity of the first rise in velocity, which with the Lee-Metford rifle is attained in about .0006 seconds. The shorter the time in which this maximum is reached, and the greater the velocity, the more violent the kick; from this it follows that the kick, though no doubt depending chiefly on the energy of recoil, cannot be said to be strictly proportional to the latter alone in various arms and with different powders . . .

"The kick is reduced by pressing the rifle firmly against the shoulder, and by letting the latter come back freely when the rifle recoils, for then part of the weight of the firer's body is added to that of the rifle, therefore, the velocity of the latter is reduced, and the kick partakes more of the nature of a push. If the rifle is held very loosely, or is fired when snap shooting, before it touches the shoulder, the kick becomes a blow, which is more damaging to the firer's shoulder than the kick from the rifle when it is properly held.

"A sportsman feels the kick of his weapon much more when firing at a target than when firing at game, for in the latter case his attention is fixed on his quarry, and he performs the required movements automatically without bracing his body to resist the recoil.

"The recoil energy of the Lee-Enfield rifle (12.75 foot pounds) is well below the maximum energy of recoil advisable for a military rifle, which should not exceed 15 foot pounds.

"The recoil of a 12 bore shotgun is double this amount, and although not excessive in the field, is very apparent when firing at a target.

"The following table, giving the particulars of the recoil of a 12 bore shotgun is taken from an article by Captain Journée in *Memorial des Poudres et Salpêtres*, Volume III. The gun was suspended by long strings, and the velocity of recoil was ascertained by attaching to the gun a tuning fork whose arm traced a wavy line on a plate placed parallel to the direction in which the weapon recoiled.

"As the time occupied by each vibration of the tuning fork is constant, and is known beforehand, the velocity of recoil at any point can be calculated by dividing the distance between vibrations at that point by the time occupied by a vibration."

Recoil of a 12 Bore Shotgun

Weight				Muzzle velocity of the shot	Velocity of recoil	Energy of recoil
Of the gun	Of the shot	Of the wads	Of the smokeless powder			
lb. oz.	oz.	grs.	grs.	f. s.	f. s.	ft. lb.
7 2½	1.37	41.66	49.4	1181	16.8	31.4

The *British Textbook of Small Arms*, 1929 edition, stated:

"As regards the sensation of recoil, it seems well established that the actual velocity of recoil is a very great factor. In shotguns weighing six to seven pounds, fifteen f.s. has been long established as a maximum above which gun-headache is sure to ensue. But with an elephant rifle weighing perhaps fifteen pounds, such a velocity is unbearable for more than one or two shots."

It will be noted that in this example the recoil velocity rather than the energy has been given; a seven pound gun with a recoil velocity of fifteen feet per second would have 24.16 foot pounds of energy, while a fifteen pound elephant rifle would have 52.47 foot pounds.

Measurement of Recoil

Figures for actual measured recoil velocity for several guns are given in the 1929 *Textbook of Small Arms*, referred to above. These were obtained by attaching the gun rigidly to a ballistic pendulum and firing it. From the swing of the pendulum the recoil velocity was then calculated. It should be noted that this method does not measure the free recoil of the weapon. Rather it measures the greatly reduced recoil of what is in effect a very heavy gun: that is, the actual gun and the pendulum bob attached rigidly to it. From the relatively small recoil thus obtained, calculations are made to find out what the results would have been had only the gun by itself been used.

This method gives a figure based on *momentum*, consisting of the weight of the gun in pounds times the recoil velocity in foot seconds. Dividing this by the weight of the gun gives the recoil velocity of the gun. Squaring this velocity and multiplying it by one-half the mass of the gun, will give the recoil energy. The order of magnitude of results obtained by this method can be seen from the following table, taken from the same work:

Gun	Measured recoil momentum lbs. x f. s.	Weight of gun lbs.	Recoil velocity f. s.	Recoil energy ft. lbs.
S. M. L. E. Rifle with .303 ctg. Mk. VII ..	81	9.0	9.0	11.0
Experimental .50 caliber rifle	285	18.0	16.0	70.0
Same with muzzle brake	212	20.0	11.0	35.0
12 gauge shotgun	97.5	6.5	15.0	22.8

Reported Values of Shotgun Recoil

Some years ago it was the practice for powder and ammunition companies to publish quite a bit more information than they are willing to turn loose at present. At that time duPont issued a leaflet giving the following information on the relation of the recoil of a shotgun to the weight of the gun, the size of the charge, the muzzle velocity, and several other factors:

Muzzle Velocity and Recoil for Weight of Gun and Load

Weight of gun lbs.	Powder, equivalent drams	Shot ozs.	Muzzle velocity f. s.	Recoil ft. lbs.
6	2 ⅞	1 ⅛	1195	24.6
6¼	3	1 ⅛	1253	25.8
6½	3¼	1 ⅛	1313	27.5
6¾	3¼	1 ⅛	1371	28.9
6¾	3	1 ¼	1210	26.8
7	3⅜	1 ⅛	1428	30.0
7	3⅛	1 ¼	1269	28.3
7¼	3⅜	1 ⅛	1487	31.4
7¼	3¼	1 ¼	1327	32.0
7½	3½	1 ⅛	1487	30.3
7½	3¼	1 ¼	1327	30.0
7¾	3½	1 ⅛	1487	29.4
7¾	3⅜	1 ¼	1384	31.0
8	3¼	1 ¼	1443	32.6
8¼	3½	1 ¼	1443	31.7
8½	3½	1 ¼	1443	30.8
8¾	3½	1 ¼	1443	28.9

Methods of Measurement Compared

The most convincing method of measurement of free recoil is that which measures the quantity directly, and requires no secondary calculations to obtain the desired result. This is best done by hanging the gun alone by parallel wires so that it can move freely to the rear when it is fired. The velocity of recoil is then measured by tuning fork or high speed camera.

Various recoil dynamometers are in use which purport to measure the free recoil by recording the compression of a spring, or the indentation made in a block of lead by a steel ball attached to the butt of the gun, etc. These are useful for quick comparative measurements, but in general they do not give the free recoil, but rather the recoil as modified by the weight of certain attachments and the resistance of the spring or lead block.

The method of measuring shotgun recoil which is standard in the industry at present is to fire the shell under test in a fifty pound gun hung by parallel wires so that it swings on a five foot arc as it moves to the rear. The results obtained are used as a basis for calculating to find what the recoil would be with any given weight of gun.

Calculation of Recoil

When a gun, such as the Model '03 Springfield rifle is fired, the pressure of the powder gas pushes on the base of the bullet, tending to drive the bullet forward, and exactly the same push is exerted on the rifle, tending to drive it back.

It is true that the rear end of the cartridge case is larger than the base of the bullet, so at first it might seem that the rearward pressure on the gun would be greater than the forward pressure on the bullet. However, the powder pressure on the inside of the body, shoulder and neck of the case gives a forward push on the sloping walls of the cartridge case body and neck which balances all the rearward pressure except that on a circle the diameter of the bore. So when the gun is fired we have at any instant a total load of a certain number of pounds pushing the bullet forward, and the same number of pounds pushing the gun back. This is the reasoning behind the statement already made that if the gun weighed just the same as the bullet, it would come back just as fast as the bullet goes forward. However, the gun weighs several hundred times as much as the bullet, and powder charge combined; hence, the bullet and powder gases go forward many hundred times as fast as the gun comes back.

Resistance by any object to motion when a force is applied depends on the mass of the object, which is simply its weight divided by the acceleration of gravity. Gravity accelerates a falling body *32.16 feet per second* for *every second* it acts; hence, the acceleration of gravity is 32.16 feet per second, per second. Not just "feet per second," but "feet per second per second."

We can call this simply 32.16 if we are careful always to stick to the units of feet, seconds, and pounds. Accordingly, if the bullet and powder weights are given in grains, we must be careful to bring them to pounds by dividing the weight in grains by the number of grains in a pound avoirdupois, which is 7,000.

Principles of Physics Involved in Recoil Calculation

Before going further, let us designate some letters to represent the various quantities we will encounter on our calculations regarding recoil, as follows:

F = Force exerted.

g = Acceleration of gravity, 32.16.

a = Acceleration due to powder pressure.

t = Time in seconds during which pressure acts.

W = Weight of gun in pounds.

M = Mass of the gun = $\dfrac{W}{32.16}$

w = Weight of the bullet in pounds = $\dfrac{7000}{\text{wt. in grains}}$

m = Mass of the bullet = $\dfrac{w}{32.16}$

c = Weight of powder charge in pounds.

z = Weight of wads in pounds.

v = Muzzle velocity of bullet in feet per second.

V = Recoil velocity of gun in feet per second.

E = Muzzle energy of bullet in foot pounds.

R = Recoil energy of gun in foot pounds.

The basic principles of physics involved in recoil calculations are based on Newton's third law of motion, which is:

Third Law: To every action there is always an equal reaction, or in other words, if a force acts to change the state of motion of a body, the body offers a resistance equal and directly opposite to the force.

The basic equations involved are as follows:

When a body which is free to move is acted on by a force F, the resulting acceleration a is equal to the force divided by the mass m of the body or $a = \dfrac{F}{m}$

The velocity v which results when an acceleration a operates for a time t is equal to the acceleration multiplied by the interval during which the acceleration operates. Stated in equations, v=at, and since $a = \dfrac{F}{m}$, $v = \dfrac{Ft}{m}$, and vm = Ft.

The quantity vm, or $\dfrac{w}{g}$ v, which is the velocity of a body times its mass, is called momentum, and is equivalent to that constant force which would bring the moving body to rest in one second.

The Three Elements of Recoil

The production of recoil in a gun is due to three separate causes.

The *first* is the reaction which accompanies the acceleration of the bullet from a state of rest to the velocity it possesses when it leaves the gun, that is, to its muzzle velocity.

The *second* is the reaction which accompanies the acceleration of the powder charge in the form of gas to a velocity in the order of half the muzzle velocity of the bullet. When the bullet leaves the muzzle, the gas occupies the whole interior of the chamber and bore. Part of the gas has moved as far as the bullet has, and has a velocity equal to the bullet's muzzle velocity. Part of the gas is in the chamber, and has not moved forward at all. The average is slightly less than half the muzzle velocity because the chamber is larger than the bore. and the gas still in the chamber and which has not moved forward is slightly higher in percentage than that which has followed the bullet all the way. Hence the average forward velocity possessed by the powder gas at the instant of bullet exit is slightly less than half the muzzle velocity of the bullet.

The *third* is the reaction due to the muzzle blast which occurs when the bullet leaves and releases the gas, which rushes out and gives the same kind of reaction or push that propels a rocket or a jet plane.

Let us consider for the moment the first element only, which is that part of the recoil that is caused by the reaction of accelerating the bullet to its muzzle velocity.

The forward push on the base of the bullet in pounds is the same as the rearward push on the gun in pounds. It acts on the bullet from the time it starts its motion until it leaves the muzzle, and it acts on the gun for exactly the same length of time. At the instant the bullet leaves the muzzle, the rearward motion of the gun in feet per second, times its mass, is the same in quantity as the muzzle velocity of the bullet times the bullet's mass. That is to say, the rearward momentum of the gun due to the push of the gas is exactly equal to the forward momentum of the bullet resulting from the same push, or $MV = mv$.

As mass equals weight divided by gravity, we also have $\dfrac{WV}{g} = \dfrac{wv}{g}$, or $WV = vw$. Stated another way, that part of the recoil velocity which is caused only by the acceleration of the bullet to its muzzle velocity varies directly with the bullet weight and inversely with the weight of the gun.

The equation $Ft = MV = mv$, shows that the same force, acting for the same length of time on two bodies which may be of different weights, will nevertheless give the same *momentum to each*. This does not, however, mean that it will give the same *kinetic energy* to each.

To make this clear, take the following example; suppose a force acts on an object weighing 100 pounds, and gives it a velocity of 10 feet per second; then the same force acting for the same length of time on an object weighing 10 pounds will give it a velocity of 100 feet per second.

The momentum mv of the first object would be $\dfrac{100}{32.16} \times 10 = 31.09$, and that of the second, $\dfrac{10}{32.16} \times 100$ is the same.

The energy, $\frac{1}{2}mv^2$ is quite different for the two cases. In the first case it is $\dfrac{1}{2} \times \dfrac{100}{32.16} \times 10 \times 10 = 156.472$ foot pounds.

In the second case it is $\dfrac{1}{2} \times \dfrac{10 \times 100 \times 100}{32.16} = 1564.72$ foot pounds, ten times as great.

That is the reason for the fortunate fact that the recoil energy is so much less than the muzzle energy of the bullet.

If a Springfield rifle weighing 8.69 pounds discharges a 150 grain bullet at 2700 feet per second, the recoil velocity of the gun due to the reaction of accelerating the bullet alone would be,

$$V = \dfrac{wv}{W} = \dfrac{150 \times 2700}{7000 \times 8.69} = 6.612 \text{ feet per second} \ldots \ldots (a)$$

Recoil Velocity Due to Accelerating the Powder Gas

Now let us look as the second element of the recoil, as mentioned above, which is that part of the recoil caused by the reaction of accelerating the powder gas to approximately half the muzzle velocity of the bullet, while the bullet is still in the bore.

In the example we have taken the powder charge weighs approximately 50 grains, or one third as much as the bullet. By the time the bullet reaches the muzzle, the powder charge in the form of gas will fill the chamber and bore. As the chamber is larger in diameter than the bore, the center of gravity of the powder charge will be nearer the breech than the muzzle at this time. It will actually be 12.7 inches short of reaching the muzzle, and will have moved forward only 10.142 inches from its former location in the center of the chamber, while the bullet was moving forward through its entire travel of 21.697 inches. This figure is arrived at as follows:

The barrel of the Springfield rifle is 24.006 inches long, and is bored out to a cone shape at the rear end, giving a space for the front end of the bolt to fit into. With normal tolerances, the front face of the bolt extends into this opening a distance of .064″, making the distance from the face of the bolt to the muzzle 23.942 inches. Depending on tolerances, the base of the 150 grain bullet may be from 2.22″ to 2.27″ forward of the base of the cartridge, when the bullet is seated and crimped into place in the cartridge. The average distance is 2.245″. Hence, for the usual situation, the base of the bullet is 2.245 inches forward of the face of the bolt when the cartridge is in place in the gun ready to fire. The face of the bolt is .064″ forward of the rear end of the barrel, so the base of the bullet is 2.309 inches forward of the rear end of the barrel. The barrel is 24.006 inches long, hence the travel of the bullet to muzzle is 21.697 inches, as given on page 65 of Ordnance Pamphlet 1923.

When the loaded cartridge lies in the chamber, the center of gravity of the powder charge lies approximately one inch in rear of the base of the bullet, or 22.697 inches from the muzzle. The cubic capacity of the powder space in the cartridge case is .251 cubic inches. The bore diameter is .300″, and the groove diameter .308″. The grooves are three times as wide as the lands. Therefore, three-fourths of the bore has a diameter of .308″, and one-fourth has a miameter of .300″; the average is .306″.

The cross section area of the bore is .07354 square inch. The cubic content of one inch length of the bore is .07354 cubic inch. The total length ahead of the powder space is 21.697″ long and has a cubic capacity of 1.5956 cubic inches, which added to the .251 cubic inch of powder space gives a total of 1.8466 cubic inches.

As the bullet reaches the muzzle, the powder gas will occupy all this space equally, and the center of the mass of gas will be in the middle of this space. There will be .9233 cubic inch of space ahead of the center of mass of the gas, and the same behind it. .9233 divided by the cubic capacity of each inch of bore gives 12.555 inches of bore between the center of the gas and the muzzle. Before the explosion it was 22.697 inches behind the muzzle; when the bullet reaches the muzzle, the center of the gas is only 12.555 from the muzzle, hence has moved forward 10.142 inches while the bullet was moving 21.697 inches.

The bullet has a muzzle velocity of 2700 feet per second acquired while it was moving 21.697 inches. During the same time the gas moved only 10.142 inches, or 46.75 per cent as much. Hence, its velocity just before bullet exit is 46.75 per cent of 2700, or 1262.0 feet per second.

That part of the recoil velocity given to the gun as a result of accelerating the powder gas from zero to 1262.0 feet per second would be $V = \dfrac{c}{7000} \times \dfrac{\text{vel. of gas in bore}}{\text{weight of gun}} = \dfrac{50 \times 1262}{7000 \times 8.69} = 1.03$ feet per second ....(b)

Third Element of Recoil

This is that part of the recoil of the gun that is caused by the muzzle blast produced when the bullet leaves and the pent up gases are free to expand into the atmospheres. The gases then rush out of the muzzle at high velocity, and give the gun the same kind of push that propels a rocket or a jet plane. In Springfield rifles, or the Garand either for that matter, the pressure of the gas at the muzzle when the bullet leaves may be anywhere from less than 3000 pounds per square inch to well over twelve thousand, depending on various factors, such, as for example, the length of barrel; the granulation of the powder and its composition; whether it is quick burning or progressive burning; etc.

With a high muzzle pressure, the rocket-like thrust of the expanding gas is much greater than with a low muzzle pressure, and the recoil is correspondingly intensified. Shortening the barrel always results in higher muzzle pressure, other things being equal, and therefore increases recoil, sometimes very noticeably.

The physics of this rocket-like thrust is very well understood these days, as a result of the large amount of work that has been done on both rockets and jet planes. The thrust on the gun at any instant from this cause is given by the equation:

Thrust = Net Gas Pressure at Exit x Area of the Exit x Mass Rate of Discharge.

The Net Gas Pressure at Exit is simply the average pressure of the gas at the muzzle, less the pressure of the atmosphere. As this starts at some such figure as mentioned above of 3000 to 12000 pounds per square inch and falls to zero in a fraction of a second, its amount for our purposes is unknown and any figure we used would be merely guesswork. The Area of the Exit, that is the cross sectional area of the bore at the muzzle is easily calculated from the known bore diameter. The Mass Rate of Discharge is, like the first term, unknown as far as our recoil calculations are concerned.

About all that this equation does tell us is that higher the atmospheric pressure, the less the recoil due to the muzzle blast, for the higher the atmospheric pressure, the less the Net Pressure at Exit. It is, of course, easily seen that if the air had a pressure equal to the gas pressure itself, the gas would not come out at all and the recoil from this cause would be zero.

This has been stated at some length in the hope of correcting a common misapprehension in this regard. So often in articles on recoil we see statements to the effect that the recoil due to the muzzle blast is caused by the pushing of the powder gas against the atmosphere. I well remember one article which, in speaking of the M 1903 Springfield, stated that "most of the recoil energy" is due to "a reaction between the base of the projectile, the circumambient atmosphere and the face of the gun breech, with the gas column as the medium of transmission."

Both the quoted statements are in error. Obviously "Most" of the recoil is not due to the ejection of the powder gas, but rather to the ejection of the bullet instead, in the proportion, for the M 1903 rifle with 150 grain service bullet, of 64 per cent of the recoil velocity caused by the bullet and 36 per cent by the gas ejection.

The atmosphere does *not* increase the recoil; it is well known even to child science fans that rockets work better in a vacuum than in the air. Nor can the thrust be transmitted to the face of the breech through the column of gas. Consider, for example, the ordinary lawn sprinkler, which rotates as a result of the reaction of the jets. The pressure of the air is not what makes it go. It would operate even better in a vacuum. Nor, when one of the streams happens to pass a tree or fence, will any additional pressure be transmitted back to the nozzle through the stream of water, any more than one can feel a reaction or increased pressure on a hose nozzle from the push of a brick wall if the hose is squirted on it. So let's get rid of this old fallacy about recoil resulting from the push of the powder gas against the surrounding atmosphere.

Practical Methods of Approximating Recoil Due to Muzzle Blast

In view of the extreme difficulty of writing a completely accurate mathematical formula that will be practical for use in everyday calculations to obtain that part of the recoil due to muzzle blast, most authorities use some approximation that gives results agreeing reasonably well with those found by actual dynamometer tests.

One approach to the problem is to consider that the gas when freed by the exit of the bullet starts to expand at a rate that is determined by the pressure and density conditions existing in the bore at that time, and that this rate falls to zero as the gas reaches atmospheric pressure. It has been considered that for modern rifles with pressures in the range of the ordinary military rifle of the past several decades, the gas starts to expand with a velocity of some 9000 feet per second, and that the rate falls to zero rapidly, with an average value of 4700 feet per second. Bevis and Donovan, in The Modern Rifle, 1917, state that experiments with a Siebert Velocimeter lead to the conclusion that a value of 4700 may be used for the exit velocity of the gases. Balleisen, in Principles of Firearms, 1945, gives the same figure.

For high powered rifles, this seems to give results that are satisfactorily close to measured values. For shotguns, it is much too high. For ultra high velocity rifles, it is most likely too low.

This figure of 4700 feet per second as the average effective velocity of the powder gases includes both the motion of the gases along the bore before the bullet leaves, and the sudden expansion to atmospheric pressure after the bullet makes its exit. Using this figure, we may now write an equation that will give us a good practical approximation to the total recoil velocity, including all three of the elements discussed above. If all weights are expressed in pounds, this formula would be:

$$V = \frac{wv + 4700\, c}{W} \qquad\dots\dots\dots\dots\dots\dots\dots\dots\dots(c)$$

A Second Method

The British Text Book of Small Arms, 1929, states that "experiments of an extensive nature with ordinary guns" indicate that the average effective velocity of the powder gases may be taken as between one and two times the muzzle velocity of the bullet, with an average value of one and a half. The same work, edition of 1909, gives a value of 2 for the Short Lee-Enfield using cartridges loaded with cordite.

In applying this approximation, a considerable degree of judgment will have to be used, as a figure approaching the higher limit must be used for very high pressure loads in short barrels, while low pressure loads, such as are used in shotguns and revolvers, require a much lower figure.

For rifles in the Krag class, a figure of 1.5 should be used, and this will work well with revolvers also, as well as with shotguns having short barrels and using full loads. For shotguns having barrels of maximum length, a figure of 1.25 gives closer results. For guns such as the M 1903 Springfield or the Garand, a value of 1.75 should be used. Using this latter figure, we can write our formula as follows;

all weights of course being in pounds; $V = \dfrac{(w + 1.75\ c)v}{W}$

........................(d)

Let's take an example and see how it works out when compared with actual measured results.

I personally own three service type Model '03 Springfield rifles, all purchased from Government Arsenals, and all three unaltered, just as they came. The old original M 1903, with straight stock, weighs 8 pounds 6 ounces. The 1903 A1, with pistol grip stock, as issued weighs 9 pounds 6 ounces. The M 1903 A3, of war manufacture, made by L. C. Smith-Corona, with stamped out parts, and no pistol grip, weighs 8 pounds 4 ounces.

Ordnance Pamphlet No. 1923 gives the wight of the rifle without bayonet as 8.69 pounds and the free recoil energy as 14.98 foot pounds. As these rifles can vary so much as to weight, principally on account of the differing densities of wood in the stocks lets take 8.69 pounds as the weight of the rifle in our example, so as to be more nearly comparable with the official pamphlet. For the same reason let's consider muzzle velocity of the 150 grain flat base 150 grain bullet to be 2700 feet per second. That was the figure to which the old M 1906 ammunition was loaded; though the present M2 ball with 150 grain bullet is rated at 2800 f.s. muzzle velocity.

A Springfield rifle, M 1903, firing a cartridge loaded with 50 grains of powder and a 150 grain bullet to give 2700 f.s. muzzle velocity would give the following results by the two formulae.

Using formula (c), we would have for the recoil velocity:

$V = \dfrac{150 \times 2700 + 4700 \times 50}{7000 \times 8.69}$ or 10.52 feet per second recoil

velocity, and the recoil energy would be $\frac{1}{2}\ MV^2$, or $\frac{1}{2} \times \dfrac{8.69}{32.16}$

$\times 10.52 \times 10.52$, or 14.95 foot pounds.

Using formula (d), we would have:

$V = \dfrac{(150 + 1.75 \times 50)\ 2700}{7000 \times 8.69}$ or 10.54 feet per second recoil

velocity, and the corresponding recoil energy would be 15.008 foot pounds.

Recoil Before the Bullet Leaves the Gun

Recently an acquaintance who is the head of a large gun business, and is a smart designer and an inveterate experimenter, told me that the recoil takes place "When the bottle is uncorked," and that the gun does not begin to move until the bullet has left the muzzle. This he said, had been determined as the result of navy experiments reported to him by a Naval Officer friend.

I asked why, in that case a revolver shoots higher with a slow heavy bullet than it does with a fast light one. That is a well known fact, and he admitted that it is so. After thinking it over, he said that in revolvers, no doubt some of the recoil must take place before the bullet leaves, but that it does not in large guns, as was proved by these navy experiments.

Be that as it may, every gun, large or small, army, navy or civilian, *starts* moving backward at the exact instant that the bullet starts moving forward.

Let's continue our experiments with that same 8.69 pound Springfield and its 150 grain 2700 foot per second bullet and 50 grain powder charge, and find out how far the gun moved back before the bullet left.

In making our calculations, let us use the figures already developed as to bullet travel and position of the center of gravity of the powder charge at the instant of bullet exit.

In its travel to the muzzle, the bullet has acquired a velocity of 2700 feet per second and the gas will have reached a velocity of $2700 \times \dfrac{10.142}{21.697}$, or 1262 feet per second. When the gun is fired, the powder pressure acts equally in all directions, driving the bullet forward and the gun back at the same time with the same force. The backward velocity of the gun times its weight is at any instant equal to the forward velocity of the bullet times its weight, plus the forward velocity of the powder gas times the weight of the gas.

The recoil velocity that the gun will have when the bullet reaches the muzzle will be:

$$V = \frac{150 \times 2700 + 50 \times 1262}{7000 \times 8.69} = 7.64 \text{ feet per second (e)}$$

As the total recoil velocity is 10.54 feet per second, we see that the part of the recoil velocity which occurs before the bullet leaves is 73 per cent of the whole, and the remainder or that part due solely to the muzzle blast would be 27 per cent, or 2.805 feet per second.

It should be noted that, since the recoil *energy* is proportional to the *square* of the recoil *velocity*, doubling the velocity will quadruple the energy. If we had two components, each of which produced 50 percent of the velocity, then what proportion of the energy would be produced by each? A little care must be used to avoid false and misleading conclusions. Suppose the bullet reaction had produced five feet per second recoil velocity, and the muzzle blast has produced exactly the same, or five feet per second.

Taking the bullet effect first, we could say that the recoil energy was one-half the mass of the gun multiplied by the velocity squared, or $\dfrac{25 \ M}{2}$ and the recoil produced by both together would be $\dfrac{100 \ M}{2}$

Thus we *could* say the bullet produced 25 per cent, and the muzzle blast 75 per cent, but if we did, we would be wrong. Each has pro-

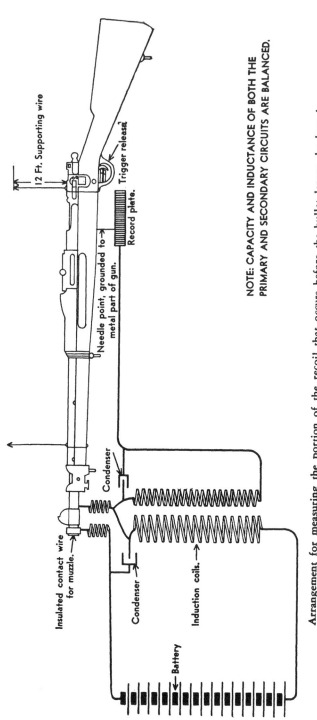

12 Ft. Supporting wire

Trigger release

Record plate.

Needle point, grounded to
metal part of gun.

Insulated contact wire
for muzzle.

Condenser

Condenser

Induction coils.

Battery

NOTE: CAPACITY AND INDUCTANCE OF BOTH THE
PRIMARY AND SECONDARY CIRCUITS ARE BALANCED.

Arrangement for measuring the portion of the recoil that occurs before the bullet leaves the barrel.

duced an equal amount of the velocity which is responsible for the energy, and if we had started with the muzzle blast first, our results would have been reversed, and we would have 25 per cent for the blast, the remaining 75 per cent for the bullet. Obviously, since each has produced an equal amount of the velocity, each is responsible for an equal amount of the energy resulting from the combined velocities.

In the case of the M 1903 rifle, mentioned above, the recoil velocity of 7.64 feet per second due to the reaction of the bullet would, by itself, give a recoil energy of 7.89 foot pounds to the gun, and the 2.805 feet per second recoil velocity due to the muzzle blast alone would give a recoil energy of 1.063 foot pounds to the gun; but both *together* would give 15.008.

Considering these figures, we see that if by the use of a muzzle brake we could suppress all of the 2.805 f.s. recoil velocity resulting from the blast effect, we would have only 8 foot pounds or recoil energy left out of 15, a reduction of nearly half.

Motion of Gun Prior to Bullet Exit

It might in some cases be of interest to know how far the gun has moved back by the time the bullet has reached the muzzle.

It follows from the equations that we have already been using that when two objects of different weights which are free to move are acted on by the same force, the product of mass times distance moved is the same for each; or more simply, since weight is proportional to mass, the weight times the distance moved in the same for each.

In the examples we have been using, the weight of the gun is 8.69 pounds, that of the bullet is 150 grains, or 150/7000ths of a pound, and the weight of the powder gas is 50/7000ths of a pound. The bullet moves 21.697 inches to reach the muzzle, and the powder gas in the same time interval moves 10.142 inches ahead of its original position in the cartridge case.

Therefore, when the bullet is at the muzzle, the gun will have moved back a distance D such that D times the weight of the gun equals bullet weight times 21.967 plus powder weight times 10.142, or

$$D \times 8.698 = \frac{150}{7000} \times 21.697 + \frac{50}{7000} \times 10.142 \text{ or}$$

$$D = \frac{150 \times 21.697 + 50 \times 10.142}{7000 \times 8.69} = .06183 \text{ inches.} \quad (F)$$

The first time I made this calculation was at Springfield Armory in 1920 in connection with the design of an automatic weapon. It seemed desirable to check the calculations by actual test, so my brother Major James L. Hatcher (now Colonel) rigged up an electrical circuit to measure it. He suspended the rifle on two parallel wires 12 feet long, so that is was free to swing straight to the rear on recoil. A point connected to the electrical circuit was attached to the muzzle, so arranged that when the bullet passed it would make contact and a spark would pass to a piece of sensitized paper placed nearby. First a spark was passed with the gun at rest, then the gun was fired. The two marks on the paper were slightly less than .07 inch apart, which was an excellent confirmation of the calculations.

To fire the gun without any disturbance from trigger pull, the trigger was tied forward with a string, and a rubber band was placed around the trigger and trigger guard. The string was then ignited with a match. When it burned away, the gun was fired with no disturbance, as the backward pull of the rubber band on the trigger was neutralized by its forward pull on the trigger guard.

The calculation performed above will readily give the *distance* the gun moves before the bullet leaves, but it does not tell us what the recoil *velocity* is, nor is there any very easy way to obtain it from the distance moved, even though we know from the interior ballistic curve for this rifle and cartridge, that the motion is accomplished in .00098 second.

The gun moves .06183 inch, which divided by 12, gives .00515 foot; it moves this distance in .00098 second, so its *average* speed over this distance is 5.276 feet per second. Since the gun started from a condition of rest, its velocity at the end of this time would be twice the average if the acceleration had been uniform. However, the acceleration was not uniform. It started high, and fell off rapidly as shown by the curve of velocity for the bullet.

Moreover, the acceleration of the powder gas, which also reacts on the gun, is quite different from that of the bullet, and is not given on the curve. Hence, as stated above, the distance the gun moves before the bullet leaves is not of much use to us in getting the recoil velocity.

From the laws of motion on which our calculations are based, it follows that in the case of a closed system, that is, up until the instant the bullet leaves, the center of gravity of the system as a whole remains in the same spot, as the different elements of the system move due to their mutual reactions. Just to check our former results, let us use this statement as a basis for determination how far back the gun moves before the bullet leaves.

The bullet has a weight of 150/7000ths of a pound, and its center of gravity moves forward 21.697 inches. The powder gas has a weight of 50/7000ths of a pound, and its center of gravity moves forward 10.142 inches. For the forward movement, we therefore have 150/7000ths x 21.697 + 50/7000ths x 10.142, or .5373 pounds-inches. The gun, weighing 8.69 pounds, must have its center of gravity move back the same number of pounds-inches if the center of gravity of the system is to remain in the same spot. To find out how far the gun moves, divide this amount by the weight of the gun;

.5375 ÷ 8.69 = .06183, which, of course, is the same figure that was found by the other method.

Effect of Recoil on the Jump of Revolvers

The handle of a revolver or pistol is below the barrel, with the result that a backward push on the barrel of a handgun in the grasp of a shooter tends to pivot the gun about the user's wrist and make the barrel swing upward.

The pressure in the chamber of the .45 caliber automatic pistol is from 14000 to 15000 pounds per square inch, and as the base of the bullet has an area of .159 square inch, that means that for an instant the pressure is driving the gun back with a force of from 2226 to 2385 pounds, or well over a ton.

Nothing that the shooter can do towards holding the gun tighter will have much effect on the motion caused by this enormous force, which, fortunately, lasts only a brief fraction of a second.

The result is that at ordinary pistol-shooting ranges not greater than 50 yards the bullet discharged from a pistol or revolver will inevitably strike above the point at which the bore of the gun was alined at the instant of discharge.

All handgun makers take this fact into account, whether consciously or not, in the way they place the sights. In order to make the bullet strike the spot aimed at, the barrel must point below this spot, so the sights are always so alined at the factory as to make the line of sight rise above the line of the bore enough to correct for the jump.

With the sights adjusted this way, the bullet hits the spot at which the sights were pointed at discharge, though not the spot at which the bore was aligned at that instant.

Users of factory loads are not too much bothered by this phenomenon; in fact, they are usually unaware of it, unless they happen, for example to use both the regular .38 Special cartridge, with the 158 grain bullet, and the .38 Special Super Police, with its 200 grain bullet, and to use them in the same gun. Or, of course, the .38 S & W and the corresponding .38 S & W Super Police. Or something of the kind.

The handloader, however, who is likely to use bullets of several different weights in the same gun, is constantly bothered by rather large changes in his point of impact. For example, I have often received letters reading something like this: "My .38 Special Revolver is sighted for the factory loads, and when I shoot the 130 grain wadcutters it groups low. Please give me a load for this bullet that will make it group with the factory load."

The answer is that it can't be done. The general impressions seem to be that if we put in more powder, we will make the jump greater and thus make the bullet hit higher on the target, but as a practical

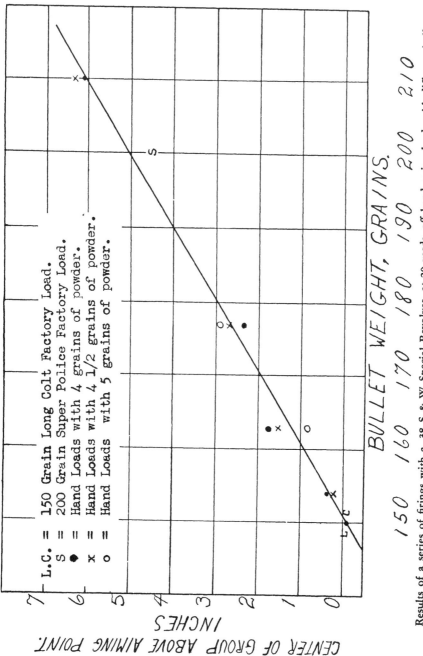

BULLET WEIGHT, GRAINS.

150   160   170   180   190   200   210

CENTER OF GROUP ABOVE AIMING POINT
INCHES

L.C. = 150 Grain Long Colt Factory Load.
S   = 200 Grain Super Police Factory Load.
●   = Hand Loads with 4 grains of powder.
×   = Hand Loads with 4 1/2 grains of powder.
o   = Hand Loads with 5 grains of powder.

Results of a series of firings with a .38 S & W Special Revolver, at 20 yards, off hand, using loads with different bullet weights from 150 to 210 grains, and with powder charges of four, four and a half, and five grains.
The heavier bullets always shot higher than the lighter ones. The heavier powder charges did not seem to make the groups any higher than the lighter charges.

matter this is not so. If we want to split hairs, we must admit that the added weight of the grain or two of powder does in theory cause the gun to jump slightly more; but this is solely on account of the added mass to be expelled from the gun along with the bullet, not because of the added velocity. The mass of the powder is so insignificant compared with that of the bullet as not to be noticeable.

To take a concrete example, it has been found by experiment that with a six inch barreled revolver, the 200 grain .38 Special Super Police bullet will strike 4½ inches higher on the target at 20 yards than will the 158 grain .38 Special with 860 feet per second muzzle velocity. While the difference in impact at 20 yards is 4½ inches, the entire drop in trajectory for the 158 grain standard velocity load at that range is only 9/10 of an inch. If we could raise the velocity of the .38 Special from 860 feet per second to 2000 feet per second, we would raise its point of impact only some ¾ of an inch, and the low velocity 200 grain Super Police bullet would still strike nearly 4 inches higher.

Of course, raising the velocity of the 158 grain bullet would greatly increase the recoil of the gun; but at the higher velocity the bullet would get away that much sooner, and these two factors balance each other, so that for a bullet of any given weight the amount the gun moves before the bullet leaves is about the same regardless of velocity.

For the standard .38 Special, the velocity of recoil will be:

$$V = \frac{(158 + 1.5 \times 3.6)\ 860}{7000 \times 2.25} = 8.92 \text{ feet per second, and recoil}$$

energy = 2.78 foot pounds.

If the powder charge were left out of the calculations, the recoil velocity would come out 8.63, and the recoil energy 2.60 foot pounds, which shows how insignificant the powder reaction and muzzle blast are with smokeless pistol and revolver loads. (With heavy black powder loads, such as the 40 grain load for the .45 Colt, the result is quite different, however.)

For the .38 Special Super Police, with 200 grain bullet we would have:

$$V = \frac{(200 + 1.5 \times 4)\ 710}{7000 \times 2.25} = 9.29 \text{ feet per second, and recoil}$$

energy = 3.02 foot pounds

We have already seen that the distance "D" that the gun moves back before the bullet leaves, multiplied by the weight of the gun is equal to the distance "L" that the bullet moves while it is in the gun, multiplied by the bullet weight, plus the distance "I" that the center of the powder gas moves, times the weight of the charge.

Or written in equation form:

$$DW = Lw + \text{1 c} \quad \text{or} \quad D = \frac{Lw + \text{1c}}{W}$$

Taking a Colt Officer's Model Revolver weighing 2.25 pounds, let us see how much it will move back before the bullet leaves with each of the two loads discussed above; the standard 158 grain load with 3.6 grains of powder at 860 feet per second, and the 200 grain Super Police with 4 grains of powder at 710 feet per second.

To figure how far the gun moves back before the bullet leaves, we must know the travel of the bullet to the muzzle. For the regular 158 grain .38 Special load in the Colt Officer's Model, this is 6.75 inches. For the 200 grain .38 Special Super Police, it is slightly greater, as the bullet is set deeper in the case, making the distance from bullet base to muzzle 6.81 inches. With the regular load the center of the powder charge is 3.56 inches forward of its original position when the bullet leaves. With the 200 grain bullet this distance is 3.62 inches.

The distance the gun would move back before bullet exit with the 158 grain load would be in inches:

$$D = \frac{6.75 \times 158 + 3.56 \times 3.6}{7000 \times 2.25} = .0685 \text{ inch.}$$

If the powder were not included in the calculation the motion would be reduced by .0008 inch.

For the 200 grain .38 Special Super Police, the distance would be:

$$D = \frac{6.81 \times 200 + 3.62 \times 4.0}{7000 \times 2.25} = .0874 \text{ and if powder were not}$$

considered this would be reduced by .0009.

It will be observed that velocity does not enter these equations, so that raising the velocity would not change the result.

Shot Gun Figures

It is usually said that the ordinary shotgun has a recoil of from one and a half to two times that of a high powered military rifle. A figure of from 28 to 30 lbs. is often mentioned. Lets see how that agrees with results calculated by the method we have used above for rifles.

My old Winchester Model 12 weighs in at just 7 lbs 12 oz., or 7¾ lbs.

A duck load of 1¼ oz. of No. 4 shot was found to have 549.29 grains of lead, or 1.256 oz., with 43.04 grains of wads, and 33.39 grains of powder.

A trap load of 1⅛ oz. of 7½ shot and 3 equivalent drams of powder actually contained 478.33 grains of lead, 53.22 grains of wads, and 24.3 grains of powder.

The muzzle velocity of neither of these loads is known, so that a very important factor in the recoil will have to be estimated. Let's call the muzzle velocity of the duck load 1350 f.s. and that of the trap load 1250.

The recoil velocity of the duck load would then figure out:

$$V = \frac{(549.29 + 43.04)\ 1350}{7000 \times 7.75} + \frac{33.39 \times 1.5 \times 1350}{7000 \times 7.75} = 14.74 + 1.25$$

= 15.99 f.s. and the recoil energy would be 30.8 ft. lbs.

For the trap load the figures would be:

$$V = \frac{(478.33 + 53.22)\ 1250}{7000 \times 7.75} + \frac{24.3 \times 1.5 \times 1250}{7000 \times 7.75} = 12.25 + 0.84$$

= 13.09 f.s. and the recoil energy would be 20.645 ft. lbs.

XIII

Notes on Gunpowder

THE name applied to military propellants is an interesting example of the way in which the original meaning of a word can be changed. "Powder" originally meant, and still does mean, fine dust; but at the present time we find substances called powder which do not in any manner resemble dust and which are not even finely divided. For example, cannon powders are ordinarily made in big grains several inches long and perforated with longitudinal holes; or flat strips an inch wide and a foot or more long, or even in tubes 4 or 5 feet in length.

The word "powder" was first applied to propellants for use in firearms because the first propellant was a black dust or powder composed of ground-up charcoal, saltpeter and sulphur.

The reason this mixture explodes when ignited is because it contains two fuels, charcoal and sulphur, which are very inflammable, and in addition, another solid substance which when heated gives off large quantities of oxygen.

If you mix charcoal and sulphur together without the saltpeter, you have a black substance which looks in all respects like the primitive gunpowder described above, and if you light it, it will burn, provided you supply plenty of air to support the combustion. The oxygen in the air enters into combination with the charcoal to form carbon dioxide gas, and with the sulphur to form sulphur dioxide gas. However, there is no explosion because these gases can be formed only as fast as air can be brought into contact with the burning powder to supply the necessary oxygen for the combustion. In other words, this mixture of sulphur and charcoal is a non-explosive powder.

Now, when we mix powdered saltpeter with it, we change its nature so that it becomes an explosive powder. The minute it is lighted it burns all at once without waiting for any air to come into contact with it. This is because the saltpeter is very rich in oxygen, which it gives up when heated. Thus the gunpowder supplies its own oxygen for combustion from within, and can burn without any outside air.

As nearly half the products of combustion of gunpowder are gases which occupy a great deal more space than the solids from which they were evolved, it is evident that the combustion of gunpowder results in a sudden expansion from the space occupied by the original powder, to the much larger space occupied by the gases which are given off. It is this sudden expansion which causes the gunpowder to exert force when it is ignited. The heat of combustion adds to this effect because hot gases occupy more space than cold ones.

Black powder relies for its explosive properties upon three qualities which are typical of all explosives. First, when ignited it will burn by itself without aid from the outside air, and this burning is very rapid. Second, in burning it gives off a large amount of gas. Third, a considerable amount of heat is evolved.

To be successful for use as an explosive, a substance must possess all three of these qualities. We have seen above that there are substances which can be burned and will give off a large amount of gas and heat, such as the mixture of charcoal and sulphur, but they do not burn without the aid of the outside air and consequently they do not burn rapidly enough.

We do have substances that will burn without the aid of outside air and burn rather rapidly, but they must also give off a large amount of gas or else there is no explosion. Thermite, which is a mixture of oxide of iron and aluminum powder, will burn rapidly without air when ignited, and gives off great heat, but it does not give off any gas, and therefore there is no explosion. When this powder is burned it forms melted iron and slag, which latter is aluminum oxide.

Even though a substance can change from a solid to a gas without the addition of oxygen from the outside air, there will be no explosion unless the change involves the liberation of heat. Some substances change into gas rather rapidly, but in doing so, instead of giving off heat they take up heat. Substances such as these do not cause an explosion when they decompose because as soon as they have started to decompose, they chill the surrounding air so much that the action comes to a stop until more heat can be supplied.

A very familiar example is the "dry-ice" in which ice cream is often packed. This is solid carbonic acid gas, and it can exist in solid form only at an extremely low temperature. The minute dry-ice is exposed to air it begins to give off great quantities of gas, but in giving off this gas it absorbs all the heat around it so that the gas can only be evolved as fast as the heat is supplied. Thus you can lay a big chunk of dry-ice on a hot stove and it will sizzle, hiss and jump around for a long time but there will be no explosion.

The backbone of gunpowder is the substance which gives off oxygen, and that is the saltpeter.

No doubt the original invention of gunpowder followed the discovery that when saltpeter is thrown into a fire, it crackles, hisses and makes the fire burn very much more brightly because of the oxygen it gives off. Then by mixing this saltpeter with inflammable materials, it was found that extremely hot fires could be made when the mixture was ignited. Finally, no doubt, the proper combination

Old fashioned gunpowder. Black sporting powder size FFG. This photograph well illustrates the characteristic grain shape of black powder. The ingredients are first made into large sized grains which are polished, then broken if too large in size. The rounded and polished surfaces of the original grains as well as the fractured surfaces can be plainly seen. Magnified 20 times.

was obtained so that when one of these mixtures was ignited it went off with a real explosion.

The actual discovery of gunpowder is variously ascribed to the Hindoos, to the Chinese, and to Roger Bacon, an English philosopher who seems to have described its composition in a manuscript written in 1249.

Whoever may be the true inventor of gunpowder, guns and cannon were known before 1350 A. D. From this time until the discovery of guncotton in 1846, black powder was the only explosive commonly known and used.

The average composition of black powder is, saltpeter 75 parts by weight, sulphur 10 parts, and charcoal 15 parts. There is, however, quite a wide variation in compositions that have been used in different years. Powders used for blasting, for example, are more effective if they do not operate quite as quickly as the ordinary gunpowder. This is for the reason that in blasting it is desired to rend the rocks and tear them out in chunks rather than to break them up in fine pieces, which a stronger powder would do. The average blasting powder would have about 70 parts saltpeter, 14 parts sulphur and 16 parts charcoal, but some powders of this kind have been made with compositions as low in saltpeter as 40 parts, with 30 parts of sulphur and 30 of charcoal.

In the manufacture of gunpowder the three ingredients are ground up very fine and then mixed together in a machine, after which the mixed material is given 2 or 3 per cent of moisture and put through a process known as incorporation. This is the most important process in the manufacture of black powder, its object being to bring the ingredients into the closest possible contact so that each particle of the resultant "cake" shall be composed of the three ingredients in the proper proportion. This incorporation is done in a mill of the edge-roller type, which is a big circular plate on which two massive rollers move round and round in circular paths.

After the incorporation, the "cake" is broken into lumps of uniform size in a machine with two pairs of grooved cylinders, arranged one pair above the other. The product of this breaking-down machine is called "powder meal."

In order that the powder may be granulated, the powder meal is first pressed into solid compact cakes, called press-cakes, which is done in a hydraulic press. The press-cake is broken up into grains by passing it through a granulating machine consisting of a series of pairs of metal cylinders with teeth of suitable size and suitably placed on the surfaces of the cylinders. There is a screen under each pair of rollers to catch the broken press-cake and conduct the large pieces to the next set of rollers.

After this granulating process, the powder is separated by a series of screens into grains of different sizes. The last process is polishing,

Black powder of medium granulation, suitable for large caliber pistol cartridges. Black powder, grain size FFG. Magnified 20 times.

which consists in placing the powder in a wooden barrel, and revolving the barrel for 5 or 6 hours. This removes all the sharp corners and produces a hard, glazed surface. Usually a little bit of graphite is included to give additional polish.

The speed of burning of black powder, and therefore to a certain degree its strength, is controlled by the size of granulation. Powder with extremely large grains burns more slowly than a fine-grain powder, and therefore is less sudden in its action. Also large-grain powder is much harder to ignite.

As the size of the granulation decreases the strength of the powder increases up to a certain point. However, when a powder is made very fine, like dust, the speed of burning is again reduced because all the spaces between the grains are filled up and hence there is no way for flame to communicate itself rapidly and ignite the whole charge at one time, as would occur with powder of larger granulation. Powder with very small grains is the easiest to ignite, however, hence this kind of powder was used for priming charges in the old muzzle loaders.

Black powder as at present made and sold to the trade comes in irregular, shiny, metallic looking black grains designated as to size by the letters Fg, FFg, FFFg, etc.; the more F's, the finer the grain. There is also a special granulation used in the Army for saluting purposes called Grade A-1. It has often been asked just what these different designations mean as to size. This is a rather difficult question because the designations vary with the different manufacturers; but taking the du Pont Company's system, the values would be as given in the table below.

The powders are measured by screening them through a coarse screen which catches all the very large lumps, letting the rest fall onto a very fine screen which allows all the very fine powder to pass through. The screens through which the different grades of powder must pass, and those on which they must be retained, are given in the table, the figures representing the number of meshes per inch in the screen.

Size	Must Pass	Must Be Retained On
Grade A-1	6	10
Fg	14	16
FFg	16	24
FFFg	24	46
FFFFg	46	60

Smokeless Powder

The discovery of nitroglycerin in 1846 opened a new field of explosives. Nitroglycerin is one of the strongest explosives known, and is the basis of many modern explosive compounds. It is a colorless,

Black powder of fine granulation, such as is used in small caliber pistol cartridges and in cap and ball pistols. Grain size FFFG. Magnified 20 times.

oily liquid formed by the action of nitric and sulphuric acids on glycerin.

Nitroglycerin differs from gunpowder in that it is not a mixture of fuels and oxidizing agents; instead, it is a chemical compound containing a large amount of oxygen, and this chemical compound is capable of rearranging itself into more stable compounds which are gases. A sharp shock will cause this rearranging process to start, and when once started it spreads almost instantly throughout the entire mass, thus resulting in a violent explosion.

Years ago when nitroglycerin was first invented, it is said that a promoter tried to get miners interested in its use, but they looked with suspicion upon this soupy substance as an explosive instead of the commonly used black powder with which everyone was thoroughly familiar. Finally in one little frontier mining town the agent ran out of money entirely and could not pay his hotel bill, so the proprietor of the hotel took his suitcase containing several quarts of nitroglycerin as security. Apparently the salesman's claims for the explosive properties of his stock in trade had not made a very great impression, for the suitcase was allowed to stand for some months in the upstairs hall, where the bootblack used it for his customers to rest their shoes on while they were being polished. Finally this gentleman noticed that some red smoke was coming out of the suitcase, and reported this to the proprietor, who then remembered that the man who left the suitcase had spoken about an explosive. It suddenly occurred to the proprietor that it might be dangerous to keep a suitcase of explosives in the house, so he promptly carried it to the back window of the hall and threw it out into a vacant lot. A two-story fall is not good for any nitroglycerin but is especially bad for nitroglycerin which has had its temper considerably sensitized by partial decomposition, and the result was that the suitcase exploded with a detonation which shook the entire neighborhood, and blew the back out of the hotel. But at least the incident gave wide publicity to the fact that the salesman was right when he claimed to have a powerful explosive.

Nitroglycerin is inconvenient to use by itself as it is subject to leakage, and thin films of nitroglycerin leaking out on the outside of containers are subject to friction which might easily cause disastrous explosions. Moreover, pure nitroglycerin is inconveniently sensitive. It was soon found that unless something could be done to overcome these disadvantages, nitroglycerin would never attain great popularity as an explosive.

The difficulty was finally overcome by the discovery that nitroglycerin absorbed into a porous substance made a much safer and more convenient explosive than the pure nitroglycerin. One of the most successful methods of using it was to allow the nitroglycerin to be absorbed in a porous earth called Kieselguhr. Nitroglycerin absorbed in a porous substance of this kind is called Dynamite.

Another very powerful explosive which, like nitroglycerin, is a chemical compound and not a mixture, is guncotton. This is formed by the action of nitric and sulphuric acids on cotton or any other kind of cellulose. Hence we often hear the term "nitrocellulose" used instead of "guncotton." Guncotton has the quality of being a substance which burns with extreme rapidity. It is said that it burns so fast that if some black powder grains are laid on guncotton and the guncotton is ignited, it may burn out from under the black powder grains without setting them on fire.

Some chemical students are said to have played a joke on their laundress by nitrating a handkerchief by soaking it in nitric and sulphuric acids. After the process the handkerchief looked just the same as it did before, the only difference being that it was then a guncotton handkerchief. They then sent it to the laundress, and when she touched it with a hot iron it simply disappeared so quickly that she did not know what had happened, and the students were much amused at her agitation when trying to explain where the handkerchief went to.

Guncotton is much too quick in exploding for use in guns. At first, attempts were made to use it in this way but they always resulted in bursting or damaging the firearm. It was finally found that by mixing nitroglycerin with guncotton a double purpose was served. First there was a substance to absorb the nitroglycerin and decrease its sensitivity the same as the Kieselguhr does in dynamite. Second, this same absorbing substance was itself a powerful explosive.

Various explosives are formed in this way. One such explosive is the English smokeless powder, Cordite, which is extensively used in Great Britain. Cordite Mark I is composed of 37 parts of guncotton, 58 parts of nitroglycerin and 5 parts of vaseline.

Another explosive formed by mixing guncotton and nitroglycerin is blasting gelatin. This mixture is a very fortunate one chemically, because guncotton contains insufficient oxygen to turn all of its carbon completely into carbon dioxide, while nitroglycerin has too much oxygen. By mixing the two substances in proper proportions the excess of oxygen in one explosive supplies the deficiency in the other, and the products of the explosion of such a mixture are nitrogen gas, carbon dioxide gas, and water (in the form of steam).

It will be remembered that gunpowder is merely a mixture of two fuels and one oxidizing agent, whereas guncotton and nitroglycerin are definite chemical compounds. Such compounds in general explode more violently than simple black powder, and are known as high explosives. Moreover, there is a big difference in the manner of explosion of a high explosive as compared with that of black powder. When black powder is ignited it burns with very great rapidity, giving off a large volume of gas, and this burning is the only explosion that occurs. On the other hand, many high explosives such as guncotton, nitroglycerin and T. N. T. can be burned without causing any explosion at all. A stick of dynamite, for example, can be cut up and thrown into a fire bit by bit with very little danger of exploding, though each piece will burn rather intensively. In the same way T. N. T. can sometimes be burned in large quantities without any explosion occurring.

What these explosives need to cause them to exert their full power is a shock which starts a chemical rearrangement of the molecules into gas instead of solids. This chemical rearrangement is called a "detonation." Once a detonation is started in a high explosive, it spreads through the entire mass with a sort of wave action with great rapidity. The speed of detonations varies in different explosives, but in some it is as high as 7000 yards in a second. A detonating fuse consisting of a long thread of T. N. T. encased in a lead covering will thus set off almost instantly a number of different charges of explosive, separated by considerable distances, if a detonating cap is exploded at one part of the fuze. Ordinarily the detonation of high explosives is started by exploding a blasting cap in contact with them. These blasting caps contain fulminate of mercury, a substance that explodes with great suddenness and which seems particularly well adapted to producing detonations.

Another method of using guncotton to make explosives besides mixing it with nitroglycerin was finally evolved, and this consists in dissolving the guncotton in a mixture of ether and alcohol, thus forming a mass called a colloid, having very much the same consistency as melted glue. This colloid is squeezed out into tubes like macaroni, and these tubes are cut into short lengths, after which the ether and alcohol used to dissolve the guncotton are evaporated off, leaving a hard substance something like dried glue. This dried-out colloid of guncotton is what most modern smokeless powders are made of. Such powders are the old Government Pyro used in 1906 for Springfield cartridges; the du Pont No. 1147 and No. 1185 powders used in the old M1 cartridges with its 172 grain boattail bullet; and the newer IMR 4895 used in World War II in the .30 Cal. M2 cartridge. Powders like these containing nitrocellulose only and no nitroglycerin are called single base powders.

Such smokeless powders are made in the form of small cylindrical grains with a hole running through the center. In other words, they are like little sections cut from a fine tube of macaroni. The object of having the hole through the center of the powder grain is to control the rate of burning so as to hold up the pressure of the powder as long as possible.

The great trouble with getting high velocity in a gun is the fact that when the powder in the cartridge is ignited it turns into gas,

A modern smokeless rifle powder. DuPont's improved military rifle powder
No. 3031. This powder is made in the form of little cylinders nearly a tenth
of an inch long with a hole through the center of each. Actual length of the
grain: seven and a half hundredths of an inch. Diameter: two and a half
hundredths. This powder is used in loading service cartridges for the Springfield rifle.

DuPont improved military rifle powder No. 4320. Magnified 20 times.

and this gas, confined in the small space of the cartridge case, creates a very high pressure which pushes the bullet along the bore of the gun. But as soon as the bullet starts to move along the bore, that leaves more space for the gas to occupy, hence there is less pressure, and the effect of the powder will rapidly fall off to nothing unless special means are taken to keep the pressure up.

One of these special means is the perforation of the powder grain, which causes it to have a larger burning surface as the combustion proceeds. This is because the primer flash ignites the inside of the tube as well as the outside of the grain. As the grain burns, the outside surface gets smaller, hence the rate of evolution of gas would tend to decrease; but at the same time the inside of the perforations burn away, and the diameter of the hole becomes larger, with a corresponding increase in the interior burning surface.

The balance between these two surfaces can be controlled by the ratio of the inside diameter to the outside diameter in the finished grain of powder. In cannon powders with their larger grains, there are usually seven perforations instead of one.

Another method of controlling the burning of the powder and making it more progressive, that is, making it hold up its pressure longer during the travel of the bullet, is by coating the powder with a substance which makes it burn slowly at first. As this coating burns off the outside of the powder, the speed of combustion increases. These progressive-burning powders tend to give a more uniformly distributed pressure, sustained longer during the travel of the bullet. Moreover, the maximum pressure is not so high because instead of being exerted all at once, the pressure is spread out more evenly during the entire travel of the bullet. The du Pont "Improved Military Rifle" powders such as I. M. R. No. 3031, I. M. R. No. 4320 and I. M. R. No. 4064 are progressive powders.

Like black powder, smokeless powders are also controlled as to their speed of burning by the grain size. Powders with very fine grains burn up in a hurry and therefore are particularly suited for short-barrel weapons. Powders with very large grains take longer to burn up, and are adapted to long-barrel weapons such as cannon.

For any given size of gun, such as the caliber .30 rifle, there is a granulation of powder that is suitable, and a larger or smaller size will either give too high pressures or will not burn up completely before leaving the barrel.

However, in the Springfield rifle the grains may be either long and slender or short and fat. In general, better results are obtained if the grains are long and slender, because this leaves larger air spaces between them for the priming flame to penetrate, and thus better ignition is obtained.

For example, when I was at Frankford Arsenal some years ago, we were loading the National Match ammunition with du Pont

No. I. M. R. No. 1147, which was similar to the modern I. M. R. No. 4320. This powder was cut into very short grains only a twenty-second of an inch long, and they would pack very uniformly in the loading machine powder measure, and the variation between the highest and the lowest charge in a test sample of cartridges would be no more than six tenths of a grain.

We then tried a very similar powder with the grains cut twice as long, that is, eleven to the inch. The charges thrown by the loading machines were not as uniform, having a maximum variation of about a grain and seven tenths from one cartridge to another from the same machine. But on machine rest tests the coarser powder made smaller groups every time. Naturally we loaded the ammunition with this more accurate powder, and the scores at Camp Perry ran exceptionally high that year. But the Ordnance Department came in for some very sarcastic and bitter criticism from a self appointed local dispenser of wisdom at the matches who carefully pulled the bullets from a number of cartridges and weighed the charges, then spread the word that the extreme variation between charges was twice as great as it had been the year before.

The critic was accusing the Department of very great stupidity, and could not understand why in the world they used a powder that did not load quite as closely as to weight variations as the finer powder. He talked loud and long and no doubt there are many who gained the impression from him that it was a matter of indifference to the makers of the ammunition whether the accuracy was good or bad.

Actually, this critic knew nothing whatever about powder or the problems of loading small-arms ammunition. He just weighed the charges in some cartridges, and found that the variation was about a grain and a half; and he heard that the variation was less with the finer powder, so he at once began to shout his discovery. I suppose it never occurred to him that the Ordnance engineers, with all their vast testing resources and their vital interest in producing the best possible ammunition, had made hundreds of tests much more elaborate than any shooter could ever afford before they finally decided to use the large-grain powder instead of the other. Truly, a little knowledge is a dangerous thing.

Besides the nitrocellulose powders described above, there are some military rifle powders containing a certain proportion of nitroglycerin as well as nitrocellulose. The old W-A (Whistler Aspinwall) powder used in the early Krag cartridges was an example. It contained about 30 per cent or more of nitroglycerin and was a good powder except that it was erosive on the barrels, as nitroglycerin powder burns at a higher temperature than nitrocellulose powder.

HiVel No. 3 is a modern nitroglycerin powder which has gained a great reputation for extreme accuracy in match loads. Bullseye is a nitroglycerin pistol powder which is still used by the Government in loading pistol cartridges. Three types of pistol powder are standard with the Government, one a nitroglycerin powder, the other a nitrocellulose powder and the third the so-called Ball Powder. The nitrocellulose powder that the Government was using in pistol cartridges during the latter part of World War II was du Pont 4768.

These pistol powders, unlike the rifle powder above mentioned, do not have tubular grains. Instead they are in the form of very fine, thin wafers, flakes, or spheres, shapes which makes them burn with the greater rapidity that is necessary to cause them to be consumed in the short-barrel weapons in which they are used.

The rate of burning of the powders, above described, such as the du Pont I. M. R. powders and the Hercules HiVel, depends not only upon the grain size but also upon the resistance that the bullet offers to being moved. If any of these powders are ignited in the open air they will burn slowly, the same as a pile of grains of celluloid, and there will be no explosion. On the other hand, when they are ignited in a gun the first grains burn and give off hot gases, and these hot gases in turn accelerate the burning of the other grains. The more the gases are confined, the hotter they are and the faster the combustion of the remaining powder will be. Thus with a heavy bullet or with the cartridge case full of powder, the combustion is more rapid than it is with a light bullet or with the cartridge case only partly filled with powder.

There are some powders which are required to burn with a large air space in the case, and a light bullet. These are powders used for reduced loads. There are also powders which are required to burn with no resistance at all in the form of a bullet to hold back the gases. This is the case with powder used in blank cartridges, where there is no bullet but only a paper wad. This powder must burn with extreme rapidity under low pressure. The powder most used for this purpose is called "E. C. Blank Fire Powder" (From the originators, the Explosives Company).

We have seen that guncotton burns with extreme rapidity. If we mix it with nitroglycerin it burns more slowly. If we should compress it, or mix it up with glue, or do anything to take away its fluffy consistency, this would tend to make it burn more slowly.

Following these principles, blank powder can be made by taking nitrocellulose or some other nitro compound such as nitro-lignin (nitrated wood) in combination with other suitable substances, and dampening the fluffy material with gum water, then rolling it into little balls or grains. Thus it is almost guncotton, but the violence of its burning is reduced by the fact that its particles are glued together by the gum water solution. Blank-cartridge powder must not be used with a bullet or charge of shot in the cartridge. The added resistance is liable to cause it to detonate and blow the gun to pieces.

A popular dense pistol powder, DuPont's Pistol Powder No. 5. It consists
of fine flakes of nitrocellulose. Magnified 20 times.

DuPont Oval. A progressive shotgun powder designed to give maximum results in long range loads.

Powder for reduced loads is midway between blank-fire powder and the regular rifle powder. It has to be fast burning because it cannot depend much upon the resistance of the bullet. It is used in small charges in big cartridge cases with lots of air space, and it is also used with very light bullets. It is difficult to make a powder that will perform well under these circumstances, but this was finally accomplished and an extremely satisfactory powder of this kind in its day was the old Sporting Rifle Powder No. 80, which was used with the gallery-practice outfits issued to the Army some years ago. This powder is no longer made, having been superseded by the tubular grain du Pont No. 4759.

Shotgun powders differ considerably from rifle powders. The shotgun is distinguished from the rifle not only in not having a rifled bore, but also in being usually of considerably greater caliber. To produce a weapon easy to handle, it is necessary to make the forward portion of the barrel very light. Therefore, there must be but little pressure except near the breech. Furthermore, distribution of the shot in a uniform pattern seems to require that comparatively little pressure be exerted on the shot in the forward portion of the barrel. For these reasons shotgun powders must burn more rapidly than rifle powders, and therefore there must be more surface exposed.

In the black powder days, the standard shotgun load was three drams weight, or 82 grains of black powder. This was always loaded by measure instead of by weight. The first smokeless powders developed for shotguns were called "bulk" powders, because they could be loaded bulk for bulk with black powder, using the same three dram charge cup. Later on a different type of shotgun powder was developed, which was much more powerful, and the three dram measure could not be used for them; a very few grains, say 24 to 30 grains of these "dense" powders would give the same velocity as a three dram measure of black or bulk smokeless. The loads of these modern dense powders are still quoted in drams, but they are actually "dram equivalents", or "equivalent drams", and bear no relation to actual dram weights or to dram measures.

The first successful bulk powder was known as Schultze, after the inventor, Captain E. Schultze of the Prussian Artillery. It was made from nitro-lignin, or nitrated wood pulp, mixed with nitrates of barium and potassium.

Modern dense shotgun powders are of both the nitroglycerine and the straight nitrocellulose types. Well known brands are Hercules Red Dot and du Pont Oval.

Semi-Smokeless Powders. Lesmok Powder

Besides the good old fashioned black powder, and the modern smokeless types, there was for years an intermediate type known as semi-smokeless, which was a mixture of black and smokeless.

Schultze powder. One of the earliest successful smokeless powders. It is of the type called "bulk" powder, and is made of nitrated wood pulp (or Nitro Lignin).

Lesmok powder, so much used in the .22 caliber match cartridges of a few years back was a mixture of guncotton and black powder. It was extremely accurate in .22 caliber loads, and while it gave much more smoke and fouling than the modern smokeless loads, the fouling was of such a nature that it did not cake or harden in the barrel, and firing did not have to be interrupted for cleaning, as it did with straight black powder.

In the days before the advent of the non-corrosive primers, the Lesmok loads were much less corrosive than were the straight smokless loads, as the powder charges were bulkier, and tended to carry away more of the primer residue. However, after the non-corrosive primers came into general use in .22 caliber ammunition, the tables were turned, and the potassium salts left by the black powder component of the Lesmok powder made it necessary to clean the bore soon after firing, regardless of the kind of primer used.

One of the great disadvantages of Lesmok powder was the extreme hazard to life involved in its manufacture. For this and other reasons it has gradually fallen into disuse. At this writing, February 1947, a lot of Lesmok loaded .22 caliber cartridges has recently been completed by Winchester, but it is said that no more will be made.

Another powder of the same general type that was formerly very popular but is now no longer made was King's Semi-Smokeless.

Ball Powder

A development of the Western Cartridge Company which was of great service during World War II was what is known as Ball Powder.

As has already been stated the ordinary tubular grain rifle or pistol powder is made of a paste or "colloid" which is squeezed through what is known as a "macaroni press". This produces tubes of powder which are cut to length by revolving knives as the tubes come through the press dies. After being extruded and cut off, the grains must then be dried.

The following brief description of the manufacture of Ball Powder was written by Lt. Commander Edwards Brown, of the NRA Technical Staff, who before he was called to active duty in 1941 was a production engineer in the Smokeless Powder & High Explosives Plant of the Western Cartridge Co.

The Western Cartridge Company, now a division of the Olin Industries Inc., has developed an unique process for the manufacture of smokeless powder having individual grains in the form of little round balls. The basic material, nitro-cellulose, is the same as that used in the older and better known extrusion process. The process, however, offers one distinct economical advantage, the nitrocellulose can be obtained either from newly nitrated material or from surplus cannon or small arms powder.

Lesmok powder, popular in .22 caliber rifle and pistol cartridges before the advent of the non-corrosive primer. It is a mixture of 85 percent black powder and 15 percent guncotton.

This new process is also a relatively safe one because the powder is wet from the beginning of the process until the finished powder grains are dried. This makes possible another economical advantage in that the nitrocellulose can be pumped as a water slurry through pipe lines from one operation to another. Trucking is thereby eliminated and handling costs are cut to a minimum. Processing and handling therefore amounts to a valve turning operation under the watchful eye of technically trained supervisors and the control laboratory.

Let's assume that Western is going to produce finished powder from a blend of fibrous guncotton and cannon powder and we will briefly follow the process from beginning to end. The first step taken is to pump the old powder, together with water, from the storage tanks through a pipeline to the beater house. Here it is pumped to a hammer mill which beats the powder into fine particles. The fine particles, suspended in water, which emerge from the mill makes a slurry which resembles mud and it is usually referred to as such.

The slurry is piped to a large storage tub where the proper quantity of guncotton is added and from whence it is pumped through a long pipeline into a large jacketed still in the hardening house.

Chalk is then added to the still to counteract the free acids present in the old powder. These acids are either entrapped during the nitration of new nitrocellulose or have been formed in the old powder during its storage over a period of years and may be the reason for its having been declared unserviceable. As smokeless powder decomposes it forms oxides of nitrogen which change to nitric acid and make the powder dangerous in a dry condition. The Western process counteracts these acids in the early stages of ball powder manufacture by completely dissolving the nitrocellulose in a solvent and washing this lacquer with chalk water to neutralize the acid.

A volatile solvent, ethyl acetate, is blown through a pipeline, from an outside storage tank, into the still with the slurry. Diphenylamine is also put into the still with the solvent and this makes the future ball powder stable for years to come because diphenylamine and chalk react with the oxides of nitrogen forming a harmless chemical. The solvent dissolves the nitrocellulose and a pliable lacquer is thus formed. Large paddles in the still are turned on to agitate the lacquer and break it up into small particles. The still, by means of hot water flowing through the jacket, is heated to facilitate this process.

A protective colloid which has been injected into the still keeps the small particles of nitrocellulose lacquer from going back together again. The agitation is continued until the particles of lacquer become spherical in shape. As soon as the grains are of the desired size and shape, the ethyl acetate is distilled out of the particles into a condenser where the solvent is recovered. When the ethyl acetate is all driven off the small spherical particles are left very hard.

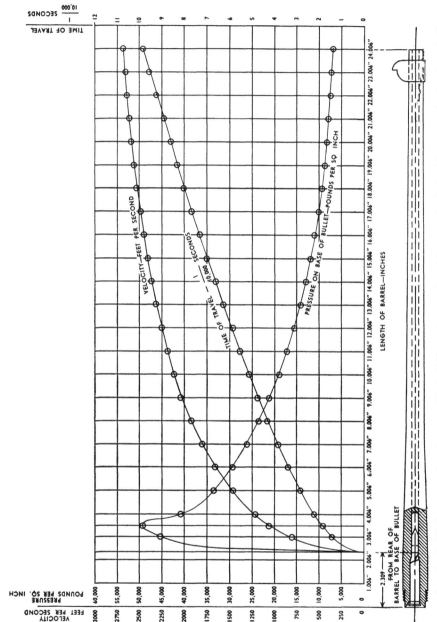

Interior ballistic curves for the 1903 U. S. Rifle, cal. 30. Cartridge was loaded with 150 grain flat base bullet, M1906, with approximately 50 grains of Pyro D. G. Powder, giving a muzzle velocity of 2700 feet per second. Note that the travel of the bullet from the start of its motion until it leaves the muzzle requires only .00098 second; the pressure of the powder gas at exit is approximately 7000 lbs; and that cutting 7 inches off the end of the barrel would reduce the velocity only 200 feet per second.

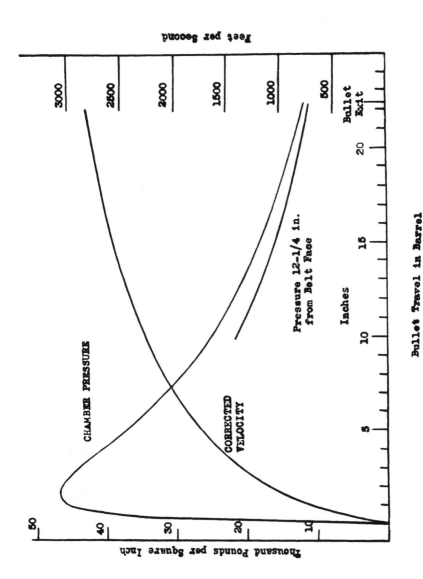

Bullet Travel in Barrel

Curves showing pressure versus travel and velocity versus travel for the cartridge, ball, caliber .30, M 2. Charge, 53 Grains IMR 4676, Army Lot 2006.

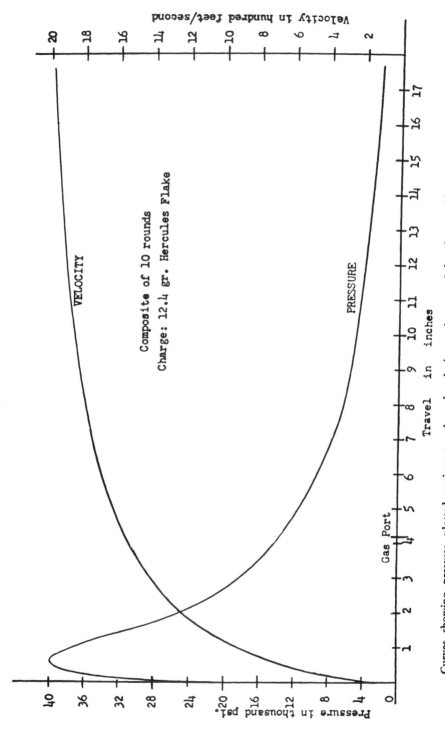

Curves showing pressure plotted against travel, and velocity against travel for the cartridge, ball, carbine, caliber .30 M 1. Composite of 10 rounds. Charge, 12.4 grains Hercules Flake.

Sodium sulphate (salt) is put into the still to aid in removing the water remaining in the otherwise solid balls. The fresh water in the balls passes through the surface of the ball into the salt. The process by which this is accomplished is known as *osmosis*. After the balls of powder are dewatered the salt water in which they are resting is exchanged for fresh water and the resulting slurry is pumped to the screen house where the various sizes of balls are segregated as to maximum and minimum diameters through rotary screens. The various segregated sizes or cuts flow from the screens into separate storage tanks designated for each particular grain size.

At this point the ballistic laboratory becomes vitally interested in the balls because the ballistic characteristics of the powder are partially determined by the size of the individual grains. Everything else being equal the smaller diameter grains result in a faster burning powder. This is by no means the only factor in controlling ballistic characteristics, as will be learned later.

Now that the balls of powder are segregated as to size and stored under water in various large wooden tubs, let's assume that the ballistic laboratory wants to make a particular powder to meet production needs for a certain cartridge. From tests of previous batches of ball powder the "lab" knows which size grain comes closest to meeting requirements. The size designated is accordingly pumped from the storage tubs through a pipeline into a large jacketed still in the coating house.

Here two coating operations are carried out in the same still. The first coating is nitroglycerine and the second is a deterrent coating. Both of these coatings are important factors in controlling the final ballistic characteristics of the powder. The nitroglycerine raises the potential or total energy in the grain. The deterrent delays the burning on the surface to provide a progressive burning powder in spite of the ball shape which would otherwise produce "degressive" burning.

After the charge of ball powder is pumped into the coating still, nitroglycerine is blown from an outside storage, through a pipeline, into the still. This is not pure nitroglycerine but it is mixed with a solvent. The solvent serves to desensitize the nitroglycerine somewhat, to make it safer during transportation to the plant and during storage. The contents of the still are agitated by large motor driven paddles to disperse the nitroglycerine throughout the water in small droplets, forming an emulsion. The still is heated slightly and the solvent together with the nitroglycerine enters the grains.

After the nitroglycerine has impregnated the grain the solvent is driven off by further heating of the still. Providing the ensuing heat treatment is properly controlled, the deterrent coating will penetrate the surface of the grain only to the proper depth. When the deterrent coating has penetrated the surface of the grain the remainder of the solvent is driven off and the individual balls are again left hard.

The unique part of the ball powder process is now complete and the powder, still in a water slurry, is pumped to a centrifuge or an Oliver filter to remove the bulk of the water. The powder, no longer in a slurry, must now be dumped into containers and hauled to the drier where all but a very small percentage of the water and solvents are removed from the grain. Western has been drying by infrared heat, a thin layer of the grains being fed from a hopper onto a continuous belt which passes under the lamps.

The next step is to transport the dry powder to a small house where it is tumbled with graphite in a large doughnut shaped container called a sweetie barrel. This gives the powder its black appearance. Since graphite is a conductor of electricity it prevents static electricity from building up in the powder on subsequent operations. Although the powder was wet screened to size it is now dry screened for final elimination of any grains which are above the maximum and below the minimum diameter for the batch specification.

After the screening operation the ballistic laboratory takes a sample of the batch to determine its ballistic characteristics. It is seldom that a batch performs exactly as desired. As in the manufacture of most products, there will be a slight variation in production units in spite of precise control methods. The ballistic expert is satisfied, however, if the results are reasonably close to his requirements. He has a record of results of other batches of the same grain size which are in magazine storage. With his batch data before him he can make up a combination of these batches which, blended together, will give him optimum results. He then furnishes instructions to the blender crew letting them know just how many pounds of each batch should be blended together to make up the finished lot of powder.

Since it is not possible to control the hardening operation to produce any one particular grain size there is of course the question of how to balance the production of the powder line to meet ammunition loading requirements. It is usually found that there is a greater need for the fine grain than there is for the coarse grain. This could be taken care of by dumping the larger sizes from the screening operation back in the hardening still and processing it over again. This would be an expensive way of getting the finer grain powder. The problem is actually solved by running the larger grain powder, in a water slurry, through rolls very much like those which you would see in a brass or steel mill. These rolls flatten out the grains which happens to make them faster burning. When rolling is called for it is done after the coating operation and before drying. By means of this rolling procedure it is therefore possible to give the large grain powder ballistic characteristics similar to the small grain powder. This

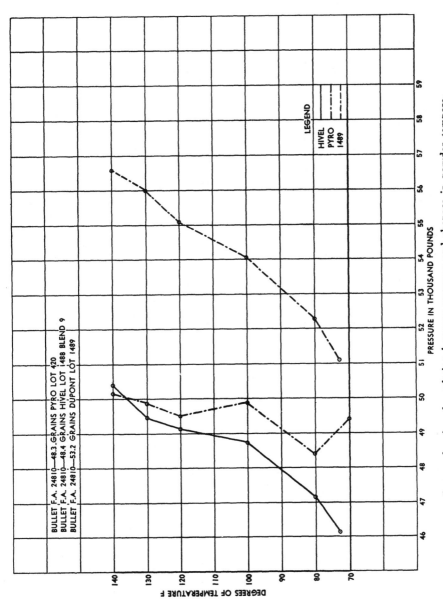

Curves showing the relation between pressure and changes in powder temperature for three types of military rifle powder.

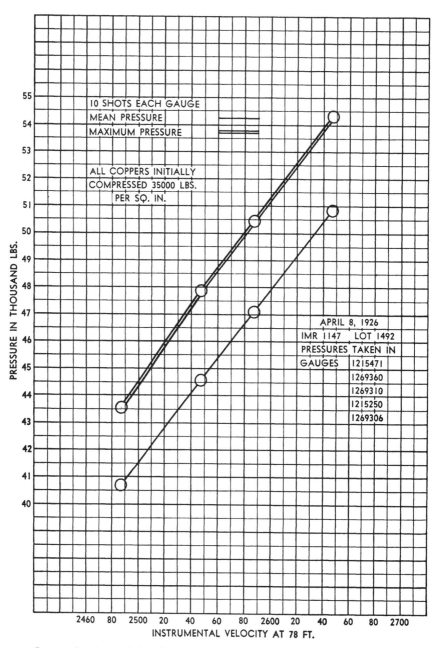

Curves showing relation between pressure and velocity for one lot of IMR powder.

permits enough flexibility to make a balanced production line possible. Consequently some "ball powder" is flat instead of spherical in its finished form.

Ball powder was used for much of the enormous production of carbine cartridges made during the World War II and was made the standard powder for those cartridges. It was also used in some of the pistol cartridge production. In addition the Western Cartridge Co. loaded several hundred million 7.92 mm cartridges for the Chinese Government with ball powder.

At this time, (1947), Ball Powder is being used in rifle, pistol and shotgun cartridges, and gives promise of having a wide and increasing use in the future.

The Use of Tin in Rifle Powders

In the period immediately following World War I, the question of metal fouling had not been solved, and the rifle shooter was constantly confronted with trouble from this source.

The French, whose artillery we used very largely in that war, were known to place metallic tinfoil in with the powder charges used for field guns, in order to prevent the depositing of copper fouling from the metal of the rotating bands on the shell.

After the end of that war, the du Pont organization obtained patents on the idea of incorporating finely powdered metallic tin in the colloid from which the gunpowder was made. Popular du Pont powders of that day were Nos. 15, 17, etc. When tin was added to the composition of one of these powders, the figure ½ was added to the number designating the powder. Thus powders No. 15½, No. 17½, etc., were the same as Nos. 15, 17, etc., except that they contained a certain percentage of tin. The first of these powders that we tried in a military loading was No. 17½, which was used in the National Match ammunition of 1921 and thereabouts. This was said to contain 4% of metallic tin. It did eliminate the old metal fouling, but at the same time it introduced another kind, though a less troublesome one. This was tin fouling, which took the shape of a dark smoky looking deposit inside the bore of the rifle near the muzzle. On close examination, this appeared to consist of minute globules of metallic tin adhering to the surface. Evidently the tin in the powder vaporized under the terrific heat of the explosion, then condensed on the comparatively cool surface near the muzzle, after the gas had also been cooled somewhat by the expansion from its first high pressure to a pressure only perhaps one tenth of the peak figure.

On cleaning a gun so afflicted, it would be found that the cloth patch would stick rather tightly on the rough surface where the tin had been deposited. Once this fouling had occurred, the only remedy was to scratch it out with a stiff wire brush, which removed it quickly and with little difficulty.

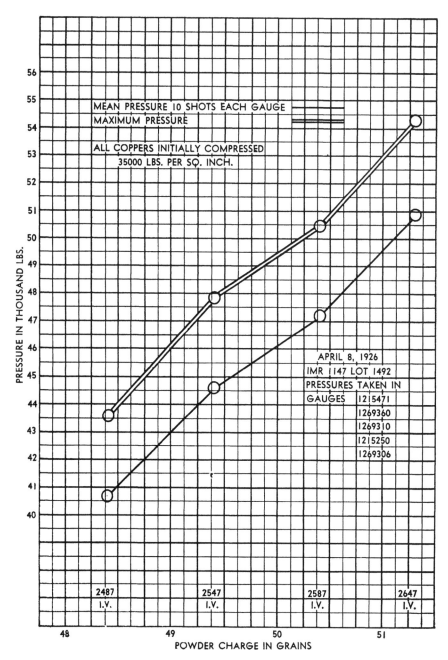

Curves showing relation between pressure and powder charge with one lot of IMR powder.

As a remedy, the percentage of tin used was reduced, first to 2½%, then to 2%, and later to 1½ percent or less.

Single Base Versus Double Base Powders

For many years there has been more less of a controversy raging as to the relative merits of single base powders as compared to the double base varieties. For years the British have mainly used Cordite, which is a typical double base powder, though this has been supplemented in times of war emergency by du Pont powders.

The old W. A., Lightning, and Sharpshooter powders used in the Krag and other arms of that day proved to be undesirably erosive, and this fact was largely responsible for a shift by the Army to a single base powder as the standard for use in the military rifle.

These powders had some 30% or more of nitroglycerine in their composition, and as it was found that the higher the percentage of nitroglycerine, the hotter the powder and the more erosive it was, the indicated remedy was to lower the nitroglycerine content.

The modern HiVel Powder, which for years has enjoyed an unexcelled reputation for accuracy, especially at long ranges has only about 20% of nitroglycerine, and is little more erosive than the best single base powders.

The Ammunition Board of 1923 made a comparative erosion test between the HiVel powder used in one of the National Match lots, and the I. M. R. No. 17 which was used in the other. The ten barrels fired with HiVel went out at an average of 4700 rounds, while those fired with No. 17 lasted but very little longer, or 5200 rounds.

A direct comparison as to accuracy between the single base and the double base powders was had in a number of the ammunition tests held in the years following World War I. Figures quoted from the tests of 1924 and 1925 are quoted below:

Year	Bullet	Powder	Velocity at 78', f.s.	Mean Pressure lbs. sq. in.	M.R. 600 yds. inches	M.R. 1000 yd. inches
1924	171 grain 9° B. T.	47 gr. HiVel	2701	49,000	2.260	5.685
1924	Same	51.5 I.M.R. 1145	2697	48740	2.676	5.706
1925	172 grain 9° B. T.	53.2 I.M.R. 1147	2716.4	49640	2.303	5.71
1925	Same	48.2 HiVel Lot 1488	2694	44020	2.592	6.887

All commercial du Pont powders are of the single base variety, while those made by the Hercules Powder Co. are double base. The ball powder made by Western Cartridge Co. is also of a double base composition.

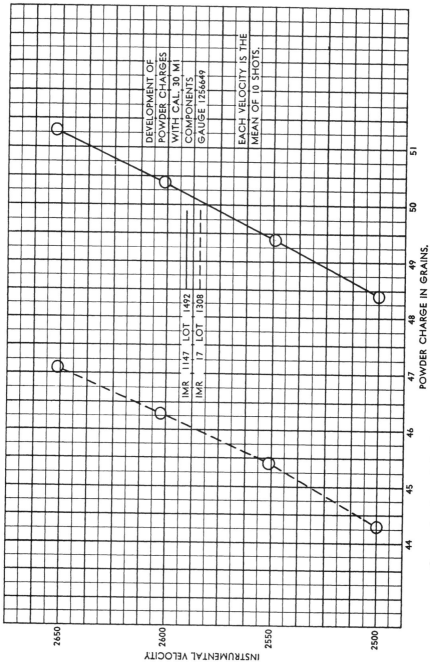

Curves showing relation between powder charge and velocity with two lots of IMR powder.

All three kinds, that is, single base, the regular double base, and the ball powder were used extensively by the Government during World War II.

As to small arms, the cal. .30 M2 cartridge was loaded with a single base powder known as du Pont No. 4895. The charge was adjusted according to lot to give 2800 feet per second muzzle velocity to the 150 grain flat base bullet. The charge varied, according to powder lot, from about 49 grains to about 51. The average pressure was about 46,700 lbs.

The pistol cartridges were loaded with either du Pont p 4768, or with ball powder; thus both single and double base powders were used.

The carbine used two kinds of powder, both double base. These were the Hercules Cal. .30 Carbine Powder, and the ball powder.

All rocket powder used in the War was of the double base variety, and it is interesting to note that owing to the high potential needed it contained a high percentage of nitroglycerine; something like 40%.

Powder for Handloaders

At the present writing there is a rather complete line of powder available for the handloader, in both the single and the double base varieties. Some of these are:

Name	Type	Intended Use.
Hercules HiVel	Double Base	Large capacity cartridges.
Hercules 2400	Double Base	Small & Medium capacity cartridges.
Bullseye	Double Base	Pistol Cartridges.
Unique	Double Base	Mid range rifle loads; super velocity pistol loads.

Some single base powders available are:

Powder	Old powder it is similar to	Intended use.
I.M.R. 4227	I.M.R. 1204	For small capacity cartridges.
I.M.R. 4198	I.M.R. No. 25½	For Medium Capacity Cartridges.
I.M.R. No. 3031	I.M.R. No. 17½	For medium sporting and military cartridges and mid-range loads.
I.M.R. No. 4320	I.M.R. No. 1147	For large capacity sporting and military cartridges.
I.M.R. No. 4064	I.M.R. No. 15½	For Magnum capacity cartridges.

XIV

Gun Corrosion and Ammunition Developments

THE shooters of a generation ago really had their troubles. In the first place, there was no such thing as a non-corrosive primer in this country, and if each and every gun were not cleaned immediately after shooting, and then cleaned again the next day, it was sure to be ruined.

Some guns were sure to be ruined anyway, no matter how much they were cleaned, for certain types of ammunition, such as .22 Short Smokeless had so much primer composition in proportion to the tiny charge of powder that corrosion seemed to get a hold before anything could be done about it, and in spite of everything that could be done.

In fact, the knowing shooter, who wanted to keep his gun accurate, just simply didn't use .22s in smokeless loads.

Another thorn in the side of the military rifle shot was the matter of metal fouling, which came in in 1903 with the Springfield rifle. This was a gun of greater power than its predecessor the Krag, and used loads of much greater intensity. Soon after the Springfield was introduced, some riflemen found it impossible to keep the bores of their guns looking right. Up near the muzzle there would be what seemed to be lumps in the bore which no amount of scrubbing could get out. At the same time the accuracy suffered.

It developed that these lumps were cupro-nickel, the material of the bullet jacket. This had a neat trick of adhering to the metal of the bore as the bullet friction developed terrific heat between the two surfaces of bullet and bore. Of course, as soon as the lump started to build, it formed a rough spot on the surface, which promptly tore off more of the next jacket. And so the vicious cycle progressed.

In those days, there was just one way in which the high powered military rifles could be kept shooting with any semblance of accuracy, and that was by the frequent and regular use of the standard Ordnance Department Metal Fouling Solution, or what was commonly called "Ammonia Dope".

The Ordnance Department formula for Ammonia Dope was

Ammonia Persulphate	1 ounce
Ammonium Carbonate	200 grains
Stronger Ammonia Water (28%)	6 ounces
Water	4 ounces

334

In using this solution the breech of the gun was corked up and a rubber tube was slipped over the muzzle, so that when the barrel was filled the muzzle could be entirely covered with no part of the metal making contact with the solution and the air at the same time. If this should occur, the solution would attack the barrel at the point where it came in contact with the air, and the barrel would be ruined in a few minutes.

After the barrel was prepared as described above, it was filled with solution and allowed to stand about twenty minutes. The solution was then taken out, and the barrel was quickly dried and oiled.

The solution had to be mixed up fresh for every use, as stale dope was corrosive to the steel. Even in spite of all precautions, the dope would sometimes unaccountably attack the steel and give it a sandblasted appearance, and a rough surface inside, which ruined it. Moreover, if any of the solution should leak past the cork into the breech mechanism, it was liable to remain there and cause serious rusting.

All this, of course, was the very worst kind of a nuisance, and it was not long before something was done about it. A theory was developed that the way to prevent metal fouling was to provide some kind of lubricant between the bullet and the bore. Various kinds of greases and vaselines, with and without graphite and other ingredients were tried. These really did help the metal fouling situation a lot, and in the period just before and after World War I, it was routine for the well equipped rifleman to carry with him a small tin pill box of grease called Mobilubricant, which was the most popular one for this use. The bullet was dipped into this just before each shot.

Just when the wheels of progress seemed to be going smoothly, Col. Whelen, down at Frankford Arsenal, threw in a bucketful of monkey wrenches. Some trouble was had at the National Matches and elsewhere with broken bolt lugs, and tests made at Frankford disclosed two sad and frightening facts: 1, Grease increased the bolt thrust dangerously; and, 2, as if that weren't enough, grease increased the chamber pressure dangerously.

When the gun is fired, the cartridge is driven back against the bolt face with the force of the powder pressure, resisted by the friction of the brass case against the chamber walls. Grease in the chamber takes away the friction of the case, and allows the entire thrust to come into the bolt head. Even if the grease were put on to the bullet alone, and great pains were taken to prevent it from getting onto the case, it would rub off the bullet onto the walls of the chamber, whence it would get onto the case anyway.

As to pressures, a test was made with 1920 National Match Ammunition, which gave the breech pressure of the dry ammunition as 51,335, while with the bullet and neck of the case carefully lubricated with vaseline the pressure averaged 59,000 lbs. per square inch.

Caliber .30 pressure gauge in use at Frankford Arsenal.

With the 1920 National Match Ammunition having the bullet and case as well as the chamber lubricated, the pressure went to 71,154 lbs. per square inch, and disastrously wrecked the pressure gage, which was considerably heavier and stronger than an ordinary rifle.

This was what was likely to happen if grease were used sparingly and properly. However, human nature being what it is, the grease was often used liberally and carelessly. After all, what's a few cents worth of cheap grease anyway? Let's jam the whole clip down in the grease pot; drop it on the ground, wipe part of the mixture of sand and grease off, and put on some more grease to cover up the sand.

So the Ordnance Department published the results of Col. Whelen's tests, and then both the Army Regulations and the National Match Rules of that year (1921) forbade the use of grease.

It was known that the French, in order to prevent deposits of copper from the rotating band of their artillery projectiles from smearing onto the bore, had placed strips of tinfoil in their powder charges. The tin seems to form an alloy with the copper that in some way prevents it from sticking to the bore. Maybe it forms a low melting alloy, and permits it to be melted and blown away. Anyway, it stopped the copper plating of the bores.

Col. Whelen, (then Major) who was making ammunition down there at Frankford Arsenal, thought this over, and conceived the idea that it might be possible to prevent lumpy metal fouling by applying tin to the bore of the rifle, and the way he did it was to tin plate the bullets. A number of experiments that he conducted showed that this would indeed do away completely with the troublesome metal fouling.

I was at that time Works Manager at Springfield Armory, busily turning out the National Match Rifles for the 1921 Matches, and naturally awaited with great impatience the first samples of the actual 1921 National Match Ammunition, so that we could see how the combination of rifle and ammunition would work.

Finally the great day arrived, and we received the first sample of the 1921 National Match Cartridges from Major Whelen. The card that came along with it gave the following information:

"*Description*. This ammunition, known as 1921 National Match Ammunition," is an experimental ammunition of the Caliber .30, Model of 1906 type, loaded at Frankford Arsenal for use in the National Matches of 1921. The bullet weighs 170 grains. The core is a composition of 30 parts lead and 1 part tin. The jacket is of cupro nickel. The base of the bullet is hollow, to prevent the lead core from extruding and making the base untrue. The assembled bullet measures .3079″ in diameter. It is then electrically tin plated so as to give a uniform coating of tin all over the bullet .0003″ thick, making the diameter of the completed bullet .3085.

The case has a special anneal so as to function at maximum efficiency in rifles. The ordinary case has a fairly soft body anneal to enable it to function in machine guns without giving ruptures from the excess headspace which so often exists in those weapons. This case has the body made much harder so as to extract more easily in rapid fire. These cases with the "Hard Rifle Anneal" are distinguished by the letter "R" placed after the year of manufacture on the head.

Frankford Arsenal No. 70 primer is used with a charge of 48.2 to 48.8 grains of du Pont Ex-1076 nitrocellulose progressive burning powder to give a muzzle velocity of 2700 feet per second with a breech pressure of 50,500 pounds per square inch.

The trajectory of this ammunition is very flat, and it requires the minimum allowance for wind. The following micrometer elevations apply

> From 200 to   300 yards, raise   2 minutes
> From 300 to   500 yards, raise   7 minutes
> From 500 to   600 yards, raise   5 minutes
> From 600 to   800 yards, raise   9 minutes
> From 800 to 1000 yards, raise 13 minutes

Competitors at the National Matches are particularly cautioned against the use of grease on the bullets. Grease will cause uneven velocities, and even when it is used carefully is liable to decrease the accuracy slightly. But more important, the use of grease with this ammunition is positively dangerous. It allows the cartridge case to slide to the rear through the greased chamber more readily, and thus increases the back thrust on the bolt head. Both the pressure and the velocity of this ammunition have been run up as high as is consistent with safety. If grease is used, the pressures will run up far above the safety limit, even running as high as 75,000 pounds per square inch. If grease should be used it will be only a question of time until with these high pressures a case with the head slightly softer than ordinary will be found which will open out and throw back and release the gas to the rear, demolishing the breech mechanism and possibly injuring the firer. Do not attempt to polish the bullets to remove the frosted appearance. The ammunition shoots more accurately with these frosted bullets than when they are polished."

A Question on Bullet Pull

When we got this new ammunition, we immediately started dissecting some of it to see what we could find. We measured and weighed it all over, then started to pull out some of the bullets so we could weigh them and the powder charges. But here we ran into a snag. The bullets just wouldn't pull. We had a very nice machine for pulling bullets from service cartridges without marring the bullets; this machine had a dial on it that read the bullet pull in pounds at the same time.

The usual bullet pull on service ammunition at that time was around 50 or 60 pounds, but the first bullet of the new lot that we pulled ran over 300 pounds, and some ran up to 600 pounds or more.

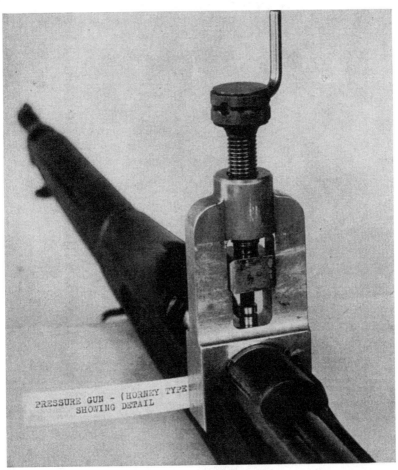

PRESSURE GUN - (HORNEY TYPE)
SHOWING DETAIL

Detail of pressure gauge, copper crusher type. The copper cylinder rests on the steel piston shown at the bottom of the yoke. This piston fits into a hole that goes down into the powder chamber. When the gun is fired, the gas pressure, acting through the piston, crushes the copper cylinder. The amount of shortening of the cylinder is compared to the dead weight required to shorten a similar cylinder a like amount.

I sat down right away and wrote to Col. Whelen, telling him what we had found, and asking him why it was, and if it would cause any trouble. He replied that apparently the tin on the bullet seemed to

An improved machine rest for the Springfield rifle, the Woodworth cradle, into which the rifle can be clamped so that it may be fired from a Mann type V-block.

have some effect that might be described as a sort of cold soldering; it more or less glued the bullet into the neck of the case. However, extensive firings had resulted in no trouble from this cause.

Col. Whelen was absolutely right. When shot dry, this was a splendid load, with exceptional accuracy. However, he had something else to reckon with, and that was the fact that some of the National Match Competitors were of the type who don't believe in signs. They evidently thought that warning about the use of grease was written just for fun.

I just happened to be in on the sequel to all this. I had been detailed as Ordnance Officer for the National Matches of that year, and was standing on the firing line during one of the first matches, when a rifle just a few feet to my left had a severe blow-back, which splintered the stock, bulged the magazine well, blew off the extractor, locked the bolt so that it couldn't be moved, and generally wrecked things. I just stepped over and noted an open pill box of grease beside the astonished competitor, so I picked up the block of cartridges he had been using, and noted that they were well daubed with grease.

A little reflection showed what could very well be the reason for the very decided reaction of this ammunition to grease on the cartridge.

Smokeless powder, as is well known burns quietly, like celluloid, if it is ignited in small quantities in the open air. If, however, it is ignited when it is confined, as it is in the cartridge, the first gas and heat that are generated cannot escape, so they cause the burning to get faster, and in a hurry. This faster burning generates more gas and heat, which makes the burning even more violent, and we have an explosion.

With this tin plated ammunition, with the bullet practically soldered in, the first thing that happened when the powder was ignited was that the initial pressure swelled the case up, and expanded the neck, and so released the bullet from its very tight seat, so it could move on down the bore and give more room for the first rush of powder gas.

However, if the bullet had been dipped in grease, this generally meant that the neck of the cartridge was greasy too. The space between the neck of the case and the neck of the chamber was filled with an incompressible substance, and the first moderate rise in pressure found it impossible to expand the neck and release the bullet. Thus the powder was strongly confined right at the beginning of its ignition, and accordingly the pressure rose disastrously.

During the matches, this "Tin-Can" ammunition, as the shooters called it, gave exceptionally fine results, and many new records were hung up; but there were also several wrecked rifles, always traced to the use of grease. One of the men on the range detail brought me a bullet that he had found on the range that had fallen there with

The author testing National Match Ammunition in the Woodworth cradle—1934.

the neck of the case of the case still attached. It had been torn off at the shoulder and had been dragged through the entire length of the barrel, becoming mashed down to bore diameter and having the rifling engraved on it during the process. The pressure generated must have been enormous.

In spite of the several blow-backs occurring during the matches, no one was hurt; at least, not to amount to anything. However, the War Department decided to ban the use of this tin-can ammunition, and all of it remaining on hand was scrapped.

Tin in the Powder; Lubaloy

While the use of tin-plated bullets had thus received a death blow, the use of tin itself for the purpose of preventing metal fouling was by no means dead. There were two other and safer approaches, and both of them were used extensively. One was the actual incorporation of tin in the propellant itself, as described in the chapter on *Powder;* and the other was the use of a bullet jacket metal which contained tin as a component part of the alloy. Such a jacket material was introduced around 1922 by the Western Cartridge Company under the trade name of Lubaloy, derived from the claim that it was a lubricating alloy. This was a compound of copper, zinc and tin.

New Jacket Materials

Up to that time the standard bullet jacket material had been, first, steel, coated with cupro-nickel, which was used from 1893 to 1902, then solid cupro-nickel, consisting of 60% copper and 40% nickel.

Gilding metal, consisting of 90% copper and 10% zinc, was a metal that was sometimes used for bullet jackets, but which was not considered stiff or strong enough to be used as the jacket for the service 150 grain flat base bullet having a core of 1 part tin to 30 parts lead. The Western Cartridge Company's Lubaloy was essentially gilding metal containing about 2% tin. The same alloy was produced by Nobel Industries in England by license agreement under the name Nobeloy.

This metal turned out to be a very good jacket material. When it was used, the lumpy metal fouling present with cupro-nickel disappeared entirely. It first came prominently to public notice when the Western Cartridge Company won the competitive test for the selection of the Palma Match long range ammunition for the 1922 matches. The winning ammunition was called Lubaloy-Palma, and had a 180 grain flat base bullet driven by 46 grains of HiVel powder at a muzzle velocity of 2625 feet per second, with a mean pressure of 46,800 pounds per square inch. The average measurements of the 24 targets shot at 1000 yards from a Mann rest gave a mean radius of 5.69 inches. The angle of departure for 1000 yards was 38 minutes. The Lubaloy jacket was composed of 90% copper, 8% zinc, and 2% tin.

In the National Match and Palma test for 1922, Frankford Arsenal for the first time introduced ammunition with gilding metal jackets.

A report of the test in *Arms and the Man* for April 1, 1922, states:

"Perhaps the most important and outstanding feature of the entire test is that gilding metal and bronze have been so improved in process of manufacture that they can now be utilized as materials for jackets of bullets that will give superior accuracy, and that these jacket materials have the great advantage of depositing no lumpy metal fouling in the bore of the rifle. These Lubaloy and gilding metal jackets are to all intents and purposes practically the same, both in composition and result."

Another innovation that appeared that year for the first time in the standard National Match ammunition was a tapered base or boat-tailed bullet. Both this year and the previous year the Western Cartridge Company had entered in the Palma Match tests a bullet with a 4 degree taper on the base. This year Frankford Arsenal entered a 6 degree boat tailed bullet as one of the three lots submitted for selection as the type for the National Matches, and the 6 degree boat tailed bullet was the one picked as a result of the accuracy test.

The National Match Ammunition to be made by Frankford Arsenal for the 1922 National Matches was described as follows:

170 grain 6 degree boat tailed gilding metal jacketed bullet, the jacket material being 90% copper and 10% zinc. Loaded with No. 70 primer, 43 grains of HiVel powder, to a muzzle velocity of 2685 feet per second and an average pressure of 48,885 pounds per square inch. Angle of departure for 1000 yards, 37½ minutes. Mean radius at 600 yards in the test, 3.16 inches.

During this development, Major Townsend Whelen, now Colonel, was in charge of the Small Arms Department at Frankford Arsenal, and he brought to both the design and manufacture of the service cartridge many years of experience in all phases of shooting, together with an open and inquisitive mind, and a tremendous capacity for hard work. His gilding metal jacket spelled the end of the metal fouling bugbear.

Barrel Corrosion

Now that metal fouling had gone out of the picture, there still remained one more big trouble to overcome, and that was the invariable tendency of every rifle and pistol barrel to rust badly unless it were cleaned thoroughly after each use.

There were many pet theories as to why gun barrels corroded. One of the most obvious and the most widely credited was the thought that the products of the powder combustion left an acid or corrosive residue in the bore of the gun.

Even the Ordnance Department at one time said "Powder fouling, because of its acid reaction, is highly corrosive." This theory came in with smokeless powder, and was responsible for the appearance of a host of so-called nitro-solvents, or simply, powder solvents. Most of these solvents are built around a base of amyl acetate or banana oil. Smokeless powder, in burning, is likely to deposit a gummy substance in the bore, and amyl acetate or acetone will dissolve this.

One such solvent, much used in past years at Springfield Armory, and in practice a most excellent gun cleaner and preservative, has the following formula:

To make ½ gallon take
    Amyl Acetate,—90 c.c., or 6 parts
    Acetone,—285 c.c., or 19 parts.
    Spirit of Turpentine,—285 c.c., or 19 parts
    Sperm Oil,—870 c.c., or 58 parts
    Pratt's Astral Oil,—390 c.c., or 26 parts

This formula was invented by the late Dr. Hudson, a famous rifle shot and experimenter of a quarter of a century ago.

The Pratt's Astral Oil was a very highly refined and acid free kerosene originally produced by Pratt & Co., of Brooklyn, and afterwards taken over by the Standard Oil Co.

This Hudson's Cleaner is an extremely satisfactory compound for both cleaning and preserving firearms. For years it was used extensively by the experimental Department of Springfield Armory. I first started to use it when I was stationed there, and the only care I ever gave my guns was to clean them very promptly with this compound just after shooting. Unless they were to be laid up for some time this was enough to keep them free from rust or corrosion, though in theory they should be cleaned again the next day then be wiped clean and lightly greased.

After-corrosion

It became well known in the old days that especially in a damp or humid climate, a gun would often show rusting in the bore starting several days after it had had a thorough cleaning. To account for this, another theory was evolved, which was called the Powder Gas Occlusion Theory, or the Sweating-Out theory.

According to this theory, the powder gases from the nitro powders were acid in reaction, and were driven by pressure into the pores of the metal while the barrel was heated. It was supposed that when the barrel cooled, these gases slowly diffused, and on coming into contact with the air, caused corrosion which would sometimes continue over long periods of time, in spite of, and following, numerous cleanings. The advocates of this theory supposed that the combustion of smokeless powder must produce oxides of nitrogen. The theory was apparently confirmed by the experience of many riflemen in having corrosion develop after careful cleaning.

Electro-chemical Theory

When two dissimilar metals touch, there is a difference of electrical potential between them, and if any chemical solution comes into contact with them, a current will flow, and the metal which is the more negative of the two will be corroded. It has been thought that the metal fouling left by a bullet would form an electrical couple with the metal of the barrel, and that in the presence of moisture, electrolysis would result, and corrode the steel. However no evidence has been produced to show that this action takes place in rifle barrels.

Metal Fouling

It was also suggested that acid residue or some other corroding agent might become imprisoned under metal fouling in the bore of the rifle, where ordinary cleaning could not reach it. After the gun had been put away and had stood for a time, it was supposed that the acid would work itself out and attack the steel. This seemed to be a reasonable explanation for after-corrosion. The fact that after-corrosion was actually prevented by doping the gun seemed to confirm this idea; it was however due entirely to another and then unsuspected reason that the metal fouling solution proved efficacious.

The Real Cause Discovered

It remained for Dr. Wilbert J. Huff of the Bureau of Mines to discover the real cause of firearms corrosion and after-corrosion, and to explode all the old favorite theories mentioned above. During World War I, in 1918, the Bureau of Mines, at the request of the War Department, undertook to investigate the cause of after-corrosion in firearms, and the work was assigned to Dr. Huff, of the Bureau's Research Staff. His brilliant work on this project was reported in Technical Papers 188—*Corrosion under Oil Films, with Special Reference to the Cause and Prevention of After-corrosion in Firearms*, by Wilbert J. Huff, published by the Government Printing Office, 1922; price, five cents.

Among other experiments, Dr. Huff placed fired rifles in humidors at different degrees of atmospheric humidity. It was found that a humidity of less than approximately 50% did not develop corrosion in fouled rifle barrels, even after exposure for a number of days. The two rifles used in this experiment were then exposed to 100% humidity, and the bores immediately developed heavy corrosion; all other metal parts remaining bright.

Carrying out this test further, sections of a barrel which had been fired were exposed at various humidities at a temperature of 30° C, and corrosion occurred at from 68% to 76% humidity.

Bullet Jacket Material Fouling

Bullets were driven by hand through unfired barrels, and cupro-nickel filings were thrown into the bores which were then exposed to 100% humidity with no resultant corrosion. Evidently, then, metal fouling is inert and will not cause corrosion.

Acid Gas Diffusion

Fired rifles were induced to corrode at 100% humidity, the bores being wiped out daily until corrosion ceased. This process lasted five days, showing that if gases were diffusing, the diffusion was completed in that time under the conditions in which the rifles were kept. Other rifles were fired and kept under the same conditions, but in less than 50% humidity, and did not corrode. If gases do diffuse and this diffusion was complete in the first case in five days, it is reasonable to suppose that it was complete in the second lot of rifles in the same time. After ten days, the second lot of rifles were exposed to 100% humidity and immediately corroded.

If corrosion were the result of gases, it might reasonably be expected to occur over the whole of the bore surface. Sections of a corroded barrel show that this is not the case, but clearly show that corrosion occurs in patches which are surrounded by clean sections of metal.

The production of corrosive acid gases by the burning of nitrocellulose powders under high pressure is not indicated by chemical examination. Carbon dioxide is produced but has little or no effect in corroding steel. Hydrogen and carbon monoxide are also formed, but when the gases are cooled from the great temperature of the explosion, 3900° F, the presence of oxides of nitrogen is impossible.

In the same way, it can be shown that the formation of nitrogen oxides from the primer is impossible, while it can be clearly demonstrated that the potassium chlorate of the primer loses oxygen and gives chloride, the salt.

Other examples can be brought to disprove the gas diffusion theory but are merely an accumulation of evidence that corrosion is not formed from this cause.

There remains the possibility that some surface residue from the powder or primer may form an acid in accord with the first theory given.

Experiments were conducted along this line, and no trace of acid could be found. The presence of acids or acid gases from powder or primer, when burned under pressure, must then be disbelieved.

It can be shown, however, that some powders burned under little or no pressure, such as in reduced loads or blanks may produce acid residue, due to incomplete combustion; but inasmuch as after-corrosion is present when no acid is formed, this cannot be the primary cause of this corrosion.

Potassium Chloride Theory

Dr. Huff knew most primers contained potassium chlorate, and when the primer is fired a certain amount of potassium chloride is formed. Potassium chloride is a salt very much of the same general chemical formula and behavior as the common table salt, sodium chloride. Potassium chloride attracts moisture.

It is well known by every one that wet salt placed on a steel surface will immediately cause rust. From a consideration of these facts, Dr. Huff conceived the idea that it might be the potassium chloride that was causing all the trouble. To test out this theory he made up a priming mixture of silver permanganate, lead sulpho-cyanide, antimony sulphide and T. N. T., and loaded some service cartridges with these primers.

Two lots of guns were first carefully made chemically clean, and then fouled by firing; one lot with the cartridges primed with the above mixture, and the other lot with a straight service cartridge and primer. The bores were coated with oil and exposed in a humidor to 100% humidity for one week. The specially primed rifles did not corrode, while those fired with the service cartridge corroded heavily under the oil.

This was indeed a great ray of light on this hitherto dark subject. It is not only demonstrated the truth of Dr. Huff's potassium chloride theory, but it further showed that oil alone is not capable of pre-venting after-corrosion by excluding air and oxygen from the salt.

A further experiment consisted of the application of chemically pure potassium chloride to sections of a barrel which had never been fired. When exposed to 100% humidity, these gave identically the same results as the fired rifle barrels.

Adherents of the old theories may object that repeated cleanings should mechanically remove the salt; that the many endorsements of non-aqueous nitro solvents can not all be in error; that after-corrosion in dry arid regions like Arizona are not explained, and similar doubts.

These objections are not at variance with the facts as found by the Bureau of Mines. Repeated cleanings may not remove every particle of salt. Microscopic examination of a barrel shows very plainly the deep tool wounds and fissures in its surface. Corrosion results in further deepening these pits or scars. When potassium chloride is deposited over the bore surfaces, it gets into these tool wounds and scars, and no amount of mechanical cleaning can insure its entire removal.

It is also a fact that while desert regions are dry in the daytime, nightfall is accompanied by a rapid cooling of the atmosphere which is frequently great enough to precipitate dew. Reports from the Weather Bureau Stations in the arid areas of Arizona, Utah and Nevada are to the effect that all these stations had observed the formation of dew.

The gas diffusion or "Sweating Out" theory is now shown up in its true colors. We have seen that humidities of over 50% are necessary to induce corrosion. After firing and mechanical cleaning and oiling, some period of time may elapse before this humidity point is encountered, and this is particularly true where guns are kept indoors and in artifically heated atmospheres. Part of the salt has probably been removed in cleaning and the remainder rubbed into the cracks and fissures of the bore surface, where it lurks, a dangerous and invisible enemy.

It may thus remain inactive until a relatively high humidity is again encountered, when corrosion sets in. This may be weeks or months after firing, and formerly, when it appeared, its presence was hard to understand, and was naturally attributed to "sweating out" of gases or acid-powder residue.

It is also true that a long period of high humidity might develop the maximum corrosion in a short time. The experiments cited show that at 100% humidity, the maximum corrosion can take place in five days, and subsequent cleanings showed that no further corrosion took place. In other words, the potassium chloride had been completely dissolved in that time by the water vapor.

This period of five days is of course not constant but depends on varying conditions. It does show, however, that a barrel may either corrode or "sweat out" on several different occasions, or the corrosion be completed at once or over a single period; and that the mechanical removal of the salt is not the sole means of stopping it. It may go on until the last of the salt is dissolved, where it stops itself for lack of fuel as it were. A gun cleaned at this stage would not show any further corrosion.

This potassium chloride, being almost the same as ordinary salt, can easily be dissolved in water and washed away where it will do no harm, whereas oil will not dissolve it and will have no effect on it.

Water as a cleaner

The Bureau of Mines pointed out that Potassium Chloride, the primary cause of after-corrosion, is soluble only in water or aqueous solutions. Manifestly, then cleaning the barrel with water will dissolve and wash away the salt, The Bureau of Mines further states, however, that "Practical riflemen seem to have a deep seated prejudice against the use of water for this purpose. . . ."

This is readily understandable, for the water must be thoroughly removed, or it will itself cause corrosion. The difficulties attending the use of water as a cleaning agent are apparent when one considers solid breech rifles, which must be cleaned from the muzzle; revolvers, where the cylinders and mechanism present numerous cracks and crevices; extractor slots in .22 caliber rifles, etc.

It can now be seen why the ammonia dope was so effective in preventing after corrosion. Certainly after this watery material had stood in the bore for twenty minutes, there would be no salt left undissolved.

As a result of the knowledge gained from this report, the standard method of cleaning guns fired with chlorate or so called "corrosive" primers is to wash out the bore thoroughly with water, hot if available, then dry and oil it. This troublesome procedure is a sure cure for after-corrosion.

Emulsions and Polarized Oils

Soon after the Huff report made the shooting world primer-salt conscious, there appeared on the market a number of cleaners designed to take advantage of the natural aversion of the shooter to the use of water for cleaning guns. A very popular one was an emulsion of water and a red oil, probably Turkey Red oil. The water dissolved the salt, and the oil left a greasy residue which stopped the compound from being in itself a rust producer, as is water alone.

The latest cleaners are based on the polarized oil. This is an oil combined with a substance of such molecular construction that it has a strong affinity for metal, and at the same time will combine readily with both oil and water. As it is explained in popular language, the molecules, besides having a powerful affinity for metal, have "hooks" on one side which will fit and take hold of the water molecules, and on the other side they have "hooks" which will fit and hold the oil molecules. When such a polarized oil compound is placed on a wet metal surface, it breaks the surface tension of the water and sinks right down through it to the metal surface and clings to it.

These polarized oil compounds have enough water in their make-up to dissolve the primer salt, and at the same time they are sufficiently oily to retard rusting.

Lanolin Mixtures

During the South Pacific Campaigns of World War II, our soldiers gained the impression that the Japanese had a gun cleaning oil that was quite superior to anything that we had, and they also gained the impression that this preservative contained lanolin, which is a grease extracted from wool. Lanolin has the property of mixing with water. In other words, it seems to have some at least of the properties of the polarized oils mentioned above.

Col. Dwight Garrison of the Ordnance Department who was at the time serving in Australia, undertook to test and analyze the Japanese gun oil, and to develop one for our own use which would be at least as good if not better. He arrived at a formula which as reported by him, performs exceptionally well. This is

Dehydrated Lanolin 15%
Green Petrolatum 35%
Motor Oil S.A.E. No. 20 Heavy (viscosity at 70 deg. = 30 S.A.E.) 50%

From the amount of talk about lanolin that was heard in connection with the Japanese oil, one might conclude that its virtues in this field were just being discovered; but this is evidently not so, for I find in

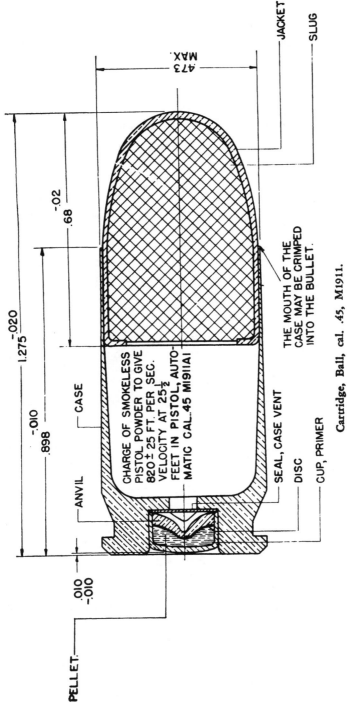

JACKET

SLUG

.473 MAX.

-.02

.68

1.275 -.020

.898 -.010

CASE

ANVIL

PELLET

.010 -.010

CHARGE OF SMOKELESS PISTOL POWDER TO GIVE 820 ± 25 FT. PER SEC. VELOCITY AT 25½ FEET IN PISTOL, AUTO-MATIC CAL. .45 M1911A1

THE MOUTH OF THE CASE MAY BE CRIMPED INTO THE BULLET.

SEAL, CASE VENT

DISC

CUP, PRIMER

Cartridge, Ball, cal. .45, M1911.

my notebook the formula, written by me in 1920, for the Frankford Arsenal Nitro-solvent Gun Cleaner No. 18. The formula as I recorded it is

Acetone ....1 part
Kerosene (Pratt's Astral Oil) ....1 part
Sperm Oil ....1 part
Mineral Spirits (turpentine) ....1 part
To every 800 c.c. add 250 grams of anhydrous lanolin.

Stir up the lanolin with mineral spirits first, add acetone last. Perfume with citronella if desired.

Oleic Acid

Another substance which has been used in gun cleaners and which may act somewhat the same as lanolin does is oleic acid. This at least seems to have a definite emulsifying effect, and may be more or less of a polarizer. As a Lieutenant in the Artillery, in 1911 I was stationed in Florida, where the hunting was very good; sometimes full sized alligators would come up from the nearby bayou into my back yard.

At that time the Remington representative for that territory was C. B. ("Cardboard") Smith, and when I obtained from him a .25 and also a .35 Remington No. 8 Autoloading Rifle, he advised me to use Hoppe's Nitro-Solvent No. 9 for cleaning them. I was quite curious as to the composition of this cleaner, and some years later had an opportunity to have it and a number of other cleaners analyzed in connection with a study of gun preservers. My notebook gives it the following probable composition:

Ammonium oleate 16%
Neutral Saponifiable oil 24%
Nitro-benzine 6%
Light Mineral Oil, such as kerosene ⎫
Amyl acetate ....⎭ 54%

The percentages are approximate. This was written down by me some 25 years ago, and may not represent the Hoppe's of today.

Soap

A gun preserver which was much in vogue in this country just after World War I was a British product known as B.S.A. Safti-Paste. The initials stand for the maker, the well known firm of Birmingham Small Arms Company. This was much praised and recommended by gun editors and experts. It was said to be a good safe preventer of corrosion, and a boon to the lazy man, as all that was necessary was to coat the bore with this after shooting and then forget the gun until the next time it was wanted for shooting. I can testify from personal experience with this product that it was exceedingly effective. Again I quote the approximate probable composition of a sample of 25 years ago from my notebook. It was

Dry soap, soluble in alcohol 43%
Mineral oil 44%
Water and Amyl Alcohol 13%

Noncorrosive Primers

When the primer was definitely identified as the culprit behind the gun corrosion trouble, it was only natural that there should at once arise a great bustle of activity directed towards finding a primer that would overcome this defect.

Let's go back a few years into primer history. For many years after the first metallic cartridges came into use, all primers had as one of their principal constituents a very sensitive explosive called fulminate of mercury, and in addition, they had more or less potassium chlorate. This mixture worked all right with black powder, which deposits some percent of its weight in the form of solids when it burns. This large amount of fouling completely masked, diluted, and washed away the small amount of solid material left by the primer combustion.

When smokeless powder came into use, the picture changed. The explosion of the cartridge left the bore of the gun and the inside of the cartridge clean and nearly free from fouling. The material deposited by the primer combustion had a fine clear place to land.

The first result was noted by the handloaders. In those days everyone was more or less used to loading his own charges from the powder horn and shot flask which hung by the old muzzle loader that stood in the corner. When guns came into use that had nice expensive brass cartridge cases to hold the charge, what was more natural than to reload the empty ones; especially as the black powder then in use was so flexible that no table of charges was necessary.

As a result, handloading was almost universal in the days of the early breech loader. When smokeless powder came into use, the handloaders noted with dismay that the brass cases cracked after being used only a very little. The cause of this cracking was finally traced by the Ordnance Department to the mercury deposited from the fulminate used in the primer composition.

This was described by the Chief of Ordnance in his report for the year 1897. The next year the Ordnance Department started loading the service Krag cartridge with a non-mercuric primer. When World War I came, the standard mixture used by Frankford Arsenal and known as FH-42, had the following composition:

Sulphur 21.97%
Potassium Chlorate 47.20%
Antimony Sulphide 30.83%

This mixture superseded the former H-48, which contained ground glass, thought by some shooters to injure the bore. This primer

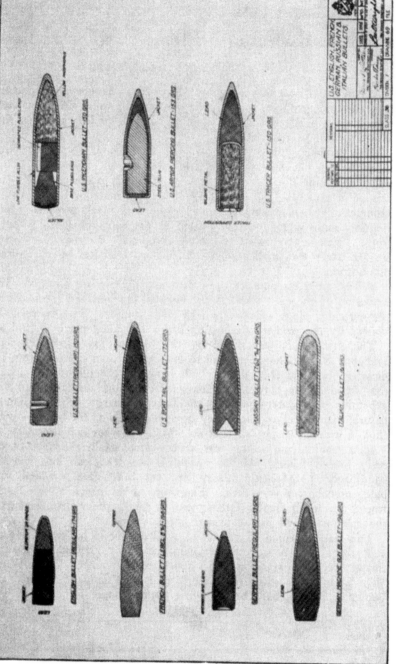

Some World War I bullets.

entirely eliminated the case cracking trouble, and was really one of the most satisfactory ever used, until an unexpected, and at the time, not understood, incident caused its sudden abandonment.

The United States entered the First World War in April, 1917, and the production of Frankford Arsenal was at once stepped up to several times what it had ever been before. Then in May, trouble began with misfires in the Frankford Service Ammunition. The trouble was so serious that the entire ammunition plant was shut down right when they needed its production worse than they had ever needed it before. The best chemists and engineers available were put to work to discover the cause of the misfires and the remedy, but in the meantime months of production were being lost, so that the Ordnance Department summarily ordered no more H-48 primers made, and directed Frankford to adopt and use forthwith the Winchester Repeating Arms Company's primer, 35-NF which was then giving very satisfactory results.

This primer mixture had the following composition:

Potassium Chlorate 53%
Antimony Sulphide 17%
Lead Sulpho-cyanide 25%
Tri-nitro-toluol (T.N.T.) 5%

After its adoption by Frankford Arsenal this primer became known as F.A. No. 70, and has been used, with minor modifications, ever since.

The trouble with the old sulphur primer was afterwards traced to the overloading of the primer drying houses that occurred when production was stepped up. The primers were loaded with the mixture in a moist condition, and the loaded cups were then put in the drying houses where steam heat was used to dry them out. When the drying houses were overloaded, the presence of so many primers in the warm room produced a condition of humidity in the air, and the primers generated sulphuric acid from the action of the moist air on the sulphur and the potassium chlorate.

At this time a typical rim fire primer used in the .22 caliber ammunition had the following composition as obtained by chemical analysis in the Frankford Arsenal Laboratory. This was from the United States Cartridge Company's "N.R.A." .22 caliber Outdoor type cartridge, loaded with Lesmok powder.

Potassium Chlorate 41.43%
Antimony Sulphide 9.53%
Copper Sulphocyanide 4.70%
Ground Glass 44.23%

The average weight of the priming in this .22 rim fire cartridge was found to be 0.237 grain.

The American ammunition companies and the shooters too, were apparently quite unconscious of any trouble from the priming composition until Dr. Huff published his findings in 1922. But evidently the Germans had been at least 20 years ahead of us in this field, for we find, as quoted by Major J. C. Gray of the Ordnance Technical Staff in his article "Lighting the Fire" in the *American Rifleman* for January 1928, that the publication *Zeitschrift fur das Gesampte Schiess-und Sprengstoffwesen* for March 15, 1914 states "Attempts to manufacture a priming composition which does not cause the barrel to rust were begun about 1900." Also, "The first rust-free primers were made in 1901 by the Rheinische-Westphalische Sprengstoff A. G. in 1901."

The German composition contained barium nitrate in the place of potassium chlorate, together with some picric acid to strengthen the mixture. The formula was as follows:

Fulminate of Mercury 39%
Barium Nitrate 41%
Antimony Sulphide 9%
Picric Acid 5%
Ground Glass 6%

It also developed that the Swiss Army had been using a non-corrosive primer since about 1911. This was based on the formula of a Swiss inventor named Ziegler. The Swiss formula was

Fulminate of Mercury 40%
Barium Nitrate 25%
Antimony Sulphide 25%
Barium Carbonate 6%
Ground Glass 4%

The barium nitrate replaced the potassium chlorate, and the barium carbonate was added, probably to neutralize the acid products of combustion.

As far as I can see, there was no attempt made on the part of the Germans or the Swiss to keep these things secret. Apparently the information was there available to anyone who had taken the trouble to read the foreign scientific journals and to realize the real significance of what he saw there.

As a matter of fact, it was quite well known in shooting circles in this country just before World War I that the Germans had been using since 1911 what was known as the Rostfrei (rustfree) primer in at least one brand of .22 caliber rim fire ammunition. However, not much notice was taken of it. There was very little foreign .22 caliber ammunition sold here, and though a few gun editors spoke of it, no one seemed to grasp the fact that a whole new idea in ammunition had been laid at their feet until Dr. Huff's report woke them up.

This German "R" primer had the following composition:

Fulminate of Mercury 55%
Antimony Sulphide 11%
Barium Peroxide 27%
T.N.T. 7%

It will be noted that there was no chlorate in this picture. But when attention had first been called to it, there were rumors that this primer was very erosive on gun bores on account of a gritty barium carbonate formed during the combustion. That is one reason why no more attention was paid to it in this country.

As soon as the Huff report was released, both Frankford Arsenal and all the commercial companies woke up and started working on the development of a non-corrosive primer. The first to place a satisfactory mixture on the market was Remington, with their Kleanbore primer. This was the development of Mr. J. E. Burns, a chemist on the Remington staff. This came on the market in 1927, and was followed in short order by other brands and makes.

All of these early primers, like the German ones, contained fulminate of mercury, and on account of this ingredient, they all suffered from the serious disadvantage of short life in storage.

Frankford Arsenal made a chemical analysis of these early non-corrosive priming mixtures, with the following result:

	Remington Kleanbore	Western	Winchester Staynless	Peters Rustless
Fulminate of Mercury	44.40%	40.79%	41.06%	38.68%
Barium Nitrate	30.54%	22.23%	26.03%	9.95%
Lead Sulphocyanide	4.20%	8.22%	5.18%	....
Ground Glass	20.66%	28.43%	26.66%	24.90%
Undetermined lead compound	....	....	....	25.91%
Binder (gum, etc.)	.20%	.33%	.58%	.56%

These mixtures all tended to become insensitive and to suffer from hangfires and misfires after storage for a year or two, especially in a warm damp place. This was due to the action of the fulminate of mercury which they contained. This lead to the eventual discovery of various substitutes for the fulminate, and all current mixtures are of the non-mercuric type.

Two typical non-mercuric primer compounds are those patented by Edmund Ritter Von Herz and Hans Rathburg, and acquired from them by the Remington Arms Company shortly after the introduction of the first Kleanbore. These formulae follow:

Composition No. 1	%	%
Guanyl Nitro-amino-guanyl-tetracene	0.5 to	15.
Lead Tri-nitro-resorcinate	20. to	45.
Barium Nitrate	30. to	50.
Antimony Sulphide or other fuel or both, as e.g. Calcium Silicide	10. to	30.

Composition No. 2

Guanyl Nitro-Amino-guanyl-tetracene	0.5 to	2.
Lead Tri-nitro-resorcinate	35. to	40.
Barium Nitrate	35. to	42.
Lead Peroxide	7. to	12.
Antimony Sulphide	0. to	5.
Calcium Silicide	0. to	12.
Glass	0. to	3.

Naturally the Ordnance Department was quite anxious to use a non-corrosive primer in the service ammunition, and a number of experiments to this end were made at Frankford Arsenal, but the mixtures tried either did not give good ignition or else failed to stand storage, or developed some other disability.

As the Swiss were using a noncorrosive primer in their regular service ammunition, there seemed no good reason why we should not do the same, especially as we knew what the Swiss composition was. A study of samples of Swiss ammunition showed that the weight of the primer pellet they used was considerably greater than that of ours. We were using about all the mixture we could get into the primer cup, and it was impossible to get in as much composition as the Swiss used. This was because we used a primer known as the Boxer type, having the anvil of the primer in the primer cup itself, while the European nations used the Berdan primer, in which there was no separate anvil; instead, there was a raised section of metal in the bottom of the primer pocket of the case which acted as an anvil.

The primer with the Berdan anvil, integral with the cartridge case, allowed more room for an increased charge of mixture. Moreover, it gave an opportunity for more direct ignition of the powder, for the flash holes lead directly from the primer to the powder, while in our Boxer type, the flash hole is located under the center of the anvil. The flash has to go through some cut out places in the edge of the anvil, then come back to the center and go down the flash hole to reach the powder. In other words, it more or less has to go around a corner to get through the flash hole.

It should be noted that the Berdan Primer is an American invention, which no doubt would be used in America today if it had not been for the fact that it is difficult to extract these primers for reloading. They have two small flash holes, located on each side of the primer pocket, instead of one large one in the center. These holes are much too small to permit the passage of a de-capping punch. The Boxer type primer with its self-contained anvil was developed to permit easy de-capping for handloading purposes.

Now the Europeans all use the Berdan primer, and moreover, the Western Cartridge Company, who made 8mm Lebel cartridges for the French during World War I, made them with the Berdan primer, and liked it. A du Pont representative for a long period kept more or less pressure on Frankford to adopt the Berdan primer, in the interest of better ignition.

All this resulted in the development of a non-corrosive primer by Frankford Arsenal, which seemed to give superb results in primer components of the Berdan type. This primer composition differed from the Swiss type in that it contained no fulminate of mercury. Fulminate has the very bad habit of deteriorating rapidly in moist humid climates, such as we encounter in our tropical possessions, though in a climate such as the mountainous one of Switzerland, it is quite satisfactory. It has another disadvantage from our viewpoint, and that is the fact that cartridge cases fired with mercuric primers become brittle.

Thus we could not do the obvious thing and copy the Swiss mixture, but we did succeed in getting another mixture which seemed even better. The first large scale trial of this was at the National Matches of 1930, where Frankford Arsenal submitted for test by the Ammunition Board a lot of National Match Ammunition loaded with non-corrosive primers in Berdan primers.

This lot of ammunition won the test with one of the best accuracy records ever achieved, and was duly issued for use in the National Matches. Shortly after the matches started, there was a spell of abnormally hot weather at Camp Perry, and it was found the ammunition was giving evidences of high pressures. The Ordnance Department thereupon withdrew this lot and substituted another which had the regular primer, and announced that experiments with Berdan primers would end forthwith.

I greatly regret that I was absent in Europe at that time with our International Rifle Team, and therefore did not see at first hand just what happened. It would seem that with every other nation in the world having used Berdan primers in every kind of climate for many years, the trouble might have been due to some other factor. The ammunition we used in Europe that year had the Berdan primer, and the team won the World Championship and almost everything else in sight. This, however, was low velocity ammunition, especially designed for best accuracy at 300 meters.

The Berdan Primer fiasco spelled the end of the non-corrosive primer in service ammunition for many years. Development proceeded feverishly, and all the commercial ammunition was changed over to the non-corrosive type, but the rigid Government specifications as to storage, hangfires, etc., could not be met by these mixtures. Frankford Arsenal developed some promising compositions, but none gave satisfactory results in the hangfire test, which was important in those days of synchronized aircraft guns.

This was the situation when mobilization occurred in 1940. Immense orders for .30 Cal. M2 ammunition were placed with the various cartridge companies, and there was quite a bit of talk about non-corrosive primers by some of the companies, who thought they were prepared to make them; but when the time came to sign on the dotted line, none of them were willing except the Canadian firm of Dominion Industries, Ltd., who in 1945 made 100,000,000 rounds of cal. .30 M 2 ammunition having a non-corrosive primer.

At the present writing, March, 1947, we are changing over slowly to a non-corrosive primer in the service cartridge, and a portion of this year's manufacture will have this type of primer. The change-over will proceed as fast as it can be done without too much of a disruption of production until all ammunition is being made that way, which should be in the very near future.

XV

The Pedersen Device

MOST of our Army's shoulder arms, be they hand operated or self loaders, have been well known to the shooting public; but there is one interesting semi-automatic fire arm that was made in great quantities for the Army during World War I that has received very little notice, for the very good reason that at the time of its manufacture, and for some years afterward, the War Department kept its existence a profound secret.

These remarks refer to the "Automatic Pistol, Caliber .30, Model of 1918," otherwise known as the "Pedersen Device," 65,000 of which were manufactured, though up to the end of the war its very existence was known to only a very few officers, one of whom was the present writer.

In spite of its name this device is not an automatic pistol at all, but is best described as an "automatic bolt" for the Springfield rifle, which can be instantly inserted in place of the regular bolt. It is constructed to receive a magazine holding 40 cartridges, which are of .30 caliber, so that they will fit the barrel of the rifle, but are of about the same size and power as the .32 automatic pistol cartridge.

When the device is fitted to the Springfield, the rifle is thus converted into a 40-shot semiautomatic, and becomes a sort of submachine gun, capable of delivering a whirlwind of rapid fire instead of single shots.

From the name of the device our readers will deduce the fact that it is the invention of Mr. J. D. Pedersen, of semiautomatic rifle fame. At the beginning of the first World War Mr. Pedersen was already well known in the firearms world from his many successful inventions, including the Remington pump-action shotgun, the Remington automatic pistol, and the Remington trombone-action rifles in both .22 caliber and high power.

In the summer of 1917, Mr. Pedersen came to the War Department and informed the chief of the Small Arms Division that he had what he considered a very important invention which he wished to have examined secretly. Because of Mr. Pedersen's prominence, this request was immediately granted, and only one or two high officials in the War Department saw his device when it was demonstrated on the Congress Heights Rifle Range in the District of Columbia.

Mr. Pedersen began his demonstration by firing the Springfield rifle which he brought with him. After firing a few shots in the ordinary way he suddenly jerked the bolt out of the rifle and dropped

The Pedersen Device in place in the rifle with 40 round magazine attached ready to fire.

it into a pouch which he had with him, and from a long scabbard which was on his belt he produced a mysterious looking piece of mechanism which he quickly slid into the rifle in place of the bolt, locking the device in the rifle in the same way that the regular bolt is held in place; that is, by turning down the cut-off. Then he snapped into place a long black magazine containing 40 small pistol-size cartridges, whose bullets were, however, of the right diameter to fit the barrel of the rifle. All this was done in an instant, and in another instant Mr. Pedersen was pulling the trigger of the rifle time after time as fast as he could work his finger, and each time he pulled the trigger the rifle fired a shot, threw out the empty cartridge, and reloaded itself.

It was really a startling demonstration. In firing the Springfield rifle as rapidly as it can be done, the soldier pulls the trigger, turns up the bolt, jerks it back and shoves it forward, turns it down, and then is ready to fire one more shot; but with this new device of Mr. Pedersen's, all that was necessary was to keep pulling the trigger, and the rifle did the rest. When the magazine of 40 rounds was empty, it was the work of but an instant to snap a new magazine into place and continue firing.

It looked as if Mr. Pedersen had converted the Springfield rifle into a one-man machine gun.

A close examination of the device showed that the cartridge he fired was only about one-fifth the size of the rifle cartridge, though the bullet was the same diameter. The automatic bolt itself was found to be very much the same thing as a straight "blowback" type automatic pistol without any stock, the dimensions of what would otherwise be a pistol being changed sufficiently to adapt it to fit in the rifle in place of the bolt. The barrel of the pistol was just the same size, shape, and length as the regular Springfield rifle cartridge (without the bullet). This little barrel is rifled with fine rifling larger in diameter than the rifling in the Springfield barrel. Thus this short barrel does not have to have the rifling match that in the regular barrel. The short barrel starts the bullet spinning, but the fine rifling does not bite in very deeply, so that when the bullet strikes the regular barrel it is not sized down too small for the regular rifling to take hold.

The device was adapted to be locked in place in the receiver by the regular magazine cut-off of the Springfield rifle. On the upper right-hand part of the device, near the front of the receiver opening in the rifle, was a spring catch to hold the long magazine, which when placed in position slanted upward, and to the right at an angle of about 45 degrees.

The ejection of the fired cartridge case is through a port on the left-hand side of the device, and a corresponding port must be cut in the receiver of the rifle, as can be seen in the picture, facing p. 369.

The Pedersen Device, shown with its ammunition, the 40 round magazine, and the metal scabbard used for carrying the device on the soldier's belt.

It will thus be seen that a specially modified Springfield rifle is required. Not only does the rifle have to have the ejection port in the receiver, but it must have two grooves in the magazine cut-off, and a little kicker in the sear.

The actual release of the firing mechanism is accomplished by pushing forward on a projection on the bottom of the device. A little pivoted lever in the sear of the rifle fits in the notch in the bottom of the device, and gives the necessary forward impulse when the trigger of the rifle is pulled.

The Springfield rifle as thus modified is called the Mark I. These modifications do not injure the rifle in any way for regular shooting with the full-powered cartridge, and the Mark I rifle is just as good for all other purposes as any other rifle. Needless to say, the Government manufactured one Mark I rifle for each Pedersen device which was produced.

Looking at the picture of the device, it will be seen that there is a little lump, or weight, on the top. Every time the gun is fired this lump, which is part of the breechblock, slides to the rear and then jumps forward again, something like a mouse running backward and forward on top of the receiver. It is the inertia of this weight which enables a powerful cartridge to be used, giving the very high velocity of 1,300 foot seconds as against 800 or 900 foot seconds of the ordinary automatic pistol of the same size.

The whole device in its metal scabbard weigh 2 pounds and 2 ounces, and the loaded magazine filled with 40 rounds weighs 1 pound.

Coming now to ballistics, the new cartridge had an 80-grain bullet driven by 3½ grains of powder, whereas the old cartridge had a 150-grain bullet driven by 45 grains of powder. In the old high-powered cartridge the bullet leaves the muzzle at a velocity of 2,700 feet per second; the Pedersen cartridge leaves the muzzle at a velocity of 1,300 feet per second.

As the energy of the bullet depends upon the square of the velocity as well as upon the bullet weight, it was found that the new bullet had a muzzle energy of about one-tenth that of the service cartridge. In other words, while the bullet of the service cartridge leaves the muzzle of the gun with an energy sufficient to lift a ton and a quarter a distance of a foot, the new bullet had only sufficient energy to lift one-eighth of a ton a foot. This is, however, quite sufficient to kill a man at any range up to 500 yards, or say a little over one-quarter of a mile.

While the service bullet will penetrate 60 inches of wood a short distance away from the gun, the new bullet will penetrate only about 8 inches, or the same that the service rifle would penetrate one-half mile away. However, a bullet which will penetrate 8 inches or 10 inches of wood will easily penetrate a man, and it was apparent at once that this system which enabled a soldier to convert his rifle at a

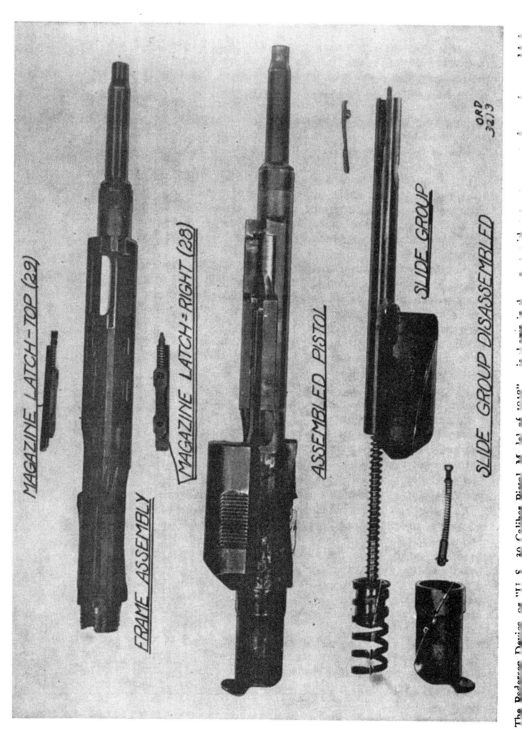

MAGAZINE LATCH—TOP (29)

MAGAZINE LATCH—RIGHT (28)

FRAME ASSEMBLY

ASSEMBLED PISTOL

SLIDE GROUP

SLIDE GROUP DISASSEMBLED

ORD
321.3

The Pedersen Device, or "U. S. .30 Caliber Pistol, Model of 1918", is largely in the same manner as the present to the upper left, and the four-moment's notice into a low-powered machine gun was indeed a most important thing.

The War Department officials who saw this test had visions of what might happen in case of an attack by the enemy on our trench system, should our men be armed with this device. As the enemy came charging across No Man's Land, each of our soldiers would begin firing with this miniature machine gun, and the entire zone in front of the trenches would be covered with such a whirlwind of fire that no attack could survive. Also it looked as if the device might have great possibilities for an attack starting from our own trenches. For one thing, there is no noticeable recoil from this Pedersen device, and it could be fired from the hip while marching or running. A line of soldiers advancing across No Man's Land, firing this device at the enemy trenches as they ran, would make it extremely dangerous for anyone in the trenches to show his head or any part of his body. Of course, fire while running or walking would not be so accurate, but the tremendous number of shots would more than make up for any inaccuracies, and the whole enemy trench system would presumably be smothered with a storm of bullets.

The inventor had made this device readily interchangeable with the regular rifle bolt so that the bolt could be put back into the rifle at any time, thus enabling the rifle to be used with the high-powered cartridge when this seemed desirable.

It was proposed that the soldier should go into battle carrying the usual high-powered cartridges, and, in addition, he would carry this device in a scabbard at his belt as well as a canvas pouch to carry the regular rifle bolt when the device was being used, and on his belt he would have a canvas case holding 10 magazines of 40 rounds each for the device.

This development appeared so important that an officer, who was sworn to secrecy, was placed on a ship to take the device over to France and explain it in person to General Pershing. The result was a code cablegram from General Pershing calling for the earliest possible production of 100,000 of these devices, and asking that the whole project be kept a profound secret.

Needless to say, the order was placed at once and the secrecy which already surrounded the development was continued. As the name "Pedersen device" seemed to be sufficiently mysterious to excite the curiosity of the people who must of necessity work on it in the various factories, a new name was adopted which was purposely made not at all descriptive of the device. This name was "Automatic Pistol, Caliber .30, Model 1918."

Of course the Pedersen device was in no sense a pistol, and one of the amusing incidents connected with the matter is the fact that some writers, who in some way heard this name, criticized the War Department severely for adopting a smaller caliber pistol, or even

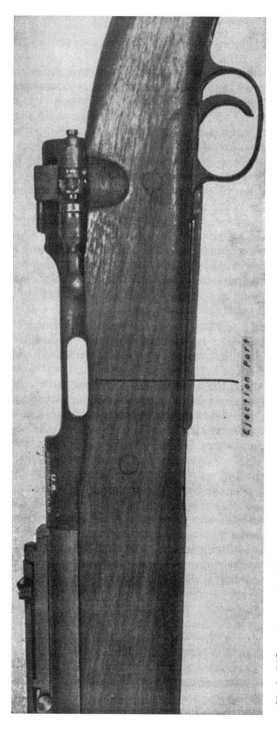

Ejection Port

U. S. Rifle, Caliber .30, M 1903 Mark I, with bolt removed to show the special ejection port for the Pedersen Device used in this Mark I Rifle.

for adopting a new pistol at all, as they contended that our .45 automatic pistol was sufficiently good, and if a new pistol were adopted it should be as large as the .45 instead of being reduced to .30 caliber.

After the first production samples of this gun came through and it began to be definitely determined what could be done in the way of manufacture, another officer was sent to France for further conference. As a result it was decided that 500,000 Pedersen devices could be ready to go on the front lines in the spring of 1919, and that they would be utilized as a surprise to be sprung on the enemy at that time.

It is an interesting speculation to think what would have occurred had our Army started to cross No Man's Land some fine morning with half a million men, each armed with an individual machine gun and 400 rounds of ammunition.

However, the old weapons we already had at hand proved sufficiently good to get the Germans out of the trenches in October, 1918, and the war ended a month later with 65,000 of the Pedersen devices completed. The remaining orders were canceled.

After the Armistice of November 11, 1918, an intensive study was made of the possibilities of this weapon for future use. One of these tests was made at LeMans, France, and was attended by General Pershing and some high officials of his staff.

In conducting this test, a competitive musketry problem was conducted between two squads of officer marksmen, one squad being armed with Springfield rifles, and the other with rifles and the Pedersen Devices.

These officers were sworn to secrecy before the test, and then were given enough practice to familiarize them with the shooting and handling of the new arm.

A number of silhouette targets were placed on the parapet of the target pit and the two squads each had a separate group of silhouettes to fire at. The squads each started from 1000 yards, lying down and firing until a certain number of hits had been attained, when the pit detail would pull down a red flag and the squad could advance to the next station. The two squads, using the .30 caliber service cartridges, advanced with about equal speed until 600 yards was reached, when the squad with the Device changed bolts, and started using the automatic bolt. Immediately they let loose such a whirlwind of fire that the flag went down and they advanced. This was repeated again and again, until they had gained the objective while the regular squad had hardly moved from 600.

All officers who saw this demonstration were strongly of the opinion that this was an epoch making innovation in shoulder weapons.

Mr. Pedersen and I had taken to France the Pedersen Devices and ammunition with which this test was conducted, and we were of course present on the ground, at the time, in charge of the Ordnance arrangements.

In September, 1946, after I had demonstrated a Pedersen Device at Camp Perry, and had described this test, a member of the Executive Staff, Col. Griswold, stepped forward and said that he had been one of the Lieutenants who had been sworn to secrecy and assigned to the target pits. The pit officers had not been given any clues as to what the device was, so they organized a G-2 committee, and after the firing, they went to the firing points and searched for an empty cartridge that might give them a clue. Alas, the fullest of precautions had been taken; the empties had been carefully picked up. Nevertheless, they continued to search, hoping that in the grassy field, at least one lone cartridge might have escaped the clean-up, and at last they were rewarded by finding one.

The author's son Lieut. Robert D. Hatcher shooting the Pedersen Device in March, 1947 with ammunition made in 1918. This view plainly shows the ejection port in the left side of the receiver of the Mark I rifle. The empty cartridges were thrown just to the left of the camera lens.

In addition, one of the officers had carefully studied the firing line from afar, using binoculars; and from these and various other fragments of information they gradually pieced together a theory of the device which was just about right. This was a new viewpoint to me on something that I saw from another angle in those days long past.

At the close of World War I, this device was seen in the light of the situation that had just been passed through; the years of intensive trench warfare on an almost completely stabilized front. Viewed thus, it looked good; but when this perspective had faded somewhat, the picture changed. It then appeared that for almost any other kind of campaign it had disadvantages which perhaps outweighed its good points.

Owing to the light weight and comparatively low power of the bullet from the Pedersen device, it is accurate against individual targets only up to about 350 yards. Beyond that range, it is difficult to hit individual targets with precision, and mass fire against mass targets must be depended on. Because of its low velocity, it has a high trajectory, and if it were sighted to hit a man at 500 yards, the bullet would pass over the head of a man at 300 yards.

Then, again, a more serious objection is that at the present time the infantry soldier has practically everything he can possibly carry loaded on him; and these things—his rifle, bayonet, ammunition, and equipment pack—are all things which cannot be discarded or reduced in any way. To make him carry in addition a metal scabbard with the Pedersen device, a canvas pouch for the bolt of his rifle, and 10 magazines full of Pedersen ammunition, would be practically impossible in any campaign of movement. Greater experience has shown that if the soldiers were called upon to advance a certain distance using their Springfield rifles with the regular ammunition at long ranges, and then at some point in their advance they had to change to the Pedersen device, they would usually reach their objective without the regular rifle bolt, as this would be lost— dropped or thrown away in their excitement.

One way in which the Pedersen device differs from the Springfield rifle is in its comparative silence. When the Springfield rifle is fired it makes a very loud noise, and moreover the bullet itself creates an air wave which causes a vicious crack whenever the bullet passes a man or an object. Any bullet or projectile which travels at a speed higher than the velocity of sound creates this air wave and makes this sharp, menacing noise when it passes. In the Pedersen device the powder charge is small in relation to the length of the barrel, so that the firing of the gun itself makes little noise, and the bullet itself does not produce the air wave that causes the bullet to "bark" when it passes.

In one of our peace-time tests, a number of soldiers in a pit were operating some targets which were being shot at by both the service rifle and the Pedersen device. While the firing was going on with the high-powered cartridges, the soldiers kept down as low as possible, entirely over-awed by the vicious and menacing snap of the high-powered .30-'06 bullets; but when the shift was made to the Pedersen device, holes began coming into the target faster than ever but without the noise, and the soldiers all got up as high as possible and wanted to look over the edge or go outside of the trenches to see what was going on. As a result it was thought by some of the observers that the lack of moral effect on account of its silence was a serious disadvantage of this weapon. Some other observers of this incident thought that this lack of noise pointed to an advantage for the Pedersen device; the enemy would be bolder about leaving their cover, and would become easier targets. However, the prevailing opinion was that the menacing noise of the Springfield rifle bullet is a decided asset owing to the moral effect it has in instilling fear into the enemy, and that any weapon which lacks this noise would place its users at a disadvantage.

The result of this gradual change of opinion was that a few years after the end of the first World War, the Army decided to waste no further funds keeping these devices in storage, and they were all destroyed, and the Mark I rifles were converted back to regular Service Rifles by the removal of the special sear and the cut-off with grooves in it to hold the device in place. The ejection port on the rifle remained, together with the wording Mark I, and the few of these rifles that have reached the hands of civilian marksmen have occasioned quite a bit of comment from the users, most of whom never heard of Pedersen's .30 caliber Pistol, Model of 1918.

XVI

Notes on Set Triggers

WHEN an individual who is not a shooter picks up a rifle, cocks it, and pulls the trigger, the trigger pull usually seems very light and easy to him. But let the same man go into a marksmanship contest, and things seem quite different. Every time he gets the front sight lined up on the bull's-eye and tries to pull the trigger, it seems to take a greatly increased amount of force to make it move. In other words, marksmanship makes the trigger pull seem heavier.

One of the first things a marksman would like to do, therefore, is to have a lighter and easier trigger pull, so that it can be touched off at just the right moment without any disturbance to the rest of the gun.

This can be accomplished to a certain extent by smoothing up the sear notch and the sear, and by making the engagement of the sear with its notch smaller and smaller, so that there will not be so much work done in disengaging the sear. There is, however, a limit to what can be done along this line, because the sear usually works into the notch on the hammer of the gun and the hammer is actuated by a strong spring. The notch in which the sear is engaged is close to the pivot of the hammer. Therefore, the pressure of the mainspring is multiplied by the time it gets to the sear notch. The work, therefore, of pulling the trigger involves sliding two metal surfaces on each other while these surfaces are being pressed together with quite a heavy force—namely, that of the mainspring, multiplied by the leverage.

In order to make the easiest possible kind of trigger pull, the set trigger or "hair trigger," as it is sometimes called, was devised. These hair trigger guns can usually be recognized by having two triggers, something like the double trigger of a shotgun. To operate them, you pull back the rear trigger until it snaps. Then when you touch the front trigger ever so lightly, the gun will go off.

Set triggers became very popular in this country over one hundred years ago, in the days of the old Kentucky squirrel rifles. In those days the standard of marksmanship in America was very high, and turkey shoots and marksmanship competitions of all kinds were popular.

Many of the old Kentucky rifles that have been handed down to the present day are fitted with set triggers, and some of these set triggers are just as good as any modern set trigger, and, in fact, would very well serve as a model for anyone who wished to build a set trigger today.

To understand the action of a set trigger, look at Fig. 1, which is a sketch showing the component parts, also the assembled view, of the set trigger of an old Kentucky rifle in possession of the author. The sear proper of the gun engages with the hammer, and is pivoted on the lock plate, which is fitted into the side of the gun. However,

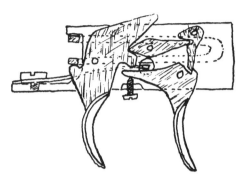

Diagram of Captain Woody's set trigger.

the sear has an arm extending right across at right angles to the lock. This arm rests just above the set trigger. Its position is noted in the sketch.

The action of the set triggers in general can very well be studied by reference to the lower drawing in Fig. 1. The rear trigger is in reality a "knock-off" for the sear. The heavy spring shown to the rear of the trigger tends to hold the rear trigger in a forward position with its forward blade kicked up into the air and resting against the sear arm.

To operate the set trigger, the gun is first cocked. Then the rear trigger is pulled back as far as possible, until it is locked down by the point on the front trigger which engages the notch on the front part of the rear trigger. The engagement is very slight at this point. Moreover, the angle is such that it is very easy to slide the parts out of engagement. The slightest touch on the front trigger will release this contact and allow the heavy spring at the back to kick the arm of the rear trigger upward, when it strikes the sear arm and suddenly disengages the sear, allowing the hammer to fall at the same instant.

The small screw between the two triggers limits the amount by which the front trigger catches onto the back one, and thereby regulates the trigger pull. There is a backward projecting blade attached to the front trigger which operates to release the sear when the front trigger is pulled without setting it. In other words, unless the rear trigger is first pulled to set the mechanism, the front trigger acts as an ordinary trigger when pulled. In this case it works with a rather hard trigger pull.

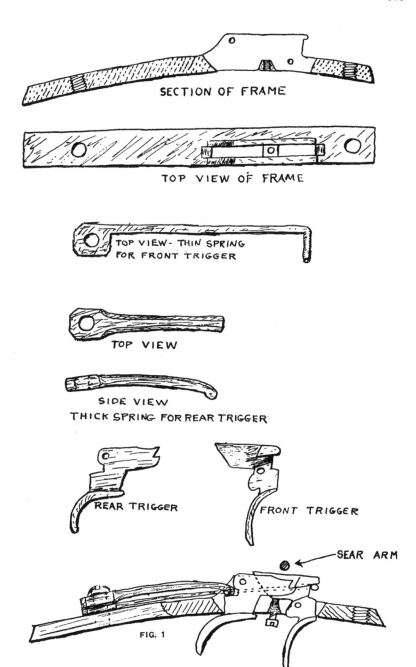

SECTION OF FRAME

TOP VIEW OF FRAME

TOP VIEW- THIN SPRING
FOR FRONT TRIGGER

TOP VIEW

SIDE VIEW
THICK SPRING FOR REAR TRIGGER

REAR TRIGGER

FRONT TRIGGER

SEAR ARM

FIG. 1

Figure 1. Set trigger from an old Kentucky rifle in the author's possession.

After the passing of the old Kentucky squirrel rifles there came a gradual lapse in marksmanship and competition shooting, during which the manufacture of set triggers was largely discontinued. However, in the latter part of the last century Schuetzen shooting became popular, and this again caused a call for set triggers.

There were two well-known makes used in the Schuetzen game, one made by Stevens and the other by Winchester. Both the Winchester and Stevens double set triggers are of exactly the same type as the old Kentucky set triggers illustrated in Fig. 1.

One of the finest modern set triggers is that on the Swiss Martini rifles our International Free Rifle Teams used in 1930. It differs very materially from the others in mechanical construction, for instead of having just two levers it has four. Each lever reduces the pressure on the operating edges of the trigger still further, until with four levers the pressure at the point where the front trigger engages the other mechanism is so light that a trigger of this kind can be made very sensitive indeed. In other words, the more levers a gunsmith puts into his set trigger the easier the trigger pull is. As the other triggers described are all two-lever triggers and this Martini trigger is a four-lever one, it will be seen that the sensitiveness is multiplied many times.

Fig. 2 shows the construction of these four-lever triggers. They can be made so sensitive that a breath of wind on the front trigger will cause them to go off, though of course it is not necessary to use it as sensitive as this at all times.

When the United States first went into the International Match shooting just after World War I the team used set triggers which were bought in Germany by members of the 1918 Army of Occupation. These set triggers, made to fit the Springfield rifle, are of the two-lever type, identical in construction with that of the Old Kentucky rifle above described.

In this German trigger there is a special cam lever placed in the sear of the Springfield rifle, and when the front trigger is touched the rear trigger flies forward and the upper arm of the rear trigger strikes upward on this sear cam, and the action causes the sear to be cammed down out of engagement with the striker. There is a certain loss of time to this reverse motion on the sear lever and sear, which is one of the disadvantages of this type of trigger. Another disadvantage is the fact that it was only the double-lever type, and therefore not as sensitive as might have been desirable.

It is this set trigger which our International Rifle Team used in the victories of 1921 and 1922. The hope of improving the set trigger used at that time led to the design of several set triggers, the most successful of which was made by Sergeant Rinkounis, of the Marine Corps, whose set trigger worked in the opposite direction and jerked the sear down instead of striking an upward blow first. Oscillographs showed that the Rinkounis trigger was faster than the German type, and it was used on the victorious American Rifle Team of 1924 by some members, while other members used the German trigger.

The Rinkounis trigger was used in 1925, but did not give satisfaction because it was a handmade job, and there was a certain amount of trouble with sloppy pieces, etc.; and besides, being only a two-lever trigger, it was not capable of as much sensitiveness as was

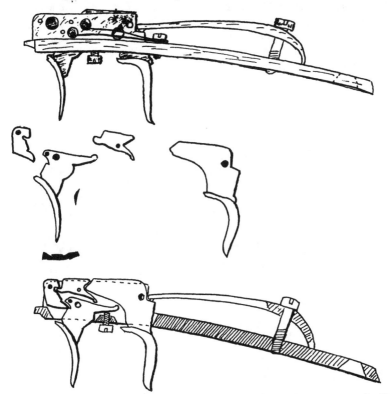

Figure 2. Four-lever set trigger from a modern Martini-type European match rifle.

thought desirable. Accordingly, the late Colonel Woody, of Frankford Arsenal, made up a set trigger for the use of the 1927 International Rifle Team. The Woody set trigger is a four-lever trigger and is an improvement on the best Swiss triggers. In the Woody trigger one of the delicate springs used in the Swiss triggers is eliminated and the leverages are improved. This trigger gives a reduction of pressure on the contact points of 40 to 1. For equal sensitivity with a two-lever trigger, the rear trigger would have to have a forward-projecting arm about 6 inches long, whereas in actual practice the forward arm of a two-lever trigger is about three-quarters of an inch long.

The view of the Woody set trigger assembled in the **Springfield** rifle is shown in Fig. 3.

Haemmerli 5-Lever Set Trigger

An excellent set trigger for the Martini rifle is the 5-lever set trigger made by Haemmerli & Co., of Switzerland. This is the trigger that was used by the Swiss team in the 1928 International Match in Holland.

The mechanism of this trigger consists of a train of five levers actuated by one heavy spring and four light springs. The arrangement is compact and ingenious and permits of very close adjustment. A set screw regulates the pressure required, which can be set down to the lightest touch or a heavy breath.

Figure 3. Woody trigger assembled in rifle action.

The trigger is extremely smooth in action. There is no creep, looseness or side play. The five levers permit a very light pressure between engaging surfaces for the last stages by which an improvement in smoothness is gained over triggers of four levers or less with no appreciable loss in the time element.

This trigger appears to be capable of being built into a trigger guard for the Springfield action, as the kick-off feature is similar to that of the various types of triggers in our heavy Springfield Match rifles.

Using a set trigger is quite different from using an ordinary trigger and requires a completely different method of handling the gun, and really requires long and persistent training to be mastered. In the first place, the set trigger is dangerous to use unless very special precautions are taken, because with the best of set triggers and the best of marksmen there are bound to be accidental discharges. For this reason special rules are made for matches in which set triggers are used. A set trigger must be "set" after the gun is loaded, because the action of closing or opening the bolt will almost certainly set off the trigger just from the jar.

Therefore, the gun is loaded with the barrel resting upon a support and pointing at the ground. While the muzzle is still resting upon this support the rear set trigger is pulled back so that the triggers are set. Sometimes accidents occur at this point and accidental discharges may be expected. The rules do not count such an accidental discharge against a marksman provided the barrel of the gun is resting upon the support when the discharge occurs; but if the barrel of the gun has left the support and an accidental discharge occurs, the marksman gets zero, or whatever his bullet makes on the target.

Using a set trigger for the first time usually makes a man who has been using only an ordinary trigger very nervous. It is like fooling with dynamite. The slightest touch makes it go off. The man using a set trigger for the first time would make a much worse score than he would with an ordinary trigger. In fact, I am not so sure that some of our International Match shots would not have done better with ordinary triggers throughout the entire match. By this I mean the old-timers of the Marine and other Service Teams, who have had years of experience with the regular trigger.

In using the set trigger the methods of different operators vary considerably. Usually the forefinger is not placed in front of the trigger but only on the side. Great care must be taken in placing the finger against the trigger not to make the set trigger go off from the mere fact of touching it. One man that I know who is very good on using a set trigger always approaches the front trigger with a forward motion of his finger, so that when the finger finally touches the trigger the tendency is that it slightly presses the front trigger forward. Then there is no danger of the guns going off when the trigger is being touched.

The next thing that happens is that the user aims at the target, and when he gets the sights into the proper position he merely relaxes his forefinger slightly, and the gun seems to go off of its own accord.

When a set trigger gun has been cocked and the trigger is set it is a rather ticklish thing to monkey with, but it is easy to unload without danger. This is done by first putting the middle finger on the rear trigger and pulling this back as far as possible, then placing the forefinger on the front trigger and pressing it to the rear. Then let the rear trigger go forward slowly. The triggers are then released. This should, of course, be done with the muzzle of the gun pointing in a safe direction.

Though all set triggers are somewhat ticklish to use, there is absolutely no doubt that with practice in their use they can help to make wonderfully high scores, especially in the standing and kneeling positions.

XVII

Random Notes on Various Subjects

1. The Men Behind the Guns

IT has been a most interesting experience through the years to have been more or less closely associated with many of the men who made the guns we have discussed.

To list some of them in alphabetical order, there are Soren Hansen Bang, of the Danish Recoil Rifle Syndicate, and Laurence V. Benet, of the Hotchkiss Company, who designed the Benet-Mercier. Still

John M. Browning, famous inventor of rifles, shotguns, pistols and machine guns. He was born in Ogden, Utah, in 1855, and died in 1926.

in the B's we have General Berthier, who lived in Springfield for some months during 1917, when I was in charge of the tests of his gun that was being modified and re-submitted from time to time.

381

John M. Browning and his brother Matthew S. Browning and his half-brother J. Edmund Browning were valued friends. "Matt" and "Ed" were mighty clever gun designers in their own rights; a semi-automatic rifle designed by Ed Browning and submitted by Winchester was a strong contender in Government tests as recently as the beginning of World War II.

John C. Garand, designer of the U. S. Rifle, Caliber .30, M 1. He pronounces his name Garand, with the G hard as in *go*, and the stress on the first syllable, to rhyme with *parent*.

Val A. Browning who inherited much of the genius of his father John M., was an Ordnance Officer with whom I was closely associated in World War I. He was the first man to fire a Browning Automatic Rifle in action in France in 1918. At this writing, 1947, he is president of the firm of J. M. & M. S. Browning which was founded by his father and uncle in Ogden, Utah.

John C. Garand, our top-notch gun designer, has personal qualities that endear him to all his acquaintances. Both my brother, Col. James L. Hatcher, himself a gun designer of great ability, and I have long counted Mr. Garand as a close and valued friend.

Gerlich, originator of the "Halger" high velocity system, Karl

Heinemann, inventor of the Parabellum Machine Gun and the Heinemann Semi-automatic Rifle, and Grant Hammond, of pistol fame were each with us only a few days during tests we made of their inventions, but even to meet and talk with them briefly was quite interesting.

J. D. Pedersen, famous arms designer. Photo by the author, April 15, 1946. (Mr. Pedersen died May 23, 1951.)

Capt. "Mel" Johnson, brilliant creator of the Johnson automatic rifle and the Johnson Light Machine Gun is another top-notch gun designer that it is a privilege to know.

The late Col. I. N. Lewis, of Lewis Gun fame was known chiefly for his Depression Position Finder when I served with him at an Artillery post many years ago.

General Liu of China brought his Semi-Automatic to Springfield for me to test in the early part of 1918. As we both spoke French pretty fluently at that time I was able to learn quite a lot from him. He was a brilliant mechanical engineer and gun expert.

J. D. Pedersen is a designer of whom Mr. Browning thought very highly. He once told me that Pedersen was the greatest gun designer in the world. My association with him dates from 1918, when work on his Pedersen Device brought us together. We took a trip to Europe together to demonstrate his device and to arrange a field trial of it for General Pershing. Just before this was written he spent an evening at my house and we had a very pleasant time dissecting and discussing a German Gew. 43.

Colonel Townsend Whelen, U. S. Army, Retired. He enjoyed a world-wide reputation as a big game hunter, author and firearms authority. Born March 6, 1877, he died December 23, 1961.

Eugene Reising has been working on guns a long time; I first knew him when he was working on his automatic .22 caliber target pistol. He is responsible for the submachinegun made by Harrington & Richardson during World War II.

Maj. Searles, who invented the Savage Automatic Pistol was an Ordnance Officer during World War I, and I saw him frequently at that time, as I did A. W. Swebilius, the talented producer of the Marlin Aircraft Machine gun. I still enjoy seeing him occasionally at his High Standard Manufacturing Co. in New Haven, where in this year of 1947 he is still doing some mighty fine gun designing.

General John T. Thompson of "Tommy Gun" fame and inventor of the Thompson Autorifle was in charge of the Small Arms Division, Ordnance Department when I first knew him.

Mr. David M. Williams, of Godwin, North Carolina, inventor of many important firearms designs and mechanisms, including the short-stroke piston principle as used in the U. S. Carbine, Cal. .30, M 1, and the floating chamber used in the U. S. .22 Caliber Machine Gun, the Colt Service Ace Pistol, and some Remington Rifles.

Captain Melvin M. Johnson, designer of the Johnson Semi-automatic Rifle and the Johnson Light Machine Gun.

There are no doubt, many more whom I have forgotten to include, even as I write these lines I recall Manning of the Murphy-Manning gun; White, who had a very promising Semi-automatic rifle; Col. Richard M. Cutts, U.S.M.C., and his son Captain Cutts, originators of the Cutts Compensator; and last but not least, Hudson Maxim, noted inventor of smokeless powders, and brother of Sir Hiram Maxim.

2. National Match Ammunition

Prior to World War I, the Government regularly obtained the then standard .30 Caliber M 1906 ammunition from Frankford Arsenal and from the large commercial cartridge companies. It was usual to hold a competition each year to determine which of the makers should furnish the ammunition to be used in the National Matches of that year.

The various makers, including Frankford Arsenal would each submit their best sample for test by the Ammunition Board. The winner would get the contract to furnish the ammunition for the matches. This was all the standard .30 Cal. M 1906, made to the regular specifications calling for a 150 grain flat base cupro-nickel jacketed bullet driven by a charge of approximately 50 grains of Pyro D. G. Powder at a muzzle velocity of 2700 feet per second, and with an average pressure which varied with the powder lot, but was usually somewhat under 50,000 pounds per square inch.

At the end of World War I, the Government was greatly overstocked with ammunition, and stopped buying it commercially. Experiments were started to develop an improved type of ammunition, and for several years the National Matches furnished a proving ground for the experimental types.

By 1925 the M1 ammunition had been standardized, with a 172 grain boat tailed bullet having a 9 degree taper at the base, and jacketed with gilding metal. At first this had a muzzle velocity of about 2700 f.s., which was later reduced to 2640.

In 1926 there were no National Matches. In 1927 the 1925 National Match ammunition remaining on hand was used. In 1928 ordinary M1 ammunition was taken from stock for the matches. This was so unsatisfactory that the production of a special lot of National Match ammunition was resumed in 1929. In 1930, National Match ammunition was made to try out the possibilities of the Berdan primer. This gave unexpectedly high and erratic pressures during a spell of unusually hot weather at the matches, so was abandoned.

National Matches since that time have been fired with service ammunition, selected from lots which show better than average accuracy in final inspection.

The National matches with the service rifle were suspended at the beginning of World War II and at this writing, March, 1947, have not been resumed.

The following recapitulation gives the characteristics of the National Match Ammunition for the various years:

CALIBER .30 NATIONAL MATCH AMMUNITION
(Frankford Arsenal)

Year	Bullet	Powder Type	Chg. Gr.	Inst. Vel. at 78 Ft.	Mean Pressure	Mean Radius 600 Yds.	Mean Radius 1000 Yds.
1919	150 Gr. F. B. CuNi.	Pyro #1406	46.5	2640	47,000	5.19"	9.65"
1920	170 Gr. F. B. CuNi.	Pyro #1406	46.5	2550	47,500	4.74"	10.24"
1921	170 Gr. F. B. CuNi. Tinned	DuPont #1076	48.2	2600	48,725	3.00"	8.52"
1922	170 Gr. 6° B.T. G.M.	Hi Vel #56-888	45.4	2652	49,440	3.18"	7.22"
1923	170 Gr. 6° B.T. G.M.	Hi Vel #59-887	45.5	2653	47,000	2.85"	6.662"
1924	170 Gr. 9° B.T. G.M.	Hi Vel #1486	46.3	2644	47,000	2.26"	5.685"
1925	170 Gr. 9° B.T. G.M.	IMR-1147 #1489	53.2	2716.4	49,640	2.30"	5.710"
1926	170 Gr. 9° B.T. G.M.	IMR-1147 #1491	52.9	2700	50,000	No Test Held	No Test Held
1927	172 Gr. 9° B.T. G.M.	IMR-1147 #1489	53.2	2716.4	49,640	*2.30"	*5.710"
1928	172 Gr. 9° B.T. G.M.	IMR-1185 #1597	50.0	2594.4	41,705	3.04"	8.00"
1929	173 Gr. 9° B.T. G.M.	IMR-1186 #1619	49.8	2692	52,000	3.06"	7.05"
1930	173 Gr. 9° B.T. G.M.	IMR-1186 #1620	50.5	2686	51,795	2.98"	5.16"
1930	173 Gr. 9° B.T. G.M.	IMR-1186 #1635	49.5	2645	47,852	2.77"	7.18"

THIS AMMUNITION CONTAINING BERDAN PRIMER NOT USED

THIS AMMUNITION USED IN MATCHES

\# Lot Number

* 1925 Over-run used in 1927

3. Caliber .30 International Match Ammunition

Up until 1930, the United States used to send a team each year to compete in the Free Rifle Matches of the International Shooting Union. As this type of shooting, with heavy barrelled Schuetzen type rifles was not popular in the United States, we always had difficulty in getting up a team that would be truly representative of a cross section of the nation's shooters, so participation in these matches was discontinued after the matches in Antwerp in 1930 when the team of which the author was manager won the World Championship and numerous individual titles.

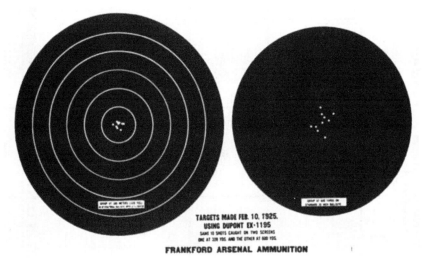

These targets were shot during the development of International and Palma Match ammunition while the author, then a major, was in charge of ammunition manufacture at Frankford Arsenal.   The center ring of the left hand target is 3.15/16 inch in diameter, and the group fired at 328 yards was 1.33 inches in diameter, or 4/10 of a minute wide.   The same ten shots caught on another screen at 600 yards are shown on a 20 inch bullseye.   The group at 600 yards was 3.17 inches in diameter, subtending just over 5/10 of a minute.

From the close of World War I until 1930, it was the custom to have a competitive test each year to select the ammunition to be used in these matches.

Particulars of ammunition with results of the tests are given below:

The author at Bisley, England, in 1931 as Captain of the United States Rifle Team.

CALIBER .30 INTERNATIONAL MATCH AMMUNITION

Year	Bullet	Powder Type	Chg. Gr.	Inst. Vel. at 78 Ft.	Mean Pressure	Mean Radius 300 Meters (Computed)	Fig. of Merit 300 Met.	Mfgr. & Remarks
1920	180 Gr. F. B. CuNi.	IMR-15½	52.5	2670	46,940	1.57"	......	Rem.
1921	....	....	......	......	......	....	......	No Test
1922	....	....	......	......	......	....	......	No Test
1923	180 Gr. F. B. CuNi.	IMR-15½	52.6	2670	46,940	1.09"	2.806"	Rem.
1924	180 Gr. F. B. CuNi.	HiVel	46.3	2610	46,200	1.02"	2.179"**	Rem.
1925	172 Gr. 9° B.T. G.M.	HiVel #2 Lot 1488 Bl. #9	37.6	2199	29,545	.844"	2.11"	F.A.
1926				No Match			No Test	
1927	172 Gr. 9° B.T. G.M.	HiVel #2 Lot 1488 -S	36.4	2203**	28,035	.982"	2.53"	F.A.
1928	172 Gr. 9° B.T. G.M.	IMR-1147 Lot 1492	51.1	2715.1***	42,650	1.10"	2.85"	F.A.
1929	173 Gr. 9° B.T. G.M.	IMR Lot 1617	52.0	2712	45,270	1.14"	2.96"	F.A.
1930	173 Gr. 9° B.T. G.M.	HiVel #2 Lot H-93 -808	33.5	2219	27,485	1.17"	2.41"	F.A.

* Figure of merit for 1924 was at 300 yards instead of meters.

** Velocity was taken in 30 inch barrel in 1928.

** Velocity was taken in 28 inch barrel in 1927

*** Velocity was taken in 28 inch barrel in 1928.

4. Palma Match Ammunition

For the long range International Palma Match, the utmost accuracy at long range is required in the ammunition. Immediately after World War I it became the custom to hold a competitive accuracy test of ammunition to determine the ammunition to be used in this match.

The particulars of the ammunition selected each year, together with the result of the official test, is given below. It will be noted that in several years there were no tests, and that in 1930, the ammunition which won the competition was afterward withdrawn from use because of high pressures which were blamed on the Berdan primers used in this lot.

Another lot without the Berdan primers was hastily substituted without any official test.

CALIBER .30 PALMA MATCH AMMUNITION

Year	Bullet	Powder Type	Chg. Gr.	Inst. Vel. at 78 Ft.	Mean Pres.	Mean Radius 1000 Yds.	Mfgr. & Remarks
1920	....	....	....	....	....	....	No Mfg.
1921	170 Gr. F.B. CuNi.	duPont Ex. No. 1076	48.5	2700	48,370	6.04"**	Remington
1922	180 Gr. F.B. Lubaloy	HiVel Lot #1	46	2625	49,865	5.69"	Western
1923	....	....	....	....	....	....	No Mfg.
1924	200 Gr. F.B. CuNi.	HiVel	44.5	2477	49,180	5.497"	Remington
1925	172 Gr. 9° B.T. G.M.	IMR-1147	54.5	2776	52,385	4.43"	Frank F.A.
1926	....	....	....	....	....	....	No Mfg.
1927	....	....	....	....	....	....	No Mfg.
1928	172 Gr. 9° B.T. G.M.	IMR-1147 Lot 1492	51.1	2715.1	42,650	5.84" (Computed)	F.A., Same as International
1929	173 Gr. 9° B.T. G.M.	IMR-1186 Lot 1619	49.8	2700	49,685	5.67"	F.A.
1930	173 Gr. 9° B.T. G.M.	IMR-1186 Lot 1620	51.2	2712.2	54,335	5.10"	F.A. (Not Used; Berdan)
1930	173 Gr. 9° B.T. G.M.	IMR-1147 Lot 1617	52.7	2643	47,130	Not Tested	F.A. (Substituted for (Berdan))
1931							National Match Used

No test; National Match Ammunition Used.

5. National Match Pistol Ammunition

The Pistol Ammunition furnished for the National Matches during the period under discussion was loaded to the regular service specifications calling for a 230 grain bullet loaded to a muzzle velocity of 810 feet per second. In the early years the bullets were jacketed with Cupro-nickel; later with gilding metal.

A typical load was that of the 1929 National Match pistol cartridge, which had a charge of 4.7 grains of Bullseye Powder, giving an instrumental velocity at 25 feet of 816 feet per second, with a mean pressure of 14,853 pounds per square inch, and a maximum pressure of 16,533 pounds per square inch.

There were no matches in 1926. In 1928, the 1927 ammunition was used. Accuracy figures for the years when tests were held were as follows:

Year	Group Diameter at 50 yards	
1920	3.15 inches	
1921	3.85 "	
1922	3.66 "	
1923	3.22 "	
1924	3.78 "	
1925	3.83 "	
1927	3.83 "	
1929	3.09 "	
1930	2.25 "	(Western Cartridge Co.)
1930	2.27 "	(Frankford Arsenal)

6. Dimensions of Cartridges

The standard overall length of the service cartridge is 3.300 to 3.350 inches. In making up ammunition to be entered in the National, International and Palma Match Ammunition tests, Frankford Arsenal endeavored to adjust the overall length so as to gain accuracy where possible by crowding the bullet up closer to the origin of the rifling. The following shows the overall length specifications to which these cartridges were loaded for the years given.

Year	Overall length, National Match Ammunition	Overall length, International and Palma Match Ammunition
1921	Flat Base, 3.337 to 3.347 inches	Flat Base, 3.350 to 3.360 inches
1922	Flat Base, 3.337 to 3.347 inches	Flat Base, 3.400 to 3.410 inches
1922	Boat Tail 3.337 to 3.347 inches	Boat Tail 3.350 to 3.360 inches
1923	Boat Tail 3.317 to 3.347 inches	Boat Tail 3.350 to 3.360 inches
1924	Boat Tail 3.317 to 3.350 inches	Boat Tail 3.390 to 3.400 inches
1925	Boat Tail 3.317 to 3.350 inches	Boat Tail 3.390 to 3.400 inches

These are some dimensions of the .30 caliber M2 cartridge.

Weight of bullet, about 152 grains.
Weight of powder, 49 to 51 grains.
Weight of primed case, 200 grains approximately.
Cubic capacity of case:

To shoulder	3.70 c.c.	.226 cu. in.
To neck	3.95 c.c.	.241 cu. in.
To top	4.40 c.c.	.269 cu. in.

7. Accuracy Specifications

Accuracy Specifications used in World War II for the purchase of Caliber .30 Ball, M2, and Caliber .30 Armor Piercing, M2.

Ammunition Type	Range at which tested	Mean Radius inches	Approximate extreme spread, inches
Cal. .30 Ball, M2	500 yards	6.5	19
Cal. .30 Ball, M2	600 yards	7.5	22½
Cal. .30 A.P., M2	500 yards	9	27
Cal. .30 A.P., M2	600 yards	10	30

8. Testing the Sensitivity of Primers; Vent Diameters of Berdan Primers

The primer under test is held in a fixture fitted with a firing pin with point of standard contour on which a ball is dropped as follows:

Caliber	No. Tested	Weight of Ball	Height of Drop	Results Required
.22 r.f.	50 cartridges	2 oz.	21 in.	All fire
.22 r.f.	50 cartridges	2 oz.	2 in.	None fire
.30 cal.	not less than 300	4 oz.	15 in.	All fire
.30 cal.	not less than 300	4 oz.	3 in.	None fire

Vent Diameter for Various Berdan Primers

Nation or Make	Caliber	Dia. of Vents
Austria	8 m/m	.040 to .080 Taper
British (Webley)	.455	.030
British	Mark VII–.303	.040
British	.50	.040
British	.276	.030
British	Mark VII–.303	.031
British (Magnum)	.303	.031
British (Bisley Match)	.303	.031
Belgian	7.65 m/m	.029
Czechoslovakia	8 m/m	.040
French	13 m/m	.031
French	8 m/m Lebel	.031
German	7 m/m	.025
German	7.9 m/m	.025
Holland	6.5 m/m	.03
Italian	6.5 m/m	.055
Siamese	8 m/m	.025
Swiss	7.5 m/m	.035

9. Nomenclature of Cartridge Defects

Blown Primer. The primer has fallen completely out of its pocket when gun is opened after firing.

Battered Cartridge. The cartridge is deformed so that it will not chamber in the gun.

Draw Mark. Straight scratch lengthwise of the case due to some foreign substance in the drawing dies.

Dropped Primer. Same as *Blown Primer.*

Gas Leak. Black marks around primer showing where gas has escaped.

Hangfire. Discharge of cartridge after an appreciable interval from fall of firing pin or hammer. This may be due to a deteriorated or defective primer, or to a weak firing pin blow.

Incipient Rupture. Partial separation of the cartridge case in a circumferential direction above the head.

Inverted Anvil. Anvil in the primer upside down. Will cause a misfire.

Laminated Case. A case which shows spots where the metal has separated in layers due to scaly inclusions.

Leaky Primer. Escape of gas around primer pocket, indicated by smoky marks around primer cup.

Light Blow. A weak firing pin blow, insufficient to discharge the primer properly.

Low Primer. A primer which is inserted too deep in its pocket. This may result in a hangfire or a misfire.

Misfire. Failure of the primer to go off when struck.

No Anvil. Absence of the anvil in the primer. Will cause a misfire.

Pierced Primer. Primer in which firing pin point has made a hole all the way through.

Punctured Primer. Same as *Pierced Primer.*

Primer Blow-Back. Primer in which gas pressure has blown out the section opposite the firing pin hole. May be due to a weak main spring or to a firing pin which is too light.

Primer Leak. Escape of gas around primer pocket.

Primer in Sideways. A rather rare defect which sometimes occurs in volume production. Primer fails to start into its pocket straight, and is crushed in sideways.

Primer Set-Back. After firing primer is partly out of its seat.

Rings. Circular marks around the case, due to poor reaming of the chamber.

Split Body. A longitudinal crack in the body of the case near the head. This is a dangerous defect, as it allows gas to escape to the rear.

Split Neck. A crack in the neck of the case. It is usually due to failure to anneal the neck sufficiently to prevent season cracking.

Season Crack. A cracking which occurs in hard brass with the passage of time. Usually seen in cartridges as Split Necks.

Soft Head. Spreading of the head and opening of the primer pocket on firing, due to over annealing of the head of the cartridge.

Stretch. A visible strain extending around the case above the head. Usually due to excess headspace.

10. Interior Ballistics

Time, from the instant of sear release to the exit of the bullet is made up of

Lock Time, that is, the interval of time from sear release until the impact of the firing pin on the primer.

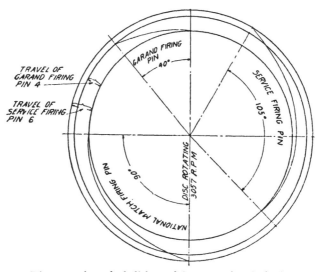

Diagram of smoked disk used in measuring lock time.

Ignition Time, the interval from impact on primer until the pressure rises enough to start the bullet from its seat.

Barrel Time, that is the interval from the time the bullet starts to leave its seat until it reaches the muzzle. For the old .30-'06 cartridge with 150 grain bullet at 2700 f.s. muzzle velocity, the barrel time has been measured at .00098 second, or just under a thousandth of a second.

Lock Time may be calculated approximately by the following formula:

Let S = length of firing pin travel.

  f = average weight of the spring.

  m = mass of the firing pin + ½ mass of the spring.

  t = time pin takes to fall.

Then $S = \dfrac{ft^2}{2\,m}$ and $t = \sqrt{\dfrac{2\,ms}{f}}$ (*Kent, Aberdeen Proving Ground*)

Actual lock time of the M 1903 rifle was measured by **John C.** Garand at Springfield Armory, using a smoked disc, turning at the rate of 3057 revolutions per minute. The firing pin was mounted alongside this disc, with a wire pointer attached to the cocking piece so as to touch the smoked surface of the rotating disc.

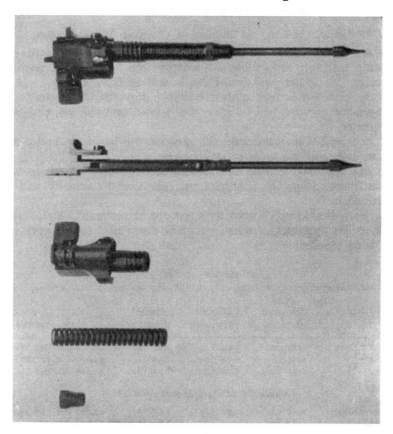

Garand super-speed firing mechanism.

With the gun cocked, this wire traced a circle on the smoke surface. When the trigger was pulled, the wire moved forward to the new position and there traced a new circle of smaller diameter. The angular length of the spiral connecting these two circles indicated the time of fall through the firing pin travel of .6 inch.

The time of fall of the service firing pin was .0057 second, and of the National Match headless firing pin, .0049 second.

Mr. Garand designed a speed firing pin with a travel of only .4 inch that had a time of fall of .0022 second.

A spring of sufficient strength was obtained by using special Chrome Vanadium steel wire which when wound, had a square cross section, and which was worked to its maximum by having it compressed solid when the mechanism was cocked.

To compensate for the distortion of the wire in winding, it was made with one edge wider than the other, a sort of keystone shape. When wound, the section became square.

11. Muzzle Velocity vs. Position of Cartridge When Loading

When the powder does not competely fill the cartridge case, the velocity will vary depending on whether the bulk of the powder is nearer the primer end or the bullet end of the case.

If the cartridge is held with the primer down before loading, the bulk of the powder will be near the primer, and the velocity will be greater.

If it is held with primer up, the powder will be in the bullet end of the case, and the velocity will be less.

If the cartridge is held horizontally and rolled, the powder will be distributed along the length of the case, and the velocity will be intermediate.

A test at Frankford Arsenal with Cal. .50 M1 ammunition also with Cal. .30 M1 ammunition with 173 grain boat tailed bullet, gave the following results:

Caliber .50 M1

	Mean Velocity at 78 ft.	Extreme Variation	Mean Variation	Mean Pressure
Primer Down	2549 f.s.	95.2 f.s.	24.2 f.s.	48,602 lbs. per sq. in.
Rolled	2524 f.s.	103.9 f.s.	24.6 f.s.	47,019 lbs. per sq. in.
Primer Up	2476 f.s.	95.0 f.s.	23.3 f.s.	44,461 lbs. per sq. in.

Caliber .30 M1. 49.4 grains IMR 1185

Primer Down	2611 f.s.	40.1 f.s.	11.1 f.s.	47,387 lbs. per sq. in.
Rolled	2589 f.s.	61.2 f.s.	15.4 f.s.	45,128 lbs. per sq. in.
Primer Up	2567 f.s.	44.4 f.s.	11.3 f.s.	43,856 lbs. per sq. in.

12. Effect of Variations in Powder Temperature on Muzzle Velocity

Velocities and pressures taken with a given charge of powder and weight of projectile vary with the temperature of the gun and powder.

The standard temperature is taken as 70 degrees F. When the gun and powder are warmer than this, the velocity will be higher; when they are cooler, the velocity will be lower.

The amount of the change depends on several variables, but can be approximated from the curve given on page 327, as developed by the Ordnance Department.

Figures which have been quoted by various authorities for this variation are shown below.

Gun	Range	Correction	Range of Powder temp-erature used	Authority
7 mm	50 meters	1.64 f.s. per degree F.	57 to 89 deg. F.	* Pachmann & Wurzle
7.9 mm	50 meters	1.09 f.s. per degree F.	not given	*Prof. Brunswig
7.9 mm	50 meters	.91 f.s. per degree F.	not given	Polish Ord. Dept.
.30-'06	150 ft.	1.66 f.s. per degree F.	not given	U. S. Ord. Dept.
.30-'06	150 ft.	1.75 f.s. per degree F.	70 to 140 deg. F.	Frankford Arsenal
.30-'06	150 ft.	1.83 f.s. per degree F.	15 to 105 deg. F.	Burnside Laboratory
.30-'06	150 ft.	1.55 f.s. per degree F.	70 to -50 deg. F.	Burnside Laboratory

In Zeitschrift für das gesampt Schiess und Sprengstoff wesen—Jan. 1928.

13. Distribution of the Heat Energy of the Powder

Each pound of modern single base smokeless powder has a potential energy of about 1,250,000 foot pounds. If this powder is fired in a .30 caliber rifle, it will supply charges for about 140 cartridges, and each will fire a 150 grain bullet at 2800 feet per second muzzle velocity, with a muzzle energy of 2612 foot-pounds.

The amount of this powder potential that has appeared in the form of muzzle energy of the bullets is therefore 140 x 2612, or 365,680 foot-pounds, or only about 29¼ percent. Where did the other 70¾ percent go to?

In 1929 the Ordnance Department set up a Technical Staff Test Program to determine this. The firing was done in a Browning Machine Rifle, with results as follows:

Heat distribution of one round in a Browning Machine Rifle.

Heat to Cartridge Case	131.0 Calories
To Kinetic Energy of Bullet	885.3 Calories
To Kinetic Energy of Gases	569.1 Calories
Heat to Barrel	679.9 Calories
Heat in Gases	598.6 Calories
Total	2864.0 Calories
Heat Generated by Friction	212.0 Calories

14. Velocity vs. Barrel Length

Tests made at Springfield Armory with various length barrels for the Browning Machine Gun gave the following comparative figures:

Length Barrel, Inches	.30 Cal. '06, Velocity, F.S.	.50 Caliber, Velocity, F.S.
24	2709	2444.9
28	2776	2567
30	2833	2673.9
32	2848	2702

The 1917 Enfield rifle with 26 inch barrel gave for an average of five shots each with 2 barrels, 2783 f.s. vs. 2700 for the 1903 rifle with 24 inch barrel.

15. Comparative Table of Remaining Velocities, Energies and Form Factors for .30 and .50 Caliber Ammunition.*

Range yards	1906 Ball Service		170 Gr. Flat Base		Experimental 1922 170 grain 6 deg. Boat Tail	
	Remaining Velocity f/s	Remaining Energy Ft. lbs.	Remaining Velocity f/s	Remaining Energy Ft. lbs.	Remaining Velocity f/s	Remaining Energy Ft. lbs.
0	2700	2429	2700	2753	2700	2753
500	1240	512	1506	860	1777	1197
1000	958	306	1083	444	1303	644
1500	763	194	815	251	960	349
2000	585	114	628	149	777	229
2500	408	55	472	84	638	154

Remaining Velocity, Range, and Energy of 172 grain Cal. .30 A. P. and Ball Ammunition M1, and 750 grain Cal. .50 A. P. and Ball Ammunition M1.

Remaining Velocity	Range—yards		Energy—ft. lb.	
	Cal. .30	Cal. .50	Cal. .30	Cal. .50
2600	26	....	2582	....
2500	79	26	2388	10411
2400	134	116	2200	9595
2300	191	209	2021	8812
2200	249	304	1849	8062
2100	310	403	1685	7346
2000	372	505	1528	6663
1900	436	611	1379	6014
1800	503	721	1238	5397
1700	573	836	1104	4814
1600	648	958	978	4264
1500	727	1088	860	3748
1400	812	1227	749	3265
1300	905	1379	648	2815
1200	1014	1558	550	2399
1100	1161	1799	462	2016
1000	1372	2145	382	1666

After the adoption in 1925 of the M1 ammunition containing the 172 grain boat-tailed bullet, an investigation was made to determine the form factor for use with Ingalls Ballistic Tables, Artillery Circular M. Results are shown below:

* (Computed from Ingall's Tables, using data from unreduced firings made at Aberdeen Proving Ground, Md., between Nov. 22, and Dec. 22, 1922.)

Table of form factors for 172 grain boat-tailed bullet Cal. .30 M1

Velocity, feet per second	Form Factor
2600	.492
2000	.514
1500	.588
1200	.744

16. Ballistic Data

Pedersen Rifle, Caliber .276,   (0.276-A-2 J
125 Gr. Bullet—P. C. 48,   (A. P. G.
Instrumental Velocity at 78 feet = 2640 f/s   (Aug. 25, 1927
B. C. for J (v) = 0.2469 when V is greater than vel. of sound
              0.4260 when V is less than vel. of sound

Yards Range	Angle of Departure Minutes	Time of Flight Seconds	Remaining Velocity ft/s	Remaining Energy ft-lbs	Maximum Ordinate Feet
0	0.0	0.000	2690	2012	.00
100	2.3	.115	2514	1758	.07
200	5.0	.239	2345	1529	.23
300	8.0	.371	2180	1322	.57
400	11.2	.514	2020	1135	1.09
500	14.6	.669	1864	966	1.82
600	18.7	.837	1711	814	2.84
700	23.1	1.021	1562	679	4.21
800	28.1	1.222	1419	560	6.00
900	33.9	1.444	1284	459	8.27
1000	40.5	1.691	1160	374	11.54
1100	48.1	1.960	1083	327	15.44
1200	56.8	2.242	1046	304	20.63

Caliber .30 Bullet, 1906 Service Ammunition,   (A. P. G., Md.
M. V. 2700 f/s. C Variable, starting with 0.410.   (April 1926
                                                    (H-1-0.30/.28

Range Yards	Angle of Departure Minutes	Time of Flight Seconds	Remaining Velocity ft/s	Remaining Energy ft-lbs	Maximum Ordinate Feet
100	2.5	0.12	2481	2051	0.06
200	5.2	0.25	2267	1712	0.27
300	8.2	0.38	2059	1412	0.62
400	11.6	0.53	1858	1150	1.1
500	15.6	0.70	1664	923	2.0
600	20.4	0.89	1481	731	3.3
700	25.9	1.11	1315	576	5.0
800	32.5	1.35	1174	459	7.4
900	40.3	1.62	1065	378	10.8
1000	49.4	1.91	989	326	15.2

U. S. Caliber .30 M1   (0.30-B-4

172 Gr. Bullet, Muzzle Velocity 2600 f/s   (A. P. G.

B. C. for J (v) Table = 0.2702 when V is greater (Sept. 7, 1927

than vel. of sound

0.3977 when V is less than vel. of sound

Range Yards	Angle of Departure Minutes	Time of Flight Seconds	Remaining		Maximum Ordinate Feet
			Velocity ft/s	Energy ft-lbs	
0	0.0	0.0	2600	2582	0.0
100	2.5	0.119	2442	2279	0.1
200	5.3	0.246	2289	2002	0.3
300	8.4	0.381	2140	1750	0.6
400	11.8	0.527	1995	1520	1.1
500	15.4	0.683	1852	1311	1.9
600	19.4	0.851	1713	1120	2.9
700	23.9	1.034	1576	949	4.3
800	29.0	1.233	1444	797	6.1
900	34.7	1.450	1320	665	8.5
1000	41.2	1.688	1203	553	11.6
1100	48.6	1.949	1102	464	15.4
1200	57.0	2.228	1057	427	20.3

U. S. Caliber .30 M1   (0.30-B-3

172 Gr. Bullet, Muzzle Velocity 2700 f/s   (A. P. G.

B. C. for J (v) Table = 0.2702 when V is greater (Sept. 7, 1927

than vel. of sound

0.3977 when V is less than vel. of sound

Range Yards	Angle of Departure Minutes	Time of Flight Seconds	Remaining		Maximum Ordinate Feet
			Velocity ft/s	Energy ft-lbs	
0	0.0	0.000	2700	2785	0.0
100	2.3	0.115	2539	2463	0.1
200	4.9	0.237	2384	2170	0.3
300	7.7	0.367	2232	1903	0.6
400	10.8	0.506	2084	1660	1.1
500	14.2	0.655	1940	1438	1.8
600	17.9	0.815	1799	1237	2.8
700	22.0	0.989	1660	1053	4.1
800	26.7	1.177	1526	889	5.8
900	31.9	1.383	1397	745	7.9
1000	37.7	1.608	1275	621	10.5
1100	44.3	1.855	1161	515	13.9
1200	52.0	2.124	1083	448	18.3

17. Rule for Computing Ordinates to Trajectory

Let y = height of desired ordinate in yards

x = horizontal distance to desired ordinate

A_r = angle of departure *in mils* for the trajectory being computed

A_x = angle of departure *in mils* for the range corresponding to x

Then $y = \dfrac{x}{1000} (A_r - A_x)$

Example:

Wanted, the 1000 yard ordinate of the 2000 yard trajectory.

Given, A_r = angle of departure for 2000 yards = 44.5 mils.

A_x = angle of departure for 1000 yards = 11.1 mils.

Then $y = \dfrac{1000}{1000} (44.5 - 11.1) = 33.4$ yards.

Note—A mil is 3.375 minutes.

18. Formula for Wind Deflection

Let D = deflection of the bullet in feet caused by wind.

W = wind velocity straight across the range in feet per second. If the wind is not straight across the range, then that component of it which acts straight across the range at right angles to the line of sight.

T = time of flight in seconds for the range at which the deflection is to be figured.

T_v = time it would take the bullet to traverse the same distance in a vacuum.

Then $D = W (T - T_v)$

Example; Find the deflection that would be caused at various ranges by a wind of 1 mile per hour acting on the 172 grain M1 boattail bullet with an initial velocity of 2700 feet per second.

Remember—1 mile per hour = 1.4667 feet per second.

Range, yards.	Time of flight.	Time to cover same range in vacuum.	Difference	Deflection, feet	Deflection, inches.
100	.115	.111	.004	.006	.07
200	.237	.222	.015	.022	.26
300	.367	.333	.034	.050	.60
400	.506	.444	.062	.091	1.09
500	.665	.555	.100	.147	1.76
600	.815	.667	.148	.217	2.60
700	.989	.778	.211	.309	3.71
800	1.117	.889	.288	.422	5.06
900	1.383	1.000	.383	.562	6.74
1000	1.608	1.111	.497	.729	8.75

19. The Relation Between Muzzle Velocity and Instrumental Velocity

When velocities are taken by chronograph, what is obtained is not the muzzle velocity, but instead, the velocity over a measured interval somewhere in front of the muzzle.

At Springfield Armory, Frankford Arsenal and Aberdeen Proving Ground, it is usual when taking the velocities of small arms ammunition to measure the time taken to pass between two screens either 100 or 150 feet apart. The first screen is usually placed 3 feet in front of the muzzle to avoid blast effects.

The time taken to traverse the distance between screens, divided by this distance gives the average velocity from the first screen to the second.

The bullet is going faster when it passes the first screen than it is when it reaches the second, but it may be assumed without much error that the average velocity between screens represents the velocity at a point halfway between the two screens.

Thus with the first screen three feet from the muzzle and the second 100 feet from the first, the velocity obtained is that at 53 feet from the muzzle. With the first screen three feet from the muzzle and the second screen 150 feet further along, the instrumental velocity obtained is that at 78 feet from the muzzle.

For velocities in the order of those obtained with the service ammunition it has been found with standard atmospheric density conditions the speed drops off at the rate of .64 foot per second for every foot from the muzzle to the mid point between screens.

Thus to find the muzzle velocity, given the instrumental velocity at 78 feet, we should add to the instrumental velocity an amount equal to 78 x .64, or 49.92 feet, which is taken as 50 feet, per second.

Likewise, to bring the instrumental velocity at 53 feet to muzzle velocity we should add 53 x .64 or 33.92, that is, 34 feet per second.

If very accurate results must be had, these figures should be corrected for any variation of the atmospheric density from the normal, which is considered as 1.2034 grams per liter.

The ratio of the density of the air at the time of firing to the normal density is designated by the Greek letter Rho; let's call it "r". Then Muzzle Velocity = Instrumental Velocity + .64 x s x r, where s is the distance in feet from the muzzle to the mid point between screens.

For values of Rho see table on page 430.

20. Mils Versus Minutes

In small arms target practice it is usual to give elevations in minutes of angle, which is convenient, as a minute equals very nearly an inch for every hundred yards of the range. Thus a minute of elevation change on the rear sight should raise or lower the point of impact an inch at 100 yards or ten inches at 1000 yards.

In military fire control work it is usual to use a different unit, the mil. The mil is the angle whose tangent is 1/1000; that is, it is the angle subtended by 1 unit at a distance of 1000 units; for example, 1 foot at 1000 feet or 1 yard at 1000 yards.

This would work out so that there are 6283 mils in a complete circle. As this number is not divisible into fractions which are whole numbers, the artillery fire control experts adopted the artillery mil, in which the circle was divided into 6400 parts, thus giving a number which is easily divisible by many other numbers, and still not changing the value of the mil to any sensible degree.

For some years the infantry used a mil of 1/6280th of a circle, called the Infantry mil, while the Artillery used 1/6400th of a circle, called the Artillery mil.

In recent years, however, the so-called Infantry mil has been dropped from use, and the Artillery mil adopted in its place.

The Artillery mil is 3' 22.5" of arc, or 3.375 minutes. As rifle elevations are given in the technical manuals in mils, this is a useful number to know. To reduce mils to minutes, multiply by 3.375.

21. Comparison of Angles of Departure (Approx) of Caliber .30 Ball M1 At Ground Level and at Elevation 10,000 ft.

Range Yards	Angle Dep. Mils Elev. 10,000 ft. Angle of site 0	Angle Dep. Mils Ground Level	Drift Right Mils (Ground Level)
0	0	0	0
100	0.7	0.7	0
200	1.5	1.5	0
300	2.2	2.4	0
400	3.1	3.3	0
500	3.9	4.3	0
600	4.7	5.3	0
700	5.6	6.5	0
800	6.6	7.8	0
900	7.6	9.3	0
1000	8.8	11.1	0
1100	10.2	13.1	0
1200	11.6	15.4	0.1
1300	13.5	18.0	0.1
1400	15.2	20.7	0.1
1500	17.3	23.9	0.1
1600	19.7	27.3	0.2
1700	22.5	31.3	0.2
1800	25.2	35.2	0.2
1900	28.5	39.9	0.3
2000	31.7	44.5	0.3

22. Bullet Penetration in Various Mediums

The Ordnance Department, U. S. Army determined that the 150 grain M2 service bullet fired into water with a velocity of 2770 f. s.

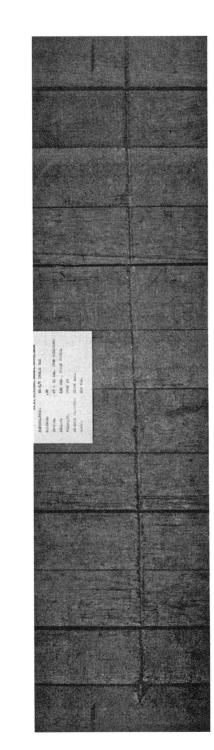

Penetration of 32½ inches of oak by .30-'06 bullet weighing 150 grains, driven at a muzzle velocity of 2700 f.s. Range, 200 yards. The range was long enough so that the bullet was sufficiently stabilized to continue point first and thus give good penetration. At shorter ranges, the penetration is likely to be much less—see photo showing results at 50 feet.

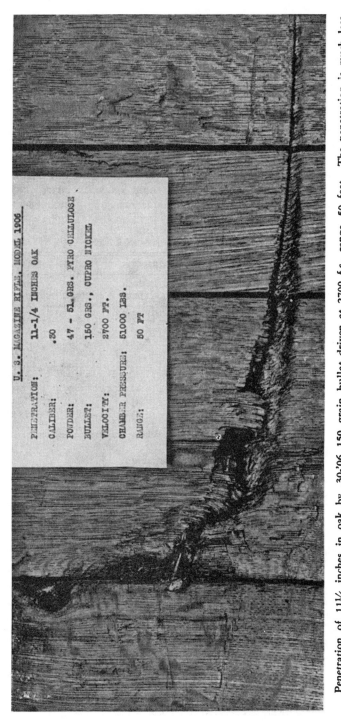

U. S. MAGAZINE RIFLE, MODEL 1906

PENETRATION:	11-1/4 INCHES OAK
CALIBER:	.30
POWDER:	47 - 51 GRS. PYRO CELLULOSE
BULLET:	150 GRS., CUPRO NICKEL
VELOCITY:	2700 FT.
CHAMBER PRESSURE:	51000 LBS.
RANGE:	50 FT

Penetration of 11¼ inches in oak by .30·'06 150 grain bullet driven at 2700 f.s., range, 50 feet.. The penetration is much less than that achieved at longer ranges. The reason is that at this short range, the bullet had not settled down to a stable flight, and when it encountered the resistance of the oak it yawed badly, and rapidly gave up all its energy.

at an angle of incidence of 90 degrees would be slowed to 140 feet per second at 3½ feet below the surface of the water. At this velocity the energy is 100 foot-pounds, which is considered the minimum to inflict a wound on the human body. Therefore a man would be safe from strafing with .30 caliber bullets if he were 4 feet beneath the surface.

The Navy Bureau of Ordnance determined, based on tests made at the Naval Proving Ground at Dahlgren, Va., that a man would be safe under 3½ to 4 feet of water from a .30-'06 projectile fired at an angle of incidence of 90 degrees to the water, and that at an angle of incidence of 30 degrees, which would be more nearly the angle at which a plane would attack a man, a man 2½ feet beneath the surface would be safe.

Penetration for Cal. .30 M 1 Ammunition

	200 yards		600 yards		1500 yards	
	Aver-age	Maxi-mum	Aver-age	Maxi-mum	Aver-age	Maxi-mum
1/4" Armor	0.1"	....	....	....	....	....
Gravel	7.0"	8.0"	4.5	5.0	4.1	5.5
Brick masonry	4.3"	6.5"	2.2	3.6	1.5	1.9
Concrete	4.0"	....	1.0	....	0.5	....
Solid Oak	13.8"	18.0"	12.0	13.6	2.1	3.8
Dry Sand	6.5"	8.2"	7.1	8.5	8.2	9.0
Moist Sand	7.3"	9.2"	9.6	11.2	8.7	9.5
Loam	24.1"	24.5"	24.0	25.0	22.7	26.2
Clay	24.6"	29.0"	22.0	23.0	14.0	15.0
Loose Earth	19.0"	....	15.8	....	....	....

23. Bullet Lubricant Formulae*

No. 1

¼ pound Japan Wax
2 heaping teaspoons Graphite (Graphite must be mechanically mixed and therefore it must be very fine, like Acheson Graphite No. 1304 or Dixon's Motor Graphite)

No. 2

Equal parts of Beeswax and Carnuba of Japan Wax, Cylinder Oil or Castor Oil, just enough to bring required flexibility

Our own lubricant consists of equal parts beeswax and paraffin tempered to a tough pliable consistency, by the trial and error method, using vaseline, or a good grade of cup grease such as Pennzoil No. 305 which contains graphite. Add fine powdered graphite if you want a black lubricant.

While the waxes are melted we add about 25% as much grease by volume. Then several samples are "tested" for consistency by

* From the National Rifle Association Technical Staff.

letting one sample cool at room temperature, and the other, in a shallow pan, is cooled in the refrigerator. If the mixture is very brittle when cool we add more grease, or more wax if too soft. Our mixture is used on both rifle and handgun bullets, and we never experience leading trouble. Our alloy consists of 96 parts lead, 2 parts tin and 2 parts antimony.

24. Identification Codes of German Arms, Ammunition and Optical Instrument Makers

During the occupation of Germany immediately after V. E. Day in 1945, our forces obtained a secret German document giving the identification code letters of various makers of arms, ammunition and optical instruments.

The document appeared somewhat garbled, and there were some duplications, indicating that some changes had been made from time to time.

Even though the list may be incomplete, it has proved to be very useful, as the makers whose products are most often seen among the souvenir weapons brought back from Europe appear on this list.

German Small Arms Manufacturers' Codes

A

aak-Waffenfabrik Brunn A. G., Prague
ac-Carl Walther, Zella-Mehlis, Thuringia
aek-F. Dusek Waffenerzeugung, Opoczno bei Nachod
amn-Mauser Works, Waldeck bei Kassel
ar-Mauser Works, Borsigwalde, Berlin
asb-Deutsche-Waffen und Munitions Fabriken A. G., Borsigwalde, Berlin
auc-Mauser Works A. G., Ehrenfeld, Cologne
awt-Wurttembergische Metallwarenfabrik A. G., Geislingen
axs-Berndorfer Metallwarenfabrik Arthur Krupp A. G., Berndorf, Niederdonau
ayf-B. Geipel, G. m. b. H., Waffenfabrik "Erma"
azg-Siemens-Schuckert Works A. G., Berlin

B

bcd-Gustloff Co., Weimar Works, Weimar
be-Berndorfer Metallwarenfabrik Arthur Krupp A. G., Berndorf, Niederdonau
bh-Brunner Waffenfabrik A. G., Brunn (Brno, Czechoslovakia)
bjv-Bohm-Mahrische Kolben-Danek A. G., Prague, Vysocan Works
bkp-Gewehrfabrik H. Burgsmüller and Sons G. m. b. H., Kreiensen, Harz
bkq-Rohrenfabrik Johannes Surmann G. m. b. H., Arnsberg
bky-Bohmische Waffenfabrik A. G., of Prague, Ung-Brod Works, Ung Brod, (Moravia)

bmv-Rheinmetall-Borsig A. G., Sömmerda Works, Sömmerda
bmz-Minerva Nahmaschinenfabrik A. G., Boscowitz
bnd-M. A. N., A. G., Nürnberg Works, Nürnberg
bnz-Steyr-Daimler Puch A. G., Steyr Works, Steyr, Austria
bpr-Johannus Grossfuss Metall and Locierwarenfabrik, Dobeln, Saxony
br-Mathias Bauerle Laufwerke G. m. b. H., St. Georgen, Schwarzwald
bvl-Th. Bergmann & Co. Abteilung Automaten u. Metallwarenfabrikation, Altona, Hamburg
bxb-Skoda Works, Pilsen
byf-Mauser Works, Oberndorf
bym-Genossenschafts Maschinenhaus der Buchsenmacher, Ferlach, Carinthia, Austria
bzt-Fritz Wolf Gewehrfabrik, Zella-Mehlis, Thuringia

C

ce-J. P. Sauer and Sons Gewehrfabrik, Suhl, Saxony
cdo-Th. Bergmann & Co. A. G., Waffen u. Munitionfabrik, Veltem Works, Veltem am Main
ch-Fabrique Nationale d'Armes de Guerre, Herstal, Liege, Belgium
chd-Berlin Industrie Werke A. G., Spandau, Berlin
cof-Carl Eickhorn, Waffenfabrik Solingen
con-Franz Stock Maschinen u. Werkzeufabrik, Berlin
cos-Merz Brothers, Frankfurt am Main
cpo-Rheinmetall-Borsig A. G., Marienfeld Works, Marienfeld, Berlin
cpp-Rheinmetall-Borsig A. G., Guben Works
cpq-Rheinmetall-Borsig A. G., Breslau Works
crs-Paul Weyersberg & Co. Waffenfabrik, Solingen
cvl-WKC Waffenfabrik G. m. b. H., Solingen
cxq-Spreewerk G. m. b. H., Metallwarenfabrik, Spandau, Berlin

D

dfb-Gustloff Co., Suhl Gun Works, Suhl, Saxony
dgl-Remo Gewehrfabrik, Rempt Brothers, Suhl, Saxony
dot-Waffenwerke Brunn A. G., Brunn (Brno, Czechoslovakia)
dou-Waffenwerke Brunn A. G., Bystrica Works
dov-Waffenwerke Brunn A. G., Vsetin Works Czechoslovakia
dow-Opticotechna, (formerly Waffenfabrik Brunn A. G.), Prerau, Czechoslovakia
dph-Interessen Gemeinschaft Farbenindustrie A. G., Autogen Works, Griesheim, Frankfurt am Main
dsh-Engineer F. Janecek, Gun Works, Prague,
duv-Berliner-Lubecker Maschinenfabriken, Lubeck Works
duw-Deutsche Rohrewerke A. G., Thyssen Works, Mulheim

E

egy-Engineer Fr. August Pfeffer, Oberlind, Thuringia

F

fnh-Bomische Waffenfabrik A. G. of Prague, Strakonitz Works
fue-Mechanische Werkstatt A. G., (formerly Dubnica Works of Skoda Co.), Dubnica
fwh-Norddeutsche Maschinenfabrik G. m. b. H., Hauptverwalting, Berlin
fxa-Eisenacher Karosseriefabrik Assmann G. m. b. H., Eisenach
fxo-C. G. Haenel Waffen u. Fahrrad Fabrik, Suhl, Saxony
fze-F. W. Holler Waffenfabrik, Solingen
fzs-Heinrich Krieghoff Waffenfabrik, Suhl, Saxony

G

ghf-Fritz Kiess & Co., G. m. b. H, Waffenfabrik, Suhl, Saxony
gsb-Rheinmetall-Borsig A. G., (formerly S. A. des Ateliers de la Dyle), Louvain, Belgium
gsc-S. A. Belge de Mécanique et de l'Armement, Monceau-sur-Sambre, Belgium
guy-Werkzeugmaschinenfabrik Oerlikon, Buhrle & Co., Oerlikon Zurich, Switzerland

H

hew-Eningeer F. Janecek, Gun Works, Prague
hhg-Rheinmetall-Borsig A. G., Tegel Works, Tegel, Berlin
hhv-Steyr-Daimler Puch A. G., Nibelungen Works, St. Valentin, Austria

J

jhv-Metallwaren Waffen u. Maschinenfabrik A. G., Budapest
jkg-Kong. Ungar. Staatliche Eisen, Stahl u. Maschinenfabrik, Budapest
jlj-Heeres Zeugamt, Ingoldstadt
jua-Danuvia Waffen u. Munitionsfabrik A. G., Budapest
jwa-Manufacture d'Armes Chatellerault, Chatellerault, France

K

kfk-Dansk Industrie Syndicat, Copenhagen, Denmark
kls-Steyr-Daimler Puch A. G., Warsaw
ksb-Manufacture Nationale d'Armes de Levallois, Levallois, Paris, France
kur-Steyr-Daimler Puch A. G., Graz Works
kwn-S. A. Fiat, Turin, Italy

L

lza-Mauser Werke A. G., Werk Karlsruhe

M

moc-Johann Springer's Erben Gewehrfabrikanten, Vienna
mpr-S. A. Hispano Suiza, Geneva, Switzerland

mrb-Aktiengesellschaft, (formerly Prague Works of Skoda Co.), Prague

myx-Rheinmetall-Borsig A. G., Sömmerda Works, Sömmerda, Thuringia

N

nec-Waffenwerke Brunn A. G., Prague

nhr-Rheinmetall-Borsig A. G., Sömmerda Works, Sömmerda, Thuringia

nyv-Rheinmetall-Borsig A. G., Werk Unterluss

nyw-Gustloff Co., Meiningen

German Small Arms Ammunition Manufacturers' Codes

A

ad-Patronen, Zundhutchen and Metallwarenfabrik A. G., (formerly Sellier and Bellot), Schoenbeck am Elbe

ak-Munitionsfabriken, (formerly Sellier and Bellot, Prague), Factory at Vlasim, Czechoslovakia

al-Deutsches Leucht and Signalmittelwerk, Dr. Feistel A. G., Berlin-Charlottenburg

am-Otto Eberhardt Patronenfabrik, of Gustloff Co., Hirtenberg, Niederdonau

an-C. Beuttenmuller & Co., G. m. b. H., Metallwarenfabrik, Bretten, Baden

ap-Otto Eberhardt Patronenfabrik, Ronsdorf Works, Wuppertal

asb-Deutsche Waffen and Munitionsfabriken A. G., Borsigwalde, Berlin

asr-HAK, (Hanseatisches Kettenwerk G. m. b. H.), Hamburg

auu-Patronenhulsen and Metallwarenfabrik A. G., Rokycany, Czechoslovakia

aux-Polte, Magdeburg Works

auy-Polte, Gruneberg Works

auz-Polte, Arnstadt Works

axq-Erfurter Laden-Industrie, Erfurt, Nord

B

bqt-Eugen Müller, Pyrotechnic Works, Vienna

byc-Aug. Klonne, Bruckenbau Anstalt, Dortmund

C

cg-Finower Industrie G. m. b. H., Finow, Mark

ch-Fabrique Nationale d'Armes de Guerre, Herstal, Liege, Belgium

cxm-Gustav Genschow & Co. A. G., Berlin

czo-Heeres Zeugamt, Geschosswerkstatt, Koenigsberg

D

dbg-Dynamit A. G., (formerly Alfred Nobel & Co.), Duneberg Works

dma-Heeres-Munitions Anstalt, Geschosswerkstatt, Zeithain

dnf-Rheinisch-Westfalische Sprengstoff A. G., Stadeln Works, Stadeln, Nürnberg

dnh-Rheinisch-Westfalische Sprengstoff A. G., Durlach Works

dph-Interessen Gemeinscaft Farbenindustrie A. G., Autogen Works, Greisheim, Frankfurt am Main

dye-Ed. Pitschmann & Co., Erste Alpenlandische Pyrotechnik, Innsbruck

E

ecc-Oskar Lunig, Pyrotechnische Fabrik, Mohringen (Fildern)

ecd-Earl Lippold, Pyrotechnische Fabrik, Wuppertal-Eberfelde

edg-J. A. Henckels Zwillinsgwerk, Solingen

edq-Deutsche Waffen and Munitionsfabriken A. G., Lubeck-Schlutup

eeg-Hermann Weihrauch, Gewehr and Fahrradteilefabrik, Zella-Mehlis, Thuringia

eel-Metallwarenfabrik, (formerly H. Wissner A. G.), Werk Brotterode, Hessen-Nassau

eem-Selve-Kornbiegel Dornheim A. G., Munitions Fabrik, Sömmerda, Saxony

eeo-Deutsche Waffen and Munitionsfabriken A. G., Posen Works

emp-Dynamit A. G., (formerly Alfred Nobel & Co.), Empelde Works

eom-H. Huck Metallwarenfabrik, Nürnberg

F

fa-Mansfield A. G., Hettstedt, Sudharz

faa-Deutsche Waffen and Munitionsfabriken A. G., Karlsruhe

fd-Stolberger Metallwerke A. G., (formerly Asten, Lynen and Schleicher), Stolberg

fde-Dynamit A. G., (formerly Alfred Nobel & Co.), Forde Works

fva-Draht and Metallwarenfabrik G. m. b. H., Salzwedel

G

gtb-J. F. Eisfeld Pulver and Pyrotechnische Fabriken Guntersberge

H

ha-Truenbritzen Metallwarenfabrik, G. m. b. H., Werke Sebaldushof

ham-Dynamit A. G., (formerly Alfred Nobel & Co.), Hamm Works

has-Pulverfabrik Hasloch, Hasloch am Main

hgs-W. C. Gustav Burmeister Pyrotechnische Fabrik and Signalmittelwerk, Hamburg

htg-Polte, Duderstadt Works

J

jtb-S. A. Tauavo, Geneva

K

k-Luch & Wagner, Suhl

kam-Hasag Eisen and Metallwerke G. m. b. H., Skarzysko-Damienna Works

kfg-Sarajevo State Arsenal

klb-L, Kiesselbach

krl-Dynamit A. G., (formerly Alfred Nobel & Co.), Werk Krummel

kry-Lignose Sprengstoff Werke G. m. b. H., Werk Kruppamuhle

kun-Werk Kunigunde

kye-Intreprinderile Metalurgie, Pumitra Voina Societate Anonima Romana, Fabrica de Armament, Brasov, Roumania

kyn-Astra, Fabrica Romana de Vagoene, Motoane Armament si Munitiuni, Brasov, Roumania

kyp-Rumanisch-Deutsche Industrie and Handels A. G., Bucharest

L

ldc-Deutsche Pyrotechnische Fabriken G. m. b. H., Cleebronn

ldb-Deutsche Pyrotechnische Fabriken G. m. b. H., Malchow, Berlin

ldn-Deutsche Pyrotechnische Fabriken G. m. b. H., Neumarkt

lge-Kugelfabrik Schulte & Co., Tente, Rhineland

lkm-Munitionsfabriken, (formerly Sellier and Bellot), Prague

N

nbe-Hasag, Eisen and Metallwerke G. m. b. H., Werk Apparatbau Tachenstochau

nfx-RWS Munitionsfabrik G. m. b. H., Warsaw-Prague

Q

qve-Carl Walther, Zella-Mehlis, Thuringia

V

Va-Kabel and Metallwerke Neumeyer A. G., Nürnberg

W

wa-Hugo Schneider A. G., Lampenfabrik Leipsig

wb-Hugo Schneider A. G., Kopenick Works, Berlin

wc-Hugo Schneider A. G., Meusewitz Works

wd-Hugo Schneider A. G., Taucha Works

we-Hugo Schneider A. G., Langeweisen Works

wf-Hasag Eisen and Metallwerke G. m. b. H., Kielce Works

wg-Hugo Schneider A. G., Altenburg Works

wh-Hugo Schneider A. G., Eisenach Works

wj-Hugo Schneider A. G., Oberweissbach Works

wk-Hugo Schneider A. G., Schlieben Works

Y

y-Jagdpatronen, Zundhutchen and Metallwarenfabrik A. G., Nagyteteny Works, Budapest

Optical Instrument Makers' Codes

B

beh-Ernst Leitz G. m. b. H., Wetzlar
bek-Hensoldt Werk für Optic and Mechanik, Herborn
blc-Zeiss Militarabteilung, Jena
bmj-Hensoldt and Sohne, Mechanische Optische Werk A. G., Wetzlar
bpd-Optische Anstalt C. P. Goerz, Vienna
byg-Joh. Wyksen, Optische and Feinmaschin, Katowitz

C

cag-Swarovski, D., Glasfabrik und Tyrolit, Wattens, Tyrol
ccx-Optische and Feinmechanische Werke Hugo Meyer and Co., Gorlitz
Cro-R. Fuess Optische Industrie, Steglitz, Berlin
ctn-Hanseatische Werkstatten für Feinmechanik and Optik, Freidricks and Co.
cxn-Emil Busch A. G., Optische Industrie, Rathenow
czn-Emil Busch A. G., Optische Industrie, Rathenow

D

ddx-Voigtlander and Sohn A. G., Braunschweig
dpw-Zeiss Ikon, Dresden; also Zeiss Ikon, Goerzwerke, Berlin-Zechlendorf
dpx-Zeiss Ikon, A. G., Stuttgart
dym-Runge and Kaulfuss, Rathenow
dzl-Optische Anstalt Oigee, Berlin

E

eaf-Mechanoptik Gesellschaft für Präzisions-technik, Aude and Reipe Optische Industrie, Babelsberg
emq-Karl Zeiss, Jena (on some range finders, etc.)
eso-Optische Werke G. Rodenstock, Munchen
eug-Optische Präzisions Werke G. m. b. H., Warsaw

F

fco-Sendlinger Optische Glaswerke G. m. b. H., Zehlendorf, Berlin
fwr-Optische Anstalt Saalfeld G. m. b. H., Saalfeld
fxp-H. Kollmorgen G. m. b. H., Berlin

G

ghp-Ruf and Co., Kassel
gug-Ungarische Optische Werke A. G., Budapest
guj-Werner D. Kuehn Optische Industrie, Steglitz, Berlin

H

hdv-Optische Werk Osterode G. m. b. H., Osterode, Harz
hkm-Carl Braun A. G., Optische Industrie, Nürnberg

J

jfp-Dr. Carl Leiss, Optische Mechanische Instrumente, Steglitz, Berlin

jnh-Hensoldt Werke für Optik und Mechanik, Herborn, Dillkress
jve-Optisches Werk Ernst Ludwig, Weixdorf
K
kjj-Seen on many binoculars but not listed in code book
krg-Emil Busch A. G., Optische Werke, Budapest
kwe-Gamma Feinmechan and Optische Werke, Budapest
L
lae-Heinrich Zeiss, Gastingen
lmg-Carl Zeiss, Jena
lwg-Optische Werk Osterode G. m. b. H., Freiheit bei Osterode (Harz)
lww-Huet & Co., Paris
lwx-O. P. L. (Optikue et Précision de Levallois), Levallois, Paris
lwy-Societe Optique et Mechanique de Haute Précision, Paris
P
pvf-Optische Werk C. Reichert, Vienna

25. Head Stamps on U. S. Service Cartridges

D A	Dominion Arsenal	
D-18	Dominion Arsenal	1918 tracer
D I	Defense Industries, Canada, Ltd.	
D E N	Denver Ordnance Plant	
E C	Evansville-Chrysler	.45 Cal. only
E C S	Evansville-Chrysler-Sunbeam	.45 Cal. only
E W	EauClaire Ordnance Plant	
F A	Frankford Arsenal	
F M	Fabrica Nacional de Municiones (Mexico).	Experimental. Non issued.
G E	General Electric Company	
K S	Allegheny Ordnance Plant	.50 Cal. only
L C	Lake City Ordnance Plant	
L M	Lowell Ordnance Plant	.50 Cal. only
M	Milwaukee Ordnance Plant	.50 Cal. only
P C	Kings Mills Ordnance Plant	
P C C	Peters Cartridge Company	
Q A	Dominion Arsenal (Quebec)	
R A	Remington Arms Company	
T R	Three Rivers (Quebec)	
T W	Twin Cities Ordnance Plant	
U, U Y	Utah Ordnance Plant	
V C	Verdun, Canada	Non-corrosive
W, W 18	Western Cartridge Company	
W C W C C	Western Cartridge Company	
W R A	Winchester Repeating Arms Company	

26. Army Test Procedure and Weapons Nomenclature

So that the reader may better understand the reason for our references to the various tests held at Aberdeen, Springfield Armory,

Fort Benning, and other places, it might be well at this point to say a few words about how the Army goes about the matter of obtaining a new weapon.

The Ordnance Department, contrary to the usual impression, does not have the say as to what weapons the Army uses. The Ordnance Department is merely a Technical Service through which the Using Service orders the fighting material that it needs.

All inventions must be sent first to the National Inventor's Council of the Department of Commerce, Washington 25, D. C. Only those that the Council decides should have Army Department action may be considered by the Army Department. These are sent to the proper agency of the Army Department for action by its Technical Committee.

Immediately after World War I, the *Ordnance Committee* was formed to co-ordinate and control the work to be done by the Ordnance Department for all of the Using Services. This Committee, which meets fortnightly, is composed of representatives of the Ground Forces, the Air Force and the Navy, the Marine Corps, and the Coast Guard, together with members from the Ordnance Department and from the other Technical Services as well.

The general function of the committee is "to consider and recommend technical action upon all matters affecting material designed for and intended to be issued to the Armed Forces, coming within the jurisdiction of the Ordnance Department."

Through this committee the using Arms of the Service express their desires and needs as to new and better equipment; have a definite voice as to the characteristics and functioning of contemplated or proposed material; and are in a position to accept or reject a newly developed item before it is standardized and goes into full production.

Frequently the Ordnance Committee has given the Ordnance Department authority to proceed with the development of an item for which no present requirement exists, but which seems to be in line with probable future progress, so that we may keep ahead of foreign developments.

Occasionally there may exist a requirement in the minds of the public or in that of an arm-chair strategist or of a newspaper columnist, when the using service thinks otherwise. Usually in such a situation the Ordnance Department comes in for severe castigation by the press for supposed backwardness. For example, in the early part of World War II, the Ordnance built and perfected a heavy tank, and had it ready for production in case a requirement should arise.

However, the using service found that such tanks were very difficult to transport over the great distances from our bases to the points where we were fighting. Bridges wouldn't carry them; especially the then existing temporary bridging that had already been procured in quantity by the Engineers. It was decided that a larger number of smaller tanks could, on account of their much greater mobility, be gotten to the needed points so much more quickly that they would be more effective. The tank sat at Aberdeen, with the designs completed, ready to be placed in production at a moment's notice if needed.

In the meantime the Germans, who were fighting right at the doors of their own factories, and thus did not have the transportation difficulties that faced us with our long lines of communication, placed a heavy tank into operation. Immediately the Ordnance Department was severely taken to task by the press, in spite of the fact our heavy tank had been ready for production months before.

At the time of the Semi-automatic Rifle Tests in 1929, the Infantry, Cavalry, Artillery, etc., each had its own Chief with an office in Washington and a Staff of his own, and a Service School and Service Board.

In attempting to produce or procure a design for a semi-automatic rifle, it therefore became necessary for the Ordnance Department to obtain, through the Ordnance Committee, the requirements of each of these using services for the Semi-automatic Rifle, together with the military characteristics desired.

The next step was to test at Springfield or Aberdeen each design prepared by our own engineers or submitted by inventors to see that they were suitable from an engineering and mechanical viewpoint for actual field test by the services. If they were, the next move was to submit samples to the Using Services, who then made their own tests to see if the gun met the military and Tactical requirements desired by them.

After the mechanical and engineering tests by the Ordnance Department, the service tests were made at the Infantry Board, Fort Benning, the Cavalry Board at Fort Riley, the Artillery Board at Fort Sill, the Engineering Board at Fort Belvoir, etc.

This clumsy, expensive, and time consuming process was greatly streamlined and shortened when the various arms were integrated into a Ground Force with one Commanding General and Staff.

When the Using Services had determined that the item met all requirements and had the necessary characteristics, the Ordnance Committee was so informed, and then recommended to the General Staff that the item be standardized.

When Standardization was actually accomplished, the item was given an M or *Model* designation, as for example, the U. S. Rifle, Caliber .30, M1. Later changes, or *Alterations* are given an A number following the M number, as for example the U. S. Carbine, Caliber .30, M 1 A 1.

Items which have not been standardized have T or *Test* numbers, followed by E or *Experimental* change numbers, as for example,

Rifle T 13 E 4 would mean that this was the 4th experimental variation of the 13th test model.

The British use the word *Mark* instead of *Model;* thus, Rifle, caliber .303 Mark I. Minor changes that we call alterations and give "A" designations they identify with a " * ", called "Star". Thus Rifle Caliber .303 Mark II *, called "Mark Two Star."

In describing Japanese Ordnance, the U. S. Army has adopted a standardized system of writing the Japanese Model Number first, followed by the year of the Christian Era in parenthesis, followed by the bore of the piece in millimeters, then the name of the item. For example, the Model 92 (1932) 6.5 mm Heavy Machine Gun.

Before the death of the Emperor Meiji in 1912, the Japanese ordnance was marked in accordance with the year of his reign, which began in 1867. Thus the Model 38 (1905) 6.5 mm rifle was adopted in the 38th year since 1867, which was 1905.

Likewise, during the reign of the Emperor Taisho, which began in 1912 and ended in 1925, weapons were marked by the year of their adoption reckoned in the Taisho era beginning with 1912. Thus the model 11 (1922) 6.5 mm light machine gun was adopted in 1922, the 11th year of the Taisho Era, and the Model 14 (1925) 8 mm Nambu Pistol was adopted in the last year of the Taisho Era.

Since the death of the Emperor Taisho, most Japanese weapons have been marked with the last two digits of the year since the founding of the Japanese Empire, which it is supposed took place 1660 years B.C. Thus when the Japanese heavy machine gun was adopted in 1932, that was the year 2592 of the Empire.

The Japanese year 2600, which in our system is 1940, is referred to by the last digit only, and becomes the year o, hence the name Zero for the famous Japanese fighter plane adopted in that year. Likewise 1941 is their year 2601, and items adopted then are Model 1 (1941); etc.

Many Japanese weapons are named with *Showa* numbers, giving the year and month of manufacture, starting with the accession of the present Emperor, Hirohito, who began his rule on the 26th of December 1925. The era of his reign has been given the name *Showa*, and accordingly the year of 1948 would be *Showa* 23. Thus a Nambu Pistol marked 14.5 was made in May 1935.

27. Methods of Measuring Chamber and Bore

It frequently becomes necessary to determine the shape and dimensions of the chamber of a gun, particularly when the weapon is of an unknown caliber, and it is desired to identify the cartridge for which it is chambered.

The common way to do this is by taking a cast of the chamber in melted sulphur, and then measuring this cast when it has cooled and hardened.

Plain sulphur does very well, but shrinkage during the cooling of the cast can be minimized by using the Frankford Arsenal mixture consisting of:

Sulphur ....2 ounces
Powdered Lampblack ....3 grains
Spirits of Camphor ....3 drops

The chamber and about 1 inch of the bore should be cleaned thoroughly and then be covered with a very light film of thin clean oil. Then the bore just ahead of the chamber should be stopped with a cork with a wire through it of the right length to project up through the chamber when the cork is in place. This wire is to act as a handle for the sulphur cast, which is quite brittle.

The sulphur mixture is then heated slowly, stirring it all the while, until it arrives at a thin pouring consistency. It is then poured into the chamber quickly, and allowed to cool before it is removed by shoving it out carefully with a cleaning rod. It must be handled carefully, as it will be quite brittle.

To obtain the dimensions of the chamber as well as its shape, the cast can then be measured with a micrometer. There is some shrinkage to this mixture, but not very much as will be seen from the note which follows giving the results of a test of this point made at Frankford Arsenal.

There is another method of making chamber or bore casts which avoids the danger of breakage which makes the sulphur cast something of a nuisance. This is to make them of a low melting metal alloy known as Woods metal, which is sold for this purpose by some dealers in gunsmiths' supplies. It is also available from the Cerro de Pasco Copper Co., and their distributors under the name of Cerrobend, for the purpose of filling thin walled pipes while bending them to keep the walls from collapsing.

This metal melts at 160 degrees F, which is less than the boiling point of water. It has the desirable characteristic of expanding slightly while cooling, which means that it forces itself tightly into all recesses, rifling grooves, etc., and does not shrink while cooling as sulphur does. This non-shrinking quality is due to the bismuth it contains.

Different compositions of this metal melt at different temperatures. Woods Metal, melting at 160 degrees F has the following composition:

Bismuth 38.4%   Lead 30.8%   Cadmium 15.4%   Tin 15.4%

A brass casting was bored to fit a standard plug gage 13/16 inch (.8125 inch) in diameter. Four sulphur casts were made in this hole, using the standard Frankford Arsenal sulphur, lampblack and camphor mixture given above. The casts were then held in a fixture so arranged as to allow precise measurements to be made without moving the cast. Measurements were made at intervals up to 72 hours without handling or moving the casts. Results were the same for all four samples, and were as follows:

Time after pouring	½ Hr.	1 Hr.	2 Hrs.	4 Hrs.	6 Hrs.	24 Hrs.	48 Hrs.	72 Hrs.
Size	.8125	.8115	.8105	.8102	.8102	.8095	.8085	.8085
Shrinkage	0	.0010	.0020	.0023	.0023	.0030	.0040	.0040

The test was repeated on three samples, which immediately after removing from the hole were laid on a cast iron fixture. Thus the initial cooling was at a faster rate that for the first four samples. These three samples all shrank slightly more than the others, probably due to the sudden change of temperature as the cast was placed on the cast iron fixture. Results were identical for these samples, and were:

Time after pouring	½ Hr.	1 Hr.	2 Hrs.	4 Hrs.	6 Hrs.	24 Hrs.	48 Hrs.	72 Hrs.
Size	.8115	.8105	.8102	.8101	.8101	.8090	.8080	.8080
Shrinkage	.0010	.0020	.0023	.0024	.0024	.0035	.0045	.0045

28. Reference List of Numbers Marking Changes in Gun Design or Manufacture

M-1903 rifles of Springfield Armory make. Rifles having serial numbers below 800,000 had receivers and bolts made of case hardened steel. While they were very strong to a steady pressure, they had low resistance to shock, and some of them have failed in service.

M 1903 rifles made at Rock Island. 285,507. Rifles having serial numbers below this figure had the same case hardened receivers and bolts as the early Springfields. Those having serial numbers between 285,507 and 319,921 have carbon steel receivers and bolts with an improved heat treatment. Those with numbers above 319,921 may be either nickel steel or carbon steel with the improved treatment.

M 1903 rifles made at Springfield Armory. 800,000 to 1,275,767. Rifles having serial numbers from 800,000 to 1,275,767 have a double heat treatment which gives them a hard skin to withstand wear, together with a relatively soft and highly tenacious core, which gives them tremendous strength and resistance to shock. These are the strongest and best receivers and bolts.

M 1903 and 1903 A1 rifles made at Springfield Armory. Rifles bearing serial numbers from 1,275,767 to 1,532,878 have nickel steel receivers and bolts. These have a somewhat "sticky" action, as the surface skin is not as hard as that of the double heat treated receivers and bolts. The strength of these nickel steel receivers and bolts, while less than that of those having the double heat treatment, is entirely satisfactory. I do not know of any report of one having been blown up in service, though in tests, a "destruction load" which will burst a nickel steel receiver will leave a double heat treated one unmoved.

M 1903 and M 1903 A 3 and A 4 rifles. Rifles bearing serial numbers from 3,000,000 to 5,784,000 inclusive were made during World War II by the Remington Arms Co., or by the L. C. Smith-Corona Typewriter Co. These have chrome nickel steel receivers and bolts.

Colt Woodsman pistols. Pistols below number 83,790 originally had mainspring housings intended for low speed ammunition. Those above this number have specially heat treated mainspring housings intended to withstand the higher shock of the stronger ammunition. New housings may be fitted to old pistols. The type of housing may be determined by the type of cross milling on the thumb spot on the rear of the housing. The old type is checkered, while the new type is milled straight across with parallel lines.

Colt automatic pistols .380 caliber. Pistols below number 98,894 do not have the magazine safety. Those of later serial numbers do. That is, they cannot be fired unless the magazine is in place.

Colt .25 Caliber automatic pistols. Pistols with serial numbers less than 141,000 do not have the magazine safety.

Colt .32 caliber automatic pistols. Pistols with serial numbers below 468,097 do not have the magazine safety.

Colt Single Action Army Revolvers. Revolvers up to number 160,000 should be used with black powder only. After this number, they have heat treated cylinders designed to use smokeless loads.

Smith & Wesson .38 M. & P. The weapon with number 241,706 was the first to have the Patent Safety Hammer Block.

Colt Woodsman pistols made before 1947 do not have the magazine safety.

29. Overloads in Revolvers

In 1914 a commission was sent to Cuba by duPont to investigate trouble reported from bursting of .45 caliber revolvers.

It was found that two bullets loaded in the same case would burst the revolver, also it was found that a double charge of powder would burst the revolver. The standard charge was 5.91 grains of Bullseye No. 2, and the commission experimented with overloads of 1, 2, 3, 4, 5, and 6 grains in addition to the regular charge.

With 5 grs. overload, total 10.91 grs. 1 revolver burst on the 3rd shot
With 5 grs. overload, total 10.91 grs. 1 revolver burst on the 4th shot
With 6 grs. overload, total 11.91 grs. 1 revolver burst on the 4th shot
With 6 grs. overload, total 11.91 grs. 1 revolver burst on the 3rd shot

30. Target Measurements

Mean Radius is the average distance of all the shots from the center of the group. It is usually about one third the group diameter.

To obtain the mean radius of a shot group, measure the heights of all shots above an arbitrarily chosen horizontal line. Average these measurements. The result is the height of the center of the group above the chosen line. Then in the same way get the horizontal distance of the center from some vertical line, such as for instance, the left edge of the target. These two measurements will locate the group center.

Now measure the distance of each shot from this center. The average of these measurements is the Mean Radius.

Group Diameter. The distance between the centers of the two most widely separated shots in the group.

Figure of Merit. A method adopted by the Ordnance Department in 1923 for evaluating very small groups. It is obtained as follows: Draw a vertical line through the lowest shot in the group, also through the shot furthest to the left. Add the distance from the bottom line to the highest shot to that from the vertical line to the shot furthest to the right. Divide by two.

Extreme Vertical. For the 1929 Ammunition Tests, the Ammunition Board adopted the Extreme Vertical, or the vertical distance between the highest and the lowest shot as the measure of ammunition performance.

31. Weights of Weapons

The weight of a rifle or other small arm is an important part of the description, but it is not a fixed and unvarying quantity, as the wood of the stock varies greatly in density from one gun to the next, so that the quoted weight of a rifle should be considered as an average.

The weight of the regular issue stocks for the Springfield M 1903 or the Garand M1 may vary from one to the next as much as a pound and a half, though the usual variation is much less.

My own three Springfields, as issued, weigh as follows:

Regular M 1903, with straight stock 8 lbs. 4 oz.

1903 A 1, with pistol grip stock, 9 lbs. 6 oz.

1903 A 3, made by Smith-Corona 8 lbs. 6 oz.

32. Weights and Measures, English and Metric

While the English speaking countries use the foot, pound and gallon as fundamental units of length, weight, and measure, most other countries use a decimal system based on the meter, which was intended to be a millionth of the quarter circumference of the Earth, but actually after it was established as a standard, was found to have missed this intended length by a small percentage.

The Metric System, besides being a decimal system, has all the various series such as length, weight, etc., connected together by the fact that the unit of weight is the weight of a cube of water at maximum density one hundredth of a meter on a side, called the gram, and the unit of volume is the volume of a cube one tenth of a meter on a side, called the liter.

UNITS OF LENGTH

In the English System, the unit of length is the foot, which is related to the other units of length in the same system as shown below:

12 inches = 1 foot
36 inches = 3 feet = 1 yard
5280 feet = 1760 yards = 1 mile

In the Metric System the fundamental unit of length is the meter, which is 39.37 inches or 3.2808 feet or 1.0936 yards. It will be seen that it is roughly 3 feet, 3 inches, and 3 tenths, which is a good way to remember it, though actually four tenths is closer. It is also about a yard and a tenth, which is handy to remember when on the range.

10 millimeters = 1 centimeter
100 millimeters = 10 centimeters = 1 **decimeter**
1000 millimeters = 100 centimeters = 10 decimeters = 1 meter
1000 meters = 1 kilometer

UNITS OF WEIGHT

In the British System the pound is the basic unit of weight, but there are three kinds of pound. For weighing ordinary merchandise, the avoirdupois pound, of 7000 grains of 16 ounces is used. The troy pound is used for weighing gold and silver, and the apothecaries pound for weighing drugs, etc. Both these have 5,760 grains and 12 ounces, but the lesser subdivisions differ.

It is indeed fortunate that the grain is the same in all three of the pounds used in the British System.

For large weights, the ton is used, but there are two kinds of ton; the long or gross ton of 2240 lbs., which is the kind used in ballistics, and the short or net ton, of 2000 lbs.

Avoirdupois Weight

24.34375 grains	= 1 dram
16 drams or 437.5 grains	= 1 ounce
16 ounces or 7000 grains	= 1 lb.
14 lbs.	= 1 stone
2 stone or 28 lbs.	= 1 quarter
4 quarters or 112 lbs.	= 1 hundredweight (cwt.)
20 cwt. or 2240 lbs.	= 1 ton (long or gross ton)
2000 lbs.	= 1 short ton (Net ton)

Note: The stone and quarter are commonly used in Great Britain but not in the U. S.

Troy Weight

24 grains	= 1 pennyweight (dwt.)
20 pennyweight or 480 gr.	= 1 ounce
12 ounces or 5760 gr.	= 1 pound

Apothecaries Weight

20 grains	= 1 scruple (Ɔ)
3 scruples, or 60 gr.	= 1 drachm (ʒ)
8 drachms or 480 gr.	= 1 ounce (℥)
12 ounces or 5,760 gr.	= 1 pound (lb.)

In the Metric System the fundamental unit of weight is the gram, which was intended to be exactly, and very nearly is, the weight in vacuum of a cubic centimeter of pure water at maximum density. It is equal to 15.432 grains. The other units are shown below:

1000 milligrams	= 1 gram
1000 grams	= 1 kilogram
1000 kilograms	= 1 tonne or metric ton

The pressure of the atmosphere, or 14.7 lbs. per sq. inch is often used as a measure of powder pressures, and is abbreviated as *atm*. In the Metric System, the unit of pressure, 1 kilogram per square centimeter, or 14.223 lbs. per square inch is sometimes called a Technical Atmosphere, abbreviated as *at*.

Comparative Tables of Weights

```
1 grain       =      64.9 milligrams =    .0649 gram
1 dram        =      1770 milligrams =    1.77  gram
1 ounce       =     28350 milligrams =   28.35  gram
1 pound       =                      =  453.59  gram =     .453 kg
1 long ton    =                                      = 1016.  kg = 1.016 tonne.
1 short ton   =                                      =  907.  kg =  .907 tonne.
1 milligram   =     .0154 grain
1 gram        =    15.432 grain =   .0353 oz.
1 kilogram    =     15432 grain =   35.3  oz. =    2.2046 lb.
1 tonne       =                               =    2204.6 lb. =  .9842 long ton
1 tonne       =                               =    2204.6 lb. = 1.023  short ton
1 lb per. sq. inch  =      .0703 kg. per sq. cm.
1 ton per sq. inch  =     157.49 kg. per sq. cm.
1 foot pound  =            .1382 kg meter
1 foot ton    =           309.7  kg. meter  =  .3097 meter ton.
1 atmosphere (14.7 lbs. per sq. in.)        = 1.033 technical atmosphere
1 kg. per sq. cm. = 14.233 lbs per sq. in. = .00635 tons per sq. in. = .967 atm.
1 kg. meter   =     7.234 ft. lbs.
1 meter tonne =     3.229 ft. tons.
```

CONVERSION FACTORS

To convert				
Grains	to Milligrams	multiply by	64.9	or divide by .0154
Grains	to Grams	multiply by	.0649	or divide by 15.43
Ounces	to Grams	multiply by	28.35	or divide by .0353
Pounds	to Kilograms	multiply by	.453	or divide by 2.205
Long Tons	to Kilograms	multiply by	1016	or divide by .000984
Short Tons	to Kilograms	multiply by	907	or divide by .001023
Milligrams	to Grains	multiply by	.0154	or divide by 64.9
Grams	to Grains	multiply by	15.432	or divide by .0649
Kilograms	to pounds	multiply by	2.205	or divide by .453
Tonnes	to Long Tons	multiply by	.9842	or divide by 1.016
Tonnes	to Short Tons	multiply by	1.023	or divide by .907
Ft. per sec.	to Meters per sec.	multiply by	.3048	or divide by 3.28
Foot pounds	to Kilogram Meters	multiply by	.1382	or divide by 7.234
Lbs. per sq. in.	to Kgs. per sq. cm.	multiply by	.0703	or divide by 14.223
Meters per sec.	to Feet per sec.	multiply by	3.28	or divide by .3048
Kilogram Meters	to Foot pounds	multiply by	7.234	or divide by .1382
Kgs. per sq. cm.	to Lbs. per sq. in.	multiply by	14.223	or divide by .0703

1 inch   = .0254 m.   = 2.54 cm. = 25.4 mm.
1 foot   = .3048 m.   = 30.48 cm. = 304.8 mm.
1 yard   = .9144 m.   = 91.44 cm.
1 mile   = 1.6093 km. = 1609.3 m.

1 sq. in.   =   =   6.45 sq. cm. 645.2 sq. mm.
1 sq. ft.   = .0929 sq. m. = 929   sq. cm.
1 cu. in.   = 16.387 c. c.

1 mm.   =   .03937 in.
1 cm.   =   .3937   in. =   .0328 ft.
1 m.   = 39.37   in. =   3.2808 ft. =   1.0936 yds.
1 km.   = 3280.8   ft. = 1093.6   yds. = .6214 mi.

1 sq. cm.   = .155729 sq. in.
1 sq. m.   = 10.765 sq. ft.

1 c. c.   = .061024 cu. in.

To convert

Inches	to Millimeters	Multiply by 25.4	or divide by	.03937
Inches	to Centimeters	Multiply by 2.54	or divide by	.3937
Feet	to Centimeters	Multiply by 30.48	or divide by	.0328
Feet	to Meters	Multiply by .3048	or divide by	3.2808
Yards	to Meters	Multiply by .9144	or divide by	1.0936
Miles	to Kilometers	Multiply by 1.609	or divide by	.6214
Sq. Ins.	to Sq. Cms.	Multiply by 6.45	or divide by	.155729
Cu. Ins.	to Cubic Cms.	Multiply by 16.387	or divide by	.061024

To convert millimeters, centimeters, etc., to inches etc., reverse the above table, multiplying where division is indicated, and dividing where multiplication is indicated. For example, to convert Millimeters to Inches, Divide by 25.4 or multiply by .03937.

In many cases multiplication or division may be avoided by reference to the following tables:

LENGTHS—MILLIMETERS TO DECIMALS OF AN INCH
From 1 to 100 Units

Millimeters	0	1	2	3	4	5	6	7	8	9
0	0	.03937	.07874	.11811	.15748	.19685	.23622	.27559	.31496	.35433
10	.39370	.43307	.47244	.51181	.55118	.59055	.62992	.66929	.70866	.74803
20	.78740	.82677	.86614	.90551	.94488	.98425	1.02362	1.06299	1.10236	1.14173
30	1.18110	1.22047	1.25984	1.29921	1.33858	1.37795	1.41732	1.45669	1.49606	1.53543
40	1.57480	1.61417	1.65354	1.69291	1.73228	1.77165	1.81102	1.85039	1.88976	1.92913
50	1.96850	2.00787	2.04724	2.08661	2.12598	2.16535	2.20472	2.24409	2.28346	2.32283
60	2.36220	2.40157	2.44094	2.48031	2.57982	2.51968	2.59842	2.63779	2.67716	2.71653
70	2.75590	2.79527	2.83464	2.87401	2.91338	2.95275	2.99212	3.03149	3.07086	3.11023
80	3.14960	3.18897	3.22834	3.26771	3.30708	3.34645	3.38582	3.42519	3.46456	3.50393
90	3.54330	3.58267	3.62204	3.66141	3.70078	3.74015	3.77952	3.81889	3.85826	3.89763

LENGTHS—HUNDREDTHS OF AN INCH TO MILLIMETERS
From 1 to 100 Hundredths

Hundredths of an Inch	0	1	2	3	4	5	6	7	8	9
0	0	.254	.508	.762	1.016	1.270	1.524	1.778	2.032	2.286
10	2.540	2.794	3.048	3.302	3.556	3.810	4.064	4.318	4.572	4.826
20	5.080	5.334	5.588	5.842	6.096	6.350	6.604	6.858	7.112	7.366
30	7.620	7.874	8.128	8.382	8.636	8.890	9.144	9.398	9.652	9.906
40	10.160	10.414	10.668	10.922	11.176	11.430	11.684	11.938	12.192	12.446
50	12.700	12.954	13.208	13.462	13.716	13.970	14.224	14.478	14.732	14.986
60	15.240	15.494	15.748	16.002	16.256	16.510	16.764	17.018	17.272	17.526
70	17.780	18.034	18.288	18.542	18.796	19.050	19.304	19.558	19.812	20.066
80	20.320	20.574	20.828	21.082	21.336	21.590	21.844	22.098	22.352	22.606
90	22.860	23.114	23.368	23.622	23.876	24.130	24.384	24.638	24.892	25.146

LIQUID MEASURE

The English Imperial Gallon is the volume of ten pounds of distilled water at 62 degrees F. It contains 277.27 cubic inches or 4.5436 liters, and is very nearly 1.2 U. S. Gallons.

The U. S. Gallon contains 231 cubic inches, or 3.7853 liters. It is almost exactly equal to the contents of a cylinder seven inches in diameter and six inches high.

The Liter, which is the metric unit of volume, is 1000 cubic centimeters. It is equal to 61.024 cubic inches.

1 gallon = 4 quarts = 8 pints
        1 quart = 2 pints
1 cubic foot = 7.48 U. S. Gallons
1 liter   = 2.1134 U. S. pints = 1.0567 quarts = .26417 U. S.
1 U. S. gallon = 3.7853 Liters   Gallons
1 U. S. quart = .9463 Liter
1 U. S. pint = .4731 Liter

To convert:
U. S. quarts to Liters   multiply by .9463   or divide by 1.0567
U. S. gallons to Liters   multiply by 3.7853 'or divide by .26417
Liters to   U.S. quarts multiply by 1.0567 or divide by .9436
Liters to   U.S. gallons multiply by .26417 or divide by 3.7853

33. American and Foreign Caliber Equivalents

The caliber of a gun is supposed to be the diameter of the *bore* of the gun in hundredths of an inch or in milimeters. The diameter of the *bullet* is usually some .008 inch larger, to fill the grooves of the rifling. However, the S. & W. .357 Magnum is named from the diameter of the bullet, not the bore, to distinguish it from the other bullets of the same diameter, called .38 caliber.

There are a number of other anomalies in the caliber designations of guns and cartridges. For example, the .303 Savage and the .32-20 are really .30 caliber guns and the .32 pistols and revolvers are really .304 to .305. .38 Pistols and revolvers are just under .35 caliber, except for the .38-40, which is nearly .40 caliber, and is just the same size as the .41 Colt.

To add considerably to the confusion, the different makers vary considerably from one to the other, in spite of the fact that they have an organization which is supposed to standardize these dimensions.

The table which follows gives the American caliber name, the representative average bore diameter both in inches and in millimeters, and the caliber name in the Metric system, when such a name is commonly used, for a number of popular weapons and their cartridges. Owing to the variation between the various makers, as well as the wide tolerances used by some of them, weapons will often be seen which may differ somewhat from these exact figures.

American Caliber Name	Average Bore Diameter, Inches	Same Bore Diameter in Millimeters Caliber	Name in Millimeters
.22 Rim Fire	.212—.218	5.38—5.53	5.6 mm
6 mm U.S.N.	.236	6.0	6 mm
.25 A.C.P.	.244	6.20	6.35 mm Pistol
.250/3000	.250	6.35	
.25 Remington	.250	6.35	
6.5 mm Mannlicher	.256	6.5	6.5 mm Mannlicher
.270 Winchester	.270	6.86	
7 mm	.276	7.0	7 mm Mauser
.30-30; .30 W.C.F.; 30 Rem.	.300	7.62	
.30-U.S. Army (.30-40 Krag)	.300	7.62	
.30-'06 (.30 U. S. Gov't)	.300	7.62	
.303 Savage	.300	7.62	
.32-20 (.32 W.C.F.)	.300	7.62	
7.63 mm Mauser Pistol	.3005	7.63	7.63 mm Mauser Pistol
7.65 mm Luger	.3001	7.65	7.65 mm Luger
.303 British	.303	7.7	7.7 mm
.32 A.C.P.	.3045	7.73	7.65 mm Pistol
.32 Colt and S. & W.	.3045	7.73	
8 mm Mauser	.312	7.92	7.92 or 7.9 mm
.32 Win. Spl.; .32 Rem.	.315	8.0	
.38 Colt and S. & W.	.3465	8.8	
.380 A.C.P.	.3475	8.83	9 mm Short
.38 A.C.P.	.3475	8.83	
9 mm Luger	.3475	8.83 *	9 mm Parabellum
.38 S. & W. Spl.	.3485	8.85	
.357 Magnum	.3475	8.85	
.38-40 (.38 W.C.F.)	.3945	10.02	
.41 Colt	.3945	10.02	
.44 S. & W. Spl.	.4185	10.62	
.45 A.C.P.	.443	11.25	11.25 mm Pistol
.455 Eley	.444	11.27	
.455 Webley & Scott Self-loading	.4505	11.44	

* Most of the Lugers that I have owned have been marked on the bottom of the barrel to indicate the exact bore size of that particular barrel. I have owned Lugers marked 8.1, 8.2, 8.3, and 8.4, indicating a range of bore sizes from .3468 inch to .3480 inch.

34. Value of $\dfrac{\delta_1}{\delta}$ For Temperature and Pressure; of Atmosphere Two Thirds Saturated With Moisture

F.	28 in.	29 in.	30 in.	31 in.	F.	28 in.	29 in.	30 in.	31 in.
0	0.945	0.912	0.882	0.853	51	1.052	1.016	.982	.951
1	.947	.914	.884	.855	52	1.054	1.018	.984	.953
2	.949	.916	.886	.857	53	1.056	1.020	.986	.954
3	.951	.918	.888	.859	54	1.058	1.022	.988	.956
4	.953	.920	.890	.861	55	1.061	1.024	.990	.958
5	.955	.922	.892	.863	56	1.063	1.026	.992	.960
6	.957	.924	.893	.865	57	1.065	1.028	.994	.962
7	.959	.926	.895	.867	58	1.067	1.030	.996	.964
8	.962	.928	.897	.869	59	1.069	1.032	.998	.966
9	.964	.930	.899	.870	60	1.071	1.034	1.000	.968
10	.966	.932	.901	.872	61	1.073	1.037	1.002	.970
11	.968	.935	.903	.874	62	1.075	1.039	1.004	.972
12	.970	.937	.905	.876	63	1.078	1.041	1.006	.974
13	.972	.939	.907	.878	64	1.080	1.043	1.008	.975
14	.974	.941	.909	.880	65	1.082	1.045	1.010	.977
15	.976	.943	.911	.882	66	1.084	1.047	1.012	.979
16	.978	.945	.913	.884	67	1.086	1.049	1.014	.981
17	.981	.947	.915	.886	68	1.088	1.051	1.016	.983
18	.983	.949	.917	.888	69	1.090	1.053	1.018	.985
19	.985	.951	.919	.890	70	1.092	1.055	1.020	.987
20	.987	.953	.921	.891	71	1.094	1.057	1.022	.989
21	.989	.955	.923	.893	72	1.097	1.059	1.024	.991
22	.991	.957	.925	.895	73	1.099	1.061	1.025	.993
23	0.993	0.959	0.927	0.897	74	1.101	1.063	1.027	0.995
24	.995	.961	.929	.899	75	1.103	1.065	1.029	.996
25	.997	.963	.931	.901	76	1.105	1.067	1.031	.998
26	1.000	.965	.933	.903	77	1.107	1.069	1.033	1.000
27	1.002	.967	.935	.905	78	1.109	1.071	1.035	1.002
28	1.004	.969	.937	.907	79	1.111	1.073	1.037	1.004
29	1.006	.971	.939	.909	80	1.113	1.075	1.039	1.006
30	1.008	.973	.941	.911	81	1.116	1.077	1.041	1.008
31	1.010	.975	.943	.912	82	1.118	1.079	1.043	1.010
32	1.012	.977	.945	.914	83	1.120	1.081	1.045	1.012
33	1.014	.979	.947	.916	84	1.122	1.083	1.047	1.014
34	1.016	.981	.949	.918	85	1.124	1.085	1.049	1.016
35	1.018	.983	.951	.920	86	1.126	1.088	1.051	1.017
36	1.021	.986	.953	.922	87	1.128	1.090	1.053	1.019
37	1.023	.988	.955	.924	88	1.130	1.092	1.055	1.021
38	1.025	.990	.957	.926	89	1.132	1.094	1.057	1.023
39	1.027	.992	.958	.928	90	1.135	1.096	1.059	1.025
40	1.029	.994	.960	.930	91	1.137	1.098	1.061	1.027
41	1.031	.996	.962	.932	92	1.139	1.100	1.063	1.029
42	1.033	.998	.964	.933	93	1.141	1.102	1.065	1.031
43	1.035	1.000	.966	.935	94	1.143	1.104	1.067	1.033
44	1.037	1.002	.968	.937	95	1.145	1.106	1.069	1.035
45	1.040	1.004	.970	.939	96	1.147	1.108	1.071	1.037
46	1.042	1.006	0.972	0.941	97	1.149	1.110	1.073	1.038
47	1.044	1.008	.974	.943	98	1.151	1.112	1.075	1.040
48	1.046	1.010	.976	.945	99	1.154	1.114	1.077	1.042
49	1.048	1.012	.978	.947	100	1.156	1.116	1.079	1.044
50	1.050	1.014	.980	.949					

35. Cartridge Dimension and Identification Tables

There are so many standard factory loaded rifle cartridges, and they are so similar in appearance and dimensions that even when a sample cartridge is known to be a standard factory load, it is sometimes a difficult matter to identify it unless the markings on the head give the caliber and type.

In recent years it has become a popular practice for individual gunsmiths or experimentors to modify standard factory cartridges by blowing them up to fit a larger chamber, or by necking them down to fit a smaller bullet. As these "wildcats" are usually made from factory loads, the markings on the case head then become meaningless, and would mislead anyone except an expert.

With the idea of aiding in the identification of cartridges, a number of standard dimensions of factory loaded cartridges have been set down below. These were prepared by first measuring a number of actual samples, then consulting such standard factory drawings as were available. Generally the actual dimensions found by measurement will differ somewhat from those given on the drawings, because a small tolerance, or variation from the exact figures is allowed as a practical manufacturing necessity.

Most modern center fire rifle cartridges are divided into the four classes of Rimmed, Rimless, Semi-rimmed, and Belted, which can easily be distinguished by simple inspection. By first placing the cartridge into the proper one of these classes the field to be examined is at once narrowed considerably.

Next the cartridge should be classified by caliber, as indicated by the bullet diameter. Caliber is the diameter of the unrifled bore of a gun in hundredths of an inch or in millimeters, and the bullet diameter is usually from .004 to .008 inch or more. Thus the U. S. Rifle Caliber .30, M1903 has a bore of .300, with grooves .004 deep, giving a groove diameter of .308, and the usual bullet diameter is .3086. It should be remembered that the caliber is the diameter of the bore, not that of the bullet. It is therefore usually .004 to .008 less than the bullet diameter.

The overall length of a cartridge is not a very definite measurement, as it varies greatly with the type of bullet, so it is not of much use for identification. For example, the .375 H & H Magnum with 235 grain Open Point Expanding bullet has an overall length of 3.515 inches, while with the 270 or 300 grain Round Nose Soft Point bullet it has an overall length of 3.600".

The case length, however, is quite constant, and should be the second dimension consulted. If the matter is still in doubt, go to the rim diameter next. This is, of course, the diameter of the extracting rim at the extreme rear end of the cartridge case.

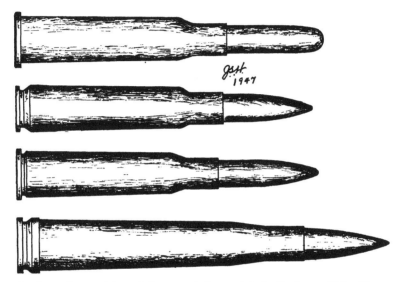

The four classes, (rim, rimless, semi-rim, and belted), into which rifle cartridges may be separated by casual inspection.

Top, a typical rimmed cartridge, the 6.5mm Dutch.

Second, the rimless 6.5mm Italian cartridge.

Third, the semi-rim 6.5mm Japanese cartridge.

Bottom, the belted .300 Holland & Holland Magnum.

Rimmed Cartridges

Cartridge name	Overall length	Case length, inches;	Case length, MM.	Body length head to shoulder	Rim diam.	Case diam. at rear	Shoulder diamerer	Neck diam.	Bullet diam.
5.5 mm Velo Dog	1.375	1.125	28.5	*	.306	.253	*	.250	.225
.218 Bee	1.68	1.345	34	.942	.408	.349	.331	.242	.2245
.22 Hornet	1.72	1.40	35.5	.825	.350	.299	.278	.244	.2235
.219 Zipper	2.260	1.938	50	1.36	.506	.421	.364	.252	.2245
.22 Sav. Hi-Power	2.51	2.05	52	1.39	.506	.461	.357	.253	.227
.25-20 Winchester	1.6	1.33	33.5	.828	.405	.349	.329	.274	.258
.20-20 Single Shot	1.8	1.633	42	1.1	.407	.315	.300	.276	.259
.25-35	2.55	2.04	52	1.37	.499	.420	.355	.280	.258
6.5 mm Netherlands	3.05	2.112	54	1.6	.526	.448	.421	.345	.263
.25-25	2.625	2.375	60.5	*	.380	.300	*	.280	.258
.30 W. C. F. (.30-30)	2.53	2.03	52	1.43	.502	.418	.402	.328	.308
7.62 Russian	3.037	2.114	54	1.475	.570	.489	.450	.336	.310
303 British	3.05	2.21	56	1.80	.530	.458	.402	.337	.312
30-40 Krag	3.089	2.314	60	1.7	.545	.457	.415	.338	.308
.32 W. C. F. (.32-20)	1.59	1.315	33.5	.903	.405	.353	.338	.326	.312
8.15 x 46 R	2.426	1.81	46	*	.481	.419	*	.344	.330
8 mm Austrian	3.000	1.99	50	1.514	.554	.492	.462	.345	.323
8 mm Lebel	2.967	1.99	50	1.457	.634	.543	.456	.350	.323
.32 Win. Spl.	2.55	2.06	52.5	1.44	.500	.419	.396	.340	.318
.32-40 Winchester	2.500	2.193	56	*	.506	.424	*	.338	.321
8 x 57 R	3.55	2.24	57	1.84	.486	.429	.375	.326	.318
8 mm Danish Krag	3.00	2.281	58	1.635	.575	.550	.457	.355	.325
.33 Winchester	2.795	2.105	53.5	1.570	.610	.508	.443	.365	.3385
.348 Winchester	2.795	2.255	57.5	1.650	.610	.553	.485	.375	.348

Rimmed Cartridges

Cartridge name	Overall length	Case length, inches	Case length, MM.	Body length head to shoulder	Rim diam.	Case diam. at rear	Shoulder diameter	Neck diam.	Bullet diam.
.38 W.C.F. (.38-40)	1.595	1.307	33	.908	.518	.466	.430	.414	.400
.38-56	2.600	2.112	44	1.210	.603	.500	.442	.402	.375
.38-55 Winchester	2.487	2.129	54	*	.506	.420	*	.392	.3775
9.3 x 72 R	3.410	2.834	72	*	.483	.426	*	.384	.3675
.40-60	2.250	1.875	48	*	.618	.503	*	.426	.408
.40-82 W. C. F.	2.765	2.390	61	1.67	.610	.508	.457	.427	.408
.405 W. C. F.	3.175	2.583	66	*	.543	.461	*	.436	.4115
.44 W. C. F. (.44-40)	1.592	1.305	33	*	.525	.471	*	.443	.429
.45-70	2.55	2.15	54	*	.600	.500	*	.475	.457
.45-85	2.80	2.40	61	*	.602	.502	*	.475	.457
Belted Cartridges									
.300 H&H Magnum	3.600	2.850	72	2.41	.532	.513	.430	.338	.3088
.375 H&H Magnum	3.600	2.85	72	2.41	.532	.513	.430	.404	.3755
Semi-Rimmed Cartridges									
6.5 mm Japanese	3.00	2.00	51	1.58	.476	.449	.414	.291	.262
.280 Ross	3.48	2.64	66	2.185	.556	.523	.404	.323	.286
.303 Savage	2.52	2.015	51	1.300	.505	.442	.390	.333	.308
7.7 Jap. Hvy M. G.	3.15	2.280	58	1.89	.499	.471	.431	.338	.311
.32 Win. S. L.	1.88	1.24	33	*	.390	.349	*	.347	.322
.35 Win. S. L.	1.65	1.154	29	*	.405	.381	*	.377	.351
.351 Win. S. L.	1.90	1.38	35	*	.410	.380	*	.377	.352
.401 Win. S. L.	2.005	1.50	38	*	.490	.433	*	.432	.407
Rimless Cartridges									
.220 Swift	2.68	2.20	56	1.75	.472	.443	.392	.260	.224
5.6 mm Vom Hofe Super Express ...	3.148	2.40	61	1.73	.477	.479	.450	.258	.226

Cartridge									
6 mm U. S. N.	3.11	2.36	60	1.76	.443	.440	.394	.276	.2435
.250-3000 Savage	2.515	1.912	49	1.52	.470	.4086	.405	.2856	.257
.25 Remington	2.53	2.05	52	1.50	.419	.417	.396	.286	.258
6.5 mm Italian	3.00	2.06	52.5	1.64	.447	.447	.425	.295	.2655
6.5 mm Mannlicher	3.02	2.12	54	1.69	.450	.447	.425	.295	.2625
6.5 mm Norway Krag	3.145	2.158	55	1.7	.479	.478	.430	.281	.262
6.5 Swedish	3.09	2.16	55	1.76	.477	.471	.431	.297	.264
6.5 x 57 mm Mauser	3.27	2.23	57	1.72	.464	.4065	.431	.296	.262
.257 Rem. Roberts	2.750	2.233	57	1.72	.473	.471	.425	.290	.2575
.276 Pedersen	2.84	2.02	51	1.68	.447	.448	.383	.311	.284
7 x 57 mm Mauser	3.00	2.235	57	1.71	.474	.471	.420	.320	.284
.270 W. C. F.	3.340	2.540	63	1.949	.473	.470	.441	.308	.278
.30 U. S. Carbine M1	1.67	1.288	33	•	.356	.354	•	.331	.308
.300 Savage	2.62	1.87	47.5	1.55	.468	.468	.443	.333	.308
.30 Remington	2.51	2.05	52	1.50	.418	.417	.396	.329	.307
7.5 mm French M29	2.995	2.124	54	1.7	.484	.481	.438	.341	.307
7.54 mm Swiss	3.044	2.19	56	1.75	.495	.494	.452	.335	.3065
7.65 mm Belgian	3.04	2.10	53.5	1.76	.472	.471	.411	.341	.310
7.7 mm Japanese	3.15	2.28	58	1.89	.474	.472	.431	.338	.311
.30-'06 U. S. Gov't	3.330	2.494	63	1.942	.469	.466	.433	.336	.3086
.30 Newton	3.356	2.495	63	2.000	.52	.525	.503	.340	.3075
7.9 Ger. Carbine	1.85	1.298	33	.955	.469	.469	.440	.352	.323
8 x 51 Short Smokeless	2.77	2.01	51	1.525	.467	.467	.430	.344	.318
.32 Remington	2.54	2.06	52	1.51	.418	.418	.394	.341	.321
8 x 56 mm Mannlicher-Schoenauer	3.040	2.218	56	1.71	.473	.467	.423	.351	.323
7.9 mm (8 mm) Mauser	3.17	2.24	57	1.82	.473	.470	.433	.349	.323
.35 Remington	2.52	1.92	49	1.53	.457	.454	.419	.4045	.359
9 x 56 mm Mann.-Sch.	3.56	2.215	56	1.832	.464	.464	.408	.378	.354
10.75 x 68	3.16	2.669	68	2.073	.488	.492	.470	.445	.422

*Case has no shoulder.

(See supplemental information on page 509).

Standard Headspace Dimensions for Various Cartridges

Rimmed Cartridges. These have heads, or rims, which are larger in diameter than the main body of the cartridge. When such a cartridge is seated in the chamber of a gun, the rim is what limits its forward motion and holds it in firing position. A space or opening must of course be provided between the front of the breech block or bolt and the rear of the barrel, for the cartridge rim to fit into, and this opening is called the headspace. Standard figures for rim thickness, headspace, bore diameter* and bullet diameter for various well known rifle cartridges are given below.

Name of cartridge	Rim thickness, Max.	Headspace Minimum	Maximum	Standard Bore Diameter	Bullet Diameter
.22 Long Rifle Rim Fire	.044″	.044″ —	.046″	.217″	.225″
.218 Bee	.065″	.065″ —	.069″	.219″	.2245″
.219 Zipper	.063″	.063″ —	.067″	.219″	.2245″
.22 Hornet	.065″	.065″ —	.069″	.217″	.2235″
.22 Savage Hi-Power	.063″	.065″ —	.069″	.221″	.226″
.25-35 W. C. F.	.063″	.063″ —	.067″	.250″	.258″
.30 W. C. F. (.30-30)	.063″	.063″ —	.067″	.300″	.308″
.30-40 Krag.	.064″	.064″ —	.067″	.300″	.3088″
7.62 mm Russian.	.064″	.064″ —	.068″	.300″	.310″
.303 Savage	.063″	.065″ —	.069″	.300″	.308″
.303 British	.063″	.064″ —	.067″	.303″	.312″
.32 W. C. F. (.32-20)	.065″	.065″ —	.069″	.305″	.311″
.32 Win. Spl.	.063″	.063″ —	.067″	.315″	.322″
.32-40 Winchester	.063″	.063″ —	.067″	.315″	.321″
8 mm Lebel	.079″	.079″ —	.083″	.314″	.323″
.33 Winchester	.070″	.070″ —	.074″	.330″	.3385″
.348 Winchester	.070″	.070″ —	.074″	.340″	.348″
.35 W. C. F.	.061″	.061″ —	.064″	.350″	.359″
.38-55 Winchester	.063″	.063″ —	.067″	.373″	.3775″
.40-82 W. C. F.	.070″	.070″ —	.074″	.402″	.4221″
.405 W. C. F.	.073″	.073″ —	.076″	.405″	.4115″
.44 W. C. F. (.44-40)	.065″	.065″ —	.069″	.4225″	.428″

* Bore diameter means the diameter of the unrifled bore, and is generally the same as the caliber. There are, however, some caliber names that have been given for special reasons, which differ from this rule. For example the .257 Remington Roberts, which is really a .25 caliber was named for the bullet diameter to distinguish it from other experimental .25 caliber cartridges of similar design.

Rimless Cartridges. Many of the modern high powered rifle cartridges are made with a groove, or cannelure, for the extractor to fit into, and the rim, or head of the cartridge is no larger in diameter than the body of the case near the head. As there is no rim to limit the forward motion of such cartridges when they are pushed into the chamber of the gun, they seat, or come to rest with the forward shoulder of the cartridge case bearing against a similar tapered shoulder or cone in the chamber. When this system of seating the cartridges is used, the distance from the face of the breech block in the locked position to some definite measuring point on the conical shoulder of the chamber is called the "headspace," though in fact it is not strictly *head*space at all, but rather *cartridge* space.

Some rimless cartridges, such as the .30 caliber carbine cartridge and the .45 automatic pistol cartridge, are nearly cylindrical, and have no such shoulder. In such cartridges, the front end of the case is left square, so that it can seat against the slight ledge or shoulder at the front of the chamber.

The tabulation which follows gives the minimum headspace dimensions for some of the better known bottlenecked rimless cartridges, together with the angle of the chamber cone, the reference diameter on the cone to which the headspace is measured, and other interesting dimensions.

While only the minimum headspace is given, the maximum may in general be taken as .004″ greater than the minimum. These figures are for new guns. The headspace may be expected to increase slightly with use. If the headspace becomes excessive, the cartridges will tend to stretch or even separate.

Name of cartridge	Body taper per inch	Angle between centerline of chamber and wall of cone	Reference diameter on cone	Headspace, breech face to reference dia., min.	Bore diameter	Bullet diameter
.220 Swift*	.0282″	21°	.335″	1.806″	.219″	.2245″
.25 Remington	.015161″	23°	.375″	1.5286″	.250″	.2575″
.250-3000 Savage	.04392″	26° 30′	.347″	1.5792″	.250″	.257″
.257 Rem. Roberts	.027278″	20° 39′	.375″	1.7937″	.250″	.2575″
.270 W. C. F.	.01658″	17° 15′	.375″	2.0479″	.270″	.278″
7 mm Mauser	.027278″	20° 39′	.375″	1.7937″	.276″	.284″
.30 Remington	.015161″	23°	.3626″	1.5432″	.300″	.307″
.300 Savage	.01768″	30°	.3968″	1.5967″	.300″	.3085″
.30-'06 U. S. Gov't	.0165″	17° 13′	.4425″	1.940″	.300″	.3086″
7.9 (8 mm) Mauser	.02386″	20° 48′ 25″	.375″	1.896″	.311″	.323″
8 mm Mann.-Schoen.	.023642″	22° 04′	.375″	1.866″	.312″	.323″
.32 Remington	.015161″	23°	.375″	1.5286″	.312″	.321″
.35 Remington	.023529″	23° 25′	.4117″	1.5504″	.349″	.359″

*Note: The .220 Swift is a sort of half breed; a semi-rim cartridge which doesn't use its rim to seat on, as do all the other semi-rim cartridges, but instead leaves it hanging out in the air and seats on the shoulder instead. This cartridge was developed from the old 6 mm U. S. Navy case, with the extractor cut and rim made larger in diameter allow more metal in the head and strengthen this weak point in the case.

(See supplemental information on page 509).

Semi-Rimmed or Semi-Rimless Cartridges. At first glance these look like rimless cartridges. They have a groove, or cannelure for the extractor to hook into, and the extracting rim appears to be about the same size as the rear end of the cartridge case body. However, on close examination the rim will be found to be just slightly larger than the rear of the case body, and this slight enlargement is enough for the cartridge to seat against when it is chambered, just as the rimmed cartridge seats against the rim.

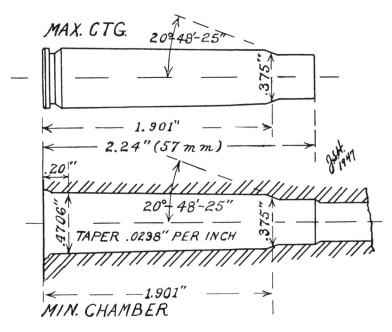

Maximum case and minimum chamber for the German service cartridge, 7.92 x 57mm J, drawn to illustrate the standard method of showing the headspace measurement in rimless bottle-necked rifle cartridges. Headspace is measured from the location of the bolt face in the locked position to a stated diameter on the cone of the chamber. In this instance, the cone has an angle of 20°-48'-25", and the .375" diameter on this cone is 1.901 inches from the bolt face when the gun has minimum headspace.

In the cartridge designation 7.92 x 57mm J, the first figure is the bore diameter, the second is the length of the case without bullet, and the J stands for Infantry (Jnfanterie), showing that it is an Army cartridge.

In semi-rim cartridges, the headspace is the distance from the face of the bolt or breechblock in the closed position to the seat against which the rim of the cartridge seats. Rim thickness and other dimensions for some semi-rim cartridges are given below.

Name of cartridge	Rim thickness	Headspace Min. Max.	Standard bore diam.	Bullet diam.
6.5 mm Japanese M 38	.06″	.060″-.064″	.256″	.262″
.280 Ross	.052″		.280″	.286″
.303 Savage	.063″	.065″-.069″	.300″	.308″
7.7 Japanese H. M. G.	.06″		.303″	.311″
.32 Win. Self Loading	.05″ max.	.05″	.315″	.322″
.35 Win. " "	.05″ "	.05″	.345″	.351″
.351 Win. " "	.05″ "	.05″	.345″	.352″
.401 Win. " "	.06″ "	.06″	.3995″	.407″

Belted Cartridges. These have a very thick seating rim, or belt, at the rear of the case, with the extractor groove cut into the rim itself. The headspace is the distance from the face of the bolt when it is locked, to the ledge in the rear part of the chamber against which the belt of the cartridge seats.

Headspace and some other dimensions are as follows:

Name of cartridge	Belt thickness Max.	Headspace Min. Max.	Bore diam.	Bullet diam.
.300 H&H Magnum ...	.220″	.220″-.223″	.300″	.3088″
.375 H&H Magnum ...	.220″	.220″-.223″	.366″	.3755″

Table of Normal Bore and Bullet Sizes

In general the bore diameters given below are intended to represent the normal minimum and the bullet diameters the normal maximum standard sizes.

The figures given below were obtained both from measurements of samples and by reference to standard drawings, checked one against the other. Wide variations between the measurements of individual samples of the same cartridge were sometimes encountered, and occasionally these measurements did not agree very well with the standard figures as given on the drawings. These discrepancies were adjusted as far as possible to give what may be taken as normal representative figures for the cartridges mentioned.

Name of cartridge	Normal minimum bore diameter	Normal maximum bullet diameter
.22 Long Rifle Rim Fire	.217″	.225″
.218 Bee	.219″	.2245″
.219 Zipper	.219″	.2245″
.22 Hornet	.217″	.2235″
.22 Savage Hi-Power	.221″	.227″
.220 Swift	.219″	.224″
5.5 mm Velo Dog	.217″	.225″
5.6 mm Vom Hofe Super Express	.220″	.226″
6 mm U. S. N.	.236″	.2435″

Name of cartridge	Normal minimum bore diameter	Normal maximum bullet diameter
.25-20 Single Shot	.250"	.256"
.25-20 Repeater	.250"	.256"
.25-25	.250"	.258"
.25-35	.250"	.258"
.25 Remington	.250"	.258"
.250-3000 Savage	.250"	.257"
.257 Remington Roberts	.250"	.2575"
6.5 x 54 mm Mannlicher	.256"	.2626"
6.5 x 57 mm Mauser	.256"	.262"
6.5 mm Japanese M 38	.256"	.262"
6.5 mm Italian Service	.256"	.2655"
6.5 mm Norwegian Krag	.256"	.262"
6.5 mm Swedish	.256"	.264"
6.5 mm Netherlands	.256"	.263"
6.5 mm Roumanian	.256"	.263"
.270 W. C. F.	.270"	.278"
.276 Pedersen	.276"	.284"
.280 Ross	.280"	.286"
7 x 57 mm Mauser	.2755"	.284"
7.5 mm French M 1929	.295"	.307"
7.54 mm Swiss	.297"	.3068"
7.65 mm Belgian	.295"	.310"
.30 W. C. F. (.30-30)	.300"	.308"
.30 Remington	.300"	.307"
.30 Cal. U. S. Carbine M1	.300"	.308"
.30-40 Krag	.300"	.3088"
.30-'06 U. S. Gov't	.300"	.3086"
.30 Newton	.300"	.3075"
.300 Savage	.300"	.308"
.300 H&H Magnum	.300"	.3088"
7.62 mm Russian	.300"	.310"
.303 Savage	.300"	.308"
.303 British	.303"	.311"
7.7 Japanese M 99	.303"	.311"
.32 W. C. F. (.32-20)	.305"	.312"
.32 Remington	.312"	.321"
.32 Winchester Special	.315"	.322"
.32-40 Winchester	.315"	.321"
.32 Winchester Self Loading	.315"	.322"
*7.9 mm (8 x 57 mm) German Spitzer	.312"	.323"
*7.9 mm (8 x 57 mm) Old, Round Nose	.312"	.318"
*8 x 57 mm Remington make for M '88 & M '98	.312"	.323"
8 x 57 R (Rimmed)	.311"	.318"
8 x 56 mm Mannlicher-Schoenauer	.312"	.323"
8 x 51 Short Smokeless	.310"	.318"
8 mm Austrian M. '95	.312"	.3228"
8 mm Danish Krag	.314"	.325"
8 mm Lebel	.314"	.323"
8.15 x 46 R	.321"	.330"-.318" (step)
.33 Winchester	.330"	.3385"

Name of cartridge	Normal minimum bore diameter	Normal maximum bullet diameter
.348 Winchester	.340″	.348″
.35 Winchester Self Loading	.345″	.351″
.351 Winchester Self Loading	.345″	.352″
.35 Remington	.349″	.359″
.375 H&H Magnum	.366″	.3755″
.38 W. C. F. (.38-40)	.394″	.400″
.38-55 Winchester	.373″	.3775″
.38-56	.370″	.375″
9 x 56 mm Mannlicher-Schoenauer	.346″	.354″
9.3 x 72 mm R	.360″	.3675″
.40-60	.400″	.407″
.40-82 W. C. F.	.402″	.408″
.401 Winchester Self Loading	.3995″	.407″
.405 W. C. F.	.405″	.4115″
.44 W. C. F. (.44-40)	.4225″	.427″
.45-70	.450″	.457″
.45-85	.450″	.4575″

*German Service Rifle M '88 has bore .312, groove diameter .321, and used the old 7.9 mm service cartridge having a bullet weighing .227 grains and with a diameter of .318. The German Service Rifle M '98 has a bore of .312 and a groove diameter of .3256, and uses the Spitzer bullet weighing 154 grains for the older flat based type, and 197.5 grains for the later boat tailed type, and both have a diameter of .323″. The hunting bullet made in America for use in both these rifles has a bullet weighing 170 grains and having a diameter of .323″.

Numerous warnings have been printed against firing the 7.9 mm Spitzer Service load in the old M '88 German Rifles, which are not as strong as the M '98 Mausers. So don't fire the German 7.9 mm Spitzer pointed service ammunition in the old Gew. '88, or in commercial rifles made on that model.

XVIII

Record of Accidents to the U.S. Rifle Cal. .30, M1903. 1917 to 1929, Incl.

During the years from 1917 to 1929 inclusive, there were 137 accidents to the U. S. Rifle, Cal. .30, M 1903 reported and made of record, the details of which are given below. These accidents were as follows:

Burst receiver 68
Blow back 23
Burst barrel due to obstruction 21
Burst barrel due to weak or seamy metal 13
Burst barrel due to burnt steel 10
Hangfire while opening bolt 1
Nature of damage not stated 1

Burst Receivers. This accident is usually caused by a failure or opening up of the cartridge head, resulting from high pressure or soft brass, thus allowing the gas under high pressure to get out into the action. If the receiver is weak or brittle, it may then rupture. These 68 burst receivers caused personal injuries as follows:

Loss of an eye .... 3 cases
Injury described as serious .... 3 "
Injury described as severe .... 3 "
Injury described as slight .... 27 "
Injury not mentioned .... 25 "
Definite report of "No Injury" .... 7 "

If shooting glasses had always been worn, it is reasonable to assume that many of these injuries would have been prevented or reduced in severity.

All but two of these accidents definitely occurred with receivers having the old heat treatment used in Springfield and Rock Island so-called low numbered receivers; that is, below No. 800,000 and No. 285,507, respectively. A Rock Island receiver reported as No. 445,136 blew up in 1918, and was later recorded in War Department records as the failure of a high numbered receiver; but it now develops that the number reported must have been in error, as the last receiver made at Rock Island in 1918 was numbered around 380,000, and receiver No. 445,136 was not made until about May, 1919. A mistake of this kind is quite easy to make, as when the receiver is shattered, the number is often blown partly or entirely off, and may have to be pieced together or more or less guessed at.

The only other case recorded as the bursting of a receiver having the improved heat treatment was Springfield receiver No. 801,540, which blew up in 1929 as the result of firing a 7.9 mm German cartridge. It is highly doubtful, however, that this was actually a receiver of the improved heat treatment, for the exact serial number of the first of the new series is not known with certainty. It is only known that this treatment was started at about the date on which receiver No. 800,000 was being made, and as over 1,000 receivers a day were being made, an error of two days in the estimated date would make the difference.

Of the 68 burst receivers reported there were 11 instances where the serial number either was not recorded or could not be ascertained with certainty. Of the remaining 57 receivers, 33 were made by Springfield and 24 by Rock Island.

Thus out of a total of 800,000 low numbered Springfield receivers, there were 33 reported burst in 13 years, or about 1 in 24,242. Of the 285,507 low numbered Rock Island receivers, there were 24 reported failures, or about 1 in 11,896. This does not of course take into account the unidentified ones, or those which may not have been reported at all.

The actual serial numbers of the receivers reported as having fractured were as follows (omitting the Rock Island receiver erroneously reported as No. 445,136, real number uncertain):

Springfield Armory Make Nos.		Rock Island Arsenal Make Nos.	
43,076	468,300	73,153	204,861
70,971	501,719	101,200	217,794
84,684	560,852	104,926	223,235
89,720	590,480	108,448	225,764
89,728	625,587	112,621	234,466
173,807	634,479	146,184	235,742
195,082	642,675	146,554	239,754
200,572	642,742	165,282	240,914
206,331	656,701	170,805	250,560
228,112	662,284	177,232	253,241
235,504	666,263	203,851	262,165
274,272	711,253		
284,086	712,763		
299,458	723,675		
312,249	770,160		
326,222	801,548		
486,640			

It is almost startling to note how sharply the failures stop about the numbers marking the change in heat treatment, that is, at approximately No. 800,000 for Springfield and No. 285,507 for Rock Island, in spite of the fact that the record continued for twelve years after this change in heat treatment went into effect.

It is also interesting to note that at least 4 of the receiver failures were due to the firing of a German 7.92 mm cartridge in the Springfield Rifle. A case will also be found where such a German cartridge was fired in a Springfield Rifle having the improved heat treatment, with no injury to the receiver.

Another fact that will bear noting is that two of the receiver failures recorded were caused by firing the guard cartridge, which is supposed to be loaded to extremely low pressure and velocity. These Guard cartridges used the regular 150 grain bullet with 9.1 grains of Bullseye Powder, to give a muzzle velocity of 1200 feet per second. The failures may have been caused by the fact that while the pressure of this small charge of Bullseye is very low, still, this is an extremely quick powder, and the unusually sudden application of the shock may have been too much for the glass-hard metal. Of course, on the other hand, a double or triple load might have occurred by some accident. This would of course give a very high pressure. However, I am inclined to lay the cause of the trouble to the sudden character of the powder rather than to high pressure, as when I investigated one of these two cases, I noted particularly that the metal showed no distortion or stretching at all, and the explosion exhibited very little energy. When the user fired the guard cartridge, the pieces of the receiver simply fell to the floor as they might have done if it had been made of glass and had been struck with a hammer.

Blow Backs. When the head of the cartridge fails as described above, and the receiver is too strong to be fractured, the escaping gas usually breaks the flanges off the front edge of the bolt, blows out or bends the extractor, and bulges the magazine well. The stock may also be more or less split and splintered around the magazine. The principal danger to the shooter is that he may get powder grains or particles of brass in the eyes; this can largely be prevented if he has on shooting glasses.

An examination of the reports shows that there were 23 accidents that were essentially cartridge head blow backs, though they are described by various terms. Many of these which occurred with receivers of the improved heat treatment would no doubt have resulted in burst receivers if the heat treatment had been of the older type. In two cases, the receivers of the improved heat treatment were damaged by such an incident. One, No. 946,508, was "deformed," while another, No. 951,718, was "bulged." However, these improved receivers held together and did not fracture.

It is not uncommon for a blow-back of the kind described above to be reported as a malfunction of the bolt, as the thin flanges at the front end of the bolt are usually broken off. For example, March 17, 1928, with rifle No. SA 276,691, it was reported that "One side of the face of bolt blown off, handle had to be driven up to extract cartridge." Again, Summer of 1927, rifle SA 201,595 "Bolt blew out, no damage to rifle proper—no mention of any injuries." This no doubt means simply that the bolt blew out around the front edges, but the wording is such that the reader might very well conclude that the entire bolt was driven out of the receiver.

Burst Barrels. Barrels may burst from firing the gun with an obstruction in the bore, which happened in 21 of the cases reported herein; from seamy, weak, or defective metal in the barrel, which happened in 13 cases; and from burnt steel in the butt end of the barrel, caused by heating the barrel blank too hot in the upsetting operation.

Unlike burst receivers, which occur only in low numbered rifles, burnt barrels usually occur only in high numbered rifles, or in low numbered guns that have been rebarrelled.

In the early Springfield production, the Armory made their own barrel blanks by rolling bars of steel in tapered rollers, so as to make the bars thinner at the muzzle end and thicker at the breech. When production was stepped up at the beginning of World War I, Springfield Armory started buying barrels from an outside source. These barrels were made by taking bars of uniform size and upsetting one end after heating it very hot, to make the thicker breech section. Some of these barrels were heated too hot in this process, with the result that the steel in the breech section was burnt, and became very weak. Several failures of this kind occurred in barrels made by the Avis Rifle Barrel Company, of New Haven, Conn. Barrels made by this company are stamped AV at the muzzle.

In the 137 accidents here reported on, burnt barrels were the cause in the guns having the following serial numbers:

Springfield Armory Make Nos.	Rock Island Arsenal Make
523,089	None
523,444	
759,943	
902,871	
1,004,623	
1,137,620	
1,145,956	
1,201,472	
1,226,267	
1,254,701	

SUMMARY OF ACCIDENTS RESULTING IN DAMAGED RECEIVERS

Rifle No.	Date	Receiver		Persons Injured	
		Heat Treatment	Type of Failure	Number	Extent of Injury
656701	7/16/1917	Old	Fractured	1	Slight
312249	7/20/1917	"	"	1	Severe
Unknown	9/19/1917	"	Shattered	1	Slight
" (2)	10/8/1917	"	Fractured	2	Slight
"	1917	"	"	1	Slight
RIA223235	9/18/1917	"	"	1	Slight
486640	1917	"	Broke		
89728	1917	"	"		
Unknown(3)	1917	"	"		
89720	8/1917	"	*Fractured*		
RIA108448	12/1917	"	Shattered		
RIA217794	1/17/1918	"	Fractured	1	Slight
RIA445136	1918	Old*	Burst		
RIA253241	1918	Old	"		
RIA262165	1918	"	"		
RIA240914	1918	"	"		
RIA239754	1918	"	"		
RIA239356	1918	"	"		
RIA225764	1918	"	"		
RIA165282	1918	"	"		
200512	6/1918	"	Shattered	1	Slight
712363	5/1918	"	Fractured	1	"
501719	2/20/18	"	Failed		
666263	2/20/19	"	Shattered	1	Not Serious
662284	2/22/19	"	"		
RIA203851	2/26/20	"	"		
RIA101200	5/23/20	"	"		
Unknown	10/24/21	"	Failed	1	Loss of Right Eye
RIA177232	5/1921	"	Shattered	1	Loss of Left Eye
326222	7/1921	"	"	0	
770160	7/13/21	"	"		
70971	8/1921	"	Fractured	1	Slight

Receiver No.	Date	Treatment	Result	No.	Severity
RIA146184	9/16/22	Old	Shattered	1	Slight
946508	1923	New	Deformed		
RIA234466	1923	Old	Shattered	0	
RIA235742	1923	"	"	1	Slight
625587	1924	"	Failed	1	"
RIA	8/1924	"	Shattered	1	Loss of Right Eye
RIA250560	10/27/23	"	"	1	Serious
284086	7/11/23	"	"	0	Slight
642742	5/9/23	"	Fractured	2	Serious
RIA104926	4/30/23	"	Shattered	4	Slight
Unknown	5/1924	"	Ruptured	1	
228112	9/15/24	"	Fractured		Slight
642675	12/5/24	"	Shattered	2	
468300	2/6/25	"	Shattered	1	Severe
195082	3/4/25	"	"	1	1 Severe, 1 Slight
206331	4/24/25	"	Fractured	2	Slight
RIA170805	6/5/25	"	Shattered	1	Severe
RIA146554	6/10/25	"	"	1	Serious
299458	11/27/25	"	Fractured	2	Slight
RIA111621	7/1/26	"	Shattered	1	Slight
84685	4/13/26	"	Fractured	1	Slight
173807	8/15/26	"	Shattered	1	Slight
RIA204801	10/21/26	"	"	1	Slight
Unknown	9/11/26	"	"	0	
43076	8/19/26	"	"	1	
560852	7/13/27	"	Fractured	0	
634479	2/3/28	"	Shattered	0	
590480	8/1928	"	Bulged	1	Slight
235501	4/21/29	"	Shattered	1	Slight
951718	5/8/29	New	Shattered	1	Slight
733675	1929	"	Shattered	1	Slight
274272	1929	"	Shattered	1	Slight
711253	8/17/29	"	Fractured		
RIA 73153	6/9/29	"	Shattered		
801548	1929	"		0	

*Evidently this number, indicating a receiver with the new heat treatment, is wrong, as the accident happened in 1918, while Rock Island Receiver No. 445136 was not made until May 1919.

July 16, 1917.

Rifle No. 656701
Reference: R 474.1/105
Location: Works of the National Brass & Copper Tube Co., Inc., Hastings-on-the-Hudson, N. Y.
Organization:
Persons Injured: One. Operator slightly scratched, bruised and scored.
Powder: Hercules K pyro D G lot 446 from Frankford Arsenal.
Nature of Failure: Splinters were broken from the edge of the bolt and the whole bolt tore back thru the pieces of the housing, including the cutoff and ejector. These were recovered. The smaller bits went thru the roof and window into the river. The face of the ejector was dented and fused and highly polished, on the extreme end. The barrel and bore were intact, the empty case from the clip cannelure forward, remained in the chamber. The bolt cut the whole receiver housing clearly away on top and the gas opened the bottom of the magazine and ripped the walnut stock away on the left side. *The line of cleavage ran thru the vent hole in the extractor chamber at the right of the rear end of the barrel and thru the pin hole directly below the ejector.* Very diverse steel structure was apparent on every broken edge. This rifle had only fired 252 rounds in all and only 28 since it had last been "doped" with a solution to remove fouling.
Note: Rifle burst while in use for proof of .30 cal. ball cartridges. (Extracted from report submitted by Mr. L. D. Van Aken, Supt. National Brass & Copper Tube Co., Inc.)
Probable Cause: It is the judgment of every one who has seen the broken edges of the receiver housing that the steel is most emphatically not properly case hardened as per specifications, that it has been heated too hot before quenching and that it is prone to burst *along the line of the vent and pin holes.*
(Lawrence R. Witsil, Asst. Inspector Ordnance)
The materiel used appears unrefined, though it apparently was heat treated, probably case hardened, but in the last heating it was overheated, creating crystallization. This resulted in the greatest weakness and there is no wonder that it burst.
(Mr. Arthur Davidson, President, The Fairley Davidson Steel Co. Inc.)
It is the opinion of this Armory that the bursts reported are primarily due to the causes indicated in this paragraph (cartridge cases not up to standard) and secondarily, to receivers somewhat below the standard. (The Springfield Armory Report)
Disposition of Rifle: Shipped to the Springfield Armory.

————————

July 20, 1917.

Rifle No. 312249
Reference: R474.1/105
Location: Works of the National Brass & Copper Tube Co., Inc., Hastings-on-the-Hudson, N. Y.
Organization:
Persons Injured: One. A piece of the receiver housing flew back and struck George Deal, the operator, in the breast piercing his lung but not lodging inside.
Powder: Hercules X pyro D G Lot 446 from Frankford Arsenal.
Nature of Failure: Rifle burst in a stripping test. The bolt held locked in place. The edges of the bolt face chipped away just like in the first rifle (656701) but the extractor was blown off and the ejector was not deformed. All of the housing except that piece which engages the bolt lug, was blown away. The barrel, chamber, and bore were not injured and all the case except the head remained in the chamber just as in the other rifle (656701). *The*

line of break ran thru the extractor chamber vent and thru the pin hole beneath the ejector, just beside the magazine cutoff. The rifle was blown clear apart. The only reason more harm was not done is that the rifle was mounted on a sliding rest, and when fired all of it, from the magazine forward, was sticking thru a port out into the gallery. The piece which injured the operator came back thru this part, the barrel group fell outside in the gallery. This rifle 312249 had fired 826 rounds in all. It burst on the 147th round of a stripping test. I personally saw that it was water cooled and cleaned every fifty shots and was right beside the operator during the test. There was no muffled or dull explosion. Every shot kicked up dust in the backshop. (Extracted from report of Lawrence R. Witsil, Asst. Inspector Ordnance).

Probable Cause: Same as for Rifle 656701.
Disposition of Rifle: Shipped to the Springfield Armory.

Sept. 19, 1917.

Rifle No. Not known.
Reference: R474.1/145
Location: Training Camp, Receiving Ship, Philadelphia, Pa.
Organization: U. S. Navy.
Persons Injured: One. Burrill Robinson, Gunner's Mate, 1st Cl. U. S. Navy. Slightly injured about forehead and face.
Ammunition: Model 1916 Ball cartridges, stamped 6-17. Manufactured by Hastings-on-the-Hudson (A.B. & C.T. Co.) lot #36-39-41.
Nature of Failure: The breech of the rifle exploded. Rifle was completely shattered around the bolt. (Report of E. F. Leiper, U. S. N. The Receiving Ship at Philadelphia, Pa.)
Probable Cause: See Report of the Springfield Armory, following—
Disposition of Rifle: Forwarded to the Bureau of Ordnance, U. S. Navy (File No. 5204-2 (8009) 9/19/1917, and later carried with four other rifles to the Springfield Armory by Lieut. J. A. Patch, O. O. R. C.

Oct. 8, 1917.

Rifle No. Not known.
Reference: R474.1/146
Location: Navy Rifle Range, Virginia Beach, Va.
Organization: Company 47, Receiving Ship, U.S.S. Richmond, U. S. N.
Persons Injured: One. Apprentice Seaman, R. R. Green, above organization, received a fragment of brass in the nose and his face was pitted with powder and badly bruised. Report of the surgeon in charge showed that he was not seriously injured.
Ammunition: Manufactured by National Brass & Copper Tube Co., Inc., Cartridges bore the dates of May, June and July 1917.
Nature of Failure: Blew off the top of the receiver, the magazine cut-off and the bridge of the receiver. Also the head of the cartridge was blown off and the stock of the rifle split from the rear sight to the grip. After the explosion the bolt was in place, fully pulled down in the correct position for firing. (Report, J. R. Hayden, U. S. N.)
Probable Cause: See report of the Springfield Armory following—
Disposition of Rifle: Delivered to the Springfield Armory with four other rifles by Lieut. J. A. Patch, O. O. R. C.

Oct. 8, 1917.

Rifle No. Not known.
Reference: R474.1/146
Location: Navy Rifle Range, Virginia Beach, Va.
Organization: U. S. Navy.
Persons Injured: One. The piece was fired by J. F. Gooch, S 2c, coach, who had fired once immediately before the explosion to test the rifle, the man under instruction having made ten consecutive misses. Gooch received several small pieces of debris in the right eye ball and his face, nose and forehead were peppered with powder and small particles of steel. One small piece also penetrated his left eye. The report of the surgeon in charge stated the man was not seriously injured.
Ammunition: Manufactured by National Brass & Copper Tube Co.
Nature of Failure: The piece was completely wrecked. The stock was shattered from the forward part of the rear sight to the grip, so that the rifle is in two parts. The receiver was broken entirely in two at the forward and where the barrel screws into it. The bolt was blown off but not injured except for a few fragments torn from the face. The right side of the cut-off was broken off and the right side of the receiver was picked up 117 feet distant. (Report of J. R. Hayden, U. S. N.)
Probable Cause: See report of the Springfield Armory following.
Disposition of Rifle: Delivered to the Springfield Armory with four other rifles by Lieut. J. A. Patch, O. O. R. C.

Date — 1917.

Rifle No. Not known.
Reference: R474.1/147
Location: Navy Rifle Range, Virginia Beach, Va.
Organization: U. S. Navy.
Record not clear—Above file refers to reports covering the bursting of five rifles, three of which have been previously covered, Reference R474.1/145, 146.

Date — 1917.

Rifle No. Not known.
Reference: R474.1/147
Location: Navy Rifle Range, Virginia Beach, Va.
Organization: U. S. Navy.
Record not clear—Above file refers to reports covering the bursting of five rifles, three of which have been previously covered, Reference R474.1/145, 146.
Concerning five rifles the Springfield Armory Reports as follows: (R474.1/148)
    1. Returned with the information that the five rifles delivered at this Armory by Lieut. J. A. Patch have been carefully examined with the result that nothing detrimental in the nature of the structure of the metal has been discovered which might be a source of the bursts. In one case, an examination of the metal of one of the receivers indicated that the heat treatment was slightly under normal but not to any degree which would be conductive to weakening the metal so that it would not withstand the required pressure.
    2. An examination has also been made of the cartridge cases taken from the rifles which were in use at the time the rifles burst. Microscopic photographs of the brass used in the manufacture of these cartridge cases are inclosed herewith together with the photograph of a case manufactured at Frankford Arsenal. A comparison of these photographs will indicate a large grain structure of the National Brass & Copper Company's case which is evidently produced through annealing the case without a final mechanical

drawing to work out the large grain structure. The cases are therefore materially weakened and softened and it is thought that undoubtedly the explosions which occurred were directly due to the ammunition and in no way chargeable to the metal used in the rifles.

Three of the five preceding rifles covered, which failed during Navy target practice were forwarded from the Springfield Armory to the Watertown Arsenal for metallurgical report on the steel used in these rifles (R-474.1/198). The following is extracted from Experimental Report #86 submitted by the Watertown Arsenal:

"The receiver on one of these rifles was not broken. One was numbered 547854. Two had receivers so badly broken the numbers could not be obtained. No cartridge fragments were found in any of these rifles. Portions of the receivers of two of the rifles have been examined. The material is exceedingly brittle and the composition is far from what would be considered desirable. Microscopic examination showed that the steel of the receivers was very streaky, and the structure was such as would indicate that the material had not been properly heat treated subsequent to the case-hardening operation. The receivers were so hard that it was necessary to anneal them before taking out samples for chemical analysis. Sulphur and Phosphorus exceeded the allowed limits. (Signed—F. C. Langenberg, Metallurgist)"

———————

Sept. 18, 1917.

Rifle No. RIA 223235.

Reference: R 474.1/149.

Location: Winchester Repeating Arms Co., New Haven, Conn.

Organization:

Persons Injured: One. Operator was slightly cut about the face.

Ammunition: W. R. A. Co. lot #20, Powder lot #486.

Nature of Failure: Receiver forging was shattered into six pieces, these pieces being driven from the gun with considerable force. The majority of the cartridge cases remained in the gun and the bolt was intact except for a small fracture on the face. Previous to the explosion rifle barrel had been fired 4242 times. Number of shots fired with the receiver may have been three or four times this number (Report of F. E. Hudley, 1st Lieut. Ord. Dept. U. S. R., Inspector at the W. R. A. Co's. plant, New Haven, Conn.)

Probable Cause: In accordance with instructions given in the 10th Ind. R. I. A. receiver No. 223235 was received attached to a rifle barrel made by the Winchester Arms Company. A careful examination reveals the fact that the receiver appears to contain an old crack in the right hand wall, which was evidently there before the explosion. Various slight hairline cracks appear in the front end and right side of the receiver, but it cannot be definitely stated whether or not these were in the receiver before the explosion. The fracture indicates a good tough structure, which is borne out by the fact that the *entire receiver was not shattered.* Since the destroyed portion is that which overhangs the bolt end of the barrel after assembling, indications are that there was a blow-back, and if the receiver had been exceptionally hard or overheated in manufacture, it would have been blown entirely from the barrel. (Report of the Rock Island Arsenal.)

Disposition of Rifle: Shipped to the Rock Island Arsenal.

Date — 1917.

Rifles Nos. **486640**
         89728
         3 numbers–No record.
References: E S 474.1/3
Location: Record indicates four were from the Navy and one from Fort D. A. Russell, Wyoming.
Organization: No record other than above.
Persons Injured: No record.
Ammunition: No record.
Nature of Failure: Receivers broke (Record of Failure, Accidents Malfunctions, Library File, No. OKD-400.43.2)
Probable Cause: Defective heat treatment (Record of Failures, accidents, Malfunctions, Library File, No. OKD-400.43.2)
Disposition of Rifles: No record.
   (Note: No further information could be obtained from the above quoted file reference.)

Date—, 1917.

Rifle No. 573014.
Reference: O. O. 474.1/186
Location: Great Lakes Naval Training Station.
Organization: U. S. Navy.
Persons Injured: One. Firer slightly injured.
Ammunition: Lot #402, Frankford Arsenal, Manufactured, April 14, 1917.
Nature of Failure: Bolts and lugs stripped, bending and damaging magazine.
Probable Causes. Ammunition.
Disposition of Rifle. No record.

Date—, 1917.

Rifle No. 573697
Reference: O. O. 474.1/186
Location: Great Lakes Naval Training Station.
Organization: U. S. Navy.
Persons Injured: One. Firer severly injured in the face.
Ammunition: Lot #402, Frankford Arsenal, Manufactured April 14, 1917.
Nature of Failure: Bolt and lugs stripped, magazine bent and stock broken.
Probable Cause: Ammunition.
Disposition of Rifle: No record.

Date—, 1917.

Rifle No. 632817
Reference: O. O. 474.1/186
Location: Great Lakes Naval Training Station.
Organization: U. S. Navy.
Persons Injured: One. Firer slightly injured.
Ammunition: Lot #407, Frankford Arsenal, Manufactured April 14, 1917.
Nature of Failure: Bolt lugs stripped, magazine bent and stock broken.
Probable Cause: Ammunition.
Disposition of Rifle: No record.

August, 1917.

Rifle No. 89720
Reference: R 474.1/277
Location: Fort D. A. Russell, Wyoming.
Organization: Troup "E" 1st Cavalry.
Persons Injured: No record.
Ammunition: No record.
Nature of Failure: Explosion separated the barrel from the receiver, completely
    destroying the latter but apparently leaving the barrel uninjured.
Probable Cause: No record. (No details obtainable. Record of Failures, Ac-
    cidents, Malfunctions, Library File No. OKD 400.43.2)
Disposition of Rifle: Shipped to the office, Chief of Ordnance.

August, 1917.

Rifle No. No Record
Reference: R 474.1/84
Location: Culver Military Academy, Culver, Ind.
Organization: No record.
Persons Injured: No record.
Ammunition: No record.
Nature of Failure: Exploded on rifle range.
Probable Cause: No record.
Disposition of Rifle: No record.

December, 1917.

Rifle No. RIA 108448
Reference: R 474.1/13
Location: Camp Shelby, Miss.
Organization: 150th Infantry.
Persons Injured:
Ammunition: U. S. Cartridge Co., marked "17".
Nature of Failure: The barrel was burst at the chamber and split over one-
    third of the distance to the muzzle.
    The portion of the receiver into which the barrel screws was shattered as
    far back as the forward end of the bolt.
                        (Col. Chas. E. Morrison)
Probable Cause: Defective material composing the barrel. High sulphur and
    phosphorus content (Watertown Arsenal, Report signed by F. C. Langen-
    bert, Metallurgist).
Disposition of Rifle: Shipped to the Watertown Arsenal.

January 17, 1918.

Rifle No. RIA 217794
Reference: E S 474.4/90,215,228
Location: U. S. Rifle Range, Mount Holly, N. C.
Organization: Co. "C" 30th U. S. Infantry.
Persons Injured: One. Corp. Floyd P. Whiting, above organization, the firer
    was slightly injured.
Ammunition: No record.
Nature of Failure: Receiver burst away from the barrel.
Probable Cause:
        a. The defective rifles have been examined in this office (O. C. of O.)
    and the reason for rifle 217794 bursting at the receiver is in all probability

in accordance with the facts as stated in report attached hereto. The firing pin rod was evidently broken and allowed the striker point to project thru the firing pin hole of the bolt. Therefore, when the bolt was thrown smartly forward, thus allowing the striker point to come in contact with the cartridge primer before the cartridge reached its position in the chamber, a premature explosion occurred, causing the rupture of the receiver. (Captain R. R. Higgins, O. R. C. office of C. of O.)

b. The receiver of this rifle had not been properly heat treated prior to being put in service, ...
The metal was very brittle under impact, as evidenced by its being readily broken when struck a light blow with a hammer. (Exp. Report #115, Watertown Arsenal, signed by F. C. Langenberg, Metallurgist, May 16, 1918).
Disposition of Rifle: Shipped to the Watertown Arsenal.

February, 1918.

Rifle No. 222223
Reference: E S 474.4/108
Location: Camp Shelby, Miss.
Organization: Battery "E", 139 F. A.
Persons Injured: Prv. Edward Copeland, the firer, slightly injured.
Ammunition: Lot 82 of lot 453 of 1817, Manufactured by the Western Cartridge Co.
Nature of Failure: Shell case was jammed fast in chamber. Portion of rim near lower lug was split off. Part of upper lug was broken off. Extractor collar ear broken off. Extractor tongue was broken in two, about one half inch from gas outlet. From point of break the tongue was bent about twenty degrees. Magazine was warped on right side and stock was split on left side. Sleeve was broken off and magazine floor plate was bent. Small bits of brass were found and that part of the head of the shell case apparently contained "rotten brass" covered by a thin outer coating. (Record of Proceedings, Board of Inquiry, Camp Shelby, Miss. February 28, 1918)
Probable Cause: Defective ammunition.
Disposition of Rifle: No record.

Date——, 1918.

Rifle No.	*Nature of Failure*
RIA 445136	Burst Receiver
SA 278671	Back Fired
RIA 253241	Burst Receiver
RIA 262165	Burst Receiver
RIA 240914	Burst Receiver
RIA 239754	Burst Receiver
RIA 239356	Burst Receiver
RIA 225764	Burst Receiver
RIA 224554	Back Fired
RIA 165282	Burst Receiver

Reference: E S 474.1/283
Location: Camp Cody, N. M.
Organization: No record.
Persons Injured: No record.
Ammunition: Winchester, lots A-117 and AO121, E S 474.1/141.
Probable Cause: (Report of the Springfield Armory, January 23, 1919, File E S 474.1/283)

1. The rifles mentioned above have been examined and the primary cause of failure was evidently due to faulty ammunition, and in every instance, the shells returned with these rifles have heads blown off.

2. The condition of the receiver steel also contributed to failure. Sufficient material could be identified for analysis of six receivers. Three of these showed abnormal analysis that would be cause for rejecting raw stock as follows:

RIA 239754	Sulphur .068	Phosphorus .068
RIA 240914	Sulphur .131	Phosphorus .036
RIA 445136	Sulphur .093	Phosphorus .114

One receiver (SA165282) showed slightly dirty steel as indicated by slag inclusions observed in the unetched metallographic specimen.

(a) The metallographic structure of these receivers (Fig. 1, 2, 3) is not uniform nor does it conform to the structure obtained in our present practice (Figs. 4 and 5). Fig. 1 shows islands of free ferrite, the results of an ineffective quench (rifles 239854 and 240914). Fig. 2 is the structure of an unhardened receiver, or one hardened at much too low a heat (Rifles 253241 and 445136.) Fig. 3, (Rifle 165282) is not only unhardened but the grain is very coarse as from high forging heat. . . . . . .

3. Rifle 278671 is a cleaned and repaired arm, the receiver being of Springfield manufacture assembled to a 1917 RIA barrel.

4. The back firing on rifles 224554 and 278671—these appeared to have been fired with cartridges having excessive pressure, the rim of the bolt being blown off and the cartridge cases showing evidence of this high pressure. (Springfield Armory)

Disposition of Rifles: Forwarded to the Springfield Armory.

June, 1918.

Rifle No. 658742
Reference: E S 474.1/151
Location: Plant of Remington U. M. C. Company, Bridgeport, Conn.
Organization:
Persons Injured: No record.
Ammunition: Remington U. S. M. Co.
Nature of Failure: Rifle burst about two inches from the muzzle. Burst while firing stripping test. Rifle had fired 10890 rounds.
Probable Cause: It is the conclusion of this laboratory that the metal used in the manufacture of this rifle barrel was very undesirable material for this purpose. The metal contained numerous long slag inclusions. Phosphorus segregation was revealed by etching with Steads reagent. Chemical analysis showed the phosphorus content of the barrel to be .088 which is above specifications and entirely too high. (The Watertown Arsenal, Report)
Disposition of Rifle: Shipped to the Watertown Arsenal.

June, 1918.

Rifle No. 200512
Reference: E S 474.1/126
Location: Camp Shelby, Miss.
Organization: Co. "D" 113th Ammunition Train.
Persons Injured: Prv. Charles Berry, the firer, slightly injured.
Ammunition: Lot #86, RA-17.
Nature of Failure: Stock split underneath from the magazine to upper band, floor plate catch broken, *receiver broken in several pieces,* bolt broken into four pieces, bolt stop spring misplaced and the cartridge is so jammed in the chamber that the barrel will have to be taken down to make further investigation. (Major Thompson Short, Inf., N. C.)
Probable Cause: No record.
Disposition of Rifle: No record.

May, 1918.

Rifle No. S A 723664
Reference: E S 474.1/107
Location: Camp Wheeler, Ga.
Organization: Co. "D" 122 Inf.
Persons Injured: No record.
Ammunition: No record.
Nature of Failure: Barrel split its entire length. (Report Major, Wm. G. Obear,
    O. R. C.)
Probable Cause: No record.
Disposition of Rifle: No record.

––––––––––––––

May, 1918.

Rifle No. S A 712363
Reference: E S 474.1/107
Location: Camp Wheeler, Ga.
Organization: Co. "M" 122nd Inf.
Persons Injured: One. Slightly.
Ammunition: No record.
Nature of Failure: Head of shell blew out, tearing off sides of receiver
    leaving remainder of shell in barrel. (Report, Major Wm. G. Obear,
    O. R. C.)
Disposition of Rifle: No record.

––––––––––––––

March, 1918.

Rifle No. S A 141157
Reference: E S 474.1/58
Location: Camp Bowie, Texas.
Organization: 111th Trench Mortar Battery.
Persons Injured: None.
Ammunition: M1906 marked for target practice in the United States only.
Nature of Failure: Barrel burst from the muzzle to a point five inches below the
    stocking swivel. (Capt. Lewis Maverick, 111th T. M. Battery.)
Probable Cause: Unknown. Accident occurred the 2nd or 3rd shot on 300
    yard range during rapid fire target practice.
    Record shows rifle had been cleaned just before firing.
Disposition of Rifle: No record.

––––––––––––––

Date––, 1918.

Rifle No. (Bolts from two Rifles)
Reference: E S 474.1/49
Location: Camp Green, N. C.
Organization: 4th Engineers.
Persons Injured:
Ammunition:
Nature of Failure: Both bolts were fractured at the forward end where they
    come in contact with the cartridge. (Exp. Rep. #100, Watertown Arsenal)
Probable Cause: The failure of both of these bolts is due to the same cause.
    Both were very hard and brittle. The existence of such a structure as that
    found in the two bolts is brought about by insufficient tempering after the
    quenching operation. (Watertown Arsenal)
Disposition of Bolts: Shipped to the Watertown Arsenal.

––––––––––––––

February 20, 1918.

Rifle No. 501719
Reference: E S 474.1/34 (E S 471.41/125)
Location: Camp McClellan, Ala.

Organization: 112th M. C. Battalion
Persons Injured: One. (Record of Failures, Accidents, Malfunctions, Library File No. O. K. D. 400.43.2)
Ammunition: No record.
Nature of Failures: No record.
Probable Cause: Defective receiver and ammunition. (Record same as quoted for Persons Injured)
Disposition of Rifle: No record.
   Note: No further information could be obtained from the above quoted file reference)

_____

February 20, 22, 1919.

Rifle Nos. 666263, 662284
Reference: MR 471.41/370, MR 474.1/57
Location: Lindsay Arsenal, Canada.
Organization:
Persons Injured: One. Not seriously.
Ammunition: Lot #L-9, Frankford Arsenal.
Nature of Failure: Stock shattered around the breech mechanism. *Receiver broken into a number of pieces.* Bolt head broken on face and one lug knocked off. Rifle failed during accuracy tests of Armor piercing cartridges.
Probable Cause: Both rifles failed because the receivers had not been given proper heat treatment. The phosphorus and sulphur content in both cases was higher than desirable. (Experimental Report No. 157, Watertown Arsenal)
Disposition of Rifle: Scrapped at the Watertown Arsenal.

_____

April, 1920.

Rifle No.
Reference: O. O. 474.1/4243
Location: Empire City and Rifle Club, 990 Trinity Avenue, Bronx, N. Y.
Organization: Rifle was property of Mr. A. P. Hahn.
Persons Injured: No record.
Ammunition: No record.
Nature of Failure: Barrel split at the muzzle for about two inches.
Probable Cause: Break in the barrel was believed to have been caused by an obstruction in the barrel. (Springfield Armory)
Disposition of Rifle: Repaired and returned to Mr. Hahn at his expense. (Springfield Armory).

_____

July 29, 1920.

Rifle No. 167204
Reference: O. O. 353.14/40
Location: Sandy Hook, N. Y.
Organization: 2nd Co.
Persons Injured: No record.
Ammunition: No record.
Nature of Failure: Barrel burst.
Probable Cause: Obstruction in bore.
Disposition of Rifle: No record.

_____

June 26, 1920.

Rifle No. RIA 203851
Reference: 471.41/1172
Location: Veilbach Rifle Range, Germany.

Organization: Headquarters Co. 8th Infantry.
Persons Injured: No record.
Ammunition: U. S. C. Co., Lots #715 and 698.
Nature of Failure: Floor plate bent forward. *Receiver shattered about the locking chamber at the forward end,* top part completely blown away. *The receiver was almost broken in two* immediately behind the safety shoulder. The bolt was broken in two at the safety lug and rested at an angle which held the front end about one inch above its normal position. All parts in rear of the chamber were more or less coated with fused brass. Barrel was uninjured. The cartridge, except the base which was blown off, remained in the chamber. There was no question about it being U. S. Ammunition. (1st Lt. W. J. Henry, 12th L. M. O. R. S.)
Probable Cause: Defective ammunition. (Lt. Henry).
Disposition of Rifle: No record.

May 23, 1920.

Rifle No. RIA 101200
Reference: O. O. 471.41/1172
Location: Wehr range, Germany.
Organization: Headquarters Co. 5th Infantry.
Persons Injured: No record.
Ammunition: W. R. A. Co., Lot A-162, 1918.
Nature of Failure: Receiver was completely demolished. Cartridge stuck in chamber with base blown off. Barrel uninjured. (Lt. Col. C. A. Schimelfenig, Ord. Dept.)
Probable Cause: Defective ammunition as it was decided to call in all ammunition, Cal. .30, manufactured by that Company, (W. R. A. Co.,) (Report of Major J. K. Crain, C. A. C., Chief Ordnance Officer, A. F. in G.) (Also orders #78, Hdqs. A. F. in G., Coblenz, Germany, 1 June 1920)
Disposition of Rifle: No record.

October 24, 1921.

Rifle No. (old receiver)
Reference: O. O. 474.1/4503
Location: Sandy Hook, N. J.
Organization: 6th Company, S. H.
Persons Injured: One. Prv. 1cl. Thomas H. Appleby, the firer. Seriously injured, resulting in the loss of the right eye and laceration of the face.
Ammunition: German, 7.9m/m (Springfield Armory)
Nature of Failure: Receiver was shattered and number was missing. Receiver was of the old single heat treatment.
Probable Cause: The cartridge which caused the explosion was still in the chamber of the gun, the head of the cartridge having been blown away. The body of the cartridge was removed from the chamber and on being examined was found to be a portion of a German 7.9m/m service cartridge . . . . The German bullet is .015 larger than our bullet. Naturally, firing a cartridge of this character in the Springfield rifle would give rise to excessive pressure. From tests that I (Major J. S. Hatcher) have made on this subject, I find that the pressure encountered in such a case is generally above 75000 lbs. per square inch. . . . Tests also indicate that the double heat treated receiver will not permit the gun to burst in spite of the excessive pressure encountered. It can, therefore, with confidence be stated that the cause of the explosion was the fact that in some way a

German service cartridge was mixed in with the ammunition being used (F. A. Lot #449, 1917) in the target practice and happened to get into a rifle with the single heat treated receiver, which is not strong enough to stand such strain. (Extracted from report of Major J. S. Hatcher, Springfield Armory, November 28, 1921.)

Disposition of Rifle: Forwarded to the Springfield Armory.

May, 1921.

Rifle No. RIA 177232
Reference: O. O. 474.1/4430, 4450
Location: Clifton, Arizona.
Organization: Clifton Rifle Club, Clifton, Arizona.
Ammunition: Powder—DuPont, lot #671, 1917 shipped from the Frankford Arsenal, March 18, 1921. Hand loaded ammunition using 48.9 grains of powder, service bullet.
Persons Injured: One. Mr. W. F. McBrayer, the firer and Sec. of the club, was seriously injured losing his left eye.
Nature of Failure: Receiver failed.
Probable Cause: 1. (a) Excessive pressure.
  (b) Failure of the cartridge head, possibly due to lamination or other defect. Some indications of a lamination were apparent.
  (c) *Very poor heat treatment in the receiver.*
  2. The chances are that a somewhat excessive pressure, combined with a defective cartridge, allowed the gas to escape into the receiver well and disrupt the receiver. With a brittle or poorly heat treated receiver a large escape of gas in this manner will frequently cause a fracture. With properly heat treated parts an escape of gas as would occur from either an excessive pressure or a defective cartridge case, or both, cannot burst the receiver or blow out the bolt. Since our new heat treatment was started in 1917, there have been no cases of the bursting of these receivers brought to the attention of Springfield Armory and every effort that we have made to burst these receivers in our experimental department has failed.
  3. The receiver in question was on a rifle made at Rock Island Arsenal in August 1910. Consequently this rifle did not have the new heat treatment.
  4. . . . .
  5. In conclusion, it may be stated that the opinion of this armory is that regardless of what causes such as defective cartridge cases may have contributed to the failure, the ultimate responsibility for the accident is due to the poor receiver, as with a good receiver the accident would not have happened. (Extracted from report of the Springfield Armory)

Disposition of Rifle: Forwarded to the Springfield Armory, and later returned to Mr. W. F. McBrayer, Secy. Clifton Rifle Club, Clifton, Arizona.

July, 1921.

Rifle No. SA 326222
Reference: O. O. 474.1/4463
Location: Camp Holabird, Md.
Organization: Co. "B" 1st Motor Repair Battalion.
Persons Injured: None
Ammunition: Guard cartridge.
Nature of Failure: Receiver shattered.

Probable Cause: The failure of the rifle had two contributing causes:

First, the fact that the receiver through *improper heat treatment* was brittle and lacked shock resisting qualities, and

Second, the improper assembly of the receiver, bolt and barrel.

Such an accident could not have happened had the heat treatment on this rifle been of the kind now in use at Springfield Armory. (Report, Springfield Armory)

Disposition of Rifle: Forward to the Springfield Armory.

––––––––––––––––

July 28, 1921.

Rifle No. SA 1,215,353
Reference: O. O. 474.1/4464-4472
Location: Fort Niagara, N. Y.
Organization: Infantry Rifle Team.
Persons Injured: Major Per Ramee, Captain, Infantry Rifle Team. Slightly injured.
Ammunition: Mixed lots of F. A. Ammunition, manufactured prior to 1917.
Nature of Failure: On the 6th or 7th shot a hang fire occurred giving time for the lifting of the bolt handle in the act of extracting the cartridge when the explosion took place, driving the bolt backward, partly shearing off the edge of the cut-off and the upper half of the split locking lug. (Extracted from Report of Board of Officers).
Probable Cause: Defective Ammunition (Report of the Frankford Arsenal.)
Disposition of Rifle:

––––––––––––––––

July 15, 1921.

Rifle No. SA 770160
Reference: O. O. 474.1/4468
Location: Camp Bullis, Texas.
Organization: Co. "D" 2nd Engineers.
Persons Injured: One. Private Frank Godea, above organization, the firer was slightly injured.
Ammunition:
Nature of Failure: Receiver broken into a number of pieces. Bolt had the small lip opposite the bottom locking lug blown away and had brass melted onto the face, indicating high pressure.
Probable Cause: In the opinion of this Armory this accident was due primarily to excessive pressure caused by a foreign substance on the forward part of the cartridge; and, secondarily, to extremely *poor heat treatment of the receiver* which was very hard, brittle and highly susceptible to shock. (Extracted from Report of the Springfield Armory.)
Disposition of Rifle: Forwarded to the Springfield Armory.

––––––––––––––––

August 12, 1921.

Rifle No.
Reference: O. O. 474.1/4472.
Location: Fort Niagara, N. Y.
Organization: Philippine Scout Rifle Team.
Persons Injured: One. Slightly.
Ammunition: Frankford Arsenal, 1921.
Nature of Failure: Magazine sides swelled out. Stock was badly broken. The magazine floor plate was blown downward and the four cartridges remaining in the magazine were blown out. The bolt held in place firmly and securely. Bolt was entirely workable after the accident.
Probable Cause: The use of greased ammunition.
Disposition of Rifle:

July 28, 1921.

Rifle No. SA 1215353
Reference: O. O. 474.1/4472
Location: Fort Niagara, N. Y.
Organization: Infantry Rifle Team.
Persons Injured: One. Capt. Alan D. Warnock, slightly.
Ammunition: 1921, National Match.
Nature of Failure: Gas escaped thru the channel cut in the frame near the receiver to admit the left locking lug on the bolt. It was thru this passage that the brass and gas passed peppering my forehead with a number of small pieces. (Capt. Warnock)
Probable Cause: Defective ammunition.
Disposition of Rifle:

––––––––––––––

August, 1921.

Rifle No. 70971
Reference: O. O. 474.1/4478
Location: Camp Grant. Illinois.
Organization: C. M. T. C.
Persons Injured:
Ammunition: Could not be identified.
Nature of Failure: Fractured receiver.
Probable Cause: From examination made thus far it is thought that the steel in this receiver was in extremely bad condition and unsuitable for the purpose for which it was used. (Extracted from Report of the Rock Island Arsenal)
 In the opinion of this office, the direct cause of the damage to the rifle was in soft cartridge head, which permitted the gas under high pressure, rather than defective material in the receiver; although the latter undoubtedly contributed to the extent of the damage done. (Ordnance Office, Chief, Small Arms Division, Major Herbert O'Leary).
Disposition of Rifle: Shipped to the Rock Island Arsenal.

––––––––––––––

June 2, 1921.

Rifle No. 607222
Reference: O. O. 474.1/4485
Location: San Juan, P. R.
Organization: Co. "B" 65th Inf.
Persons Injured:
Ammunition: R. A.–18
Nature of Failure: Barrel burst, causing a tear of about 1½ inches under the front sight.
Probable Cause: Obstruction in bore. (Report of the Springfield Armory.)
Disposition of Rifle: Forwarded to the Springfield Armory.

––––––––––––––

Date––, 1921.

Rifle No. SA 608498
Reference: O. O. 474.1/4384, 4393.
Location: Hawaiian Department.
Organization: Hawaiian Ordnance Detachment.
Persons Injured:
Ammunition: Overhauled locally.
Nature of Failure: Barrel burst.
Probable Cause: Due to continuous slag streaks in barrel. (Report, Springfield Armory.)
Disposition of Rifle: Forwarded to the Springfield Armory.

Date——, 1922.

Rifle Nos. 459881, 379004
Reference: O. O. 474.1/4540
Location: Fort Crook, Nebr.
Organization: Troop "E" 14th Cavalry.
Persons Injured:
Ammunition: R. A. H-18, Gallery practice cartridge, Reloaded, Feb. 1922.
Nature of Failure: Barrels split.
Probable Cause: Obstructions in the bores.
Disposition of Rifles:

————————————

September 16, 1922.

Rifle No. RIA 146184
Reference: O. O. 474.1/4602
Location: Atlanta, Ga. During civic demonstration.
Organization: U. S. Army.
Persons Injured: One, The firer, slightly.
Ammunition: Pyro blank cartridges and combination rifle and hand grenade "White Phosphorus."
Nature of Failure: Shattered receiver.
Probable Cause: Excessive pressure. Receiver not properly heat treated, was too brittle to be suitable for this component. It cannot be said that any receiver would have held, although no broken receivers of Springfield Armory's late manufacture have been returned to this establishment. (Report, Springfield Armory.)
Disposition of Rifle: Forwarded to the Springfield Armory.

————————————

August 16, 1922.

Rifle No. 759943
Reference: O. O. 474.1/4573
Location: Sea Girt, N. Y.
Organization: Hqs. Co., 104th Engineers, N. J. N. G.
Persons Injured: None.
Ammunition: Winchester, Lot A-377, 1918.
Nature of Failure: Barrel burst, blowing a piece of steel about three inches long out of the right hand side of the barrel one half of these three inches being the chamber holding the cartridge. (Extracted from report of Captain George C. Bonstelle, Co. "A" 104th Engineers, N. J. N. G. firer of the rifle.)
Probable Cause: Barrel contained burnt steel. The failure of this barrel is due to weakness that was produced by excessive heating in the upsetting operation. The excessive heat caused internal oxidation or burning of the metal rendering it entirely unfit for use as a rifle barrel. (Extracted from report of E. L. Wood, Metallurgist, Springfield Armory.)
Disposition of Rifle: Forwarded to the Springfield Armory.

————————————

Date——, 1923.

Rifle No. 946508
Reference: O. O. 474.1/4574
Location: U. S. Naval Academy, Annapolis, Md.
Organization: U. S. Naval Academy Corps of Midshipmen.
Persons Injured:
Ammunition:
Nature of Failure: Bolt and receiver deformed. Barrel showed no indication of bulging or deformation. (Report of Springfield Armory)
Cause of Failure: Excessive Pressure, (Springfield Armory)
Disposition of Rifle: Forwarded to the Springfield Armory.

Date——, 1923.

Rifle Nos. RIA 234466, 235742
Reference: O. O. 474.1/4720, 4726, 4727, 4735
Location: Coalinga, Calif.
Organization: Coalinga Rifle Club, Coalinga, Calif.
Persons Injured:
Ammunition: Lot #397, R. A. 18.
Nature of Failure: Receivers shattered.
Probable Cause: Defective ammunition (Frankford Arsenal) It is concluded that the bursting of each rifle was due primarily to failure of the cartridge head, the cause of such failure is not known, combined with weakness and brittleness of the receiver, and possibly aggravated by excessive pressure. (Springfield Armory)
Disposition of Rifle: Forwarded to the Springfield Armory.

Date——, 1924.

Rifle No. 625587
Reference: O. O. 474.1/4727
Location: The Frankford Arsenal, Philadelphia, Pa.
Organization: This rifle blew up at the Frankford Arsenal while making a surveillance test of ammunition used in rifles nos. RIA 234446 and RIA 235742 which exploded while being used by a civilian rifle team and are described next above.
Persons Injured: None
Ammunition: Lot #397, R. A. 18
Nature of Failure: Receiver failed. Bolt held in place.
Probable Cause: Defective ammunition. (Frankford Arsenal)
Disposition of Rifle: Forwarded to the Springfield Armory by the Frankford Arsenal.

April 23, 1923.

Rifle No. 970762
Reference: O. O. 474.1/4652
Location: U. S. S. Nevada (at anchor) San Pedro, Calif.
Organization: U. S. Navy.
Persons Injured:
Ammunition: Lot #1227, U. S. Cartridge Co., 1918.
Nature of Failure: Split Barrel.
Probable Cause: Damage was caused by a bullet being stuck in the bore due to an insufficient powder charge. (Office C. of O.)
Disposition of Rifle:

Date——

Rifle No. 971779
Reference: O. O. 474.1/4655
Location: Fort McPherson, Ga.
Organization: Co. "M" 22nd Inf.
Persons Injured:
Ammunition: Lot #172, U. S. C., 1917.
Nature of Failure: Barrel failed.
Probable Cause: Due to a longitudinal seam, or lap, in the metal located about 7½ inches forward of the butt end. (Springfield Armory.)
Disposition of Rifle: Forward to the Springfield Armory.

August 26, 1924.

Rifle No. RIA (Old heat treated receiver)
Reference: O. O. 600.913/1226, 1230
Location: Plattsburg Barracks, N. Y.
Organization: Co. "E" C. M. T. C.
Persons Injured: Candidate Erlis Mesher, above organization, slightly injured.
Ammunition: Lot # D-1424, U. S. Cartridge Co., 1918.
Nature of Failure: Receiver blown in several places. The explosion caused the receiver lugs the rear of the receiver and the bolt to be blown from the rifle with considerable force.
Probable Cause: Defective ammunition. Cases are overannealed and consequently liable to give cut-offs or blown heads in firing. (Frankford Arsenal)
Failure was caused primarily by a cartridge case having a soft head. Failure of the head subjecting the forward end of the receiver to gas pressure sufficient to burst it. The failure is typical of these conditions but is a somewhat aggravated case due to the receiver being rather brittle. It is noted that this rifle is a Rock Island manufacture and that its receiver had been given a heat treatment as used for rifles up to the number eight hundred thousand. (Springfield Armory)
Disposition of Rifle: Forwarded to the Springfield Armory.

––––––––––––––––

Sept. 8, 1924.

Rifle No. SA 78745
Reference: O.O. 474.1/4885
Location: Camp Bullis, Texas.
Organization:
Persons Injured:
Ammunition: W. R. A. Lot #A-116.
Nature of Failure: Barrel was split from the breech to a point approximately three inches ahead of the forcing cone. *Receiver slightly split.* (O.O. 8th C. A.)
Probable Cause: Seam in barrel caused by a "pipe." (Springfield Armory)
Disposition of Rifle: Forwarded to the Springfield Armory.

––––––––––––––––

Date –– 1924.

Rifle No. 335258
Reference: O. O. 474.1/4800
Location: Ft. McPherson, Ga.
Organization: Co. "A" 22nd Inf.
Ammunition:
Nature of Failure: Barrel bulged considerably and split slightly just forward of the front sight stud.
Probable Cause: Obstruction in the bore (Springfield Armory)
Disposition of Rifle: Forwarded to the Springfield Armory.

––––––––––––––––

Date –– 1923.

Rifle No. SA 1093941
Reference: O. O. 474.1/4719
Location: Elgin, Illinois
Organization: Elgin Rifle Club, 413 Mill Street, Elgin, Ill.
Persons Injured:
Ammunition: F A 21-R
Nature of Failure: Bolt lugs set back about 1/64th inch into the receiver. Flange of bolt head blown off. (Springfield Armory)
Probable Cause: Excessive pressure (Springfield Armory).
Disposition of Rifle: Forwarded to the Springfield Armory. Rifle replaced without charge to the club member.

Oct. 27, 1923.

Rifle No. RIA 250560
Reference: O.O. 474.1/4709
Location: Fort McPherson, Ga.
Organization:
Persons Injured: One. Slightly.
Ammunition: RA Co. Lot #118.
Nature of Failure: Receiver shattered. The receiver broke off clear around even with the end of the rifle barrel.
Probable Cause: Due to soft cartridge case or excessively high pressure, accompanied by a brittle receiver. (Springfield Armory)
Disposition of Rifle: Forwarded to the Springfield Armory.

———————————

July 11, 1923.

Rifle No. 284086
Reference: O. O. 474.1/4672
Location: Fort Sill, Oklahoma
Organization: Co. "C" 179th Inf. Okla. N. G.
Persons Injured: Sergeant Blair, slightly injured.
Ammunition:
Nature of Failure: Receiver failed.
Probable Cause: The indications are that failure of the receiver was due to the combination of excessive headspace and a brittle receiver, possibly aggravated by a soft case or excessive pressure or both. (Springfield Armory)
Disposition of Rifle: Forwarded to the Springfield Armory.

———————————

July 24, 1923.

Rifle No. 655360
Reference: O. O. 474.1/4677, O. O. 471.41/2037, 2057, 2058
Location: State Camp, Peekskill, N. Y.
Organization: 14th Inf. N. Y. N. G.
Persons Injured: One. Slightly.
Ammunition: W. R. A. Co., Lot A-364.
Nature of Failure: Barrel burst.
Probable Cause: No defect in rifle. Caused by an obstruction in the bore. (Springfield Armory)
Disposition of Rifle: Forwarded to the Springfield Armory.

———————————

May 9, 1923.

Rifle No. SA 642742
Reference: O. O. 471.41/2082
Location: Hawaiian Department.
Organization: Co. "I" 35th Inf.
Persons Injured: Private Manley, above organization, seriously injured, losing his right eye.
Ammunition: U. S. Cartridge Co., Lot D-1410
Nature of Failure: Top of the *receiver* blown off. It is probable that the receiver gave way over the threaded section of the barrel first. (D.O.O. Hawaiian Dept., Maj. W. L. Clay)
Probable Cause: Excessive headspace and insufficient strength and ductility of the receiver accompanied by unusually high pressure. Examination of the fracture of the receiver show a complete lack of ductility and a condition not suited to withstand the pressure exerted on the face of the bolt in abnormal cases produced by excessive headspace or undue high chamber pressure. (Springfield Armory)
Disposition of Rifle: Forwarded to the Springfield Armory.

May 18, 1923.

Rifle No. SA 1254701
Reference: O. O. 600.913/948
Location: West Point, N. Y.
Organization: U. S. Military Academy.
Persons Injured: None.
Ammunition: W. R. A. Co. Lot A-377.
Nature of Failure: Barrel burst at powder chamber.
Probable Cause: Burnt metal in the butt section of the barrel. (Springfield Armory)
Disposition of Rifle: Forwarded to the Springfield Armory.

June, 1924.

Rifle No. RIA 90101
Reference: O. O. 474.1/4863, 4884
Location: Camp Stephen D. Little, Nogales, Arizona.
Organization: Co. "F" 25th Infantry.
Persons Injured:
Ammunition: W. R. A. Co., Lot A-435
Nature of Failure: Barrel split about five inches from the muzzle.
Probable Cause: Failure of the barrel was caused by a seam which evidently did not show in manufacture. (Springfield Armory.)
Disposition of Rifle: Forwarded to the Springfield Armory.

April 30, 1923.

Rifle No. RIA 104926
Reference: O. O. 600.913/970, 1094
Location: Fort Wm. McKinley, P. I.
Organization: Co. "G" 31st Infantry.
Persons Injured: Major Heisington, 31st Inf. Seriously.
Ammunition: U. S. C. Co., Lot D-1100, Powder Lot 983 B 1039-1058
Nature of Failure: The barrel and receiver of this rifle were separated at the place they screw together. The barrel appeared to be uninjured but the *Receiver was blown all to pieces.* The bolt was picked up about twenty paces to the right and was slightly bent. The locking lugs and safety lugs showed that they were subjected to an enormous pressure. (Proceedings, Board of Officers.)
Probable Cause: The cause of failure in this case lies in the *weakness* of the receiver under abnormal conditions. It is quite possible that a receiver of recent manufacture would have held under the same conditions. Receiver does not possess the ductility desired and obtained by the latest method of heat treating. (Extract from Report of Springfield Armory)
Disposition of Rifle: Forwarded to the Springfield Armory.

May 1, 1923.

Rifle No. SA 523089
Reference: O. O. 600.913/970, 1094
Location: Fort Wm. McKinley, P. I.
Organization: Co. "C" 31st Infantry.
Persons Injured: None.

Ammunition: U. S. C. Co., Lot D-1100, Powder Lot 985 B 1039-1058.

Nature of Failure: Rear sight blown off. Fixed base split longitudinally about two inches, the movable base was forced upward about its center and broken in half. (Proceedings of a Board of Officers) Barrel split about one-inch long immediately under the fixed base of the rear sight. (Springfield Armory).

Probable Cause: Metal in the barrel when polished indicating that the metal is burnt, so weakening the barrel that the accident followed. (Springfield Armory).

Disposition of Rifle: Forwarded to the Springfield Armory.

––––––––––––––––

May, 1924.

Rifle No.

Reference: O. O. 600.913/1251

Location: Dona Ana Target Range, N. M.

Organization: 1st Sqd. 7th Cavalry.

Persons Injured: Sgt. Rufus O. Ervin, Troop "C," 7th Cav. Slightly.

Ammunition: W. R. A. Co., Lot #453

Nature of Failure: Bolt blown from rifle. Receiver ruptured.

Probable Cause: I inspected Sgt. Ervin's rifle after the accident, the steel of the receiver appeared brittle and crystalized. Witness stated to me that one of the upper holding lugs of the bolt was broken. This bolt could not be found for presentation as evidence, when I investigated this case. (Major R. H. Lee, Ord. Dept., Post Ordnance Officer testifying before a Board of Officers.)

Disposition of Rifle:

––––––––––––––––

Sept. 15, 1924.

Rifle No. 228112

Reference: O. O. 600.913/1253

Location: Bay Range, Fort Humphrie, Va.

Organization: Co. "A" 13th Engineers.

Persons Injured: None.

Ammunition: F. A. Lot #449 of 1917.

Nature of Failure: Burst receiver.

Probable Cause: An examination of the damaged rifle indicates that the accident took place just as the locking lugs on the bolt were beginning to engage with the corresponding locking shoulders on the receiver. The bolt was recovered after the accident and it was found that the firing pin was protruding from the face of the bolt and was stuck fast in that position. These circumstances appear to indicate that the firing pin was damaged by the shot fired previous to the one which disrupted the rifle and that it was protruding from the bolt in such a manner that it fired the cartridge before the bolt was fully locked as it was being pushed into the chamber during the operation of loading. (Sub-Committee, The Ordnance Committee, Tech. Staff, Jan. 22, 1925.)

Disposition of Rifle:

––––––––––––––––

Oct. 28, 1924.

Rifle No. 90489

Reference: O. O. 600.913/1305

Location: Fort Washington, Md.

Organization: Co. "K" 12th Inf.

Persons Injured: None.

Ammunition: F. A. E. C. Powder, Lot No. 5 (blank)

Nature of Failure: Barrel split from chamber to the upper band.
Probable Cause: During tactical exercise Private Jones was advancing from one one position to another and it is thought the muzzle of the rifle accidently struck the ground thus fouling the bore. (O. O. Fort Washington)
Disposition of Rifle:

Dec. 5, 1924.

Rifle No. SA 642675
Reference: O. O. 474.1/4915, 4932, O. O. 600.913/1321
Location: Hawaiian Department.
Organization: Co. "G" 35th Inf.
Persons Injured: Private James C. Pickett, 35th Inf. Seriously.
Ammunition: U. S. Cartridge Co., Lot No. D-1437.
Nature of Failure: Receiver shattered. Top blown completely off. Cracked at junction with barrel in lower half. Bolt was blown to rear shearing safety stop on receiver. No evidence of obstruction in bore. (Major James Kirk)
Probable Cause: Excessive pressure and brittle receiver. (Springfield Armory)
Disposition of Rifle: Forwarded to the Springfield Armory.

Feb. 26, 1925.

Rifle No. SA 468300
Reference: O. O. 600.913/1342, 1356, 1393
Location: Camp Lewis, Washington.
Organization: Co. "A," 6th Engineers, 3rd Div.
Persons Injured: Two enlisted men injured.
Ammunition: Firing rifle grenades, Lachrymatory, C. N., Lot 7-27-22. Blank Ammunition used.
Nature of Failure: Receiver demolished.
Probable Cause: Failure resulted from a *brittle receiver* subjected to high gas pressure by failure of the cartridge head. (Springfield Armory)
Disposition of Rifle: Forwarded to the Springfield Armory.

March 4, 1925.

Rifle No. SA 195082
Reference: O. O. 600.913/1361/1383
Location: Fort Wm. McKinley, P. I.
Organization: Headquarters Company, 31st Infantry.
Persons Injured: Four, Slightly.
Ammunition: U. S. Cartridge Co., Lot No. 978.
Nature of Failure: Receiver shattered, Bolt blown out.
Probable Cause: Excessive chamber pressure and brittle receiver . . . Metal of coarse structure . . . If properly heat treated and tough, the receiver is not likely to shatter although it is almost certain to be split, but a brittle receiver will invariably shatter. (Springfield Armory)
Disposition of Rifle: Forwarded to the Springfield Armory.

March 20, 1925.

Rifle No. SA 613496
Reference: O. O. 474.811/260
Location: Fort Sill, Oklahoma
Organization: Co. "I" 20th Infantry.
Persons Injured: None.
Ammunition: Tracer. Lot number not known.
Nature of Failure: Barrel burst.

Probable Cause: The evidence indicates that the soldier who had the rifle was firing tracer ammunition when one round failed to explode properly, causing the bullet to lodge in the bore about six inches from the muzzle. The soldier did not investigate the malfunction, particularly to determine whether the bore was clear, consequently on the next shot the barrel burst. (Major A. J. Stuart, Ord. Dept.)

Disposition of Rifle: Turned in locally for exchange.

'April 24, 1925.

Rifle No. 206331
Reference: O. O. 600.913/1384, 1410, 1446
Location: Fort Huachuca, Arizona.
Organization: 1st Sqd. 10th Cavalry.
Persons Injured:
Ammunition: Peters Cartridge Co., Lot No. A-139.
Nature of Failure: Receiver shattered. The receiver was sheared off at the bolt locking lug recess on the lower side of the receiver in a downward backward direction. The left side of the receiver also fractured at the base of the safety shoulder. The right side of the receiver was fractured underneath and to the point equal to the rear face of the cut-off thumb piece. The top portion of the receiver both front and rear when fractured.
Probable Cause: The failure of the above mentioned rifle was undoubtedly due primarily to the breaking out of the cartridge head. This is the result of a weak or soft cartridge head, excessive head space due to setting back of the bolt or to a combination of both of these. The receiver was one of the earlier single heat treated type any of which are almost certain to *shatter* when the cartridge head fails. (Springfield Armory).
Disposition of Rifle: Forwarded to the Springfield Armory.

May 21, 1925.

Rifle No. SA 523444
Reference: O. O. 800.913/1442, 1444, 1454.
Location: Fort Wm. McKinley, Rizal, P. I.
Organization: Co. "A" 15th Infantry.
Persons Injured: None.
Ammunition: Western Cartridge Co., Lot # S-55.
Nature of Failure: Portion of the barrel 3″ long and one-half the circumference was blown away.
Probable Cause: Barrel failed because the steel was burned during manufacture of the barrel blank. (Springfield Armory)
Disposition of Rifle: Forwarded to the Springfield Armory.

June 5, 1925.

Rifle No. RIA 170805
Reference: O. O. 600.913/1440, 1441
Location: Fort Wm. McKinley, Rizal, P. I.
Organization: Co. "C" 14th Engineers, P. S.
Persons Injured: Staff Sgt. Felix Armada, Slightly.
Ammunition: U. S. Cartridge Co., Lot No. 744.
Nature of Failure: Upper front locking lug stripped. Upper front face of bolt fractured. Top of receiver containing the serial number blown off. The bolt was picked up off the ground directly under the rifle. (Capt. David W. Craig, Ord. Dept., O. O. Fort McKinley.)
Probable Cause: Defective ammunition and receiver of old heat treatment. (Record)
Disposition of Rifle: Forwarded to the Springfield Armory.

June 10, 1925.

Rifle No. RIA 146554
Reference: O. O. 600.913/1400, 1407, 1408
Location: Camp McClellan, Ala.
Organization: Co. "A," 22nd Infantry.
Persons Injured: Private Charles A. Vick, above organization, slightly.
Ammunition: Peters Cartridge Co., Lot B-1, 1918 Grade E.
Nature of Failure: Receiver blown to pieces. Bolt and pieces of receiver were found twenty steps from where the rifle exploded. (O. O. 22nd Inf. Camp McClellan, Ala.)
Probable Cause: An examination of barrel and ruptured case would seem to indicate that the misfired case was withdrawn from the chamber, leaving the bullet in the bore. The next cartridge was forced on to the bullet, seating the bullet onto the powder charge. This with the added resistance of the first bullet caused sufficient pressure to blow up the rifle. The *excessive shattering* was due to the *receiver* being of the *old single heat treatment.* (Springfield)
Disposition of Rifle: Forwarded to the Springfield Armory.

————————————

Aug. 13, 1925.

Rifle No. SA 858256
Reference: O. O. 600.913/1465, 1496
Location: Fort Ruger, T. H.
Organization: Hdq. Det. & C. T., 2nd Bat. 55th C. A.
Persons Injured: None.
Ammunition: Reloaded gallery practice.
Nature of Failure: Barrel split and bulged.
Probable Cause: Obstruction in the Barrel. (Springfield Armory)
Disposition of Rifle: Forwarded to the Springfield Armory.

————————————

Date —— 1925.

Rifle No. SA 1004623
Reference: O. O. 474.1/5090
Location: U. S. Naval Academy, Annapolis, Md.
Organization: U. S. Navy.
Persons Injured: None.
Ammunition: Remington, U. S. M. C. Co. Lot E-1114. Manuf. Nov. 23, 1918.
Nature of Failure: Barrel split under the fixed base sight band, showing a crack starting about two inches forward of the receiver and extending longitudinally towards the muzzle for about 1½ inches. (Navy Dept., Bureau of Ordnance)
Probable Cause: Defective heat treatment. (Springfield Armory.)
Disposition of Rifle: Forwarded to the Springfield Armory.

————————————

Oct. 27, 1925.

Rifle No. SA 1198207
Reference: O. O. 600.913/1499, 1521
Location: Fort Benning, Ga.
Organization: Firing by recruits. Hqs. Co., 2nd Bat. 29th Inf.
Persons Injured: Two. Slightly.
Ammunition: Unknown. (O. O. Fort Benning)
Nature of Failure: Magazine floor plate and firing pin rod were blown out and stock was broken on both sides opposite magazine. (O. O. Fort Benning)
Probable Cause: Due to the firing of an 8 m/m German cartridge. (Springfield Armory)
Disposition of Rifle: Forwarded to the Springfield Armory.

Nov. 20, 1925.

Rifle No. SA 1201472
Reference: O. O. 600.913/1505
Location: Fort Benning, Ga.
Organization:
Persons Injured: One. Slightly.
Ammunition: Tracer. F. A. Lot No. 282, Mod. 1923.
Nature of Failure: Barrel ruptured longitudinally for about four inches just forward of the receiver. (O. O. Fort Benning)
Probable Cause: Defective heat treatment (O. C. M. Item No. 5346)
Disposition of Rifle: Forwarded to the Springfield Armory.

Nov. 27, 1925.

Rifle No. SA 299458
Reference: O. O. 600.913/1506, 1510, 1526
Location: Fort Sill, Okla.
Organization: Co. "L" 20th Inf.
Persons Injured: Private Holt, above organization, severely wounded. Did not recover sufficiently to be questioned until Jan. 25, 1926.
Ammunition: Blank and C. H. Grenades.
Nature of Failure: Receiver burst.
Probable Cause: Rupture of cartridge case. Gas vent in the side of the receiver not large enough to carry off this increase of escaping gas, and the gas lifted over the top of the receiver at the point where the locking lugs engage. Probably excessive headspace. Brittle receiver of old heat treatment. (Frankford Arsenal and Springfield Armory)
Disposition of Rifle: Shipped to the Frankford Arsenal and then to the Springfield Armory.

July 1, 1926.

Rifle No. RIA 111621
Reference: O. O. 600.913/1574, 1714
Location: Camp Stephen D. Little.
Organization: Co. "I" 25th Inf.
Persons Injured: Two. Private Vernon Duncan, above organization, the firer, had part of third finger of left hand blown off. Corp. Albert Hamilton, above organization, who was about nine paces away received an injury to one of his eyes.
Ammunition: W. R. A. Co., Lot No. A-436. Not defective. (Frankford Arsenal)
Nature of Failure: Left side of receiver blown off.
Probable Cause: Examination by the Springfield Armory indicates that the *receiver was very hard and brittle.* The bullet being still in the barrel indicates that the receiver burst before much pressure was developed. Evidence seems to support the opinion that the cartridge was fired before the bolt was locked. Test of the ammunition at Frankford Arsenal revealed no defects. (O. C. of O.)
Disposition of Rifle: Forwarded to the Springfield Armory.

Apr. 13, 1926.

Rifle No. 84685
Reference: O. O. 600.913/1667
Location: Fort McKinley, Rizal, P. I.
Organization: Co. "E" 45th Inf. (P. I.)
Persons Injured: One. Private Paulino Mina, slightly.
Ammunition: Lot # D-755.

Nature of Failure: Receiver blown away and part of exploded shell remained in the rifle barrel. (Proceedings Board of Officers)
Probable Cause: Excessive pressure and brittle receiver. (Proceedings Board of Officers.)
Disposition of Rifle:

June 28, 1926.

Rifle No.: SA 735791
Reference: O.O. 600.913/1681, 1715, 1785.
Locations Fort Clark, Texas.
Organization: R. O. T. C. Texas A. & M. College.
Persons Injured: None.
Ammunition: R. A. Lot # E-1474.
Nature of Failure: Barrel split four inches in rear of upper band to the muzzle.
Probable Cause: Defective steel. (Springfield Armory)
Disposition of Rifle: Forwarded to the Springfield Armory.

Aug. 15, 1926.

Rifle No. 173807
Reference: O. O. 600.913/1718, 1725, 1782
Location: Camp Logan, Illinois.
Organization: 202nd Artillery, Illinois N. G.
Persons Injured: One. Seriously. Both eyes injured. Injury to right eye considered serious. Loss of eye is not expected. (Capt. G. H. Drewry, Ord. Dept.)
Ammunitions R. A. Lot No. C-576
Nature of Failure: Receiver completely broken from rifle. Break occurred around the threaded part where barrel joins the receiver. (Capt. Drewry)
Probable Cause: Excessive headspace. Heat treatment of receiver below standard. (Springfield Armory)
Disposition of Rifle: Forwarded to the Springfield Armory.

Oct. 21, 1926.

Rifle No. RIA 204801
Reference: O. O. 600.913/1792, 1795
Location: Fort Des Moines, Iowa
Organization: Detachment 14th Cavalry.
Persons Injured: Private Martin Hangeveld, Troop C. 14th Cavalry, seriously injured.
Ammunition: Old model guard cartridge. (Springfield Armory)
Nature of Failure: Receiver blown out on both sides. Receiver was picked up in about three pieces. Many small pieces were never found. Receiver was entirely separated from the barrel. (O. O. Fort Des Moines)
Probable Cause: Excessive pressure and *receiver* of old heat treatment. (Springfield Armory)
Disposition of Rifle: Forwarded to the Springfield Armory.

Sept. 11, 1926.

Rifle No.
Reference: O. O. 600.913/1750, 1755, 1756
Location: Camp Bullis, Texas
Organization: Service Co. 9th Infantry.
Persons Injured: One. Slightly.
Ammunition: Peters Cartridge Co., Lot A-156. Declared unserviceable.

Nature of Failure: Bullet lodged in barrel close to muzzle and on next shot *Receiver* was blown out. (O. O. Fort Sam Houston, Texas)

Probable Cause: High pressure in combination with a rifle having a receiver of old single heat treatment. (O. C. of O. and O. C. M.)

Disposition of Rifle: Forwarded to the Springfield Armory.

───────────────

Date — 1926.

Rifle No. 107317
Reference: O. O. 600.913/1803, 1810
Location: Fort Sill, Okla.
Organization: Field Artillery School.
Persons Injured:
Ammunition: Unknown.
Nature of Failure: Barrel bulged about twelve inches from muzzle, increasing the diameter of the barrel approximately 50%.
Probable Cause: Obstruction in the bore. (Springfield Armory)
Disposition of Rifle: Forwarded to the Springfield Armory.

───────────────

July 11, 1926.

Rifle No. 863426
Reference: O. O. 600.913/1816
Location: Ann Arbor, Mich.
Organization: Co. "A" 125th Inf. Michigan, N. G.
Persons Injured: None.
Ammunition: Unknown.
Nature of Failure: Barrel burst near the breech. Receiver damaged.
Probable Cause: Obstruction in bore. (Springfield Armory)
Disposition of Rifle: Forwarded to the Springfield Armory.

───────────────

Nov. 14, 1926.

Rifle No. SA 1216644
Reference: O. O. 600.913/1839, 1842, 1843
Location: Ann Arbor, Mich.
Organization: R. O. T. C. University of Michigan.
Persons Injured: One. Slightly.
Ammunition: National Match, Lot No. 6, FA-21R, Grade B-1.
Nature of Failure: Stock shattered from point on line with front of rear sight to approximately the center of small of stock. Floor plate blown out and bent. (Proceedings Board of Officers.)
Probable Cause: Rifle was damaged due to the presence of an undue amount of oil in the chamber of the weapon when fired, and that a round of 1921 National Match Ammunition may have been a contributary cause. . . . The receiver was heat treated in accordance with the present practice of this armory and was undamaged other than the set back of the locking shoulders. Had the receiver been one of those numbered under 800,000 it undoubtedly would have been badly broken. (Springfield Armory)
Disposition of Rifle: Forwarded to the Springfield Armory.

───────────────

Aug. 19, 1926.

Rifle No. 43076
Reference: O. O. 600.913/1853, 1860, 1869
Location: Fort Sam Houston, Texas
Organization: Co. "F" 2nd Engineer.
Persons Injured: One. Probably slightly.

Ammunition: (see below)
Nature of Failure: Receiver was very badly shattered. Flange was blown from the bolt.
Probable Cause: This armory is very positive that this rifle was damaged by the firing of a round of German Ball Ammunition therein. (Springfield Armory)
Disposition of Rifle: Forwarded to the Springfield Armory.

Date —— 1927.

Rifle No. RIA 186047
Reference: O. O. 600.913/1849
Location: Fort Huachuca, Arizona
Organization: Rifle was damaged while being used by a member of the 10th Cavalry for hunting purposes.
Persons Injured:
Ammunition:
Nature of Failure: Barrel bulged under the upper band and cracked for a distance of about 12-inches toward the breech end.
Probable Cause: Obstruction in the bore. (Springfield Armory)
Disposition of Rifle: Forwarded to the Springfield Armory.

Date —— 1927.

Rifle No. 745779
Reference: O. O. 600.913/1863
Location: Gardnerville, Nevada
Organization: Kit Carson Rifle Club.
Persons Injured:
Ammunition: "B01, Lot A-484" 'Incomplete information)
Nature of Failure: Barrel split.
Probable Cause: Obstruction in bore. (Springfield Armory)
Disposition of Rifle: Forwarded to the Springfield Armory.

May 7, 1927.

Rifle No. SA 857791
Reference: O. O. 600.913/1904, 1910
Location: Fort McPherson, Georgia
Organization: Co. "A" 22nd Infantry.
Persons Injured: One. Slightly.
Ammunition: U. S. Cartridge Co., Lot B-1361.
Nature of Failure: Base of cartridge gave way, blew out the magazine floor plate, bulged out the magazine walls and shattered the stock. No damage to the Receiver is apparent.
Probable Cause: Excessive pressure developed by a probable obstruction in the bore. (O. C. of O.)
Disposition of Rifle: Forwarded to the Springfield Armory.

May 23, 1927.

Rifle No. 816284
Reference: O. O. 600.913/1917, 1922, 1925
Location: Fort Washington, Md.
Organization: 12th Infantry.
Persons Injured: One. Slightly.
Ammunition: F. A., C. P. Pyro., Lot, 451 of 1917.
Nature of Failure: Stock shattered. Magazine walls bulged. Floor plate bulged. Bolt head flange broken. (Springfield Armory)
Probable Cause: Excessive pressure. (Springfield Armory)
Disposition of Rifle: Forwarded to the Springfield Armory.

Rifle No. 874345   July 6, 1927.
Reference: O. O. 600.913/1927, 1935, O. O. 474./93
Organization: West Point, N. Y.
Persons Injured: One. Slightly.
Ammunition: U. S. Cartridge Co., Lot 998-2R
Nature of Failure: Bulged magazine walls. Bent floor plate. Split stock. Receiver
    received no injury.
Probable Cause: Failure of cartridge case.
Disposition of Rifle: Forwarded to the Springfield Armory.

————————————

                                                                   June 30, 1927.

Rifle No. SA 1248143
Reference: O. O. 600.913/1956, 1970, 1976
Location: Fort Amador, Canal Zone.
Organization: Battery "G" 4th C. A.
Persons Injured: One. Slightly.
Ammunition: R. A. Lot, E-896.
Nature of Failure: Floor plate blew down and out. (Proceeding, Board of
    Officers.)
Probable Cause: Soft head case combined with a bolt on which there was a
    broken flange on the bolt face (Ordnance Committee)
Disposition of Rifle:

————————————

                                                              Date (Summer) 1927.

Rifle No. SA 201595
Reference: O. O. 600.913/1981, 2049
Location: Camp Glenn, N. C.
Organization: Co. "I", 120th Inf. N. C. N. G.
Persons Injured: No mention in report of anyone injured.
Ammunition: U. S. C. Co. Lot #1199.
Nature of Failure: Bolt blew out. No damage to rifle proper.
Probable Cause: Defective material in bolt. Bolt was of very brittle structure.
Disposition of Rifle: Forwarded to the Springfield Armory.

————————————

                                                                   May 21, 1927.

Rifle No. RIA 138978
Reference: O. O. 600.913/1931, 1934, 1983
Location: Knoxville, Tenn.
Organization: R. O. T. C. Knoxville, High School.
Persons Injured:
Ammunition:
Nature of Failure: Barrel of rifle badly shattered at the muzzle and has two
    cracks which extend the whole length of the barrel. Stock and guard badly
    splintered. (Springfield Armory)
Probable Cause: Obstruction in the bore. (Springfield Armory)
Disposition of Rifle: Forwarded to the Springfield Armory.

————————————

Rifle No. 460371   July, 1927.
Reference: O. O. 600.913/2030
Location: Corozal, Canal Zone.
Organization: Hqs. & Service Co., 11th Engineers.
Persons Injured: None.
Ammunition: Gallery Practice loaded locally, by organization.
Nature of Failure: Barrel burst 9¾ inches from the muzzle.
Probable Cause: Obstruction in bore. (Proceedings Board of Officers.)
Disposition of Rifle:

July 13, 1927.

Rifle No. 560852 SA
Reference: O. O. 600.913/2048
Location: Camp Glenn, N. C.
Organization: Hqs. Co. 120th Inf. N. C. N. G.
Persons Injured: None reported.
Ammunition: See below.
Nature of Failure: Receiver shattered.
Probable Cause: Firing of an 8mm German cartridge (Springfield Armory)
Disposition of Rifle: Forwarded to the Springfield Armory.

June 13, 1927.

Rifle No. SA 600988
Reference: O. O. 600.913/2086, 2085, 2108
Location: Fort Sheridan, Illinois.
Organization: Troop B., 14th Cavalry.
Persons Injured: None reported.
Ammunition: Could not be determined.
Nature of Failure: Enlargement of the barrel at the muzzle end directly in front of the fixed stud.
Probable Cause: Obstruction in the bore.
Disposition of Rifle: Forwarded to the Springfield Armory.

December 2, 1927.

Rifle No. RIA 16224
Reference: O. O. 600.913/2084
Location: San Francisco, Calif.
Organization: Ordnance Detachment.
Persons Injured: One. Slightly.
Nature of Failure: Barrel burst at muzzle.
Probable Cause: Obstruction in bore.
Disposition of Rifle:

February 3, 1928.

Rifle No. SA 634479
Reference: O. O. 600.913/2239
Location: Fort Wm. McKinley, Rizal, P. I.
Organization: 23rd Wagon Co. (P. I.)
Persons Injured: One. Slightly.
Ammunition: Lot, # D-748.
Nature of Failure: Receiver shattered.
Probable Cause: The board finds that the explosion was caused by the breaking of the neck of the firing pin while the bolt was being pushed home and after the cartridge had arrived at its position on the face of the bolt, the bolt having arrived completely home, and being pushed down, the force and friction thus created caused the cartridge to explode before the bolt was completely locked. (Proceedings, Board of Officers.)
Disposition of Rifle: No record of it being sent to the Springfield Armory.

March 17, 1928.

Rifle No. SA 276691
Reference: O. O. 600.913/2271, 2277, (CCM 7170, 8/1/28)
Location: Camp Stotsenburg, Pampangas, P. I.
Organization: Troop "A" 26th Cavalry, (P. I.)
Persons Injured: One. Slightly.
Ammunition: U. S. Cartridge Co., Lot, #D-1057.

Nature of Failure: One side of face bolt blown off, headspace minimum, no
  obstruction in bore, bolt handle had to be driven up to extract cartridge.
Probable Cause: Soft Cartridge head.
Disposition of Rifle:

———————————

May 25, 1928.

Rifle No. SA 1145956
Reference: O. O. 600.913/2279, 2282
Location: Gatun, Canal Zone.
Organization: Co. "B" 14th Inf.
Persons Injured: One. Slightly.
Ammunition: Retained in service.
Nature of Failure: A piece of steel ½″ x 1½″ was blown from the barrel just
  forward of the fixed base.
Probable Cause: Barrel was manufactured by the Avis Gun Barrel Mfg. Co.,
  New Haven, Conn., and has every indication that it was not properly heat
  treated. (Springfield Armory)
Disposition of Rifle: Forwarded to the Springfield Armory.

———————————

Date——, 1928.

Rifle No. 467324
Reference: O. O. 600.913/2306, 2312, (O. C. M. 7136, 7/17/28)
Location: N. C. State College, College Station, N. C.
Organization: R. O. T. C.
Persons Injured: One. Slightly.
Ammunition: N. M. DuPont Powder, EX1076, Lot 6, 170 Grain, tinned bullet,
  Frankford Arsenal, #34121.
Nature of Failure: Barrel Split.
Probable Cause: Ammunition. It had been placed in grade 3 and no authority
  existed for its use in this weapon. (O. C. M. 7136, July 17, 1928.)
Disposition of Rifle:

———————————

August, 1929.

Rifle No. SA 590480
Reference: O. O. 600.913/2405, O. O. 474.1/172 (O. C. M. 7395, 1/3/29)
Location: Fort Riley, Kansas.
Organization: Co. "C" 137th Inf. Kansas N. G.
Persons Injured: None reported.
Ammunition: R. A. Lot #729 (Placed in grade M. G.)
Nature of Failure: The *receiver* which bears a number below 800,000 has a very
  thin hard case and carbon core; its top right half at the forward end, including the bridge, are blown off. The locking lugs of the bolt are upset
  but the bolt does not appear to be sprung or otherwise damaged. The
  floor plate is bent out, caused apparently by a violent escape of gas. About
  half of the base of the cartridge case, which was in the rifle when the
  accident occurred is blown out. . . . *The complete fracture of the receiver,*
  with no apparent stretch or elongation is characteristic of the old single
  heated receiver when subjected to excessive stress. (Springfield Armory)
Probable Cause: It is the opinion of this armory that the damage was caused
  by the cartridge developing a higher pressure than this type of receiver
  would stand. (Springfield Armory)
Disposition of Rifle: Forwarded to the Springfield Armory.

September 23, 1928.

Rifle No. SA 1137620
Reference: O. O. 600.913/2423, 2431, 2434
Location: Plattsmouth, Nebraska.
Organization: Co. "K" 17th Infantry.
Persons Injured: None.
Ammunition: W. R. A. Co. Lot, #112, Grade 2M.
Nature of Failure: Barrel ruptured 3¼" long on left side under the rear sight
    fixed base. (Springfield Armory)
Probable Cause: Due to overheating of the barrel during manufacture. (Spring-
    field Armory)
Disposition of Rifle: Forwarded to the Springfield Armory.

-- -------------

September, 1928.

Rifle No. 267305
Reference: O. O. 600.913/2432, 2444, 2451, 2453. (O. C. M. 7428 1/24/1929)
Location: Camp McCoy, Sparta, Wisc.
Organization: Troop "A" 14th Cavalry.
Persons Injured: None reported.
Ammunition: W. R. A. Co., Lot #318.
Nature of Failure: Bulge about 1½" from muzzle. Barrel split from muzzle to
    rear sight base.
Probable Cause: Obstruction in bore. (Springfield Armory)
Disposition of Rifle: Forwarded to the Springfield Armory.

August, 1928.

Rifle No. 500348
Reference: O. O. 143.8/65, O. O. 600.913/2471, 2474 (O. C. M. 7468 2/14/29)
Location: Fort Oglethorpe, Ga.
Organization: Reserve officers, 310 Cavalry and 504 Sqd. (Non-Div.)
Persons Injured: None reported.
Ammunition: Western Cartridge Co., Lot #A-79.
Nature of Failure: Barrel bulged 3½-inches from muzzle and split a distance of
    9-inches from the muzzle.
Probable Cause: Obstruction in the bore. (Springfield Armory)
Disposition of Rifle: Forwarded to the Springfield Armory.

April 21, 1929.

Rifle No. SA 235501
Reference: O. O. 400.43/35 (O. C. M. 7949, 11/7/1929)
Location: Near Macon, Ga.
Organization: Co. "C" 121st Infantry, Ga. N. G.
Persons Injured: None reported.
Ammunition: U. S. Cartridge, Lot #488 or Peters, Lot #A-48.
Nature of Failure: Rear and top of receiver blown off, front end of floor plate
    blown down, rear still in place and held by catch. (O. O. 4th C. A.)
Probable Cause: Obstruction in bore immediately forward of the chamber,
    causing excessive pressure which a receiver of the old heat treatment could
    not withstand. Receiver shattered badly. (Springfield Armory)
Disposition of Rifle: Forwarded to the Springfield Armory.

May 8, 1929.

Rifle No. 951718
Reference: O. O. 400.43/37
Location: Plattsburg, Barracks.
Organization: Co. "C" 26th Infantry.
Persons Injured: One. Private John Martens, above organization, Not seriously.
Ammunition: U. S. C. Co., Lot #708.
Nature of Failure: Cartridge case ruptured. *Receiver bulged outward at a point near the center of the magazine.* Bolt broken. Sides of the magazine bent outward. (Proceedings, Board of Officers)
Probable Cause: Damage was caused by excessive pressure which was sufficiently high to cause the cartridge case to fail suddenly and allow gas, under very high pressure to escape into the action. *The receiver* was evidently properly heat treated because *it did not fracture.* (O. C. of O.)
Disposition of Rifle:

June 4, 1929.

Rifle No. RIA 297591
Reference: O. O. 400.43/39, 67, 69 (O. C. M. 7936, 10/31/29)
Location: Fort Sill. Okla.
Organization: Co. "C" 38th Infantry.
Persons Injured: None.
Ammunition: Blank cartridges. F. A. Smokeless Powder E. C., Lot #9.
Nature of Failure: Barrel split in two from about 14-inches in front of the breech.
Probable Cause: Obstruction in the bore.
Disposition of Rifle: Forwarded to the Springfield Armory.

July 16, 1929.

Rifle No. RIA 870557
Reference: O. O. 400.43/68, 80 (O. C. M. 7938, 10/19/1929)
Location: Fort D. A. Russell, Wyoming.
Organization: Co. "E" 1st Infantry.
Persons Injured: One. Probably slightly.
Ammunition: Remington, Lot #E-1081.
Nature of Failure: Malfunction of ammunition.
Probable Cause: Rifle was not damaged by this accident. Receiver had been bent subsequent to its manufacture. (Springfield Armory)
Disposition of Rifle: Forwarded to the Springfield Armory.

August 16, 1929.

Rifle No. 219855
Reference: O. O. 400.43/113,118
Location: Ft. Douglas, Utah
Organization: Co. "F" 38th Infantry.
Persons Injured: None.
Ammunition: R. A. Lot. #E-1203.
Nature of Failure: Barrel split from the muzzle to within four inches of the breech with a decided bulge at a point approximately three inches from the muzzle.
Probable Cause: Bullet lodged in the bore at a point about three inches from the muzzle, (Springfield Armory)
Disposition of Rifle: Forwarded to the Springfield Armory.

Date (Summer) 1929.

Rifle No. 723675
Reference: O. O. 40.43/85
Location: Camp Grayling, Michigan.
Organization: 107 Ordnance Company, (M) Mich. N. G.
Persons Injured: One. Slightly.
Ammunition: U. S. C. Co., Lot #D-415.
Nature of Failure: Receiver badly shattered. Bolt flanges blown off the bolt. Extractor blown off and stock shattered. Safety lugs of the bolt upset. Head of cartridge case blown off. (Springfield Armory)
Probable Cause: Excessive pressure probably caused by an obstruction in the bore just forward of the bullet seat. *The Complete fracture of the receiver* with no apparent stretch is characteristic of the old single heat treated receivers when subjected to very high pressure. (Springfield Armory)
Disposition of Rifle: Forwarded to the Springfield Armory.

———————————

Date (Summer) 1929.

Rifle No. 274272
Reference: O. O. 400.43/85
Location: Camp Grayling, Mich.
Organization: Co. "A", 126th Inf. Mich. N. G.
Persons Injured: One. Slightly.
Ammunition: U. S. Car. Co., Lot #D-415
Nature of Failure: Receiver badly shattered. Bolt flanges blown off the bolt. Extractor blown off and stock shattered. Safety lugs of the bolt upset. Head of cartridge case blown off. (Springfield Armory)
Probable Cause: Excessive pressure probably caused by an obstruction in the bore just forward of the bullet seat. *The complete fracture of the receiver,* with no apparent stretch is characteristic of the old single heat treated receivers when subjected to very high pressure. (Springfield Armory)
Disposition of Rifle: Forwarded to the Springfield Armory.

———————————

August 17, 1929.

Rifle No. SA 711253
Reference: O. O. 400.43/117,129
Location: Schofield Barracks, T. H.
Organization: 11th Ordnance Co.
Persons Injured: One. Private Teddy Gattz, not seriously.
Ammunition: U. S. C. Co., Lot #956.
Nature of Failure: Receiver shattered. Parts of the receiver were found 50 yards away. (Major R. H. Hannum, Ord. Dept.)
Bolt head damaged, flange blown off, extractor hook broken off and stock shattered. Guard broken. *Receiver badly shattered.* (Springfield Armory)
Probable Cause: High pressure. Grease on the case and the concave indications disclose that there was grease in the bore when the rifle was fired . . . *The complete fracture of the receiver with no apparent stretch is characteristic* of the old single heat treated receiver when subjected to a greater pressure than it will stand. (Springfield Armory)
Disposition of Receiver: Forwarded to the Springfield Armory.

———————————

August 26, 1929.

Rifle No. SA 1255473
Reference: O. O. 400.43/116, 127, 134, 165. (O. C. M. 7990 11/29/1929)
Location: Fort Sam Houston, Texas.
Organization: Co. "I", 9th Inf.

Persons Injured: Two. Slightly.
Ammunition: Peters B-75.
Nature of Failure: Base of cartridge blown out. Right magazine wall bulged. Floor plate bent. Extractor hook and tongue broken off. Extractor collar torn off. The tips of the slotted locking lug and the metal in front of the extractor tongue groove blown to bits. Safety lock thumb piece was also knocked off. (O. O. Fort Sam Houston, Texas.)
Probable Cause: Obstruction in the bore. (Springfield Armory.)
Disposition of Rifle: Forwarded to the Springfield Armory.

September 3, 1929.

Rifle No. SA 1271923
Reference: O. O. 400.413/121, 135, 150 (O. C. M. 7971, 11/14/1929)
Location: Camp Perry, Ohio.
Organization: R. O. T. C. Rifle Team. 2nd Corps Area.
Persons Injured: One. Slightly.
Ammunition: 1929 National Match.
Nature of Failure: Barrel burst at the breech, opening up for about a distance of one foot, piece of the barrel breaking off completely. (O. O. National Matches 1929)
Probable Cause: Slag in the barrel (Springfield Armory)
Disposition of Rifle: Forwarded to the Springfield Armory.

June 9, 1929.

Rifle No. RIA 73153
Reference: O. O. 400.43/5706
Location: Calcium, N. Y.
Organization: Co. "A" 108th Inf. N. Y. N. G.
Persons Injured: One. Extent of injury not known.
Ammunition: R. A. Lot. #B-1, D727, 1918.
Nature of Failure: Cartridge burst causing fracture of rifle. (8th Ind. C. O. Co. "A", 108th Inf. N. Y. N. G.).
It is believed that the receiver fractured. (J. A. B. G.)
Note: No further information available.
Investigation pending.
Original file in Small Arms Division, Manufacturing Service. (Feb. 5, 1929.)

October 29, 1929.

Rifle No. SA 902871
Reference: O. O. 400.43/176, 182.
Location: Fort Benning, Ga.
Organization: 29th Infantry.
Persons Injured: One. Hand slightly injured.
Ammunition: U. S. C. Co., Lot #1166.
Nature of Failure: Upper half of the barrel for a length of about three inches and just in front of the chamber had been entirely blown out also at the forward end of this break the barrel was broken off. (O. O. Fort Benning)
Probable Cause: Due to overheating of barrel blank during the process of manufacturing. (Springfield Armory)
Disposition of Rifle: Forwarded to the Springfield Armory.

Date——, 1929.

Rifle No. SA 1226267
Reference: O. O. 600.913/2584 (O. C. M. 7714, 5/27/29)
Location: California.
Organization: 250th C. A., California, N. G.
Persons Injured: None reported.
Ammunition:
Nature of Failure: Section of barrel approximately 2-inches long and ½-inches wide blown out of the top just forward of the front end of the chamber.
Probable Cause: Burnt stock in barrel blank resulting from over-heating during manufacture. (Springfield Armory)
Disposition of Rifle: Forwarded to the Springfield Armory.

————————————

Date——, 1929.

Rifle No. 801548
Reference: O. O. 400.3294/7897
Location: Braintree, Mass.
Organization: Braintree Guards Association Rifle Club, Braintree, Mass.
Persons Injured: None reported.
Ammunition: German Service.
Nature of Failure: Shattered receiver, shattered stock, both flanges blown off, extractor, follower, floor plate, magazine spring missing.
Probable Cause: Damage was due to the firing of an 8m/m German cartridge. (Springfield Armory)
Disposition of Rifle: Forwarded to the Springfield Armory.

PART TWO

XIX

Recent Developments

THE announcement on May 1, 1957, of the adoption by the Army of a new Infantry rifle, the M14, and a new heavy barrelled automatic rifle, the M15, points up the fact that during the nine years since Hatcher's Notebook was first published in 1948, progress has been made which should be recorded in the book to keep it reasonably up-to-date.

Items that should be mentioned include the adoption by the Army of a non-corrosive, non-chlorate primer mixture for all small arms primers manufactured after January, 1950; the standardization by the Army of a new cartridge in August, 1954; the adoption early in 1957 of a new general purpose machine gun, the M60; and the adoption on May 1, 1957 of the M14 and M15 rifles as noted above.

In addition, several new hunting cartridges have been designed and introduced by the several arms and ammunition manufacturers, and the dimensions of these new cartridges are included to supplement the lists of cartridge dimensions on pages 433, 434, and 435.

Non-Corrosive Primers

As will be seen by reference to pages 347, 348 and 349, the cause of the destructive corrosion which had for so many years plagued gun users was finally traced to salt deposited in the gun barrel by the decomposition of potassium chlorate which had been used for many years as one of the principal ingredients of most small arms primers. Knowing that some European nations, notably the Swiss and the Germans had developed primers which were said to be completely non-corrosive, I made a trip to various European cartridge factories and arsenals in 1927, and obtained the formula for the non-corrosive primers that were then in use there. On my return to Frankford Arsenal, where I was then stationed, the laboratory at that place embarked on an extensive development program to produce a non-chlorate primer that would be satisfactory for military use.

The first move was to duplicate the very successful Swiss primer. It was found, however, that their primer mixture was less concentrated and more bulky than ours, and so required more room in the primer cup than was available in primer cups of the standard American design, containing a separate anvil. Consequently, to use the Swiss mixture, or any of several variations of it that we developed, it became necessary to go to the type of primer used in Europe, which has an integral anvil, formed from the brass of the cartridge case at the bottom of the primer pocket, and having two (or three) small flash holes at the sides instead of one large one in the center, as is the practice with the American primer.

For the National Matches of 1930, an experimental lot of non-corrosive primers was made up using the Berdan type of primer construction. However, that year the weather was excessively hot at Camp Perry (the site of the National Rifle Matches), and trouble was experienced with high pressures. As a result, the Ordnance Office in Washington ordered that experiments with the Berdan type of primer be discontinued.

During further experiments with the Swiss type of primer mixture (see p. 356), it was found that it has a serious defect, which is the fact that it uses fulminate of mercury as an important ingredient. Fulminate of mercury has two disadvantages for use in primers. One is the fact that a cartridge case in which a fulminate of mercury primer has been fired is adversely affected by the mercury released, so that the case is no longer suitable for reloading or any other reuse as a cartridge. An even more serious disadvantage of mercury fulminate is the fact that primers containing it are likely to deteriorate with storage. Some of the commercial ammunition companies when they first produced non-corrosive 22 caliber rim fire ammunition used mercury fulminate as a primer ingredient, and found that after several years on the shelf the ammunition gave bad hang-fires or mis-fires, or even became completely dead and insensitive.

No doubt the Swiss did not have that trouble because in their comparatively cool and dry climate such deterioration was greatly retarded, or perhaps never occurred at all.

Meanwhile, the Remington Arms Co., originators of the non-corrosive priming known as Kleanbore, had obtained the services of James E. Burns, a chemist who had about the mid-1920's demonstrated to them an experimental non-corrosive primer that he had made in which he had found it possible to omit potassium chlorate. An important ingredient in his primer was lead tri-nitro-resorcinate, usually called lead styphnate.

It had also been found that instead of the troublesome fulminate of mercury, it was possible to use a substance called tetracene, a product of the reaction of amino-guanidine nitrate with sodium nitrite. This is otherwise known as guanyl-nitros-amino-guanyltetracene or guanyl-diazo-guanyltetracene, and an application for a U. S. patent on its use in primers had already been filed by Hans Rathbürg, of Furth, Germany, in 1923.

The Remington Arms Co. purchased this patent, No. 1,586,380, dated May 25, 1926, and also acquired patent No. 1,859,225, for which application had been filed Jan. 5, 1929 by Edmund Von Herz of

Cologne-Dellburg, Germany, and which covered the use of lead styphnate in primers.

Enjoying the protection afforded them by these patents, Remington produced the highly successful Kleanbore non-corrosive primers. Other companies made up their own non-corrosive primer formulas, and some of the early ones came to grief through deterioration of the fulminate of mercury used in them; but before long, all companies had discarded fulminate, and all had come up with highly satisfactory non-corrosive small arms primers.

Finally, the patents mentioned above ran out, and other companies besides Remington used the styphnate primer mixtures with various proportions of the different ingredients.

Meanwhile, Frankford Arsenal was continuing its development work on the problem of developing a non-corrosive primer which would meet the stringent requirements imposed by its use in service ammunition. A highly important requirement is the ability of the ammunition to undergo long periods of storage in tropical climates without deterioration. Another requirement, and a most important one from the viewpoint of the ammunition maker, is ease of production and the absence of any tricky idiosyncrasies making it necessary to demand extraordinary purity of the ingredients.

A burnt child dreads the fire, and Frankford Arsenal was still smarting from the experience of World War I (see p. 355), when, due to a certain combination of circumstances connected with rush of war production plus the difficulty of obtaining completely pure ingredients, the whole primer production of the Arsenal went bad just when it was needed most. The F.A. No. 70 primer mixture, adopted at that time, was so free from any such trouble, and so utterly reliable, that the Ordnance Department, and Frankford Arsenal in particular, dreaded any change in the primer composition, and leaned over backward in making doubly sure that any new mixture adopted would be satisfactory from every viewpoint. Thus the adoption of a non-corrosive primer seemed to lag during a seemingly interminable search for perfection.

About 1940 when the carbine had been adopted by the Army and large contracts were about to be awarded to commercial ammunition makers for caliber 30 carbine ammunition, Col. E. H. Harrison, Ord. Dept., USA, was the officer in charge of preparing the specifications on which this ammunition was to be purchased. He decided that the piston arrangement of the carbine was too vulnerable and too difficult to get at to risk primer corrosion, so he simply put in the specifications the requirement that the primer must be "non-corrosive" without specifying any primer mixture or type.

By this time, every one of the companies which was awarded a contract for the manufacture of carbine ammunition had developed a satisfactory non-corrosive primer composition of its own, using a lead styphnate mixture, the basic patents above mentioned having by then expired.

Thus each company making carbine ammunition used its regular primer, and as far as anyone in the service could determine, they all worked equally well. Through this far-sighted action on the part of Col. Harrison it came about that all carbine ammunition has non-corrosive primers.

Meanwhile Frankford Arsenal's search for a perfect non-corrosive primer for other service ammunition had been progressing, and they had come up with a non-corrosive primer mixture consisting of barium nitrate and red phosphorus, and started its manufacture.

While this was in many ways an excellent primer, it had two dis-advantages. The red phosphorus suitable for use in this primer had to be of such extraordinary purity that it turned out to be a problem to obtain it of the right quality and in sufficient quantity; and moreover if the phosphorus came in contact with the metal parts, an undesirable reaction occurred, so that the metal components had to be protected against such contact with the phosphorus.

This primer mixture was used for a time (about 1949) with succcess; but it was finally decided to adopt a lead styphnate primer mixture for all service small arms primers, and such a non-corrosive small arms primer based on lead styphnate was standardized by Ordnance Committee action in August, 1949. The new mixture was put into production as soon as possible, and as a consequence all small arms ammunition made since January, 1950, has primers of the non-corrosive type. Incidentally, they are also non-fulminate, as fulminate of mercury was dropped as a primer constituent about 1899 on account of the fact that at that time it was the practice to return fired cartridge cases to Frankford Arsenal to be reloaded, and the use of fulminate of mercury in primers ruined the brass of the cartridge cases for this purpose.

The New Army (NATO) Cartridge

During its continuing study of small arms and small arms ammunition design, the Army Ordnance Corps found that the service .30M2 cartridge when loaded with modern smokeless ball powder, does not utilize all the space in the cartridge case, and could be shortened a full half inch and still have space for enough powder to retain the present bullet weight and still get the same velocity and energy.

Obviously a shorter cartridge case would require less brass, thus making for important savings in critical raw material; it would occupy less volume, permitting economy in storage and shipping space; and perhaps most important of all, its reduced length would permit any newly designed rifle to be made about an inch shorter in length, and correspondingly lighter.

Accordingly the Ordnance Corps designed a new service cartridge which is simply a shortened 30-06, and which greatly resembles the well-known 300 Savage. The case for the new cartridge was called the T65; it was modified several times, and the latest type of case, with a lengthened neck and a sharper shoulder than the first version, was called the T65E3 case.

Using this new T65E3 cartridge case, several new experimental cartridges were made up, designated as follows:

Cartridge, Armor Piercing	T93E1
Cartridge, Ball, with soft steel core	T104E1
Cartridge, Dummy	T70E4
Cartridge, Grenade Launching	T116E2
Cartridge, Spotting	T103E1
Cartridge, Armor Piercing Incendiary	T101E1

The 7.62 mm NATO Cartridge

After the North Atlantic Treaty Organization (NATO) was formed, it was decided that it would be important for all the allies forming that organization to have weapons and ammunition that would be interchangeable, thus greatly simplifying supply and logistics problems.

An early contender for the honor of NATO adoption was a cartridge of .280″ caliber proposed in 1947 by a "Small Arms Ideal Caliber Panel" which had been convened in Great Britain in 1945. This small light cartridge had a 140 grain bullet with a muzzle velocity of 2300 f.s. The British offered it to the United States, but our authorities decided that it did not have as much power as was desirable for our service cartridge, and declined to adopt it.

In refusing to go along with the British in adopting the .280 cartridge, our authorities were thinking not simply of a cartridge for an infantry rifle, but rather of a cartridge to be used in an arm taking the place of all shoulder weapons—rifle, carbine, sub machine gun, and automatic rifle—and also to be used in all rifle-caliber machine guns as well. In other words, from the thinking of our authorities on the subject, there was beginning to emerge a broad new concept of an entirely new weapons system for the armed services, which was finally embodied in an announcement by the Secretary of the Army on May 1, 1957, and will be quoted later in connection with the story of rifle development.

Our officials admitted that for uses of the rifle in cases where only the carbine or submachine gun would now be employed, the light and comparatively low powered British .280 cartridge with its 140 grain bullet at 2300 f.s. muzzle velocity would be adequate, and would even be advantageous; but for the rifle proper and for the substitute BAR and the machine gun they considered that it would be entirely inadequate. But it was considered that our T65 cartridge would be

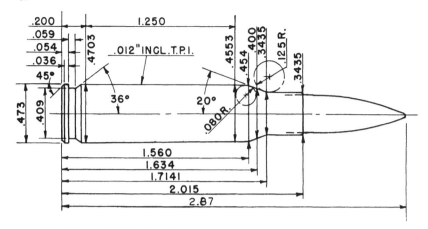

The 7.62mm NATO Cartridge, showing maximum cartridge dimensions.

adequate for machine gun use and not too burdensome for the lighter duties mentioned above.

The official U. S. view is further indicated in the following quotation from an official statement released in 1951:

"The Army is firmly opposed to the adoption of any less effective smaller caliber cartridge for use in either its present rifle or in the new weapons being developed. Any new rifle cartridge must have wounding power, penetration performance, and ballistics at least equal to that in use today. Battle experience has proven beyond question the effectiveness of the present rifle and ammunition, and there have been no changes in combat tactics that would justify a reduction of rifle caliber and power."

The North Atlantic Treaty Organization had previously prepared a statement of the military characteristics desired in a rifle and machine gun cartridge, and as these seemed to be met by cartridges based on our T65 case, such cartridges were adopted as a common standard by a NATO announcement on Dec. 15, 1953. The NATO powers agreed on detailed specifications in February, 1954, and in August, 1954, the Ordnance Committee formally standardized this cartridge for the U. S. service under the official name of *Cartridge, NATO, Caliber 7.62 mm.*

Army Weapons Developments

During World War II, the U. S. 30 caliber rifle M1 (Garand) proved to be a highly satisfactory battle weapon, though most of the soldiers complained of its weight of nearly 10 lbs., and would have liked a lighter gun. A demand also arose for a semi-automatic rifle that could on occasion be changed over to full-automatic fire. Such a rifle would need a greater magazine capacity than the 8 rounds of the

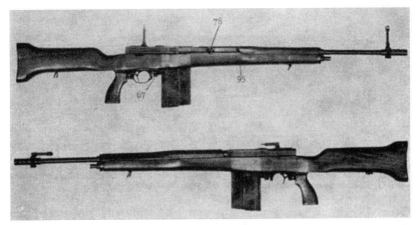

The experimental rifle T25. This radical design was one of those extensively tested prior to the adoption of the T44. Made to fire the T65 cartridge, it weighed about 7½ pounds.

Garand, and because of the tendency of the muzzle to climb in full-automatic fire, would need a muzzle brake.

Such a rifle was designed by the Army toward the end of the War. It was simply an M1 which had a change lever for permitting full-automatic fire, a detachable 20-round box magazine, and a muzzle brake. It was called the T20 rifle, but because the war ended before it had been standardized, it never was put into production.

After the war was over, it began to be realized that before any new rifle was designed, the whole subject of a weapons system for the army and other services should be the subject of a comprehensive study. Looking ahead, it was decided to put first things first, and start with the cartridge. The ultimate result was the adoption by the U. S. and the other NATO nations of the 7.62 mm NATO cartridge, as has already been described. As soon as it was decided there must eventually be a new cartridge, it became obvious that any design for a new rifle or machine gun should be for a gun to use the new cartridge.

The first new rifle tested was known as the T25, a gas operated rifle with a non-rotating bolt, developed at Springfield Armory from a design originated in the Ordnance Office. It had a 20-round detachable box magazine, a selective firing switch, and a muzzle brake. Made to fire a cartridge based on the T65 case, the forerunner of the NATO cartridge, this gun weighed about 7½ lbs. By 1950 this development had progressed so far that a pilot procurement of about 5000 T25 rifles was about to be made, but as a result of some international developments and complications, this procurement was cancelled and was never reinstated.

These international complications revolved around developments in

The British EM2 Rifle. Made for the British .280 cartridge, it weighs 7 pounds, 15 ounces; is 35 inches long overall, and has a 24.7 inch barrel. The one-power optical sight is mounted on top of the carrying handle.

Great Britain, where a radically new and different gun called the EM 2 had been produced in record time as a result of a crash program; an astonishingly fine performance, for which the British should be given great credit.

The British EM 2 rifle was most unusual in design and appearance. It had a straight stock, with a one-power telescope sight located high above the barrel, and this sight was also arranged to serve as a handle for carrying the gun. It used the newly developed .280 short cartridge, already mentioned.

In addition, the Belgian firm of Fabrique Nationale d'Armes de Guerre ("F N"), at Herstal, near Liège, Belgium, had produced a most promising new rifle, also using the British .280 cartridge.

About the time we were ready to go ahead with the procurement of a quantity of T25 rifles, the British told us they had decided to adopt the EM 2, and asked us to test it in competitive trials before going ahead with our procurement of the T25.

These trials were held at Fort Benning, Georgia, and included the new FN rifle as well as the EM 2. The T25 performed disappointingly, and none of the three rifles did as well as had been hoped. The net result was a decision by the U. S. to stick to the .30 caliber (7.62 mm), and to make intensive efforts to correct the deficiencies that showed up in the T25.

After this decision, the British went ahead and adopted the EM 2 rifle and the .280 cartridge as the standard infantry weapon. However, a change of government occurred soon afterward, and the new Prime Minister, Sir Winston Churchill, insisted on unity between his country and the U. S., and took steps to have the adoption of the EM 2 and the .280 cartridge countermanded. This was duly accomplished, but not without difficulty and embarrassment.

The United States then proceeded with further developments, dropping the T25 and replacing it by a similar gun called the T47, which was much the same as the T25, but with a more conventional type of stock, and entering another rifle made at Springfield Armory, called the T44. This has a mechanism which is largely the same as that of the Garand M1, though it is simplified in certain details; has a 20 round detachable box magazine, a change lever to permit full-automatic fire, and has a skeleton type flash hider. This new rifle weighs about a pound less than the regular M1, or approximately 8½ to 9 lbs. as against 9½ to 10 lbs. for the Garand.

A new turn of events occurred when the FN officials appeared with a model of their rifle made to use the T65 cartridge. Preliminary tests showed this gun had great promise, and it was therefore decided to obtain a number of the FN rifles to test against our own preferred model, the T44; the T47 was dropped from consideration in 1952. It was further decided that each rifle was to be tested in two barrel weights, a light barrel version to replace the M1 and the Carbine, and a heavy barrel version to replace the Browning Automatic Rifle (BAR).

In spite of all efforts to make the rifles as light as possible, and in spite of the fact that these rifles were made for the shorter NATO cartridge, it was found impossible to accomplish much reduction in weight, principally because of the very drastic performance demands made on the rifles by the using services.

In the tests which followed, the Belgian FN rifle using our T65 cartridge was called the T48, and it was tested in comparison with the T44. After preliminary tests had shown that both rifles performed well, arrangements were made to have 500 of each rifle built by mass production methods to see whether the rifles would perform satis-

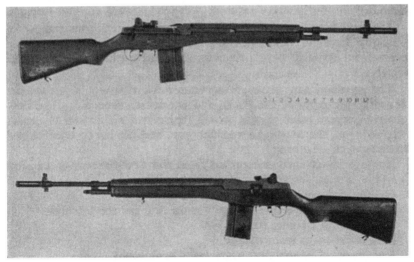

U. S. Rifle, Caliber 7.62mm, M14. During the test this rifle was known as the T44.

Another view of the Belgian designed T48 rifle. Note that the carrying handle, shown in the using position in the upper photograph, is normally folded down as shown in the lower picture.

factorily when mass produced. The T44 rifles were made by Springfield Armory, and the T48, or FN rifles were made by Harrington & Richardson Arms Co., Worcester, Mass.

In addition, the Army purchased 3000 FN rifles of the light barreled type, and 200 of the heavy barrel type for a tactical test of the practicability of the newly conceived weapons system for the services.

The new idea as to what different types of small arms the Army ought to have for best efficiency contemplated cutting the existing types from seven to two; 1 machine gun and 1 rifle with two barrel weights.

The proposed new automatic-semiautomatic rifle would replace the M1 rifle, the carbine, the BAR, and the submachine gun. The new general purpose machine gun would replace the air cooled M1919A4 machine gun, the M1919A6 machine gun, and the heavy watercooled machine gun, M1917A1.

Among the advantages expected from this new concept of an ideal weapons system for small arms were the following:

Greater fire power for the Infantry.

A better individual rifle and automatic rifle for the Infantry.

Reduction in training time.

Simplification in maintenance.

Reduction of supply and spare parts problems.

During the summer of 1954 deliveries started on the FN rifles pur-

Experimental rifle, caliber 7.62mm, T48. This Belgian designed rifle, commonly known as the FN, was a strong contender in the tests.

chased for these tactical studies, and the studies and tests proceeded at the various service schools and combat units, both in the continental U. S., and in tropical and Arctic locations. The results indicated a definite advantage for the new single rifle-single-machine gun idea.

Arctic tests held during the winter of 1953-54 had shown that while the T44 rifle performed well, the T48 (or FN) did not. This was disturbing, for early in 1954 Great Britain, Belgium, Canada, and Australia had already adopted the FN rifle made for the 7.62 mm NATO cartridge, which was the same as the T48 that was now performing badly in extreme cold. A project was immediately initiated to correct all deficiencies that had developed and repeat the tests the following winter.

The additional Arctic tests thus required were made during the winter of 1954-55, using new rifles made up for that purpose after the previous winter's test. This time the rifles both performed well, and were found suitable for use in very cold conditions.

The same rifles that had just completed the second Arctic test satisfactorily were then tested at Fort Benning by an Army Field Forces board. In a special "Combat Course Test" devised to established the performance of a rifle under very severe combat conditions, the T48 rifles performed badly, and the board stopped the test before it was completed. The British and Canadians, who, as stated above, had already adopted this rifle, were advised of this and invited to submit samples of their latest rifles for test. The British did so, and the FN firm also sent in their latest and most improved samples.

The T48 rifles that had been used in the test were modified at Springfield Armory on the basis of recommendations by the British and by the FN firm for correction of certain deficiencies, and based also on experience gained by the British during tests in the Sudan.

With these corrected T48 rifles available, the tests at Fort Benning were resumed in April, 1956, and carried on to completion.

Both rifles were found suitable for adoption, but the T44 was preferred both because of the fact that it was about 1 pound lighter than the T48 and also because it was considered to be better suited to U. S. mass production and training methods.

Accordingly on May 1, 1957, the Secretary of the Army announced the adoption of the T44 rifle in a light barrel version, standardized as the *Rifle, Caliber 7.62 mm, M14* and in a heavy barrel version, the *Automatic Rifle, Caliber 7.62 mm, M15.*

The following tabulation of comparative weights is interesting:

Light barrel rifles		Heavy barrel automatic rifles	
M1 Garand	9.6 lbs.	BAR (M1918A2)	20.8 lbs.
M14 (T44)	8.7 lbs.	M15 (T44)	14.1 lbs.
T48	9.7 lbs.	T48	13.4 lbs.

The M14 rifle is designed so that it can be produced either with or without a change lever to switch from semiautomatic to full automatic fire. It has been announced that the first M14 rifles will not have this change lever, and so can be used for semiautomatic fire only.

The new rifle has a 22 inch barrel, and a 20 round detachable box magazine. The rear sight is of the peep variety, of the same design and construction as that on the latest M1 rifle, with both windage and elevation adjustments having good positive 1-minute clicks. A slotted flash hider extends forward of the front sight.

Rifle automatic, caliber 7.62mm, M15. The mechanism is the same as that of the M14, the differences being the heavier barrel and the provision of a bipod support for the muzzle.

The M60 Machine Gun, 7.62mm on M91 Mount.

The M15 is similar in construction, except that the barrel is thicker and heavier, and a bipod is provided. The M15 has the change lever for full automatic fire, and will not be furnished without this feature.

New Machine Gun

On January 30, 1957, the Army announced the adoption of a new lightweight general purpose machine gun, intended to replace the M1919A4 and M1919A6 air cooled machine guns, and the M1917A1

U. S. Machine Gun, caliber 7.62mm, M60. This lightweight, general purpose Machine gun was developed to replace all three of the present U. S. Army Caliber .30 Machine Guns. It can be fired from the shoulder, from the hip, or from a newly developed aluminum tripod mount. (U. S. Army photo.)

The all-purpose Machine Gun, caliber 7.62mm, M60, adopted January 30, 1957.

heavy water cooled machine gun, generally called the Heavy Browning. This new machine gun is made for the 7.62 mm NATO cartridge, and is designated the M60. It weighs only 23 lbs. with bipod.

The new gun is gas operated and air cooled, and is fed from a disintegrating metal link belt. Besides the bipod, which enables it to be fired from a steady position close to the ground, the new gun may be fired from the usual tripod generally used with heavy type machine guns.

A feature of the new gun that renders it more suitable to replace the water cooled gun for sustained fire is the fact that the barrel and gas system may be removed and replaced with a cool one in a few seconds.

Further barrel life and heat resistance is provided by the use of a stellite liner and by chromium plating the bore.

It is expected that initial issue to troops will be in 1959.

New Commercial and Hunting Cartridges

Besides the new Army developments that have been described, there have been several new items of commercial ammunition put on the market since the first edition of this book. The new cartridges that have been announced to date will be described briefly, and a tabulation will be included at the end of the chapter giving important cartridge dimensions to supplement the list of dimensions on pp. 433, 434, and 435.

The 222 Remington Cartridge

The first of the several new cartridges to appear in the interval between the first edition of this book and the present time was the 222 Remington cartridge, announced in January, 1950.

When the first samples of the 222 Remington appeared, the expert handloaders and wildcat cartridge enthusiasts eagerly looked to see what well known wildcat cartridge had been copied, or had formed the basis for the new cartridge; to their surprise, they found it was like nothing they had ever seen before. Actually, it looked most like a 30-06 scaled down. Quite evidently it represents a completely new and original effort on the part of its designers.

It has a 50 grain .224" diameter bullet with 3200 f.s. muzzle velocity, driven by a charge of about 17.6 grains of a smokeless powder very similar in appearance to the powder known as Hercules No. 2400. The case is rimless, with a maximum head diameter of .378" and a maximum case length of 1.700", or 43 mm. The maximum overall length of the loaded cartridge is 2.130".

The 222 Remington has turned out to be an exceptionally successful and popular varmint cartridge.

A short time after this cartridge came on the market, the makers published rather complete ballistic data on it up to and including 500 yards range. This is given below:

222 Remington—50 Grain Soft Point Bullet

Range yds.	Velocity ft. per sec.	Energy ft. lbs.	Angle of departure minutes	Bullet drop inches
0	3200	1135	0	0.0
50	2920	945	1	0.5
100	2650	780	2	2.0
150	2400	640	3	4.7
200	2170	520	4	8.9
250	1950	420	6	15.0
300	1750	340	7.5	23.5
350	1570	275	9.5	34.5
400	1400	215	12.	50.0
450	1260	175	15.	69.5
500	1150	145	18.	94.5

The 308 Winchester Cartridge

Soon after the Army began to experiment with the shortened version of the 30-06 case called the T65, and later, in a slightly improved version, the T65E3, the Winchester Repeating Arms Division of Olin Mathieson Chemical Corporation decided to bring out a hunting cartridge using this same case; and in August, 1952, they announced the 308 Winchester cartridge, which is simply the commercial version of the Army cartridge that later became the 7.62 mm NATO cartridge. The Winchester Model 70, the lever action Winchester Model 88, and many other fine rifles are now made for this very efficient cartridge. Factory announced ballistics are given in the table on the following page.

The .243 Winchester and the .358 Winchester

The .308 Winchester turned out to be so popular and successful that the company soon decided to add 2 more hunting cartridges

Winchester .308 Ballistic Data

Bullet	Range	Velocity (ft/sec)	Energy (ft/pounds)	Mid-Range Trajectory (in)
110 Grain Soft Point	Muzzle	3340	2730	
	15'	3300		
	100 yds.	2810	1930	.5
	200 "	2340	1340	2.2
	300 "	1920	900	6.0
	400 "	1550	590	13.0
	500 "	1260	390	
159 Grain Silvertip	Muzzle	2860	2730	
	15'	2845		
	100 yds.	2570	2200	.6
	200 "	2300	1760	2.6
	300 "	2050	1400	6.5
	400 "	1810	1090	13.4
	500 "	1590	840	23.0
180 Grain Silvertip	Muzzle	2610	2720	
	15'	2600		
	100 yds.	2390	2280	.8
	200 "	2170	1870	3.1
	300 "	1970	1540	7.4
	400 "	1780	1260	15.0
	500 "	1600	1010	26.0

based on the same case, one of smaller caliber for varmint and medium game shooting, and one of larger caliber for larger game. This they accomplished by necking down the .308 Winchester case on the one hand, and by expanding it on the other. The necked down version is called the .243 Winchester; it has a 6 mm or .243" bullet of 80 grains weight at 3500 f.s. muzzle velocity, or a 100 grain bullet at 3070 f.s. This cartridge, first announced in September, 1955, and described by me on pp. 28-32 of the *American Rifleman* for August, 1955, has proved to be a highly efficient game cartridge, and is very popular. Warren Page, the gun editor of *Field and Stream*, did much experimental work on such a cartridge, and some of the factory personnel told me that his work had much to do with causing them to bring it out.

The .358 Winchester cartridge, announced at the same time, and made from the .308 Winchester case with an expanded neck, has either a 200 grain bullet and 2530 f.s. muzzle velocity or a 250 grain bullet with 2250 f.s. muzzle velocity.

Another new cartridge announced at the same time and described in the same article in the Sept. 1955 *American Rifleman* is the .244 Remington, another 6 mm based on a necked down .257 Roberts cartridge. It has either a 75 grain bullet at 3500 f.s. muzzle velocity, or a 90 grain bullet at 3200 f.s. muzzle velocity.

Factory ballistics for these two cartridges are as follows:

Winchester .243 and .358 Ballistic Data.

	Muzzle	100 yds.	200 yds.	300 yds.	400 yds.	500 yds.
VELOCITY, F. P. S.						
.244 Rem. 75 gr.	3,500	3,070	2,660	2,290	1,960	1,670
.243 Win. 80 gr.	3,500	3,080	2,720	2,410	2,140	1,910
.244 Rem. 90 gr.	3,200	2,850	2,530	2,230	1,960	1,710
.243 Win. 100 gr.	3,070	2,790	2,540	2,320	2,120	1,940
ENERGY, FT. LBS.						
.244 Rem. 75 gr.	2,040	1,570	1,180	875	640	465
.243 Win. 80 gr.	2,180	1,690	1,320	1,030	810	645
.244 Rem. 90 gr.	2,050	1,630	1,280	995	765	584
.243 Win. 100 gr.	2,090	1,730	1,430	1,190	995	835
MID-RANGE TRAJECTORY, INCHES						
.244 Rem. 75 gr.		0.4	1.9	4.9	10.0	18.5
.243 Win. 80 gr.		0.4	1.8	4.7	9.4	16.5
.244 Rem. 90 gr.		0.5	2.1	5.5	11.0	20.0
.243 Win. 100 gr.		0.5	2.2	5.5	11.0	18.5

The .458 Winchester Cartridge

Late in 1955, the Winchester Repeating Arms Division of Olin Mathieson Chemical Corporation completed the pilot models of a newly designed large caliber cartridge for heavy game which represented the most powerful big game cartridge manufactured in the United States, the .458 Winchester. As Technical Editor of the *American Rifleman*, I received for examination and test a sample rifle and ammunition of this caliber, on November 8, 1955.

During my shooting tests the rifle developed a few difficulties in feeding cartridges from the magazine with rapidity and certainty, and the first sample rifle was returned to the factory, where it underwent further development, during which the cause of the trouble was discovered and remedied.

In July, 1956, I received the improved model, with all the former troubles eliminated. This gun and its ammunition was described by me in an article in the *American Rifleman* for August, 1956.

This big gun shoots either a 500 grain full metal patch, or "solid" bullet, or a 510 grain soft point bullet. The muzzle velocity is 2125 f.s., giving a bit over 5000 ft. lbs. of energy. In my tests of the rifle I fired the full jacketed bullet into an oak log, which it penetrated to a distance of over 33 inches.

This gun and its ammunition are suitable for the largest and most dangerous African game. The jacket of the "solid" ball is made of steel coated with gilding metal, and is 1/10 inch thick at the point and .067" thick along the sides. The jacket weighs 222 grains, and would make a formidable projectile in itself. With this thick and strong jacket there is no danger that this bullet will break up or rivet over, and deep penetration can be counted on with certainty.

The 510 grain soft point bullet is intended for the very largest and most dangerous soft-skinned game.

Based on a muzzle velocity of 2125 f.s. and a ballistic coefficient for Ingalls tables of approximately .40 we can figure the following ballistics:

.458 Winchester Cartridge Ballistic Data.

Range yds.	Velocity f.s.	Energy ft. lbs.	Mid-range trajectory inches
Muzzle	2125	5014	
100	1932	4145	1.13
200	1751	3404	5.03
300	1587	2797	11.83

The .280 Remington Cartridge

On June 1, 1957, the Remington Arms Co. announced a new hunting cartridge, the 280 Remington. It listed in three bullet weights; the 125 grain pointed soft point Core-Lokt, the 150 grain pointed soft point Core-Lokt, and the 165 grain soft point Core-Lokt. Announced muzzle velocity is 3140 f.s. for the 125 grain bullet, 2810 f.s. for the 150 grain, and 2770 f.s. for the 165 grain.

The new cartridge is exactly the same as the .270 Winchester except for the fact that the shoulder is moved forward approximately .052 inch and the bullet is .005″ larger in diameter.

The company claims a better pressure-velocity ratio for the new .280 than is possible with the .270. They say it is difficult to load the .270 to specified velocity and stay within pressure limits, whereas they say that with the new .280, due to its slightly larger base area of the bullet−, (1.036% that of the .270) and its slightly greater case capacity −the pressure is less for the same velocity. Announced ballistics are as follows:

.280 Remington Cartridge Ballistic Data.

Bullet	Muzzle	100 yds.	200 yds.	300 yds.	400 yds.
		Velocity, feet per second			
125 grain	3140	2870	2600	2330	2070
150 grain	2810	2580	2360	2130	1920
165 grain	2770	2460	2180	1930	1700
		Energy, ft. lbs.			
125 grain	2740	2290	1880	1510	1190
150 grain	2630	2220	1850	1510	1230
165 grain	2810	2220	1740	1630	1060
		Mid-range trajectory, inches			
125 grain	0.0	0.5	2.2	5.5	11.0
150 grain	0.0	0.0	0.6	6.5	13.0
165 grain	0.0	0.7	2.9	7.4	14.5

The .44 Remington Magnum Cartridge

For many years handloaders and particularly big game hunter Elmer Keith, of Salmon, Idaho, have been loading the .44 S & W Special cartridge to velocities up to around 1200 feet per second with bullets weighing up to 240 grains.

Mr. C. G. Peterson of the Remington Arms Company has been interested for some time in the possibility of a commercial high velocity load for the .44 Special, and the company carried out experiments looking to the production of such a cartridge, but were discouraged because the pressures of the experimental cartridges were higher than they were willing to recommend for use in old revolvers, so for a time the matter was dropped. However, when Smith & Wesson found out that Remington was seriously interested in producing such a cartridge, they decided to construct a .44 caliber revolver of superior strength expressly for the new cartridge. At the same time, the cartridge was made longer than the existing .44's to eliminate the possibility of its use in old guns which might not have sufficient strength.

In February, 1956, Smith & Wesson announced a new .44 Magnum revolver, and the Remington Arms announced their .44 Magnum cartridge. It has a 240 grain gas check bullet, and is said by the makers to have a muzzle velocity of 1570 feet per second with 1,314 foot pounds of energy.

In order to prevent its use in old guns, the case of the .44 Magnum is made 1/8 inch longer than that of the regular .44 Special.

Experiments with Reduced Caliber Rifles

After the adoption of the M14 rifle to supersede the M1 on May 1, 1957, the Army continued to look to the future, and instituted a project called "Salvo" to study possible improvements in the small arms weapon system in terms of better hitting ability, superior wounding capacity, and lightening the load to be carried by the soldier. Among the several widely differing approaches to the problem, one idea which had some strong supporters was in the direction of a radical reduction in caliber of the service small arm from .30 caliber down

Winchester Caliber .224 Light Weight Military Rifle.

to a high velocity .22 caliber in the same general category as the
.220 Swift, the .219 Zipper, the .222 Remington, and the like.

Under the direction of the U.S. Continental Army Command in
1957, two high powered .22 caliber center fire rifles were designed for
test in connection with this program. One of these, called the Winchester Light Weight Military Rifle, caliber .224, is the product
of the Winchester-Western Division of the Olin Mathieson Chemical
Corporation. It has an overall length of 37.6 inches and a 20-inch
barrel. The 20-round box magazine is inserted from below, and there
is a change lever to permit either full automatic or semiautomatic
fire, as desired. The rifle weighs 5.3 lbs. with empty magazine in
place. Its cartridge, called the .224 Winchester, has a 53 grain full
jacketed spitzer bullet, driven at 3300 f.s. muzzle velocity to give
1280 ft.-lbs. of muzzle energy.

AR-15 Lightweight Military and Police Rifle Caliber .223.

Another rifle which resulted from this program is the AR-15, a
design of the Armalite Division of the Fairchild Engine & Airplane
Corporation. This rifle exhibits a rather advanced and unusual design,
with the barrel being made of steel, but most of the other metal parts
being of aluminum alloy, while the stock, fore end, and separate
pistol grip are of plastic. The frame is hinged like that of the T48
rifle submitted by Fabrique Nationale of Belgium as a contender for
adoption at the time of the M14 trials. The action is operated by gas
transmitted to the bolt through a tube on top of the barrel, and the
gun can be fired either full- or semiautomatically according to the
position of a change lever. The rifle weighs 6 pounds, 3 ounces, with
the empty 20-round magazine in place. Its cartridge, called the .223
Remington, has a 55 grain bullet driven at 3300 f.s. muzzle velocity
for a muzzle energy of 1330 ft.-lbs. In general this cartridge has much
the same dimensions as the .224 Winchester, but there is a slight difference in neck length and it turns out that it can be fired in the

AR-15 but not in the Light Weight Winchester, while the .224 Winchester will operate in both rifles.

At this writing (January, 1962), work on project Salvo is continuing, though along less conventional lines than those indicated above, and it does not appear likely that either of the two experimental rifles described will ever be adopted for military use by our services. However, the owners of the AR-15 design have had some of these guns made up for them by the Colt's Patent Firearms Manufacturing Co., and an effort is being made to interest foreign governments as well as to promote the use of these guns in the U.S. for use by law enforcement agencies.

New Hunting Cartridges

The .222 Remington Magnum. The start on designing ammunition for project Salvo was made by necking down the U.S. caliber .30 carbine cartridge to .22 caliber, but this effort was dropped when it was found that the necked down version did not have enough powder space to permit it to be loaded to the desired velocity.

In a further exploration of this subject, Springfield Armory gave a contract to the Remington Arms Co. to develop a high intensity center fire .22 caliber cartridge, and their design showed real promise, but at the time was thought to be too long for the rifles being designed, so the Army offered no objection when the company requested permission to bring out the new cartridge in sporting form. Christened the .222 Remington Magnum, it was first announced in a full-page advertisement in the American Rifleman for May 1958. It has the same head diameter as the .222 Remington, but is .15 inch longer overall, and has a shorter neck but more powder capacity. It has a 55-grain bullet at 3300 f.s.

The .222 Remington Magnum has a heavier bullet than the .222 Remington (55 grains as against 50 grains for the .222 Remington), and a higher muzzle velocity (3300 f.s. as against 3200 f.s. for the .222 Remington). Corresponding muzzle energies are 1330 ft.-lbs. for the .222 Remington Magnum and 1137 ft.-lbs. for the .222 Remington.

Comparative dimensions taken from sample cartridges by micrometer are as given below:

Cartridge Dimensions, .222 Remington Magnum Compared with Others

Cartridge name	Overall length	Case length	Length to shoulder	Neck length	Head diameter
.222 Remington	2.130	1.700	1.2966	.436	.378
.222 Remington Magnum	2.280	1.850	1.4637	.264	.378
.223 Remington*	2.25	1.755	1.433	.190	.378
.224 Winchester*	2.170	1.780	1.438	.223	.378

* Experimental.

The .22 Winchester Magnum Rim Fire. At the annual meetings of the National Rifle Association in Washington, March, 1959, the Winchester-Western Division of Olin Mathieson Chemical Co. first showed a new rim fire .22 of greatly increased power over any previous rim fire .22, and named it the .22 Winchester Magnum Rim Fire.

With a 40-grain jacketed soft nosed hollow point bullet driven at a specified 2000 f.s. muzzle velocity to give 335 ft.-lbs. of muzzle energy, this new rim fire .22 has over twice the energy of the ordinary .22 long rifle cartridge, and thus fills the gap between the high velocity .22 long rifle with its 37 grain plain lead bullet at 1365 f.s. and 149 ft.-lbs. of energy and the center fire .22 Hornet with a 45 grain jacketed bullet at 2690 f.s. and 720 ft.-lbs. of energy.

An appealing feature of the new rim fire cartridge is the fact that it provides a fairly effective varmint cartridge at about half the cost of the .22 Hornet.

Previously the most powerful .22 rim fire was the .22 Winchester Rim Fire (.22 W.R.F.), known to the older generation of shooters as the 22-7-45 because of its 45 grain bullet and former charge of 7 grains of black powder. A ballistic comparison of the .22 long rifle, the .22 W.R.F., and the .22 W.M.R. with the .22 Hornet is given below:

Ballistic Data, .22 LR, .22 WRF, .22 WMR, and .22 Hornet

Cartridge name	Velocity, f.s. muzzle:	100 yds.:	Energy, ft.-lbs. muzzle:	100 yds.:	100 yd. mid-range trajectory
.22 L.R. HP, 37 grs.	1365	1040	149	86	3.3″
.22 WRF HV, 45 grs.	1460	1110	210	123	2.7″
.22 WMR HP, 40 grs.	2000	1390	355	170	1.6″
.22 Hornet HV, 45 grs. ..	2690	2030	720	410	0.8″
(HP means hollow point; HV means high velocity.)					

Later Belted Cartridges

As already mentioned on p. 501, the Winchester-Western Division of Olin Mathieson Chemical Corporation in 1955 brought out the .458 Winchester Magnum cartridge with a belted case having the same head and belt dimensions as the .375 H. & H. Magnum.

Since that time the Winchester-Western Division has produced and marketed two more big game cartridges with belted cases. These have the same head and belt dimensions, the same case length, and the same overall length as the .458 Winchester Magnum.

They will be described briefly below.

The .338 Winchester Magnum Cartridge. About mid-1959 the Winchester-Western Division announced the .338 Winchester Magnum, described as a medium caliber high velocity hunting cartridge powerful enough for the largest big game, yet short enough to function through the standard length box magazines of popular bolt action hunting rifles.

Like the .458 Winchester Magnum, the .338 Winchester Magnum is of the belted type, with headspacing on the front edge of the belt. Rim, belt, and head dimensions are identical to those of the .300 H. & H. Magnum and the .375 H. & H. Magnum cartridges, as well as those of the .458 Winchester Magnum. This cartridge is necked down to form a shoulder which is sharp and which appears to be sufficiently broad to form the stop to limit the forward motion of the cartridge in chambering. However, it is not used for this, as the front rim of the belt performs the headspacing function.

This potent big game cartridge comes with either a 200 grain Power Point bullet at a specified muzzle velocity of 3000 f.s., or a 250 grain Silvertip at 2700 f.s. muzzle velocity. Muzzle energy is 4000 ft.-lbs. for the 200 grain bullet and 4050 ft.-lbs. for the 250 grain bullet. Both bullets are .338 inch in diameter and are of the flat base type with gilding metal jackets.

The .264 Winchester Magnum Cartridge. In 1960 the Winchester-Western Division of Olin Mathieson Chemical Corporation announced a high velocity hunting cartridge with a bullet .264 inch in diameter which they named the .264 Winchester Magnum. This new cartridge was stated to be designed primarily for long range flat trajectory shooting, and to be suitable for hunting such thin skinned game as antelope, elk, deer, mountain sheep, goats, and the like. The cartridge is of the belted Holland & Holland type, with the same head dimensions, case length, and overall length as those of the .458 Winchester Magnum and the .338 Winchester Magnum, and like those cartridges, it is designed to work in standard length magazines of the usual bolt action hunting rifle. Two bullet weights are available, a 100-grain flat base pointed soft point varmint load with exposed lead tip and a specified muzzle velocity of 3700 f.s. to give 3040 ft.-lbs. of muzzle energy; and a 140-grain big game bullet at 3200 f.s. muzzle velocity corresponding to 3180 ft.-lbs. of muzzle energy.

New Small Caliber High Velocity Pistol Cartridges

For several years makers of handguns have noted a demand for a handgun shooting small caliber high velocity reloadable cartridges suitable for varmint shooting, and a few gunsmiths have from time to time made on special order single shot pistols chambered for high velocity wildcat cartridges, and occasionally revolvers have been re-barrelled and fitted with new cylinders to shoot such cartridges.

To meet the demand for a handgun cartridge of this general type, both the Remington Arms Co. and the Winchester-Western Division of the Olin Mathieson Chemical Corporation have announced that they will manufacture a very high velocity (for handguns) small caliber revolver cartridge of the center fire type with a rim type case. The announcements were made and the two cartridges were first shown to the public at the annual meetings of The National Rifle Association of America at St. Louis in March, 1961.

The Remington entry is called the Remington .22 Jet, based on a necked down .357 Magnum case. It has a semi-spitzer jacketed soft-point bullet weighing 40 grains, for which the makers claim a muzzle velocity of 2640 f.s. in an 8 inch barrel, giving it a muzzle energy of 619 ft.-lbs. Remaining velocities are given as 1780 f.s. at 100 yards, 1280 f.s. at 200 yards, and 1020 f.s. at 300 yards.

At the same time that the cartridge was announced, Smith & Wesson offered a revolver chambered for this new cartridge, and with an adapter system permitting the shooting of the ordinary .22 long rifle rim fire cartridge in the same revolver if desired. This involves the furnishing of cylinder inserts chambered for the .22 long rifle cartridge, plus a system of changing the striker from center fire to rim fire.

The Winchester entry has a somewhat larger caliber, .258 inch as against .22, and a somewhat heavier bullet, 60 grains as against 40 grains, but necessarily a somewhat lower velocity. This new Winchester high velocity revolver cartridge is called the .256 Winchester Magnum cartridge. The makers claim a muzzle velocity of 2200 f.s. for the 60 grain jacketed bullet, which would give it 650 ft.-lbs. of muzzle energy; slightly more than the 619 ft.-lbs. claimed for the Remington .22 Jet. Remaining velocities claimed for the .256 Winchester Magnum are 1890 f.s. at 50 yards, 1630 f.s. at 100 yards, and 1420 f.s. at 150 yards.

At the time of the announcement of this new revolver cartridge, it was said that a Ruger revolver would be produced to shoot it, but nothing further has been heard on that subject up until this writing.

Cartridge Dimensions, Later Cartridges, Rimless Type. To supplement tables on pp. 433, 434, and 435.

Ctg. name	Overall length	Case length, inches	Case length, mm.	Lgth. to shoulder	Case dia., at rear	Shoulder diameter	Neck dia.	Bullet diameter
222 Rem.	2.130	1.700	43	1.2644	.3759	.3584	.253	.2245
222 Rem. Magnum	2.280	1.850	47	1.4637	.3754	.358	.253	.2245
243 Win.	2.710	2.045	52	1.560	.4703	.454	.276	.2435
244 Rem.	2.750	2.233	57	1.7240	.4711	.4294	.276	.243
280 Rem.	3.33	2.54	64	2.0	.470	.4412	.315	.2835
308 Win.	2.750	2.015	51	1.560	.4703	.454	.3435	.309
358 Win.	2.780	2.015	51	1.560	.4703	.454	.388	.3585

Headspace Data on the Later Rimless Cartridges. To supplement table on p. 437.

Name of Cartridge	Body taper inches per inch	Angle between centerline and wall of cone	Reference diameter on cone	Headspace diameter breech face to ref. dia. (Min.)	Rim dia.	Case dia., rear	Bore dia.	Bullet dia.
222 Remington	.01746	23 deg.	.330	1.296			.219	.2245
222 Rem. Magnum	.01454	23 deg.	.330	1.4925			.219	.2245
243 Winchester	.012	20 deg.	.400	1.6300			.237	.2435
244 Remington	.02734	26 deg.	.375	1.7767			.237	.243
280 Remington	.01641	17 deg. 15'	.375	2.100			.277	.2835
308 Winchester	.012	20 deg.	.400	1.6300			.300	.3088
358 Winchester	.012	20 deg.	.420	1.6027			.350	.3588

Dimensional data on later Belted Case Cartridges

Ctg. Name	Overall lgth.	Case lgth.	Rim dia.	Case dia., rear	Bore dia.	Bullet dia.
264 Winchester Magnum	3.340	2.50	.532	.513	.256	.265
338 Winchester Magnum	3.340	2.50	.532	.513	.330	.339
458 Winchester Magnum	3.340	2.50	.532	.513	.450	.4505

Dimensions of the 44 Remington Magnum Pistol Cartridge

44 Remington Magnum.... Overall lgth., 1.610; Case lgth., 1.285; Rim dia., .514; Case dia., .457; Bore dia., .420; Bullet dia., .429

XX

Bullets from the Sky

MANY people who own a rifle have wondered what would happen if they fired the gun straight up into the air, so the bullet would fall back to earth nearby. Some have even tried it; but mighty few have ever had any luck hearing the bullet come back.

Dr. F. W. Mann, a famous firearms experimenter who spent his lifetime and a fortune trying to find out all he could about firearms, tells in his book "The Bullet's Flight From Powder To Target" about making such an experiment. He had obtained a Model 1895 Winchester lever action gun, chambered for the U.S. Army .30-40 Krag cartridge, having a 220-grain jacketed bullet. It was in 1900 that he made the experiment described below. He says: "A curious desire to ascertain, if possible, the length of time required by one of these Krag bullets to make its perpendicular flight and return to earth, instigated the next experiment. From the end of a boat landing reaching out into a pond that was about 440 by 200 yards in size, half surrounded by a grove of pines, during a perfectly calm day, the test was made.

"Plumb lines were attached to outstretching limbs above, the butt of the rifle being placed upon the landing and so held as to cause the barrel to assume as nearly perpendicular position as possible, by sighting from the lines, in the effort to cause the returning bullet to drop into the placid lake.

"Eight shots were made from this carefully plumbed position, and any returning bullets would surely make a splash that could be seen, or if striking in the grove of pines, the day was so still they could be heard. With all these precautions, however, as not a splash was seen in the water nor a sound heard of any one of the returning eight bullets."

When I was stationed by the Gulf of Mexico in Florida before World War I, I had also tried this experiment of shooting straight up, and, like Dr. Mann, I got no results. By shooting along the beach I had also become convinced that the 4700-yard maximum range given in the handbooks for the .30-'06 Service ammunition was incorrect; I could never get a bullet to go anything like that far.

During World War I, when I was Chief of the Engineering Division of Ordnance for Small Arms and Machine Guns, we received

Ballistic Station at Miami, Florida where bullets were recovered after vertical firing.

complaints from the troops in France that the machine gun fire control tables were incorrect at long ranges. This caused me to establish a ballistic research station headed by one of my assistants, the late Lt. Col. Glenn P. Wilhelm.

This station operated at Borden Brook, Mass., in 1918; at Miami, Fla., in the fall of 1919; and at Daytona Beach, Fla., in 1920. In my official capacity I visited all three of these stations and saw much of the work being done.

Before undertaking any work on this subject at Miami, the literature was studied to see what had been done before. It was found that one of the earliest references to this subject was made by the great English ballistician, Benjamin Robins, in a book called *Mathematical Tracts*, which he published in 1761. In this he told about some vertical firing that he did with a smoothbore gun shooting lead balls 6 to the pound. That would be 1167 grains, and would require a gun with a bore of about .92 inch.

Robins "set the piece nearly perpendicular, sloping it only 3 or 4 degrees" toward the wind; when fired thus "the bullet continued about half a minute in the air, it rising by computation nearly three-quarters of a mile, perpendicular height." He also found that the bullet usually came to the ground "to the leeward of the piece, at such a distance as nearly corresponded to its angle of inclination and to the effort of the wind; it usually falling not nearer to the piece than a hundred nor farther from it than a hundred and fifty yards."

John W. Hicks, in *The Theory of the Rifle and Rifle Shooting*, published in London in 1919, notes the experiments of the British Major Hardcastle, as reported by that officer in *The Field* of October 23, 1909. He found the time of return of the British .303-inch Mk VI bullet when fired vertically to be from 52 to 57 seconds, and that of the .303 Mk VII to be 48 to 51 seconds, agreeing with figures previously obtained by calculations from ballistic tables. (In this connection it should be remember that the round nosed Mk VI bullet weighs 215 grains and has a muzzle velocity of 2060 feet per second and the pointed Mk VII weighs 174 grains and has a muzzle velocity of 2440 feet per second).

To quote from Hicks: "Major Hardcastle informs the present writer that his experiments were carried out on the river Stour at Manningtree. His boatman—probably a theorist, and unaware of the vagaries of the vertically fired bullet—insisted upon carrying a *Kelly's Directory* on his head. Not one of the returning bullets fell within a hundred yards of the boat. Some of them fell a quarter of a mile away and others were lost altogether."

Another experimenter, Mr. R. L. Tippins, as described by Hicks, carried out vertical firings on the tidal mud of the Suffolk side of the River Stour, at several different times. In the autumn of 1910 he fired two series of about 30 shots of Mk VI ammunition from a Maxim Machine Gun. In his own words: "We had no head cover, but trusted to the wind to carry them away far enough to miss us. The bullets fell on the shallow water and mud on the shore, between 100 and 200 yards away. We did not see where the first lot fell. We heard them come back in regular sequence, striking like they had started. We timed them with a stop watch, and the time of flight was over 50 seconds, and less than 60 seconds; 55 seconds was practically as near as we could get, because one cannot be certain till one has heard a few shots strike, whether the sound is really that of the bullets."

Mr. Tippins recovered two bullets which had struck on sand base first. Experiments in which the gun was tipped showed there was a critical angle in which it was practically a toss-up whether the bullets would reach the ground base first or point first.

From calculations and experiments, the British concluded that their Mk VII bullet when fired vertically rises to about 9000 feet, taking 19 seconds to go up, and 36 to come down, total time of flight up and back 55 seconds. The Germans gave similar figures for 7.9 mm, their 153-grain flat base spitzer bullet having a muzzle velocity of 2882 feet per second. It is supposed to rise 9000 feet, taking 19 seconds to go up and 38 seconds to come down; total, 57 seconds.

Among the many experiments carried out at Miami and at Daytona, was this same one of vertical firing. It was desired to find out how fast a bullet returned to earth and how dangerous such a bullet would be if it struck a soldier after dropping from a great height, such as would be the case in very high angle fire with machine guns. Many interesting things were learned from this test, and they are given in detail in the Official Report of Vertical Time of Flight for Small Arms Ammunition, in the files of the Ordnance Office. Much of the information given below is from that source.

At Miami the firing was done from a platform built in the shallow water of a protected inlet, where the water was often very calm. A frame was built to hold a machine gun tripod so that the barrel pointed vertically. Instruments were provided to check the angle of the barrel, and the tripod controls permitted any necessary changes in the barrel inclination to be made with ease and precision.

By firing a burst from the machine gun, it was fairly easy to locate the return of the shots in the calm water which surrounded the tower on all sides. The gun could then be adjusted to bring the shots close in to the tower, and then single shots could be fired and timed. A fixture for holding a rifle or a heavy Mann Barrel could be substituted for the machine gun, to permit the firing of other than the Service cartridge.

While it was comparatively easy to locate the shots at the Miami station, it was a different story when more experiments were attempted the next year at Daytona, where the firing position was on a sandy beach. Here it proved impossible to locate any of the returning shots, until a system of sounding balloons was used to plot the winds aloft, which were usually found to be reversed in direction from what they were at the ground level.

The firing platform at Miami was about ten feet square. There was a shield of thin armor plate over the heads of the men at the gun.

Out of more than 500 shots fired after adjusting the gun so as to bring the shots as nearly as possible onto the platform, only 4 shots hit it, and one more fell into the boat.

One of the shots that hit the platform was a Service .30-'06, 150-grain flat based bullet, which came down base first, (as that bullet usually does), and bounced into the water after striking the edge of the lower platform. It left a mark about 1/16 inch deep in the soft pine board.

Two more bullets struck in a pail of water beside the machine gun, and left a barely perceptible dent in the bottom of the pail, showing the bullet had landed on its side. One struck the edge of the thwart in the boat, and left a shallow indent. The shape of this indent showed the bullet was at an angle of about 45 degrees from the vertical when it hit. These last two bullets were experimental boat-tailed bullets Model of 1919, weighing 175 grains. This bullet was not very stable, and often turned over in flight instead of coming down base first, as did the Service 150-grain bullet.

It was concluded from these tests that the return velocity was about 300 feet per second. With the 150-grain bullet, this corresponds to an energy of 30 foot pounds. Previously the Army had decided that on the average, an energy of 60 foot pounds is required to produce a disabling wound. Thus Service bullets returning from extreme heights cannot be considered lethal by this standard.

Most .30 caliber bullets seem to attain about this same final velocity, and it doesn't make any difference how far they fall. Even if a bullet were fired downward from a very high plane, it still would reach the ground at about this same velocity. That is because the air resistance increases very rapidly indeed with increases in speed. If the air resists the motion of a bullet a certain amount at 300 feet per second, it will resist three times as much at 600 feet per second, and nearly nine times as much at 1000 feet per second.

A 150-grain bullet weighs .021 pounds, and when, in falling, it reaches a velocity where the air resistance balances the weight, the velocity of the fall will no longer increase.

Many expensive experiments have been made on the drag, or air retardation of a moving bullet, and amount of the air resistance is well known. For a .30 caliber bullet of standard experimental shape, having a pointed nose of two caliber radius, the air resistance on the nose at 2700 feet per second would be about 2.3 lbs.; at 2000 feet per second, 1.5 lbs.; at 1500 feet per second, .89 lb.; at 1000 feet per second, .17 lbs.; at 500 feet per second, .04 lbs.; at 350 feet per second, .025 lbs.; and at 320 feet per second, .021 lb., balancing the weight of the bullet, and stopping any further increase in velocity in case of a falling bullet.

With a very sharply pointed bullet, the resistance on the point will be less, and on the square base much greater, so that bullets coming down nose first fall faster than those that fall base first; but even so, a 150-grain .30-caliber bullet tends to balance its weight against the air resistance at some speed not too far from 300 feet per second.

For larger calibers, the terminal velocity of fall is higher, as the weight is greater in relation to the diameter. An ordinary .50 caliber machine gun bullet having a weight of 718 grains would have a terminal velocity of fall of nearly 500 feet per second, and a final energy of something less than 400 foot pounds. A 12-inch shell weighing 1000 pounds and fired straight up would return with a speed of between 1300 and 1400 feet per second, and over 28,000,000 ft. lbs. of striking energy.

Of course a heavy shell plunging down from the heights onto the deck of a vessel would be frightfully destructive. Before air power made fixed coast defenses obsolete, 12-inch and 16-inch mortars were an important part of such defenses. A mortar fires from an elevation of 45 degrees for maximum range up to elevations of as much as 85 degrees for shorter ranges. The higher the gun is elevated, the closer in the shell falls. At angles of elevation of less than about 85 degrees, the action of the air keeps the shells flying point forward; at higher elevations they are likely to fall base first.

Something over half a century ago I happened to have command of a battery of 12-inch mortars in the coast defenses of Pensacola, Florida, and I knew from first hand experience that there was no mystery about where the shells would come down, such as there is with small arms bullets. The weight of the shell, and its enormously greater ballistic coefficient make all the difference. With our fire control instruments and our range tables, we knew exactly where the shells would fall, and could fire these guns with great accuracy at moving targets distant 10,000 yards or more. The very long time of flight, 30 seconds or more, had to be allowed for, but we had instruments to do it, and the results were good.

Like the mortar shells, airplane bombs have a high ballistic coefficient, and fall with high speed, making possible the use of deck-piercing bombs for use with delayed fuses against naval vessels.

Another class of weapons with great weight and a high ballistic coefficient are the rocket missiles. General Walter Dornberger, in his book, "V-2," says that the German V-2 rocket, with a diameter of 5 feet 5 inches, and weighing 8818 lbs. (empty, but with war head), rose to a height of 56 miles and returned to earth with a velocity of 3000 to 3600 feet per second, and striking energy in the order of fourteen hundred million foot pounds.

The Miami and Daytona tests showed many other interesting facts about bullets fired straight up. For example, the flat based 150-grain Service bullet fired straight up at 2700 feet per second took 49.2 seconds to return, while the same bullet fired from the guard cartridge, having only 1200 feet per second muzzle velocity, took 40.8 seconds for the round trip. Thus initial velocity makes less difference than might be supposed, as in this case, the guard cartridge gave its bullet only 44 percent of the velocity that the Service cartridge did, but it took 83 percent as much time to go up and back.

It is interesting to speculate that when a bullet is fired upward at 2700 feet per second, the air resistance slows it down about 60 times as fast as gravity does. When the speed falls off, air resistance weakens, and has less effect. Gravity always reduces the upward velocity at the rate of 32 f.s. per second until the bullet has stopped its upward flight; then gravity starts it toward the earth at 32 feet per second and increases the downward speed at 32 feet per second for each second of the fall, less the amount that air resistance holds it back.

When the bullet reaches the top of its flight, then stops and starts back, it is still spinning, and if it is stable and well balanced, it will come down base first. However, one type of bullet, the 175 grain experimental boat-tail Model of 1919 that was fired at Miami and Daytona, was not well stabilized, and this one gave two different times for the trip up and down. When a burst of shots was fired straight up from a machine gun, some of the bullets would come down in 1 minute and 6 seconds, followed by another group that took 40 seconds longer; 1 minute and 46 seconds. Calculations showed that bullets of this type and muzzle velocity coming down base first should take 1 minute and 6 seconds, so the others were evidently those that wobbled and turned over.

Machine gun bursts of ten shots generally came down in a group not over 25 yards across, but when a bullet came down more slowly than normal, it was usually 75 of 100 yards away from the group, and sometimes so far away that it was not seen or heard.

It was found that the shape of the point on the bullet does not seem to make much difference in the time of return in vertical firing. A 160-grain .30-30 hunting bullet with a blunt nose fired upward at 2600 feet per second took 50.4 seconds to return, while a 175-grain pencil pointed match bullet with the same velocity took nearly the same time, or 51.4 seconds. It should be realized, however, that the shape of the point did not help much on the downward flight, which takes most of the time; the flat base of the bullet had to buck the air resistance in both cases.

When the Service bullet was reversed in the case and fired base first, the time of return was greatly reduced, to 30.4 seconds, agreeing closely with results reported some years before by the Germans who performed the same experiments with their 153-grain flat based spitzer bullet. In this instance, there are two factors to consider. In the first place, the flat base had to buck the air at high speed at the beginning of the upward flight, hence the height to which the bullet rose was reduced. Then, again, the bullet was coming down point first, and the pointed end, wedging its way through the air on the way down made the bullet fall faster, and gave it a higher terminal velocity.

Calculations indicate that the 150-grain .30- caliber Service bullet fired straight up at a muzzle velocity of 2700 feet per second will rise 9000 feet, taking about 18 seconds to do it; and that it takes 31 seconds to return to earth, the last few thousand feet of the fall being at a nearly constant speed of a bit over 300 feet per second.

If this same bullet, (or any other bullet, for that matter) were fired in a vacuum upward at the same velocity, it would rise a height of over 113,000 feet, or nearly 21½ miles. It would take nearly 84 seconds to make the ascent, and exactly the same time to come back, and it would return with the same velocity it had when it started up. That gives a good idea of what air resistance does to a bullet in flight. Looking at it another way, if the bullet were fired at an elevation of 45 degrees in a vacuum at 2700 feet per second, it would have a range of nearly 43 miles, and would take a minute and 59 seconds to go. But with the air to contend with, the .30-caliber Service bullet at

2700 feet per second muzzle velocity has a maximum range of only a mile and nine tenths, and to reach this range it must be fired at an elevation of 29 degrees.

In the Miami and Daytona firings, much was learned about the effect of winds aloft. Wind velocities were measured with anemometers, sounding balloons, etc., and it was found that the wind could be blowing in several different directions at the same time at different heights above the earth. Very often the wind aloft might be in just the opposite direction from that on the ground.

When a bullet is fired upward, it finally reaches a point where it has only 32 feet per second of upward velocity left. It will take this slow-moving bullet another whole second to rise 16 feet and come to a stop. Then it will start to fall, and it will take another second for it to fall 16 feet. Thus there is an interval of 2 seconds during which the bullet is poised 9000 feet above the earth, and during which it moves only 16 feet up and 16 feet down. During that time and all the rest of the time it takes the bullet to fall the gale of wind that often blows at these heights will be pushing the bullet before it. That makes it quite easy to see why it is hard to get a bullet to come back to earth near its starting place without first checking the upper winds.

Escape Velocity

The amount of written material we see on space travel these days has introduced us to the term "escape velocity," which is simply the speed with which a projectile would have to leave the earth and its surrounding air to insure that it would never return.

As the attraction of gravity is inversely proportional to the distance from the center of the earth, it will be seen that if a bullet were fired upward fast enough to reach a height of 4000 miles, it would then be twice as far from the center of the earth as it was when it started from the surface; and gravity would be only ¼ as great. At such a distance, the bullet would have an acceleration toward the earth of 8 feet per second per second, and would fall only 4 feet in the first second.

If the rising bullet got to a point as far away as the moon is, which is about 240,000 miles, or 60 times the radius of the earth, the earth's gravity would be only about 1/112 of what it is at the surface; a bullet dropped from such a point would have an acceleration of only .2844 feet per second per second, and would fall a little less than an inch and three quarters in the first second. This will illustrate how very rapidly the attraction of the earth falls off as an object recedes into outer space.

If an object, such as a meteorite, were located in far distant space, with no motion relative to the earth, the faint attraction that the earth has at that distant point would start the body moving toward the earth ("falling") at an almost imperceptibly slow rate. Eventually, as the distance between the earth and the body became less, the attraction would become stronger, and the speed of "fall" would increase. Astronomy books tell us that such an object would finally reach the earth with a speed of about 7 miles per second. Conversely, if a body were projected from the earth with a speed greater than this, it would never come back, but would keep on receding farther into space forever.

The much quoted figure of 7 miles per second for the escape velocity is obviously an approximation. It would be interesting to work this out for ourselves, and see how close this approximation is.

A bit of integration gives us the formula $v = {}^2\sqrt{2gR}$, where g is the acceleration of gravity, which we will take as 32 feet per second per second; R is the radius of the earth, which we will take as 4000 miles; and v is the quantity sought, which is the escape velocity.

Working it out, we come up with 36,765.25 feet per second, or 6.96 miles per second, showing that the quoted figure of 7 miles per second is sufficiently close to the truth.

XXI

Explosions and Powder Fires

Powder and Ammunition Fires

THE purpose of this chapter is to explore the question of how much danger there is in having a cartridge go off in a fire, as in burning trash; how much of a risk there is in keeping small quantities of powder or small arms ammunition in a home in case of a fire; and other related questions. In an endeavor to find out the answers, I have over a period of years made a large number of actual tests and experiments along these lines, and the results will give facts, not guesswork.

It is necessary to distinguish between *high explosives,* such as t.n.t., tetryl, dynamite, nitroglycerine, guncotton, etc., which *detonate,* and ordinary black or smokeless gunpowders, which simply burn when in the open, or explode when confined.

Some high explosives, such as dynamite or t.n.t., when ignited in the open in small quantities, simply burn like rubber, and usually do not explode, though there have been disastrous exceptions, which will be discussed presently.

To make a high explosive detonate, it is usually necessary to employ a substance with great *brisance,* or shattering effect, such as fulminate of mercury to start the action. A detonation seems to be an actual rearrangement of the molecules to form a new compound or compounds which occupy many times the space formerly required. Some high explosives, such as nitroglycerine, complete the detonation in as little as 1/25,000th of a second. Such substances strike such a sudden blow that no confinement is necessary for them to wreak great destruction. Nitroglycerine dynamite, when simply laid on a rock and detonated, will shatter the rock even though there is no tamping or covering of the explosive. Some high explosives, such as nitroglycerine or dynamite, are sensitive to shock, while others such as t.n.t. will stand great abuse without exploding. Some such explosives may be pounded, sawed or cut with very little risk of explosion, but if a fulminate of mercury cap is embedded in a block of t.n.t. or tetryl, and fired, the explosive will detonate if a strong enough cap is used; however, if the cap is too weak, the t.n.t. or tetryl block may simply shatter or be pulverized without exploding.

As stated above, dynamite or t.n.t. may often be burned in small quantities without an explosion, but when large quantities are in-

Explosion at Lake Denmark Naval Ammunition Depot, July 10, 1926
This crater marks the site of Building No. 8, where the first detonation occurred. This building contained over a million pounds of cast t.n.t. The ground
was still smoking when I supervised the taking of this photo.

volved in a fire, the danger is extreme, and a detonation usually takes
place when the heat and disturbance of the burning become considerable.

An example of such an explosion occurred Dec. 6, 1917, in the
harbor of Halifax, Nova Scotia, when the ship Mont Blanc, carrying
some 3,000 tons of t.n.t. caught fire after a collision with the Belgian
relief steamer Imo. A fire started among some oil drums on the fore-
castle, and soon communicated itself to the cargo. The crew took
to the boats and rowed rapidly away. In a few minutes a frightful
detonation occurred, devastating the entire northern part of the city,
with the loss of about 1600 lives and some $50,000,000 property
damage.

Another classic example of a massive explosion of bulk t.n.t. following a fire occurred at the Lake Denmark Naval Ammunition
Depot near Dover, N. J., on the afternoon of Saturday, July 10, 1926.

At about 5:15 p. m., during a heavy thunder storm, a bolt of
lightning was seen to descend at or near the location of temporary
magazine #8, which contained over a million pounds of cast t.n.t.
for depth charges and airplane bombs. In spite of the fact that this
building was protected with lighting rods, a thick column of black
smoke was seen issuing from the south end of the building. At about
5:20 p. m., a colossal detonation occurred, and building #8 com-

Lake Denmark Explosion. Site of building No. 9, the second to go.

pletely disappeared, leaving only a deep crater, and instantly killing the members of the post fire department who had arrived to fight the fire. Five minutes later, building #9, adjoining, also detonated, leaving a similar crater. Steel girders were blown a distance of 5000 ft., and it was reported to me on the site the next day that a smoking wooden beam had fallen on a farm about 3½ miles away.

At 5:45 p. m., shell house #22, containing similar material detonated, also disappearing completely and leaving a crater. Fires started up in various places and detonations continued at intervals for 10 hours or more.

The Army Smokeless Powder Factory, Picatinny Arsenal, adjoins the Lake Denmark establishment, and its personnel escaped heavy casualties because at that time only half a day was worked on Saturday, and the Arsenal had closed for the day several hours before the explosion took place.

Col. (later Brigadier General) N. F. Ramsay, the commanding officer of Picatinny Arsenal, heard the fire alarm at Lake Denmark, and ordered a phone call made to see if help might be needed. The operator reported that he couldn't get through, and Col. Ramsay ordered him to keep trying, meanwhile watching the column of smoke on the hill about ⅝ of a mile distant. Suddenly he saw an enormous flash, and with excellent judgment, he threw himself flat. A few seconds later, when the blast hit, portions of the glass from the window through which he had been looking were blown across the room and embedded deeply in an oak door.

At the time of this explosion, I happened to be the executive officer of Frankford Arsenal, at Philadelphia, about 60 miles away, and accompanied by Brig. Gen. O. C. Horney, commanding officer of Frankford, I got into an official car and hurried to the scene. I was therefore able to get a first hand impression of just what happens in a major explosion of this magnitude, and my photographer, who accompanied us obtained some excellent pictures.

In this great explosion both the two adjoining establishments of Lake Denmark Naval Ammunition Depot and Picatinny Arsenal were practically wiped out. The initial detonation of building #8, with its contents of over a million pounds of bulk t.n.t., completely demolished every unshielded building within a radius of 2700 feet, and heavily damaged buildings as far away as 8000 feet.

It is notable, however, that one building containing about 2,500,000 pounds of a shell filling called Dunnite (ammonium picrate, invented by the late Col. B. W. Dunn) burned quietly with no explosion, thus confirming the claims that it was unusually safe to handle or store.

The army magazines at Picatinny were located along a winding ravine with strict attention to safety distances, and while many were smashed flat, they neither burned nor exploded. Likewise a number of partly buried magazines similar to the modern "igloo" magazine, at Lake Denmark also escaped damage.

Explosion at Lake Denmark, July 10, 1926

Effect of the blast on a building at Picatinny Arsenal. Every building within 2700 feet of the big detonations which was not behind an intervening hill or was not shielded in some way was completely demolished.

Lake Denmark Explosion, July 10, 1926
Picatinny Arsenal, an army installation a mile or so distant from the Lake
Denmark Ammunition Depot, was practically wiped out. This shows one of the
Picatinny buildings after the explosion. Picture taken under my supervision
right after the disaster.

Explosion at Lake Denmark Naval Ammunition Depot, July 10, 1926
Main section of the post after the disaster. The car in the foreground was
occupied by fire fighting personnel approaching the blaze. All were killed.

Lake Denmark Explosion

This car was just leaving the post when the fire started, and had gone about ½ to ¾ of a mile when the first blast occurred. The occupants were killed.

The exhaustive study of this disaster which was made right after it happened had a most important influence on later magazine and ammunition depot construction.

Initiators

Another class of explosives which is extremely dangerous is the initiators, such as the dynamite caps and small arms primers. Fulminate of mercury, lead azide, tetracene, and several other substances are in this class. They are very sensitive to shock, and when they do go off, they explode with great violence—or in other words, their explosion is always very rapid, taking place in perhaps a ten thousandth of a second or less.

The dynamite cap is a little copper tube about the same diameter as a .22 caliber cartridge, and a bit longer, open on one end, and slightly rounded on the other. Such caps are used around construction projects, and sometimes are dropped, to be picked up by youngsters playing around. Usually the next thing is that a boy has lost some fingers or his eyesight by pounding such a cap, holding a match to it, or some other such unfortunate procedure. Dynamite caps are deadly, for when exploded in the open, the closed end of the little tube will be blown off and will be projected with great velocity and with force enough to penetrate deeply into any object struck. The velocity of such a fragment has been found to be 4000 feet per second or more. This is in marked contrast to the action of small arms cartridges, which when exploded outside of a gun, and unconfined, are relatively harmless, as will be shown later.

The Briscoe case. Early in January, 1934, I was asked by Rear Admiral W. S. Pye, to give an opinion on the strange death of his sister-in-law, Miss Katherine Briscoe. She had gone to the cellar of her Baltimore home to put some coal on the furnace fire. A few moments later she staggered up the cellar stairs, clutching a wound in her chest, and gasped out that she had been hurt. A physician was called by telephone, and found her dead. Neither the physician or the coroner could determine the nature of her injuries. An autopsy revealed that a tiny bit of metal had severed a large blood vessel near her heart. On examination of the disc of metal, I decided it was the end off of a blasting cap, and thereupon, searched the ashes of the furnace, which had already been sifted by the police without result. In the ashes the tell-tale evidence was plainly visible, having previously been overlooked simply because the searchers didn't know what to look for, and had passed it by as unimportant. This bit of evidence was the lead wires of an electric blasting cap, such as is used in coal mines. Such a cap had evidently failed to go off, and had been in the shovel of coal Miss Briscoe had thrown on the fire.

Small Arms Primers

Like dynamite caps, small arms primers are quite brisant, that is, they go off suddenly. However, any one primer has too little mixture in it to make it very dangerous by itself, though it could be dangerous to eyesight if handled carelessly. However, a large quantity of primers in bulk can be deadly. Some years ago I was told about an accident that happened at one of the cartridge factories, where a laboratory technician was carrying a large quantity, perhaps a quart or more, of loose primers in a metal bucket. As he walked along. he bounced the bucket up and down, to hear the primers shake. But suddenly the entire quantity detonated, and he was killed instantly Fortunately, primers as they are now furnished to handloaders aie immune to shock, as they are packed in grooves in small wooden blocks, and hence never get together in bulk. Moreover, this method of packing removes the risk of having them cause damage in case of fire. I saw a gunsmith's shop which had burned, and while there was a biq pile of charred boxes of primers found in the ruins, none of them had gone off.

Powder Fires

Gunpowder is of two general varieties, black and smokeless. Black powder is a mixture of charcoal, sulphur, and saltpeter. The charcoal and the sulphur are fuels and the saltpeter, (potassium nitrate), is an oxygen supplier. When heat is applied, the saltpeter decomposes, releasing free oxygen and so the combustion can proceed without the need of any outside air being supplied.

Black powder burns with an almost instantaneous flash even when burned in the open and unconfined. Moreover it is easily ignited by even a very slight spark, and hence it is much more dangerous to handle than smokeless powder is. Persons working around black powder must wear shoes with no nails, and iron or steel tools of any kind are forbidden, any necessary tools being of copper.

An almost unbelievable violation of the most elementary precautions necessary in handling black powder occurred at Nansemond Ordnance Depot some years ago when a freight car containing cans of black powder was being unloaded into a magazine. An explosion of all the powder in both car and magazine wiped out the crew with the exception of one survivor who was temporarily away from the immediate vicinity. From his testimony it was learned that the lids of the cans were rusty, and could not be opened in the usual manner, and that the man in charge had set the crew to opening them by slashing the lids with a hatchet, as is often done in army kitchens with canned foods, condensed milk, etc.

Smokeless powder as we know it today is a colloid, or glue-like substance formed by dissolving gun-cotton in a solvent, usually a mixture of ether and alcohol, and then evaporating the solvent. It looks much like celluloid, and burns in the same manner when ignited in the open. In a gun it burns so much faster because all the heat and pressure generated by the burning of the first few grains is retained, and therefore builds up in intensity with extreme rapidity; and the higher the heat and pressure, the faster the powder burns.

If a small amount of smokeless powder is to be disposed of, it is safe to place it in a heap in the open, and ignite it by a trail of paper or otherwise from a distance. However, do not underestimate the rapidity with which heat can build up if there is a respectable amount of powder involved. At Camp Dix, N. J., just after World War I, it became necessary to dispose of a relatively large quantity of howitzer powder which was in the magazines there, and which was showing signs of deterioration, and was considered unsafe to keep in the magazines. When the situation was reported to Washington, it was ordered that the powder be burned in an open field, a very proper recommendation under the circumstances, but one that needed to be carried out with due regard to the necessity of destroying reasonably small quantities at a time.

However, this was not done. It was all emptied out at one time and formed a pile several feet deep and some yards across. A train of powder was laid to the main pile, and after the spectators withdrew to what they estimated to be a safe distance, the powder train was ignited. All went well for a few seconds, but then the flame and heat mounted so fast that it became apparent that the distance was far too short for safety. The heat suddenly became unbearable; clothes began to scorch and faces to blister, and the persons involved threw themselves flat and fortunately escaped serious injury, but learned a sharp lesson in powder behavior.

Curtis Bay Powder Fire

During 1928, when I was Ordnance Officer of the Third Corps Area of the U. S. Army, a magazine containing 600,000 lbs. of small arms rifle powder burned at Curtis Bay Ordnance Depot, only a short distance from my office, and I had a chance to see what happened.

The magazines were situated in rows, no magazine being closer than 400 feet to the next, according to the Army tables of distances for magazines in force at the time.

Two laborers with a team of mules were about to start some earth moving operations with a scraper, and they stopped by a magazine, set their bags of lunch on the ground, stood their shovels against the magazine wall and hung their overalls on them. About that time they heard a loud rushing sound from the magazine next in line, which was 400 feet away. This was described as sounding like the lifting of the safety valve on a locomotive. Almost instantly flames burst out of the doomed building, and the men started to run, but the heat became so intense that they fell to the ground, fortunately in a small depression, which shielded them slightly, and they escaped with blisters on the backs of their necks but no serious injury. The team of mules simply trotted around the corner of the building, where they stood, shielded from the direct rays of the heat. The men's lunch bags and overalls burst into flame, and the shovel handles were charred.

The whole thing was over almost as suddenly as it began. In a minute and 50 seconds the fire was out, and where a magazine had stood containing 600,000 lbs. of powder, there was only a concrete foundation strewn round with seared and twisted sheets of steel which a few minutes before had been the walls and roof of the building.

An airplane was flying nearby at the time at an altitude of 1600 feet, and the pilot said that a yellow pencil of flame shot up an estimated 2000 feet higher than he was, then slowly died down. The recording thermometer on the outside of the headquarters building over half a mile away showed a sharp rise in temperature lasting a minute and fifty seconds, from which the duration of the fire was deduced. This fire was thought to be due to spontaneous combustion of the powder, sometimes possible when powder is stored in bulk, but which does not occur when it is in small cans such as are used by handloaders, where any incipient rise in temperature can easily be dissipated.

Ignition of Powder by Rifle Bullets

Right after World War I some mysterious magazine fires occurred, which were laid to bullets from careless hunters, and it was decided to see if a rifle bullet fired into a large can of rifle powder could set it off. Some experiments were conducted in which large cans (150 lbs.) of smokeless powder were fired at with Springfield rifles. It was found that sometimes such a bullet would ignite the powder. In one such test, the firer got a surprise, for this time he seated himself about 100 feet away and fired into the very bottom of the can. Instead of igniting, it exploded with great violence, and turned the startled firer end over end. It seems that if there is more than about 2 feet of powder above the point of entrance of the bullet, the powder may explode instead of simply burning.

The Bushnell Smith Case

J. Bushnell Smith was a well-known gunsmith and custom ammunition loader, who had a residence with an adjoining 4 room frame shop at Weybridge, Vermont. At 11 a. m. on July 16, 1948, I received a wire from his father stating that Bushnell Smith had died in a fire at his shop at about 10 that forenoon. I phoned the Director of Public Safety of Vermont and asked him to let me know what had happened when his men had finished their investigation. A short time later he phoned me stating that his investigators were "on the ropes," and inviting me to come and see for myself and help his men find out the answers. The Chief Fire Marshal of the State met my plane at Burlington and I was at the scene of the fire by 6 p. m., with still some daylight left.

Smith's body was found in the lathe room of his shop, in or near the doorway to a room where he had five 150 lb. cans of surplus small arms powder stored, or 750 lbs. altogether. The shelves in another room were stacked with 20 lb., 5 lb., and 1 lb. cans of various kinds of small arms powder, and a shed against the wall contained large drums of kerosene or fuel oil. It is needless to point out that the powder in such quantities should have been in a magazine.

Smith had been adjusting a trigger mechanism which had been giving him premature discharges, and a few moments before the accident had been firing through an open window at a target in the woods behind the shop. The rifle, a .30-06, was found under his body.

From a careful evaluation of all the evidence it became apparent that Smith had had an accidental discharge, and that the bullet had gone through the open door into the next room and into one of the 150-lb. cans of rifle powder, which had ignited instantly and had set off the other 4 cans. The resulting burst of flame through the open door had simply cooked Smith before he could move, and had dropped him in his tracks.

Other members of his household phoned the fire department, which arrived about 15 minutes later. At that time loaded cartridges were popping off, and they were rather afraid to go near, but in spite of that fact they quickly got two streams of water on the fire, and extinguished it with much of the shop still standing.

An examination of the rooms where the powder was stored revealed no sign of any explosion. The powder cans were mostly split open along the seam or bulged, but the only damage to the building was from fire.

Smith used a large number of primers in his reloading operations, and the room where he died had the shelves stacked with them, in the original containers, just as they came from the maker. Some of the shelves containing the primers had burned through and collapsed, and the packages were charred, but apparently none of the primers had gone off, indicating that as they are packed for sale to handloaders, they do not constitute a hazard.

Experimental Powder Fires

While experiences such as the Bushnell Smith case and others had led me to a fixed opinion that the small 1-lb. cans of powder such as are used by handloaders do not constitute any particular fire hazard, it was felt that it would be desirable to suplement or confirm these opinions by actual tests, so that I could say "I have tried it."

Accordingly a number of 1-lb cans of small arms powder of various kinds were obtained, including both black and smokeless, and nitroglycerine as well as nitrocellulose varieties, in both rifle and pistol granulations.

Taking along the powder, matches, kindling wood, and several witnesses, we went out into a safe place in the country, piled up a small stack of sticks, and placed on top of them a 1-lb. can of I.M.R. (Improved Military Rifle) powder no. 4895, such as was used for loading the .30 caliber service cartridges during World War II. Shoving some crumpled paper under the pile of sticks, I lighted it with a match and stepped back about 20 feet to wait results.

The fire flamed up quickly, and in spite of the fact that the can was evidently being subjected to a considerable degree of heat, it was 1½ minutes before the can burst open with a very mild report, and with a yellowish white flame about 4 feet in diameter and lasting about 1½ seconds. The can was bulged and the bottom seam was opened about half way around. The pile of sticks was not disturbed, and all spectators agreed that the burning of a closed 1-lb. can full of rifle powder was a very mild performance.

Next we tried a container of 11 ounces of Bullseye powder, a nitroglycerine powder of very fine granulation, used in pistols and revolvers. This is about the fastest small arms smokeless powder in existence, and if any one of them would be likely to produce anything resembling an explosion, this would be it.

This can was made of cardboard in several layers, and had a crimped-on metal bottom and a metal top with screw type lid. This can stood in the flames for a minute and 45 seconds before it opened up and gave out a bright yellowish white flame about three feet in diameter. There was practically no noise at all; only a soft hissing sound. Again the pile of sticks was undisturbed.

The same test was tried on several other types of small arms powder, with practically identical results. Powders included Red Dot, Hercules No. 2400, DuPont No. 3031, DuPont No. 4064, and rifle powder No. 4676.

It was then decided to try the one powder we had some doubts about, black powder. We tried both DuPont Fg and DuPont FFg, in the usual DuPont oval cans of flattened elliptical section, about 5 ¾ inches high, 4 inches wide, and 1 ¾ inches thick, with a screw top. From this we expected more action, so we stood back farther, but the result, while more pronounced than that with the smokeless powder, was on the whole less than we had feared. After five minutes on the fire, the can exploded with a heavy dull thud, and a dense cloud of white smoke rose upward in a mushroom shape. The can was blown about 35 feet to one side and was opened out nearly flat, separating along the seam and having the bottom blown out. Even so, the pile of sticks was not disturbed.

The powder burning tests were now over, but one member of the party had brought along a small Chinese firecracker which he said boys were using in his neighborhood, and which seemed to him to be very potent. We took an empty one pound powder can, removed the lid, punched a small hole in it, then put the fuse of the firecracker through the hole, leaving the end outside, and screwed the lid back on, leaving the firecracker hanging inside the can. About 2 seconds after the fuse was lighted, the firecracker exploded with a tremendous report, many times as loud as that of any of the cans of powder, and the can was blown wide open, and flattened into a single sheet of tin, and blown about 30 feet away. This little firecracker was only ¼ inch in diameter by about 1 ½ inches long, and must have been loaded with some substance like fulminate of mercury. Such firecrackers are extremely dangerous, and this experiment points up a common misconception, which is the mistaken belief that smokeless powder is an unusually powerful and destructive explosive. Actually, it is a weak one, and does not compare with common gasoline or cleaning fluid in destructive potential. By no stretch of the imagination could a 1-lb. can of smokeless powder pack enough of a punch to demolish a whole dwelling house, but a similar quantity of gasoline can, if it is distributed throughout the house and allowed to mix with the air. The reason is that the powder, which is designed to be fired in a closed chamber, must supply within itself both the fuel and the oxydizing agent, while the gasoline is all fuel, and mixes with a large volume of air to form a much more destructive mass of explosive.

Again, powder as compared to gasoline, especially if the latter is in glass jugs, as is so often the case, is negligible as a fire hazard. In case of a fire, nothing can happen until the flames actually lick the container for some time; then all that happens is a ball of flame several feet in diameter, and lasting not much over a second. Should flames come in contact with a gallon jug of gasoline, the jug will eventually crack, the gasoline will run out, and there will be an enormous volume of flame which will last long enough to ignite everything on that floor with great thoroughness.

An acquaintance of mine told me, with some embarrassment, of a gasoline incident that happened to him. He had gasoline for a power lawnmower in a 1-gallon glass jug. Desiring to clean some tools with it, he brought it into the basement workshop where he had been doing some handloading. As he tipped the jug up to pour out some gasoline, the jug struck lightly against a bench vise, and cracked wide open, and the gasoline poured out on the basement floor and ran over toward the furnace. In just an instant, there was a loud pouff, and the basement floor was covered with a sheet of flame, the gasoline vapor having ignited from the furnace. My friend rushed out of the room, closed the door, and phoned the fire department. After the fire was out, it was found that the handloads that had been left standing base down on the bench had been burned, and had gone off, but a sheet aluminum air duct just above them was unmarked.

To sum up; small arms powder properly packed in the factory containers, and in small quantities is not a fire hazard. It is however, smart to keep it where fire cannot get at it. My friend W. E. McNellis, of Gallup, N. M., an avid handloader, keeps his powder in old abandoned refrigerators which he purchases for a few dollars from the local junkman. He knocks off the latch, so no children can lock themselves in, then fits a hasp and padlock, and keeps these refrigerators with powder in them in his back yard. This method has the advantage of keeping the powder temperature even. A short time after he adopted this system a fire occurred which burned several buildings adjoining his back yard, but the powder was safe inside the refrigerators.

Small Arms Ammunition as a Fire or Explosion Hazard

Enough experiments have been made on this subject so that almost any question that might arise can be answered with definite information based on tests. As for any possible explosion hazard from small arms ammunition, even in large quantities, it can be said with confidence that there is no such danger. Much information on this subject is contained in a small but highly authoritative pamphlet issued Jan. 12, 1956, by the Sporting Arms and Ammunition Manufacturers' Institute, 250 East 43rd Street, New York 17, N. Y.

As stated on the title page of this pamphlet, it illustrates and describes a series of very severe and thorough tests made for the purpose ascertaining whether or not small arms ammunition is dangerous to handle in warehouses or freight stations, on docks and wharves, or in transit by rail, water truck, and by air, when subjected to rough or careless handling, falls, shock or fire.

A large shipping container full of cartridges was hoisted up to a height of 30 feet over a solid concrete block, and dropped. The wooden case was shattered to pieces, but no explosion occurred, though some of the cartridges were mutilated by the sheer force of the impact.

A freight car with the entire floor covered with cases of .22 caliber cartridges, 10,000 to a case, was subjected to such rough treatment that many of the wooden cases were broken open or shattered: but there was no explosion.

The ability of small arms ammunition to take a terrific shock without exploding was shown by firing a .30 caliber rifle bullet into a full case of the blank cartridges used for actuating stud drivers and similar powder operated tools. These do not contain bullets; the space otherwise occupied by the bullet contains extra powder instead, so these cartridges would seem to be the most likely to cause trouble in such a test.

There was a small burst of flame at the instant of impact, but no explosion or fire occurred though the case was burst open and the cartridges were scattered around from the impact of the bullet. This test was made on both fibreboard and wooden packing cases full of ammunition, with the same result. Out of the 10,000 cartridges contained in one case, 176 were damaged by the impact of the bullet; 130 fired; and 9694 were completely unaffected.

A standard shipping case containing 500 12-gauge shotgun shells had 2 .30 caliber bullets fired into it from a distance of 50 feet. Both bullets penetrated into the first and second cartons nearest the point of entrance, causing several of the cartridges in these two cartons to burn. White smoke issued from the case for an instant after each bullet hit, but the case was not distorted, and there was no communication of fire to the rest of the case.

A case of 10,000 .22 caliber rim fire cartridges was fired into by a high powered rifle from a distance of 100 yards. The case was burst open by the impact, and some cartridges were strewn around, but no explosion occurred.

A fibreboard case containing 500 12-gauge shotgun shells was placed on a metal rack over a pile of kindling wood, and the wood was ignited. After the case was burning, the blazing wood was dragged away. The burning continued until the case and all the shells had burned. At no time did any of the shells explode with violence. The powder charges burned quietly, and barely opened the crimped shells. No propelling of shot charges could be detected. However, some of the primers did pop off audibly.

Moreover, in other tests by the same organization, a large number of metallic cartridges and shotgun shells were burned in a fire of oil-soaked wood. The cartridges and shells exploded from time to time, but there was no general explosion or propulsion of shot or bullets with any great force or to any great distance. Throughout the test, the men conducting it remained within 20 feet without injury. This test showed that small arms cartridges, whether they are metallic cartridges or shotgun shells, when involved in a fire, will not explode simultaneously but rather piece by piece; that the bullets or the shot are not projected with any great velocity; and that the material of which the cartridges or shells are made will usually not fly more than a few feet.

Newspaper Accounts Often Misleading

In spite of the fact that people who are acquainted with ammunition know these facts, they are not commonly realized by the public, and distorted or inaccurate newspaper accounts of incidents involving ammunition in a trash fire or the like have spread a contrary impression. Many times such erroneous reports originate when some individual tries to explain an unwise or illegal action by blaming it on a cartridge in the fire for which he could not have been responsible.

A boy is forbidden to play with firearms, but he sneaks a gun out when nobody is looking, and manages by bad luck to wound himself or a companion; so he evades punishment or a scolding by saying they were burning some leaves and an explosion occurred and he was hit by a bullet from a cartridge which must have gotten in the fire in some way. In one such case in which I was consulted, I pointed out that the bullet recovered from the boy's leg showed rifling marks. He then admitted the fire story was invented, and that he and a friend had been playing with a cheap revolver his friend had acquired in a trade.

A fairly common occurrence is for a youngster to find a .22 cartridge, and then lay it on a rock and pound it with a hammer. In such a case the powder may be more or less confined at the moment of ignition between the hammer and the rock, and the bullet may be projected with enough force to penetrate flesh.

In a case reported in the papers, a hunter was said to have been shot through the arm by the bullet from a cartridge which exploded in his shirt pocket; when an attempt was made to pin down the exact facts, the victim became highly evasive. The facts were that he didn't want to admit that he had been shot with his own rifle because in that state it is illegal to have a loaded rifle in an automobile, so what was easier than simply to say that the cartridge had exploded in the shirt. It was when we insisted in seeing how much damage the cartridge did to the shirt pocket that the story came out.

It was a newspaper account of the accidental death of a prominent South Carolina hunter that caused me to make a whole series of experiments which will be described presently. According to the item,

1   2   3   4

1. Piece of brass removed from eye of boy who exploded 22 cartridge in vise with screwdriver.

2. 22 l.r. cartridge exploded by heating on hot-plate while covered with cardboard box. No piece penetrated.

3. Black powder cartridge (.41 rim fire) exploded on hot-plate under cardboard box. No piece penetrated.

4. 38 S & W revolver cartridge exploded on hot-plate under cardboard box. No piece penetrated the box.

the hunter died when the gun he was leaning on collapsed from a broken stock, and the gun struck a shotgun shell in his shirt pocket, causing it to explode and blow his head off. Investigation showed that the gun did indeed collapse while he was leaning on it, from the breaking of a weak plastic stock. As the stock folded, the trigger guard bent inward, pressing on the trigger; and as the muzzle of the gun was pointing up under the victim's chin, part of his head was blown off. At the same time the charge of shot did graze the shell in his pocket, and ripped it open, but it did not explode.

Actually, if the gun had been empty, and the shell in his pocket had been exploded as described, the hunter might have had a good scare, and might have imagined he had experienced a close call, but he would have been in no real danger, because while it would be unpleasant to have such a thing happen, it would not be dangerous to life.

What actually happens. To get some reliable first-hand information on what really happens when a 12-gauge shotgun shell is exploded while not in a gun, and when it is separated from the flesh only by a thin layer of cloth, as it would be in a shirt pocket, I took a bar of laundry soap, covered it with a piece of a white sheet, and laid a shell on the sheet. Over the shell I laid a piece of bath towel to represent a coat. White cloth was used to make it easier to see how much scorching occurred, if any. The shell contained an ounce and an eighth of No. 7½ shot and 3 drams equivalent of powder.

A wire attached to one electrode of an electric welding torch was twisted around the metal base of the shell, and the carbon rod in the other electrode was laid against the primer of the shell.

To see what a cartridge would do if it were accidentally discharged in a shirt pocket, soap was used to simulate flesh. White sheeting simulated the shirt, and bath toweling the outer coat. Cartridge was laid on the sheeting, covered with the toweling, and fired.

In this way, as soon as the electricity was connected to the welder, heat would be applied to the primer, and the shell would be fired. An ordinary corrugated cardboard box was then inverted over the arrangement just described, to catch any fragments, and to indicate what force they might have.

On closing the switch, the pop of the exploding primer was heard, followed by the rattle of shot inside the cardboard box. On lifting the box, I found that the end crimp of the shell had opened up, and the shot was scattered all around, together with the wads and some unburned powder. There were no marks on the inside of the box, and no scorch or burn on the cloth, and the soap was not dented or bruised.

The next thing I did was to explode a .45 Automatic Colt pistol cartridge in the same way. There was only a dull pop, something like a champagne cork being pulled, and again, there was no bruising of the soap or scorching of the cloth. The bullet made a slight mark on the wall of the cardboard box, just a little polished place that could not be called a dent. Most of the powder was lying around unburned, and the empty case had not even moved out of the wire loop.

Next cartridge fired was a .30-06. This made a dent on the soap about a quarter of an inch deep. That would have been a mean bruise. We found that the cartridge case had burst open and thrown some bits of brass around, and had left a smoky smudge about an inch long on the cloth. The only damage suffered by the cardboard box was a slight mark where the bullet had struck.

Next we tried a .32 caliber pistol cartridge loaded with black powder. It went off like a very sick firecracker, and there was no damage.

During all the firing, the pasteboard box was penetrated only once,

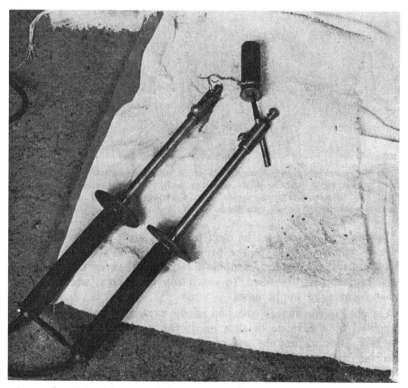

Set-up for firing shotgun shell experimentally. The entire arrangement was then covered with an inverted cardboard box.

The shotgun shell after firing. The carboard box covering it was not even dented. The sound of the explosion was so mild it did not sound like an explosion at all, but more like a marble dropping into a dishpan.

and that was by the primer, when we tried firing the shell by heating the metal and not the primer. In this case, the electrode was laid against the side of the brass case, and the current applied. Instantly the brass melted at that spot, and the powder flamed through the hole for 7 seconds with a loud hissing sound, while flame shot out of a hole in the side of the case. It was about three seconds after the powder was all burned out that the primer went off. This test shows also that if the powder is to be burned in any snappy fashion at all, it takes the primer to do it.

In another exhaustive series of experiments, I took various cartridges for both rifle and pistol, loaded with smokeless powder and with black powder, and placed them base downward in a lead melting pot that was arranged to be heated by electricity. On top of the pot I laid a piece of corrugated cardboard, with the cartridge standing on its base underneath so the bullet was pointing directly at the cardboard. Then the heat was turned on until the cartridge exploded. In no case did the bullet pierce the cardboard, or even dent it deeply.

A slightly different type of test was instituted after I read an item in the Washington, D. C. daily papers of July 22, 1955, about two boys who had been playing in the park when, as they told it, they heard a shot, and one of them was wounded in the neck. Later, a piece of thin brass, evidently a fragment of a cartridge case, as taken from the boy's neck. Under close questioning, he then admitted that they had found a .22 caliber cartridge, and that one of them had held a match under it until it had exploded.

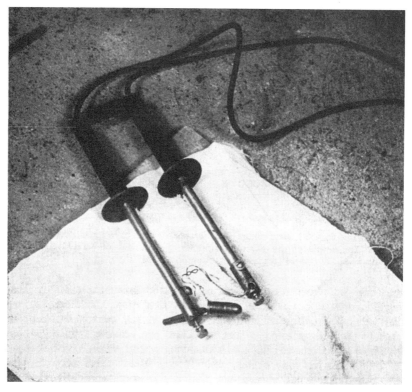

To fire the cartridge experimentally, it was arranged as shown, with the electrode of an electric welding torch in contact with the primer.

To see just exactly what would happen in such a case, I took a high speed .22 long rifle cartridge and suspended it by looping a wire around the case just behind the bullet. I then arranged a small birthday candle on a sliding piece so it could be pushed precisely under the rim of the cartridge. Lighting the candle, I placed a corrugated cardboard box over the arrangement, and pushed the lighted candle under the cartridge rim, at the same time starting a stop-watch.

It took 10 seconds for the cartridge to go off. No piece came

When .45 pistol cartridge was fired lying on the cake of soap, the only effect was a slight dent on the soap, corresponding to a minor bruise in flesh. The cloth was very slightly scorched.

through the cardboard box; when the box was lifted, it was found that the bullet had made a very slight dent in the cardboard. The case was blown to fragments, and the head of the case was stuck into the cardboard with just sufficient force to cause it to break the outer surface. Had this fragment struck flesh, it would have broken the skin. Such a piece would be dangerous to eyesight.

The experiment was repeated with a .22 short of the type which has a very light frangible bullet, with a muzzle velocity of about 1600 f.s. This cartridge took 15 seconds to go off. The bullet made a deep dent, about halfway through the corrugated cardboard. The head of the case made a dent about half as deep as that made by the bullet, or about 1/32 inch. Two slivers of brass from the case made an edgewise penetration of about ⅛ inch and just broke the far surface of the cardboard. The main piece of the case struck a small piece of wood that was lying inside the cardboard box, and penetrated the board about 1/16 inch and stuck in it. Again, this fragment would have broken the skin, but at a few feet distance its velocity could have been much reduced, so that a person would have to be quite close to the explosion to be in any danger of injury.

In this test we found that an ordinary pasteboard match will burn for about 20 seconds, while the .22 long rifle cartridge took only 10 seconds to explode with a flame under the rim. Thus it would be quite possible for a boy to lay such a cartridge down with the rim exposed, and **hold** a match to it long enough to explode it, and in such a case **he would** most likely be injured by pieces of the case.

XXII

How Far Will My Gun Shoot?

IT is very important for any shooter to have a good idea of just how far the bullet from his gun could go if it were discharged at a high angle, and just how much space should be allowed beyond the target as a danger space.

Most users of a high-powered rifle know that it will shoot well up to perhaps a thousand yards, and they also are aware of the fact that if it should go off when pointed upwards at a high angle, the bullet will go much farther; but just how much? The ordinary cal. .22 long-rifle cartridge box carries a statement that the bullet is dangerous to one mile, and it is self-evident that higher powered rifles will have a much greater range.

The easiest way to ascertain the maximum range of a large shell is to observe the splash it makes when it is fired on a large body of water, but it is hard to obtain the maximum range of small-arms ammunition in this way because, while the large shell makes a big, easily-observed splash, the small-arms bullet at maximum range has a low velocity and drops into the water or onto the ground with little observable disturbance. One way to overcome this difficulty is to fire a prolonged burst from a machine gun, and in fact this is the way that the actual maximum range of the .30-06 service bullet was first determined. This method is available with military ammunition for which machine guns are made, but not with most hunting cartridges.

Some years ago an attempt was made by the National Rifle Association to verify the actual range of cal. .22 rim-fire ammunition by firing on a smooth body of water, such as a canal or small lake, with an observer in a sheltered position near where the bullet is expected to strike. However, it proved very difficult to find a body of water free from small ripples or wavelets which could easily hide the small splash of a cal. .22 bullet dropping quietly into the water at low velocity. Moreover, at extreme ranges, there is such a big variation in distance between succeeding shots fired with identical elevation and azimuth that it is hard to station an observer within sight of all points of fall. As a result, the experiments gave very unsatisfactory results, doing little more than to confirm that the one mile distance on the cal. .22 ammunition boxes is a safe figure.

This difficulty in observing the fall of small-arms bullets at extreme range as compared to the difficulty of making similar observations on artillery shells is due primarily to the fact that at the far end of their trajectory, these bullets have quite low velocities, and fall steeply. Their low velocity and steep fall at the end of their trajectory are largely due to the fact that the resistance of the air has such a relatively great effect on a small-arms bullet as compared to its effect on a heavy shell. If there were no air, the maximum range would depend on one thing only, and that is the muzzle velocity, and would always be obtained at an elevation of 45°.

In such a case, a bullet with the velocity of the Service cal. .30 M2 would go about 43 miles, which is about 22 times as far as it actually goes in air. Projectiles of relatively heavy weight and low velocity, such as rifle grenades and trench-mortar shells, actually go nearly as far in air as they would in its absence.

Years ago our seacoast defenses included heavy mortar batteries and the big, low-velocity shells required an elevation of 45° to attain maximum range. To shoot at nearer targets they were elevated higher, and the shells fell closer. The 12″ coast-defense mortar shell, weighing 824 lbs., gave a maximum range of about 12,000 yards when fired with a muzzle velocity of nearly 1300 feet per second (f.s.); this is about 71% of its vacuum range.

With a small-arms bullet, the effect of air resistance is so great that maximum range is attained at an elevation of about 29°, and there is little change as the gun is given more elevation up to about 35°, after which the bullets will begin to fall closer. A study of this question is presented in the *British Textbook of Small Arms, 1929*, in which there is given a chart of the trajectories of the boat-tail Swiss bullet of approximately cal. .30 weighing 174 grs., and with ballistic coefficient of .406 and a muzzle velocity of 2600 f.s.

The chart shows that this bullet attains its maximum range of 4457 yards at an angle of departure of 34° 42 minutes. Table 1 shows the range attained, time of flight, terminal velocity, and angle of fall at various angles of departure from 5° up to 40°.

TABLE 1. Elevations & Ranges for 174 Grain Swiss Bullet at 2600 f.s.

Elevation (deg.)	Range (yds.)	Flight time (sec.)	Final velocity (f.s.)	Angle of fall (deg.)
5	2464	7.56	588	11.25
10	3273	12.65	447	24.3
20	4097	20.95	390	47.68
30	4423	27.91	405	62.40
34	4455	30.2	416	66.15
35	4456	31.06	417	67.4
40	4413	34.01	429	71.35

Maximum Range in Vacuum Easily Approximated

A good approximation to the maximum distance in yards that a projectile of any shape or weight would travel if there were no air on earth and it were fired at an elevation of 45° can be obtained by dividing the muzzle velocity by 10 and squaring the result. Thus under vacuum conditions a projectile, whatever its shape or weight, if fired at a muzzle velocity of 1000 f.s. would go about 10,000 yards.

Heavy bullets fired from low-velocity, large-caliber rifles will go about 15% to 20% of their theoretical vacuum range when fired in air as can be seen from Table 2, from figures given in the *British Textbook of Small Arms, 1909* and the U. S. *Handbook for the Cal. .45-70 Springfield Rifle.*

TABLE 2. Extreme Ranges of Old Large Caliber Military Rifles

Country	Name of rifle	Caliber (ins.)	Bullet wt. (grs.)	Muzzle vel. (f.s.)	Extreme range (meters)	(yds.)	Pct. of vacuum range
France	Gras	.433 (11 mm.)	386	1493	2900	3171	14%
Germany	Mauser	.433 (11 mm.)	386	1427	3000	3281	16%
Italy	Vetterli	.40	313	1430	2750	3007	14%
Netherlands	Beaumont	.433 (11 mm.)	386	1476	3000	3281	15%
Servia	Mauser	.40	355	1580	3250	3554	14%
Spain	Remington	.433 (11 mm.)	387	1340	2800	3062	17%
U. S.	Springfield	.45	500	1315	....	3500	20%
U. S.	Springfield Carbine	.45	405	1150	....	2800	21%

The lower the velocity and the higher the ballistic coefficient, the closer the bullet will come to its vacuum range. An extreme case as regards small arms is the British cal. .455 Webley revolver, with a 265-gr. bullet having only 600 f.s. muzzle velocity, which will go 1300 yards when fired at 35° elevation. This is 36% of its theoretical maximum vacuum range.

The disproportionate effect of higher velocities in taking away velocity from a moving bullet can be appreciated by considering how far the 152-gr. cal. .30 M2 bullet with ballistic coefficient of .40 would travel in air at various speeds to lose 1 f.s. These distances are as follows: at a speed of 500 f.s., 17 ft.; at 1000 f.s., 6.3 ft.; at 1500 f.s., 2 ft.; at 2000 f.s., 1.5 ft.; at 2500 f.s., 1.3 ft.; at 3000 f.s., 1.2 ft.; at 3500 f.s., 1.1 ft.; and at 4000 f.s., 1.02 ft. The big change comes at the velocity of sound in air, or 1050 to 1100 f.s.

Game Bullets

Modern hunting rifles with their relatively light bullets at high velocity may be expected to attain only about 4% to 10% of their theoretical maximum vacuum range when fired in air; pistol bullets lower in velocity, 10% to 20% of the vacuum maximum.

A number of small-arms cartridges, particularly the military ones, have had their maximum range in air determined by actual test, and

Relation of Velocity Loss to Length of Bullet Travel.

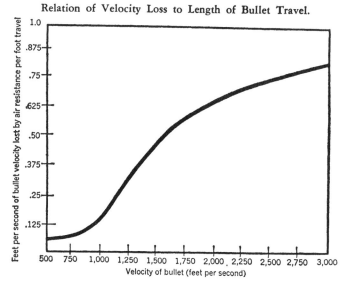

Curve showing how the amount of velocity lost per foot of travel varies with the velocity of the bullet. This is for a bullet with ballistic coefficient of .40, such as the flat-base 152-gr. .30-'06.

by searching through various manuals and other publications we have found records of these as given in Table 3.

TABLE 3. Maximum Ranges as Given in Ordnance Publications, etc.

Bullet name	Bullet wt. (grs.)	Muzzle vel. (f.s.)	Ballistic co-efficient	Extreme range (yds.) (miles)		Percent of max. vacuum range
Cal. .22 long rifle	40	1145	.128	1500	.85	12%
Cal. .380 ACP	95	970	.08	1089	.62	12%
Cal. .45 ACP in pistol	234	820	.16	1640	.93	24%
Same in submachine gun	234	970	.16	1760	1.0	21%
Cal. .30 carbine M1	111	1970	.179	2200	1.25	6%
Same, tracer M16	107	1910	.154	1680	.95	5%
Cal. .30 ball, M2	152	2800	.40	3500	1.99	4½%
Cal. .30 boattail M1	172	2600	.56	5500	3.12	8%
Same in sub-caliber gun	172	1990	.56	4300	2.44	11%
Cal. .30-40 Krag	220	2000	.34	4050	2.3	10%
Same in carbine	220	1920	.34	4000	2.27	10%
Cal. .50 AP M2	718	2840	.84	7275	4.13	9%

Table 3 gives some practical reference points for the shooter who wants to be certain that he has enough safety space in front of his gun. One such reference point is the demonstrated range of 1500 yards for the cal. .22 long rifle with standard velocity of 1145 f.s. In this connection, a natural question is how much farther will it go if we raise the velocity 190 f.s. to the 1335 f.s. of the high-velocity cal. .22 long rifle. Ballistic tables show us that its muzzle velocity is reduced to 1145 f.s. after only 65 yards flight, so obviously if the higher-velocity bullet were fired from 65 yards behind the firing line of the standard velocity .22 long rifle bullet, it would pass that firing point with the same velocity and would go to the same spot, so that we may merely add the 65 yards to the figure for the standard-velocity cartridge.

In the same manner, the very well proven 3500 yards maximum range for the cal. .30-'06 M2 ball gives us another reference point. For any bullet of about the same power or less, we can use this figure and be pretty safe. If the bullet has a higher velocity, as for example, the 150-gr. bullet in the cal. .300 H&H Magnum, with its 390 f.s. higher velocity of 3190 f.s., we can find how far it will take air resistance to absorb this extra velocity—which in this case turns out to be about 156 yards, assuming the ballistic coefficient to be about the same for the two bullets. But this still does not mean that it will go that much farther, because that is figured on the level; while for maximum range we must fire at an elevation of 30° or more, so we must multiply this figure by the cosine of 30°, or .866, if we want a closer approximation—giving us 135 yards for the extra range of the cal. .300 Magnum beyond the cal. .30-'06 M2. To get much extra distance it would be necessary to go to an entirely different category of ammunition, namely one having a much larger and heavier bullet, such as the ammunition for the cal. .50 machine gun.

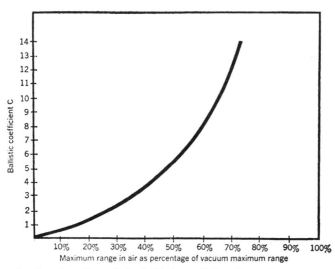

Curve showing the effect of the ballistic coefficient C on the percentage which the maximum range in air of a projectile at 2800 f.s. muzzle velocity bears to the theoretical maximum vacuum range. Small-arms bullets, most of which have C of less than .5, would be in the left hand ⅛″ of curve.

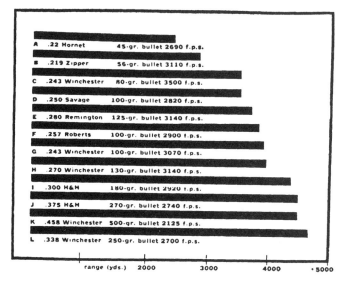

Maximum Ranges Which Rifle Bullets Could Attain If They Had Long Sharp Points (see text).

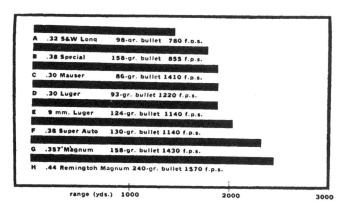

Maximum Ranges Which Pistol Bullets Could Attain If They Had Long Sharp Points (see text).

Some calculations have been made showing how far most of the modern hunting bullets would go at 30° elevation, and as a factor of safety because the shape of the bullet nose can vary so widely and is seldom surely known, the calculations have assumed a shape of point that would give the longest extreme range. *In other words, a shape similar to that of the spitzer-pointed cal. .30-'06 has been assumed.*

On this assumption, some calculated extreme ranges in yards are given in Table 4.

TABLE 4. Calculated Maximum Ranges Assuming Bullets Have Sharp Points

Bullet name	Bullet wt. (grs.)	Assumed M. V. (f.s.)	Calculated max. range (yds.)	(Miles)
Cal. .22 WRF	45	1450	1950	1.11
Cal. .22 WMR	40	2000	1900	1.08
Cal. .30 Mauser Pistol	86	1410	1900	1.08
Cal. .30 Luger	93	1220	1900	1.08
Cal. .32 S&W Long	98	780	1450	.82
Cal. .38 Special	158	855	1800	1.02
Cal. .357 S&W Magnum	158	1430	2350	1.34
Cal. .38 Super Auto	130	1140	2050	1.26
9 mm. Luger	124	1140	1900	1.08
Cal. .44 Remington Magnum	240	1570	2500	1.42
Cal. .219 Zipper	56	3110	2850	1.62
Cal. .22 Hornet	45	2690	2350	1.33
Cal. .243 Winchester	100	3070	4000	2.27
Same	80	3500	3500	1.99
Cal. .250 Savage	100	2820	3500	1.99
Cal. .257 Roberts	100	2900	3850	2.18
Cal. .270 Winchester	130	3140	4000	2.27
Cal. .280 Remington	125	3140	3700	2.10
Cal. .300 H&H Magnum	180	2920	4350	2.47
Cal. .338 Winchester Magnum	250	2700	4660	2.64
Cal. .375 H&H Magnum	270	2740	4500	2.56
Cal. .458 Winchester F.M.J.	500	2125	4500	2.56

By reference to Table 4, it should be quite easy to estimate just about how many yards behind the target must be considered as a danger space for any given bullet. If a particular bullet is not listed, take another of as nearly the same caliber and weight as can be found in the tabulation. If a bullet is heavier than the example, or if it has more velocity, it will tend to go a bit farther, but not much.

Shotgun Ranges

Because round balls have a much smaller ballistic coefficient than do elongated and pointed bullets, the range of all shotguns is comparatively limited. Ordnance Technical Manual 9-1990 gives the following distances as the maximum ranges attained by standard shot loads when fired in full-choke guns: No. 00 Buckshot, 600 yards; No. 8 shot, 230 yards; and No. 9 shot, 210 yards.

T.M. 9-1990 also gives a formula, called "Journée's Formula," for determining the approximate maximum ranges for a shotgun. This formula states that the maximum range in yards is roughly 2200 times the shot diameter in inches. This would give the results shown in Table 5.

Rifled Shotgun Slugs

Rifled shotgun slugs start out with a fairly high velocity of about 1600 f.s., but they have poor sectional density and a low ballistic coefficient (C), usually less than half that of the ordinary cal. .22

long rifle which has a C of about .128 and goes to a maximum range of about 1500 yards when fired at 30° elevation with 1145 f.s. muzzle velocity. The C of the 12-gauge rifled slug is only .058, and it loses 40% of its initial velocity in traveling the first 100 yards, so it can reasonably be assumed that it will not have as great an extreme range as the cal. .22 long rifle, in spite of its higher starting velocity. Then

TABLE 5

MAXIMUM RANGES OF SHOT
BASED ON JOURNÉE'S FORMULA

Shot size	Diameter (ins)	Maximum range (yds.)
12-ga. round ball	.645	1420
16-ga. " "	.610	1340
20-ga. " "	.545	1200
410-ga. " "	.38	850
00 buckshot	.34	748
0 "	.32	704
1 "	.30	660
#1 shot	.16	352
#2 "	.15	330
#3 "	.14	308
#4 "	.13	286
#5 "	.12	264
#6 "	.11	242
#7½ "	.095	209
#8 "	.09	198
#9 "	.08	176
#12 " (cal. .22 shot cartridges)	.05	110

the 16-gauge rifled slug, with a somewhat higher C of .069 loses 36% of its velocity in 100 yards, the 20-gauge rifled slug with a C of .054 loses 41%, and the .410 with a C of only .045 loses 45% of its velocity in the first 100 yards, so that it can be assumed that no rifled slug can be projected from a shotgun to more than 1500 yards at the outside.

XXIII

Exterior Ballistics

THE main object of this chapter is to include in this book a set of
ballistic tables, together with simple directions for using them,
so that without using any mathematics other than simple addition,
subtraction, multiplication and addition, and without going at all
into the theory of the subject, the shooter can make a number of
useful and interesting calculations to show what his bullet will do
and how it compares with other bullets in time of flight, remaining
velocity, flatness of trajectory, etc.

There are numerous ballistic tables in existence, which differ
mainly in the fact that they were calculated from retardation data
obtained from firings of experimental projectiles which differed from
each other in shape. No one table will be perfect for both very blunt
nosed projectiles and very sharp pointed ones. Ideally, a different
set of tables should be used for each distinct class of bullet shapes.

However as a practical matter, any one of the several tables mentioned in this book will give acceptable results if it is used with the
proper multiplier, (or *ballistic coefficient*). One of the best for use
with small arms bullets, considering the average shape of a small
arms bullet and the comparatively low angle of departure at which
it is fired, is the set of ballistic tables published in Artillery Circular
M, which is now out of print and generally unobtainable.

These tables were computed a number of years ago by the late
Col. James M. Ingalls, U. S. Army, with whom I had the pleasure
of serving at an artillery post soon after I first entered the Army.

Ingalls' Table I, which gives the time and space functions, is reprinted at the end of this chapter, together with an abridgement of
his very lengthy Table II.

By the use of Table I the ballistic coefficient, time of flight, and
remaining velocity at various ranges may be computed, given the
muzzle velocity and the remaining velocity at some one point along
the trajectory; or given the ballistic coefficient and the velocity at
some one point, the velocity and time of flight for any range may be
computed.

By the use of Table II, the angle of departure for any range may
be computed, given the muzzle velocity and the ballistic coefficient.

Because the Ingalls tables go no higher in velocity than 3600 feet

549

per second, and because some wildcat cartridges and at least one factory cartridge (the 220 Swift @ 4110 f.s. muzzle velocity) go higher than this, I have included the time and space function tables of the British 1909 ballistic tables which are based on the same shape of projectile as Ingalls, and which give practically identical results, but which in the published form go to 4000 f.s., and have been extrapolated by me to 4200 f.s. For optional use I also include an extension of Ingalls' tables to 5000 f.s., using negative values for the time and space functions above the 3600 f.s. zero point.

Because the Ingalls tables start at 3600 f.s. and proceed downward in velocity to 100 f.s., while the British tables start at 0 and go upwards, there is a very slight difference in the instructions for using the two tables; in some cases where a quantity is subtracted in the Ingalls tables it is added in the British tables. Also, there is a very slight difference in the ballistic coefficient for these two tables; the proper one must be used with each. Otherwise, they are almost identical, and the results are extremely close together. Nevertheless, each has its own instructions, and the proper instructions must be used with each.

Those who merely wish to make ballistic computations are referred directly to the tables at the end of this chapter, and to the appropriate instructions printed with each table. For others who may wish to go more into history and basic principle, a few pages of simplified material on the subject of Exterior Ballistics follows.

Some Basic Principles

When a bullet leaves a gun, it has kinetic energy which tries to make it move in a straight line with its original velocity. However, gravity pulls it toward the ground, and air resistance tries to hold it back. The result is that it follows a drooping curve called the *trajectory*, and soon strikes the earth.

A very good idea of the shape of the trajectory in air may be gained by watching the flight of a well-hit golf ball when driven off the tee on a golf course. The ball seems to go straight out for a while, in a slightly rising almost flat curve. Soon, the curvature becomes more pronounced, and the ball comes down much more steeply than it went up. The same sort of curve may be seen when a stream of water leaves a garden hose at a small upward angle. The trajectory of the golf ball is longer and flatter than that of the stream from the hose, and the trajectory of the bullet is many times longer and flatter than that of the golf ball, but the fundamental shape is the same for all three.

The greater curvature, or steepening, of the trajectory at its distant end, is entirely due to air resistance. Without it, the shape would be the same at both ends.

If space travel dreams ever come true, we may some day be

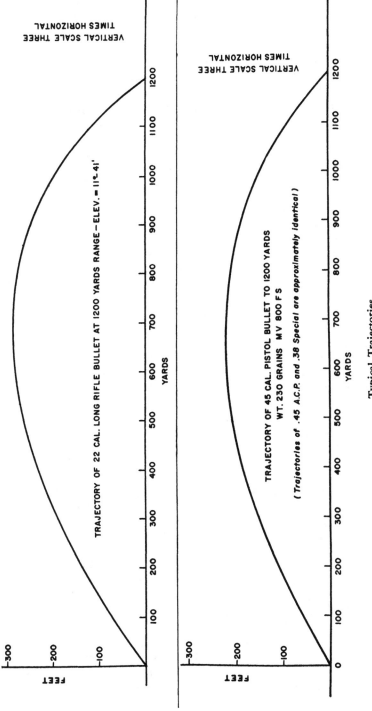

Typical Trajectories.

shooting on the moon, where there is no air. In that case, we would find the trajectory very different from what it is on the earth, both because of the absence of air resistance, and because of the reduced effect of gravity on a body smaller than the earth. There would be no drift, and no wind deflection, because both these effects are caused by the action of the atmosphere.

If the earth had no air, the trajectory would depend on muzzle velocity alone, and would be the same for all weights and shapes of bullet. As soon as the ball left the gun, it would in effect become a small satellite of the earth, and would follow a curve which would be an ellipse with one of its two foci at the earth's center. In general, this elliptical orbit would lie partly inside the earth, so that soon after it started its flight, the bullet, in attempting to follow its orbit, would arrive at the surface of the earth; in other words, it would strike the ground.

An exception would occur if and when the bullet were fired horizontally, or parallel to the surface, and at just the right speed so that the drop due to gravity would be equal to the amount the surface of the earth drops away from the original line of departure due to its curvature. At the end of the first second of horizontally directed flight, the bullet will have dropped 16 feet; if in that second, it had traveled far enough so that the curvature of the earth had depressed the surface by the same amount below the original horizontal direction of the bullet, then the bullet would be no closer to the ground and no farther away than it was when it was fired; and unless some obstruction should get in the way, it would continue to orbit around the earth forever. In this case its orbit would still be an ellipse, but of the specialized kind in which the foci both coincide; such an ellipse is called a circle.

Measurement on bodies falling in a vacuum have shown that in the absence of air resistance, any falling body will acquire a speed of about 32.16 feet per second in the first second of its fall, and will increase its speed by the same amount during each succeeding second of its fall. Thus it is said that gravity produces an acceleration of 32.16 feet per second per second. (Note that velocities are always given in feet per second, and that accelerations are given in feet per second per second.)

For simplicity taking gravity as 32, and the radius of the earth as 4000 miles instead of the actual figure of 3959 miles, the orbiting bullet mentioned above would have to be fired at a speed of 25,999 f.s., and would make the trip around the world in 1 hour 25 minutes 4 seconds.

We can figure this out by another method if we care to. In high school physics we were taught that if a weight is whirled around in a circle on the end of a string, it exerts a pull which equals v^2/r where v is the velocity of the object, and r is the radius of the circle in which it swings. Taking the radius of the earth r as 4000 miles, or 4000x5280 feet, we find that the velocity v necessary to give an outward pull equal to the acceleration of gravity is the same 25,999 f.s. we obtained before for the minimum orbital speed around a supposed airless earth.

If the firing speed were a little faster than these minimum figures, the orbit would become an elongated ellipse instead of a circle; but the bullet would still travel in an elliptical orbit having one focus at the earth's center. As the speed of firing was increased, the ellipse would become more elongated, and the projectile would travel farther from the earth at the most distant end of its orbit. On each return trip it would again pass close to the surface, just as some comets in the solar system swing far out into space, then return to pivot around the sun and repeat the trip.

If the speed of the bullet reached a figure of about 36,000 feet per second, known as the *escape velocity* (see p. 517), it would go off into space, never to return. In this case its orbit would be a parabola, which is essentially an ellipse with its two foci an infinite distance apart; or, practically a very elongated ellipse open at the far end. This is similar to what occurs occasionally in the solar system when a stray comet and the sun approach each other with a relative speed greater than the escape velocity of an object on the sun. As the comet passes near the sun, the intense gravitational field of that great body alters the comet's direction of travel so that it swings around the sun as a racing plane rounds a pylon, and is then whirled off into outer space like a stone thrown from a giant sling. Such comets, approaching the sun in parabolic or hyperbolic orbits, go away and never come back, and that is what the bullet in a vacuum would do at speeds greater than the escape velocity from the earth.

While such projectiles as the Intercontinental Ballistic Missile may rise above the upper reaches of the atmosphere and fly in a vacuum for part of their flight, we cannot fire small arms bullets in a vacuum, and never will until space travel becomes a reality. Nevertheless, certain objects such as rifle grenades, which are heavy in relation to their surface area and are only projected at low velocities, have such low air resistance that they behave about as they would if air were not present. Because speculations and calculations regarding the vacuum trajectory are quite applicable to such missiles, and also because such speculations and calculations serve a useful purpose in teaching the basic principles of exterior ballistics we will consider it briefly.

The Vacuum Trajectory

Let R=range in feet.
V=initial velocity in f.s.
E=the angle of departure

g=the acceleration of gravity
t=the time of flight
Then, referring to the figure,

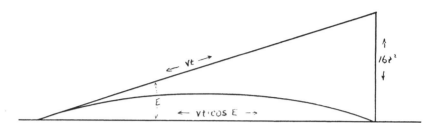

(a)   R=Vt cos E
      Vt sin E   =½ gt²   hence t=$\frac{2V \sin E}{g}$

      and substituting the value of t in (a)
      R=$\frac{2V^2 \sin E \cos E}{g}$

      and as 2 sin E cos E=sin 2 E, we have
(b)   R=$\frac{V^2 \sin 2E}{g}$

The British Textbook of Small Arms, 1929, gives the following, which, it will be noted, is consistent with the above:

Range in yards=$\frac{V^2 \sin 2E}{3g}$

and as sin 90 deg.=1, and as max. range in vacuum occurs at 45 deg. elevation, and as 3 g is nearly 100, we have:

Maximum range in vacuum in yards=$(v/10)^2$ approximately.

from (b) the range in feet, R=$\frac{V^2 \sin 2E}{g}$ hence sin 2E=$\frac{Rg}{V^2}$

and as sin 1 minute=1/3438, this formula becomes

angle of elevation in vacuum=$\frac{55,238 \, R}{V^2}$ minutes.

Also, H, the maximum height of the trajectory=$\frac{R \tan E}{4}$

The amount a body falls in a vacuum is 16 t² feet, or 192 t² inches. In a vacuum trajectory, the bullet would be that far below its original line of departure at any instant.

Action of the Air

The air not only tries to hold the bullet back, but also causes it to drift in the direction of the spin. The action is as follows: as the bullet starts to fall from the action of gravity after it has started its flight, the air pressure under its point causes the point to deviate in the direction of rotation, because of the fact that the rapidly rotating bullet acts as a gyroscope, and any pressure causes the axis of rotation to swing at right angles to the direction of the pressure. Thus if the bullet is rotating to the right, the upward pressure on the nose causes it to swing very slightly toward the right, and as the bullet presents its elongated surface to the air resistance, it is shoved bodily over to the right. The amount of drift is not great; in the service .30 M2 bullet it amounts to 6.7 inches to the right at 1000 yards.

While the most important effect of air resistance in exterior ballistic calculations has to do with the retardation of the bullet, the action of the air also makes necessary the provision of rifling, so that subject will be discussed here to get it out of the way before studying the effects of retardation of the bullet by the air.

Rifling

One result if the action of the air on the bullet is the necessity of giving the bullet a spin around an axis coinciding with its initial line of flight if serious deviations and inaccuracies are to be avoided.

Round balls in smooth bore muskets are very inaccurate. A certain amount of clearance is necessary between the ball and the wall of the bore, to permit loading from the muzzle. When it is fired, the ball bounces along down the bore, striking first one side, then another, and when it leaves, it has a spin or rotation about an undetermined axis. If the barrel is bent to one side or the other near the muzzle, that might give the ball a spin as it rubs against one side of the bore, and then it would act much as a golf ball does when it is sliced or hooked. Perhaps the most usual condition is for the ball to roll along the bottom of the bore, and leave the gun with a tendency to dive downward, or drop more than the normal amount caused by gravity and air retardation.

Even if the ball should be a very tight fit in the smooth bore, so that it slides along without getting any spin at all, it still may be erratic; a small pile of compressed air may be pushed along by the ball until something causes it to deviate to one side a slight amount, when it may then "break" from its former path. This is seen in baseball with the so-called spit ball, which has no spin, and therefore breaks erratically at some point in its flight.

All this trouble is avoided if the ball is given a definite spin on an axis coinciding with the line of the bore, and this is the reason rifling was used with round balls.

In the case of elongated bullets, rifling is even more necessary than it was with round balls, for in the absence of rifling, an elongated bullet will tumble end over end, and no sort of accuracy is possible.

The Greenhill Formula

A method for determining mathematically the amount of spin necessary to stabilize an elongated bullet was worked out in 1879 by Sir Alfred George Greenhill (1847-1927), who was at that time Professor of Mathematics to the advanced class of artillery officers at Woolwich. A discussion of this formula will be found on pp 288 and 289 of the British Textbook of Small Arms, 1929.

The abstruse mathematical work done by Greenhill resulted in a simple method of obtaining the spin required to overcome instability in an elongated projectile. A figure that for all practical purposes is satisfactory for bullets having a specific gravity of 10.9 can be obtained from the following rule:

The twist required (in calibers) equals 150 divided by the length of the bullet (in calibers). Note that lead itself has a specific gravity of 11.35; a jacketed lead bullet has specific gravity about 10.9.

To check out this formula, let's apply it to the 220 grain .30 caliber bullet such as was used in the old Krag rifle, and in the first M-1903 rifles. At that time it was determined that the necessary twist for this bullet was 1 turn in 10 inches, and that twist was adopted. Later, when the sharp pointed and shorter spitzer bullet was adopted, in 1906, the same twist was retained; while it might be slightly more twist than was required for the shorter bullet, it still enabled the use of heavier bullets should that become necessary. Let's see what twist the Greenhill formula says should have been adopted.

The length of the 220 grain .30 caliber bullet is 1.35 inches, or 1.35/.30=4.5 calibers, so the twist given by the formula would be 150/4.5=33 1/3 calibers, or 33 1/3 times the diameter of the bullet. 33 1/3 x .30=9.99 or in round numbers, 10 inches.

For bullets made of other materials than lead, the spin as given by the formula should be multiplied by the square root of the number found by dividing the specific gravity on which the formula is based (10.9), by the specific gravity of the material of which the bullet is made. Thus if it is made of aluminum, whose specific gravity is 2.7 we would divide 10.9 by 2.7, obtaining 4. Then take the square root of this number, which is 2, and multiply the spin by that, showing that the aluminum bullet would require twice as much spin as the usual jacketed lead one.

Another point to be considered is the fact that the Greenhill formula gives the spin necessary to stabilize the flight of the bullet in air; in denser materials, more spin is required. For a bullet to have a stable flight in any material other than air, the spin as worked out for air must be multiplied by the square root of a number found by dividing the density of the material in question by the density of air. Water has a specific gravity about 900 times that of air, so that to be stable in penetrating water, the bullet would require a twist as given by Greenhill's formula, multiplied by the square root of 900, or 30. Thus the twist for stable flight in water would be 30 times as great as that for flight in air.

Note—To obtain the specific gravity of a bullet, proceed as follows:

1. Suspend the bullet by a thin light wire or thread from the pan of a balance.

2. Weigh the bullet while it is hanging this way.

3. Place a container of water under the scale so the bullet hangs in the water, and take the weight.

4. Subtract the second weight from the first.

5. Divide the weight of the bullet as obtained in (2) by the difference as obtained in (4). This result is the specific gravity.

Retardation of the Bullet by Air Resistance

One of the most noticeable results of air resistance on a bullet's flight is to slow the bullet down and thus reduce its maximum range. An idea of the magnitude of this effect may be gained by figuring how far a bullet at a given speed would go in a vacuum, then comparing it with the actual maximum range in air. Thus a bullet of any weight, size or shape, if fired in a vacuum at a muzzle velocity of 2700 f.s. and an angle of elevation of 45 degrees, would have a maximum range of 226,397 feet, or nearly 43 miles, while a 150 grain flat base .30 caliber M2 bullet at 2700 f.s. has a maximum range of only 3400 yards or 10,200 feet, or about 4½% of the distance it would go if air resistance did not hold it back. Moreover, in a vacuum, the maximum range is obtained at an elevation or angle of departure of 45 degrees, while in air the maximum range of the .30 caliber M2 bullet is obtained at an angle of departure of 29 degrees.

On p. 401 there will be found a table of fire for the .30 cal. 1906 ammunition, which is equally applicable to the 152 grain flat base .30 caliber M2. It will be seen that over the first 300 feet of its flight this bullet starting at 2700 f.s. loses 219 f.s. of its initial velocity during its .12 second time of flight. If it loses velocity at the rate of 219 f.s. in .12 second, that would be at the rate of 1825 f.s. in each second, and the backward acceleration of the bullet would be equal to that caused by a pressure of over 56 times its own weight against its nose, holding it back. In other words, the negative acceleration caused by air resistance at the average speed the bullet had in the first 100 yards of its flight is equal to over 56 times the acceleration of gravity. This retardation is greater at higher speeds, less at lower ones. From 900 to 1000 yards where the speed of the bullet has dropped to about the velocity of sound, it loses only 76 f.s. over 300 feet of flight, and takes .29 second to do it, which is at the rate of 262 f.s. per second or 8 times gravity.

The way this retardation varies at other points and at other bullet speeds can be seen from the tabulation which follows:

152 grain flat base .30 cal. M2 bullet, 2700 f.s.

Range Yards	Remaining Velocity f.s.	Loss in 100 yards	Time required sec.	Rate of loss f.s. per sec.	Neg. acceleration —times gravity
0	2700	. . .	. .	. . . .	. . . .
100	2481	219	.12	1825	56.67
200	2267	214	.13	1643	51.
300	2059	208	.14	1485	46.1
400	1858	201	.15	1340	41.6
500	1664	194	.17	1141	35.4
600	1481	183	.19	963	29.9
700	1315	166	.22	754	23.4
800	1174	141	.24	587	18.2
900	1065	109	.27	403	12.6
1000	989	76	.29	262	8.1

It will be noted that if the bullet continued to lose speed at the same rate that it does during the first 100 yards of its flight, it would be completely stopped in less than 1½ seconds; however, the loss in velocity gets less and less as the speed diminishes, so that actually it has over 1100 f.s. of velocity left at the end of 1½ seconds. This tabulation shows clearly how much greater the retardation is at higher than at lower velocities.

Formula for Air Resistance

Sir Isaac Newton (1642-1727), turned his attention to this subject, and after making experiments by dropping glass spheres filled with air, water and mercury from the dome of St. Paul's Cathedral, he concluded that the air resistance was proportional to the square of the velocity. His experiments were of course at lower velocities than are usual with small arms bullets.

Later experiments made in various countries and by various governmental bodies and scientific commissions gave results that seemed to show that Newton's assumption of the square law was not true, as at certain speeds, especially those in the neighborhood of the velocity of sound, the resistance increased much faster than this rule provided.

Such experiments and studies were carried out in England (1866-1880); in Russia (1868-69); in Germany (1881); in Holland (1883); and especially by the Commission d'Experience de Gavre in France (1873-1898). The earlier of these studies were largely confined to obtaining remaining velocities at various velocities and over different distances, and from them attempting to derive a mathematical formula for the relation between velocity in the air and retardation.

Notable work in this field was done by the Russian Colonel Mayevski from a study of firings done by Krupp at Meppen in Germany in 1881, using a projectile about 3 calibers long with a flat base and an ogival head with a 2 caliber radius.

From this study, Mayevski concluded that it was possible to express the retardation as proportional to some power of the velocity in a restricted zone of velocities, using another power of the velocity in the next zone of velocities, and so on.

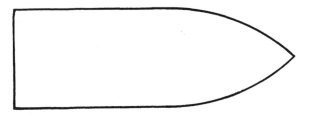

General shape of projectile used in the Krupp and Gavre firings. It is 3 calibers long and has an ogival head with 2 caliber radius.

He found a good agreement with the results of the experimental firings could be obtained if the retardation were expressed in the form Av^n where both A and n are constant in a restricted velocity zone, but where the values of both A and n change when this velocity zone is passed.

Values for both A and n were computed for the standard projectile mentioned above, and the results were applied to other projectiles of other sizes and weights by means of a constant multiplier called the ballistic coefficient, and designated as C. The ballistic coefficient and its meaning and use will be more fully discussed later.

Col. Ingalls converted Mayevski's results into English units, and based his famous ballistic tables on them.

Following are Mayevski's functions, where R is the retardation of the standard projectile in f.s. per second. R divided by the proper ballistic coefficient gives the retardation r for any other projectile.

$R = Cr = Av^2$ for velocities from 0 f.s. to 790 f.s. In this range log A = 5.6698914-10
$R = Cr = Av^3$ for velocities from 790 f.s. to 970 f.s. In this range log A = 2.7734430-10
$R = Cr = Av^5$ for velocities from 970 f.s. to 1230 f.s. In this range lot A = 6.8018712-20
$R = Cr = Av^3$ for velocities from 1230 f.s. to 1370 f.s. In this range log A = 2.9809023-10
$R = Cr = Av^2$ for velocities from 1370 f.s. to 1800 f.s. In this range log A = 6.1192596-10
$R = Cr = Av^{1.7}$ for velocities from 1800 f.s. to 2600 f.s. In this range log A = 7.0961978-10
$R = Cr = Av^{1.55}$ for velocities from 2600 f.s. to 3600 f.s. In this range log A = 7.6090480-10

In 1904-1906, the British, using elaborate apparatus, carried out retardation firing experiments up to very high velocities, and from the results deduced a formula very similar to that announced some years previously by Mayevski. They concluded that for the standard

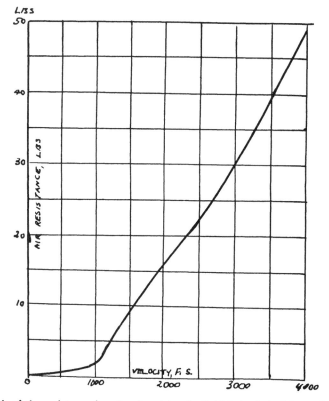

Graph of the resistance function found by the British in their firings of 1904-06.

Type of projectile for which British 1909 tables are computed. It has an ogival head with 2 caliber radius, is 1 inch in diameter, and weighs 1 lb.

experimental projectile of unit diameter and weight and with a 2 caliber ogive, the retardation can be obtained from this formula:

$$R = Av^m; \text{ also } R = Cr = pg; \text{ where}$$

R = retardation of the standard projectile in f.s. per second.

r = retardation of any other projectile of ballistic coefficient C.

v = the velocity of the projectile.

m = the index of a power of the velocity in a restricted zone of velocities.

A = a constant modifying m, and applying only in a restricted zone of velocities.

C = the ballistic coefficient of any projectile as compared with the standard.

p = air resistance in pounds on the nose of the standard projectile.

g = the gravitational constant.

The values of A and m for various zones of velocity under normal conditions of projectile stability and of atmospheric density are as follows:

Limits of velocity. f. s.		Value of A	Value of m
0	to 840	$\dfrac{74,422}{10^7}$	1.6
840	1040	$\dfrac{59,939}{10^{12}}$	3
1040	1190	$\dfrac{23,385}{10^{22}}$	6.45
1190	1460	$\dfrac{95,408}{10^{12}}$	3
1460	2000	$\dfrac{59,814}{10^8}$	1.8
2000	2600	$\dfrac{58,495}{10^7}$	1.5
2600	4000	$\dfrac{15,366}{10^7}$	1.67

It was as a result of these firings that the British computed their ballistic Tables of 1909, which are almost identical with those of Ingalls.

Let us return now to the Gâvre Commission, which, as stated above, carried out a series of firings and studies lasting from about 1873 to 1898. They made firings of their own up to the previously unattained velocity of 6000 f.s., and in doing this, they anticipated the device the Germans used to obtain very high velocities with the

Paris long range gun of 1918, which was a long smooth bored extension attached to the muzzle of a cannon.

The Gâvre Commission not only carried out their own firing
experiments, but also they reviewed and studied all previous resistance
firings in all countries, of which the records were available; and in
1898, they formulated and published the results of their own experiments and of their study of the previously reported experiments.
Their report showed conclusively that the resistance of the air could
not simply be taken as proportional to the square of the velocity, or
to any other one power.

Instead of announcing their results in the form of a formula, the
Gâvre Commission reduced them to a table showing retardations for
each velocity, and this relation became known as the Gâvre function,
and was accepted extensively both here and abroad as the basis
of ballistic calculations. In general its publication marked the end of
the long search for a single formula for calculating air resistance,
and substituted instead a table of actual values for each velocity
found from experiment.

In the United States, a slightly modified form of the Gâvre function, usually referred to as the G-function, and later designated by

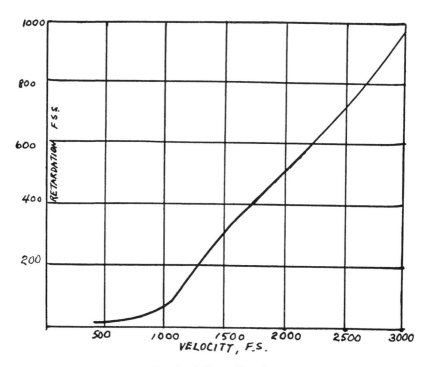

Graph of Gavre Function.

the Ballistic Section of Aberdeen Proving Ground as G_1, has been widely used in the computation of trajectories.

In effect, the G-function is a table showing the relation between velocity and retardation; that is, a table from which may be found directly the retardation corresponding to any given velocity for any projectile having the same shape as the standard projectile used in the Gâvre firings and studies a flat based projectile having an ogival head with a 2 caliber radius.

A graph of the G-function is included here. Note the sharp rise in retardation just at the velocity of sound.

An individual effort that should be mentioned here mainly because it was directed specifically at small arms resistance functions was a series of firings carried out in England in 1897 and 1898 by the late Col. Henry Mellish and the late Lord Cottesloe, (T. F. Fremantle, author of The Book of the Rifle, 1901, who died June 1956).

Col. Mellish and Lord Cottesloe, (with whom I was personally acquainted), set up a specially designed ballistic pendulum behind the 8-inch hole in the center of the bullseye of a heavy iron target, and with it obtained actual striking velocities at 1000 yards with the .461 Gibbs bullet of 570 grains weight. From these striking velocities

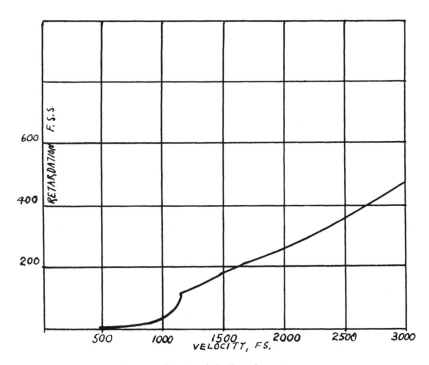

Graph of J Function.

an attempt was made to deduce a formula for air resistance vs velocity, but without success.

Further notable resistance firings were made at Aberdeen Proving Ground by the Ordnance Department in 1922-26, using several different shapes of projectile, as by this time long capped projectiles had come into use by heavy Army & Navy cannon, and it had become obvious that for such shells range tables computed from resistance functions based on a rather blunt ogive left something to be desired.

One of the several projectiles used in the Aberdeen firings had a long pencil-pointed nose and a boat tail or tapered base. This projectile, labelled "J" in the tests, was the basis for the Army's ballistic tables for boat tailed and sharp pointed projectiles, called the "J" tables, and based on what was at first called the "j"-function of resistance, (afterward called by Aberdeen the G_2 function).

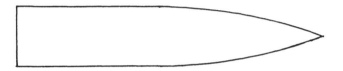

Projectile for which the British 1929 Tables were computed. It is one inch in diameter, weighs one pound, and has an ogival head of 8 calibers radius.

In 1921 firings were carried out by Mr. F. W. Jones, at Hodsock, in England, with a .303 caliber flat based spitzer bullet, using the same 1000-yd. ballistic pendulum arrangement that has just been described as having been used by Col. Mellish and Lord Cottesloe. In 1922, Mr. Jones carried out further experiments with a similar bullet having a boat tail or tapered base.

From these firings by Mr. Jones a set of resistance functions for spitzer pointed small arms bullets was developed, and from them a set of ballistic tables was worked out, which were known as the Hodsock tables. They were published, but eventually went out of print. However, they have now been reprinted in a revised and improved form as a final chapter in the book, Notes on Sporting Rifles by Major Sir Gerald Burrard, D.S.O., 4th Edition, 1953. (Edward Arnold & Co., London).

Additional firings for retardation were made by the British War Office with a flat based projectile having a long ogive point of 8 calibers radius, and the tables for sharp pointed projectiles that were printed in the British Textbook of Small Arms, 1929 were computed from these firings.

Thus it will be seen that there are several different sets of ballistic tables available that may be used with small arms bullets. The Ingalls tables, and the almost identical British 1909 tables are most suitable for the ordinary hunting bullet, either the rounded nose type such as the full metal cased .30-30, or the modified spitzer shapes, such as the 222 Remington soft point; while the Hodsock tables or the British "Sharp Point" tables of 1929 give slightly closer results with very sharp pointed spitzers, such as the military .30-06. The Ordnance Department's J tables give closer results for boat-tailed spitzer bullets, though it should be observed that at velocities above the speed of sound it makes little difference whether the base of the bullet is boat-tailed or not.

Comparison of Retardation Functions

At this point it may be of interest to compare the retardations obtained in several of the various resistance firings previously referred to. Accordingly a tabulation is included here, giving velocities in one column, and listing in adjacent columns the results of— (a) the Krupp firings at Meppen in 1881, on which Mayevski's formula and the Ingalls tables were based; (b) the Gâvre function; (c) results of the British firings of 1904-06 using the same shape of projectile as was used by Krupp and at Gâvre; (d) the Aberdeen firings with the "J" projectile; (e) firings by the Germans with a flat based spitzer; (f) firings made by Jones at Hodsock in 1921 with a flat based spitzer; and (g) firings made in 1922 by Jones at Hodsock with a boat-tailed spitzer bullet of .303 inch caliber.

Construction of a Ballistic Table

For those who may be curious about how a set of ballistic tables can be made up from only a formula for air resistance, the following brief explanation is included.

Mayevski's formula for the retardation in f.s. per second of the standard projectile of unit weight and diameter and with a 2 caliber radius of ogive, gives the retardation as Av^n where A and n have different values in different velocity zones as shown on page 559.

Suppose we decide to find the space traversed by the standard projectile while it is being retarded from 3600 f.s. to 3580 f.s., which is the first interval covered in Ingalls' tables.

The average velocity over this space is evidently close to $\frac{3600 + 3580}{2}$ or 3590 f.s., so the first step is to find the retardation of the standard projectile for this velocity.

We see by Mayevski's formula, as already quoted, that in the velocity zone from 2600 f.s. to 3600 f.s., n is 1.55 and A is the number whose logarithm is 7.609,048—10.

First we take the logarithm of 3590 which is 3.555094 and multiply it by 1.55, getting 5.510,396. To it we add log A, which is 7.609,048—10,

RESULTS OF SOME HISTORIC RETARDATION FIRING TESTS

Retardation, f.s. per second for standard projectiles 1 inch in diameter and 1 lb. in weight.

Velocity f.s.	Krupp	Gavre	British 1904-06	Aberdeen "J"	German Spitzer	Hodsock flat base	Hodsock boat-tail
800	26.2	28.8	32.8	22	24.1	...	...
850	30.6	34.7	36.76	25	27.3	...	...
900	36.2	42.6	43.75	28	31.2	...	...
950	43.3	53.3	51.45	32	36.2	...	...
1000	54.2	68.0	59.81	38	44.7	...	...
1050	73.3	88.2	72.14	48	60.3	...	...
1100	107.0	112.7	96.8	95	87	...	...
1120	120	123.4	108.74	102	99	...	...
1150	141	139.6	128.96	111	116	...	...
1200	175	166.4	164.86	122	141	128	125
1250	195	191.8	186.34	132	152	135	135
1300	213	216.2	209.36	141	164	150	143
1400	258	261.6	261.76	160	187	176	159
1600	343	347.1	349.90	195	233	222	195
1800	426	429.2	432.23	225	280	268	230
2000	509	516.5	522.60	265	325	303	263
2200	598	593.0	603.00	295	371	364	296
2400	692	678.5	686.93	337	407	410	328
2600	795	769.3	774.73	375	464	454	359
2800	904	867.1	876.68	423	509	502	390
3000	1015	973.0	983.77	463	555	523	420
3200	1135	1087.5	1095.69	514	601	...	...
3400	1265	1213.2	1212.75	...	...	...	...
3600	1410	1349.3	1333.99	...	...	...	...
3800	1565	1495.5	1460.06	...	...	...	...
4000	1730	1649.6	1590.63	...	...	...	...

getting 3.119,444. The number corresponding to this logarithm is found to be 1316.5, which is the retardation in f.s.s. for the standard projectile at 3590 f.s.

The usual formula for the space passed over by a uniformly accelerated (or retarded) body in passing from speed V to speed v is

$$\frac{V^2 - v^2}{2\,r}$$ which in this case is $$\frac{3600^2 - 3580^2}{2 \times 1316.5} = 54.5 \text{ feet.}$$

Looking now at Ingalls tables, p. 583, we see that this is indeed the first entry in column S (u), the space function. This represents the actual distance in feet that would have been traversed by the standard projectile while its speed fell from 3600 f.s. to 3580 f.s. if it had been projected with an initial velocity of 3600 f.s., and its path had remained horizontal throughout.

The quantity u used in the expression S(u) is the *pseudo-velocity*, which is the projection of the actual velocity along the trajectory onto the horizontal. With the very small angles of departure used in small arms firing, it differs so little from the actual velocity v that u is disregarded, and v is used instead without introducing any noticeable error.

Dividing the space passed over, which is 54.5 feet, by the average speed over this distance, or 3590 f.s., we get 0.015 for the time required for the projectile to have its speed changed from 3600 f.s. to 3580 f.s. by the air resistance encountered at that speed.

Thus we see that using only Mayevski's formula, and without recourse to higher mathematics, we have been able to fill in the first two values in the space function and time function columns of the ballistic tables. The entire table could be completed that way without any great error, providing only that the intervals between each two calculations are taken small enough.

What the Ballistic Tables Mean

To the average user of ballistic tables, they are just a seemingly interminable string of figures with the magical property of giving good ballistic information when used according to directions. Actually, however, when in the form of Ingall's tables they are rather simple when considered from the viewpoint of what the figures actually are.

As was seen above, the figures in the Space function column simply indicate spaces passed over by the bullet while its velocity is changing, (or being retarded by the air resistance), from some starting velocity to the velocity to which the particular figures apply; and the difference between the S figure for any one velocity and any other velocity represents the space passed over by the projectile while its speed is changing from one of the two velocities to the other. Likewise, the figures in the T or time function column represent the time occupied by the projectile in changing its speed from one velocity to the other.

It may be noted that the Ingalls tables, as well as most other American ballistic tables, start at the high velocity end of the velocity scale, and consider that the bullet is started off at 3600 f.s., and for the first increment of the space function and time function columns give the space and time required for the velocity to drop to the next lower figure.

The British, on the other hand, start their tables with 100 f.s. velocity, and for the first increment of the time and space function columns they give the time and space required by the bullet to be slowed down to 100 f.s. from some slightly higher velocity, say, 110 f.s.

The American system seems more logical, for it follows what the bullet actually does when fired; that is, it starts out with some high speed (the muzzle velocity), and then slows down.

Moreover, there is necessarily a great uncertainty as to just exactly what the retardation is at low velocities, for as a practical matter it is almost impossible to measure retardations experimentally at these low velocities. For example, according to Ingalls' tables, it takes the standard projectile only 274.4 feet to slow down from 3600 f.s. to 3500 f.s., and according to the British 1909 tables, it takes 272.2 feet, and requires 0.07 seconds.

However, the space required to slow down from 200 f.s. to 100 f.s. as given in the British 1909 tables is 6672 feet, while in Ingalls' tables it is 14,822 feet, and requires 23 seconds. In 23 seconds the bullet would drop 8464 feet, so it can readily be seen that it would be impossible to chronograph a bullet at the beginning and end of this interval.

This situation was impressed on my mind when I once plotted both the Ingalls tables and the supposedly almost identical British 1909 tables on cross-section paper, starting with 100 feet as the origin of the plot. The two curves were for the most part identical in shape, but the Ingalls curve lay considerably farther to the right. I puzzled over this for a while, then remembered the facts mentioned above, and repeated the work, but this time took 3600 f.s. as the origin of the plot. This time the curves practically coincided everywhere until the very low velocities were reached.

In view of the fact that the very low velocities are of no importance in the usual ballistic calculations, and that the thing that matters is the *difference* between the space or time function for some velocity under consideration and the space or time function for some other velocity, this discrepancy in the very low velocity ranges makes no difference at all to the average user of these tables.

Pressure in Pounds on the Nose of the Projectile

If a force of p pounds acts on a body of mass m, it will cause an acceleration of p/m f.s. per second. Mass is weight divided by gravity, so the retardation of the projectile by the air resistance of p pounds on its nose will be pw/g. However, with the standard projectile of unit weight which was used in making up the ballistic tables, w is 1, and the formula for retardation becomes r = pg, and from this we have p = r/g. Thus we can find p simply by dividing the retardation by 32.16.

As the retardation of the standard projectile at a velocity of 3590 f.s. was found to be 1316.5 f.s. per second, the actual force on the nose at that speed is 1316.5/32.16, or 40.95 pounds.

Proceeding in this way, we can make up a table of retardations and nose pressures for Mayevski's standard projectile for several different velocities, as follows:

Velocity f.s.	Retardation f.s. per second	Pressure p lbs. on nose of projectile
3600	1323.5	41.15
3500	1271.0	39.51
3400	1203.9	37.43
3300	1152.1	35.82
3200	1097.9	34.1
3100	1045.6	32.51
3000	995.0	30.93
2500	708.0	22.01
2000	508.9	15.82
1500	293.1	9.1
1200	154.3	4.7
1100	99.7	3.10
1000	61.2	1.90
900	42.53	1.32

As was stated above, this table is for a projectile of unit diameter; in other words, the diameter is 1 inch, and consequently the diameter squared is also unity. This fact makes it extremely simple to find the rearward pressure in pounds for any other projectile of the same nose shape, but of a different diameter; for to convert the figures in the table to another projectile of the same shape it is only necessary to multiply the figures in the table by the square of the diameter of the projectile.

Thus for a .30 caliber projectile having an effective diameter of the caliber plus the depth of 1 groove, or .304, and a shape of nose similar to that of the standard projectile, the pounds rearward force on the nose at any speed would be that in the table multiplied by .304 x .304, or .0924.

Thus for a .30 caliber bullet with about a 2 caliber ogive, at 2500 f.s., we would expect to have a nose resistance of 22.01 x .0924 = 2.034 lbs.

Form Factor

Now considering the .30-06 service bullet, we know from the way it acts when chronographed that it actually experiences a nose pressure at 2500 f.s. of about 1.14 lbs. The fact that the pressure is less should be no surprise, however, for this bullet has a much sharper point than the standard projectile for which the Ingalls tables were computed. Instead of a 2 caliber radius, it has one of 7 calibers, which obviously would pierce the air much more easily.

We see therefore, that to compensate for the sharper point of the .30-06 spitzer as compared to the standard Ingalls shape, we must multiply the figures given in our resistance table above by .56.

This multiplier is called the coefficient of reduction, or form factor, and is variously designated by different ballistics writers as c, (as distinguished from C, the ballistic coefficient), as n, and as i.

This book will follow the practice of Artillery Circular M and call it the form factor, designated by i.

It should be understood, and firmly borne in mind, that there is no *absolute* form factor for any bullet; the form factor is always for a *particular ballistic table,* and is determined by comparison of the retardation of the bullet in question with the retardation of the standard projectile for which the ballistic table was made.

While the form factor is best found by experimental firing, there are ways of estimating it fairly closely from the shape. One simple way is by comparing the bullet with a chart of bullet shapes, each with its coefficient of form marked thereon. Such a chart, by Edgar Bugless and Wallace H. Coxe, Ballistic Engineers of the DuPont Co. formed a part of a series of ballistic charts called "A Short Cut to Ballistics" published by the DuPont Co. By permission of the DuPont Company, this chart is reproduced herewith.

Instructions for using the chart.

Given a bullet; to estimate the coefficient of form, i.

1. Lay the bullet on the group of ogive curves marked with the proper caliber for the bullet.

2. Slide the bullet along until it matches one of the ogive curves as closely as possible.

3. Refer to the instruction page and read off the coefficient of form.

As an example, to estimate the coefficient of form for the .30 M2 bullet which has a 7 caliber ogive and a point which has a small blunt point about .03″ in diameter, lay the bullet on the set of curves marked .30, and slide it along until it seems to match an ogive curve. It will be seen that it is a bit too slim for the ogive 6 and a bit too fat for ogive 8, so the ogive evidently has a 7 caliber radius.

Referring to the instruction page, we see that for velocities over 2000 f.s. an 8 caliber ogive with a 0.1 caliber flat point has a coefficient of form of 0.55, and one with a 6 caliber ogive has a coefficient of form of 0.60. Hence one with a 7 caliber ogive will have a coefficient of form equal to the average of these two, or about .575.

BULLET FORM	NORMAL POINT	VALUE OF i — Diam. of Hollow Point or Flat Nose in Calibers				
		0.1	0.2	0.3	0.4	0.5
Blunt Projectile, Cylindrical	2.30					
Blunt Projectile, Taper Sides 0.9 Cal	1.85					
Blunt Projectile, Taper Sides 0.8 Cal	1.50					
Blunt Projectile, Taper Sides 0.7 Cal	1.30					
Blunt Projectile, Taper Sides 0.6 Cal	1.10					
Head Radius of 0.5 Cal	1.40					
Head Radius of 1.0 Cal	1.10	1.15	1.20	1.25	1.30	1.40
Head Radius of 1.5 Cal	0.95	1.00	1.10	1.15	1.25	1.35
Head Radius of 2.0 Cal	0.85	0.90	0.95	1.00	1.10	1.25
Head Radius of 3.0 Cal. M.V. 2000–3500 f.s.	0.70	0.75	0.80	0.90	1.00	1.10
Head Radius of 3.0 Cal. M.V. under 2000 f.s.	0.75	0.80	0.85	0.95	1.05	1.15
Head Radius of 4.0 Cal. M.V. 2000–3500 f.s.	0.60	0.65	0.70	0.75	0.85	1.00
Head Radius of 4.0 Cal. M.V. under 2000 f.s.	0.70	0.75	0.80	0.85	0.95	1.10
Head Radius of 6.0 Cal. M.V. 2000–3500 f.s.	0.55	0.60	0.65	0.70	0.80	0.95
Head Radius of 6.0 Cal. M.V. under 2000 f.s.	0.65	0.70	0.80	0.85	0.95	1.10
Head Radius of 8.0 Cal. M.V. 2000–3500 f.s.	0.49	0.55	0.60	0.65	0.75	0.90
Head Radius of 8.0 Cal. M.V. under 2000 f.s.	0.60	0.65	0.70	0.75	0.85	1.00
Head Radius of 10.0 Cal. M.V. 2000–3500 f.s.	0.44	0.50	0.55	0.60	0.70	0.85
Head Radius of 10.0 Cal. M.V. under 2000 f.s.	0.55	0.60	0.65	0.70	0.80	0.95
Balls with M.V. under 1000 f.s.	2.00					
Balls with M.V. between 1000–1300 f.s.	1.70					
Balls with M.V. over 1300 f.s.	1.40					

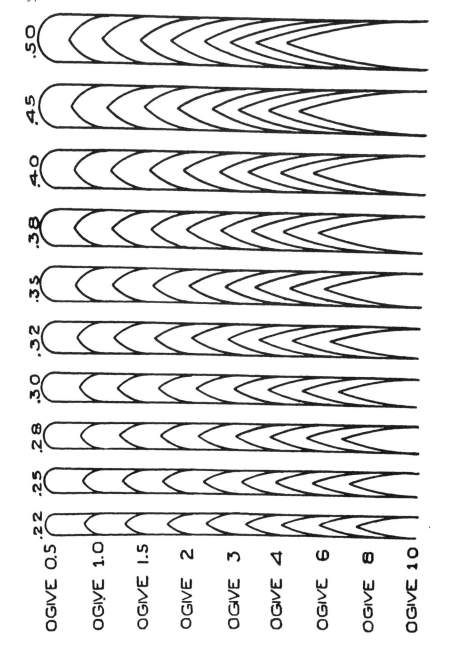

The British Textbook of Small Arms, 1909, gives a formula for caluculating the form factor for ogival pointed bullets, such as the

.30-06 spitzer, which gives close results. It is $i = \dfrac{2}{n} \sqrt{\dfrac{4n-1}{7}}$

where i is the form factor, and n is the radius of the ogive expressed in calibers.

Thus the .30-06 bullet has an ogive with a radius of 2.1 inches, or 7 calibers, and the form factor computed by that formula comes out .56

For ogival pointed bullets the radius of the ogive, n, can be determined rather easily by first measuring the diameter and the length

of head of the bullet, and then using the formula $n = \dfrac{4 L^2 + 1}{4}$

where L represents the length of the head of the bullet expressed in calibers.

The Ballistic Coefficient

The ballistic tables given in this book are made for a standard projectile of 1 inch diameter, 1 lb. weight, and with a shape corresponding to that of the projectile used in the resistance firings on which the particular table is based. As stated above the space and time functions in the tables represent actual spaces and times required by *this projectile* to pass from one velocity to another. If any other projectile is used, the spaces and times will be different.

Of course, the heavier the projectile is, all other things being equal, the less it will be retarded. If we want to use the tables with a projectile having the same shape and diameter, but twice the weight, we must multiply all figures in the table by 2, for it will go twice as far and take twice as long in slowing down from one velocity to another as will the standard projectile.

Again, suppose that we have a projectile of the same shape of nose and same weight as the standard projectile for which the tables were made, but of half the diameter. As cross-sectional area varies with the square of the diameter, this projectile will have only one-quarter the cross-sectional area of the standard projectile, and will meet only one-quarter the air resistance, so it will slow down only one-quarter as fast, and all figures in the table will have to be multiplied by 4. Such a multiplier is what is called the *Ballistic Coefficient* of the projectile for the particular ballistic table to be used. The ballistic coefficient of any bullet takes into account the weight, cross-section area, and shape of the bullet as compared to those qualities for the standard projectile on which the table is based, and also it takes into account the density of the air at the time of firing as compared to the standard density for which the tables were computed.

As will be seen from what has been said about the effect of weight and cross section, the ballistic coefficient is proportional to w/d²where w is the weight of the bullet in pounds, and d is its diameter in inches. The quantity w/d² is called the *Sectional Density*.

Use of the Form Factor

Obviously, the form factor of the bullet under consideration as compared to the standard projectile for which the tables were computed enters importantly into the ballistic coefficient, for the shape of the point of the bullet has a large effect on the magnitude of the air resistance it encounters in flight; the sharper the point and the smaller the form factor, the more easily the bullet can bore its way through the air.

Thus when the form factor is included, the ballistic coefficient

becomes $C = \dfrac{w}{i\ d^2}$ where w is the weight of the bullet in pounds,

d is its effective diameter (usually taken as the caliber plus the depth of 1 groove) and i is the form factor.

Correction of C for Changes in Air Density

There is another factor that enters into the complete expression for the ballistic coefficient, and that is a correction for variations in the density of the air from standard. The density of the air is affected by variations in temperature, in moisture content of the air, and in barometric pressure. The density is considered to be standard for ballistic calculations when the temperature is 60 deg. F., the barometer is 30 inches, and the air is two-thirds saturated with moisture.

It is usual to represent the density of the air by the symbol delta (δ). δ represents the actual density at the time and place of firing, while δ_1 represents the standard density. On p. 430 will be found a table of

$\dfrac{\delta_1}{\delta}$ for various temperatures and barometer readings. While such

corrections are vitally important in long range artillery firing, they are relatively unimportant in small arms firing at the usual ranges used in hunting or target practice, and hence may be disregarded.

However if it is desired to use them, it is only necessary to

multiply the ballistic coefficient by $\dfrac{\delta_1}{\delta}$ as found from the table

on p. 430 for the temperature and barometer at the time of firing.

Drag Coefficient

The reader who merely desires to use the ballistic tables at the end of the chapter may skip what follows, and turn directly to the tables.

However, for those who may desire as a matter of interest to study the subject of air resistance further, there follow a few paragraphs on the subject of the drag coefficient.

It was said above that Sir Isaac Newton decided that air resistance to a moving body is proportional to the square of the velocity, and that resistance firings seemed to show that this is not so. Further light is thrown on this subject by the following, quoted from the Ordnance School Text on Ballistics, prepared by Dr. L. S. Dederick for use in the Ordnance School in 1939 at the time when I was head of that school. The direct quotation starts here—

Dimensional Analysis

Before it is possible to give a complete and intelligible account of the assumptions made at the present time about the laws of air resistance, it is necessary to make a digression into a rather general subject of physical theory, that of dimensional analysis.

In order to specify the magnitude of any physical quantity, it is necessary to name the unit as well as the numerical measure. Thus a length of 5 is not determined unless we know whether it is 5 inches, 5 feet, or 5 of some other unit of length. The same is true of an area or a volume, but the three things are related. We know that if we change our unit of length from feet to inches, the number of units in a given length is multiplied by 12, the number of units in a given area is multiplied by the square of 12, and that in a given volume by the cube of 12.

This is briefly expressed by saying that the dimensions of area and volume are respectively two and three in length, or that the dimensional formulas for area and volume are L^2 and L^3. In the same way, most physical units can be expressed in terms of a small number of fundamental units, the most commonly used being length, mass, and time, and denoted by L, M, and T respectively. Thus we may say the dimensional formula for velocity is LT^{-1}, since velocity is obtained as a distance divided by a time. Since an acceleration is a velocity divided by a time, its dimensional formula is LT^{-2}.

Again, since a force is determined as a mass multiplied by an acceleration its dimensional formula is MLT^{-2}. Likewise the formula for density is ML^{-3} since density is mass divided by volume.

If any mathematical equation involves terms representing physical quantities, it must be homogeneous in the dimensional formulas of these quantities; that is, the degree of any one of the letters M, L, and T in the dimensional form of one term of the equation must be the same as that in any other term. The reason is that the equation may be supposed to represent a physical fact which is independent of the units used. A change of any unit will multiply every term by the same factor and so preserve the equality if the equation is homogeneous, but will not in the contrary case. This principle is commonly used as a check, but may also be used to discover new facts.

A very commonly used example of this procedure is the following. The time of oscillation t of a pendulum for a given amplitude may be supposed to depend conceivably on its length L, its mass M, and the intensity of gravity g. We write an equation in the form

$$t = kL^\alpha M^\beta g^\gamma$$

where k is a constant, assumed to be dimensionless, and the exponents α, β, and γ are to be determined.

The dimensional formula for the left side is of course T. For the right side it is

$$L^\alpha M^\beta (MT^{-2})^\gamma$$

Comparing the exponents of L, M, and t respectively in the two formulas, we get $\alpha + \gamma = 0, \beta = 0, -2\gamma = 1$. Hence $\alpha = \frac{1}{2}, \beta = 0$, and $\gamma = -\frac{1}{2}$, and we can infer that $t = k\sqrt{l/g}$

While the value of k is not given by this process, the result is rather substantial for the small amount of labor involved.

Of course in this sort of investigation we must take account of all relevant considerations. We assumed here that the oscillations were of a given amplitude. Dimensional analysis will tell us nothing about angles, since they are dimensionless, that is, they are independent of the units of length, mass, and time used.

Application to Air Resistance

We shall now apply the method of dimensional analysis to the law of air resistance. We have already assumed that the drag depends on the velocity of the projectile, the air density, and the shape and size of the projectile. Since we have seen that there is experimental evidence that there are different drag functions for different shapes, we need only consider size, which is then determined by any one linear dimension, such as diameter. We may write then

$$D = K_D d^\delta u^\beta \rho^\gamma$$

where D is in the air resistance, or drag, K_D is the coefficient of drag, d is the diameter of the projectile, u its velocity with respect to the air, and ρ the air density.

Now the dimensional formula for D is MLT^{-2}, that for d is L, that for u is LT^{-1}, and that for ρ is ML^{-3}. We have then

$$MLT^{-2} = L^\alpha (LT^{-1})^\beta (ML^{-3})^\gamma$$

and hence, by comparing the exponents of L, M, and T, respectively,

$$1 = \gamma$$
$$1 = \alpha + \beta - 3\gamma$$
$$-2 = -\beta$$

Hence $\gamma = 1$, $\beta = 2$, and $\alpha = 2$. We have then that the drag is proportional to the air density, to the square of the diameter, and to the square of the velocity of the bullet through the air. If we replace α, β, and γ, by their numerical values, the equation for drag becomes

$$D = K_D d^2 u^2$$

where the quantity K_D is called the *drag coefficient*, and is a quantity of dimensions zero. The implication of this last is that the value of the drag coefficient is entirely independent of the other quantities in the equation, provided of course, that these are consistent. Thus if d is expressed in feet, u in feet per second, p in pounds per cubic foot, and the corresponding value of D in poundals, the value of K_D will be the same as if d were in centimeters, u in centimeters per second, p in grams per cubic centimeter, and the corresponding value of D in dynes. Of course the unit of force must be absolute and not gravitational; the use of a pound force or a gram force would arbitrarily introduce the units of g. Not only is K_D of dimensions zero, but any quantity on which it depends must also be of dimensions zero.

The indication that D is proportional to u^2 appears to be a very astonishing result, for it apparently brings us back to Newton's law of resistance, which had been discredited by all the firings made by the Gâvre commission, and the resistance firings performed at Aberdeen.

Any such inference as this, however, overlooks the fact pointed out previously, that dimensional analysis throws no light on the influence of a dimensionless quantity, such as an angle or any other number in the form of the ratio of two quantities of the same dimensions. Thus while dimensional analysis shows that the drag is proportional to the square of the velocity, the drag may depend on any way whatever on the ratio of the projectile velocity to some other independent velocity.

If the drag were actually dependent on the square of the velocity, and not dependent on the velocity in any other way, we should have D/u^2 equal to a constant for any particular projectile and air density. For a standard projectile, this will be proportional to G/u, (where G is the Gâvre function, which is the particular drag function based on the experimental evidence collected by the Gâvre commission, practically all of which pertained to projectiles of conventional pre-World War I shape,) and also to K_D.

If then we compute G/u as a function of u from a G table, we may learn the mode of variation of K_D as a function of u.

If now we plot or tabulate this result based on the Gâvre function

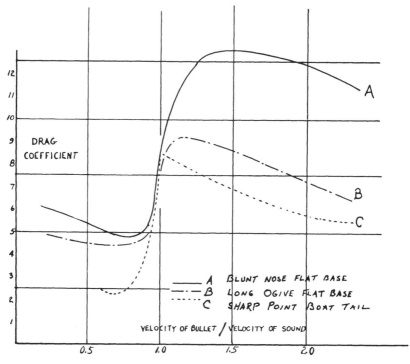

Drag coefficient plotted against ratio of bullet velocity to velocity of sound for three projectile shapes.

or any of the other drag functions, we get a function of u with the following properties. For small values of u it is nearly constant or decreases slightly; in the neighborhood of 1100 f.s. it increases very rapidly; it reaches a maximum shortly beyond this, and then decreases, but remains considerably larger than the value first mentioned.

For the different drag functions—that is for the drag functions pertaining to different projectile shapes—the abruptness of the increase, and the amount of the increase differ, but the value of u for which the increase is most rapid shows very little variation. This suggests forcibly that the rise is connected with the velocity of sound in air.

A set of three curves is given herewith, in which the drag function K_D is plotted against u/a for three different shapes of projectile. Curve A is for the Gâvre projectile, and the other two are for projectiles used in the Aberdeen firings of 1922. Projectile B has a long ogival point and a flat base, while projectile C, called the "J" projectile, has a long pencil-pointed nose and a tapered or "boat-tailed" base.

The fact that K_D has been made to depend on u/a rather than on u itself conforms to the requirement that K_D is not only of dimensions zero itself, but must also depend on arguments which are dimensionless.

Only one argument has been mentioned so far, namely u/a. This is called Mach's number. A full treatment would require the consideration of the cross-wind force and the overturning moment and stability factor, but in this very brief chapter they will have to be omitted.

Change of Ballistic Coefficient With Velocity.

It will be noticed in working with ballistic tables that the ballistic coefficient often changes with changes in velocity. Theoretically the

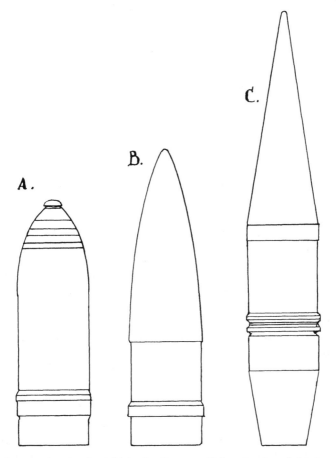

The three projectiles for which the Drag coefficient is plotted in the accompanying graph. Projectile A is similar to the Gavre type, while C is the Aberdeen "J" projectile.

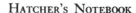

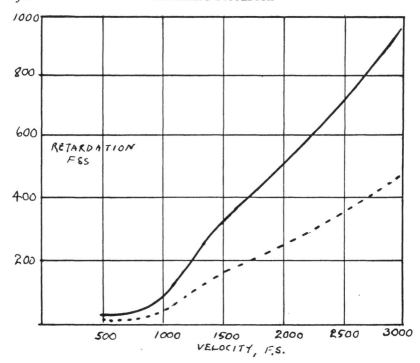

Full line shows Gavre function and dotted line shows resistance function for a projectile with Gavre shape and a ballistic coefficient of 2.0.

ballistic coefficient should remain constant regardless of velocity, but this is only so when the shape of the bullet is exactly similar to that of the standard projectile for which the ballistic table was computed.

Looking at the curve of K_D given herewith it can be seen that a projectile having a shape like that of projectile A will by no means follow a ballistic table computed for a projectile having a shape like that of projectile C.

Looking now at the sketch above, we see a graph of the G function, together with a graph of the retardation function of a projectile having the same form and weight but half the cross section area. It will have a ballistic coefficient of 2.0 and that will not change with velocity when used with tables computed for the Gâvre projectile.

Now refer to the sketch on the next page to see what happens when a projectile having a shape similar to the J projectile is used with tables computed from the G functions. At about 2100 f.s. velocity, where the two curves are together, the projectile will have the same ballistic coefficient when referred to ballistic tables computed from the G function as it will for those computed from the J function. Where the two curves coincide, it will make no difference which tables are used, but at other points, the ballistic coefficient will change when the G tables are used, while it will not change at any velocity if the J tables are used, because the projectile, being of the J shape, will follow the J function curve of resistance.

Comparison of the different Ballistic Tables

During many years work with ballistic tables, I have used the Ingalls tables, the British 1909 tables, (which are almost the same as the Ingalls), the British 1929 tables, based on a spitzer pointed flat based bullet with 8 calibers radius of point, and the Hodsock tables, which are also based on a spitzer shape.

We have several methods of judging which tables give the most nearly accurate results for any particular small arms bullet. For flat based spitzer bullets, such as the .30-06 or the .30 M2, we have a complete table calculated by the Ordnance Department up to 1000 yards, given on p. 401. Of all the tables we have used, the Hodsock tables give the closest results for *this* bullet, but the others are not

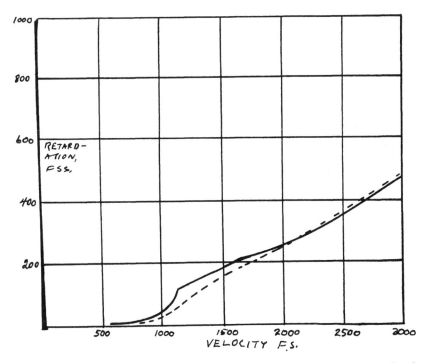

Solid line is the J function, while the dotted line is the G function reduced ½ as for a projectile having a ballistic coefficient of 2.0 referred to the G projectile.

far off. This is not surprising, for the Hodsock firings were done with a bullet of almost exactly the same shape.

The tabulation given below lists the Ordnance figures, together with those obtained with the 4 different ballistic tables mentioned in the second paragraph above.

150 Grain .30-06 Flat Based Spitzer Pointed Bullet at 2700 f.s.

Ordnance figures		Hodsock Tables C = .2507 i = .92	British 1929 Tables C = .2346 i = 1.0	Ingalls' Tables C = .4107 i = .56	British 1909 Tables C = .4083 i = .56
Range yds.	Remaining Veloc- ity, f.s.				
100	2481	....	....	....	....
200	2267	2268	2263	2275	2272
300	2059	2057	2048	2081	2071
400	1858	1853	1838	1892	1881
500	1664	1658	1638	1720	1705
600	1448	1477	1448	1565	1543
700	1315	1316	1279	1421	1395
800	1174	1180	1150	1295	1240

In connection with this tabulation attention is invited to the different values of C for the different tables. This difference is entirely due to the difference in the form factor as referred to the particular standard projectile on which each table was based. Both the Hodsock and the British 1929 tables were based on a sharp pointed bullet not far from the shape of the .30-06, hence the form factor for each of these tables is close to 1.0, which means that the ballistic coefficient does not change much with velocity with these tables for this particular bullet.

On the other hand, the Ingalls tables and the British 1909 tables are both made for a much blunter bullet, and it will be seen that the form factor for both these tables is .56, and the ballistic coefficient of the .30-06 bullet changes considerably with changes in velocity with these tables.

Most of our modern hunting bullets are much closer to the form of the Ingalls shape; even a small blunting of the point of a spitzer bullet will greatly increase its form factor, and make the Ingalls tables give more consistent results for it.

To check this out, I have taken the .222 Remington cartridge with 50 grain bullet at 3200 f.s. muzzle velocity, for which the factory has run ballistic tests and furnished trajectory figures up to 500 yards. This comparison follows:

222 Remington with 50 grain bullet at 3200 f.s. Muzzle velocity

Factory figures		Ingalls Tables $C = .1819$ $i = .78$	British 1909 Tables $C = .1792$ $i = .80$	British 1929 Tables $C = .0974$ $i = 1.47$	Hodsock Tables $C = .1025$ $i = 1.4$
Range yds.	Remaining velocity				
0	3200	....	....	....	....
100	2660	....	....	....	....
200	2170	2180	2178	2143	2131
300	1750	1765	1750	1642	1637
400	1400	1420	1393	1227	1234
500	1150	1163	1143	1009	1031

It will be seen that with this bullet, as is the case with most modern American hunting bullets, the form factor is closer to unity as referred to the Ingalls tables than when referred to the British 1929 and the Hodsock tables, both of which were made for sharp pointed spitzer type bullets. It is true that the 222 Remington has the general shape of a spitzer with about a 6 caliber radius but the lead point of the soft nose bullet has a flat on it of about a tenth of a caliber, which greatly increases the form factor. Looking at the DuPont chart of form factors, we would estimate a form factor of about .80 for this bullet for the Ingalls tables, and this is close to what it turns out to be.

Thus for this bullet, as for most others commonly used in our present day small arms shooting, the Ingalls tables are closer than the others.

A number of spot checks on other bullets included in the ammunition maker's published ballistic data all show close agreement with the results of calculations made with Ingalls tables. This includes even the boat-tailed full metal jacketed .30-06 bullet of 180 grains weight, figures for which are included below.

Western Cartridge Company's 180 gr. full metal jacketed .30-06

Company's published ballistics		Ingalls Tables $C = .512$ $i = .56$	British 1909 Tables $C = .50$ $i = .56$	British 1929 Tables $C = .286$ $i = .97$	Hodsock Tables $C = .305$ $i = .91$
Range yds.	Remaining velocity				
Muzzle	2700	....	....	....	....
100	2520	....	....	....	....
200	2350	2348	2346	2341	2392
300	2190	2185	2179	2163	2166

These comparisons, together with many others I have made all add up to the fact that the Ingalls tables are about the most generally satisfactory ones available today for use in small arms ballistic calculations.

Acknowledgment

In preparing this chapter, I have received invaluable assistance from Colonel E. H. Harrison, Ordnance Corps, USA, retired, of the Editorial Staff of the *American Rifleman*, and from Mr. Homer S. Powley, Shaker Heights, Ohio. Both of these authorities are highly qualified in this field, and both have been most generous in making the results of their knowledge available to me. To both I desire to express my thanks and deep appreciation.

USE OF INGALLS' BALLISTIC TABLES

The space function S tabulated opposite a velocity V is the actual distance in feet that would have been traversed by the *standard projectile* of unit weight and unit diameter while its speed fell from 3600 f.s: to V f.s. if it had been projected horizontally with an initial velocity of 3600 f.s., and if its path had remained horizontal throughout. The letter u used in the expression S(u) represents the pseudo-velocity, which is the projection of the actual velocity onto the horizontal plane. For the small angles of departure used in small arms firing, u can be taken as equal to V.

The symbols have the following meaning:
X is the range in feet.
V is the initial velocity for range X (refer to column headed u).
v is the terminal velocity for range X.
T is the time of flight for range X.
C is the ballistic coefficient.
i is the form factor.
H is the maximum height of the trajectory in feet.
S(V) is the velocity function (from S(u) in the table) for V.
S(v) is the velocity function (form S(u) in the table) for v.
T(V) is the time function (from the table) for V.
T(v) is the time function (from the table) for v.
w is the bullet weight in pounds.
d is the bullet diameter in inches.

Formulas and Examples of How to Use the Tables

PROBLEM 1:

Given the muzzle velocity V, the range X, and the remaining velocity v at the end of range X, to determine the ballistic coefficient C.

Formula: $C = \dfrac{X}{S(v) - S(V)}$ where S(v) and S(V) are space

functions for velocities V and v as taken from column S(u) in Table I.

Example 1. The 50 grain bullet for the Remington 222 cartridge has a muzzle velocity of 3200 f.s., and a remaining velocity of 2660 f.s. at 100 yds. Find the ballistic coefficient.

$$v = 2660 \text{ f.s. and } S(v) = 2772.9$$
$$V = 3200 \text{ f.s. and } S(V) = 1124.4$$

$$S(v) - S(V) = 1648.5$$
$$X = 100 \text{ yds}, = 300 \text{ feet, and } 300/1648.5 = .1819 = C$$

PROBLEM 2:

Given the muzzle velocity V, and the remaining velocity at the end of the range X, to find the form factor i.

Formula: $C = w/id^2$, hence $i = w/Cd^2$ where w is the weight of the bullet in pounds, and d is the diameter of the bullet in inches, generally taken as bore diameter plus the depth of 1 rifling groove.

Example 2. The 50 grain 222 Remington bullet has a muzzle velocity of 3200 f.s., a remaining velocity at 100 yds of 2660 f.s., and an effective diameter of .224 inch. Find the form factor.

First find the ballistic coefficient, as in problem 1. It was found be be .1819. Now find w/d^2 thus; $\dfrac{50}{.224 \text{ X } .224 \text{ X } 7000} = .1423$. This divided by the ballistic coefficient will give the form factor, thus .1423/.1819 = .78.

PROBLEM 3:

Given the muzzle velocity V, the ballistic coefficient C, and the range X; to find the remaining velocity v at the end of range X.

Formula: $S(v) = S(V) + \dfrac{X}{C}$

Example 3. Find the remaining velocity v at the end of 200 yards for the 50 grain 222 Remington bullet which has a muzzle velocity of 3200 f.s. and a ballistic coefficient of .1819.

$$\frac{X}{C} = \frac{600}{.1819} = 3298.5$$
$$V = 3200 \text{ f.s., and } S(V) = 1124.4$$
$$\text{Add } X/C = 3298.5$$

$$S(v) = 4422.9$$
$$v = 2180 \text{ f.s.}$$

PROBLEM 4:

Given the muzzle velocity V, and the remaining velocity v at 100 yards, to find the remaining velocity at 200 yards, 300 yards, and so on.

Formula: S(v) for 200 yd = S(V) + twice $\left\{ S(v) - S(V) \right\}$

also S(v) for 300 yd = S(v) + three times $\left\{ S(v) - S(V) \right\}$

and so on. This is simply a short cut which follows from a consideration of problems 1 and 3.

Example 4. Find the remaining velocity at 200, 300, 400, and 500 yards for the 50 grain 222 Remington bullet which has a muzzle velocity of 3200 f.s. and a remaining velocity of 2660 f.s. at 100 yds.

$$v = 2660 \qquad S(v) = 2772.9$$
$$V = 3200 \qquad S(V) = 1124.4$$
$$S(v) - S(V) \quad = 1648.5$$

$$S(V) \qquad\qquad = 1124.4$$
$$S(v) - S(V) \quad = 1648.5$$
$$S(v) \text{ for } 100 \text{ yd} = 2772.9$$
$$\text{Add} \qquad\qquad \underline{\;1648.5\;}$$

S(v) for 200 yds = 4421.4   Velocity at 200 yds = 2180 f.s.
Add $\underline{1648.5}$

S(v) for 300 yds = 6069.9   Velocity at 300 yds = 1765 f.s.
Add $\underline{1648.5}$

S(v) for 400 yds = 7718.4   Velocity at 400 yds = 1420 f.s.
Add $\underline{1648.5}$

                   9366.9   Velocity at 500 yds = 1163 f.s.

PROBLEM 5: Given the intial velocity V, the ballistic coefficient C and the range X, to find the time of flight for range X.

Formula: T = C $\left\{ T(v) - T(V) \right\}$ where T(v) and T(V) are taken from the column of time functions headed T(u) in Table I.

Example 5. Find the time of flight over a range of 500 yds for the 50 grain 222 Remington bullet having a ballistic coefficient of .1819.

First find the remaining velocity for 1500 feet as in problem 3. This is found to be 1163 f.s.

$$v = 1163 \text{ f.s.} \qquad\qquad T(v) = 4.7655$$
$$V = 3200 \text{ f.s.} \qquad\qquad T(V) = 0.3310$$

$$T(v) - T(V) \qquad\qquad\qquad = 4.4345$$
$$T = 4.4345 \times C = 4.4345 \times .1819 = .79 \text{ sec.}$$

PROBLEM 6:

Given the muzzle velocity, the range, and the ballistic coefficient, to find the maximum height of trajectory for the range X.

Formula: H in feet $= (2T)^2 = 4T^2$ and H in inches $= 48\ T^2$

Example 6: For a range of 300 yards, find the maximum ordinate H for the 50 grain 222 Remington bullet.

First find the remaining velocity at 300 yards. In problem 4 this was found to be 1765 f.s. Use this value to find the time of flight, as in problem 5. This is found to be .380 second, which is T. T^2 is .1444, which multiplied by 48 gives 6.93 inches as the maximum height of trajectory for 300 yards. Reference to the Western Ammunition Handbook shows that the maker's figure for this is 7 inches. (Note—ammunition maker's published ballistic tables give what is called MID-RANGE trajectory. The maximum ordinate occurs just a bit further along than mid-range, and is just a bit greater, but the difference is so small that the maximum ordinate as calculated above may be taken as mid-range trajectory without much error.

PROBLEM 7:

Given the maximum ordinate H for any range, find the time of flight for that range.

Formula: $T = \frac{1}{2}\ \sqrt{H}$ where H is in feet, or $T = \frac{1}{4}\ \dfrac{\sqrt{H}}{3}$ where

H is in inches.

Example 7: Given that the 300 yard mid range trajectory of the 50 grain 222 Remington is 7 inches, find the approximate time of flight.

$$T = \frac{1}{4}\frac{\sqrt{7}}{3} = \frac{1}{4}\sqrt{2.333} = \frac{1.527}{4} = .38 \text{ seconds}$$

PROBLEM 8:

Given the velocity of a bullet at any point, and the bullet weight in grains, to find the energy of the bullet in foot-pounds at that point.

Formula: Energy in foot-pounds $= \frac{1}{2} mv^2 = \frac{1}{2} \frac{wv^2}{g} = \frac{wv^2}{2g}$

where w is the bullet weight *in pounds* and g is the value of the acceleration of gravity, 32.16 f.s. per second.

As there are 7000 grains in a pound avoirdupois, the bullet weight in grains must be divided by 7000 to bring it to pounds, and must also be divided by gravity to bring it to mass instead of weight. The formula thus becomes $\frac{wv^2}{2g \times 7000}$ And as 2×32.16 × 7000 = 450,240, the formula simplifies down to bullet weight in grains times velocity squared divided by 450,240, or simply $\frac{wv^2}{450,240}$. If multiplication instead of division is preferred, it will be found that 1 divided by 450,240 = 0.000002221, so in this case the formula becomes Energy in foot pounds = 0.000002221 wv^2

Example 8: The 50 grain 222 Remington bullet has a remaining velocity at 100 yards of 2660 f.s.; find the energy at that point in foot pounds.

$$\frac{50 \times 2660 \times 2660}{450,240} = \frac{50 \times 7,075,600}{450,240} = 785 \text{ ft. lbs.}$$

Use of Table A

This table is used to find the angle of departure. The following example will show how it is used.

PROBLEM 8: Given the muzzle velocity V, and the ballistic coefficient C, find the angle of departure a, for range X.

Formula: Sin 2a = A x C, where A is the quantity found in Table A under the proper velocity heading and opposite Z, where $Z = \frac{X}{C}$.

Example 8: Find the angle of departure for a range of 400 yards with the 150 gr. .30-06 bullet with a muzzle velocity of 2700 f.s., if the ballistic coefficient is .41

X = 400 x 3 = 1200 feet.

$\frac{X}{C} = \frac{1200}{.41} = 2926.8$

Look at Table A under 2700 f.s. velocity, and under column Z.

We find no value for 2926.7 in the Z column, and as values for 2800 and 3000 are both given, it is necessary to interpolate.

A for Z of 3000 = 0.01708
A for Z of 2800 = 0.01565

Difference   = 0.00143   0.00143 x 126.7/200 = 90.6

A for Z of 2800 = 0.01565
Diff. to be added =   91

A for Z of 2926.7 = 0.01656

Sin 2 a = 0.01656 x .41 = .0067896
2 a = 23.91′ hence a = 11.5′

Checking with the table on p. 401, we see that the Ordnance range tables give the angle of departure for this bullet at 400 yards as 11.6′

BALLISTIC TABLES

The following tables will be found immediately following:

On pp. 590 to 616, incl., Ingalls' Table I, from Artillery Circular M.

On p. 617, an extension of Table I to 5000 f.s.

On pp. 619 to 624, incl., Ingalls' Table II from Artillery Circular M, ABRIDGED, and hence called Table A. It is used to find angles of elevation.

On pp. 624 & 625, a table of Natural Sines from 0 to 4 deg.

On pp. 626 to 628, Instructions and table for finding bullet drop.

On pp. 629 to 632, incl., the time and space functions from the British 1909 Ballistic Tables.

TABLE I.

u	$S(u)$	Δ	$A(u)$	Δ	$I(u)$	Δ	$T(u)$	Δ
3600	0.0	54.5	0.00	1.72	0.03138	0.00027	0.000	0.015
3580	54.5	54.7	1.72	1.74	0.03165	0.00028	0.015	0.015
3560	109.2	54.9	3.46	1.76	0.03193	0.00028	0.030	0.016
3540	164.1	55.1	5.22	1.78	0.03221	0.00028	0.046	0.016
3520	219.2	55.2	7.00	1.80	0.03249	0.00029	0.062	0.015
3500	274.4	55.4	8.80	1.82	0.03278	0.00030	0.077	0.016
3480	329.8	55.5	10.62	1.85	0.03308	0.00029	0.093	0.016
3460	385.3	55.8	12.47	1.87	0.03337	0.00030	0.109	0.016
3440	441.1	55.9	14.34	1.89	0.03367	0.00031	0.125	0.017
3420	497.0	56.1	16.23	1.92	0.03398	0.00031	0.142	0.016
3400	553.1	28.2	18.15	0.96	0.03429	0.00016	0.158	0.008
3390	581.3	28.1	19.11	0.97	0.03445	0.00016	0.166	0.008
3380	609.4	28.2	20.08	0.98	0.03461	0.00016	0.175	0.008
3370	637.6	28.2	21.06	0.98	0.03477	0.00016	0.183	0.009
3360	665.8	28.3	22.04	0.99	0.03493	0.00016	0.192	0.008
3350	794.1	28.4	23.03	1.00	0.03450	0.00016	0.200	0.008
3340	722.5	28.4	24.03	1.01	0.03525	0.00016	0.208	0.009
3330	750.9	28.4	25.04	1.01	0.03541	0.00017	0.217	0.008
3320	779.3	28.5	26.05	1.02	0.03558	0.00016	0.225	0.009
3310	807.8	28.6	27.07	1.02	0.03574	0.00017	0.234	0.009
3300	836.4	28.6	28.09	1.03	0.03591	0.00017	0.243	0.008
3290	865.0	28.6	29.12	1.03	0.03608	0.00017	0.251	0.009
3280	893.6	28.7	30.15	1.04	0.03625	0.00017	0.260	0.009
3270	922.3	28.7	31.19	1.05	0.03642	0.00018	0.269	0.009
3260	951.0	28.8	32.24	1.06	0.03660	0.00017	0.278	0.008
3250	979.8	28.8	33.30	1.06	0.03677	0.00018	0.286	0.009
3240	1008.6	28.9	34.36	1.07	0.03695	0.00018	0.295	0.009
3230	1037.5	28.9	35.43	1.08	0.03713	0.00018	0.304	0.009
3220	1066.4	29.0	36.51	1.08	0.03731	0.00018	0.313	0.009
3210	1095.4	29.0	37.59	1.09	0.03749	0.00018	0.322	0.009
3200	1124.4	29.1	38.68	1.10	0.03767	0.00018	0.331	0.009
3190	1153.5	29.1	39.78	1.10	0.03785	0.00019	0.340	0.009
3180	1182.6	29.2	40.88	1.12	0.03804	0.00018	0.349	0.010
3170	1211.8	29.2	42.00	1.12	0.03822	0.00019	0.359	0.009
3160	1241.0	29.3	43.12	1.13	0.03841	0.00019	0.368	0.009
3150	1270.3	29.3	44.25	1.13	0.03860	0.00019	0.377	0.009
3140	1299.6	29.4	45.38	1.14	0.03879	0.00019	0.386	0.010
3130	1329.0	29.4	46.52	1.15	0.03898	0.00020	0.396	0.009
3120	1358.4	29.5	47.67	1.16	0.03918	0.00019	0.405	0.010
3110	1387.9	29.5	48.83	1.16	0.03937	0.00020	0.415	0.009
3100	1417.4	29.6	49.99	1.18	0.03957	0.00020	0.424	0.010
3090	1447.0	29.6	51.17	1.18	0.03977	0.00020	0.434	0.009
3080	1476.6	29.7	52.35	1.19	0.03997	0.00020	0.443	0.010
3070	1506.3	29.8	53.54	1.20	0.04017	0.00020	0.453	0.010
3060	1536.1	29.8	54.74	1.21	0.04037	0.00021	0.463	0.009
3050	1565.9	29.8	55.95	1.21	0.04058	0.00021	0.472	0.010
3040	1595.7	29.9	57.16	1.22	0.04079	0.00021	0.482	0.010
3030	1625.6	30.0	58.38	1.23	0.04100	0.00021	0.492	0.010
3020	1655.6	30.0	59.61	1.24	0.04121	0.00021	0.502	0.010
3010	1685.6	30.1	60.85	1.25	0.04122	0.00021	0.512	0.010
3000	1715.7	30.1	62.10	1.26	0.04163	0.00022	0.522	0.010

TABLE I.—Continued.

u	$S(u)$	Δ	$A(u)$	Δ	$I(u)$	Δ	$T(u)$	Δ
3000	1715.7	30.1	62.10	1.26	0.04163	0.00022	0.522	0.010
2990	1745.8	30.2	63.36	1.27	0.04185	0.00022	0.532	0.010
2980	1776.0	30.2	64.63	1.28	0.04207	0.00022	0.542	0.010
2970	1806.2	30.3	65.91	1.28	0.04229	0.00022	0.552	0.011
2960	1836.5	30.3	67.19	1.29	0.04251	0.00022	0.563	0.010
2950	1866.8	30.4	68.48	1.30	0.04273	0.00023	0.573	0.010
2940	1897.2	30.5	69.78	1.32	0.04296	0.00022	0.583	0.010
2930	1927.7	30.5	71.10	1.32	0.04318	0.00023	0.593	0.011
2920	1958.2	30.6	72.42	1.33	0.04341	0.00023	0.604	0.010
2910	1988.8	30.6	73.75	,1.34	0.04364	0.00024	0.614	0.011
2900	2019.4	30.7	75.09	1.35	0.04388	0.00023	0.625	0.010
2890	2050.1	30.8	76.44	1.36	0.04411	0.00024	0.635	0.011
2880	2080.9	30.8	77.80	1.37	0.04435	0.00024	0.646	0.011
2870	2111.7	30.9	79.17	· 1.38	0.04456·	0.00024	0.657	0.011
2860	2142.6	30.9	80.55	1.39	0.04483	0.00024	0.668	0.011
2850	2173.5	31.0	81.94	1.40	0.04507	0.00025	0.679	0.011
2840	2204.5	31.1	83.34	1.41	0.04532	0.00025	0.690	0.011
2830	2235.6	31.1	84.75	1.42	0.04557	0.00025	0.701	0.011
2820	2266.7	31.2	86.17	1.43	0.04582	0.00025	0.712	0.011
2810	2297.9	31.2	87.60	1.44	0.04607	0.00026	0.723	0.011
2800	2329.1	31.3	89.04	1.46	0.04633	0.00026	0.734	0.011
2790	2360.4	31.3	90.50	1.47	0.04659	0.00026	0.745	0.011
2780	2391.7	31.4	91.97	1.48	0.04685	0.00026	0.756	0.011
2770	2423.1	31.5	93.45	1.48	0.04711	0.00027	0.767	0.012
2760	2454.6	31.5	94.93	1.50	0.04738	0.00026	0.779	0.011
2750	2486.1	31.6	96.43	1.51	0.04764	0.00027	0.790	0.012
2740	2517.7	31.7	97.94	1.52	0.04791	0.00027	0.802	0.011
2730	2549.4	31.7	99.46	1.53	0.04818	0.00028	0.813	0.012
2720	2581.1	31.8	100.99	1.54	0.04846	0.00028	0.825	0.012
2710	2612.9	31.9	102.53	1.56	0.04874	0.00028	0.837	0.012
2700	2644.8	31.9	104.09	1.57	0.04902	0.00028	0.849	0.011
2690	2676.7	32.0	105.66	1.59	0.04930	0.00029	0.860	0.012
2680	2708.7	32.1	107.25	1.60	0.04959	0.00029	0.872	0.012
2670	2740.8	32.1	108.85	1.60	0.04988	0.00029	0.884	0.012
2660	2772.9	32.2	110.45	1.62	0.05017	0.00029	0.896	0.012
2650	2805.1	32.3	112.07	1.63	0.05046	0.00030	0.908	0.013
2640	2837.4	32.3	113.70	1.64	0.05076	0.00030	0.921	0.012
2630	2869.7	32.4	115.34	1.66	0.05106	0.00030	0.933	0.012
2620	2902.1	32.5	117.00	1.67	0.05136	0.00030	0.945	0.012
2610	2934.6	32.5	118.67	1.69	0.05166	0.00031	0.957	0.013
2600	2967.1	32.6	120.36	1.72	0.05197	0.00031	0.970	0.013
2590	2999.7	32.7	122.08	1.72	0.05228	0.00032	0.983	0.012
2580	3032.4	32.9	123.80	1.73	0.05260	0.00031	0.995	0.013
2570	3065.3	32.9	125.53	1.75	0.05291	0.00032	1.008	0.013
2560	3098.2	33.0	127.28	1.76	0.05323	0.00033	1.021	0.013
2550	3131.2	33.1	129.04	1.77	0.05356	0.00033	1.034	0.013
2540	3164.3	33.2	130.81	1.78	0.05389	0.00033	1.047	0.013
2530	3197.5	33.3	132.59	1.81	0.05422	0.00034	1.060	0.013
2520	3230.8	33.3	134.40	1.83	0.05456	0.00034	1.073	0.014
2510	3264.1	33.5	136.23	1.84	0.05490	0.00034	1.087	0.013
2500	3297.6	33.6	138.07	1.86	0.05524	0.00035	1.100	0.013

TABLE I—Continued.

u	$S(u)$	Δ	$A(u)$	Δ	$I(u)$	Δ	$T(u)$	Δ
2500	3297.6	33.6	138.07	1.86	0.05524	0.00035	1.100	0.013
2490	3331.2	33.6	139.93	1.88	0.05559	0.00035	1.113	0.014
2480	3364.8	33.8	141.81	1.89	0.05594	0.00035	1.127	0.014
2470	3398.6	33.8	143.70	1.91	0,05629	0.00036	1.141	0.013
2460	3432.4	34.0	145.61	1.93	0.05665	0.00036	1.154	0.014
2450	3466.4	34.0	147.54	1.95	0.05701	0.00037	1.168	0.014
2440	3500.4	34.2	149.49	1.97	0.05738	0.00037	1.182	0.014
2430	3534.6	34.2	151.46	1.98	0.05775	0.00038	1.196	0.014
2420	3568.8	34.3	153.44	2.00	0.05813	0.00038	1.210	0.015
2410	3603.1	34.5	155.44	2.02	0.05851	0.00038	1.225	0.014
2400	3637.6	34.5	157.46	2.04	0.05889	0.00039	1.239	0.014
2390	3672.1	34.6	159.50	2.06	0.05928	0.00039	1.253	0.015
2380	3706.7	34.8	161.56	2.08	0.05967	0.00040	1.268	0.014
2370	3741.5	34.8	163.64	2.10	0.06007	0.00040	1.282	0.015
2360	3776.3	35.0	165.74	2.12	0.06047	0.00040	1.297	0.015
2350	3811.3	35.0	167.86	2.14	0.06087	0.00041	1.312	0.015
2340	3846.3	35.2	170.00	2.16	0.06128	0.00042	1.327	0.015
2330	3881.5	35.3	172.16	2.18	0.06170	0.00042	1.342	0.015
2320	3916.8	35.3	174.34	2.21	0.06212	0.00042	1.357	0.016
2310	3952.1	35.5	176.55	2.23	0.06254	0.00043	1.373	0.015
2300	3987.6	35.6	178.78	2.25	0.06297	0.00043	1.388	0.015
2290	4023.2	35.7	181.03	2.27	0.06340	0.00044	1.403	0.016
2280	4058.9	35.8	183.30	2.30	0.06384	0.00044	1.419	0.016
2270	4094.7	35.9	185.60	2.32	0.06428	0.00045	1.435	0.015
2260	4130.6	36.0	187.92	2.34	0.06473	0.00046	1.450	0.016
2250	4166.6	36.2	190.26	2.36	0.06519	0.00046	1.466	0.016
2240	4202.8	36.2	192.62	2.39	0.06565	0.00047	1.482	0.017
2230	4239.0	36.4	195.01	2.41	0.06612	0.00047	1.499	0.016
2220	4275.4	36.4	197.42	2.44	0.06659	0.00048	1.515	0.016
2210	4311.8	36.6	199.86	2.46	0.06707	0.00048	1.531	0.017
2200	4348.4	36.7	202.32	2.50	0.06755	0.00049	1.548	0.017
2190	4385.1	36.9	204.82	2.52	0.06804	0.00050	1.565	0.016
2180	4422.0	36.9	207.34	2.54	0.06854	0.00050	1.581	0.017
2170	4458.9	37.1	209.88	2.57	0.06904	0.00051	1.598	0.017
2160	4496.0	37.2	212.45	2.60	0.06955	0.00052	1.615	0.018
2150	4533.2	37.3	215.05	2.62	0.07007	0.00052	1.633	0.017
2140	4570.5	37.4	217.67	2.65	0.07059	0.00053	1.650	0.017
2130	4607.9	37.6	220.32	2.68	0.07112	0.00053	1.667	0.018
2120	4645.5	37.6	223.00	2.70	0.07165	0.00054	1.685	0.018
2110	4683.1	37.8	225.70	2.73	0.07219	0.00055	1.703	0.018
2100	4720.9	38.0	228.43	2.77	0.07274	0.00056	1.721	0.018
2090	4758.9	38.1	231.20	2.80	0.07330	0.00056	1.739	0.018
2080	4797.0	38.2	234.00	2.83	0.07386	0.00057	1.757	0.019
2070	4835.2	38.3	236.83	2.86	0.07443	0.00058	1.776	0.018
2060	4873.5	38.4	239.69	2.90	0.07501	0.00058	1.794	0.019
2050	4911.9	38.6	242.59	2.93	0.07559	0.00060	1.813	0.019
2040	4950.5	38.7	245.52	2.96	0.07619	0.00060	1.832	0.019
2030	4989.2	38.9	248.48	2.99	0.07679	0.00061	1.851	0.019
2020	5028.1	38.9	251.47	3.03	0.07740	0.00062	1.870	0.019
2010	5067.0	39.1	254.50	3.07	0.07802	0.00062	1.889	0.020
2000	5106.1	39.2	257.57	3.10	0.07864	0.00064	1.909	0.020

TABLE I—Continued.

u	S (u)	Δ	A (v)	Δ	I (v)	Δ	T (u)	Δ
2000	5106.1	39.2	257.57	3.10	0.07864	0.00064	1.909	0.020
1990	5145.3	39.4	260.67	3.14	0.07928	0.00064	1.929	0.019
1980	5184.7	39.6	263.81	3.17	0.07992	0.00066	1.948	0.020
1970	5224.3	39.6	266.98	3.21	0.08058	0.00066	1.968	0.021
1960	5263.9	39.8	270.19	3.25	0.08124	0.00067	1.989	0.020
1950	5303.7	40.0	273.44	3.29	0.08191	0.00068	2.009	0.021
1940	5343.7	40.1	276.73	3.32	0.08259	0.00069	2.030	0.020
1930	5383.8	40.2	280.05	3.36	0.08328	0.00070	2.050	0.021
1920	5424.0	40.4	283.41	3.40	0.08398	0.00071	2.071	0.022
1910	5464.4	40.6	286.81	3.45	0.08469	0.00071	2.093	0.021
1900	5505.0	40.7	290.26	3.49	0.08540	0.00073	2.114	0.021
1890	5545.7	40.8	293.75	3.53	0.08613	0.00074	2.135	0.022
1880	5586.5	41.0	297.28	3.58	0.08687	0.00075	2.157	0.022
1870	5627.5	41.1	300.86	3.62	0.08762	0.00076	2.179	0.022
1860	5668.6	41.3	304.48	3.67	0.08838	0.00077	2.201	0.022
1850	5709.9	41.5	308.15	3.71	0.08915	0.00078	2.223	0.023
1840	5751.4	41.6	311.86	3.76	0.08993	0.00080	2.246	0.022
1830	5793.0	41.8	315.62	3.81	0.09073	0.00080	2.268	0.023
1820	5834.8	41.9	319.43	3.85	0.09153	0.00082	2.291	0.024
1810	5876.7	42.1	323.28	3.90	0.09235	0.00083	2.315	0.023
1800	5918.8	42.3	327.18	3.96	0.09318	0.00084	2.338	0.024
1790	5961.1	42.6	331.14	4.02	0.09402	0.00086	2.362	0.024
1780	6003.7	42.8	335.16	4.08	0.09488	0.00088	2.386	0.024
1770	6046.5	43.1	339.24	4.14	0.09576	0.00089	2.410	0.024
1760	6089.6	43.3	343.38	4.21	0.09665	0.00090	2.434	0.024
1750	6132.9	43.5	347.59	4.27	0.09755	0.00092	2.458	0.025
1740	6176.4	43.8	351.86	4.33	0.09847	0.00094	2.483	0.025
1730	6220.2	44.1	356.19	4.40	0.09941	0.00095	2.508	0.026
1720	6264.3	44.3	360.59	4.47	0.10036	0.00097	2.534	0.026
1710	6308.6	44.5	365.06	4.54	0.10133	0.00099	2.560	0.026
1700	6353.1	44.8	369.60	4.61	0.10232	0.00100	2.586	0.026
1690	6397.9	45.1	374.21	4.68	0.10332	0.00102	2.612	0.027
1680	6443.0	45.4	378.89	4.76	0.10434	0.00104	2.639	0.027
1670	6488.4	45.7	383.65	4.83	0.10538	0.00106	2.666	0.027
1660	6534.1	45.9	388.48	4.91	0.10644	0.00108	2.693	0.028
1650	6580.0	46.2	393.39	4.99	0.10752	0.00110	2.721	0.028
1640	6626.2	46.5	398.38	5.08	0.10862	0.00112	2.749	0.028
1630	6672.7	46.7	403.46	5.16	0.10974	0.00113	2.777	0.029
1620	6719.4	47.1	408.62	5.24	0.11087	0.00116	2.806	0.029
1610	6766.5	47.3	413.86	5.33	0.11203	0.00119	2.835	0.030
1600	6813.8	23.8	419.19	2.70	0.11322	0.00060	2.865	0.015
1595	6837.6	23.9	421.89	2.72	0.11382	0.00060	2.880	0.015
1590	6861.5	23.9	424.61	2.75	0.11442	0.00061	2.895	0.015
1585	6885.4	24.0	427.36	2.77	0.11503	0.00062	2.910	0.016
1580	6909.4	24.1	430.13	2.79	0.11565	0.00062	2.926	0.015
1575	6933.5	24.1	432.92	2.82	0.11627	0.00063	2.941	0.015
1570	6957.6	24.3	435.74	2.84	0.11690	0.00063	2.956	0.016
1565	6981.9	24.3	438.58	2.87	0.11753	0.00064	2.972	0.015
1560	7006.2	24.4	441.45	2.89	0.11817	0.00065	2.987	0.016
1555	7030.6	24.5	444.34	2.91	0.11882	0.00065	3.003	0.016
1550	7055.1	24.6	447.25	2.94	0.11947	0.00066	3.019	0.016

TABLE I—Continued.

u	$S(u)$	Δ	$A(u)$	Δ	$I(u)$	Δ	$T(u)$	Δ
1550	7055.1	24.6	447.25	2.94	0.11947	0.00066	3.019	0.016
1545	7079.7	24.6	450.19	2.97	0.12013	0.00067	3.035	0.016
1540	7104.3	24.7	453.16	2.99	0.12080	0.00067	3.051	0.016
1535	7129.0	24.8	456.15	3.02	0.12147	0.00068	3.067	0.016
1530	7153.8	24.9	459.17	3.05	0.12215	0.00069	3.083	0.016
1525	7178.7	24.9	462.22	3.08	0.12284	0.00069	3.099	0.016
1520	7203.6	25.0	465.30	3.10	0.12353	0.00070	3.115	0.017
1515	7228.6	25.1	468.40	3.13	0.12423	0.00071	3.132	0.016
1510	7253.7	25.2	471.53	3.16	0.12494	0.00071	3.148	0.017
1505	7278.9	25.3	474.69	3.18	0.12565	0.00072	3.165	0.017
1500	7304.2	25.5	477.87	3.21	0.12637	0.00073	3.182	0.017
1495	7329.7	25.5	481.08	3.25	0.12710	0.00073	3.199	0.017
1490	7355.2	25.6	484.33	3.27	0.12783	0.00075	3.216	0.017
1485	7380.8	25.6	487.60	3.31	0.12858	0.00075	3.233	0.018
1480	7406.4	25.7	490.91	3.33	0.12933	0.00075	3.251	0.017
1475	7432.1	25.8	494.24	3.37	0.13008	0.00077	3.268	0.018
1470	7457.9	25.9	497.61	3.40	0.13085	0.00077	3.286	0.017
1465	7483.8	26.0	501.01	3.43	0.13162	0.00078	3.303	0.018
1460	7509.8	26.1	504.44	3.46	0.13240	0.00079	3.321	0.018
1455	7535.9	26.1	507.90	3.49	0.13319	0.00080	3.339	0.018
1450	7562.0	26.3	511.39	3.53	0.13399	0.00081	3.357	0.018
1445	7588.3	26.3	514.92	3.56	0.13480	0.00081	3.375	0.018
1440	7614.6	26.4	518.48	3.59	0.13561	0.00082	3.393	0.019
1435	7641.0	26.5	522.07	3.63	0.13643	0.00083	3.412	0.018
1430	7667.5	26.7	525.70	3.67	0.13726	0.00084	3.430	0.019
1425	7694.2	26.7	529.37	3.70	0.13810	0.00085	3.449	0.018
1420	7720.9	26.8	533.07	3.74	0.13895	0.00086	3.467	0.019
1415	7747.7	26.9	536.81	3.77	0.13981	0.00087	3.486	0.020
1410	7774.6	26.9	540.58	3.81	0.14068	0.00087	3.506	0.019
1405	7801.5	27.0	544.39	3.84	0.14155	0.00089	3.525	0.019
1400	7828.5	27.2	548.23	3.88	0.14244	0.00090	3.544	0.019
1395	7855.7	27.3	552.11	3.93	0.14334	0.00090	3.563	0.020
1390	7883.0	27.4	556.04	3.96	0.14424	0.00092	3.583	0.020
1385	7910.4	27.5	560.00	4.00	0.14516	0.00092	3.603	0.020
1380	7937.9	27.6	564.00	4.05	0.14608	0.00094	3.623	0.020
1375	7965.5	27.6	568.05	4.08	0.14702	0.00094	3.643	0.020
1370	7993.1	27.9	572.13	4.15	0.14796	0.00096	3.663	0.020
1365	8021.0	28.1	576.28	4.20	0.14892	0.00097	3.683	0.021
1360	8049.1	28.4	580.48	4.27	0.14989	0.00099	3.704	0.021
1355	8077.5	28.6	584.75	4.32	0.15088	0.00101	3.725	0.021
1350	8106.1	28.8	589.07	4.38	0.15189	0.00102	3.746	0.021
1345	8134.9	29.0	593.45	4.45	0.15291	0.00103	3.767	0.022
1340	8163.9	29.2	597.90	4.51	0.15394	0.00105	3.789	0.022
1335	8193.1	29.4	602.41	4.58	0.15499	0.00107	3.811	0.022
1330	8222.5	29.6	606.99	4.64	0.15606	0.00108	3.833	0.022
1325	8252.1	29.9	611.63	4.71	0.15714	0.00110	3.855	0.023
1320	8282.0	30.1	616.34	4.78	0.15824	0.00112	3.878	0.023
1315	8312.1	30.3	621.12	4.85	0.15936	0.00113	3.901	0.023
1310	8342.4	30.6	625.97	4.92	0.16049	0.00115	3.924	0.023
1305	8373.0	30.8	630.89	5.00	0.16164	0.00116	3.947	0.024
1300	8403.8	12.4	635.89	2.02	0.16280	0.00047	3.971	0.009

TABLE I.—Continued.

u	S (u)	Δ	A (u)	Δ	I (u)	Δ	T (u)	Δ
1300	8403.8	12.4	635.89	2.02	0.16280	0.00047	3.971	0.009
1298	8416.2	12.4	637.91	2.03	0.16327	0.00048	3.980	0.010
1296	8428.6	12.5	639.94	2.04	0.16375	0.00048	3.990	0.010
1294	8441.1	12.5	641.98	2.06	0.16423	0.00048	4.000	0.009
1292	8453.6	12.5	644.04	2.07	0.16471	0.00048	4.009	0.010
1290	8466.1	12.6	646.11	2.08	0.16519	0.00049	4.019	0.010
1288	8478.7	12.6	648.19	2.09	0.16568	0.00049	4.029	0.009
1286	8491.3	12.7	650.28	2.11	0.16617	0.00049	4.038	0.010
1284	8504.0	12.7	652.39	2.12	0.16666	0.00050	4.048	0.010
1282	8516.7	12.7	654.51	2.13	0.16716	0.00050	4.058	0.010
1280	8529.4	12.8	656.64	2.14	0.16766	0.00050	4.068	0.010
1278	8542.2	12.8	658.78	2.16	0.16816	0.00051	4.078	0.010
1276	8555.0	12.9	660.94	2.17	0.16867	0.00050	4.088	0.010
1274	8567.9	12.9	663.11	2.19	0.16917	0.00051	4.098	0.010
1272	8580.8	12.9	665.30	2.20	0.16968	0.00052	4.108	0.010
1270	8593.7	13.0	667.50	2.21	0.17020	0.00052	4.118	0.010
1268	8606.7	13.0	669.71	2.23	0.17072	0.00052	4.128	0.011
1266	8619.7	13.1	671.94	2.24	0.17124	0.00053	4.139	0.010
1264	8632.8	13.1	674.18	2.25	0.17177	0.00053	4.149	0.010
1262	8645.9	13.1	676.43	2.27	0.17230	0.00053	4.159	0.011
1260	8659.0	13.2	678.70	2.28	0.17283	0.00053	4.170	0.010
1258	8672.2	13.2	680.98	2.30	0.17336	0.00054	4.180	0.011
1256	8685.4	13.2	683.28	2.31	0.17390	0.00055	4.191	0.011
1254	8698.6	13.3	685.59	2.33	0.17445	0.00054	4.202	0.010
1252	8711.9	13.4	687.92	2.34	0.17499	0.00055	4.212	0.011
1250	8725.3	13.4	690.26	2.36	0.17554	0.00056	4.223	0.011
1248	8738.7	13.4	692.62	2.37	0.17610	0.00055	4.234	0.010
1246	8752.1	13.5	694.99	2.38	0.17665	0.00056	4.244	0.011
1244	8765.6	13.5	697.37	2.40	0.17721	0.00057	4.255	0.011
1242	8779.1	13.6	699.77	2.42	0.17778	0.00056	4.266	0.011
1240	8792.7	13.6	702.19	2.43	0.17834	0.00057	4.277	0.011
1238	8806.3	13.7	704.62	2.45	0.17891	0.00057	4.288	0.011
1236	8820.0	13.7	707.07	2.46	0.17948	0.00057	4.299	0.012
1234	8833.7	13.8	709.53	2.48	0.18005	0.00058	4.311	0.011
1232	8847.5	13.8	712.01	2.49	0.18063	0.00059	4.322	0.011
1230	8861.3	13.8	714.50	2.51	0.18122	0.00059	4.333	0.011
1228	8875.1	13.9	717.01	2.54	0.18181	0.00060	4.344	0.012
1226	8880.0	14.0	719.55	2.56	0.18241	0.00060	4.356	0.011
1224	8903.0	14.1	722.11	2.59	0.18301	0.00061	4.367	0.011
1222	8917.1	14.2	724.70	2.61	0.18362	0.00061	4.378	0.012
1220	8931.3	14.3	727.31	2.64	0.18423	0.00062	4.390	0.012
1218	8945.6	14.4	729.95	2.67	0.18485	0.00062	4.402	0.011
1216	8960.0	14.5	732.62	2.69	0.18547	0.00063	4.413	0.012
1214	8974.5	14.6	735.31	2.72	0.18610	0.00064	4.425	0.012
1212	8989.1	14.7	738.03	2.74	0.18674	0.00064	4.437	0.012
1210	9003.8	14.7	740.77	2.77	0.18738	0.00065	4.449	0.012
1208	9018.5	14.9	743.54	2.80	0.18803	0.00066	4.461	0.013
1206	9033.4	15.0	746.34	2.83	0.18869	0.00066	4.474	0.012
1204	9048.4	15.0	749.17	2.86	0.18935	0.00067	4.486	0.012
1202	9063.4	15.2	752.03	2.89	0.19002	0.00068	4.498	0.013
1200	9078.6	15.3	754.92	2.92	0.19070	0.00068	4.511	0.013

TABLE I.—Continued.

u	S (u)	Δ	A (u)	Δ	I (u)	Δ	T (u)	Δ
1200	9078.6	15.3	754.92	2.92	0.19070	0.00068	4.511	0.013
1198	9093.9	15.4	757.84	2.94	0.19138	0.00069	4.524	0.013
1196	9109.3	15.4	760.78	2.98	0.19207	0.00070	4.537	0.013
1194	9124.7	15.6	763.76	3.01	0.19277	0.00071	4.550	0.013
1192	9140.3	15.7	766.77	3.04	0.19348	0.00071	4.563	0.013
1190	9156.0	15.8	769.81	3.07	0.19419	0.00072	4.576	0.013
1188	9171.8	15.9	772.88	3.11	0.19491	0.00072	4.589	0.014
1186	9187.7	16.0	775.99	3.14	0.19563	0.00073	4.603	0.013
1184	9203.7	16.1	779.13	3.17	0.19636	0.00074	4.616	0.014
1182	9219.8	16.2	782.30	3.20	0.19710	0.00075	4.630	0.014
1180	9236.0	16.3	785.50	3.24	0.19785	0.00075	4.644	0.014
1178	9252.3	16.5	788.74	3.27	0.19860	0.00076	4.658	0.014
1176	9268.8	16.5	792.01	3.31	0.19936	0.00077	4.672	0.014
1174	9285.3	16.7	795.32	3.34	0.20013	0.00078	4.686	0.014
1172	9302.0	16.8	798.66	3.38	0.20091	0 00079	4.700	0.014
1170	9318.8	16.9	802.04	3.42	0.20170	0.00080	4.714	0.015
1168	9335.7	17.0	805.46	3.45	0.20250	0.00080	4.729	0.014
1166	9352.7	17.2	808.91	3.49	0.20330	0 00082	4.743	0.015
1164	9369.9	17.2	812.40	3.53	0.20412	0.00082	4.758	0.015
1162	9387.1	17.4	815.93	3.57	0.20494	0.00083	4.773	0.015
1160	9404.5	17.5	· 819.50	3.60	0.20577	0.00084	4.788	0.015
1158	9422.0	17.6	823.10	3.65	0.20661	0.00084	4.803	0.016
1156	9439.6	17.7	826.75	3.68	0.20745	0.00086	4.819	0.015
1154	9457.3	17.9	830.43	3.73	0.20831	0.00087	4.834	0.015
1152	9475.2	18.0	834.16	3.77	0.20918	0.00087	4.849	0.016
1150	9493.2	18.1	837.93	3.81	0.21005	0.00088	4.865	0.016
1148	9511.3	18.2	841.74	3.86	0.21093	0.00089	4.881	0.016
1146	9529.5	18.4	845.60	3.90	0.21182	0.00090	4.897	0.016
1144	9547.9	18.5	849.50	3.94	0.21272	0.00091	4.913	0.016
1142	9566.4	18.6	853.44	3.98	0.21363	0.00092	4.929	0.016
1140	9585.0	18.7	857.42	4.03	0.21455	0.00093	4.945	0.017
1138	9603.7	18.9	861.45	4.08	0.21548	0.00094	4.962	0.016
1136	9622.6	19.0	865.53	4.13	0.21642	0.00095	4.978	0.017
1134	9641.6	19.2	869.66	4.17	0.21737	0.00096	4.995	0.017
1132	9660.8	19.3	873.83	4.22	0.21833	0.00097	5.012	0.017
1130	9680.1	19.4	878.05	4.27	0.21930	0.00098	5.029	0.017
1128	9699.5	19.6	882.32	4.32	0.22028	0.00099	5.046	0.017
1126	9719.1	19.7	886.64	4.38	0.22127	0.00100	5.063	0.018
1124	9738.8	19.8	891.02	4.42	0.22227	0.00102	5.081	0.017
1122	9758.6	20.0	895.44	4.48	0.22329	0.00102	5.098	0.018
1120	9778.6	20.1	899.92	4.52	0.22431	0.00103	5.116	0.018
1118	9798.7	20.3	904.44	4.58	0.22534	0.00105	5.134	0.01
1116	9819.0	20.4	909.02	4.63	0.22639	0.00105	5.152	0.019
1114	9839.4	20.6	913.65	4.69	0.22744	0.00107	5.171	0.018
1112	9860.0	20.7	918.34	4.74	0.22851	0.00108	5.189	0.019
1110	9880.7	20.9	923.08	4.80	0.22959	0.00109	5.208	0.019
1108	9901.6	21.0	927.88	4.86	0.23068	0.00110	5.227	0.019
1106	9922.6	21.2	932.74	4.91	0.23178	0.00112	5.246	0.019
1104	9943.8	21.3	937.65	4.98	0.23290	0.00113	5.265	0.019
1102	9965.1	21.5	942.63	5.04	0.23403	0.00114	5.284	0.020
1100	9986.6	10.8	947.67	2.54	0.23517	0.00057	5.304	0.010

TABLE I.—Continued.

u	$S(u)$	Δ	$A(u)$	Δ	$I(u)$	Δ	$T(u)$	Δ
1100	9986.6	10.8	947.67	2.54	0.23517	0.00057	5.304	0.010
1099	9997.4	10.9	950.21	2.56	0.23574	0.00058	5.314	0.010
1098	10008.3	10.9	952.77	2.58	0.23632	0.00058	5.324	0.009
1097	10019.2	10.9	955.35	2.59	0.23690	0.00059	5.333	0.010
1096	10030.1	10.9	957.94	2.60	0.23749	0.00058	5.343	0.010
1095	10041.0	11.0	960.54	2.62	0.23807	0.00059	5.353	0.010
1094	10052.0	11.0	963.16	2.64	0.23866	0.00060	5.363	0.011
1093	10063.0	11.1	965.80	2.65	0.23926	0.00060	5.374	0.010
1092	10074.1	11.1	968.45	2.67	0.23986	0.00060	5.384	0.010
1091	10085.2	11.2	971.12	2.69	0.24046	0.00060	5.394	0.010
1090	10096.4	11.2	973.81	2.70	0.24106	0.00061	5.404	0.010
1089	10107.6	11.2	976.51	2.72	0.24167	0.00061	5.414	0.011
1088	10118.8	11.3	979.23	2.74	0.24228	0.00061	5.425	0.010
1087	10130.1	11.3	981.97	2.75	0.24289	0.00062	5.435	0.010
1086	10141.4	11.3	984.72	2.77	0.24351	0.00062	5.445	0.011
1085	10152.7	11.4	987.49	2.79	0.24413	0.00062	5.456	0.010
1084	10164.1	11.5	990.28	2.81	0.24475	0.00063	5.466	0.011
1083	10175.6	11.5	993.09	2.82	0.24538	0.00063	5.477	0.011
1082	10187.1	11.5	995.91	2.84	0.24601	0.00063	5.488	0.010
1081	10198.6	11.6	998.75	2.86	0.24664	0.00064	5.498	0.011
1080	10210.2	11.6	1001.61	2.88	0.24728	0.00064	5.509	0.011
1079	10221.8	11.7	1004.49	2.89	0.24792	0.00065	5.520	0.011
1078	10233.5	11.7	1007.38	2.92	0.24857	0.00065	5.531	0.010
1077	10245.2	11.8	1010.30	2.93	0.24922	0.00065	5.541	0.011
1076	10257.0	11.8	1013.23	2.95	0.24987	0.00065	5.552	0.011
1075	10268.8	11.8	1016.18	2.97	0.25052	0.00066	5.563	0.011
1074	10280.6	11.9	1019.15	2.99	0.25118	0.00067	5.574	0.012
1073	10292.5	11.9	1022.14	3.01	0.25185	0.00066	5.586	0.011
1072	10304.4	12.0	1025.15	3.02	0.25251	0.00067	5.597	0.011
1071	10316.4	12.0	1028.17	3.05	0.25318	0.00068	5.608	0.011
1070	10328.4	12.1	1031.22	3.07	0.25386	0.00068	5.619	0.011
1069	10340.5	12.1	1034.29	3.08	0.25454	0.00068	5.630	0.012
1068	10352.6	12.1	1037.37	3.11	0.25522	0.00068	5.642	0.011
1067	10364.7	12.2	1040.48	3.13	0.25590	0.00069	5.653	0.011
1066	10376.9	12.3	1043.61	3.14	0.25659	0.00069	5.664	0.012
1065	10389.2	12.3	1046.75	3.17	0.25728	0.00070	5.676	0.011
1064	10401.5	12.3	1049.92	3.18	0.25798	0.00070	5.687	0.012
1063	10413.8	12.4	1053.10	3.21	0.25868	0.00071	5.699	0.011
1062	10426.2	12.4	1056.31	3.23	0.25939	0.00071	5.710	0.012
1061	10438.6	12.5	1059.54	3.25	0.26010	0.00071	5.722	0.012
1060	10451.1	12.5	1062.79	3.27	0.26081	0.00072	5.734	0.012
1059	10463.6	12.6	1066.06	3.29	0.26153	0.00072	5.746	0.012
1058	10476.2	12.6	1069.35	3.31	0.26225	0.00073	5.758	0.012
1057	10488.8	12.7	1072.66	3.34	0.26298	0.00073	5.770	0.012
1056	10501.5	12.7	1076.00	3.36	0.26371	0.00073	5.782	0.012
1055	10514.2	12.8	1079.36	3.38	0.26444	0.00074	5.794	0.012
1054	10527.0	12.8	1082.74	3.40	0.26518	0.00074	5.806	0.012
1053	10539.8	12.8	1086.14	3.42	0.26592	0.00075	5.818	0.012
1052	10552.6	12.9	1089.56	3.45	0.26667	0.00075	5.830	0.013
1051	10565.5	13.0	1093.01	3.47	0.26742	0.00076	5.843	0.012
1050	10578.5	13.0	1096.48	3.49	0.26818	0.00076	5.855	0.012

TABLE I.—Continued.

u	S (u)	Δ	A (u)	Δ	I (u)	Δ	T (u)	Δ
1050	10578.5	13.0	1096.48	3.49	0.26818	0.00076	5.855	0.012
1049	10591.5	13.0	1099.97	3.52	0.26894	0.00076	5.867	0.013
1048	10604.5	13.1	1103.49	3.54	0.26970	0.00077	5.880	0.012
1047	10617.6	13.2	1107.03	3.57	0.27047	0.00077	5.892	0.013
1046	10630.8	13.2	1110.60	3.59	0.27124	0.00078	5.905	0.012
1045	10644.0	13.2	1114.19	3.61	0.27202	0.00078	5.917	0.013
1044	10657.2	13.3	1117.80	3.63	0.27280	0.00078	5.930	0.012
1043	10670.5	13.4	1121.43	3.66	0.27358	0.00079	5.942	0.013
1042	10683.9	13.4	1125.09	3.69	0.27437	0.00080	5.955	0.013
1041	10697.3	13.5	1128.78	3.71	0.27517	0.00080	5.968	0.013
1040	10710.8	13.5	1132.49	3.73	0.27597	0.00080	5.981	0.013
1039	10724.3	13.6	1136.22	3.76	0.27677	0.00081	5.994	0.013
1038	10737.9	13.6	1139.98	3.79	0.27758	0.00082	6.007	0.013
1037	10751.5	13.7	1143.77	3.81	0.27840	0.00082	6.020	0.013
1036	10765.2	13.8	1147.58	3.84	0.27922	0.00082	6.033	0.014
1035	10779.0	13.8	1151.42	3.87	0.28004	0.00083	6.047	0.013
1034	10792.8	13.8	1155.29	3.89	0.28087	0.00083	6.060	0.013
1033	10806.6	13.9	1159.18	3.92	0.28170	0.00084	6.073	0.014
1032	10820.5	13.9	1163.10	3.94	0.28254	0.00084	6.087	0.013
1031	10834.4	14.0	1167.04	3.97	0.28338	0.00085	6.100	0.014
1030	10848.4	14.0	1171.01	4.00	0.28423	0.00085	6.114	0.014
1029	10862.4	14.1	1175.01	4.03	0.28508	0.00086	6.128	0.013
1028	10876.5	14.2	1179.04	4.06	0.28594	0.00086	6.141	0.014
1027	10890.7	14.2	1183.10	4.08	0.28680	0.00087	6.155	0.014
1026	10904.9	14.2	1187.18	4.11	0.28767	0.00087	6.169	0.014
1025	10919.1	14.3	1191.29	4.14	0.28854	0.00088	6.183	0.014
1024	10933.4	14.4	1195.43	4.17	0.28942	0.00088	6.197	0.014
1023	10947.8	14.4	1199.60	4.19	0.29030	0.00089	6.211	0.015
1022	10962.2	14.5	1203.79	4.23	0.29119	0.00089	6.226	0.014
1021	10976.7	14.6	1208.02	4.25	0.29208	0.00090	6.240	0.014
1020	10991.3	14.6	1212.27	4.29	0.29298	0.00090	6.254	0.014
1019	11005.9	14.7	1216.56	4.31	0.29388	0.00091	6.268	0.015
1018	11020.6	14.7	1220.87	4.35	0.29479	0.00092	6.283	0.014
1017	11035.3	14.8	1225.22	4.38	0.29571	0.00092	6.297	0.014
1016	11050.1	14.8	1229.60	4.41	0.29663	0.00093	6.311	0.015
1015	11064.9	14.9	1234.01	4.44	0.29756	0.00093	6.326	0.015
1014	11079.8	15.0	1238.45	4.47	0.29849	0.00094	6.341	0.014
1013	11094.8	15.0	1242.92	4.51	0.29943	0.00094	6.355	0.015
1012	11109.8	15.1	1247.43	4.53	0.30037	0.00095	6.370	0.015
1011	11124.9	15.1	1251.96	4.57	0.30132	0.00095	6.385	0.015
1010	11140.0	15.2	1256.53	4.60	0.30227	0.00096	6.400	0.015
1009	11155.2	15.2	1261.13	4.63	0.30323	0.00096	6.415	0.015
1008	11170.4	15.3	1265.76	4.67	0.30419	0.00097	6.430	0.015
1007	11185.7	15.4	1270.43	4.70	0.30516	0.00098	6.445	0.016
1006	11201.1	15.4	1275.13	4.73	0.30614	0.00098	6.461	0.015
1005	11216.5	15.5	1279.86	4.77	0.30712	0.00099	6.476	0.015
1004	11232.0	15.6	1284.63	4.80	0.30811	0.00099	6.491	0.016
1003	11247.6	15.6	1289.43	4.84	0.30910	0.00100	6.507	0.015
1002	11263.2	15.7	1294.27	4.87	0.31010	0.00101	6.522	0.016
1001	11278.9	15.8	1299.14	4.91	0.31111	0.00101	6.538	0.016
1000	11294.7	15.8	1304.05	4.94	0.31212	0.00102	6.554	0.016

TABLE I—Continued.

u	$S(u)$	Δ	$A(u)$	Δ	$I(u)$	Δ	$T(u)$	Δ
1000	11294.7	15.8	1304.05	4.94	0.31212	0.00102	6.554	0.016
999	11310.5	15.9	1308.99	4.98	0.31314	0.00102	6.570	0.016
998	11326.4	16.0	1313.97	5.02	0.31416	0.00103	6.586	0.016
997	11342.4	16.0	1318.99	5.05	0.31519	0.00104	6.602	0.016
996	11358.4	16.1	1324.04	5.09	0.31623	0.00104	6.618	0.016
995	11374.5	16.1	1329.13	5.12	0.31727	0.00105	6.634	0.016
994	11390.6	16.2	1334.25	5.17	0.31832	0.00105	6.650	0.017
993	11406.8	16.3	1339.42	5.20	0.31937	0.00106	6.667	0.016
992	11423.1	16.3	1344.62	5.24	0.32043	0.00107	6.683	0.016
991	11439.4	16.4	1349.86	5.28	0.32150	0.00108	6.699	0.017
990	11455.8	16.5	1355.14	5.32	0.32258	0.00108	6.716	0.017
989	11472.3	16.5	1360.46	5.36	0.32366	0.00109	6.733	0.016
988	11488.8	16.6	1365.82	5.40	0.32475	0.00109	6.749	0.017
987	11505.4	16.6	1371.22	5.44	0.32584	0.00110	6.766	0.017
986	11522.0	16.7	1376.66	5.48	0.32694	0.00111	6.783	0.017
985	11538.7	16.8	1382.14	5.52	0.32805	0.00112	6.800	0.017
984	11555.5	16.9	1387.66	5.56	0.32917	0.00112	6.817	0.017
983	11572.4	16.9	1393.22	5.61	0.33029	0.00113	6.834	0.017
982	11589.3	17.0	1398.83	5.64	0.33142	0.00114	6.851	0.018
981	11606.3	17.1	1404.47	5.69	0.33256	0.00114	6.869	0.017
980	11623.4	17.2	1410.16	5.73	0.33370	0.00115	6.886	0.017
979	11640.6	17.2	1415.89	5.77	0.33485	0.00115	6.903	0.018
978	11657.8	17.3	1421.66	5.82	0.33600	0.00117	6.921	0.018
977	11675.1	17.3	1427.48	5.86	0.33717	0.00117	6.939	0.018
976	11692.4	17.4	1433.34	5.91	0.33834	0.00118	6.957	0.017
975	11709.8	17.5	1439.25	5.95	0.33952	0.00118	6.974	0.018
974	11727.3	17.6	1445.20	6.00	0.34070	0.00119	6.992	0.018
973	11744.9	17.7	1451.20	6.04	0.34189	0.00120	7.010	0.019
972	11762.6	17.7	1457.24	6.09	0.34309	0.00121	7.029	0.018
971	11780.3	17.8	1463.33	6.13	0.34430	0.00122	7.047	0.018
970	11798.1	17.9	1469.46	6.19	0.34552	0.00122	7.065	0.019
969	11816.0	18.0	1475.65	6.24	0.34674	0.00123	7.084	0.018
968	11834.0	18.0	1481.89	6.28	0.34797	0.00124	7.102	0.019
967	11852.0	18.0	1488.17	6.31	0.34921	0.00124	7.121	0.019
966	11870.0	18.1	1494.48	6.35	0.35045	0.00125	7.140	0.018
965	11888.1	18.1	1500.83	6.38	0.35170	0.00125	7.158	0.019
964	11906.2	18.1	1507.21	6.42	0.35295	0.00126	7.177	0.019
963	11924.3	18.2	1513.63	6.45	0.35421	0.00126	7.196	0.019
962	11942.5	18.2	1520.08	6.49	0.35547	0.00127	7.215	0.019
961	11960.7	18.3	1526.57	6.53	0.35674	0.00127	7.234	0.01
960	11979.0	18.3	1533.10	6.56	0.35801	0.00128	7.253	0.019
959	11997.3	18.3	1539.66	6.61	0.35929	0.00128	7.272	0.019
958	12015.6	18.4	1546.27	6.64	0.36057	0.00129	7.291	0.019
957	12034.0	18.4	1552.91	6.67	0.36186	0.00129	7.310	0.019
956	12052.4	18.4	1559.58	6.72	0.36315	0.00130	7.329	0.020
955	12070.8	18.5	1566.30	6.75	0.36445	0.00131	7.349	0.019
954	12089.3	18.6	1573.05	6.79	0.36576	0.00131	7.368	0.019
953	12107.9	18.5	1579.84	6.83	0.36707	0.00132	7.387	0.020
952	12126.4	18.6	1586.67	6.87	0.36839	0.00132	7.407	0.019
951	12145.0	18.7	1593.54	6.90	0.36971	0.00133	7.426	0.020
950	12163.7	18.7	1600.44	6.94	0.37104	0.00133	7.446	0.020

TABLE I—Continued.

u	$S(u)$	Δ	$A(u)$	Δ	$I(u)$	Δ	$T(u)$	Δ
950	12163.7	18.7	1600.44	6.94	0.37104	0.00133	7.446	0.020
949	12182.4	18.7	1607.38	6.99	0.37237	0.00134	7.466	0.019
948	12201.1	18.8	1614.37	7.03	0.37371	0.00134	7.485	0.020
947	12219.9	18.8	1621.40	7.06	0.37505	0.00135	7.505	0.020
946	12238.7	18.8	1628.46	7.11	0.37640	0.00136	7.525	0.020
945	12257.5	18.9	1635.57	7.15	0.37776	0.00136	7.545	0.020
944	12276.4	19.0	1642.72	7.19	0.37912	0.00137	7.565	0.020
943	12295.4	18.9	1649.91	7.23	0.38049	0.00137	7.585	0.021
942	12314.3	19.0	1657.14	7.27	0.38186	0.00138	7.606	0.020
941	12333.3	19.1	1664.41	7.31	0.38324	0.00139	7.626	0.020
940	12352.4	19.1	1671.72	7.36	0.38463	0.00139	7.646	0.020
939	12371.5	19.1	1679.08	7.40	0.38602	0.00140	7.666	0.021
938	12390.6	19.2	1686.48	7.44	0.38742	0.00140	7.687	0.020
937	12409.8	19.2	1693.92	7.48	0.38882	0.00141	7.707	0.021
936	12429.0	19.2	1701.40	7.53	0.39023	0.00142	7.728	0.020
935	12448.2	19.3	1708.93	7.57	0.39165	0.00142	7.748	0.021
934	12467.5	19.3	1716.50	7.62	0.39307	0.00143	7.769	0.020
933	12486.8	19.4	1724.12	7.66	0.39450	0.00143	7.789	0.021
932	12506.2	19.4	1731.78	7.70	0.39593	0.00144	7.810	0.021
931	12525.6	19.5	1739.48	7.74	0.39737	0.00145	7.831	0.021
930	12545.1	19.5	1747.22	7.79	0.39882	0.00145	7.852	0.021
929	12564.6	19.6	1755.01	7.84	0.40027	0.00146	7.873	0.021
928	12584.2	19.6	1762.85	7.88	0.40173	0.00146	7.894	0.021
927	12603.8	19.6	1770.73	7.92	0.40319	0.00147	7.915	0.021
926	12623.4	19.7	1778.65	7.98	0.40466	0.00148	7.936	0.022
925	12643.1	19.7	1786.63	8.02	0.40614	0.00148	7.958	0.021
924	12662.8	19.8	1794.65	8.07	0.40762	0.00149	7.979	0.021
923	12682.6	19.8	1802.72	8.11	0.40911	0.00150	8.000	0.022
922	12702.4	19.8	1810.83	8.16	0.41061	0.00150	8.022	0.021
921	12722.2	19.9	1818.99	8.21	0.41211	0.00151	8.043	0.022
920	12742.1	19.9	1827.20	8.25	0.41362	0.00152	8.065	0.022
919	12762.0	20.0	1835.45	8.31	0.41514	0.00152	8.087	0.021
918	12782.0	20.0	1843.76	8.36	0.41666	0.00153	8.108	0.022
917	12802.0	20.0	1852.12	8.40	0.41819	0.00153	8.130	0.022
916	12822.0	20.1	1860.52	8.45	0.41972	0.00154	8.152	0.022
915	12842.1	20.2	1868.97	8.51	0.42126	0.00155	8.174	0.022
914	12862.3	20.2	1877.48	8.55	0.42281	0.00156	8.196	0.022
913	12882.5	20.2	1886.03	8.60	0.42437	0.00156	8.218	0.023
912	12902.7	20.3	1894.63	8.66	0.42593	0.00157	8.241	0.022
911	12923.0	20.3	1903.29	8.70	0.42750	0.00158	8.263	0.022
910	12943.3	20.4	1911.99	8.76	0.42908	0.00158	8.285	0.022
909	12963.7	20.4	1920.75	8.81	0.43066	0.00159	8.307	0.023
908	12984.1	20.4	1929.56	8.86	0.43225	0.00160	8.330	0.022
907	13004.5	20.5	1938.42	8.91	0.43385	0.00161	8.352	0.023
906	13025.0	20.6	1947.33	8.97	0.43546	0.00161	8.375	0.022
905	13045.6	20.6	1956.30	9.02	0.43707	0.00162	8.397	0.023
904	13066.2	20.6	1965.32	9.07	0.43869	0.00163	8.420	0.023
903	13086.8	20.7	1974.39	9.12	0.44032	0.00163	8.443	0.023
902	13107.5	20.7	1983.51	9.18	0.44195	0.00164	8.466	0.023
901	13128.2	20.8	1992.69	9.23	0.44359	0.00165	8.489	0.023
900	13149.0	20.8	2001.92	9.28	0.44524	0.00165	8.512	0.023

TABLE I—Continued.

u	$S(u)$	Δ	$A(u)$	Δ	$I(u)$	Δ	$T(u)$	Δ
900	13149.0	20.8	2001.92	9.28	0.44524	0.00165	8.512	0.023
899	13169.8	20.9	2011.20	9.34	0.44689	0.00167	8.535	0.023
898	13190.7	20.9	2020.54	9.40	0.44856	0.00167	8.558	0.024
897	13211.6	21.0	2029.94	9.46	0.45023	0.00167	8.582	0.023
896	13232.6	21.0	2039.40	9.51	0.45190	0.00169	8.605	0.023
895	13253.6	21.1	2048.91	9.57	0.45359	0.00169	8.628	0.024
894	13274.7	21.1	2058.48	9.63	0.45528	0.00170	8.652	0.024
893	13295.8	21.1	2068.11	9.68	0.45698	0.00171	8.676	0.023
892	13316.9	21.2	2077.79	9.74	0.45869	0.00172	8.699	0.024
891	13338.1	21.3	2087.53	9.80	0.46041	0.00172	8.723	0.024
890	13359.4	21.3	2097.33	9.86	0.46213	0.00173	8.747	0.024
889	13380.7	21.3	2107.19	9.92	0.46386	0.00174	8.771	0.024
888	13402.0	21.4	2117.11	9.98	0.46560	0.00174	8.795	0.024
887	13423.4	21.5	2127.09	10.04	0.46734	0.00176	8.819	0.024
886	13444.9	21.5	2137.13	10.10	0.46910	0.00176	8.843	0.025
885	13466.4	21.5	2147.23	10.17	0.47086	0.00177	8.868	0.024
884	13487.9	21.6	2157.40	10.22	0.47263	0.00177	8.892	0.024
883	13509.5	21.6	2167.62	10.28	0.47440	0.00179	8.916	0.025
882	13531.1	21.7	2177.90	10.34	0.47619	0.00180	8.941	0.024
881	13552.8	21.7	2188.24	10.41	0.47799	0.00180	8.965	0.025
880	13574.5	21.8	2198.65	10.47	0.47979	0.00181	8.990	0.025
879	13596.3	21.8	2209.12	10.53	0.48160	0.00182	9.015	0.025
878	13618.1	21.9	2219.65	10.60	0.48342	0.00183	9.040	0.025
877	13640.0	21.9	2230.25	10.66	0.48525	0.00183	9.065	0.025
876	13661.9	22.0	2240.91	10.73	0.48708	0.00185	9.090	0.025
875	13683.9	22.0	2251.64	10.79	0.48893	0.00185	9.115	0.025
874	13705.9	22.1	2262.43	10.86	0.49078	0.00186	9.140	0.026
873	13728.0	22.1	2273.29	10.92	0.49264	0.00187	9.166	0.025
872	13750.1	22.2	2284.21	10.99	0.49451	0.00188	9.191	0.025
871	13772.3	22.2	2295.20	11.06	0.49639	0.00189	9.216	0.026
870	13794.5	22.3	2306.26	11.12	0.49828	0.00190	9.242	0.026
869	13816.8	22.3	2317.38	11.19	0.50018	0.00190	9.268	0.025
868	13839.1	22.4	2328.57	11.26	0.50208	0.00191	9.293	0.026
867	13861.5	22.4	2339.83	11.33	0.50399	0.00192	9.319	0.026
866	13883.9	22.5	2351.16	11.41	0.50591	0.00193	9.345	0.026
865	13906.4	22.6	2362.57	11.47	0.50784	0.00195	9.371	0.026
864	13929.0	22.6	2374.04	11.54	0.50979	0.00195	9.397	0.026
863	13951.6	22.6	2385.58	11.61	0.51174	0.00195	9.423	0.026
862	13974.2	22.7	2397.19	11.69	0.51369	0.00197	9.449	0.026
861	13996.9	22.8	2408.88	11.75	0.51566	0.00198	9.475	0.027
860	14019.7	22.8	2420.63	11.83	0.51764	0.00198	9.502	0.027
859	14042.5	22.9	2432.46	11.90	0.51962	0.00200	9.529	0.026
858	14065.4	22.9	2444.36	11.98	0.52162	0.00200	9.555	0.027
857	14088.3	23.0	2456.34	12.05	0.52362	0.00202	9.582	0.027
856	14111.3	23.0	2468.39	12.13	0.52564	0.00202	9.609	0.027
855	14134.3	23.1	2480.52	12.20	0.52766	0.00203	9.636	0.027
854	14157.4	23.1	2492.72	12.28	0.52969	0.00204	9.663	0.027
853	14180.5	23.2	2505.00	12.35	0.53173	0.00206	9.690	0.027
852	14203.7	23.2	2517.35	12.43	0.53379	0.00206	9.717	0.028
851	14226.9	23.3	2529.78	12.50	0.53585	0.00207	9.745	0.027
850	14250.2	23.3	2542.28	12.58	0.53792	0.00208	9.772	0.027

TABLE I—Continued.

u	$S(u)$	Δ	$A(u)$	Δ	$I(u)$	Δ	$T(u)$	Δ
850	14250.2	23.3	2542.28	12.58	0.53792	0.00208	9.772	0.027
849	14273.5	23.4	2554.86	12.66	0.54000	0.00209	9.799	0.028
848	14296.9	23.5	2567.52	12.74	0.54209	0.00210	9.827	0.028
847	14320.4	23.5	2580.26	12.83	0.54419	0.00211	9.855	0.027
846	14343.9	23.6	2593.09	12.90	0.54630	0.00212	9.882	0.028
845	14367.5	23.6	2605.99	12.98	0.54842	0.00213	9.910	0.028
844	14391.1	23.7	2618.97	13.07	0.55055	0.00214	9.938	0.028
843	14414.8	23.7	2632.04	13.14	0.55269	0.00216	9.966	0.028
842	14438.5	23.8	2645.18	13.22	0.55485	0.00216	9.994	0.029
841	14462.3	23.9	2658.40	13.31	0.55701	0.00217	10.023	0.028
840	14486.2	23.9	2671.71	13.39	0.55918	0.00218	10.051	0.028
839	14510.1	23.9	2685.10	13.48	0.56136	0.00219	10.079	0.029
838	14534.0	24.0	2698.58	13.56	0.56355	0.00221	10.108	0.028
837	14558.0	24.1	2712.14	13.65	0.56576	0.00221	10.136	0.029
836	14582.1	24.1	2725.79	13.74	0.56797	0.00222	10.165	0.029
835	14606.2	24.2	2739.53	13.82	0.57019	0.00224	10.194	0.029
834	14630.4	24.3	2753.35	13.91	0.57243	0.00225	10.223	0.029
833	14654.7	24.3	2767.26	14.00	0.57468	0.00225	10.252	0.029
832	14679.0	24.4	2781.26	14.09	0.57693	0.00227	10.281	0.030
831	14703.4	24.4	2795.35	14.17	0.57920	0.00228	10.311	0.029
830	14727.8	24.5	2809.52	14.26	0.58148	0.00229	10.340	0.029
829	14752.3	24.5	2823.78	14.36	0.58377	0.00229	10.369	0.030
828	14776.8	24.6	2838.14	14.45	0.58606	0.00231	10.399	0.030
827	14801.4	24.7	2852.59	14.54	0.58837	0.00233	10.429	0.030
826	14826.1	24.7	2867.13	14.64	0.59070	0.00233	10.459	0.030
825	14850.8	24.8	2881.77	14.73	0.59303	0.00234	10.489	0.030
824	14875.6	24.9	2896.50	14.82	0.59537	0.00236	10.519	0.030
823	14900.5	24.9	2911.32	14.92	0.59773	0.00237	10.549	0.030
822	14925.4	25.0	2926.24	15.01	0.60010	0.00238	10.579	0.030
821	14950.4	25.0	2941.25	15.10	0.60248	0.00239	10.609	0.031
820	14975.4	25.1	2956.35	15.20	0.60487	0.00240	10.640	0.031
819	15000.5	25.1	2971.55	15.30	0.60727	0.00241	10.671	0.030
818	15025.6	25.2	2986.85	15.41	0.60968	0.00243	10.701	0.031
817	15050.8	25.3	3002.26	15.50	0.61211	0.00244	10.732	0.031
816	15076.1	25.4	3017.76	15.60	0.61455	0.00245	10.763	0.032
815	15101.5	25.4	3033.36	15.71	0.61700	0.00246	10.795	0.031
814	15126.9	25.5	3049.07	15.80	0.61946	0.00248	10.826	0.031
813	15152.4	25.5	3064.87	15.91	0.62194	0.00249	10.857	0.032
812	15177.9	25.6	3080.78	16.00	0.62443	0.00250	10.889	0.031
811	15203.5	25.6	3096.78	16.11	0.62693	0.00251	10.920	0.032
810	15229.1	25.7	3112.89	16.21	0.62944	0.00252	10.952	0.032
809	15254.8	25.8	3129.10	16.32	0.63196	0.00254	10.984	0.032
808	15280.6	25.8	3145.42	16.43	0.63450	0.00255	11.016	0.032
807	15306.4	25.9	3161.85	16.54	0.63705	0.00256	11.048	0.032
806	15332.3	26.0	3178.39	16.65	0.63961	0.00257	11.080	0.032
805	15358.3	26.0	3195.04	16.75	0.64218	0.00259	11.112	0.032
804	15384.3	26.1	3211.79	16.86	0.64477	0.00260	11.144	0.033
803	15410.4	26.2	3228.65	16.97	0.64737	0.00261	11.177	0.032
802	15436.6	26.2	3245.62	17.08	0.64998	0.00263	11.209	0.033
801	15462.8	26.3	3262.70	17.19	0.65261	0.00264	11.242	0.033
800	15489.1	26.4	3279.89	17.30	0.65525	0.00265	11.275	0.033

TABLE I—Continued.

u	S (u)	Δ	A (u)	Δ	I (u)	Δ	T (u)	Δ
800	15489.1	26.4	3279.89	17.30	0.65525	0.00265	11.275	0.033
799	15515.5	26.4	3297.19	17.42	0.65790	0.00266	11.308	0.033
798	15541.9	26.5	3314.61	17.53	0.66056	0.00268	11.341	0.033
797	15568.4	26.5	3332.14	17.65	0.66324	0.00269	11.374	0.033
796	15594.9	26.6	3349.79	17.77	0.66593	0.00271	11.407	0.034
795	15621.5	26.7	3367.56	17.89	0.66864	0.00272	11.441	0.033
794	15648.2	26.8	3385.45	18.00	0.67136	0.00273	11.474	0.034
793	15675.0	26.8	3403.45	18.12	0.67409	0.00275	11.508	0.034
792	15701.8	26.9	3421.57	18.24	0.67684	0.00276	11.542	0.034
791	15728.7	26.9	3439.81	18.36	0.67960	0.00278	11.576	0.034
790	15755.6	27.1	3458.17	18.52	0.68238	0.00280	11.610	0.034
789	15782.7	27.1	3476.69	18.62	0.68518	0.00280	11.644	0.035
788	15809.8	27.1	3495.31	18.71	0.68798	0.00282	11.679	0.034
787	15836.9	27.2	3514.02	18.83	0.69080	0.00283	11.713	0.035
786	15864.1	27.2	3532.85	18.92	0.69363	0.00284	11.748	0.034
785	15891.3	27.3	3551.77	19.02	0.69647	0.00285	11.782	0.035
784	15918.6	27.3	3570.79	19.13	0.69932	0.00286	11.817	0.035
783	15945.9	27.3	3589.92	19.23	0.70218	0.00287	11.852	0.035
782	15973.2	27.4	3609.15	19.33	0.70505	0.00288	11.887	0.035
781	16000.6	27.4	3628.48	19.44	0.70793	0.00289	11.922	0.035
780	16028.0	27.4	3647.92	19.54	0.71082	0.00290	11.957	0.035
779	16055.4	27.5	3667.46	19.65	0.71372	0.00292	11.992	0.035
778	16082.9	27.5	3687.11	19.75	0.71664	0.00292	12.027	0.036
777	16110.4	27.5	3706.86	19.86	0.71956	0.00294	12.063	0.035
776	16137.9	27.6	3726.72	19.97	0.72250	0 00295	12.098	0.035
775	16165.5	27.6	3746.69	20.07	0.72545	0.00296	12.133	0.036
774	16193.1	27.6	3766.76	20.18	0.72841	0.00297	12.169	0.036
773	16220.7	27.7	3786.94	20.29	0.73138	0.00299	12.205	0.036
772	16248.4	27.7	3807.23	20.39	0.73437	0.00299	12.241	0.036
771	16276.1	27.8	3827.62	20.51	0.73736	0.00301	12.277	0.036
770	16303.9	27.8	3848.13	20.62	0.74037	0.00302	12.313	0.036
769	16331.7	27.8	3868.75	20.72	0.74339	0.00303	12.349	0.037
768	16359.5	27.9	3889.47	20.84	0.74642	0.00304	12.386	0.036
767	16387.4	27.9	3910.31	20.95	0.74946	0.00306	12.422	0.036
766	16415.3	27.9	3931.26	21.07	0.75252	0.00307	12.458	0.037
765	16443.2	28.0	3952.33	21.17	0.75559	0.00308	12.495	0.037
764	16471.2	28.0	3973.50	21.29	0.75867	0.00309	12.532	0.036
763	16499.2	28.1	3994.79	21.41	0.76176	0.00310	12.568	0.037
762	16527.3	28.1	4016.20	21.52	0.76486	0.00311	12.605	0.037
761	16555.4	28.1	4037.72	21.64	0.76797	0.00313	12.642	0.037
760	16583.5	28.1	4059.36	21.76	0.77110	0.00314	12.679	0.037
759	16611.6	28.2	4081.12	21.88	0.77424	0.00315	12.716	0.037
758	16639.8	28.2	4103.00	22.00	0.77739	0.00316	12.753	0.038
757	16668.0	28.3	4125.00	22.11	0.78055	0.00318	12.791	0.037
756	16696.3	28.3	4147.11	22.23	0.78373	0.00319	12.828	0.037
755	16724.6	28.3	4169.34	22.35	0.78692	0.00320	12.865	0.038
754	16752.9	28.4	4191.69	22.47	0.79012	0.00322	12.903	0.038
753	16781.3	28.4	4214.16	22.59	0.79334	0.00322	12.941	0.037
752	16809.7	28.5	4236.75	22.70	0.79656	0.00324	12.978	0.038
751	16838.2	28.5	4259.45	22.83	0.79980	0.00326	13.016	0.038
750	16866.7	28.5	4282.28	22.96	0.80306	0.00327	13.054	0.038

TABLE I—Continued.

u	S (u)	Δ	A (u)	Δ	I (u)	Δ	T (u)	Δ
750	16866. 7	28. 5	4282. 28	22. 96	0. 80306	0. 00327	13. 054	0. 038
749	16895. 2	28. 6	4305. 24	23. 09	0. 80633	0. 00328	13. 092	0. 038
748	16923. 8	28. 6	4328. 33	23. 21	0. 80961	0. 00329	13. 130	0. 038
747	16952. 4	28. 7	4351. 54	23. 33	0. 81290	0. 00331	13. 168	0. 039
746	16981. 1	28. 7	4374. 87	23. 46	0. 81621	0. 00332	13. 207	0. 038
745	17009. 8	28. 7	4398. 33	23. 59	0. 81953	0. 00333	13. 245	0. 039
744	17038. 5	28. 8	4421. 92	23. 72	0. 82286	0. 00335	13. 284	0. 038
743	17067. 3	28. 8	4445. 64	23. 84	0. 82621	0. 00336	13. 322	0. 039
742	17096. 1	28. 8	4469. 48	23. 98	0. 82957	0. 00337	13. 361	0. 039
741	17124. 9	28. 9	4493. 46	24. 10	0. 83294	0. 00339	13. 400	0. 039
740	17153. 8	28. 9	4517. 56	24. 23	0. 83633	0. 00340	13. 439	0. 039
739	17182. 7	29. 0	4541. 79	24. 37	0. 83973	0. 00341	13. 478	0. 039
738	17211. 7	29. 0	4566. 16	24. 50	0. 84314	0. 00343	13. 517	0. 040
737	17240. 7	29. 0	4590. 66	24. 63	0. 84657	0. 00344	13. 557	0. 039
736	17269. 7	29. 1	4615. 29	24. 76	0. 85001	0. 00346	13. 596	0. 039
735	17298. 8	29. 1	4640. 05	24. 90	0. 85347	0. 00347	13. 635	0. 040
734	17327. 9	29. 1	4664. 95	25. 04	0. 85694	0. 00349	13. 675	0. 040
733	17357. 0	29. 2	4689. 99	25. 17	0. 86043	0. 00350	13. 715	0. 040
732	17386. 2	29. 2	4715. 16	25. 30	0. 86393	0. 00351	13. 755	0. 040
731	17415. 4	29. 3	4740. 46	25. 45	0. 86744	0. 00353	13. 795	0. 040
730	17444. 7	29. 3	4765. 91	25. 59	0. 87097	0. 00354	13. 835	0. 040
729	17474. 0	29. 3	4791. 50	25. 72	0. 87451	0. 00356	13. 875	0. 041
728	17503. 3	29. 4	4817. 22	25. 87	0. 87807	0. 00358	13. 916	0. 040
727	17532. 7	29. 4	4843. 09	26. 00	0. 88165	0. 00359	13. 956	0. 040
726	17562. 2	29. 5	4869. 09	26. 15	0. 88524	0. 00360	13. 996	0. 041
725	17591. 7	29. 5	4895. 24	26. 29	0. 88884	0. 00361	14. 037	0. 041
724	17621. 2	29. 5	4921. 53	26. 43	0. 89245	0. 00363	14. 078	0. 041
723	17650. 7	29. 6	4947. 96	26. 57	0. 89608	0. 00365	14. 119	0. 041
722	17680. 3	29. 7	4974. 53	26. 72	0. 89973	0. 00366	14. 160	0. 041
721	17710. 0	29. 7	5001. 25	26. 87	0. 90339	0. 00368	14. 201	0. 041
720	17739. 7	29. 8	5028. 12	27. 01	0. 90707	0. 00369	14. 242	0. 041
719	17769. 5	29. 8	5055. 13	27. 16	0. 91076	0. 00371	14. 283	0. 042
718	17799. 3	29. 8	5082. 29	27. 31	0. 91447	0. 00372	14. 325	0. 041
717	17829. 1	29. 9	5109. 60	27. 46	0. 91819	0. 00374	14. 366	0. 042
716	17859. 0	29. 9	5137. 06	27. 61	0. 92193	0. 00376	14. 408	0. 041
715	17888. 9	30. 0	5164. 67	27. 76	0. 92569	0. 00377	14. 449	0. 042
714	17918. 9	30. 0	5192. 43	27. 92	0. 92946	0. 00379	14. 491	0. 042
713	17948. 9	30. 0	5220. 35	28. 06	0. 93325	0. 00380	14. 533	0. 043
712	17978. 9	30. 1	5248. 41	28. 22	0. 93705	0. 00382	14. 576	0. 042
711	18009. 0	30. 1	5276. 63	28. 38	0. 94087	0. 00383	14. 618	0. 042
710	18039. 1	30. 1	5305. 01	28. 53	0. 94470	0. 00385	14. 660	0. 042
709	18069. 2	30. 1	5333. 54	28. 69	0. 94855	0. 00387	14. 702	0. 043
708	18099. 3	30. 2	5362. 23	28. 85	0. 95242	0. 00388	14. 745	0. 043
707	18129. 5	30. 3	5391. 08	29. 01	0. 95630	0. 00390	14. 788	0. 042
706	18159. 8	30. 3	5420. 09	29. 16	0. 96020	0. 00392	14. 830	0. 043
705	18190. 1	30. 3	5449. 25	29. 33	0. 96412	0. 00394	14. 873	0. 043
704	18220. 4	30. 4	5478. 58	29. 49	0. 96806	0. 00395	14. 916	0. 043
703	18250. 8	30. 4	5508. 07	29. 65	0. 97201	0. 00397	14. 959	0. 044
702	18281. 2	30. 5	5537. 72	29. 81	0. 97598	0. 00398	15. 003	0. 043
701	18311. 7	30. 5	5567. 53	29. 98	0. 97996	0. 00400	15. 046	0. 044
700	18342. 2	30. 6	5597. 51	30. 15	0. 98396	0. 00402	15. 090	0. 044

TABLE I—Continued.

u	$S(u)$	Δ	$A(u)$	Δ	$I(u)$	Δ	$T(u)$	Δ
700	18342.2	30.6	5597.51	30.15	0.98396	0.00402	15.090	0.044
699	18372.8	30.6	5627.66	30.31	0.98798	0.00404	15.134	0.043
698	18403.4	30.6	5657.97	30.48	0.99202	0.00405	15.177	0.044
697	18434.0	30.7	5688.45	30.64	0.99607	0.00407	15.221	0.044
696	18464.7	30.8	5719.09	30.82	1.00014	0.00409	15.266	0.045
695	18495.5	30.8	5749.91	30.99	1.00423	0.00411	15.310	0.041
694	18526.3	30.8	5780.90	31.15	1.00834	0.00412	15.354	0.044
693	18557.1	30.9	5812.05	31.33	1.01246	0.00414	15.399	0.045
692	18588.0	30.9	5843.38	31.50	1.01660	0.00416	15.443	0.044
691	18618.9	31.0	5874.88	31.68	1.02076	0.00418	15.488	0.045
690	18649.9	31.0	5906.56	31.85	1.02494	0.00420	15.533	0.045
689	18680.9	31.0	5938.41	32.03	1.02914	0.00421	15.578	0.045
688	18711.9	31.1	5970.44	32.21	1.03335	0.00423	15.623	0.045
687	18743.0	31.1	6002.65	32.39	1.03758	0.00425	15.669	0.046
686	18774.1	31.2	6035.04	32.57	1.04183	0.00427	15.714	0.045
685	18805.3	31.3	6067.61	32.74	1.04610	0.00429	15.759	0.045
684	18836.6	31.3	6100.35	32.93	1.05039	0.00431	15.805	0.046
683	18867.9	31.3	6133.28	33.12	1.05470	0.00433	15.851	0.046
682	18899.2	31.4	6166.40	33.30	1.05903	0.00434	15.897	0.046
681	18930.6	31.4	6199.70	33.48	1.06337	0.00437	15.943	0.046
680	18962.0	31.5	6233.18	33.67	1.06774	0.00438	15.989	0.046
679	18993.5	31.5	6266.85	33.86	1.07212	0.00441	16.035	0.047
678	19025.0	31.6	6300.71	34.05	1.07653	0.00442	16.082	0.046
677	19056.6	31.6	6334.76	34.25	1.08095	0.00445	16.128	0.047
676	19088.2	31.7	6369.01	34.43	1.08540	0.00446	16.175	0.046
675	19119.9	31.7	6403.44	34.62	1.08986	0.00448	16.221	0.047
674	19151.6	31.7	6438.06	34.82	1.09434	0.00450	16.268	0.048
673	19183.3	31.8	6472.88	35.01	1.09884	0.00453	16.316	0.047
672	19215.1	31.9	6507.89	35.21	1.10337	0.00454	16.363	0.047
671	19247.0	31.9	6543.10	35.41	1.10791	0.00456	16.410	0.048
670	19278.9	31.9	6578.51	35.61	1.11247	0.00458	16.458	0.048
669	19310.8	32.0	6614.12	35.81	1.11705	0.00460	16.506	0.048
668	19342.8	32.0	6649.93	36.01	1.12165	0.00462	16.554	0.048
667	19374.8	32.1	6685.94	36.21	1.12627	0.00465	16.602	0.048
666	19406.9	32.1	6722.15	36.42	1.13092	0.00467	16.650	0.048
665	19439.0	32.2	6758.57	36.62	1.13559	0.00468	16.698	0.049
664	19471.2	32.2	6795.19	36.83	1.14027	0.00471	16.747	0.048
663	19503.4	32.3	6832.02	37.03	1.14498	0.00473	16.795	0.049
662	19535.7	32.3	6869.05	37.24	1.14971	0.00475	16.844	0.049
661	19568.0	32.4	6906.29	37.46	1.15446	0.00478	16.893	0.049
660	19600.4	32.4	6943.75	37.67	1.15924	0.00480	16.942	0.049
659	19632.8	32.5	6981.42	37.88	1.16404	0.00482	16.991	0.049
658	19665.3	32.5	7019.30	38.10	1.16886	0.00484	17.040	0.050
657	19697.8	32.6	7057.40	38.31	1.17370	0.00486	17.090	0.049
656	19730.4	32.6	7095.71	38.53	1.17856	0.00488	17.139	0.050
655	19763.0	32.7	7134.24	38.75	1.18344	0.00491	17.189	0.050
654	19795.7	32.7	7172.99	38.97	1.18835	0.00493	17.239	0.050
653	19828.4	32.8	7211.96	39.18	1.19328	0.00495	17.289	0.050
652	19861.2	32.8	7251.14	39.41	1.19823	0.00497	17.339	0.050
651	19894.0	32.9	7290.55	39.64	1.20320	0.00500	17.389	0.051
650	19926.9	32.9	7330.19	39.86	1.20820	0.00502	17.440	0.051

TABLE 1—Continued.

u	$S(u)$	Δ	$A(u)$	Δ	$I(u)$	Δ	$T(u)$	Δ
650	19926.9	32.9	7330.19	39.86	1.20820	0.00502	17.440	0.051
649	19959.8	33.0	7370.05	40.09	1.21322	0.00504	17.491	0.051
648	19992.8	33.0	7410.14	40.32	1.21826	0.00507	17.542	0.051
647	20025.8	33.1	7450.46	40.56	1.22333	0.00509	17.593	0.051
646	20058.9	33.1	7491.02	40.78	1.22842	0.00511	17.644	0.052
645	20092.0	33.2	7531.80	41.01	1.23353	0.00514	17.696	0.051
644	20125.2	33.3	7572.81	41.25	1.23867	0.00516	17.747	0.052
643	20158.5	33.3	7614.06	41.49	1.24383	0.00518	17.799	0.052
642	20191.8	33.3	7655.55	41.72	1.24901	0.00521	17.851	0.052
641	20225.1	33.4	7697.27	41.96	1.25422	0.00524	17.903	0.052
640	20258.5	33.4	7739.23	42.21	1.25946	0.00526	17.955	0.052
639	20291.9	33.5	7781.44	42.44	1.26472	0.00528	18.007	0.053
638	20325.4	33.6	7823.88	42.69	1.27000	0.00531	18.060	0.052
637	20359.0	33.6	7866.57	42.94	1.27531	0.00534	18.112	0.053
636	20392.6	33.6	7909.51	43.19	1.28065	0.00536	18.165	0.053
635	20426.2	33.7	7952.70	43.43	1.28601	0.00538	18.218	0.053
634	20459.9	33.8	7996.13	43.68	1.29139	0.00541	18.271	0.053
633	20493.7	33.8	8039.81	43.94	1.29680	0.00544	18.324	0.054
632	20527.5	33.9	8083.75	44.18	1.30224	0.00546	18.378	0.053
631	20561.4	33.9	8127.93	44.45	1.30770	0.00549	18.431	0.054
630	20595.3	34.0	8172.38	44.70	1.31319	0.00551	18.485	0.054
629	20629.3	34.0	8217.08	44.96	1.31870	0.00554	18.539	0.054
628	20663.3	34.1	8262.04	45.22	1.32424	0.00557	18.593	0.054
627	20697.4	34.1	8307.26	45.49	1.32981	0.00560	18.647	0.054
626	20731.5	34.2	8352.75	45.75	1.33541	0.00562	18.701	0.055
625	20765.7	34.3	8398.50	46.02	1.34103	0.00564	18.756	0.055
624	20800.0	34.3	8444.52	46.28	1.34667	0.00568	18.811	0.055
623	20834.3	34.3	8490.80	46.56	1.35235	0.00570	18.866	0.055
622	20868.6	34.4	8537.36	46.83	1.35805	0.00573	18.921	0.055
621	20903.0	34.5	8584.19	47.10	1.36378	0.00576	18.976	0.056
620	20937.5	34.5	8631.29	47.38	1.36954	0.00579	19.032	0.056
619	20972.0	34.6	8678.67	47.66	1.37533	0.00581	19.088	0.056
618	21006.6	34.6	8726.33	47.93	1.38114	0.00584	19.144	0.056
617	21041.2	34.7	8774.26	48.22	1.38698	0.00587	19.200	0.056
616	21075.9	34.7	8822.48	48.49	1.39285	0.00590	19.256	0.057
615	21110.6	34.8	8870.97	48.78	1.39875	0.00593	19.313	0.056
614	21145.4	34.9	8919.75	49.07	1.40468	0.00596	19.369	0.057
613	21180.3	34.9	8968.82	49.36	1.41064	0.00598	19.426	0.057
612	21215.2	35.0	9018.18	49.64	1.41662	0.00602	19.483	0.058
611	21250.2	35.0	9067.82	49.94	1.42264	0.00604	19.541	0.057
610	21285.2	35.1	9117.76	50.23	1.42868	0.00607	19.598	0.057
609	21320.3	35.1	9167.99	50.53	1.43475	0.00611	19.655	0.058
608	21355.4	35.2	9218.52	50.82	1.44086	0.00613	19.713	0.058
607	21390.6	35.3	9269.34	51.13	1.44699	0.00617	19.771	0.058
606	21425.9	35.3	9320.47	51.43	1.45316	0.00619	19.829	0.058
605	21461.2	35.4	9371.90	51.74	1.45935	0.00623	19.887	0.059
604	21496.6	35.4	9423.64	52.04	1.46558	0.00626	19.946	0.059
603	21532.0	35.5	9475.68	52.36	1.47184	0.00629	20.005	0.059
602	21567.5	35.6	9528.04	52.66	1.47813	0.00632	20.064	0.059
601	21603.1	35.6	9580.70	52.98	1.48445	0.00635	20.123	0.059
600	21638.7	35.7	9633.68	53.30	1.49080	0.00638	20.182	0.059

TABLE I—Continued.

u	$S(u)$	Δ	$A(u)$	Δ	$I(u)$	Δ	$T(u)$	Δ
600	21638.7	35.7	9633.68	53.30	1.49080	0.00638	20.182	0.059
599	21674.4	35.7	9686.98	53.62	1.49718	0.00642	20.241	0.060
598	21710.1	35.8	9740.60	53.94	1.50360	0.00645	20.301	0.060
597	21745.9	35.8	9794.54	54.25	1.51005	0.00648	20.361	0.060
596	21781.7	35.9	9848.79	54.58	1.51653	0.00652	20.421	0.060
595	21817.6	36.0	9903.37	54.91	1.52305	0.00654	20.481	0.061
594	21853.6	36.0	9958.28	55.23	1.52959	0.00658	20.542	0.061
593	21889.6	36.1	10013.50	55.6	1.53617	0.00661	20.603	0.061
592	21925.7	36.2	10069.10	55.9	1.54278	0.00665	20.664	0.061
591	21961.9	36.2	10125.00	56.2	1.54943	0.00668	20.725	0.061
590	21998.1	36.3	10181.20	56.6	1.55611	0.00671	20.786	0.061
589	22034.4	36.3	10237.80	56.9	1.56282	0.00675	20.847	0.062
588	22070.7	36.4	10294.70	57.2	1.56957	0.00679	20.909	0.062
587	22107.1	36.4	10351.90	57.6	1.57636	0.00681	20.971	0.062
586	22143.5	36.5	10409.50	58.0	1.58317	0.00685	21.033	0.063
585	22180.0	36.6	10467.50	58.3	1.59002	0.00689	21.096	0.062
584	22216.6	36.7	10525.80	58.6	1.59691	0.00693	21.158	0.063
583	22253.3	36.7	10584.40	59.0	1.60384	0.00696	21.221	0.063
582	22290.0	36.8	10643.40	59.4	1.61080	0.00699	21.284	0.063
581	22326.8	36.8	10702.80	59.7	1.61779	0.00703	21.347	0.064
580	22363.6	36.9	10762.50	60.1	1.62482	0.00707	21.411	0.064
579	22400.5	37.0	10822.60	60.4	1.63189	0.00710	21.475	0.064
578	22437.5	37.0	10883.00	60.9	1.63899	0.00714	21.539	0.064
577	22474.5	37.1	10943.90	61.2	1.64613	0.00718	21.603	0.064
576	22511.6	37.1	11005.10	61.5	1.65331	0.00721	21.667	0.065
575	22548.7	37.2	11066.60	62.0	1.66052	0.00726	21.732	0.064
574	22585.9	37.3	11128.60	62.3	1.66778	0.00729	21.796	0.065
573	22623.2	37.4	11190.90	62.7	1.67507	0.00733	21.861	0.066
572	22660.6	37.4	11253.60	63.1	1.68240	0.00737	21.927	0.065
571	22698.0	37.5	11316.70	63.5	1.68977	0.00741	21.992	0.066
570	22735.5	37.6	11380.20	63.9	1.69718	0.00745	22.058	0.066
569	22773.1	37.6	11444.10	64.2	1.70463	0.00748	22.124	0.066
568	22810.7	37.7	11508.30	64.7	1.71211	0.00753	22.190	0.067
567	22848.4	37.7	11573.00	65.0	1.71964	0.00757	22.257	0.066
566	22886.1	37.9	11638.00	65.5	1.72721	0.00761	22.323	0.067
565	22924.0	37.9	11703.50	65.8	1.73482	0.00764	22.390	0.067
564	22961.9	37.9	11769.30	66.3	1.74246	0.00769	22.457	0.068
563	22999.8	38.0	11835.6	66.7	1.75015	0.00773	22.525	0.067
562	23037.8	38.1	11902.3	67.1	1.75788	0.00777	22.592	0.068
561	23075.9	38.2	11969.4	67.5	1.76565	0.00781	22.660	0.068
560	23114.1	38.2	12036.9	67.9	1.77346	0.00785	22.728	0.068
559	23152.3	38.3	12104.8	68.4	1.78131	0.00790	22.796	0.069
558	23190.6	38.3	12173.2	68.8	1.78921	0.00794	22.865	0.069
557	23228.9	38.4	12242.0	69.2	1.79715	0.00798	22.934	0.069
556	23267.3	38.5	12311.2	69.7	1.80513	0.00802	23.003	0.069
555	23305.8	38.6	12380.9	70.1	1.81315	0.00807	23.072	0.069
554	23344.4	38.7	12451.0	70.5	1.82122	0.00811	23.141	0.070
553	23383.1	38.7	12521.5	70.9	1.82933	0.00816	23.211	0.070
552	23421.8	38.7	12592.4	71.4	1.83749	0.00820	23.281	0.070
551	23460.5	38.9	12663.8	71.9	1.84569	0.00824	23.351	0.071
550	23499.4	38.9	12735.7	72.3	1.85393	0.00829	23.422	0.071

HATCHER'S NOTEBOOK

TABLE I—Continued.

u	$S(u)$	Δ	$A(u)$	Δ	$I(u)$	Δ	$T(u)$	Δ
550	23499.4	38.9	12735.7	72.3	1.85393	0.00829	23.422	0.071
549	23538.3	39.0	12808.0	72.8	1.86222	0.00833	23.493	0.071
548	23577.3	39.1	12880.8	73.2	1.87055	0.00838	23.564	0.071
547	23616.4	39.1	12954.0	73.7	1.87893	0.00843	23.635	0.072
546	23655.5	39.2	13027.7	74.1	1.88736	0.00847	23.707	0.072
545	23694.7	39.3	13101.8	74.6	1.89583	0.00852	23.779	0.072
544	23734.0	39.3	13176.4	75.1	1.90435	0.00857	23.851	0.072
543	23773.3	39.4	13251.5	75.6	1.91292	0.00861	23.923	0.073
542	23812.7	39.5	13327.1	76.0	1.92153	0.00867	23.996	0.073
541	23852.2	39.6	13403.1	76.6	1.93020	0.00871	24.069	0.073
540	23891.8	39.6	13479.7	77.0	1.93891	0.00878	24.142	0.073
539	23931.4	39.7	13556.7	77.6	1.94767	0.00881	24.215	0.074
538	23971.1	39.8	13634.3	78.0	1.95648	0.00886	24.289	0.074
537	24010.9	39.9	13712.3	78.5	1.96534	0.00891	24.363	0.074
536	24050.8	39.9	13790.8	79.0	1.97425	0.00896	24.437	0.075
535	24090.7	40.0	13869.8	79.5	1.98321	0.00901	24.512	0.075
534	24130.7	40.1	13949.3	80.1	1.99222	0.00905	24.587	0.075
533	24170.8	40.1	14029.4	80.5	2.00127	0.00912	24.662	0.075
532	24210.9	40.3	14109.9	81.1	2.01039	0.00916	24.737	0.076
531	24251.2	40.3	14191.0	81.6	2.01955	0.00921	24.813	0.076
530	24291.5	40.4	14272.6	82.1	2.02876	0.00926	24.889	0.076
529	24331.9	40.5	14354.7	82.7	2.03802	0.00932	24.965	0.077
528	24372.4	40.5	14437.4	83.2	2.04734	0.00937	25.042	0.077
527	24412.9	40.6	14520.6	83.7	2.05671	0.00942	25.119	0.077
526	24453.5	40.7	14604.3	84.3	2.06613	0.00948	25.196	0.077
525	24494.2	40.8	14688.6	84.9	2.07561	0.00954	25.273	0.078
524	24535.0	40.9	14773.5	85.4	2.08515	0.00959	25.351	0.078
523	24575.9	40.9	14858.9	85.9	2.09474	0.00964	25.429	0.078
522	24616.8	41.0	14944.8	86.5	2.10438	0.00970	25.507	0.079
521	24657.8	41.1	15031.3	87.0	2.11408	0.00975	25.586	0.079
520	24698.9	41.1	15118.3	87.6	2.12383	0.00981	25.665	0.079
519	24740.0	41.2	15205.9	88.2	2.13364	0.00987	25.744	0.080
518	24781.2	41.3	15294.1	88.8	2.14351	0.00992	25.824	0.080
517	24822.5	41.4	15382.9	89.4	2.15343	0.00999	25.904	0.080
516	24863.9	41.5	15472.3	90.0	2.16342	0.01004	25.984	0.081
515	24905.4	41.5	15562.3	90.5	2.17346	0.01010	26.065	0.081
514	24946.9	41.7	15652.8	91.2	2.18356	0.01015	26.146	0.081
513	24988.6	41.7	15744.0	91.7	2.19371	0.01022	26.227	0.081
512	25030.3	41.8	15835.7	92.3	2.20393	0.01028	26.308	0.082
511	25072.1	41.9	15928.0	93.0	2.21421	0.01034	26.390	0.082
510	25114.0	42.0	16021.0	93.6	2.22455	0.01040	26.472	0.082
509	25156.0	42.0	16114.6	94.2	2.23495	0.01046	26.554	0.083
508	25198.0	42.2	16208.8	94.8	2.24541	0.01052	26.637	0.083
507	25240.2	42.2	16303.6	95.5	2.25593	0.01059	26.720	0.083
506	25282.4	42.3	16399.1	96.1	2.26652	0.01065	26.803	0.084
505	25324.7	42.4	16495.2	96.8	2.27717	0.01071	26.887	0.084
504	25367.1	42.5	16592.0	97.4	2.28788	0.01077	26.971	0.084
503	25409.6	42.6	16689.4	98.0	2.29865	0.01084	27.055	0.085
502	25452.2	42.7	16787.4	98.7	2.30949	0.01091	27.140	0.085
501	25494.9	42.7	16886.1	99.4	2.32040	0.01097	27.225	0.085
500	25537.6	42.8	16985.5	100.1	2.33137	0.01104	27.310	0.086

TABLE I—Continued.

u	S (u)	Δ	A (u)	Δ	I (u)	Δ	T (u)	Δ
500	25537.6	42.8	16985.5	100.1	2.33137	0.01104	27.310	0.086
499	25580.4	42.9	17085.6	100.7	2.34241	0.01110	27.396	0.086
498	25623.3	43.0	17186.3	101.4	2.35351	0.01117	27.482	0.086
497	25666.3	43.0	17287.7	102.1	2.36468	0.01124	27.568	0.087
496	25709.3	43.2	17389.8	102.8	2.37592	0.01131	27.655	0.087
495	25752.5	43.2	17492.6	103.5	2.38723	0.01137	27.742	0.088
494	25795.7	43.4	17596.1	104.2	2.39860	0.01145	27.830	0.088
493	25839.1	43.4	17700.3	104.9	2.41005	0.01151	27.918	0.088
492	25882.5	43.5	17805.2	105.6	2.42156	0.01158	28.006	0.088
491	25926.0	43.6	17910.8	106.3	2.43314	0.01166	28.094	0.089
490	25969.6	43.7	18017.1	107.1	2.44480	0.01173	28.183	0.089
489	26013.3	43.8	18124.2	107.8	2.45653	0.01180	28.272	0.090
488	26057.1	43.8	18232.0	108.5	2.46833	0.01187	28.362	0.090
487	26100.9	44.0	18340.5	109.3	2.48020	0.01194	28.452	0.090
486	26144.9	44.0	18449.8	110.0	2.49214	0.01202	28.542	0.091
485	26188.9	44.2	18559.8	110.8	2.50416	0.01210	28.633	0.091
484	26233.1	44.2	18670.6	111.6	2.51626	0.01216	28.724	0.091
483	26277.3	44.4	18782.2	112.3	2.52842	0.01225	28.815	0.092
482	26321.7	44.4	18894.5	113.1	2.54067	0.01232	28.907	0.092
481	26366.1	44.5	19007.6	113.9	2.55299	0.01240	28.999	0.093
480	26410.6	44.6	19121.5	114.7	2.56539	0.01248	29.092	0.093
479	26455.2	44.7	19236.2	115.5	2.57787	0.01255	29.185	0.093
478	26499.9	44.7	19351.7	116.3	2.59042	0.01263	29.278	0.094
477	26544.6	44.9	19468.0	117.1	2.60305	0.01272	29.372	0.094
476	26589.5	45.0	19585.1	117.9	2.61577	0.01279	29.466	0.095
475	26634.5	45.0	19703.0	118.8	2.62856	0.01287	29.561	0.095
474	26679.5	45.2	19821.8	119.6	2.64143	0.01296	29.656	0.095
473	26724.7	45.3	19941.4	120.4	2.65439	0.01304	29.751	0.096
472	26770.0	45.3	20061.8	121.3	2.66743	0.01312	29.847	0.096
471	26815.3	45.5	20183.1	122.1	2.68055	0.01321	29.943	0.097
470	26860.8	45.5	20305.2	123.0	2.69376	0.01329	30.040	0.097
469	26906.3	45.7	20428.2	123.9	2.70705	0.01338	30.137	0.098
468	26952.0	45.7	20552.1	124.7	2.72043	0.01346	30.235	0.098
467	26997.7	45.9	20676.8	125.7	2.73389	0.01355	30.333	0.098
466	27043.6	45.9	20802.5	126.5	2.74744	0.01364	30.431	0.099
465	27089.5	46.0	20929.0	127.4	2.76108	0.01372	30.530	0.099
464	27135.5	46.2	21056.4	128.4	2.77480	0.01382	30.629	0.100
463	27181.7	46.2	21184.8	129.2	2.78862	0.01390	30.729	0.100
462	27227.9	46.4	21314.0	130.2	2.80252	0.01399	30.829	0.100
461	27274.3	46.4	21444.2	131.1	2.81651	0.01409	30.929	0.101
460	27320.7	46.5	21575.3	132.1	2.83060	0.01418	31.030	0.101
459	27367.2	46.7	21707.4	133.0	2.84478	0.01427	31.131	0.102
458	27413.9	46.7	21840.4	134.0	2.85905	0.01436	31.233	0.102
457	27460.6	46.8	21974.4	134.9	2.87341	0.01446	31.335	0.103
456	27507.4	47.0	22109.3	135.9	2.88787	0.01456	31.438	0.103
455	27554.4	47.0	22245.2	136.9	2.90243	0.01465	31.541	0.103
454	27601.4	47.2	22382.1	137.9	2.91708	0.01474	31.644	0.104
453	27648.6	47.2	22520.0	139.0	2.93182	0.01485	31.748	0.105
452	27695.8	47.4	22659.0	139.9	2.94667	0.01494	31.853	0.105
451	27743.2	47.5	22798.9	140.9	2.96161	0.01505	31.958	0.105
450	27790.7	47.6	22939.8	142.0	2.97666	0.01515	32.063	0.106

TABLE I—Continued.

u	S (u)	Δ	A (u)	Δ	I (u)	Δ	T (u)	Δ
450	27790.7	47.6	22939.8	142.0	2.97666	0.01515	32.063	0.106
449	27838.3	47.6	23081.8	143.0	2.99181	0.01524	32.169	0.106
448	27885.9	47.8	23224.8	144.1	3.00705	0.01535	32.275	0.107
447	27933.7	47.9	23368.9	145.1	3.02240	0.01545	32.382	0.107
446	27981.6	48.0	23514.0	146.2	3.03785	0.01556	32.489	0.108
445	28029.6	48.1	23660.2	147.3	3.05341	0.01566	32.597	0.108
444	28077.7	48.2	23807.5	148.4	3.06907	0.01577	32.705	0.109
443	28125.9	48.4	23955.9	149.4	3.08484	0.01588	32.814	0.109
442	28174.3	48.4	24105.3	150.6	3.10072	0.01598	32.923	0.110
441	28222.7	48.6	24255.9	151.7	3.11670	0.01609	33.033	0.110
440	28271.3	48.7	24407.6	152.8	3.13279	0.01620	33.143	0.111
439	28320.0	48.7	24560.4	154.0	3.14899	0.01631	33.254	0.111
438	28368.7	48.9	24714.4	155.2	3.16530	0.01643	33.365	0.112
437	28417.6	49.0	24869.6	156.3	3.18173	0.01654	33.477	0.112
436	28466.6	49.1	25025.9	157.4	3.19827	0.01665	33.589	0.113
435	28515.7	49.3	25183.3	158.7	3.21492	0.01677	33.702	0.113
434	28565.0	49.3	25342.0	159.8	3.23169	0.01688	33.815	0.114
433	28614.3	49.4	25501.8	161.0	3.24857	0.01700	33.929	0.114
432	28663.7	49.6	25662.8	162.3	3.26557	0.01712	34.043	0.115
431	28713.3	49.7	25825.1	163.5	3.28269	0.01724	34.158	0.115
430	28763.0	49.8	25988.6	164.7	3.29993	0.01736	34.273	0.116
429	28812.8	49.8	26153.3	166.0	3.31729	0.01748	34.389	0.116
428	28862.6	50.0	26319.3	167.3	3.33477	0.01761	34.505	0.117
427	28912.6	50.2	26486.6	168.5	3.35238	0.01773	34.622	0.118
426	28962.8	50.2	26655.1	169.8	3.37011	0.01785	34.740	0.118
425	29013.0	50.4	26824.9	171.1	3.38796	0.01798	34.858	0.119
424	29063.4	50.5	26996.0	172.5	3.40594	0.01811	34.977	0.119
423	29113.9	50.6	27168.5	173.7	3.42405	0.01824	35.096	0.120
422	29164.5	50.7	27342.2	175.1	3.44229	0.01837	35.216	0.120
421	29215.2	50.9	27517.3	176.5	3.46066	0.01850	35.336	0.121
420	29266.1	51.0	27693.8	177.8	3.47916	0.01863	35.457	0.122
419	29317.1	51.1	27871.6	179.2	3.49779	0.01877	35.579	0.122
418	29368.2	51.2	28050.8	180.6	3.51656	0.01890	35.701	0.123
417	29419.4	51.3	28231.4	182.0	3.53546	0.01904	34.824	0.123
416	29470.7	51.5	28413.4	183.5	3.55450	0.01917	35.947	0.124
415	29522.2	51.6	28596.9	184.9	3.57367	0.01932	36.071	0.124
414	29573.8	51.8	28781.8	186.3	3.59299	0.01945	36.195	0.125
413	29625.6	51.8	28968.1	187.8	3.61244	0.01960	36.320	0.126
412	29677.4	52.0	29155.9	189.2	3.63204	0.01974	36.446	0.126
411	29729.4	52.1	29345.1	190.8	3.65178	0.01989	36.572	0.127
410	29781.5	52.2	29535.9	192.3	3.67167	0.02003	36.699	0.128
409	29833.7	52.3	29728.2	193.8	3.69170	0.02018	36.827	0.128
408	29886.0	52.5	29922.0	195.3	3.71188	0.02033	36.955	0.129
407	29938.5	52.6	30117.3	196.9	3.73221	0.20048	37.084	0.129
406	29991.1	52.7	30314.2	198.5	3.75269	0.02063	37.213	0.130
405	30043.8	52.9	30512.7	200.0	3.77332	0.02078	37.343	0.131
404	30096.7	53.0	30712.7	201.7	3.79410	0.02094	37.474	0.131
403	30149.7	53.1	30914.4	203.2	3.81504	0.02109	37.605	0.132
402	30202.8	53.3	31117.6	204.9	3.83613	0.02125	37.737	0.133
401	30256.1	53.4	31322.5	206.5	3.85738	0.02141	37.870	0.133
400	30309.5	53.5	31529.0	208.2	3.87879	0.02157	38.003	0.134

TABLE I—Continued.

u	S (u)	Δ	A (u)	Δ	I (u)	Δ	T (u)	Δ
400	30309.5	53.5	31529.0	208.2	3.87879	0.02157	38.003	0.134
399	30363.0	53.7	31737.2	209.9	3.90036	0.02174	38.137	0.135
398	30416.7	53.8	31947.1	211.7	3.92210	0.02190	38.272	0.135
397	30470.5	53.9	32158.8	213.3	3.94400	0.02207	38.407	0.136
396	30524.4	54.1	32372.1	215.1	3.96607	0.02223	38.543	0.137
395	30578.5	54.2	32587.2	216.8	3.98830	0.02240	38.680	0.138
394	30632.7	54.3	32804.0	218.5	4.01070	0.02257	38.818	0.138
393	30687.0	54.5	33022.5	220.4	4.03327	0.02275	38.956	0.139
392	30741.5	54.6	33242.9	222.2	4.05602	0.02292	39.095	0.139
391	30796.1	54.8	33465.1	223.9	4.07894	0.02310	39.234	0.140
390	30850.9	54.9	33689.0	225.9	4.10204	0.02328	39.374	0.141
389	30905.8	55.1	33914.9	227.7	4.12532	0.02345	39.515	0.142
388	30960.9	55.2	34142.6	229.6	4.14877	0.02364	39.657	0.142
387	31016.1	55.3	34372.2	231.5	4.17241	0.02382	39.799	0.143
386	31071.4	55.5	34603.7	233.5	4.19623	0.02401	39.942	0.144
385	31126.9	55.6	34837.2	235.4	4.22024	0.02420	40.086	0.145
384	31182.5	55.7	35072.6	237.3	4.24444	0.02439	40.231	0.145
383	31238.2	55.9	35309.9	239.4	4.26883	0.02458	40.376	0.146
382	31294.1	56.1	35549.3	241.3	4.29341	0.02477	40.522	0.147
381	31350.2	56.2	35790.6	243.4	4.31818	0.02497	40.669	0.148
380	31406.4	56.3	36034.0	245.4	4.34315	0.02517	40.817	0.149
379	31462.7	56.5	36279.4	247.6	4.36832	0.02537	40.966	0.149
378	31519.2	56.7	36527.0	249.6	4.39369	0.02557	41.115	0.150
377	31575.9	56.8	36776.6	251.7	4.41926	0.02577	41.265	0.151
376	31632.7	56.9	37028.3	253.9	4.44503	0.02598	41.416	0.152
375	31689.6	57.1	37282.2	256.0	4.47101	0.02619	41.568	0.152
374	31746.7	57.3	37538.2	258.3	4.49720	0.02640	41.720	0.153
373	31804.0	57.4	37796.5	260.4	4.52360	0.02661	41.873	0.154
372	31861.4	57.6	38056.9	262.7	4.55021	0.02682	42.027	0.155
371	31919.0	57.7	38319.6	265.0	4.57703	0.02705	42.182	0.156
370	31976.7	57.9	38584.6	267.2	4.60408	0.02726	42.338	0.157
369	32034.6	58.0	38851.8	269.6	4.63134	0.02749	42.495	0.157
368	32092.6	58.2	39121.4	271.9	4.65883	0.02771	42.652	0.158
367	32150.8	58.3	39393.3	274.3	5.68654	0.02794	42.810	0.159
366	32209.1	58.5	39667.6	276.6	4.71448	0.02818	42.969	0.160
365	32267.6	58.7	39944.2	279.1	4.74266	0.02840	43.129	0.161
364	32326.3	58.8	40223.3	281.6	4.77106	0.02864	43.290	0.162
363	32385.1	59.0	40504.9	284.0	4.79970	0.02887	43.452	0.163
362	32444.1	59.2	40788.9	286.5	4.82857	0.02912	43.615	0.163
361	32503.3	59.3	41075.4	289.0	4.85769	0.02936	43.778	0.165
360	32562.6	59.5	41364.4	291.6	4.88705	0.02961	43.943	0.165
359	32622.1	59.7	41656.0	294.2	4.91666	0.02985	44.108	0.167
358	32681.8	59.8	41950.2	296.8	4.94651	0.03011	44.275	0.167
357	32741.6	60.0	42247.0	299.4	4.97662	0.03036	44.442	0.168
356	32801.6	60.2	42546.4	302.1	5.00698	0.03061	44.610	0.170
355	32861.8	60.3	42848.5	304.8	5.03759	0.03087	44.780	0.170
354	32922.1	60.5	43153.3	307.6	5.06846	0.03114	44.950	0.171
353	32982.6	60.7	43460.9	310.3	5.09960	0.03141	45.121	0.172
352	33043.3	60.8	43771.2	313.1	5.13101	0.03167	45.293	0.173
351	33104.1	61.0	44084.3	316.0	5.16268	0.03194	45.466	0.174
350	33165.1	61.2	44400.3	318.8	5.19462	0.03222	45.640	0.175

TABLE I—Continued.

u	S (u)	Δ	A (u)	Δ	I (u)	Δ	T (u)	Δ
350	33165.1	61.2	44400.3	318.8	5.19462	0.03222	45.640	0.175
349	33226.3	61.4	44719.1	321.7	5.22684	0.03249	45.815	0.176
348	33287.7	61.5	45040.8	324.7	5.25933	0.03278	45.991	0.177
347	33349.2	61.7	45365.5	327.6	5.29211	0.03306	46.168	0.178
346	33410.9	61.9	45693.1	330.7	5.32517	0.03335	46.346	0.180
345	33472.8	62.1	46023.8	333.6	5.35852	0.03364	46.526	0.180
344	33534.9	62.3	46357.4	336.8	5.39216	0.03394	46.706	0.181
343	33597.2	62.4	46694.2	339.9	5.42610	0.03424	46.887	0.182
342	33659.6	62.6	47034.1	343.0	5.46034	0.03454	47.069	0.184
341	33722.2	62.8	47377.1	346.2	5.49488	0.03484	47.253	0.184
340	33785.0	63.0	47723.3	349.5	5.52972	0.03515	47.437	0.185
339	33848.0	63.2	48072.8	352.7	5.56487	0.03547	47.622	0.187
338	33911.2	63.3	48425.5	356.0	5.60034	0.03578	47.809	0.188
337	33974.5	63.5	48781.5	359.3	5.63612	0.03610	47.997	0.189
336	34038.0	63.8	49140.8	362.7	5.67222	0.03643	48.186	0.190
335	34101.8	63.9	49503.5	366.1	5.70865	0.03675	48.376	0.191
334	34165.7	64.2	49869.6	369.6	5.74540	0.03708	48.567	0.192
333	34229.9	64.3	50239.2	373.1	5.78248	0.03741	48.759	0.194
332	34294.2	64.5	50612.3	376.6	5.81989	0.03776	48.953	0.194
331	34358.7	64.7	50988.9	380.3	5.85765	0.03810	49.147	0.196
330	34423.4	64.9	51369.2	383.9	5.89575	0.03845	49.343	0.197
329	34488.3	65.1	51753.1	387.5	5.93420	0.03880	49.540	0.198
328	34553.4	65.3	52140.6	391.3	5.97300	0.03916	49.738	0.199
327	34618.7	65.5	52531.9	395.0	6.01216	0.03951	49.937	0.201
326	34684.2	65.7	52926.9	398.9	6.05167	0.03988	50.138	0.202
325	34749.9	66.0	53325.8	402.8	6.09155	0.04026	50.340	0.203
324	34815.9	66.1	53728.6	406.7	6.13181	0.04063	50.543	0.204
323	34882.0	66.3	54135.3	410.7	6.17244	0.04101	50.749	0.206
322	34948.3	66.5	54546.0	414.6	6.21345	0.04139	50.953	0.207
321	35014.8	66.7	54960.6	418.8	6.25484	0.04178	51.160	0.208
320	35081.5	66.9	55379.4	422.9	6.29662	0.04218	51.368	0.209
319	35148.4	67.2	55802.3	427.1	6.33880	0.04257	51.577	0.211
318	35215.6	67.3	56229.4	431.3	6.38137	0.04298	51.788	0.212
317	35282.9	67.6	56660.7	435.5	6.42435	0.04338	52.000	0.214
316	35350.5	67.8	57096.2	439.9	6.46773	0.04380	52.214	0.215
315	35418.3	68.0	57536.1	444.2	6.51153	0.04422	52.429	0.216
314	35486.3	68.2	57980.3	448.7	6.55575	0.04464	52.645	0.218
313	35554.5	68.4	58429.0	453.2	6.60039	0.04507	52.863	0.219
312	35622.9	68.6	58882.2	457.8	6.64546	0.04551	53.082	0.220
311	35691.5	68.9	59340.0	462.4	6.69097	0.04595	53.302	0.222
310	35760.4	69.1	59802.4	467.1	6.73692	0.04640	53.524	0.223
309	35829.5	69.3	60269.5	471.8	6.78332	0.04684	53.747	0.225
308	35898.8	69.5	60741.3	476.6	6.83016	0.04731	53.972	0.226
307	35968.3	69.8	61217.9	481.5	6.87747	0.04777	54.198	0.228
306	36038.1	70.0	61699.4	486.4	6.92524	0.04824	54.426	0.229
305	36108.1	70.2	62185.8	491.5	6.97348	0.04872	54.655	0.231
304	36178.3	70.5	62677.3	496.5	7.02220	0.04920	54.886	0.232
303	36248.8	70.7	63173.8	501.7	7.07140	0.04969	55.118	0.234
302	36319.5	70.9	63675.5	506.9	7.12109	0.05019	55.352	0.235
301	36390.4	71.2	64182.4	512.1	7.17128	0.05069	55.587	0.237
300	36461.6	71.4	64694.5	517.5	7.22197	0.05120	55.824	0.238

TABLE I—Continued.

u	S (u)	Δ	A (u)	Δ	I (u)	Δ	T (u)	Δ
300	36461.6	71.4	64694.5	517.5	7.22197	0.05120	55.824	0.238
299	36533.0	71.7	65212.0	523.0	7.27317	0.05172	56.062	0.240
298	36604.7	71.9	65735.0	528.4	7.32489	0.05223	56.302	0.242
297	36676.6	72.1	66263.4	534.0	7.37712	0.05277	56.544	0.243
296	36748.7	72.4	66797.4	539.6	7.42989	0.05331	56.787	0.245
295	36821.1	72.6	67337.0	545.3	7.48320	0.05385	57.032	0.217
294	36893.7	72.8	67882.3	551.2	7.53705	0.05441	57.279	0.248
293	36966.5	73.1	68433.5	557.0	7.59146	0.05496	57.527	0.250
292	37039.6	73.4	68990.5	563.0	7.64642	0.05553	57.777	0.252
291	37113.0	73.6	69553.5	569.0	7.70195	0.05611	58.029	0.253
290	37186.6	73.9	70122.5	575.2	7.75806	0.05669	58.282	0.255
289	37260.5	74.1	70697.7	581.4	7.81475	0.05728	58.537	0.257
288	37334.6	74.4	71279.1	587.7	7.87203	0.05788	58.794	0.258
287	37409.0	74.6	71866.8	594.0	7.92991	0.05849	59.052	0.261
286	37483.6	74.9	72460.8	600.6	7.98840	0.05911	59.313	0.262
285	37558.5	75.2	73061.4	607.1	8.04751	0.05973	59.575	0.264
284	37633.7	75.4	73668.5	613.8	8.10724	0.06037	59.839	0.266
283	37709.1	75.7	74282.3	620.6	8.16761	0.06101	60.105	0.268
282	37784.8	76.0	74902.9	627.5	8.22862	0.06166	60.373	0.270
281	37860.8	76.2	75530.4	634.4	8.29028	0.06233	60.643	0.272
280	37937.0	76.5	76164.8	641.5	8.35261	0.06299	60.915	0.274
279	38013.5	76.8	76806.3	648.7	8.41560	0.06368	61.189	0.276
278	38090.3	77.0	77455.0	655.9	8.47928	0.06437	61.465	0.277
277	38167.3	77.4	78110.9	663.3	8.54365	0.06507	61.742	0.280
276	38244.7	77.6	78774.2	670.7	8.60872	0.06578	62.022	0.282
275	38322.3	77.9	79444.9	678.4	8.67450	0.06651	62.304	0.284
274	38400.2	78.2	80123.3	686.1	8.74101	0.06723	62.588	0.286
273	38478.4	78.5	80809.4	693.9	8.80824	0.06798	62.874	0.288
272	38556.9	78.7	81503.3	701.9	8.87622	0.06873	63.162	0.290
271	38635.6	79.1	82205.2	709.9	8.94495	0.06949	63.452	0.292
270	38714.7	79.4	82915.1	718.1	9.01444	0.07027	63.744	0.294
269	38794.1	79.6	83633.2	726.5	9.08471	0.07105	64.038	0.297
268	38873.7	80.0	84359.7	734.8	9.15576	0.07186	64.335	0.299
267	38953.7	80.2	85094.5	743.3	9.22762	0.07267	64.634	0.301
266	39033.9	80.6	85837.8	752.1	9.30029	0.07350	64.935	0.303
265	39114.5	80.8	86589.9	760.9	9.37379	0.07434	65.238	0.306
264	39195.3	81.2	87350.8	769.8	9.44813	0.07518	65.544	0.308
263	39276.5	81.4	88120.6	778.9	9.52331	0.07605	65.852	0.310
262	39357.9	81.8	88899.5	788.2	9.59936	0.07692	66.162	0.313
261	39439.7	82.1	89687.7	797.5	9.67628	0.07781	66.475	0.315
260	39521.8	82.4	90485.2	807.1	9.75409	0.07871	66.790	0.318
259	39604.2	82.7	91292.3	816.8	9.83280	0.07962	67.108	0.320
258	39686.9	83.1	92109.1	826.5	9.91242	0.08056	67.428	0.322
257	39770.0	83.4	92935.6	836.5	9.99298	0.08151	67.750	0.325
256	39853.4	83.7	93772.1	846.6	10.0745	0.0825	68.075	0.328
255	39937.1	84.0	94618.7	857.0	10.1570	0.0835	68.403	0.330
254	40021.1	84.3	95475.7	867.4	10.2405	0.0844	68.733	0.333
253	40105.4	84.7	96343.1	878.0	10.3249	0.0854	69.066	0.335
252	40190.1	85.0	97221.1	888.9	10.4103	0.0865	69.401	0 338
251	40275.1	85.4	98110.0	899.8	10.4968	0.0875	69.739	0.341
250	40360.5	85.7	99009.8	911.1	10.5843	0.0886	70.080	0.344

HATCHER'S NOTEBOOK

TABLE I—Continued.

u	$S(u)$	Δ	$A(u)$	Δ	$I(u)$	Δ	$T(u)$	Δ
250	40360.5	85.7	99009.8	911.1	10.5843	0.0886	70.080	0.344
249	40446.2	86.1	99920.9	922.1	10.6729	0.0896	70.424	0.346
248	40532.3	86.4	100843.	934.	10.7625	0.0907	70.770	0.350
247	40618.7	86.8	101777.	946.	10.8532	0.0918	71.120	0.352
246	40705.5	87.1	102723.	957.	10.9450	0.0930	71.472	0.354
245	40792.6	87.4	103680.	969.	11.0380	0.0941	71.826	0.358
244	40880.0	87.8	104649.	982.	11.1321	0.0953	72.184	0.361
243	40967.8	88.2	105631.	995.	11.2274	0.0965	72.545	0.363
242	41056.0	88.6	106626.	1007.	11.3239	0.0976	72.908	0.367
241	41144.6	88.9	107633.	1020.	11.4215	0.0989	73.275	0.369
240	41233.5	89.3	108653.	1033.	11.5204	0.1001	73.644	0.372
239	41322.8	89.7	109686.	1046.	11.6205	0.1013	74.016	0.376
238	41412.5	90.0	110732.	1060.	11.7218	0.1027	74.392	0.379
237	41502.5	90.4	111792.	1074.	11.8245	0.1040	74.771	0.382
236	41592.9	90.8	112866.	1088.	11.9285	0.1053	75.153	0.385
235	41683.7	91.2	113954.	1103.	12.0338	0.1067	75.538	0.389
234	41774.9	91.6	115057.	1117.	12.1405	0.1081	75.927	0.392
233	41866.5	92.0	116174.	1132.	12.2486	0.1094	76.319	0.396
232	41958.5	92.4	117306.	1146.	12.3580	0.1109	76.715	0.399
231	42050.9	92.8	118452.	1162.	12.4689	0.1123	77.114	0.403
230	42143.7	93.2	119614.	1178.	12.5812	0.1138	77.517	0.406
229	42236.9	93.7	120792.	1193.	12.6950	0.1153	77.923	0.410
228	42330.6	94.0	121985.	1209.	12.8103	0.1168	78.333	0.413
227	42424.6	94.5	123194.	1226.	12.9271	0.1184	78.746	0.417
226	42519.1	94.8	124420.	1243.	13.0455	0.1199	79.163	0.421
225	42613.9	95.1	125663.	1260.	13.1654	0.1216	79.584	0.425
224	42709.0	95.6	126923.	1277.	13.2870	0.1232	80.009	0.428
223	42804.6	96.1	128200.	1295.	13.4102	0.1249	80.437	0.432
222	42900.7	96.5	129495.	1313.	13.5351	0.1265	80.869	0.436
221	42997.2	97.0	130808.	1331.	13.6616	0.1283	81.305	0.440
220	43094.2	97.4	132139.	1351.	13.7899	0.1301	81.745	0.444
219	43191.6	97.9	133490.	1369.	13.9200	0.1318	82.189	0.448
218	43289.5	98.4	134859.	1388.	14.0518	0.1337	82.637	0.452
217	43387.9	98.8	136247.	1407.	14.1855	0.1356	83.089	0.456
216	43486.7	99.2	137654.	1428.	14.3211	0.1374	83.545	0.461
215	43585.9	99.7	139082.	1447.	14.4585	0.1394	84.006	0.465
214	43685.6	100.2	140529.	1469.	14.5979	0.1413	84.471	0.469
213	43785.8	100.6	141998.	1491.	14.7392	0.1433	84.940	0.473
212	43886.4	101.1	143489.	1512.	14.8825	0.1454	85.413	0.478
211	43987.5	101.6	145001.	1535.	15.0279	0.1475	85.891	0.483
210	44089.1	102.1	146536.	1558.	15.1754	0.1496	86.374	0.487
209	44191.2	102.5	148094.	1580.	15.3250	0.1518	86.861	0.492
208	44293.7	103.1	149674.	1603.	15.4768	0.1539	87.353	0.496
207	44396.8	103.5	151277.	1626.	15.6307	0.1562	87.849	0.501
206	44500.3	104.1	152903.	1651.	15.7869	0.1585	88.350	0.507
205	44604.4	104.5	154554.	1675.	15.9454	0.1608	88.857	0.511
204	44708.9	105.1	156229.	1701.	16.1062	0.1632	89.368	0.517
203	44814.0	105.6	157930.	1727.	16.2694	0.1657	89.885	0.521
202	44919.6	106.1	159657.	1753.	16.4351	0.1681	90.406	0.527
201	45025.7	106.7	161410.	1780.	16.6032	0.1707	90.933	0.532
200	45132.4	107.2	163190.	1808.	16.7739	0.1733	91.465	0.537

TABLE I—Continued.

u	S (u)	Δ	A (u)	Δ	I (u)	Δ	T (u)	Δ
200	45132.4	107.2	163190	1808	16.7739	0.1733	91.465	0.537
199	45239.6	107.8	164998	1835	16.9472	0.1759	92.002	0.543
198	45347.4	108.3	166833	1864	17.1231	0.1785	92.545	0.548
197	45455.7	108.8	168697	1893	17.3016	0.1813	93.093	0.554
196	45564.5	109.4	170590	1922	17.4829	0.1841	93.647	0.560
195	45673.9	110.0	172512	1953	17.6670	0.1869	94.207	0.565
194	45783.9	110.5	174465	1984	17.8539	0.1899	94.772	0.571
193	45894.4	111.1	176449	2015	18.0438	0.1928	95.343	0.578
192	46005.5	111.6	178464	2047	18.2366	0.1958	95.921	0.583
191	46117.1	112.3	180511	2080	18.4324	0.1990	96.504	0.589
190	46229.4	112.8	182591	2114	18.6314	0.2021	97.093	0.592
189	46342.2	113.5	184705	2148	18.8335	0.2053	97.689	0.606
188	46455.7	114.1	186853	2183	19.0388	0.2087	98.291	0.608
187	46569.8	114.6	189036	2219	19.2475	0.2121	98.899	0.614
186	46684.4	115.3	191255	2256	19.4596	0.2155	99.514	0.621
185	46799.7	115.9	193511	2294	19.6751	0.2191	100.13	0.63
184	46915.6	116.5	195805	2331	19.8942	0.2226	100.76	0.64
183	47032.1	117.2	198136	2371	20.1168	0.2263	101.40	0.64
182	47149.3	117.8	200507	2410	20.3431	0.2300	102.04	0.65
181	47267.1	118.5	202917	2451	20.5731	0.2339	102.69	0.66
180	47385.6	119.2	205368	2492	20.8070	0.2378	103.35	0.66
179	47504.8	119.8	207860	2536	21.0448	0.2418	104.01	0.67
178	47624.6	120.5	210396	2580	21.2866	0.2459	104.68	0.68
177	47745.1	121.1	212976	2624	21.5325	0.2502	105.36	0.69
176	47866.2	121.8	215600	2670	21.7827	0.2545	106.05	0.69
175	47988.0	122.4	218270	2717	22.0372	0.2589	106.74	0.70
174	48110.4	123.2	220987	2765	22.2961	0.2634	107.44	0.71
173	48233.6	124.0	223752	2814	22.5595	0.2680	108.15	0.72
172	48357.6	124.8	226566	2863	22.8275	0.2727	108.87	0.73
171	48482.4	125.5	229429	2914	23.1002	0.2775	109.60	0.73
170	48607.9	126.2	232343	2966	23.3777	0.2824	110.33	0.75
169	48734.1	126.9	235309	3021	23.6601	0.2875	111.08	0.75
168	48861.0	127.6	238330	3076	23.9476	0.2927	111.83	0.76
167	48988.6	128.5	241406	3133	24.2403	0.2981	112.59	0.78
166	49117.1	129.2	244539	3190	24.5384	0.3034	113.37	0.78
165	49246.3	130.0	247729	3250	24.8418	0.3091	114.15	0.79
164	49376.3	130.8	250979	3311	25.1509	0.3147	114.94	0.80
163	49507.1	131.7	254290	3372	25.4656	0.3205	115.74	0.81
162	49638.8	132.4	257662	3436	25.7861	0.3265	116.55	0.82
161	49771.2	133.2	261098	3501	26.1126	0.3327	117.37	0.83
160	49904.4	134.1	264599	3568	26.4453	0.3389	118.20	0.84
159	50038.5	134.9	268167	3637	26.7842	0.3454	119.04	0.85
158	50173.4	135.8	271804	3707	27.1296	0.3521	119.89	0.86
157	50309.2	136.6	275511	3780	27.4817	0.3588	120.75	0.87
156	50445.8	137.5	279291	3854	27.8405	0.3659	121.62	0.89
155	50583.3	138.4	283145	3931	28.2064	0.3730	122.51	0.89
154	50721.7	139.3	287076	4008	28.5794	0.3804	123.40	0.91
153	50861.0	140.2	291084	4088	28.9598	0.3878	124.31	0.92
152	51001.2	141.2	295172	4170	29.3476	0.3956	125.23	0.93
151	51142.4	142.1	299342	4255	29.7432	0.4035	126.16	0.95
150	51284.5	143.1	303597	4342	30.1467	0.4117	127.11	0.95

TABLE I—Continued.

u	S (u)	Δ	A (u)	Δ	I (u)	Δ	T (u)	Δ
150	51284.5	143.1	303597	4342	30.1467	0.4117	127.11	0.95
149	51427.6	144.0	307939	4430	30.5584	0.4200	128.06	0.97
148	51571.6	145.0	312369	4523	30.9784	0.4286	129.03	0.99
147	51716.6	145.9	316892	4616	31.4070	0.4374	130.02	0.99
146	51862.5	147.0	321508	4713	31.8444	0.4466	131.01	1.01
145	52009.5	148.0	326221	4813	32.2910	0.4559	132.02	1.03
144	52157.5	149.0	331034	4914	32.7469	0.4655	133.05	1.04
143	52306.5	150.1	335948	5020	33.2124	0.4754	134.09	1.05
142	52456.6	151.1	340968	5128	33.6878	0.4855	135.14	1.07
141	52607.7	152.2	346096	5239	34.1733	0.4959	136.21	1.08
140	52759.9	153.3	351335	5354	34.6692	0.5067	137.29	1.10
139	52913.2	154.4	356689	5471	35.1759	0.5177	138.39	1.11
138	53067.6	155.5	362160	5593	35.6936	0.5291	139.50	1.13
137	53223.1	156.7	367753	5717	36.2227	0.5409	140.63	1.15
136	53379.8	157.8	373470	5845	36.7636	0.5529	141.78	1.17
135	53537.6	159.0	379315	5978	37.3165	0.5654	142.95	1.18
134	53696.6	160.2	385293	6114	37.8819	0.5781	144.13	1.20
133	53856.8	161.4	391407	6255	38.4600	0.5913	145.33	1.22
132	54018.2	162.6	397662	6400	39.0513	0.6049	146.55	1.23
131	54180.8	163.9	404062	6549	39.6562	0.6189	147.78	1.26
130	54344.7	165.2	410611	6703	40.2751	0.6334	149.04	1.27
129	54509.9	166.4	417314	6862	40.9085	0.6483	150.31	1.30
128	54676.3	167.8	424176	7026	41.5568	0.6636	151.61	1.32
127	54844.1	169.0	431202	7195	42.2204	0.6795	152.93	1.33
126	55013.1	170.4	438397	7369	42.8999	0.6959	154.26	1.36
125	55183.5	171.7	445766	7550	43.5958	0.7128	155.62	1.38
124	55355.2	173.2	453316	7736	44.3086	0.7303	157.00	1.40
123	55528.4	174.5	461052	7927	45.0389	0.7483	158.40	1.43
122	55702.9	176.0	468979	8126	45.7872	0.7669	159.83	1.45
121	55878.9	177.5	477105	8331	46.5541	0.7861	161.28	1.47
120	56056.4	179.0	485436	8544	47.3402	0.8060	162.75	1.50
119	56235.4	180.5	493980	8763	48.1462	0.8267	164.25	1.52
118	56415.9	182.0	502743	8990	48.9729	0.8479	165.77	1.55
117	56597.9	183.6	511733	9224	49.8208	0.8699	167.32	1.57
116	56781.5	185.1	520957	9468	50.6907	0.8928	168.89	1.61
115	56966.6	186.8	530425	9720	51.5835	0.9163	170.50	1.63
114	57153.4	188.4	540145	9980	52.4998	0.9408	172.13	1.66
113	57341.8	190.1	550125	10250	53.4406	0.9661	173.79	1.69
112	57531.9	191.8	560375	10530	54.4067	0.9923	175.48	1.72
111	57723.7	193.5	570905	10820	55.3990	1.0195	177.20	1.75
110	57917.2	195.3	581725	11120	56.4185	1.0477	178.95	1.78
109	58112.5	197.1	592845	11432	57.4662	1.0769	180.73	1.82
108	58309.6	198.9	604277	11756	58.5431	1.1072	182.55	1.85
107	58508.5	200.8	616033	12093	59.6503	1.1388	184.40	1.89
106	58709.3	202.7	628126	12439	60.7891	1.1714	186.29	1.92
105	58912.0	204.7	640565	12803	61.9605	1.2054	188.21	1.95
104	59116.7	206.6	653368	13179	63.1659	1.2407	190.16	2.00
103	59323.3	208.6	666547	13571	64.4066	1.2773	192.16	2.04
102	59531.9	210.7	680118	13977	65.6839	1.3155	194.20	2.07
101	59742.6	212.8	694095	14400	66.9994	1.3551	196.27	2.12
100	59955.4	215.0	708495	14840	68.3545	1.3963	198.39	2.16

EXTENSION OF INGALLS' TABLE I TO 5000 FEET VELOCITY

Ingalls ballistic tables as contained in Artillery Circular M start at 3600 feet per second velocity. However, a few cartridges such as the 220 Swift and some wildcat cartridges have velocities higher than 3600 f.s.; and to permit ballistic calculations to be made for such cartridges, there is included here an extension of the space functions and time functions of Ingalls' Table I to 5000 f.s.

Because Ingalls' tables start with zero space and time at 3600 f.s., and the values get larger as the velocity decreases, it has been found convenient to assign negative values to the time and space functions for velocities above 3600 f.s.; the alternative would be to start with zero at 5000 f.s. and then increase every other time and space function figure in the entire Table I accordingly.

The instructions for using this extension to Table I are exactly the same as those for using Table I itself, remembering only that if one of two numbers to be added has a minus sign it must actually be subtracted, and that if a number to be subtracted already has a minus sign, then the two minus signs cancel, and the number actually must be added.

For example, consider the 220 Swift cartridge, which has a 48 grain bullet at 4110 f.s. muzzle velocity and 3490 f.s. remaining at 100 yards. To find the ballistic coefficient C, use the formula $C = \dfrac{S(v) - S(V)}{X}$.

$$X = 100 \text{ yd.} = 300 \text{ ft.}$$
$$v = 3490, \text{ and } S(v) = 302.1 \quad \text{from the Table}$$
$$V = 4110 \text{ and } S(V) = (-)\ 1337.9$$

$$S(v) \quad -S(V) = 1640.0$$

$$C = 300/1640 = .1828$$

To find the remaining velocity at 200 yards use the formula
$$S(v) = S(V) + \frac{X}{C} \qquad X = 600 \text{ ft. and } \frac{600}{.1828} = 3292.3$$

$$V = 4110 \text{ and } S(V) = (-)1337.9$$
$$X/C = 3293.3$$

$$S(v) = 1954.4$$

and hence v = 2921 f.s. from the table.

HATCHER'S NOTEBOOK

TABLE OF SPACE AND TIME FUNCTIONS
S(u) and T(u)
u=5000 f. s. to 3600 f. s.
An Extension of Table I, Artillery Circular M

u	S(u)	Δ	T(u)	Δ	u	S(u)	Δ	T(u)	Δ
5000	(−)3740.0	45.5	(−)0.818	9	4300	(−)1813.0	49.4	(−)0.461	12
4980	(−)3424.5	45.6	(−)0.809	9	4280	(−)1763.6	49.6	(−)0.449	11
4960	(−)3378.9	45.7	(−)0.800	9	4260	(−)1714.0	49.7	(−)0.438	12
4940	(−)3333.2	45.8	(−)0.791	10	4240	(−)1664.3	49.8	(−)0.426	12
4920	(−)3287.4	46.0	(−)0.781	9	4220	(−)1614.5	50.0	(−)0.414	12
4900	(−)3241.4	46.0	(−)0.722	10	4200	(−)1564.5	50.2	(−)0.402	12
4880	(−)3195.4	46.1	(−)0.762	9	4180	(−)1514.3	50.2	(−)0.390	12
4860	(−)3149.3	46.2	(−)0.753	10	4160	(−)1464.1	50.4	(−)0.378	12
4840	(−)3103.1	46.3	(−)0.743	9	4140	(−)1413.7	50.5	(−)0.366	12
4820	(−)3056.8	46.5	(−)0.734	10	4120	(−)1363.2	50.5	(−)0.354	12
4800	(−)3010.3	46.5	(−)0.724	10	4100	(−)1312.7	50.8	(−)0.342	12
4780	(−)2963.8	46.6	(−)0.714	9	4080	(−)1261.9	50.9	(−)0.330	13
4760	(−)2917.2	46.8	(−)0.705	10	4060	(−)1211.0	51.0	(−)0.317	12
4740	(−)2870.4	46.8	(−)0.695	10	4040	(−)1160.0	51.2	(−)0.305	13
4720	(−)2823.6	47.0	(−)0.685	10	4020	(−)1108.0	51.3	(−)0.292	13
4700	(−)2776.6	47.1	(−)0.675	10	4000	(−)1057.5	51.4	(−)0.279	13
4680	(−)2729.5	47.2	(−)0.665	10	3980	(−)1006.1	51.6	(−)0.266	13
4660	(−)2682.3	47.3	(−)0.655	10	3960	(−) 954.5	51.7	(−)0.253	13
4640	(−)2635.0	47.4	(−)0.645	11	3940	(−) 902.8	51.9	(−)0.240	14
4620	(−)2587.6	47.5	(−)0.634	10	3920	(−) 850.9	52.1	(−)0.226	13
4600	(−)2540.1	47.7	(−)0.624	10	3900	(−) 798.8	52.2	(−)0.213	13
4580	(−)2492.4	47.7	(−)0.614	10	3880	(−) 746.6	52.3	(−)0.200	14
4560	(−)2444.7	47.9	(−)0.604	11	3860	(−) 694.4	52.5	(−)0.186	13
4540	(−)2396.8	47.9	(−)0.593	10	3840	(−) 641.8	52.6	(−)0.173	14
4520	(−)2348.9	48.2	(−)0.583	11	3820	(−) 589.2	52.8	(−)0.159	14
4500	(−)2300.7	48.2	(−)0.572	11	3800	(−) 536.4	52.9	(−)0.145	14
4480	(−)2252.5	48.4	(−)0.561	11	3780	(−) 483.5	53.1	(−)0.131	14
4460	(−)2204.1	48.4	(−)0.550	11	3760	(−) 430.4	53.2	(−)0.117	14
4440	(−)2155.7	48.6	(−)0.539	11	3740	(−) 377.2	53.4	(−)0.103	15
4420	(−)2107.1	48.7	(−)0.528	11	3720	(−) 323.8	53.6	(−)0.088	14
4400	(−)2058.4	48.8	(−)0.517	11	3700	(−) 270.2	53.7	(−)0.074	15
4380	(−)2009.6	49.0	(−)0.506	11	3680	(−) 216.5	53.9	(−)0.059	14
4360	(−)1960.6	49.1	(−)0.495	11	3660	(−) 162.6	54.0	(−)0.045	15
4340	(−)1911.5	49.2	(−)0.484	12	3640	(−) 108.6	54.2	(−)0.030	15
4320	(−)1862.3	49.3	(−)0.472	11	3620	(−) 54.4	54.4	(−)0.015	15
					3600	0.0	54.5	0.000	15

$Z = \dfrac{X}{C}$ TABLE A—(Continued) $A = \dfrac{\text{Sin } 2a}{C}$

Velocity Z	2000 A	2100 A	2200 A	2300 A	2400 A
5600	0.07736	0.07027	0.06394	0.05831	0.05331
5800	0.08170	0.07428	0.06763	0.06171	0.05643
6000	0.08615	0.07840	0.07144	0.06522	0.05966
6200	0.09073	0.08264	0.07536	0.06885	0.06300
6400	0.09542	0.08700	0.07941	0.07259	0.06646
6600	0.10022	0.09147	0.08357	0.07645	0.07004
6800	0.10513	0.09606	0.08784	0.08043	0.07373
7000	0.11016	0.10077	0.09224	0.08452	0.07754
7200	0.11531	0.10560	0.09675	0.08873	0.08146
7400	0.12057	0.11053	0.10138	0.09305	0.08550
7600	0.12594	0.11558	0.10612	0.09749	0.08965
7800	0.13142	0.12075	0.11097	0.10204	0.09391
8000	0.13702	0.12602	0.11593	0.10671	0.09829
8200	0.14273	0.13141	0.12101	0.11149	0.10278
8400	0.14856	0.13691	0.12620	0.11638	0.10739
8600	0.15449	0.14252	0.13150	0.12139	0.11211
8800	0.16054	0.14825	0.13691	0.12650	0.11694
9000	0.16670	0.15408	0.14244	0.13173	0.12188
9200	0.17298	0.16003	0.14808	0.13707	0.12693
9400	0.17937	0.16610	0.15383	0.14252	0.13210
9600	0.18588	0.17228	0.15970	0.14808	0.13738
9800	0.19249	0.17857	0.16568	0.15376	0.14277
10000	0.19922	0.18497	0.17177	0.15954	0.14827
10200	0.20607	0.19148	0.17798	0.16545	0.15388
10400	0.21304	0.19811	0.18429	0.17147	0.15961
10600	0.22013	0.20486	0.19072	0.17760	0.16545
10800	0.22733	0.21173	0.19727	0.18385	0.17140

$Z = \dfrac{X}{C}$ TABLE A Abridged from Ingalls' $A = \dfrac{\text{Sin } 2a}{C}$

Velocity Z	2000 A	2100 A	2200 A	2300 A	2400 A
200	0.00163	0.00148	0.00134	0.00123	0.00114
400	0.00333	0.00301	0.00274	0.00251	0.00231
600	0.00509	0.00460	0.00419	0.00384	0.00353
800	0.00690	0.00625	0.00568	0.00520	0.00478
1000	0.00878	0.00795	0.00723	0.00661	0.00607
1200	0.01073	0.00971	0.00883	0.00807	0.00741
1400	0.01275	0.01154	0.01050	0.00958	0.00879
1600	0.01485	0.01344	0.01222	0.01115	0.01023
1800	0.01702	0.01541	0.01400	0.01278	0.01172
2000	0.01927	0.01744	0.01585	0.01446	0.01325
2200	0.02160	0.01955	0.01776	0.01620	0.01484
2400	0.02402	0.02175	0.01976	0.01802	0.01650
2600	0.02654	0.02403	0.02182	0.01990	0.01821
2800	0.02915	0.02638	0.02396	0.02184	0.01999
3000	0.03186	0.02882	0.02617	0.02386	0.02183
3200	0.03468	0.03135	0.02847	0.02596	0.02374
3400	0.03761	0.03399	0.03086	0.02813	0.02573
3600	0.04064	0.03673	0.03335	0.03040	0.02779
3800	0.04377	0.03957	0.03593	0.03274	0.02993
4000	0.04701	0.04252	0.03860	0.03517	0.03215
4200	0.05038	0.04557	0.04138	0.03770	0.03445
4400	0.05388	0.04875	0.04427	0.04033	0.03684
4600	0.05749	0.05204	0.04726	0.04306	0.03934
4800	0.06123	0.05545	0.05037	0.04589	0.04193
5000	0.06508	0.05898	0.05359	0.04883	0.04462
5200	0.06905	0.06263	0.05692	0.05187	0.04740
5400	0.07315	0.06639	0.06037	0.05504	0.05030

$Z = \dfrac{X}{C}$ TABLE A—(Continued) $A = \dfrac{\text{Sin } 2a}{C}$

Velocity	2500	2600	2700	2800	2900
Z	A	A	A	A	A
200	0.00105	0.00097	0.00090	0.00083	0.00078
400	0.00212	0.00197	0.00183	0.00170	0.00158
600	0.00324	0.00300	0.00278	0.00259	0.00241
800	0.00439	0.00406	0.00377	0.00350	0.00326
1000	0.00558	0.00516	0.00478	0.00444	0.00413
1200	0.00681	0.00629	0.00583	0.00541	0.00504
1400	0.00808	0.00747	0.00691	0.00642	0.00597
1600	0.00940	0.00869	0.00803	0.00747	0.00694
1800	0.01077	0.00994	0.00920	0.00854	0.00794
2000	0.01218	0.01124	0.01040	0.00965	0.00897
2200	0.01364	0.01259	0.01165	0.01080	0.01004
2400	0.01516	0.01399	0.01294	0.01199	0.01115
2600	0.01673	0.01543	0.01427	0.01322	0.01229
2800	0.01836	0.01693	0.01565	0.01450	0.01348
3000	0.02005	0.01848	0.01708	0.01582	0.01470
3200	0.02180	0.02009	0.01856	0.01719	0.01597
3400	0.02362	0.02176	0.02009	0.01861	0.01728
3600	0.02551	0.02349	0.02169	0.02008	0.01865
3800	0.02747	0.02529	0.02334	0.02161	0.02006
4000	0.02950	0.02715	0.02506	0.02319	0.02152
4200	0.03161	0.02908	0.02684	0.02483	0.02305
4400	0.03381	0.03110	0.02870	0.02654	0.02463
4600	0.03609	0.03319	0.03063	0.02832	0.02627
4800	0.03845	0.03537	0.03263	0.03016	0.02796
5000	0.04091	0.03762	0.03469	0.03206	0.02971
5200	0.04346	0.03995	0.03684	0.03404	0.03154
5400	0.04611	0.04239	0.03908	0.03611	0.03344

$Z = \dfrac{X}{C}$ TABLE A—(Continued) $A = \dfrac{\text{Sin } 2a}{C}$

Velocity	2000	2100	2200	2300	2400
Z	A	A	A	A	A
11000	0.23465	0.21872	0.20394	0.19021	0.17747
11200	0.24209	0.22582	0.21072	0.19668	0.18365
11400	0.24966	0.23305	0.21762	0.20327	0.18995
11600	0.25734	0.24039	0.22463	0.20997	0.19636
11800	0.26513	0.24785	0.23177	0.21680	0.20288
12000	0.27305	0.25543	0.23902	0.22374	0.20952
12200	0.28109	0.26313	0.24639	0.23079	0.21628
12400	0.28926	0.27096	0.25389	0.23796	0.22315
12600	0.29755	0.27890	0.26150	0.24526	0.23014
12800	0.30598	0.28697	0.26924	0.25268	0.23725
13000	0.31453	0.29516	0.27709	0.26022	0.24448
13200	0.32321	0.30348	0.28506	0.26786	0.25183
13400	0.33203	0.31193	0.29317	0.27564	0.25930
13600	0.34098	0.32051	0.30140	0.28354	0.26690
13800	0.35006	0.32922	0.30977	0.29157	0.27461
14000	0.35928	0.33806	0.31826	0.29973	0.28245
14200	0.36864	0.34704	0.32689	0.30802	0.29041
14400	0.37814	0.35615	0.33565	0.31644	0.29850
14600	0.38778	0.36541	0.34454	0.32499	0.30672
14800	0.39755	0.37480	0.35337	0.33367	0.31507
15000	0.40747	0.38433	0.36272	0.34248	0.32355
15200	0.41754	0.39400	0.37201	0.35142	0.33216
15400	0.42776	0.40382	0.38145	0.36051	0.34091
15600	0.43812	0.41378	0.39103	0.36973	0.34979
15800	0.44864	0.42389	0.40075	0.37909	0.35881
16000	0.45930	$.43415	0.41062	0.38859	0.36796

$Z = \dfrac{X}{C}$ TABLE A—(Continued) $A = \dfrac{\text{Sin } 2a}{C}$

Velocity	2500	2600	2700	2800	2900
Z	A	A	A	A	A
11000	0.16565	0.15468	0.14448	0.13497	0.12610
11200	0.17155	0.16031	0.14985	0.14009	0.13098
11400	0.17756	0.16604	0.15533	0.14532	0.13596
11600	0.18368	0.17189	0.16092	0.15066	0.14106
11800	0.18993	0.17786	0.16663	0.15611	0.14626
12000	0.19628	0.18394	0.17244	0.16167	0.15157
12200	0.20275	0.19014	0.17836	0.16733	0.15699
12400	0.20934	0.19645	0.18441	0.17312	0.16252
12600	0.21604	0.20288	0.19056	0.17901	0.16817
12800	0.22286	0.20942	0.19683	0.18502	0.17394
13000	0.22979	0.21607	0.20322	0.19115	0.17981
13200	0.23684	0.22285	0.20972	0.19739	0.18580
13400	0.24402	0.22974	0.21635	0.20375	0.19190
13600	0.25131	0.23675	0.22308	0.21022	0.19812
13800	0.25872	0.24387	0.22993	0.21681	0.20445
14000	0.26626	0.25111	0.23690	0.22351	0.21089
14200	0.27392	0.25847	0.24399	0.23033	0.21745
14400	0.28170	0.26596	0.25120	0.23727	0.22413
14600	0.28961	0.27357	0.25853	0.24433	0.23092
14800	0.29765	0.28130	0.26598	0.25150	0.23783
15000	0.30581	0.28916	0.27355	0.25880	0.24486
15200	0.31410	0.29715	0.28125	0.26622	0.25201
15400	0.32252	0.30527	0.28907	0.27376	0.25928
15600	0.33108	0.31352	0.29703	0.28143	0.26668
15800	0.33977	0.32191	0.30510	0.28922	0.27419
16000	0.34859	0.33042	0.31331	0.29714	0.28183

$Z = \dfrac{X}{C}$ TABLE A—(Continued) $A = \dfrac{\text{Sin } 2a}{C}$

Velocity	2500	2600	2700	2800	2900
Z	A	A	A	A	A
5600	0.04887	0.04492	0.04141	0.03826	0.03542
5800	0.05174	0.04756	0.04383	0.04049	0.03748
6000	0.05471	0.05029	0.04634	0.04280	0.03961
6200	0.05779	0.05312	0.04895	0.04520	0.04183
6400	0.06098	0.05606	0.05167	0.04770	0.04414
6600	0.06429	0.05912	0.05449	0.05030	0.04655
6800	0.06771	0.06228	0.05742	0.05301	0.04905
7000	0.07124	0.06556	0.06045	0.05582	0.05164
7200	0.07489	0.06894	0.06359	0.05873	0.05433
7400	0.07866	0.07244	0.06684	0.06176	0.05713
7600	0.08253	0.07606	0.07021	0.06489	0.06004
7800	0.08652	0.07979	0.07368	0.06812	0.06305
8000	0.09062	0.08363	0.07727	0.07146	0.06616
8200	0.09484	0.08758	0.08097	0.07491	0.06939
8400	0.09917	0.09165	0.08478	0.07847	0.07272
8600	0.10361	0.09583	0.08871	0.08214	0.07617
8800	0.10816	0.10012	0.09275	0.08593	0.07972
9000	0.11283	0.10453	0.09690	0.08982	0.08339
9200	0.11761	0.10904	0.10116	0.09382	0.08717
9400	0.12250	0.11367	0.10553	0.09796	0.09106
9600	0.12751	0.11841	0.11001	0.10220	0.09506
9800	0.13262	0.12325	0.11460	0.10656	0.09917
10000	0.13785	0.12821	0.11931	0.11104	0.10338
10200	0.14318	0.13328	0.12412	0.11560	0.10771
10400	0.14863	0.13847	0.12905	0.12028	0.11214
10600	0.15419	0.14376	0.13408	0.12506	0.11668
10800	0.15986	0.14917	0.13923	0.12996	0.12133

TABLE A—(Continued)

$Z = \dfrac{X}{C}$ $A = \dfrac{\text{Sin } 2a}{C}$

Velocity Z	3000 A	3100 A	3200 A	3300 A	3400 A
5600	0.03287	0.03058	0.02848	0.02661	0.02489
5800	0.03477	0.03234	0.03012	0.02812	0.02630
6000	0.03674	0.03416	0.03182	0.02969	0.02777
6200	0.03874	0.03606	0.03361	0.03133	0.02929
6400	0.04084	0.03804	0.03546	0.03304	0.03088
6600	0.04304	0.04010	0.03737	0.03480	0.03252
6800	0.04535	0.04223	0.03934	0.03664	0.03423
7000	0.04776	0.04445	0.04136	0.03856	0.03601
7200	0.05030	0.04675	0.04345	0.04054	0.03785
7400	0.05293	0.04916	0.04565	0.04261	0.03978
7600	0.05564	0.05166	0.04795	0.04475	0.04178
7800	0.05844	0.05425	0.05036	0.04699	0.04386
8000	0.06134	0.05695	0.05288	0.04932	0.04602
8200	0.06436	0.05975	0.05551	0.05174	0.04827
8400	0.06747	0.06265	0.05824	0.05425	0.05061
8600	0.07068	0.06566	0.06106	0.05687	0.05305
8800	0.07401	0.06877	0.06398	0.05959	0.05558
9000	0.07745	0.07199	0.06699	0.06240	0.05821
9200	0.08100	0.07532	0.07010	0.06532	0.06093
9400	0.08465	0.07875	0.07332	0.06834	0.06376
9600	0.08842	0.08230	0.07665	0.07147	0.06669
9800	0.09230	0.08595	0.08009	0.07471	0.06973
10000	0.09628	0.08971	0.08364	0.07804	0.07286
10200	0.10037	0.09358	0.08729	0.08149	0.07611
10400	0.10458	0.09756	0.09106	0.08505	0.07946
10600	0.10889	0.10165	0.09493	0.08870	0.08291
10800	0.11331	0.10585	0.99890	0.09246	0.08647

TABLE A—(Continued)

$Z = \dfrac{X}{C}$ $A = \dfrac{\text{Sin } 2a}{C}$

Velocity Z	3000 A	3100 A	3200 A	3300 A	3400 A
200	0.00072	0.00068	0.00063	0.00060	0.00056
400	0.00147	0.00138	0.00129	0.00122	0.00114
600	0.00224	0.00210	0.00197	0.00185	0.00174
800	0.00304	0.00285	0.00266	0.00250	0.00236
1000	0.00386	0.00361	0.00338	0.00318	0.00299
1200	0.00470	0.00440	0.00412	0.00387	0.00364
1400	0.00557	0.00521	0.00488	0.00458	0.00431
1600	0.00647	0.00606	0.00567	0.00532	0.00500
1800	0.00740	0.00693	0.00648	0.00608	0.00572
2000	0.00836	0.00782	0.00732	0.00687	0.00645
2200	0.00935	0.00785	0.00819	0.00768	0.00721
2400	0.01037	0.00970	0.00908	0.00851	0.00800
2600	0.01143	0.01069	0.01000	0.00938	0.00881
2800	0.01253	0.01171	0.01095	0.01027	0.00964
3000	0.01367	0.01277	0.01194	0.01119	0.01051
3200	0.01485	0.01387	0.01296	0.01214	0.01140
3400	0.01607	0.01501	0.01401	0.01313	0.01232
3600	0.01733	0.01618	0.01511	0.01414	0.01327
3800	0.01864	0.01740	0.01624	0.01520	0.01426
4000	0.01999	0.01865	0.01741	0.01629	0.01527
4200	0.02139	0.01995	0.01862	0.01743	0.01633
4400	0.02285	0.02130	0.01989	0.01860	0.01743
4600	0.02437	0.02270	0.02120	0.01981	0.01856
4800	0.02594	0.02416	0.02255	0.02107	0.01974
5000	0.02758	0.02567	0.02395	0.02238	0.02096
5200	0.02927	0.02724	0.02539	0.02374	0.02222
5400	0.03103	0.02888	0.02690	0.02515	0.02353

$Z = \dfrac{X}{C}$ TABLE A—(Continued) $A = \dfrac{\sin 2a}{C}$

Velocity	3500	3600	Velocity	3500	3600
Z	A	A	Z	A	A
200	0.00053	0.00050	5600	0.02333	0.02192
400	0.00108	0.00102	5800	0.02465	0.02314
600	0.00164	0.00155	6000	0.02602	0.02442
800	0.00222	0.00210	6200	0.02744	0.02575
1000	0.00282	0.00266	6400	0.02891	0.02712
1200	0.00343	0.00324	6600	0.03044	0.02855
1400	0.00406	0.00384	6800	0.03203	0.03003
1600	0.00472	0.00445	7000	0.03369	0.03158
1800	0.00539	0.00508	7200	0.03541	0.03318
2000	0.00608	0.00573	7400	0.03720	0.03485
2200	0.00679	0.00641	7600	0.03906	0.03658
2400	0.00753	0.00710	7800	0.04100	0.03838
2600	0.00829	0.00781	8000	0.04300	0.04026
2800	0.00907	0.00855	8200	0.04510	0.04222
3000	0.00988	0.00931	8400	0.04728	0.04424
3200	0.01071	0.01009	8600	0.04955	0.04636
3400	0.01158	0.01090	8800	0.05191	0.04856
3600	0.01247	0.01174	9000	0.05436	0.05084
3800	0.01340	0.01261	9200	0.05691	0.05322
4000	0.01435	0.01351	9400	0.05956	0.05570
4200	0.01534	0.01444	9600	0.06230	0.05827
4400	0.01637	0.01530	9800	0.06514	0.06093
4600	0.01742	0.01639	10000	0.06809	0.06370
4800	0.01852	0.01742	10200	0.07114	0.06657
5000	0.01966	0.01848	10400	0.07430	0.06954
5200	0.02084	0.01958	10600	0.07756	0.07261
5400	0.02207	0.02073	10800	0.08092	0.07578

$Z = \dfrac{X}{C}$ TABLE A—(Continued) $A = \dfrac{\sin 2a}{C}$

Velocity	3000	3100	3200	3300	3400
Z	A	A	A	A	A
11000	0.11784	0.11015	0.10299	0.09633	0.09014
11200	0.12248	0.11456	0.10718	0.10030	0.09391
11400	0.12723	0.11908	0.11148	0.10438	0.09779
11600	0.13209	0.12371	0.11589	0.10858	0.10177
11800	0.13706	0.12845	0.12040	0.11289	0.10586
12000	0.14213	0.13329	0.12502	0.11731	0.11006
12200	0.14732	0.13824	0.12975	0.12183	0.11437
12400	0.15262	0.14330	0.13459	0.12644	0.11878
12600	0.15803	0.14847	0.13954	0.13115	0.12329
12800	0.16354	0.15376	0.14459	0.13598	0.12792
13000	0.16917	0.15916	0.14976	0.14093	0.13265
13200	0.17491	0.16467	0.15504	0.14598	0.13749
13400	0.18076	0.17030	0.16043	0.15115	0.14244
13600	0.18673	0.17603	0.16592	0.15643	0.14750
13800	0.19281	0.18187	0.17153	0.16182	0.15266
14000	0.19900	0.18782	0.17725	0.16731	0.15793
14200	0.20531	0.19388	0.18308	0.17292	0.16332
14400	0.21174	0.20006	0.18903	0.17865	0.16882
14600	0.21828	0.20635	0.19508	0.18448	0.17443
14800	0.22494	0.21276	0.20125	0.19043	0.18014
15000	0.23172	0.21928	0.20754	0.19650	0.18597
15200	0.23862	0.22592	0.21394	0.20268	0.19192
15400	0.24563	0.23268	0.22046	0.20897	0.19797
15600	0.25277	0.23956	0.22710	0.21536	0.20444
15800	0.26002	0.24657	0.23385	0.22187	0.21043
16000	0.26739	0.25369	0.24072	0.22850	0.21683

TABLE S.
Natural Sines.

	0°	1°	2°	3°	4°
0	.00000	.01745	.03490	.05234	.06976
1	29	774	519	263	.07005
2	58	803	548	292	034
3	87	832	577	321	063
4	116	862	606	350	092
5	.00145	.01891	.03635	.05378	.07121
6	175	920	664	408	150
7	204	949	693	437	179
8	233	.01978	723	466	208
9	262	.02007	752	495	237
10	.00291	.02036	.03781	.05524	.07266
11	320	065	810	553	295
12	349	094	839	582	324
13	378	123	868	611	353
14	407	152	897	640	382
15	.00436	.02181	.03926	.05669	.07411
16	465	211	955	698	440
17	495	240	.03984	727	469
18	524	269	.04013	756	498
19	553	298	042	785	527
20	.00582	.02327	.04071	.05814	.07556

$Z = \dfrac{X}{C}$ TABLE A—(Concluded) $A = \dfrac{\text{Sin } 2a}{C}$

Velocity	3500	3600	Velocity	3500	3600
Z	A	A	Z	A	A
11000	0.08439	0.07905	14000	0.14911	0.14079
11200	0.08796	0.08244	14200	0.15428	0.14579
11400	0.09164	0.08593	14400	0.15957	0.15083
11600	0.09543	0.08952	14600	0.16496	0.15602
11800	0.09932	0.09322	14800	0.17046	0.16131
12000	0.10331	0.09701	15000	0.17607	0.16670
12200	0.10741	0.10091	15200	0.18180	0.17221
12400	0.11162	0.10492	15400	0.18763	0.17784
12600	0.11593	0.10903	15600	0.19358	0.18357
12800	0.12035	0.11325	15800	0.19964	0.18942
13000	0.12488	0.11758	16000	0.20581	0.19537
13200	0.12951	0.12201			
13400	0.13425	0.12655			
13600	0.13910	0.13119			
13800	0.14405	0.13594			

TABLE S—(Continued)

Natural Sines.

	0°	1°	2°	3°	4°
21	611	356	100	844	585
22	640	385	129	873	614
23	669	414	159	902	643
24	698	443	188	931	672
25	.00727	.02472	.04217	.05960	.07701
26	756	501	246	989	730
27	785	530	275	.06018	759
28	814	560	304	047	788
29	844	589	333	076	817
30	.00873	.02618	.04362	.06105	.07846
31	902	647	391	134	875
32	931	676	420	163	904
33	960	705	449	192	933
34	989	734	478	221	962
35	.01018	.02763	.04507	.06250	.07991
36	047	792	536	279	.08020
37	076	821	565	308	049
38	105	850	594	337	078
39	134	879	623	366	107
40	.01164	.02908	.04653	.06395	.08136

TABLE S—(Concluded)

Natural Sines.

	0°	1°	2°	3°	4°
41	193	938	682	424	165
42	222	967	711	453	194
43	251	996	740	482	223
44	280	.03025	769	511	252
45	.01309	.03054	.04798	.06540	.08281
46	338	083	827	569	310
47	367	112	856	598	339
48	396	141	885	627	368
49	425	170	914	656	397
50	.01454	.03199	.04943	.06685	.08426
51	483	228	972	714	455
52	513	257	.05001	743	484
53	542	286	030	773	513
54	571	316	059	802	542
55	.01600	.03345	.05088	.06831	.08571
56	629	374	117	860	600
57	658	403	146	889	629
58	687	432	175	918	658
59	716	461	205	947	687
60	.01745	.03490	.05234	.06976	.08716

BULLET DROP

It is of interest to know how much a bullet will drop below the line of departure at various ranges.

An object falls a distance of $\frac{1}{2}gt^2$ where g is the acceleration of gravity and t is the time of fall. Calling gravity 32.16 this gives the distance of fall in feet as $16.08t^2$ or in inches as $193\ t^2$.

In a vacuum trajectory we could simply use the time of flight for any range as t to calculate the drop for that range. However, in actual practice, the effect of the air resistance on the bullet is to cause it to drop less than the amount given by the vacuum trajectory calculation. The British Textbook of Small Arms 1929, p. 309, says that it is very much as if the value of g were to fall off from 32 at the muzzle to 28 at 500 yards and 24 at 1000 yards.

On page 310 of that book, a formula by Mr. F. W. Jones gives a method of obtaining an adjusted value of g which he calls f. According to his formula, $f = g \left\{ \dfrac{1-b\ (V-v)}{V} \right.$, and he suggest that taking b as 3/7 gives suitable values of f for small arms down to v=V/3.

McShane, Kelly & Reno, in their book *Exterior Ballistics* (University of Denver Press, 1953) give a formula for bullet drop which makes it possible to construct a table for obtaining the bullet drop for any range when the initial velocity, the terminal velocity and the time of flight are known. Such a table is given here.

The procedure is first to find the ratio of the remaining velocity at the range in question to the muzzle velocity. Simply divide the remaining velocity by the muzzle velocity to get this quantity, which is shown in the left hand column of the table under the heading V/V_0.

Then find the time of flight for the range under consideration, using the appropriate ballistic table. In the table, under the column for the appropriate time of flight, and opposite the proper value of V/V_0 find the drop in inches.

As an example, let us find the drop for the 222 Remington bullet at 500 yards. Referring to the maker's ballistics for this cartridge, given on p. 505, it will be seen that the muzzle velocity is 3200 f.s. and the remaining velocity at 500 yards is 1150 f.s., from which V/V_0 is .36. From the ballistic tables we find the time of flight for this bullet to 500 yards is .812 sec.

Opposite .36 in the left hand column of the drop table we see that for a time of flight of .80 sec. the drop is 90 inches and for a time of flight of .89 sec. it is 112 inches. Interpolating, we find the drop for a time of flight of .812 sec. would be 93 inches, which agrees with the figure given by Remington in their published ballistics.

Instead of interpolating, as was just done, we can, if desired, simply square the time of flight and multiply by the figure in the column headed f, which is opposite the proper value of V/V_0.

The square of .812 is .659, and this multiplied by 142 gives 93.5.

DROP, IN INCHES

Time of Flight, Seconds

V/V₀	f	0.14	0.20	0.28	0.34	0.40	0.49	0.57	0.69	0.80	0.89	1.13	1.20
1.00	193	3.78	7.72	15.1	22.4	30.9	46.3	62.7	91.9	123	153	247	278
0.98	192	3.76	7.68	15.0	22.3	30.7	46.1	62.4	91.4	123	152	246	276
0.96	191	3.74	7.64	15.0	22.2	30.6	45.8	62.0	90.0	122	151	244	275
0.94	190	3.72	7.60	14.9	22.0	30.4	45.8	62.0	90.9	122	151	244	274
0.92	187	3.67	7.48	14.7	21.7	29.9	44.9	60.8	89.0	120	148	239	269
0.90	186	3.64	7.44	14.6	21.6	29.8	44.6	60.5	88.5	119	147	238	268
0.88	185	3.63	7.40	14.5	21.5	29.6	44.4	60.1	88.1	118	146	237	266
0.86	184	3.61	7.36	14.4	21.3	29.4	44.2	59.8	87.6	118	146	236	265
0.84	182	3.57	7.28	14.3	21.1	29.1	43.7	59.2	86.6	116	144	233	262
0.82	181	3.55	7.24	14.2	21.0	29.0	43.4	58.8	86.2	116	143	232	261
0.80	180	3.53	7.20	14.1	20.9	28.8	43.2	58.5	85.7	115	142	230	259
0.78	178	3.49	7.12	14.0	20.6	28.5	42.7	57.9	84.7	114	141	228	256
0.76	176	3.45	7.04	13.8	20.4	28.2	42.2	57.2	83.8	113	139	225	253
0.74	175	3.43	7.00	13.7	20.3	28.0	42.0	56.8	83.3	112	139	224	252
0.72	174	3.41	6.96	13.6	20.2	27.8	41.8	56.6	82.8	111	138	223	251
0.70	172	3.37	6.88	13.5	20.0	27.5	41.0	55.9	81.8	110	136	220	248
0.68	170	3.33	6.80	13.3	19.7	27.2	40.8	55.3	80.9	109	135	218	245
0.66	169	3.31	6.76	13.2	19.6	27.0	40.6	54.9	80.4	108	134	216	243
0.64	167	3.27	6.68	13.1	19.4	26.7	40.1	54.3	79.4	107	132	214	240
0.62	166	3.25	6.64	13.0	19.3	26.6	39.8	54.0	79.0	106	131	212	239
0.60	164	3.21	6.56	12.8	19.0	26.2	39.4	53.3	78.0	105	130	210	236

DROP, IN INCHES, *Continued*

Time of Flight, Seconds

V/V₀	f	0.14	0.20	0.28	0.34	0.40	0.49	0.57	0.69	0.80	0.89	1.13	1.20
0.58	162	3.18	6.48	12.7	18.8	25.9	38.9	52.7	77.1	104	128	207	233
0.56	161	3.16	6.44	12.6	18.7	25.8	38.6	52.3	76.6	103	128	206	232
0.54	160	3.14	6.40	12.5	18.6	25.6	38.4	52.0	76.1	102	127	205	230
0.52	157	3.08	6.28	12.3	18.2	25.1	37.7	51.0	74.7	101	125	201	226
0.50	156	3.06	6.24	12.2	18.1	25.0	37.4	50.7	74.3	100	124	200	225
0.48	154	3.02	6.16	12.1	17.9	24.6	37.0	50.1	73.3	98	122	197	222
0.46	152	2.98	6.08	11.9	17.6	24.3	36.5	49.4	72.4	97	120	195	219
0.44	150	2.94	6.00	11.8	17.4	24.0	36.0	48.4	71.4	96	119	192	216
0.42	148	2.90	5.92	11.6	17.1	23.7	35.5	48.1	70.4	95	117	189	213
0.40	145	2.84	5.80	11.4	16.8	23.2	34.8	47.1	69.0	93	115	186	209
0.38	144	2.82	5.76	11.3	16.7	23.0	34.6	46.8	68.5	92	114	184	207
0.36	142	2.78	5.68	11.1	16.5	22.7	34.1	46.2	67.6	90	112	182	204
0.34	139	2.72	5.56	10.9	16.1	22.2	33.4	45.2	66.2	89	110	178	200
0.32	137	2.69	5.48	10.7	15.9	21.8	32.6	44.2	64.7	87	108	174	197

Instructions for use of

TIME AND SPACE FUNCTIONS FROM BRITISH 1909 BALLISTIC TABLES

The British Ballistic Tables of 1909 are almost identical with Ingalls' tables, but they go up to velocities of 4200 f.s. whereas Ingalls' tables stop at 3600; therefore these are convenient for use with any cartridges that may give velocities above the highest included in Ingalls.

Functions up to and including 4000 f.s. are taken directly from the official British tables; values from 4000 f.s. to 4200 f.s. have been computed by the author.

Formulae for use with these tables are similar to those for use with Ingalls with the exception that, unlike the Ingalls tables, these start at 100 f.s. and go up instead of starting at 3600 f.s. and going down; therefore in these tables we find that functions of v are smaller than those of V, and instead of subtracting functions of V from those of v as in Ingalls' tables, we subtract functions of v from those of V. Thus the formulae already given for use with Ingalls Tables are changed as follows:

Formula 1 become $C = \dfrac{X}{S(V) - S(v)}$

Formula 2 is unchanged.

Formula 3 becomes $S(v) = S(V) - \dfrac{X}{C}$

Formula 4 becomes S(v) for 200 yd $= S(V) -$ twice $\{ S(V) - S(v) \}$

Formula 5 becomes $T = C \{ T(V) - T(v) \}$

Formulae 6, 7, and 8 remain unchanged.

Time and Space functions extracted from
BRITISH 1909 BALLISTIC TABLES

Velocity f.s.	Space Function S	Difference For 1 f.s.	Time Function T	Difference for 1 f.s.
100	3,571.5	80.17	0.186	.7321
120	5,175.0	72.51	14,828	.5594
140	6,625.0	66.52	26.017	.4445
160	7,955.4	61.70	34.908	.3635
180	9,189.4	57.71	42.179	.3042
200	10,343.6	54.34	48.263	.2591
220	11,430.4	51.45	53.445	.2239
240	12,459.4	48.94	57.932	.1959
260	13,438.2	46.72	61.842	.1730
280	14,372.7	44.76	65.305	.1544
300	15,268.0	43.01	68.394	.1388
320	16,128.2	41.42	71.171	.1256
340	16,956.7	39.98	73.683	.1143
360	17,756.4	38.67	75.969	.1040
380	18,529.9	37.47	78.060	.0961
400	19,279.3	36.36	79.982	.0887

Velocity f.s.	Space Function S	Difference For 1 f.s.	Time Function T	Difference for 1 f.s.
420	20,006.6	35.34	81.757	.0822
440	20,713.4	34.39	83.401	.0764
460	21,401.2	33.50	84.930	.0713
480	22,071.2	32.67	86.356	.0666
500	22,724.7	31.90	87.689	.0626
520	23,362.7	31.17	88.941	.0588
540	23,986.1	30.48	90.117	.0554
560	24,595.8	29.84	91.226	.0520
580	25,192.6	29.23	92.273	.0495
600	25,777.2	28.65	93.264	.0470
620	26,350.2	28.10	94.204	.0446
640	26,912.2	27.58	95.096	.0424
660	27,463.8	27.08	95.944	.0404
680	28,005.4	26.60	96.753	.0385
700	28,537.5	26.15	97.524	.0370
720	29,060.6	25.72	98.261	.0351
740	29,575.1	25.31	98.966	.0337
760	30,081.3	24.91	99.641	.0324
780	30,579.5	24.53	100.288	.0310
800	31,070.2	24.16	100.909	.0298
820	31,553.5	23.81	101.506	.0287
840	32,029.8	23.09	102.080	.0271
860	32,491.7	22.05	102.623	.0253
880	32,932.6	21.06	103.130	.0237
900	33,353.9	20.15	103.604	.0221
920	33,756.9	19.29	104.047	.0207
940	34,142.7	18.48	104.461	.0195
960	34,512.4	17.73	104.851	.0182
980	34,867.1	17.02	105.216	.0172
1000	35,207.6	16.36	105.560	.0162
1020	35,534.8	15.72	105.884	.0153
1040	35,849.3	14.64	106.190	.0139
1060	36,142.2	13.22	106.469	.0123
1080	36,406.6	11.95	106.716	.0109
1100	36,645.6	10.82	106.935	.0097
1120	36,862.0	9.815	107.130	.0087
1140	37,058.3	8.920	107.304	.0077
1160	37,236.7	8.125	107.459	.0069
1180	37,399.2	7.455	107.598	.0062
1200	37,548.3	7.160	107.723	.0059
1220	37,691.5	6.930	107.842	.0056
1240	37,830.1	6.705	107.954	.0054
1260	37,964.2	6.500	108.062	.0051
1280	38,094.2	6.300	108.164	.0049
1300	38,220.2	6.100	108.262	.0046
1320	38,342.2	5.935	108.355	.0044
1340	38,460.9	5.750	108.444	.0042
1360	38,575.9	5.585	108.529	.0041
1380	38,687.6	5.425	108.611	.0039
1400	38,796.1	5.270	108.689	.0037
1420	38,901.5	5.130	108.764	.0035
1440	39,004.1	4.985	108.835	.0034
1460	39,103.8	4.890	108.904	.0033
1480	39,201.6	4.835	108.971	.0032
1500	39,298.3	4.790	109.036	.0031
1520	39,394.1	4.735	109.099	.0031
1540	39,488.8	4.685	109.161	.0030
1560	39,582.5	4.640	109.221	.0029
1580	39,675.3	4.595	109.280	.0029
1600	39,767.2	4.545	109.338	.0028
1620	39,858.1	4.505	109.395	.0027
1640	39,948.2	4.460	109.450	.0027
1660	40,037.4	4.415	109.504	.0026
1680	40,125.7	4.375	109.557	.0026
1700	40,213.2	4.330	109.609	.0025
1720	40,299.8	4.295	109.660	.0025
1740	40,385.7	4.255	109.709	.0024
1760	40,470.8	4.215	109.758	.0024
1780	40,555.1	4.175	109.805	.0023
1800	40,638.6	4.140	109.852	.0023
1820	40,721.4	4.105	109.898	.0022
1840	40,803.5	4.070	109.942	.0022
1860	40,884.9	4.035	109.987	.0021
1880	40,965.6	3.995	110.030	.0021
1900	41,045.5	3.970	110.072	.0021
1920	41,124.9	3.930	110.113	.0020
1940	41,203.5	3.905	110.154	.0020

Velocity f.s.	Space Function S	Difference For 1 f.s.	Time Function T	Difference for 1 f.s.
1960	41,281.6	3.870	110.194	.0020
1980	41,359.0	3.835	110.234	.0019
2000	41,435.7	3.815	110.272	.0019
2020	41,512.0	3.795	110.310	.0019
2040	41,587.9	3.775	110.347	.0018
2060	41,663.4	3.755	110.384	.0018
2080	41,738.5	3.740	110.421	.0018
2100	41,813.3	3.720	110.456	.0017
2120	41,887.7	3.705	110.492	.0017
2140	41,961.8	3.690	110.526	.0017
2160	42,035.6	3.670	110.561	.0017
2180	42,109.0	3.650	110.595	.0016
2200	42,182.0	3.640	110.628	.0016
2220	42,254.8	3.620	110.661	.0016
2240	42,327.2	3.600	110.693	.0016
2260	42,399.2	3.590	110.725	.0016
2280	42,471.0	3.575	110.757	.0015
2300	42,542.5	3.555	110.788	.0015
2320	42,613.6	3.540	110.819	.0015
2340	42,684.4	3.530	110.849	.0015
2360	42,755.0	3.510	110.879	.0015
2380	42,825.2	3.495	110.909	.0014
2400	42,895.1	3.485	110.938	.0014
2420	42,964.8	3.465	110.967	.0014
2440	43,034.1	3.455	110.996	.0014
2460	43,103.2	3.440	111.024	.0014
2480	43,172.0	3.425	111.052	.0014
2500	43,240.5	3.415	111.079	.0014
2520	43,308.8	3.400	111.106	.0013
2540	43,376.8	3.385	111.133	.0013
2560	43,444.5	3.370	111.160	.0013
2580	43,511.9	3.360	111.186	.0013
2600	43,579.1	3.345	111.212	.0013
2620	43,646.0	3.325	111.238	.0012
2640	43,712.5	3.310	111.263	.0012
2660	43,778.7	3.295	111.288	.0012
2680	43,844.6	3.275	111.313	.0012
2700	43,910.1	3.265	111.337	.0012
2720	43,975.4	3.245	111.361	.0012
2740	44,040.3	3.225	111.385	.0011
2760	44,104.8	3.215	111.408	.0011
2780	44,169.1	3.200	111.432	.0011
2800	44,233.1	3.180	111.454	.0011
2820	44,296.7	3.170	111.477	.0011
2840	44,360.1	3.150	111.500	.0011
2860	44,423.1	3.140	111.522	.0011
2880	44,485.9	3.125	111.544	.0010
2900	44,548.4	3.105	111.565	.0010
2920	44,610.5	3.095	111.586	.0010
2940	44,672.4	3.080	111.608	.0010
2960	44,734.0	3.070	111.629	.0010
2980	44,795.4	3.050	111.649	.0010
3000	44,856.4	3.040	111.670	.0010
3020	44,917.2	3.025	111.690	.0010
3040	44,977.7	3.015	111.710	.0010
3060	45,038.0	2.995	111.730	.0095
3080	45,097.9	2.990	111.749	.0095
3100	45,157.7	2.975	111.768	.0095
3120	45,217.2	2.960	111.787	.0095
3140	45,276.4	2.950	111.806	.0095
3160	45,335.4	2.935	111.825	.0095
3180	45,394.1	2.925	111.844	.0090
3200	45,452.6	2.910	111.862	.0090
3220	45,510.8	2.900	111.880	.0090
3240	45,568.8	2.885	111.898	.0090
3260	45,625.5	2.875	111.916	.0090
3280	45,684.0	2.865	111.933	.0085
3300	45,741.3	2.850	111.951	.0085
3320	45,798.3	2.840	111.968	.0085
3340	45,855.1	2.830	111.985	.0085
3360	45,911.7	2.810	112.002	.0085
3380	45,968.1	2.905	112.019	.0085
3400	46,024.2	2.795	112.035	.0080
3420	46,080.1	2.785	112.052	.0080
3440	46,135.8	2.775	112.068	.0080
3460	46,191.3	2.765	112.084	.0080
3480	46,246.6	2.750	112.100	.0080
3500	46,301.6	2.745	112.116	.0080
3520	46,356.5	2.730	112.132	.0075
3540	46,411.1	2.720	112.147	.0075

Velocity f.s.	Space Function S	Difference For 1 f.s.	Time Function T	Difference for 1 f.s.
3560	46,465.5	2.710	112.162	.0075
3580	46,519.7	2.705	112.177	.0075
3600	46,573.8	2.690	112.192	.0075
3620	46,627.6	2.680	112.207	.0075
3640	46,681.2	2.670	112.222	.0075
3660	46,734.6	2.660	112.237	.0070
3680	46,787.8	2.655	112.251	.0070
3700	46,840.9	2.640	112.266	.0070
3720	46,893.7	2.635	112.280	.0070
3740	46,946.4	2.620	112.294	.0070
3760	46,998.8	2.615	112.308	.0070
3780	47,051.1	2.605	112.322	.0070
3800	47,103.2	2.595	112.336	.0070
3820	47,155.1	2.585	112.349	.0070
3840	47,206.8	2.580	112.363	.0065
3860	47,258.4	2.570	112.376	.0065
3880	47,309.8	2.550	112.389	.0065
3900	47,360.9	2.550	112.402	.0065
3920	47,412.0	2.540	112.416	.0065
3940	47,462.8	2.535	112.428	.0065
3960	47,513.5	2.525	112.441	.0065
3980	47,564.0	2.515	112.454	.0065
4000	47,614.3	2.505	112.467	.0065
4020	47,664.4	2.495	112.480	.0065
4040	47,714.3	2.485	112.493	.0060
4060	47,764.0	2.475	112.506	.0060
4080	47,813.5	2.465	112.519	.0060
4100	47,862.8	2.455	112.531	.0060
4120	47,911.9	2.445	112.543	.0060
4140	47,960.8	2.435	112.555	.0060
4160	48,009.5	2.425	112.567	.0060
4180	48,058.0	2.415	112.579	.0060
4200	48,106.3		112.591	

Index